Morality of the Market

Morality of the Market:

Religious and Economic Perspectives

Contributors
include:

Kenneth E. Boulding
Milton Friedman
Edward R. Norman
Michael Novak
James M. Wall
J. Philip Wogaman

Edited by:
Walter Block
Geoffrey Brennan
Kenneth Elzinga

THE FRASER INSTITUTE

HB 72. I57 1985t

Proceedings of an International Symposium on Religion, Economics and Social Thought, held August 9-11, 1982 in Vancouver, British Columbia, Canada. This event is part of the program of Liberty Fund Inc., under the direction of its President, Dr. Neil McLeod. It was managed by the Centre for the Study of Economics and Religion, a division of the Fraser Institute. It was organized by CSER Director, Dr. Walter Block, Professor Paul Heyne of the University of Washington, Seattle and Professor Anthony Waterman of St. John's College, the University of Manitoba.

Canadian Cataloguing in Publication Data

International Symposium on Religion, Economics and
    Social Thought (1982: Vancouver, B.C.)
    The morality of the market

"Proceedings of an International Symposium on
    Religion, Economics and Social Thought, held
    August 9-11, 1982, in Vancouver, British Columbia,
    Canada."
Includes index.
ISBN 0-88975-074-2

1. Economics – Religious aspects – Congresses.
2. Religion and politics – Congresses. 3. Religion
and sociology – Congresses. 4. Capitalism –
Religious aspects – Congresses. I. Boulding,
Kenneth E. (Kenneth Ewart), 1910 –   II. Block,
Walter, 1941 –   III. Brennan, H. Geoffrey, 1944 –
IV. Elzinga, Kenneth G. V. Fraser Institute
(Vancouver, B.C.) VI. Title.
HB72.I57 1982   291.1'785   C85-091253-9

Printed in Canada

Contents

Participants

Dr. Richard Baepler
Professor of Theology and Law, and Vice President for Academic Affairs, Valparaiso University, Indiana. Member, Advisory Committee of *The Journal of Law and Theology.* Co-author and Editor: *Changing American Lifestyles; The Quest for a Viable Saga.*

Dr. John C. Bennett
President Emeritus and Reinhold Niebuhr Professor of Social Ethics Emeritus, Union Theological Seminary, New York City; Minister of the United Church of Christ. Author of *Christian Ethics and Social Policy; Christians and the State; Foreign Policy in Christian Perspective;* and *The Radical Imperative.* Senior Contributing Editor of *Christianity and Crisis.*

Dr. Walter Berns
Resident Scholar, American Enterprise Institute, Washington, D.C. Author of *The First Amendment and the Future of American Democracy; For Capital Punishment: Crime and the Morality of the Death Penalty;* and *The Defense of Liberal Democracy.*

Dr. Walter Block
Director, Centre for the Study of Economics and Religion; Senior Economist, The Fraser Institute. Author of *Amending the Combines Investigation Act;* and *Focus: On Economics and the Canadian Bishops.* Editor: *Zoning: Its Cost and Relevance for the 1980s; Rent Control: Myths and Realities; Discrimination, Affirmative Action, and Equal Opportunity;* and *Taxation: An International Perspective.*

Dr. Kenneth E. Boulding
Distinguished Professor of Economics Emeritus, University of Colorado, Boulder; Project Director and Research Associate, Program of Research on Political and Economic Change at the University's Institute of Behavioral Science. Author of *Ecodynamics: A New Theory of Societal Evolution; Evolutionary Economics and Human Betterment;* and *The Economics of Love and Fear.*

Dr. H. Geoffrey Brennan
Professor of Economics, Australian National University. Author, with James Buchanan, of *The Power to Tax.* Author of *The Christian*

and the State. Contributor to *American Economic Review; Economic Journal; Journal of Political Economy;* and other professional economic journals.

Dr. John W. Cooper
Academic Dean and Professor of Religion, Bridgewater College, Virginia. Author of *The Theology of Freedom: The Legacy of Jacques Maritain and Reinhold Niebuhr.* Co-editor, with Michael Novak, *The Corporation: A Theological Inquiry.* Author of numerous articles, including "A Christian Theology of Economics"; "Islamic Economic Justice"; and "The Cuban Revolution and Liberation Theology."

Dr. Kenneth G. Elzinga
Professor of Economics, University of Virginia. Author, with William Breit, of *The Antitrust Penalties* and *The Fatal Equilibrium.* Editorial Board: *The Antitrust Bulletin;* Series Editor, *Political Economy and Public Policy.*

Dr. S. Herbert Frankel
Chairman, Board of Governors, Oxford Centre for Postgraduate Hebrew Studies, Oxford, and author of *Money, Two Philosophies: The Conflict of Trust and Authority* and *Money and Liberty.*

Dr. David Friedman
Associate Professor, A.B. Freeman School of Business, Tulane University. Author of *The Machinery of Freedom* and *Thomas Aquinas and the Just Price.* Contributor to *Human Events; The New Guard; and Ripon Quarterly.*

Dr. Milton Friedman
Senior Research Fellow, Hoover Institution, Stanford University; Professor of Economics Emeritus, University of Chicago; 1976 Nobel Laureate in Economic Sciences. Author of numerous books including *A Theory on the Consumption Function; Capitalism and Freedom; The Optimum Quantity of Money; Free to Choose;* and *Tyranny of the Status Quo.*

Dr. Paul Heyne
Lecturer in Economics, University of Washington, Seattle. Author of *Private Keepers of the Public Interest* and *The Economic Way of Thinking.* Contributor to numerous journals of economics and theology.

Dr. Aaron Levine
Professor and Chairman, Department of Economics, Yeshiva University; Rabbi, Young Israel of Ave. J, Brooklyn, New York. Author of *Free Enterprise and Jewish Law* and numerous articles on economics and Judaism.

Dr. David Martin
Professor of Religious Sociology, London School of Economics. Author of *A General Theory of Secularization* and *Contemporary Dilemmas of Religion.* Contributor to numerous journals of theology.

Dr. Murdith R. McLean
Warden, St. John's College, University of Manitoba; Priest of the Anglican Church of Canada. Contributor to *Canadian Journal of Theology; Canadian Journal of Philosophy; Scottish Journal of Theology;* and *The Philosophical Quarterly.*

Dr. David I. Meiselman
Professor of Economics, Virginia Polytechnic Institute. Chairman, American Jewish Forum, Editorial Board, *Policy Review.* Adjunct Scholar, American Enterprise Institute, Heritage Foundation. Author of *The Phenomenon of World Wide Inflation.*

Dr. Ezra J. Mishan
Author of *Costs of Economic Growth; 21 Popular Economic Fallacies; The Economic Growth Debate; Cost-Benefit Analysis; Introduction to Normative Economics; What Political Economy Is All About; Economic Efficiency and Social Welfare; Pornography, Psychedelics and Technology;* and several other books.

Reverend Dr. Edward R. Norman
Dean of Peterhouse, Cambridge. Author of *The Catholic Church and Ireland; The Conscience of the State in North America; A History of Modern Ireland; Church and Society in Modern England;* and *The English Catholic Church in the Nineteenth Century.*

Dr. Michael Novak
George Frederick Jewett Chair in Religion, Philosophy, and Public Policy at the American Enterprise Institute, Washington, D.C.; Founding Editor, *Catholicism in Crisis.* Author of *Freedom with Jus-*

tice: Catholic Social Thought and Liberal Institutions; The Spirit of Democratic Capitalism; Confession of a Catholic; and numerous other works.

Reverend Edmund A. Opitz
Congregational minister and economist, Foundation for Economic Education; Book Editor, *The Freeman.* Author of *Religion and Capitalism: Friends or Foes?; The Powers that Be;* and *The Kingdom Without God.*

Dr. Ronald Preston
Professor Emeritus of Social and Pastoral Theology, University of Manchester, and Canon Emeritus of Manchester Cathedral. Author of *Religion and the Persistence of Capitalism; Explorations in Theology No. 9; Church and Society in the Late Twentieth Century;* and Editor of *Technology and Social Justice.*

Dr. Lance Roberts
Associate Professor of Sociology, University of Manitoba. Contributor to *Journal of the Scientific Study of Religion; Canadian Public Policy;* and *Canadian Journal of Sociology.*

Mr. Arthur A. Shenfield
Professor of Economics at the University of London, University of Chicago Graduate School of Business, and lately Ludwig von Mises Distinguished Professor of Economics, Hillsdale College. Author of *Capitalism Under the Test of Ethics* and former President of the Mont Pèlerin Society.

Dr. Roger L. Shinn
Reinhold Niebuhr Professor of Social Ethics, Union Theological Seminary, New York. Adjunct Professor of Religion and Society, Columbia University. Author of *Tangled World; Wars and Rumors of Wars;* and *Forced Options: Social Decisions for the 21st Century.* Contributing Editor of *Christianity and Crisis.*

Rabbi Seymour Siegel
Professor of Ethics and Theology, Jewish Theological Seminary, New York City, and Executive Director, United States Holocaust Memorial Council, Washington, D.C. Author of *Conservative Judaism and Jewish Law;* Editor of *Encyclopedia Judaica;* co-editor of *This World: A Journal of Religion and Politics.* Contributor to *Conservative Judaism.*

Reverend James M. Wall
Editor of *The Christian Century* magazine. Ordained Methodist minister and author of *Three European Directors; Church and Cinema; Biblical Spectaculars and Secular Man;* and *Theologians in Transition.*

Dr. Anthony Waterman
Fellow of St. John's College, Winnipeg and Professor of Economics, University of Manitoba. Formerly Chairman, Anglican National Task Force on the Economy. Author of *Poverty in Canada: A Christian Perspective* and contributor to both economic and theological literature.

Dr. J. Philip Wogaman
Professor of Christian Social Ethics, Wesley Theological Seminary, Washington, D.C.; Ordained minister, the United Methodist Church. Past President, the Society of Christian Ethics. Author of *The Great Economic Debate: An Ethical Analysis* and other books and articles.

Bennett, Frankel, Martin, Norman and Novak have made significant contributions to the book, but were not in attendance at the conference—eds.

Preface

Religious convictions

This book is based on the proceedings of a conference held in Vancouver, like its companion volume *Religion, Economics and Social Thought,* under the auspices of Dr. Neil McLeod of the Liberty Fund Inc. It was administered by the Centre for the Study of Economics and Religion, a division of the Fraser Institute. The entire project grew out of a perception that there is some useful purpose to be served by dialogue between theologians and economists on the virtues and vices of the free market order. The particular stimulus for the conference, and now the present volume, was a growing conviction among the organizers that an anti-market orientation now predominates within the ecclesiastical establishment—that the "high ground" within the churches is occupied by those whose political positions would properly be described as left of centre. For those who both hold religious convictions and espouse non-leftist political philosophies, this is a troubling state of affairs. It is troubling because when the church or synagogue speaks out on social/political/economic issues, the moral authority of the institution tends to lie behind what is said. There is the implication, plausibly drawn, that the social/political/economic position taken is a logical outgrowth of the religious conviction.

A nexus between religious conviction and policy prescription raises an immediate set of questions: does Judaism—does Christianity—, properly understood, and faithfully applied, have direct implications for social/political/economic organization? Are such implications independent of judgements of fact about the workings of alternative institutional orders? And if not, can the empirical judgements and social theories used by theologians and ecclesial officials sustain the critical scrutiny of prevailing social science orthodoxy?

These are big questions, and should not be allowed to be answered by default. But, in addition, there is another question that naturally arises: since the churches and synagogues appear not to have always held the views that now seem to be in the ascendancy, what has caused the change? Is there a new and more vigorous grasp on religious truth — a new attentiveness to socio-political implications that has always been there? Or is it a response to external forces in the social order itself? And are these alternatives mutually exclusive?

Spontaneous order

Nominally, the conference was supposed to be focused on this latter set of questions. In fact, most of what went on dealt with the former set. This drifting of the domain of discourse is rather in the nature of the beast. A gathering such as this is necessarily an exercise in what we might term "non-teleological constructivism": one puts together an interesting group of people under a given agenda and a given set of rules for debate, and then one must simply allow things to take their course. What emerges is necessarily a creature of the participants, rather than of the organizers, and there is often chaos, much talking at cross purposes, and some detouring along the way. But there is also much serious attention to interesting and important issues, and much genuine intellectual engagement as people with quite different views seek to articulate their own positions and grapple with the perspectives of others. The result makes, in our view, quite fascinating reading.

Apart from anything else, professional economists and professional theologians rarely confront one another in a context where there can be an engagement of minds. This conference provided that context. And served to reveal an intellectual territory that cries out to be explored. The debate here reported makes a beginning.

Although this project grew out of one particular set of political concerns, in selecting conference participants — indeed in framing the entire enterprise — the organizers made a conscientious effort to put together a group which would represent a variety of viewpoints. No stone was left unturned in an effort to include spokespersons from all points on the political/economic/ideological/religious spectrum. The conviction was that representatives of the differing ideological and theological positions should be given an opportunity to engage with each other in meaningful dialogue. Equally, in editing the papers and the transcript of the discussion, we have tried to exercise a light touch — to allow all points of view to be heard. A similar balance is reflected in the selection of two major protagonists in the debate to provide an overview of these conference proceedings. Michael Novak and John Bennett represent quite different positions on the central issues addressed. We are grateful to them both for their commentaries. Their contributions mark the conclusion of the book — not to represent any sort of coming to a mind, but rather to indicate that the debate is necessarily an ongoing affair. The broad representation of disparate views is a unique feature of this book, and we value that broadness highly.

Extemporaneous discussion

At most academic conferences, a transcript of the conferees' extemporaneous discussion is neither produced nor published. The reason, presumably, is that such a record is generally too costly relative to the value of the remarks. We believe this conference to be an exception. Consequently interspersed among the formal papers and commissioned responses is much of the informal dialogue by the conference participants.

The format of this conference entailed the advance submission to all the participants of ten major papers and one or two written critiques of each paper. Except for minor editing, these ten papers and the prepared responses to them are published in this volume, largely as they were submitted prior to the assembly in Vancouver. The one exception: happily, we were able to secure the publication rights to Professor S. Herbert Frankel's, "Modern Capitalism and the Jews," a paper written several years earlier (but not at that time published) in response to the work done by Milton Friedman on this subject. Professor Friedman's paper is one of the ten papers around which this conference was structured. We count it a privilege to add Professor Frankel's paper* to the volume, though he was not present in Vancouver.

The format of the volume is thus as follows: 1) the major paper; 2) the written comments; 3) the author's reply (in several cases); 4) the informal discussion which includes:

a) the oral remarks (strictly limited by a time constraint) of the commentators;
b) the oral response of the author of the major paper (each paper-

---

* The paper has been published recently as an occasional paper of the Oxford Centre for Postgraduate Hebrew Studies — eds.

giver was allowed five to ten minutes for this purpose);
c)   the discussion that followed the opening of the floor to all participants.

At this juncture, both the paper-givers and the commentators were
treated by the moderator on a par with other participants. Often the
oral response of the major paper-giver proved to be one of the most
valuable portions of the conference, for the speaker was then responding, in his own words, to the criticism or praise that had just been
uttered.

An exception to this format occurs with the first paper, "Introduction: Religious Belief and Political Bias" by Anthony Waterman. This
session did not begin with the commentator of Waterman's paper. Instead Professor Waterman opened the session with a brief assessment
of the issue of characterizing bias in the context of religious belief.
This was done to set the introductory tone for the conference. A final
note on the conference format: the much regretted absence of David
Martin and Edward R. Norman, whose papers were two of the major
ones at the conference, meant that we did not have the benefit of their
oral responses to their commentators, nor their additions to the dialogue.

To meet the page constraints of this volume, a portion of the transcript has not been published. Exercising the editorial discretion for
this excising task was at times difficult. But in what follows, we
believe we have retained the substance of the issues discussed and the
positions that were staked out and defended.

Tasting economics

Sir Dennis Robertson used to advise his economics students that the
best way to learn about pudding was to taste it. He believed this counsel had relevance to the learning of economics as well. Sir Dennis's
advice also applies to learning from this book; it is best to start by tasting it. Hence our Preface presents no lengthy summary of each article.
Nor is an annotation of the transcript attempted. Instead, what we
have done, for the assistance of the reader who will dip selectively into
this book, is to only highlight the various contributions.

In Part One the Introduction sets out the question, can there be a
mapping or correlation between religious beliefs and political convictions. In his remarks, Professor Waterman defends the proposition

that religious belief does not imply a preference for any particular form of social organization. Therefore an externalist conception of faith and political bias may be necessary to explain any correlation between religious dogma and a preference for a particular economic/political policy, i.e., the explanation for the correlation is external to religion, not intrinsic to it.

The discussion moves around several issues, such as whether disagreement on social policies between people of like faith is a function of differences in their level of understanding and sophistication in economics. Also addressed is whether religion, by inherently dealing in symbols, cuts against any clear, uniform derivation of economic policy. A portion of the discussion concerns the possibility of testing the proposition that a particular faith determines a political belief, and whether such a test requires that the particular religion alone must entail that particular policy orientation. A division arises, which surfaces again and again: the economists generally holding to a cleavage between questions of fact and questions of value; the theologians (generally) disagreeing that such a line could be drawn. The discussion becomes spirited on epistemological issues, e.g., is there such a thing as a fact, or are these only tautologies, and how can religions deal with the mixing of facts and values. All this establishes a starting point for more specific topics that are addressed in later sessions.

Stewardship, vocation, charity

In Part Two the paper entitled "Theological Perspective on Economics" by Professor Philip Wogaman introduces the theological concepts of stewardship, vocation, and charity. The commentators on this paper take rather different tacks. Professor John Cooper addresses the paper as an exercise in taxonomy, while Dr. Walter Block disagrees starkly with the ends that would result from the policy means commended in the paper. In his reply, Wogaman insists upon the primacy of theological commitments, over and above that to which is owed to economic theology—a point neglected by both his critics. Perhaps in no other session does the disparity between a theologian's communitarian approach to social issues and an economist's individualistic approach to social issues become more apparent. Also striking is the agreement between the (friendly) disputants on the *ends* to be sought. This is the source of many interesting discussions. For example most religions hold ethical conduct to be an obligation but should the state enforce moral behaviour? Is good conduct a religious act only if carried out voluntarily? The answer to these questions divides several of the participants, and of course has enormous implications for the merits or demerits of different social policies. Several case examples of ethical issues that might arise through the operation of a market system are cited, with respondents commenting (but not uniformly) as to the implications of each from the perspective of Christianity and Judaism. The discussion ranges widely, from the question of unionized farm labour to the current Law of the Sea negotiations.

Perhaps the most narrowly focused discussion of the entire assembly concerns Edmund Opitz's paper, *"The Christian Century* on Religion and Society."* His sole commentator, the *Century's* current editor, Dr. James Wall, was able to offer an insider's response to Opitz's negative assessment of this influential journal of U.S. Protestantism. In his rejoinder, Opitz defends against the charge that his view of *The Christian Century* sets up an artifical straw man: Marxian collectivism. The subsequent debate about the bias and influence of *The Christian Century* is augmented by the intimate knowledge of the journal by several of the other conferees. The remarks during this session came mostly, but not exclusively, from the theologians (rather than the economic professionals). For some of the economists, this was their introduction to the tremendous influence of Reinhold Niebuhr, whose name surfaced again and again as the question of the political orientation of this periodical was examined.

Interface

Professor Roger Shinn's paper on the interface between theology and the social sciences is well placed on the agenda. By the time it was discussed, the character of the debate as to what forces, if any, determined the social policies that stemmed from religious belief and activity, was taking shape. It was as if the foundation of a house had been laid; now the framing-in of the structure could begin. In the discussion, respondents returned to the issue: are theologians sufficiently trained in economics to pronounce intelligently on economic policy? Further prodding the debate was the deeper philosophical question of whether the search for social justice itself could be rendered identifiable, or desirable.

In addition to this very fundamental issue, several conferees voice disagreement over the *right* (apart from the competence) of theologians to pronounce upon economic policy matters. As a corollary, more than one economist argues the position that the economist *qua* economist has no right (possibly even competence) to pronounce upon economic policy matters. Once again, during this colloquy, the question was raised as to whether one can separate the positive analysis of a problem from the ideological presuppositions the analyst brings to the problem; and if not, does this not tend to bias the results of the purportedly positive-scientific analysis? This was the matter of methodology that often provoked a very helpful and illuminating dialogue. On a different level of discourse, that of ethics, the question of whether ethical behaviour was, at root, social or individual, is a running issue throughout; it comes up pointedly in this section.

Internalist explanations

Part Three is concerned with internalist explanations of policy bias in religious thought. It begins with Geoffrey Brennan's paper on "Markets and Majorities." Professor Brennan's contribution, a public choice explanation of why religious bodies and individuals may prefer collective political action over and above market action, provoked comments by his discussants, Professors Kenneth Boulding and David Meiselman, on the character and rationality of voting. The notable analogy was drawn more than once that voting is akin to a religious or liturgical act. Part of the discussion involved pondering the question: does the economist's model of voting behaviour explain why the church might be overtly hostile to the market system or might instead only choose to ignore it. Another matter of concern to both economists and theologians is whether voting for a particular social policy was simply a form of cheap grace, i.e., perceived as being virtuous at little personal cost or sacrifice.

Also under the heading of internalist explanations is Professor E. J. Mishan's paper on "Religon, Culture and Technology." Professors Kenneth Elzinga and David Friedman criticize Professor Mishan's thesis that technology and mass advertising ineluctably lead to decadence and a decline in religious fervour and influence. Mishan begins his response with an analysis of sexual gadgetry such as the vibrator, and goes on to condemn other aspects of our "liberative" society. The ensuing dialogue concerns the relationship between the advance in science and the alleged decline in religion, as well as the connection between the role of myth and religion in modern society. The role of the market system in eroding society's ethical consensus is debated. More than one discussant raises the question, not of causal relationship, but of what is factually known about the decline in morals and the decline in religious influence. An important footnote to this entire section is whether intellectuals have a propensity to decry their age and culture, regardless of the actual level and trends of integrity and ethics in existence at the time.

Sociological issues

In Part Four the discussion turns to sociological issues, beginning with David Martin's paper on "The Clergy, Secularization and Politics." His discussant, Professor Ronald Preston, raises the possibility that those who purport to disapprove of the church pronouncing on social issues are either those with only nominal commitments to their faith (hence they dislike any changes), or those who simply disagree with the particular pronouncements (witness the fact that these individuals are not vocal when the church sanctions the *status quo)*. The discussion also returns to the basic methodological question of the validity of both internalist and externalist explanations of religion's political orientation. An unanswered question is whether an externalist account of a social phenomenon, such as the alleged tilt of clergy to the left, can be offered up in any way other than to dismiss the validity of that particular policy orientation. A historical dimension to this subject is also cited, by reference to the tension (at least in the U.S.) between the Puritan tradition of trying to save society versus the Pietistic tradition of trying to save souls. The evolving modern day resolution of this tension may help explain the increasing politicization of the clergy—both right and left.

Professor Milton Friedman's paper, "Capitalism and the Jews," explores the thesis that Jews, who benefited and were even protected by the economic system of capitalism, nevertheless are often the market system's most penetrating critics. Professor Friedman's commentator, Professor Aaron Levine, examines the ancient traditions of Judaism, to further explore the dimensions and roots of this alleged antipathy. He concludes that any antagonism need not exist out of adherence to the structures of Jewish faith. Professor Frankel takes Milton Friedman's views strongly to task for being "a-historical and indefensible," and guilty of the "fallacy that races of people can be regarded as having identifiable general social characteristics or attitudes which determine their behaviours." For his part, Friedman totally rejects the Frankel criticism, holding it to be really a critique of Sombart, not of his own views. As can be seen by a perusal of the text, the fur really flies when these two intellectual giants take the hammer and tongs to each other's theories. It is no exaggeration to say this controversy alone is worth the entire price of admission.

In the informal discussion which follows, it is maintained that Judaism never contemplated a *laissez-faire* economic order. The ensuing dialogue addresses the empirical issue of the extent, if at all, that *religious* Jews are or ever were anti-market (as opposed to Jews who left their community of faith). The deliberation also turns to the manner in which liberal democracy, the political system in which Jews are most likely to prosper, requires the market system as a necessary corollary to its existence. The dialogue also embraces the place of Jewish intellectuals in the neo-conservative movement, with disagreement being voiced as to whether these individuals can be construed as being friends of the market system or not. Keen interest is also shown in the economic policy orientation of the Zionists and of modern Israel.

Economic justice

Part Five begins with Paul Heyne's paper on "The Concept of Economic Justice in Religious Discussion." Professor Heyne, whose formal training is in both theology and economics, chose to wear his economist's hat in drafting this paper, though his commentator, Professor Richard Baepler, perceives remnants of Heyne's theological training in the work. The endeavour to derive a working concept of justice from the concept of property rights provokes lively discussion on the subject of the original delineation of the rights to property. The dialogue turns from the Lockean and Humean approach to this problem to the modification of Locke proposed by Robert Nozick and the libertarian concept of self-ownership. The just determination of property rights is seen by most participants as very basic to the moral foundations of the market system. The task of applying the property rights approach to the Third World generally, and to groups such as the latifundia in particular, evidences a disagreement even among defenders of the market system on this subject. Conferees differ as to whether there is a normative solution to the problem of rights delineation, either through Locke or James Buchanan's explication of a social contract, or whether the search for such a solution involves an infinite regress.

Further enlivening the session were debates about the merits of impersonal rules versus personal benevolence, and which of these categories were closer to the ideal of rendering justice, particularly for the unfortunate. The colloquy was further stimulated by the defense of the proposition that justice was not a definable concept for a society to pursue; hence the desirability of an alternative policy: the protection of the pursuit of individual liberty.

Religious secularization?

The final paper in Part Five entails a discussion of "Where We Are Today." This is Professor Edward R. Norman's, "Religion, Ethics and Politics in the 1980s." The dialogue in this session focuses very directly on the factual issues discussed and explored conceptually: have Christian religious organizations become secularized, and if so, is their secularization virtually indistinguishable from the political left-wing? The commentator, Professor Walter Berns, agrees with Norman's empirical assessment of this situation, and offers evidence gathered by himself on this subject, though he differs in his assessment of the character of this problem. Other participants at the conference disagree sharply that mainline religious groups have an affinity with Marxist or leftist groups, and further argue a rationale for religious groups in North America adopting a double standard in criticizing the actions of democracies rather than left-wing totalitarian regimes. Critics of the Norman position, such as James Wall and Philip Wogaman, suggest that a distinction must be made between position papers of mainline churches and working papers that do not carry the endorsement of these groups. In addition to a divergence of opinion over the actual teachings of what is being advocated within various church documents, there is an informative discussion over the Hobbesian doctrine of separating the government from the "intellectuals and priests," a doctrine designed to minimize the influence of the latter on the former. Some participants such as Geoffrey Brennan find the discussion of Hobbes disturbing, because of the implication that the Christian faith and a society based on libertarian principles is potentially inconsistent. This provokes a discussion of whether a society with a civil government, Hobbesian in structure, can ever foster the religious principles arguably necessary for its sustenance. One of the closing points proffered is the prediction (perhaps made hopefully) that with the increasing ascendancy of free market thinking among economists today, it could be expected that this analysis will eventually permeate the thinking of politicians, journalists, and eventually the clergy as well. If so, then even this latter group will return to their previous position of support for a system of natural liberty based on private property and voluntary exchange under a democratic political order.

The arguments, confrontations and strongly held positions maintained in this book range widely over the spheres of economics, politics, sociology and theology. The Fraser Institute is pleased to publish the findings of our panel of scholars as a signal contribution to each of these fields. However, due to the independence of each participant, their views may or may not conform, severally or collectively to the views of the members of the Fraser Institute.

Walter Block
H. Geoffrey Brennan
Kenneth G. Elzinga

PART ONE

INTRODUCTION

Chapter 1

Religious Belief and Political Bias

Anthony Waterman

"To think of God's concern for this world really means that we are committed, in some form, to the idea that certain solutions to problems are more a reflection of God's unbounded love than are others: and that is also where our biases had better be." This proposition, contained in a recent book by Phillip Wogaman [1977, p. 32], is widely entertained by religious believers of many different kinds. A correlation is believed to exist between a given set of religious beliefs and theological interpretations on the one hand, and a particular set of political commitments on the other. Moreover, the correlation is held to be rationally defensible in terms of the ethical and epistemological assumptions embodied in the religious beliefs, and not merely a social phenomenon explicable in terms of some exogenous cause. As William Temple was once incautious enough to say: "The alternative stands before us — socialism or heresy . . . socialism . . . is the economic realization of the Christian Gospel" [Preston, 1976, p. 23].

The purpose of this conference is to elucidate the theological and scientific content of Wogaman's proposition, and to subject it to critical examination. In this introductory paper I will attempt to define the issues: first, whether the putative biases imparted by religious belief are worth talking about; secondly, how these might be explained; and thirdly, whether an "internalist" explanation might suffice as a rational justification of bias. "Bias" is understood to mean a predisposition to prefer one of a number of possible economic and political systems, leaving the onus of proof with those who dissent.

I. THE EXISTENCE AND SIGNIFICANCE OF BIAS

The very idea of an option between alternative systems is revolutionary and modern. And so, therefore, is that of political bias. It follows that a discussion of the relation between religious belief and political bias must be based to a large extent upon the experience of industrial society in the liberal-democratic West.

Social thought in the Church to the seventeenth century

Viner and others have maintained that the early Christian church, not only in Apostolic and sub-Apostolic times but also well into the patristic period, had no recognizable body of social thought [Viner, 1978, pp. 9–13]. It is true that Clement of Alexandria (c. 200) earned the title "Consoler of the Rich" for his denial of the heretics' claim that the rich could not be saved; that Lactantius (c. 310) attacked communism on the grounds that it was unjust to take away one man's property to give it to another; and that Theodoretus (c. 435) wrote a reasoned defence of social inequality that anticipated eighteenth century Anglican apologetic [Viner, pp. 18–20]. It is equally true that Ambrose (c. 380) and many others of the Fathers before and after condemned the rich in the harshest terms for their selfish misuse of wealth and power at the expense of the poor [McGuire, 1967, p. 374]. It is the case, moreover, that Augustine (c. 420), the greatest and most influential of the Fathers, argued that since private property originated in a sharing by Man of God's gifts to the whole human race, its ultimate distribution must rest with the state. But Augustine drew no reformist or socialist inferences from this, for he, like all the Fathers, was profoundly "other-worldly," thought little of any scheme for social and economic progress, and would have echoed the words of his fellow-African Tertullian (c. 200): "I have no concern in this life except to depart from it as speedily as possible" [Viner, p. 2].

Quentin Skinner has argued that it was the influence of Augustine in particular which long inhibited such discussion of political questions as might have been possible in a static, subsistence-level, agrarian economy. Aristotle had established the position that politics — as the art of government — ought to be subject to rational inquiry. "The idea was lost to view, however, with Augustine's immensely influential insistence in *The City of God* that the true Christian ought not to concern himself with the problems of this temporal life, but ought to keep his gaze entirely fixed on the everlasting blessings that are promised for the future" [Skinner, 1978, II, p. 349]. The revival of Roman law at Bologna by the end of the eleventh century, and the ideological needs first of the Italian cities in their struggle with the Empire, then of the Empire in its contest with the Papacy, produced a rebirth of political thought in Europe by the fourteenth century [Skinner, 1978, I, chap. 2]. By the end of the seventeenth century, under the impact of the Reformation and its political aftermath, a fully developed political philosophy had emerged with a theory of the state as its centrepiece. Two points must be noted in connection with the theme of this paper.

First, there was as yet no distinction between a secular, or academic "political philosophy" and a specifically ecclesiastical "Christian Social Thought." The church did not stand aside from society, judging and admonishing. Church and society were generally regarded as one and the same thing, and in the work of extreme statists such as Hobbes, of course, the church was actually subsumed under the state. Secondly, despite the existence of revolutionary elements in some Reformation political thought there was little, if any, conception of alternative political and economic systems. Locke was remarkable in justifying the English revolution of the seventeenth century not by the usual Whig appeal to the ancient constitution but with an abstract theory of rights and obligations [Tully, 1980, passim]. Yet there is no trace in Locke of that pluralistic view of political possibilities which is characteristic of modern thought and which provides the opportunity for, if not the necessity of, "bias."

Eighteenth century Christian political economy

Three interrelated phenomena of the second half of the eighteenth century afforded the conditions of modern political thought: the Enlightenment; the collapse of the *ancien régime;* and the beginnings of industrialization. The Enlightenment — specifically the French, as distinct from the Anglo-Scottish, Enlightenment [Kristol, 1979, pp. 17–19] — by driving a wedge between the "religious" and "secular" ways of perceiving reality, created the intellectual possibility of a distinctly "Christian Social Thought." The destruction of the *ancien régime* by the French Revolution detached the Church of Rome from its age-old alliance with European feudalism and set it loose to find a new social and political role in an increasingly bourgeois world. And industrialization, by opening the possibility of continuously rising living standards, the defeat of scarcity and rational control of the human environment, engendered an attitude of mind capable of conceiving alternative states of society as serious political options. The three together are necessary and sufficient for a relation to exist between religious belief and political bias.

The earliest occurrence of such a relation is found in the school of "Christian Political Economy," which originated in the first *Essay on Population* of T. R. Malthus [1798] and which flourished during the first third of the nineteenth century through the work of J. B. Sumner, Richard Whately and Thomas Chalmers [Waterman, 1983]. Despite the seeming radicalism of classical Political Economy, its Christian practitioners succeeded in welding certain of its theorems to late eighteenth century Protestant theology so as to construct a powerful ideological defence of the economic and social *status quo*. As against the romantic anarchism of Godwin, Rousseau and Condorcet, and later the revolutionary and reformist workers' movements of early nineteenth century Britain, Malthus and his followers sought to show the inevitability of poverty, inequality, competition, private property, marriage and wage labour: and to exhibit these as examples of the goodness, wisdom and "contrivance" of God. At the very outset of modern "Christian Social Thought," the political bias imparted by religious belief was very definitely to the right.

It is important to distinguish this conservative tendency of Christian Political Economy from the superficially similar conservatism of nineteenth century Papal social teaching. The former was essentially modern in spirit, intellectually radical, coherent and sophisticated. The latter was merely a sign of the cultural lag which then existed between the Church of Rome and industrializing Europe, epitomized in the eightieth anathema of Pius IX's *Syllabus* (December 8, 1864) condemning the proposition that "the Roman Pontiff can, and ought to, reconcile himself, and come to terms with progress, liberalism and modern civilization" [Denzinger, 1937, para. 1780; Corrigan, 1937, p. 295].

Modern thought and the anti-capitalist trend

Before the appearance of the *Syllabus* and the strongly conservative encyclical *Rerum Novarum* (1891) of Leo XIII, the current of thought in English Christianity had turned away from acquiescence in capitalism and its putative consequences, poverty and inequality, and begun to run in a reformist and even socialist direction. "Christian Socialism" first appeared in England from 1848 to 1855 in the work of Maurice, Ludlow, Kingsley and others, and was in part a response to the economic conditions of the "Hungry Forties" [Norman, 1976, pp. 167–75]. After a temporary eclipse it reappeared in the 1870s and ever since that time, though with continued development, has exercised a growing influence upon the intellectual elite in English-speaking Christianity. Though the doctrines of Christian Political Economy were never entirely forgotten, and have to this day afforded support for such articulate conservatives as Margaret Thatcher [1978] and Enoch Powell [1977], there is a widely-held belief that a certain Leftward bias — not so much pro-socialist as anti-capitalist — is an unquestioned orthodoxy among Christian intellectuals of virtually every Protestant tradition, European and American no less than British. Meanwhile the social teaching of the Roman Church which in *Quadragesimo Anno* (1931) recognized a species of socialism with some claim to consideration [Chaigne, 1965, pp. 157–161], has moved since *Gaudiam et Spes* (1962) of the Second Vatican Council and *Populorum Progressio* (1967) of Paul VI to the (partially) "Marxist perspective" of John Paul II's encyclical *Laborem Exercens* (1981) [Baum, 1981b, p. 1]. In this the Roman hierarchy has been influenced by the revolutionary experience of the church in Latin America and elsewhere in the Third World, and by the semi-Marxist "Liberation Theology" which is its rationale. Liberation Theology has also been influential among Protestants and especially within the World Council of Churches, an official of which acknowledged lately that its staff were "nearly all socialists" [Norman, 1979, p. 26, n. 50].

Whether the bias exhibited by Christian intellectuals and church leaders is now in fact Marxist, or whether it is the more moderate "democratic socialism" preferred by Wogaman [1977] and asserted by E. R. Norman to be more characteristic of ecclesiastical elites [Norman, 1976, pp. 461–74] cannot be determined here. Nor can the extent of the Rightward bias increasingly to be found among theologically literate Christians, especially in the United States [Baum, 1981a]. The existence of various biases, claiming justification in some version of Christianity (or other religion) seems beyond doubt. The question to be settled is that of their significance.

The epistemological kernel

The most important issue is epistemological. Does religious belief supply the "values," and an autonomous social science the "facts": — as will be assumed in the second section of this paper? or can religion actually enhance our perception of the facts themselves? The latter was the view entertained by the Papacy, at any rate, down to the 1930s at least. In *Rerum Novarum* Leo XIII did not hesitate to assert empirical judgements in the same breath as theological pronouncements [Waterman, 1982]. In the account of that encyclical supplied by Pius XI, "the eyes of all, as often in the past, turned towards the Chair of Peter, that sacred depository of all truth," whereupon "the venerable Pontiff taught mankind new methods of dealing with social problems" [Pius XI, 1931, paras. 7, 9]. *Mutatis mutandis,* a similar view of the intellectual sovereignty of theology is not unknown among Protestants, especially those of the Neo-Calvinist, Kuyperian philosophical school [e.g., Vickers, 1975, p. 13]. Though the more liberal-minded Christians (most likely to exhibit a Leftward bias) have been less willing to assert the epistemic primacy of theology, something of this kind is sometimes implied by a willingness to ascribe political preferences to religious belief.

Even where this is not the case, the question of whether religious belief can properly determine political judgements is of the highest importance for believers, and of considerable interest to all students of politics. The former must discover what "biases," if any, their beliefs about God and the universe ought to dictate. The latter can never be indifferent to the springs of political behaviour.

II.   POSSIBLE EXPLANATIONS OF BIAS

It is useful to apply to the history of ideas a distinction between "internalist" and "externalist" explanations first developed to analyse rival methodological approaches in the history of science [Lakatos, 1978, I, pp. 102ff].

The internalist-externalist distinction

The distinction between "internal" and "external" history had been employed by Kuhn and others in a way which implied their complementarity. "Internal" history abstracted from the social matrix within which scientific inquiry took place, and concentrated solely upon the sequential development of ideas and theories. "External" history attempted "to set Science in a cultural context which might enhance understanding both of its development and of its effects" [Kuhn, 1968, p. 78]. Popper had attempted to show that "progress" in Science (as distinct from mere change) could and ought to be explained "internally" by reference to the "Logic of Scientific Discovery." Kuhn, however, seemed to commit himself to the view that explanation of change must be sought in the "external," sociological and psychological circumstances which brought about "Scientific Revolutions" and the triumph of new "paradigms" [Popper, 1959; Kuhn, 1962; Lakatos and Musgrave, 1970]. Lakatos therefore proposed an "unorthodox, new demarcation between 'internal' and 'external' history" [1978, I, p. 102, n. 1]: the former being an attempt to explain development in scientific understanding in terms of "normative methodologies" provided by the philosophy of science; the latter being at best a supplementary, at worst a rival attempt to explain the same phenomena by means of "empirical (socio-psychological)" investigations. "Internal" history is autonomous and primary: if a scientific development can be explained in terms of the rationality of the procedures which led to it, an "external" explanation, even if plausible, is redundant and ought to be excised by Ockham's razor.

In the spirit of this usage I shall employ the adjectives "internalist" and "externalist" to label the alternative explanations of any observed correlation between intellectual principles and political bias. An "internalist" explanation is one which displays a rational connection between a given set of principles and a particular set of political preferences sufficiently cogent to permit us to say that the former can account for the latter. An "externalist" explanation is one which discovers the causes of bias not in rational inference from coherent principles but in social and psychological determinants of human behaviour.

What if both internalist and externalist explanations exist, either of which is sufficient to account for a political preference? One must be redundant; to which ought the razor be applied? Suppose, for example, that a wealthy man produces intellectually satisfactory reasons for preferring a capitalist to a socialist order of society. Suppose his critics provide convincing evidence that his (though not most peoples') material interests are better served by capitalism than by socialism, and alleged that the "real" reason for his preference is the desire to maintain a privileged position. Does the latter show that the reasons given for preferring capitalism are merely "rationalization" or "ideology?" Or does the former make the externalist explanation unnecessary, as Lakatos argued that it did in the history of science?

The primacy of internalist explanation

Though Lakatos's reasons for asserting the sufficiency of internalist explanations are not available in this case, I shall suggest that here too a good internalist explanation makes otiose any externalist alternative. In the first place, as Schumpeter insists, "it cannot be emphasized too strongly that, like individual rationalizations, ideologies are not lies" [Schumpeter, 1954, p. 36]. Our ability to explain why a person supplied a particular reason for some action implies nothing, of itself, about the validity of that reason. It may be valid or invalid: and if valid, can be regarded as a satisfactory explanation of the action. Provided that generally accepted procedures exist for appraising the arguments themselves, it is simply irrelevant to speculate upon the social and psychological factors which entered into the mental processes of the person formulating those arguments. In the second place, to assert — when a satisfactory internalist explanation exists — that an equally satisfactory externalist explanation should be preferred is to incur the risk of self-refutation. For if a reason is supplied for the assertion, then he who makes it is committed to an internalist account of his own actions while denying it to others. But if no reason is given, the assertion is empty.

I shall take it, therefore, that internalist explanations of political preference have priority over externalist ones. The onus of proof will be taken to lie with those who urge the latter. Only if it appears that no coherent internalist explanation is or can be forthcoming is it helpful to explain political preference by external, non-rational causes. Before considering whether such might be the case, we must analyse further the concept of an internalist explanation as it applies to the particular case of a correlation between religious belief and political bias.

The application to religious belief and political bias

The existence of an internalist explanation of political bias is necessary but not sufficient to demonstrate that a set of political preferences has been determined by some set of religious beliefs. Three possibilities exist. In the first place, the political preferences could be shown to be deducible from principles not in conflict with, but not required by, the religious beliefs. Secondly, they could be shown to be deducible from any of several different sets of principles of which the religious beliefs were one. Finally, the political preferences could be shown to be uniquely deducible from the religious beliefs, such that no other set of intellectual principles could have given rise to those preferences.

If what I have so far argued is correct, the proper strategy for investigating the relation between religious belief and political bias is clear. First, we must inquire whether a set of religious beliefs can uniquely determine a set of political preferences. If so we need look no further for justifications of bias and can concern ourselves solely with the question of how variation in the latter is related to variation in the former. (What difference will it make to our political biases if we are Catholic rather than Protestant; Christian rather than Jew; believer rather than atheist?) If we fail to establish at least the possibility of a unique determination, we must turn secondly to other internalist explanations. Only in the event of our being unable to establish *any* convincing rationale for political preferences need we resort at last to externalist explanations of the kind suggested by Bryan Wilson [1966, 1976], Peter Berger [1977] and E. R. Norman [1976, 1979].

In the remainder of this paper I intend to make a start on this program by raising some of the more obvious difficulties in the way of establishing a unique causal relation between religious belief and political bias.

III.   THE NEXUS BETWEEN RELIGIOUS BELIEF AND POLITICAL BIAS

Is it possible in principle to make the judgement: "right understanding of some particular religious belief involves a rational preference for some particular form of social or economic organization?" If we can answer this question in the affirmative, then the way is open for those who wish to demonstrate that their own political biases are derived from their religious beliefs. It does not guarantee the success of their enterprise, of course, for it is still necessary to show that their biases are compatible only with the religious beliefs they themselves hold, and with no other beliefs, religious or secular. But it makes the task worth beginning.

The fact-value distinction

Consider the following assumptions.

i)   Suppose, for the time being at any rate, that judgements about the way in which society actually behaves ("factual judgements") can be distinguished, in principle at least, from judgements about the way in which it *ought* to behave ("normative judgements") and evaluations of actual behaviour ("value judgements"). For simplicity of exposition only, suppose that "normative judgements" can be subsumed under "value judgements."

ii) Assume that the procedures for arriving at factual judgements are independent, in principle at least, of the procedures for arriving at value judgements, in the sense that agreement could be reached about some social "fact" (e.g., that the rate of price inflation is 11 per cent p.a.) by those who differ about the evaluation of that fact (e.g., that it ought or ought not to be allowed to persist).

iii) Assume that the procedures for arriving at value judgements include the application ("theology") of an authoritative teaching of revealed religion ("belief"), but are not exhausted by it. Hence agreement upon values may be possible among those who disagree upon theology. The possibility of disagreement upon values among those who agree upon theology is ruled out by definition of "theology" in this context. But believers in the same body of authoritative teaching may differ in theology, and so in values.

Suppose that individuals entertain various "goals" for society as a whole, where a "goal" is some state of society preferred to all other possible states which are alternative to it (e.g., inflation at 2 per cent p.a. is preferred to inflation at any other higher or lower rate). Goals may or may not be independent of each other, and if independent may or may not conflict. Choice of goals necessitates value judgements.

The rational pursuit of goals requires the appropriate matching of means to ends. This in turn requires a *factual* judgement to be made about the outcomes to be expected, respectively, from the use of each of the set of possible means; and a *value* judgement about the worth of each possible outcome. When the outcomes of all possible alternative means have been estimated and evaluated, the most "efficient" set of means may be selected; meaning by that the set of means affording the most highly valued (net) outcome.

An illustration

An illustration may help. Suppose enough individuals agree that energy self-sufficiency is a proper goal for Canada for it to become an object of national policy. Value judgements must have entered into the selection of that goal (e.g., "Canadians ought not to be dependent upon foreigners for energy"). Suppose there is a choice of three means of achieving that goal: expansion of either hydro-electric or nuclear power production, or reduction of domestic demand for energy. Factual judgements are needed in estimating the full social consequences of each of these three means, and further value judgements in making these outcomes commensurate thus permitting rational choice.

Now, if we suppose that society may be organized in a number of different ways, it is clear that any particular form of social organization may afford the most efficient means of pursuing some goals but not others. A military hierarchy might afford the most efficient means of achieving the goal of national security, for example, but not the goals of rising real incomes or political freedom. The more interdependent are all goals the less likely is this to be the case. In an extreme Hobbesian world where one goal (peace) is taken to be necessary for all other possible goals, that form of social organization which is most efficient for the pursuit of peace is *ipso facto* the most efficient means to all other ends. But if goals are believed to be to any extent independent, then except where one form of social organization is judged to be the most efficient means of pursuing *all* goals, the choice of any one form of social organization will impose a cost defined as the value forgone by pursuing some goals by means other than the most efficient. Rational choice of the form of social organization will thus require a further complex fact-value judgement of the kind described above. The net value of the benefits of pursuing some goals under one form of social organization, and the costs of pursuing others under that form, must be compared with the corresponding costs and benefits of pursuing those goals under all other possible forms of social organization.

It will be seen that value judgements must enter into at least two and possibly three stages of the process of rational choice of alternative forms of social organization. The selection of goals must itself involve some value judgement, even if here too there is a mixture of fact and value judgement. The assignment of means to ends requires the evaluation of expected outcomes. And except where *either* the attainment of one goal is necessary for the attainment of all others *or* one form of social organization affords the most efficient means of pursuing all goals, the costs and benefits associated with each possible form of social organization must be evaluated and compared.

Value judgements and theology

Now, theology may, but need not, enter into the formation of value judgements (assumption iii above). The selection of full employment as a social goal, for example, might depend upon a particular understanding of the biblical account of Creation and Fall. Demand management as a means of achieving full employment might be preferred to import restrictions because of some theological understanding of the unity and interdependence of mankind (or, alternatively, because of a willingness to see economic efficiency as a corollary of the theological concept of "stewardship"). The market economy might be preferred to socialism (etc.) because although the latter is judged to afford the more efficient means of pursuing full employment, the value of this is outweighed by the sacrifice of political freedeom believed to be associated with the former. And this comparative evaluation of "work" and "freedom" might be based upon some understanding of biblical, or patristic, or papal (etc.), teaching about the nature of God and Man. But all these judgements might also be arrived at (and often are) without conscious or explicit recourse to any religious belief or theological system.

It would seem from this that in order to be able to say that some particular religious belief *is* compatible with rational preference for some particular form of social organization, it is only necessary that the following conditions be met:

(a) A set of social goals must be entertained;
(b) One particular form of social organization must be judged superior to any other in the pursuit of this set; in that the net value of all outcomes, good and bad, expected from the employment of this means must exceed the net value of all outcomes expected from the employment of any other means.

If theology plays no part in the value judgement required by (a) and (b), then *any* possible form of social organization is equally compatible (or incompatible) with the specifically *religious* beliefs of an individual who takes such a view. His choice between the various possibilities is made in the light of values derived from sources other than what he regards as the authoritative teaching of a revealed religion.

If theology enters into the choice of ends, or the evaluation of alternative expected outcomes, or both, then rational preference for this particular form of social organization is compatible with his religious beliefs.

Theology as a filter

It is clear from this that in order to be able to say that some particular religious belief *is not* compatible with rational preference for some particular form of social organization, a third condition must be satisfied, in addition to those specified in (a) and (b) above:

(c) Theology must play a part in the determination of value judgements required for (a) and (b).

A person who regards theology as relevant to the value judgements required in the rational choice of social organizations may be in agreement with those who differ from him in belief or theology; and may be in disagreement with those who profess the same beliefs and accept the same theology. In the first case he may agree with those of different belief or theology because the values relevant to the choice and appraisal of social ends and means are common to more than one belief, or more than one theology. In the second case, he may disagree with those of the same belief because he differs from them in theology (Ultramontane Catholics might differ from Liberation Theology Catholics); or because he differs in the factual judgements required in the estimation of alternative possible outcomes; or both.

Theology as a determinant

It may be noted that the conditions which permit the negative judgement, "this particular religious belief is *not* compatible with rational preference for this particular form of social organization" leave open the question of whether theology is necessary for the value judgements entailed by it. Two alternatives exist:

A. The value judgements resulting in the preference of some other form of social organization to the one in question could not have been made except by one professing the particular religious belief and accepting the same theology;

B. Those same value judgements, though determined wholly or in part by theological considerations, could equally have been determined without reference to this particular theology, or indeed to any theology at all.

On the face of it, it might seem that alternative A is the "strong" case of a unique correspondance between a particular theology and preference for a particular social organization, whereas B is the "weak" case permitting the compatibility of political preference with more than one theological position. On examination, this distinction disappears. This is because judgements of fact, as well as judgements of *value,* are required for rational preference. Under case A, all who hold religious belief B1, accept theology T1 and agree upon the set of necessary factual judgements F1 will prefer social organization S1 to all other. But it is logically possible that some who hold different beliefs B2 and theology T2 could nevertheless prefer S1 because they make a different set of factual judgements F2. As an example, consider the following: F1 "Socialism results in more equality than capitalism"; B1, T1 "For theological reasons the benefits of equality when taken together with the disadvantages of socialism outweigh the advantages of capitalism"; F2 "Socialism results in less equality than capitalism"; B2, T2 "For theological reasons the benefits of inequality when taken together with the disadvantages of socialism outweigh the advantages of capitalism." It is evident that both (F1, B1, T1) and (F2, B2, T2) are consistent with rational preference for S1.

Now if it were possible for there to be agreement on F, this case could be ruled out. Except in what seems to be the unlikely event of this agreement, however, it would seem that although it is possible to assert that a particular set of religious beliefs is or is not compatible with rational preference for a particular form of social organization, *it cannot be maintained that belief and theology can ever require such a preference.* Moreover, it may easily be the case in practice:

First: that those who agree on belief differ on theology, and who therefore, even if they agree on matters of fact, will differ in their social preference;

Secondly: that those who agree on belief and theology may differ in matters of fact, and therefore in their social preference;

Thirdly: that those who differ on belief or theology may also disagree on matters of fact in such a way as to agree in their social preferences.

A possible objection

At this point, it is appropriate to consider a possible objection to the analysis so far. People do not usually assert a compatibility (or incompatibility) between religious belief and *rational preference* for a particular social organization, but between the former and the particular social organization itself. They rather say, for example, as in the dictum quoted from William Temple at the beginning of this paper, that for the Christian, the choice is "socialism or heresy," implying that right understanding of religious belief is incompatible with any other form of social organization. Aside from the counter that this strong assertion is virtually denied by the argument so far — as Temple himself realized by 1942, when he conceded that it is of the utmost importance that the church acting corporately should not commit itself to any particular policy [Temple, 1976, p. 40] — this way of speaking is difficult to justify. All that can be meant by saying that S1 is incompatible with B1 would seem to be that given the theological understanding T1 and the relevant factual judgements F1, the net value of the expected outcomes of S1 is exceeded by that of some other possibility S2. Suppose, therefore, one is treated to an assertion such as the following: "Both constitutional monarchy and republican socialism are compatible with Christianity but fascism is not." The only way to make any sense of this is to translate as: "Given my theological understanding of Christianity and my judgement of the relevant facts, it is rational for me to prefer either constitutional monarchy or republican socialism to fascism, but not to prefer either of the first two to the other."

IV. A RECAPITULATION

The tendency of my argument in the previous section has been to cast doubt upon the possibility of being able to say that a particular set of religious beliefs entails a particular set of political preferences or "biases." I ought to conclude by reminding the reader of the more important assumptions and factual judgements on which my conclusions depend. First and foremost, of course, is the distinction between judgements of "fact" and judgements of "value."

The fact-value disjunction is under attack from at least three different schools of thought. Marxists and others influenced by Hegelian metaphysics speak of the "dialectical" nature of thought and action, regard the distinction between fact and value as "static" and therefore unsatisfactory, and assert that all "facts" are "value-laden" and at least potentially "ideological." Neo-Calvinists of the Dooyeweerdian school take the view that true knowledge—of any kind—is possible only to those who accept a "biblical" (and/or "Reformational") faith, and hence that "positive economics" (etc.) is an illusion and must be replaced by "Christian economics" (etc.). And within the mainstream, English-speaking school of analytical philosophy, Hume's Law ("ought" cannot be deduced from "is"—a primary source of the fact-value disjunction) is at least a matter of debate. It is easier for those who hold such views to disparage the kind of analysis presented here than to offer any coherent alternative. Until such emerges it seems reasonable to maintain—provisionally, of course—some kind of autonomy for scientific inquiry, not only into "Nature" conceived as distinct from the human investigator, but also into "Nature" conceived to include human societies and individuals. Though in one sense it may still be true that Theology is "Queen of the Sciences," the onus of proof would seem to lie with those who claim that without Theology (etc.) no scientific knowledge is possible.

In the second place, the analysis of political judgements I have elaborated assumes as a matter of fact that the costs and benefits associated with alternative social organizations must be evaluated and compared. As I acknowledge, this will not be so either when the attainment of one goal is necessary for the attainment of all others (the Hobbesian case), or when one form of social organization is the most satisfactory means of pursuing all goals. In either of these cases, of course, there can be no disagreement among rational persons, whatever their religious or ethical beliefs, about political preference.

Finally, even when none of these objections to my argument apply, it would still be proper to assert a necessary connection between religious belief and political bias if it were possible in principle for there to be agreement about all the relevant facts. An argument might be constructed to rule this out if it could be shown that "scientific" or empirical knowledge was of its nature less certain, more tentative and corrigible than "dogmatic" or religious knowledge. But to do so would take us too far afield and I will resist the temptation to try.

REFERENCES

Baum, G. "Neo-Conservative Critics of the Churches," *Concilium* 141 (1981a).
_____. "John Paul II's Encyclical on Labor," *The Ecumenist* 20:1 (November/December 1981): 1–4.
Berger, P. L. *Facing Up to Modernity.* New York: Basic Books, 1977.
Chaigne, Herve. "The Catholic Church and Socialism," *Cross-Currents* (Spring, 1965).
Corrigan, Raymond. *The Church and the Nineteenth Century.* Milwaukee: Bruce, 1938.
Denzinger, H. *Enchiridion Symbolorum.* Frigburgi: Herder, 1937.
Kuhn, T. S. "Science: the History of Science," in Sills, D. L. (ed.) *International Encyclopedia of the Social Sciences.* New York: Macmillan, 1968, Vol. 14, pp. 74–83.
Kristol, Irving. "The Disaffection from Capitalism," in Novak, M. (ed.), *Capitalism and Socialism.* Washington, D.C.: A.E.I., 1979.
Lakatos, Imre. *The Methodology of Scientific Research Programmes.* Philosophical Papers, Vol. I (Worral, J. and Currie, G., eds.). Cambridge: Cambridge University Press, 1978.
Lakatos, Imre and Musgrave, A. (eds.). *Criticism and the Growth of Knowledge.* Cambridge: Cambridge University Press, 1970.
McGuire, M.R.P. "Ambrose," in *New Catholic Encyclopedia.* New York: McGraw-Hill, 1967, Vol. I, pp. 373–75.
Norman, E. R. *Church and Society in England, 1770–1970.* Oxford: Clarendon, 1976.
_____. *Christianity and World Order.* Oxford: Oxford University Press, 1979.
Pius XI, Pope. *Quadragesimo Anno.* On Reconstructing the Social Order... in Commemoration of the Fortieth Anniversary of the Encyclical "Rerum Novarum." Oxford: Catholic Truth Society, 1931.
Popper, K. *The Logic of Scientific Discovery.* London: Hutchinson, 1959.
Powell, Enoch. *Wrestling with the Angel.* London: Sheldon, 1977.
Preston, R. H. "Introduction" to Temple (1976).

Schumpeter, J. A. *History of Economic Analysis.* London: Allen and Unwin, 1954.

Skinner, Quentin. *The Foundations of Modern Political Thought.* Cambridge: Cambridge University Press, 1978.

Temple, William. *Christianity and Social Order.* London: S.P.C.K., 1976.

Thatcher, Margaret. "'I Believe': a Speech on Christianity and Politics" at St. Lawrence Jewry, Next Guildhall, London, Thursday, 30th March, 1978. (Conservative Central Office Press Release 442/78).

Tully, James. *A Discourse on Property: John Locke and His Adversaries.* Cambridge: Cambridge University Press, 1980.

Vickers, Douglas. *Man in the Maelstrom of Modern Thought.* Nutley, N.J.: Presbyterian and Reformed Publishing Co., 1975.

Viner, Jacob. *Religious Thought and Economic Society: Four Chapters of an Unfinished Work.* (Melitz, J. and Winch, Donald, eds.). Durham, N. C.: Duke University Press, 1978.

Waterman, A. M. C. "The Ideological Alliance of Political Economy and Christian Theology." *Journal of Ecclesiastical History,* 1983.

_____. "John Locke's Theory of Property and Christian Social Thought," *Review of Social Economy,* 1982.

Wilson, B. R. *Religion in a Secular Society: a Sociological Comment.* London: Watts, 1966.

_____. *Contemporary Transformations of Religion.* London: Oxford University Press, 1976.

Wogaman, J. P. *Christians and the Great Economic Debate.* London: S.C.M., 1977.

Discussion

Edited by: Kenneth G. Elzinga

Anthony Waterman: When I prepared these remarks, I never supposed that I would actually have Philip Wogaman sitting on my immediate left side. And I hope he doesn't mind being used as a peg on which to hang them.

When Walter Block and Paul Heyne and I first got together nearly two years ago to plan this conference, one of the questions in our minds was whether or not the kind of explanation of political bias, thought to be observable among various ecclesiastical dignitaries, could in fact be explained, as E. R. Norman was proposing to explain, in terms of their sociology. In other words, could one say that theologians were taking a particular political stand merely because they were ecclesiastical bureaucrats, or members of a new class, or something of that kind? Or, as against what Norman seemed to be arguing, could there be a valid connection established between the religious beliefs they expressed and the political biases they exhibited?

What my paper was intended to do was to set out what you might call the logical structure of the question. How far is it possible in general, without reference to any particular religious belief, to establish some kind of necessary connection between religious belief and political bias?

My first point is that the idea of an option between alternative systems is quite modern and revolutionary; and therefore, that in an important sense, what is sometimes called "Christian social thought" is necessarily a post-Enlightenment and post-industrialization phenomenon. So, what I'm thinking of as Christian or, more generally, as religious social thought, is for reasons I explain in the first part of my paper, a novel thing in human history. This is something which belongs essentially to modern times, and to the history of the industrialized West. That's my first point, and you may well wish to debate that.

The second thing I want to underline is this. I have taken a particular stand here, for purposes of constructing my argument, which I'm well aware is vulnerable to objection. I try to answer some of those objections in the last part of the paper. But it's quite important to realize that my argument rests crucially upon the assumption that, for purposes of this discussion at any rate, we can draw some kind of distinction between questions of fact and questions of value.

The third point I want to underline is the particular way in which I'm going to employ two terms, "internalist" and "externalist," which I have lifted from a different discourse from Imre Lakatos's — discussion of the Kuhn-Popper debate on certain important questions concerned with the history and philosophy of science.

It seems to me that the distinction between "internalist" and "externalist" explanations of scientific progress, which Lakatos and Feyerabend and Kuhn discuss in that particular debate, are not irrelevant to the kinds of questions we want to discuss here. It seems to me that E. R. Norman, for example, is saying that an externalist explanation was sufficient to explain the behaviour of leftist, ecclesiastical bureaucrats, and therefore we need not take it seriously.

The last point I want to underline is what I thought was the most significant. I attempted in Part II of my paper to argue that although it is possible to assert that a particular set of religious beliefs is or is not compatible with rational preference for a particular form of social organization, it cannot be maintained that belief and theology can ever require such a preference.

Seymour Siegel: I want to say that the distinction between internal and external explanations is very relevant to our discussion. In theological discussion, the internal/external explanations are understood in the reverse way. That is, the internal explanation is something that a person who is participating fully in something gives, whereas an external one is just a spectator. And the participant in a faith community understands things differently while he's participating in them, than someone who is looking at it from the outside — the distinction made by Richard Niebuhr and other important theologians.

In understanding and discussing this question, we have to make a distinction between "faith," "religion," and "theology." Faith is understood, as Buber put it, as the central idea of a life system, I'm quoting him:

> In distinction to a thought system which illuminates and eluci-
> dates the spheres of being from a central idea, a life system is the

real unit in which again and again, the spheres of existence or historical group build up around a supreme principle.

And the assertion is that no great, or even not so great, civilization or culture can function and live without being built around (in Buber's words), "a supreme principle." What the supreme principle of this civilization is becomes one of the most important questions you can ask.

Or consider the celebrated definition of Tillich that "faith is being ultimately concerned"; and that no human existence can continue to function without having some concern that is above all other concerns; and since "faith is being ultimately concerned," this means that either a collective or an individual cannot function without a faith. And that this faith does colour all preferences and all interpretations of existence and world views; and that therefore given the structure of individuals and societies, or civilizations (to use Buber's phrase), all explanations of religious preferences have to be (in terms of Professor Waterman) "internalist," because they are the expressions of these basic orientations, which are part of human existence and social existence.

Religion, which is a symbolic expression in an institutional form of this ultimate concern or faith, is partially influenced by the faith itself, and by external factors in the way it is symbolized; and therefore participates in both alternatives as they were presented to us by Dr. Waterman.

Theology, which is of course a rational or at least putatively rational explanation, both of the faith principle and of religion, is partially internal insofar as it expressed the original faith, and external insofar as the faith has to be expressed in terms which are known to the cultural situation of the time.

Therefore in our strategies that we may develop out of this conference, to set the theological agenda right (that is in the economic sphere), we will have to stress a campaign of education for people to speak about theology in economics, and the basic truth of economics. And that people who speak about economics and don't know what it's all about are just speaking about what they don't know. And therefore, it may be entertaining, but not the least bit useful.

In other words, what I'm saying is that everybody has some kind of faith, and every great civilization has some kind of faith; and that therefore, the internalist explanations are always right. The only question is whether they are the total truth or just the partial truth. This depends on historical developments and the capacity of human beings, which is apparently limitless, to deceive themselves and to speak in a name, in their own, or self-interest when they say they are speaking in God's name or the Divine's interest.

Philip Wogaman: I'm reminded reading through many of the papers of a statement by John Courtney Murray that "genuine disagreement is a rare achievement." I would imagine that over the course of three days, we will arrive even closer at genuine disagreement than we have now. I cite this only to say that I'm not sure I understand Anthony Waterman's paper well enough to be sure that I disagree at every point where I think perhaps I do, and I appreciate many aspects of the paper.

I did want, however, to rescue the quotation from my book, *The Great Economic Debate,* and relate it to a couple of points which may or may not be fundamental to the thesis of the paper. First of all, my use of the term "bias" is in the context of my discussion of "presumption" in the world of judgement. It's my thesis that most of our thinking in ethical matters is structured by certain presumptions to which we accord the benefit of the doubt, and require the burden of proof to be placed against it.

I think that the term "bias" often is used colloquially to suggest an irrational view of things, or even racial bias, or something of that sort; but the use of the word "bias" here is not in that sense.

Now I have used the term bias in the passage that Anthony Waterman cited in his paper, particularly to suggest that religious views can significantly affect our thinking, but that their initial bias or presumption always ought to be checked against other realities (including the factual, or externalist dimension).

Christians and Buddhists of different kinds can agree on some things and disagree on some things. A Christian may agree with a Buddhist and disagree with a fellow Christian on another point, and so on. But that doesn't mean that a religious view is not functioning significantly to determine the ethical outcome. I make this point to rescue the thought that religious conceptions of society are very important, and that all of us probably operate with them consciously or unconsciously — and that we do well if we do it consciously.

Roger Shinn: I want to find out how much genuine disagreement there is between Anthony Waterman and Seymour Siegel. Their language might appear to lead to a direct clash, but I'm not sure it does. Anthony Waterman doubts that a particular set of religious beliefs entails a particular set of political preferences; Seymour Siegel says faith *must* involve political preferences. The presence and then absence of the word "particular" may mean that there is not so big a disagreement as there may seem to be. But to put it in terms of a test question to each of you: to Anthony Waterman, you'll recall the time when the German confessing church came to the judgement, it had to say "no" to the Nazi system. It was a very particular path not shared by all German Christians, and in fact opposed by the party called German Christians. But the confessing church said, "Our religious faith entails opposition here." And I would wonder if you would rule that out, in your doubt that religious belief in that instance entailed political preferences.

And then to Seymour Siegel, I'd ask the reverse of it. How much room would you allow for a faithful Jew or Christian to differ from the social conclusions that you've come to in your paper? That is, are you in the position of saying, "One who comes to different positions, really is not being a faithful Jew or Christian?" Are you saying that that person might be as faithful as you or I, but understands the situation differently?

Anthony Waterman: I grant that it's logically possible that one set of religious beliefs can determine a particular political response, say to Hitler's Germany; and that another set of beliefs, religious or otherwise, can also determine the same response. There are others besides Christians who said "no" in Germany, who said "no" to Nazism, you see.

What I want to ask, is whether or not Christian theology has anything particular to say about this. I think that unless a unique correspondence can be established, then one is bound to be skeptical about the claims of the religious believers to say that their position is in fact actuated by religious belief, and not in fact unwittingly, perhaps, by other circumstances.

Seymour Siegel: I think the question, if I can recast Roger Shinn's*

---

*All conference participants invariably referred to each other by their first names. For ease of identification, however, surnames have been added — eds.

question, is one that puzzles people—both laymen and professional clerics. That is, "How is it possible for someone to profess the same tradition—to be a Jew, or Christian, or Moslem, or a Buddhist as you mentioned—and come to diametrically opposite conclusions on important issues?"

And the liberal response to this is that each view is right. And then the old response to the obvious question, "How can they both be right?" is "So, you're right too." (laughter)

Now that, I think, makes everything more or less irrelevant, because if everybody's right, nobody's right. I think it was Gilbert who said, "If everybody is somebody, no one is anybody." (laughter)

But I think to a certain extent it isn't wrong, too, because a lot of it has to do with interpretation of the main symbols of and teachings of the religious community. And a lot has to do with the assessment of the *facts,* both as they now exist and as they might unfold in the future.

So, to take one example, if people thought that the conquest of Vietnam on the part of the communists would lead to greater troubles for the world, then you have one view on the Vietnam war. Or if you think it would not lead to greater troubles, then you would have another view. Whereas you could both share the same value, even the same symbol and the same faith, but come to different conclusions on the basis of assessment—true or false assessments—of the facts.

Now I think what we have been preaching here, more or less, is that when it comes to economics that the preachments of a lot of people on economics suffer from the fact that the economic realities are neither assessed nor understood, nor properly predicted.

And then the other strategy, which is a very difficult one (which I call the "strategy of truth") is to say to the person who disagrees with you, that you are not expressing your faith, you're expressing some other interest. And that you better shape up and study, or pray or do something, so that you understand and commit yourself more fully to your faith principle.

Murdith McLean: I think Anthony Waterman is making far too high a requirement on the believer, and I'm going to speculate why. But first of all, I want to show why it's too high a requirement. Surely, it's simply a mistake to argue that in order to show that faith could entail some political conviction, or some political position, you must show that it alone should entail that position. There's simply and clearly a difference between saying, "religious position A entails political stance B," and saying that "it entails it uniquely—that A alone entails B." And when I read the paper through, I wondered why Anthony made that claim. Now, as a matter of fact I think the way the paper goes, not much rests on it.

I think that the reason Anthony is making that claim, is that he wants to discuss, at least in general terms, a larger question than whether faith entails a certain political position or commitment. He wants to explore the question as to whether the faith has something really specific to say. And by specific he means something that nobody else is saying.

Now I don't think in order to find that out, we've got to say that a faith condition is going to entail any specific political stance. We would then have to explore a whole range of questions about what the faith commits us to. Not just a stand on this political issue, or this political party in this setting, but a whole bunch of things. I don't think anyone will question the fact that a faith commitment entails a political commitment, just because it doesn't entail it uniquely.

David Friedman: The comments that Murdith McLean made at the beginning were roughly the ones I wanted to start with, for I was also puzzled about why, in order to say that religious faith implied political views, you had to have political views that nothing else could imply. And looking at the paper, it seemed to me that the argument is not one of logical necessity, but somehow practical necessity. If I understand what the author is saying correctly, it is not that it couldn't be that your religious faith implied a political conclusion which other people reached for other reasons, but only that if you observe other people reaching these conclusions who don't have your religious faith, that makes you suspect that perhaps your claim that you reached it from the religious faith is wrong.

And from that standpoint, it would seem to me, the crucial question is whether the other people who reached the same conclusions have things other than the religious faith in common. That is, if we observe that a Christian who is also an American liberal intellectual reaches the same conclusions as an atheist who is an American liberal intellectual, that casts reasonable suspicion on his claim that it's a Christian conclusion, although it might be.

On the other hand, if you observe that an American who is a liberal intellectual reached the same conclusion as a Buddhist who is an anarcho-capitalist, it would seem to me you have a fairly clear case of simply two different arguments that happen to lead to the same conclusion; and there's no reason to suspect either of the people in this regard.

Edmund Opitz: I suspect that the referent for the phrase "religious belief" has not been adequately pinned down. People may assume that John Doe's religious beliefs are the creeds he repeats, sometimes thoughtlessly, every Sunday or at least periodically; and John Doe may think that those are his religious beliefs. But, in fact, are not his religious beliefs the assumptions or the premises upon which he habitually acts in given situations?

Ronald Preston: It seems to me that religious beliefs must in some way bear on political and economic issues, or they become unreal. The problem is that within the religious beliefs themselves, there is a plurality of articulation of their significance. And also, you cannot make any judgement about their bearing without making some judgement about the world itself at the time. You are involved in making some judgements for which you depend upon information, other people's opinions, expertise, and your own life experience.

A very subtle situation arises at this point, because whilst part of the time you're coming up against what one might properly call "bare facts," there are, however, very few "bare facts," and the weighting of the "facts" in your own mind is going to be affected by your religious belief. Therefore, we have this continually indeterminate situation with wide varieties of interpretation. And I don't see that we'll ever get out of it. I think one might make some judgements that some facts are more plausible than others. And often that's what a lot of inter-disciplinary discussion is about. But I don't think we're ever going to do more than that.

Anthony Waterman: In order to make a political judgement, both a value commitment and a factual judgement have to be made. And insofar as those who share value commitments may differ on factual judgements, we can have the situation in which two people starting from the same beliefs can differ; or alternatively, as I tried to show in my paper, we can have a situation in which two people of widely differing value commitments can, because of correspondingly differing factual judgements, arrive at the same belief. Unless one can establish a unique correspondence, then one hasn't said very much to that point about the cash value of religious commitment, as a determinant of a political position.

David Friedman: I noticed that everybody seems implicitly to be agreeing that religions are mostly about values, and while that may be a reasonable normative statement, it's not a true empirical statement. The Mormon religion, for example, includes some propositions about the early history of the New World. I think this is typical of religions, that they include positive propositions. In general it seems to me that a lot of this talk is distinguishing between, as it were, value systems and sets of positive propositions, and not recognizing that religions as we meet them in the real world are generally a mix of those two things.

Geoffrey Brennan: I think that David Friedman is absolutely right when he says that Christianity does involve a set of factual propositions which have the status of facts. But I'm not sure that's a very profitable intervention in one important sense, because I don't think that the facts that Christianity offers, together with the values (if we can in any sense compartmentalize those things), are sufficient, by common consent to generate necessarily any particular or specific political belief. The question that Roger Shinn was raising seems to me to be germane here. If we take the set of possible religious positions, however we understand those, including perhaps certain embodied facts or particular theological positions and certain particularized facts, then it seems clear that different understandings of either or both can result in different sorts of political positions.

The question that I think might reveal something useful is, "Is it true that the set of propositions that are involved in Christianity, although being congruent with possibly a range of particular positions, nevertheless excludes some?" It seems to me that we could argue that certain political positions are, at base, incompatible with Christianity, because those political positions contain some amalgam of values and facts which are logically inconsistent with those central to Christian understanding. If so, I think we can say something about the compatibility, or otherwise, between particular religious positions and particular political positions, without necessarily saying that Christianity logically implies a single political position. I mean, it's just a more modest exercise of delineating a range.

Kenneth Boulding: One of the interesting questions of this conference is whether there is such a thing as error in evaluations. The situation is that our evaluations may be just as unstable as our images of facts. Our valuations are also going to depend on our images of facts.

Let me give you an illustration. I once asked a group of church people to write down what they thought was the proportion of the national income going to labour. And their answers ranged all the way from 10 per cent to 90 per cent. And obviously if you thought 10 per cent was going to labour, you'd have rather a different political view than if you thought 90 per cent, I'm sure. Now, this fact is something that is reasonably in the public domain. The proportion is about 75–80 per cent. This is one of the many facts which are in the public domain that most people don't know. And yet this profoundly affects their evaluations. I don't think you can separate the images of fact from the images of value. I look on this process of learning as the process of the detection of error by testing, whether casual or organized, and which gradually reduces the proportion of error and increases the proportion of truth.

I'm not at all sure that the real world conforms to any simple logic, at least if Einstein's right, so that if we try to impose formal logic on the real world, we are apt to find ourselves in very real serious error. I have very little faith in it, really. However, I do have a certain amount of faith in identities or what you might call tautologies. I think all we really know are tautologies. And yet it is very important to find these out.

Murdith McLean: I'm going to attempt to impose a view as to what the central issue is in Anthony Waterman's paper, and try an attack on it. I think the central position is this. Anthony is suggesting to us that it is in principle impossible that a faith position by itself should entail a political commitment; because in any political commitment two components are involved, only one of which can be provided by a religious conviction. The two components are, namely, values of preference, or whatever you want to call them, and another part which we'll call "factual judgements."

And the reason why it's in principle impossible that religious convictions by themselves should lead to political convictions is that they cannot by themselves supply the matters of judgement about empirical matters — a point that Professor Shinn made in his paper as well.

I think if Anthony is right about that, then he's right in his conclusion. I mean, then he's got his paper's position. That is, if it's true that people who share a religious commitment but could, with all rationality continue to disagree about the facts, then it is, in principle, impossible that a religious position by itself should entail a political commitment.

But it's not bad to remind people that there are some facts that it's pretty hard to dispute. I know, in principle, it's possible we might come to doubt the spherical shape of the earth, and the general distribution of material in the solar system. And I know, in principle, that it is possible, but it's not likely; and at least those people right now who are making judgements about this matter are likely to agree. Let's at least settle for that.

Now I want to say in principle — and maybe we could come down to the practicalities of our present situation later on, because I know economics is in a tortured state — but, in principle, it seems to me possible anyway, that we might well come to several judgements that the facts in question are of a kind that rational people are more than likely to agree about. And where that's the case, political convictions will follow from religious convictions.

Anthony Waterman: What I mean by values are evaluations which have proceeded via religious belief from commitment to some set of supposed facts, which are generally described in Christian discourse, at least, as *revelation.* To be sure, ultimately, Christian values come from supposed facts about what God did or said. In that sense, I admit to the blurring of the distinction between fact and value.

And what I call "facts," roughly speaking, correspond to at least a systematization of those observations which we can all make of what the eighteenth century and natural theologians called "nature."

So, I'm pinning my colours here to the mast of the traditional distinction between revelation and nature, as sources of information relevant to this kind of discussion.

My other point is to thank Murdith McLean, not only for what he has just said, but for his help in constructing this paper at a much earlier stage. I do in fact concede his point, as he well knows, for I say in my paper, "If it were possible, in principle, for there to be agreement about all the relevant facts, then indeed it might be possible, in principle, for there to be the kind of special correspondence (which I am discussing) between religious faith and political belief." So those, I would say, those who want to take issue with my scepticism, would be those who think that it is possible, in principle, for there to be agreement about the relevant facts; those who want to side with the sceptics would be those who think that it is difficult, if not impossible, in principle, for there to be agreement about the relevant facts—facts as I have now defined them.

PART TWO

INTERNALIST EXPLANATIONS: THEOLOGICAL ISSUES

Chapter 2

Theological Perspective on Economics

J. Philip Wogaman

I. INTRODUCTION

Does theology have any particular contribution to make to economic thought and policy-making? Generations of economists have thought not. Economists as diverse as Adam Smith and Karl Marx or Kenneth Galbraith and Milton Friedman have done their work as though theology were completely irrelevant. At the same time, of course, many theologians have managed to write theology as if economics didn't matter either. It is beyond the scope of this paper to struggle with the reasons why Western thought has been so fragmented in the past couple of centuries. But this fragmentation has made it difficult for all of us to relate our economic decisions to other aspects of life, and it has perpetuated the notion that theology pertains to a very specialized "religious" sphere of our existence.

Properly understood, theology can never be specialized in that sense. Theology is concerned about those things we value most — the objects of our worship. It is preeminently occupied, as H. R. Niebuhr observed, with our centre of value: the supreme good on the basis of which we evaluate all other things.[1] It is concerned with what we take to be ultimate in good, with the good that we consider to be self-evidently good. If this is so, then theology absolutely cannot be bypassed by those who wish to think responsibly about any human values. For theology contains the answers we must come to finally when asked why certain values are preferable to others and why we have designated some things as good and others as evil. Theology is inevitable, even in treating "problems," for problems presuppose values and values presuppose their theological validation. Problems are defined by purposes or goals which, in turn, reflect values. There can be no such thing as pure pragmatism. Problem-solving practicality is measured by utility in achieving purposes and fulfilling values.[2]

Broadly speaking, economics refers to the production and distribution of scarce goods. The dynamics of production and distribution can be detailed in more or less value-free terms once the values to be produced are given and the purposes of distribution set forth. But without that value frame of reference in the background, economics is nearly meaningless. It is difficult enough to measure the accomplishments of an economic policy or system in achieving its stated value goals. There is only confusion when we try to measure economic performance in the absence of *any* value goals. Nor is it much help to treat the value goals as things we all agree upon. Attitudes vary even on such things as inflation, recession, full employment, increasing the gross national product (inflation is a problem to most of us, but it may be more a *solution* to some people with large mortgages or indexed incomes). Efforts to quantify units of "utility" generally flounder on the fact that utility means so many different things to different people. Paul Samuelson's self-evident but highly misleading formula that "happiness equals material consumption over desire"[3] seems to suggest that a net increase in material consumption increases overall happiness. Yet those who see material consumption in social as well as individual terms and those who advocate "small is beautiful" may have a very different perspective from those who measure their own fulfillment in terms of personal consumption.[4]

In any event, the theological frame of reference is ultimately very important — even decisive — in determining what matters to us in economic life. To accept this, we need not be believers in any one particular theological viewpoint. But everybody believes in something; everyone has some values which supersede and give point to other values; everyone has a centre of value, which is to say, a theological orientation. Sometimes that theological orientation is not the creedal tradition to which one formally subscribes; sometimes it is. But whatever one's acknowledged religious views, the decisive question which serves to locate our *real* theology is, What do we value most?

II. THEOLOGICAL ENTRY POINTS

How are we to "apply" theology to economics? Often enough Christians have thought they could find specific biblical texts to apply directly to specific contemporary problems. The Parable of the Talents (Matt. 25:14–30) could be taken as a mandate for capitalistic enterprise and St. Paul's "If any one will not work, let him not eat" (2 Thess. 3:10b) could be treated as a judgement against welfare programs. (Of course, one would then have to deal with the many biblical passages condemning love of wealth and failure to fulfil obligations to the poor.) Such specific texts may be important parts of the tradition: but applying them directly to contemporary problems can greatly distort our perspective. Some of the particular passages now quoted to settle contemporary issues were never intended to have that kind of use, even at the time of writing. And those passages that did speak to such problems in their own time may be misleading when applied too directly to current issues today. It is debatable, for instance, whether St. Paul actually supported the institution of slavery (some passages suggest that he did, or at least that he did not challenge it in his advice to slaves). But whether he did or not, it would greatly distort our understanding of how Christianity should be related to economics if we were to use such passages to justify slavery in our own time. Biblical writings are on different levels. Some convey the core meanings of the faith while others apply those meanings to the ancient situation.

Those who wish to apply the faith tradition to contemporary issues as profoundly as possible will struggle first to understand the core meanings and then reflect creatively on how those meanings illuminate contemporary issues.

To do this, we need to seek the theological "entry points" which help relate the core meanings of faith to the most important underlying economic issues. These entry points are refractions from the central light; they are ways of seeing the core theological truth when we allow contemporary issues to pose important questions for theological response. Such an approach to theological application is largely intuitive and creative, but that does not mean that it is just subjective. The faith tradition and factual world are objective reference points. But the faith tradition is profound — which means it challenges ever deepening levels of insight. And the factual world is almost infinitely complex — which means we should be always modest about the finality of our judgements.

Bearing this in mind, I wish to suggest six useful theological entry points into the meaning of economic life. These six points are not offered as a complete "theology of economics," nor can this paper exhaust the meaning of even these points. Nevertheless, such entry points can help us work toward a theological perspective on the economic issues of our time.

Physical existence as God's creation

Were theology to be committed to an altogether other-worldly conception of life, it could dispense readily enough with economics. At best, the material world would be completely neutral or a kind of necessary evil. There would be no point in pursuing its meaning on a theological plane. But the main stream of Christianity has persistently rejected an exclusively *spiritualistic* self-understanding, from the time of early Gnosticism to the present. Against spiritualism it has affirmed the doctrine of creation.[5] The material world is good because God created it to reflect good purposes. The theme is struck forcefully in the Genesis accounts of creation, in a number of the great Psalms, in the Sermon on the Mount, and elsewhere in scripture. While the goodness of the created material world is affected by recognition of evil, the doctrine of creation commits theology to a basically positive attitude toward economic life and material well-being. Material life is not evil; it is a good to be embraced and enhanced and celebrated as God's gift.

The priority of grace to works

Biblical faith is covenantal, through and through, which means that it understands human life to be in personal relationship with the source of all being. It is this personal relationship that confers ultimate meaning upon both individual and social existence. We matter because we matter to God; and we are brothers and sisters in a moral community because we are the family of God. Our relationship with God and our relationships with one another are moral in quality. They are in fact the essence of morality. Yet they are not moral because of our own moral action in the first instance; rather they are moral because of God's gift. As expressed most profoundly in the parables of Jesus and the writings of St. Paul, God's love is the "given" with which we start. It is not something we have to earn in order to receive: "for he makes his sun rise on the evil and on the good, and sends rain on the just and on the unjust." (Matthew 5:45) St. Paul uses the juridical metaphor to say that we are saved by grace and not by works of the law. We are affirmed by God even before we have done anything to deserve it. Indeed, Paul argues that none of us *do* deserve what we receive. Those who take pride in their moral accomplishments tend to be self-righteous, and self-righteousness is in fact the most insidious spiritual danger of all. When we are self-righteous we are unable to respond gratefully to the goodness of life as a gift and we are estranged from our brothers and sisters whom we judge morally inferior to ourselves.

While the pertinence of this to economics might not appear self-evident the relationship of "grace" to "works" is in fact an issue of watershed importance. If, in the ultimate moral perspective, justice is the proper rewarding of behaviour, then we have a clear paradigm for economic organization. People should get what they "deserve," nothing more, nothing less. But if justice is patterned in accordance with the priority of grace, then economic goods should be distributed in such a way as to enhance human well-being and self-acceptance and communal fellow-feeling without asking first whether people have deserved what they receive. The pertinence of this issue to welfare policy is especially clear. If we think of poverty as a morally deserved condition, then we might be inclined to accept George Gilder's judgement that a good welfare system should be "unattractive and even a bit demeaning"; and we might agree with his further observation that "in order to succeed, the poor need most of all the spur of their poverty."[6] But if we accept instead the theological notion that *none* of us are morally deserving and *all* of us are dependent upon God's free gift of love, then we are more likely to see and treat poor people as less fortunate sisters and brothers. The latter view may not in itself be an economic policy, but it could scarcely escape affecting economic policy where it is believed.[7]

Physical well-being and relational wholeness

An important corollary of the foregoing points is that economics must be concerned about two things at once: the physical needs of people and the effect of economic organization upon relationships. Both are important. Physical deprivation obviously frustrates human fulfillment. Without adequate food, clothing, shelter, and medical care people suffer and die; and one does not have to be an economist or a theologian to recognize that the purposes of human life are threatened. But economic life can also be structured in such a way that barriers are created between people, frustrating the higher ends of human community. Both are important, and each is, to some extent, independent of the other. The poorest members of a community may be well enough off economically that they are not suffering physically while, at the same time, they are so much poorer than others that it is nearly impossible to relate as brother and sister to the affluent. On the other hand, it is at least theoretically possible for everybody in the community to be deprived to the point of physical suffering while the bonds of community itself remain intact. So it is not even possible to establish a lexical ordering of priorities, with physical well-being *necessarily* first. A case can be made that without physical well-being nothing else is possible. But a case can also be made that the moral quality of life in community is worth considerable sacrifice in physical well-being. Of course, from a theological standpoint it is highly desirable to have *both* physical well-being and relational wholeness within the community.

Vocation

The doctrine of vocation is a particularly good theological entry point to the significance of work. The term means "calling," of course; and the traditional implication of vocation was that it reflected one's call from God. Post-Reformation Christianity generally understood this to mean that everyone has a particular calling from God. Stated most generally, the meaning is that we should be active in our grateful response to God's gifts of life and love, and that our response should involve our dedication to the realization of God's loving purposes. Hebrew faith and Christian faith are, alike, activist. The theme of peaceful rest is also biblical, but rest is always related to work in the portrayal of human fulfillment. We rest in order to work as much as we work in order to rest. It is the doctrine of vocation, indeed, that saves the Christian conception of grace from leading to merely passive conceptions of existence. We are not just passive receptacles of God's goodness; we are invited, through grace, into creative activity. St. Paul is particularly careful not to push this to the opposite extreme of seeing "salvation" as something we accomplish through our own efforts. We do not have to earn or deserve God's grace; but God's grace remains unfulfilled in our lives without our active response.

The connection point between this and economics is obvious, in light of the importance of work for production and distribution. But the theological understanding of vocation is both narrower and broader than a purely economic conception of work. It is narrower in that some economic activities are so injurious to the life and well-being of the community that they could never be regarded as vocational in the theological sense. But it is also broader in that some vocational activity falls outside usual definitions of gainful employment. It is a good thing when, within the normal working of the economy, all people are challenged to contribute their best creative efforts to the betterment of all.

Stewardship

The doctrine of stewardship has traditionally spoken to the question of ownership and use of property. A more limited Protestant conception of stewardship has seen this as the giving of a certain portion of one's income, perhaps 10 per cent, to ecclesiastical institutions. But the doctrine of stewardship is more sweeping than that; it is recognition that everything belongs to God: "The earth is the Lord's and the fulness thereof, the world and those who dwell therein." (Psalm 24) All other property claims are relativized by that very basic one. An orderly society will, of course, define and protect the property rights of individuals and groups. But the theological perspective of stewardship does not permit us to treat those socially defined property rights as absolute. They are morally, if not legally, subordinated to the purposes of the Creator. Property is to be enjoyed; but understood as stewardship, it is to be used for loving purposes, not selfishness, and with an eye toward the future and not only the present. Stewardship does not permit the impertinent question, What has posterity ever done for me?[8] For stewardship recognizes the linkage of all generations through the common source of all being, and it accepts responsibility to the ultimate design of things and not only to oneself and a narrow frame of loyalties.

Original sin

There is, finally, the theological recognition that human nature is corrupted by self-centredness. All people are presumed to be sinners. This does not mean that people are *exclusively* sinful; they are also capable

of generosity and love. But the tendency toward selfishness is painfully and persistently a part of our makeup. The most persuasive theological accounts of original sin do not attribute this to our created nature nor to moral weakness, as such, but rather to our despair accompanied by a frantic drive to find personal fulfillment.[9] Loving requires
a "letting go" in faith, and that is difficult until we find ourselves
grasped by a reality larger than ourselves. In any event, the tendency
toward self-centredness has important implications for economics. It
suggests that no economic system predicated entirely upon human
goodness is likely to be successful and that economics, as well as politics, needs to institutionalize protections against the destructive possibilities of self-centred behaviour. It also suggests that we do well not
to separate the world between "good" people and "bad" people. Original sin means that all of us have this tendency and that none should
be presumed to have a corner on goodness. Self-righteousness, besides
exhibiting the subtlest forms of sin, is often the root of the most
demonic social practices. Economically successful people need to be
especially on guard lest they attribute their success to their own goodness while blaming poverty on the character deficiencies of poor
people.

III. THEOLOGICAL DANGER SIGNALS

Even the brief foregoing theological characterizations serve to remind
us of points where contemporary economic attitudes can be challenged. I
wish to suggest three such points.

Materialistic idolatry

First, there is the persistent idolatry of materialism or of particular
economic systems. The material realm becomes idolatry when it is
treated as an end and not as means. Seen through the eyes of theology,
there is a good deal of idolatry in all economic systems and in economic views expressed on all sides of the ideological spectrum. Inflated assessments of capitalism or socialism may contain much truth,
but it is ludicrous to treat them as absolute truth. Humanity is not here
to serve economics; rather the function of economics is to serve humanity, in accordance with God's loving purposes. This is not to say
that all economic systems or ideologies are not themselves ultimate objects of loyalty. Recognition of this should give us reason to be some-

what open concerning the outcome of the worldwide debate between contending economic ideologies.

Self-centredness in property concepts

The second point concerns property. A purely natural theory of property may have all the force of self-evident truth, yet be in serious tension with the theological conception of stewardship. The Lockean view of property has been particularly influential in Western economic thought over the past two or three centuries. According to Locke, property is constituted when we mix our labour with nature, withdrawing things from the state of nature by transforming them into useful objects.[10] The self-evident claim of this view of property is contained in the observation that had somebody not made it it wouldn't exist. The *prima facie* claim of ownership rests upon the fact that one should not be forced to give up what one has made. Certainly nobody else has any kind of claim upon the object that would not exist were it not for the labour of another person. We may hope people will be generous with their possessions, but it is unjust to deprive them of property against their will.

Whatever may be said for this understanding of property, it is a thoroughly self-centred view. In its individualism it is neglectful of the grand design. Curiously, the underlying view of what constitutes property is also suggested by Marxism, but there is a more social form. The Marxist criticism of alienation or exploitation is very much dependent on the judgement that something one has created has been taken away.[11] But whether in Marxist or Lockean form, the view that one's labour constitutes property treats nature itself simply as a given. But nature isn't just given. It is not unlimited. Those who control it have a much better opportunity to create property in the sense of mixing their labour with it. And in any event a theological view of nature requires us to come to terms with the enduring source of nature's existence.

Inflated claims of moral motivation in social life

A third theological problem is suggested by inflated theological images of the motivations presupposed by free market activity or by socialism. Thus, George Gilder attributes capitalism ultimately to acts of outgoing, self-giving love.[12] The capitalist entrepreneur is committed to making something to fill the needs of others even before he or she is certain there will be a market for the product. The basic motivation is not self-seeking, but generosity. Similarly, Michael Novak writes of the corporation as sacramental in character and uses the biblical imagery of "suffering servant" to characterize the faithful corporation leaders who persist in their good works despite the ill-founded abuse of corporate critics.[13] But how much truth is there, really, in such characterizations? Do businesspersons work fundamentally for the sake of others? Is there no hint of desire for reward to cloud their motives? Are they willing to do all, to give all, without any specific material incentives? No doubt, there are numbers of businesspeople whose motives include loving kindness and concern for others. But are there not also those who are profoundly corrupted by materialism? And which of us, indeed, is altogether free of self-seeking? Can businesspeople claim to be?

Similarly one must question the inflated conceptions of socialist morality that one sometimes hears — the new socialist man or woman of China or Cuba or wherever. For in such places, too, one may be infected by selfishness, in relation to the possession of power and prestige if not of wealth. For what it may be worth, my own journeyings to socialist countries have not revealed any startling new developments in human nature. It is a risky thing to assume that any people will, by virtue of their roles in systems and institutions, be wholly free of selfishness — whether those institutions are socialist or capitalist in character. A more modest expectation is that some institutions may help more than others in bringing out the best in people and in subordinating the destructive aspects of human sinfulness. A persuasive case can be mounted for both socialism and capitalism along these lines, but in neither instance would the case be dependent upon fundamental changes in human nature itself.

IV. ECONOMIC ALLOCATION

Most of the struggles over economic organization in recent times have centred around the relative claims of two competing approaches to the allocation of goods and services: the (more or less) free market and the (more or less) democratic government.[14] Where the free market is dominant, the prices of goods and services are established by the market and the role of government in economics is limited to the protection of property and the maintenance of agreed rules of the game.

Where government is dominant, economic activity is planned by central authority, and the pricing function of the market is sharply reduced. Most societies make use of both mechanisms for allocation; but the possibilities and limitations of each need to be explored.

Free market allocation

A strong case can be made for the efficiency of the market mechanism where genuine competition exists.[15] (George Gilder argues that even monopoly conditions do not basically frustrate the workings of market forces since even monopolies must compete against other alternatives for the spending of money.)[16] The prices that people are willing to pay for goods and services in the open market provide us with the best possible barometer of relative values as the buyers perceive them. The market mechanism, especially under competitive conditions, maximizes material incentive to produce and deliver goods at the lowest possible cost, relative to other goods. Those whose costs are substantially above their competitors are either forced to change quickly or to go out of business. The market mechanism also provides considerable incentive and freedom for those who wish to pursue new inventions and the development of new product lines. It is therefore a spur to dynamic, productive economic behaviour.

There are, to be sure, certain moral drawbacks to the market system, which have long been noted by the critics of capitalism. The very great focus upon material incentives may lead to the enthronement of materialistic greed in a culture and to the subordination of vocation and stewardship to personal selfishness. The competitive character of economic life may lead to divisive individualism, particularly evident during times of economic crisis and unemployment. There may be too much exploitativeness of nature and fellow humanity. The system may be too vulnerable to the contrasting problems of inflation and recession. It may lead to too great inequalities.

Such points can be answered, with arguments that include the claim that the market mechanism helps subordinate greed to the common good, since the only way one can make money is by offering goods and services that people want. It may also be claimed that the dynamic forces of the market keep the social status structure relatively fluid, there always being room for new entrants to the market who have new, saleable ideas. The effect of the system upon the cultural values of a people may not easily be assessed. Certainly the free enterprise system has appeared to spawn a good deal of plain, old-fashioned greed. Certainly it has also given rise to a good deal of creativity, and it has provided an arena for a considerable amount of voluntary generosity. No doubt the social and cultural consequences of free enterprise will continue to be debated by persons of opposite, though equally enthusiastic conviction.

Efficiency versus other social ends

The point where the market mechanism, per se, appears to create gravest difficulties is, ironically, the point of its greatest supposed strength. The very fact that the market rewards efficiency so admirably creates a conflict wherever market efficiency is at odds with social justice, or ecological responsibility, or other important moral purposes. An important aspect of the market's efficiency is its unfailing reward for those who can cut costs the most. Lower costs of production and marketing translate into lower prices, and lower prices normally translate into more sales. Conversely, those who cannot match the lower prices because their costs are too high must either find ways to cut their costs or, ultimately, be threatened with ruin. This is taking the market as it is defined by its strongest advocates.

The problem is that the market, thus defined, is largely blind to the *ways* in which enterprises manage to cut their costs. Firms are rewarded for cutting out waste and finding new, more efficient productive processes. But firms are also rewarded by the market for keeping wages as low as possible, avoiding unnecessary costs to improve employee working conditions, dumping wastes into rivers, and anything else that will lower the cost of doing business. Over the short run (which, for various reasons, may be the extent of a particular businessperson's interest) it may even prove advantageous to sell shoddy merchandise and misrepresent products sold. It is difficult for morally sensitive people to do moral things insofar as they must compete in the market against the less scrupulous. Many high-minded growers in Central California complained bitterly during the 1960s that their churches were turning against them to support the farm labour movement of Cesar Chavez. Their plea was that they were already doing the best they could in providing improved wages and living conditions for the migrant workers, and no union was needed. But that was exactly the point. Without some external force to regularize wages and working conditions throughout the whole industry these good Christian growers were quite unable to do better by the workers. Any who raised their labour costs unilaterally quickly discovered that they were pricing themselves out of the market! The market mechanism enforces prices at the level established by those able to cut their costs to the lowest levels. Clearly mechanisms of intervention into the workings of the market must be contemplated by those who are unwilling to settle for such consequences.

Bias towards private goods

There is another problem with exclusive reliance upon the free market. The market system emphasizes individual, private decision-making. Consequently, its bias is toward those goods and services we consume privately. It may indeed be fairly efficient in translating the individual preferences of millions of people into productive allocations by a whole economy, without much intervention from the standpoint of society as a whole.[17] But it is much less efficient in determining goods and services needed by society as a whole. The free market could theoretically provide for security needs (police and military and fire protection), education, transportation, parks, museums, and public works projects.[18] But is that really the most efficient way to deal with such social needs? Is there not a need for mechanisms of social planning and allocation which permit the community as a whole to determine priorities and assemble the resources needed to accomplish social objectives? And are there not some kinds of consumption where it is better not to try to assess consumers precisely the costs of their consumption? And, given the great differences in wealth and income, should not some forms of economic decision-making for society be on the basis of one-person-one-vote rather than one-dollar-one-vote?

Governmental allocation

Such questions have led many people to conclude that the government should play a dominant role in economic planning and allocation. Substantial numbers of people worldwide have concluded in fact that government should own the whole economy and distribute through central planning institutions. Socialist writers tend to present this alternative as though it were clearly superior morally to the market mechanism — as, on the face of it, it may be. Socialism promises social justice and cooperation as direct objectives, not byproducts, of economic activity. Some socialist writers, such as Ota Sik and Oskar Lange, have even suggested a prominent use of the market mechanism in a socialist economy — thus hoping to capitalize on the strengths of a market economy while avoiding its weaknesses.

But it needs to be said that governmental management of economic life is not a morally risk-free alternative to the free market. A very large number of governments around the world are authoritarian and oppressive. Such governments are not made less oppressive by control of economic life. Michael Harrington comments wisely that if the state owns the economy, it matters all the more who owns the state. If the state is not "owned" democratically, then its control of the economy will only fit it to be more oppressive. Even if the state is democratic it may, through corrupt or oppressive majorities, do evil things.

The democratic ideal

Still, democratic governmental institutions are uniquely the instruments of common purpose. They are able to regulate economic life for the common good, to maintain public institutions, and to provide protection of all citizens through programs of redistribution. While even a democratic government can make mistakes, its actions will be based upon a publicly argued-out conception of the kind of community the majority of the people want it to be. It provides a forum for serious debate of serious issues, with the prospect that the results of the debate can register in determining the character of the community. Through democratic decision-making people have an opportunity to participate more directly in the definition of their own on-going history. While market allocation may appear to place greater premium upon individual decision-making and may appear to maximize freedom of choice in one's economic life, this freedom can be illusory if the net result of individual decisions is to create social conditions that undermine one's intentions. Individuals may desire the freedom afforded by use of private automobiles, but if too many people opt for that same freedom before there is an adequate system of roads the result may simply be congestion and smog — which nobody would have chosen deliberately. Garrett Hardin neatly refers to the irony of this in his essay, "The Tragedy of the Commons."[19] Where a number of sheepherders are using the same grazing land, he writes, it may be in the interest of each to increase the number of animals in his/her flock. But if all the sheepherders increase the size of their flocks, the result may be the over-grazing of the commons, thereby undermining its value to each one. Only when a common decision is made to regulate the number of sheep can a rational decision be made that is in the interest of all. The sum total of private decisions may *not* be the well-being of all. The decision-making process may, in some instances, need to be corporate, leading toward corporate ends. We may appear to be free to choose our own destiny in a market economy. But that freedom is only illusory to the extent that we are locked into a common destiny. Governmental decisions, taken in behalf of the whole community, may in such cases be the avenue to real freedom. Then it is a matter of whether or not we are free to share in corporate decision-making, and thereby to share in determining the overall character of community life.

Democratic decision-making and theological understanding

An impressive theological case can be made for the importance of democratic decision-making in economics. We live, after all, in community. Under God, we are a family—not just solitary individuals relating, one at a time, to God. Through democratic politics, we can share in the common stewardship of earth. Even those who find themselves voting with a minority on an important issue can affect outcomes; and in a true democracy they remain free to speak out and organize for change. Each person is formally equal to every other; no one is treated as a mere object. From a theological standpoint, each is seen to stand in equal relationship before God and to be able to contribute out of that transcendent source of meaning to the issues of the day. In democratic decision-making it is the power of one's mind and soul that is recognized—whereas in the marketplace it is one's wealth and saleable skills.

Critics of pure socialism note the residual dangers, however, in combining economic and political power under an all-powerful government. While such a government may theoretically be democratic, it may prove difficult to keep it that way. Arthur Okun remarks that "a market economy helps to safeguard political rights against encroachment by the state. Private ownership and decision-making circumscribe the power of the government . . . and hence its ability to infringe on the domain of rights. If," he continues, "the government commanded all the productive resources of the society, it could suppress dissent, enforce conformity, and snuff out democracy."[20] It is theoretically possible for a state to be organized very democratically even though there existed no concentrations of private economic power independent of the state. Such a state would have to protect, by law and tradition, the right of each person to dissent and to organize for political action. It would also have to make provision for utterly neutral public channels of communication. Such protections and provisions do exist in all democratic societies. In a socialist democracy there might be more temptations to those in power to make their power permanent.

The debate between those who favour market allocation and those who support governmental allocation must remain somewhat inconclusive. We may lean more toward one than toward the other; but both have potential flaws as well as strengths.[21] Those of us who are currently living in the capitalist (or mixed-economy) democracies face three broad issues which challenge us as we try to sort out our attitudes toward the relative claims of the marketplace and government.

Our attitude toward the economic role of government in a predominantly capitalistic society

The election of conservative governments in the United States and the United Kingdom in recent years has raised anew the question of the legitimacy of a substantial economic role of government. The Thatcher government in Britain has attempted to stem what it perceived to be a rising tide of socialism. The Reagan administration in the United States has attempted to break the momentum of fifty years of political economy based upon the assumptions of the New Deal. President Reagan may have spoken for both governments in this remark from his first economic address to the nation in February, 1981: "The taxing power of Government must be used to provide revenues for legitimate Government purposes. It must not be used to regulate the economy or bring about social change. We've tried that and surely must be able to see it doesn't work." There may be sufficient ambiguity in this remark to protect its meaning from harsher interpretations. But by any interpretation it is negative in its assessment of the economic role of government as practised over the past fifty years.

The failure of *laissez-faire*

Yet if we have learned anything over the past it is that unrestrained *laissez-faire* market economics is what does not work. At least it does not work to protect the weaker members of the community nor the common environmental inheritance of all. We may be in some danger of forgetting *why* the New Deal developed fifty years ago. The *laissez-faire* assumptions that guided economic policy before 1933 were impotent to prevent or deal with the greatest economic catastrophe in American history. The market simply could not correct itself. Even if *laissez-faire* economic policies had not brought a massive breakdown to the system they would have perpetuated vast disparities of income and wealth in American society. Such disparities are a profound threat to the health of society and democratic institutions. To the extent that taxation has helped redistribute American wealth and income and to place an economic floor beneath most people in the United States, it has clearly "worked" to bring about beneficent social change. Use of tax dollars to expand educational opportunity (including higher education), to improve recreational facilities, and to strengthen the arts has also contributed to useful social change. One does not have to defend all governmental programs of the past fifty years to observe that in the main and on the whole the country is better because of them. From a theological perspective, it seems clear that it is easier for more people to be what God has intended them to be as participants in the life of community because of active interventions by government. The fact that many such programs are weak or wasteful should lead to criticism and improvement — not to the abandonment of governmental responsibility.

I do not take these observations, in and of themselves, as arguments for socialism, even though I find the case for out-and-out socialism more persuasive than the case for out-and-out *laissez-faire* capitalism. There may well be a need for private centres of economic power. And whether or not there is such a need, there is no question but that we shall continue to have them for the foreseeable future. The real question is whether private centres of economic power will be kept subordinate to governmental power, which alone can uphold the order of justice. Opinions will continue to vary over what is the best mix of private and public sector responsibilities in the economy. But there should be no doubt that the private sector should be accountable to society through law and government, just as there should be no doubt that government and law should be accountable to the people through free democratic processes. The people of a society should have the capacity, through responsible government, to define the nature of the community in which they live.

Needed international structures for economic accountability

Notwithstanding recent developments, most of the Western capitalist democracies are in fact mixed economies with well-established traditions of economic accountability to government. That is not true of international economics. The past two decades have witnessed startling increases in the scope and activity of multinational corporations; but they have not seen comparable development of transnational institutions to regulate and govern international economic activity. A considerable debate has developed in recent years over the role of multinational corporations, with much disagreement over their relative merits in economic development and social justice.[22] Some see them as a positive and dynamic source of much-needed development in the less-developed countries of Africa, Asia, and Latin America, organizing production and markets, stimulating world trade and even redistributing wealth and income in the direction of the poorer countries by growth of investments and better jobs in those areas. Others perceive them as basically exploitative devices to increase control over the Third World by the industrialized countries and in fact to increase poverty as well. In either case there seems little doubt that they will remain an important factor in the years to come. The real issue may not be whether we will or will not have multinationals but whether they can be made more accountable. Presently their great power makes it difficult for relatively weak countries to control them, and in some instances they may escape local control by corrupting public officials. They are international in scope; the governmental agencies available to make them accountable are national or local.

A key question in the next few years is, therefore, whether we can evolve responsible international agencies and a corresponding body of international regulation to achieve the needed balance of public control and private initiative. In some fields, such as telecommunications and aviation, the character of economic activity has virtually mandated the development of international regulation, and much has been accomplished. In some other fields (notably petroleum) it has been possible for a number of Third World countries to band together to improve their bargaining hand. But in most cases, there is simply a political-legal vacuum at the international level.

The Law of the Sea

The problem and the possibilities have been dramatized in recent years by two interesting developments. One is the Law of the Sea negotiations which commenced over a decade ago to bring some semblance of order into the anarchy of efforts to exploit the world's offshore fisheries and the mineral deposits in the deep seabeds.[23] The Law of the Sea negotiations took as their basis the conviction that the oceans are the "common heritage of mankind." They envisage a fully international ownership of that heritage, with an international "enterprise" to do some deep-seabed mining and a franchise system to regulate and tax the mining endeavours of private corporations. Proceeds from these international ventures and franchises would be used largely to assist in the development efforts of poorer countries. If successful, the Law of the Sea precedent could prepare the way for similar international control of Antarctica and the moon.

Breast-milk substitutes

The other development has been the adoption of a recommended set of international guidelines to govern the marketing of breast-milk substitutes (infant formula). In 1979, after several years of intense international controversy over the methods used by infant formula companies to increase sales in Third World countries, the World Health Organization and UNICEF began the development of a marketing code to correct abuses.[24] After two years of negotiations the code was in fact adopted overwhelmingly by the World Health Assembly in May 1981 (with only the United States voting against it). The code was adopted purely as a recommendation for national law and company policy, but its adoption by the international body gave it considerable moral weight, and it has become the basis for legislation in a number of countries. It is believed that this precedent could inspire similar efforts in governing the practices of transnational pharmaceutical companies.

Such efforts are very modest in scope in face of the enormous size and diversity of multinational corporations, but they may still be pointing in the right direction. Many companies resist such regulation (the infant formula companies did so quite vigorously). But sensible international regulation may be a very welcome thing for those companies seeking a world in which it is possible to carry on business responsibly. Resistance to such regulation invites suspicion that businesses wish to escape moral accountability.

V. THE ATTITUDE TOWARD SOCIALISM

The third broad issue facing capitalist democracies in the closing decades of the twentieth century is their attitude toward socialism in other parts of the world—particularly the socialism emerging in several Third World countries. Socialist rhetoric is pervasive in the speeches and writings of many Third World intellectual leaders and in the announced programs of revolutionary movements. And the number of Third World countries officially committed to some form of socialism increases almost yearly. Some of these countries, such as Cuba, Angola and Mozambique, are more or less explicitly Marxist in their ideological commitments; others, such as Tanzania and Zambia, are attempting to develop their own indigenous forms of socialism. Still others, while greatly influenced by socialism, are yet difficult to define. Revolutionary movements in such countries as El Salvador and Guatemala are likely to develop socialist states if they succeed in capturing power.

Capitalism and democracy

People who are deeply committed to free enterprise or to mixed economy conceptions of political economy tend to view these developments with skepticism or downright hostility. At best, such developments may be viewed as economically foolish; at worst, they may be considered the root cause of creeping totalitarianism. Such writers as Michael Novak[25] and Richard John Neuhaus have even argued recently that capitalism may be a necessary condition for democracy. According to Neuhaus and his Institute on Religion and Democracy colleagues, "We note as a matter of historical fact that democratic governance exists only where the free market plays a large part in a society's economy."[26] This claim is a dubious one historically (even primitive tribes and nomadic peoples have been known to develop democratic societies, and subgroups within capitalist or mixed economies combine highly socialistic life-styles with profoundly democratic approaches to internal government), although it must be acknowledged that there is not yet a really good illustration of a thoroughly socialist country that is, at the same time, thoroughly democratic. Czechoslovakia gave brief promise of this during the Dubcek reform period of 1968—before the crushing blow of Soviet invasion, and Chile embarked on a democratic Marxist venture before the regime of President Salvador Allende was replaced by coup d'etat (possibly encouraged by the United States). Two or three Third World countries—one thinks of Zimbabwe and Nicaragua especially—may yet take that turn. But no thoroughly socialist country could today also be described as completely democratic. Most Marxists would of course argue that democracy in capitalist countries is itself a sham, a one-dimensional form lacking the substance of real self-rule. So there are both capitalists and Marxists who agree that a particular kind of economic system is absolutely essential to democracy, they just disagree as to which economic system!

But they may both be wrong. Reinhold Niebuhr wrestled with the relationship between bourgeois civilization and democracy in his classic work, *The Children of Light and the Children of Darkness.* That book responded to challenges to democracy in the ideological movements of the 1930s and in World War II. Niebuhr was anxious to establish a theological basis for democracy independent of those movements and of the bourgeois culture which had provided the matrix for democracy during the preceding two centuries. "The democratic ideal is thus more valid than the libertarian and individualistic version of it which bourgeois civilization elaborated. Since the bourgeois version has been discredited by the events of contemporary history and since, in any event, bourgeois civilization is in process of disintegration, it becomes important to distinguish and save what is permanently valid from what is ephemeral in the democratic order."[27] Whether or not Niebuhr correctly assessed the prospects for what he called bourgeois civilization, we need to take seriously his implication that the case for democracy transcends any particular economic system. Niebuhr himself offered a powerful theological statement of that case, based primarily on the assessment of human creativity and human sinfulness—the one making democracy possible, the other making it necessary.

The primacy of democracy

If, as I believe, the theological case for democratic social order sur-
passes in importance the case for any particular economic system,
then it would seem important not to over-react to socialism as though
it must be opposed to democracy. Some countries, such as Zimbabwe
and Angola, are almost bound to be socialist. The real question is
whether they will also be democratic. If I may personalize this a bit,
the chief of state of the new nation of Zimbabwe happens to be a
graduate of the theological institution with which I am associated. In a
1981 lecture at his alma mater, President Canaan Banana made clear
his judgement that Zimbabwe must be socialist in its basic approach to
economic questions.[28] At the same time that country has also preserved the traditions of parliamentary democracy. The issue in the
mind of the government of Zimbabwe is evidently not whether socialism should or should not be tried, but rather whether the commitment
to democracy should be maintained. Those who, like Novak and
Neuhaus, seriously question the possibility of democracy apart from
capitalism appear to have abandoned the hope of persuading the
leadership of countries like Zimbabwe that democracy is also an
important thing for socialists.

Perhaps what is needed in the world today is a healthier sense of
economic pluralism. Neither socialism nor capitalism has yet provided
humanity with conclusive evidence that it alone best serves the cause
of economic justice and human well-being. Our basic commitments
should be deeper than any economic system, and then we can be free
to evaluate various economic practices and experiments more lucidly.
We may then see that socialists have managed to solve some kinds of
problems more successfully than capitalists and vice versa.

Above all, we need to be cautious in the use of military power and
covert activities to curb socialism. It is, in fact, in the deeper interest
of the capitalist democracies that there *be* successful experiments with
democratic socialism in various parts of the world — for that would
greatly enhance the attractiveness of democracy in the more oppressive socialist countries. The coup d'etat in Chile regrettably conveyed
exactly the opposite impression in Marxist circles. Marxists today are
typically critical of Allende for maintaining his democratic commitments after assuming power, for this made him vulnerable to the military coup that in fact occurred. Had events been permitted to follow
their course, Chile might or might not be a socialist country. But
Marxists would not have been supplied with concrete evidence that

capitalists will not tolerate democracy when it conflicts with their economic interests.

VI. CONCLUSION

Theology has an important, even indispensable, role to play in contributing perspective to economic life. Theological clarity lends clarity to those ultimate values by which we measure all lesser goods, including the lesser goods with which economics deals. Because theology reminds us that we do not live by bread alone it helps us understand the importance of bread in sustaining the totality of our being. Because it saves us from making a god of any economic ideology, it helps us better to understand how economic systems serve or impede God's deeper purposes for humanity. And because it reminds us of the limits and moral ambiguities of our vision, it helps us to make our contributions to the economic debate of our time with greater humility.

NOTES

1. H. Richard Niebuhr, *Radical Monotheism and Western Culture* (New York: Harper and Row, 1960).

2. A pragmatic style is often contrasted with ideological thinking, but "practicality" generally presupposes acceptance of an ideological frame of reference. There is a sense in which we are all "ideologues," or even "true believers"; but much depends upon the ideologies we do accept and what we do believe to be true. Much also depends upon our openness to new truth and our acceptance of the humanity of persons with whom we disagree.

3. Paul A. Samuelson, *Economics,* Ninth Edition (New York: McGraw-Hill, 1973), p. 770.

4. E. F. Schumacher, *Small is Beautiful: A Study of Economics as if People Mattered* (London: Blond and Briggs, 1973).

5. See esp. Karl Barth, *Church Dogmatics,* III/1 (Edinburgh: T. and T. Clark, 1958).

6. George Gilder, *Wealth and Poverty* (New York: Basic Books, 1981), pp. 117–118.

7. Acceptance of this religious belief may also contribute to greater lucidity in viewing the actual facts of wealth and poverty. For wealth is sometimes based upon sheer accidents of birth and sometimes upon dishonesty and exploitation, as poverty is not infrequently the result of misfortune and oppression.

8. Robert L. Heilbroner, *An Inquiry into the Human Prospect* (New York: W. W. Norton, 1975), pp. 169 ff.

9. See esp. Reinhold Niebuhr, *The Nature and Destiny of Man* (New York: Scribner's, 1941). This is perhaps the best twentieth century account of the doctrine of original sin.

10. John Locke, *2nd Treatise on Civil Government* (1690), Chapter V.

11. See esp. Marx's *Economic and Philosophical Manuscripts of 1844* and Erich Fromm, *Marx's Concept of Man* (New York: Frederick Ungar, 1961).

12. Gilder, *Wealth and Poverty,* pp. 24–27.

13. Michael Novak, *Toward a Theology of the Corporation* (Washington, D.C.: The American Enterprise Institute, 1981), p. 33.

14. J. Philip Wogaman, *The Great Economic Debate* (Philadelphia: Westminster, 1977).

15. The maximum case for this is provided in the writings of Friedrich A. Von Hayek and Ludwig Von Mises. A sweeping contemporary expression of the case is provided by Milton Friedman, *Capitalism and Freedom* (Chicago: University of Chicago Press, 1962).

16. Gilder, *Wealth and Poverty,* pp. 37–38.

17. See also Arthur M. Okun, *Equality and Efficiency: The Big Tradeoff* (Washington, D.C.: The Brookings Institution, 1975) for a good brief statement of the efficiency of the market by one who was commited to a mixed economy perspective.

18. See Friedman, *Capitalism and Freedom,* for a maximum — some would say extreme — statement of the case for market allocation in what is now widely accepted as government's sphere of responsibility.

19. Garrett Hardin, "The Tragedy of the Commons," *Science,* CLXII (December 13, 1968), pp. 1243–48.

20. Okun, *Equality and Efficiency,* pp. 38–39.

21. See Wogaman, *The Great Economic Debate,* for more extended discussion.

22. An interesting contrast is provided by Richard J. Barnet and Ronald E. Muller, *Global Reach: The Power of the Multinational Corporations*

(New York: Simon and Schuster, 1974) and Michael Novak, *Toward a Theology of the Corporation.*

23. *Soundings: Law of the Sea News and Comment,* Vol. 7, No. 1 (November, 1981-February, 1982).

24. World Health Organization, *International Code of Marketing of Breastmilk Substitutes* (Geneva, World Health Organization, 1981).

25. Novak, *Toward a Theology of the Corporation* and *The Denigration of Capitalism* (Washington, D.C.: American Enterprise Institute, 1979).

26. Richard John Neuhaus, *Christianity and Democracy* (Washington, D.C.: Institute on Religion and Democracy), pp. 6-7.

27. Niebuhr, *The Children of Light and the Children of Darkness* (New York: Scribner's, 1944) p. 5.

28. Canaan Sodindo Banana, "In Search of Human Justice" (unpublished lecture, Wesley Theological Seminary, October 22, 1981).

Comment

John W. Cooper

The variety of theologies of economics

J. Philip Wogaman's "Theological Perspective on Economics" is in my view one of the most significant but flawed recent contributions to a growing list of theologies of economics, a relatively rare species until the late 1970s. Today there are theologies of economics of all kinds—leftist and rightist, staid and chic, but most important of all, socialist and capitalist. Among those American theologians who write from a "democratic capitalist" point of view, Wogaman mentions Michael Novak and Richard John Neuhaus (George Gilder is not a theologian, although his *Wealth and Poverty* is at least quasi-theological). One could add Robert Benne to this list. On the "democratic socialist" side of the theology-of-economics debate are such notable figures as John C. Bennett, Robert McAfee Brown, William Sloan Coffin, Jr., Robert Bellah, Harvey Cox, and M. Douglas Meeks. It is uncertain which group and which viewpoint is predominant among theologians. The anti-capitalist bias is quite apparent in many circles. The pro-socialism view is much less common and has greater credibility among professionals than among ordinary citizens.

Wogaman's position in the spectrum:

Wogaman's essay clearly places him among the more numerous "democratic socialist" theologians and in opposition to the relative handful of democratic capitalist theologians. That a fragmentation of professional theologians and ethicists into differing ideological camps is desirable in the first place is doubtful. But there it is. And Wogaman has added his voice to the chorus of American churchmen who argue that government command of the economy is preferable to a market-oriented approach.

The author begins on solid ground by rehearsing some basic themes of theological ethics, his main point being the importance of the economic sphere as a matrix of values, and therefore an appropriate subject matter for ethics and theology. Next, he sets up a dichotomy between the "free market" and "democratic government" as models for organizing society—a weighted phraseology. In fact, these terms signify the classic "markets-vs.-planning" debate. Wogaman breaks no new ground in his argument. Along the way, Wogaman uncovers some interesting relationships, but in the end he makes a rather conventional argument for the preferability of a state-run economy to a market economy. Does he have in mind some model socialist state which America could emulate? Well, no. There is "not yet a . . . thoroughly socialist country that is, at the same time, thoroughly democratic." The annual Freedom House report, *Freedom in the World,* suggests an inverse relationship between socialism and democracy. Perhaps he dreams that America could be the first nation to have a socialist revolution that is truly "democratic."

What is "democratic socialism"?

If Wogaman means by "democratic socialism" the current transformations in Nicaragua and Zimbabwe, for example, then his dream is in jeopardy. History is open-ended and anything can happen. But the news from these countries does not suggest the eschatological inbreaking of the new. It looks like the same old gradual social and political regimentation which Marxism brings in its train. If Wogaman means by "democratic socialism" the mixed economies of Western Europe and Israel, for example, then we might all be content as "democratic socialists." But these lands enjoy essentially market-oriented economic arrangements using more or less government *regulation,* not, ordinarily, direct management. Furthermore, so does the United States, although the United States generally chooses to regulate its economy less. Therefore, America's dreamed-of socialist horizon is somewhat illusive.

Destination Stockholm or Managua?

Wogaman's case for socialism rests not only on the illusive *democratic* socialist state, but also on the failure of *"laissez-faire* capitalism." This is a typical case of the comparison of ideals with realities. The caring, "revolutionary," communal bonds of the socialist myth are infinitely more appealing than the mundane and unjust realities of nineteenth-century industrialism. A truer account would compare ideals with ideals and realities with realities. Where is there more freedom and more prosperity — in East or West Germany, North or South Korea, Tanzania or Kenya, Cuba or Costa Rica, Libya or Egypt?

The problem with *laissez-faire* capitalism, as Wogaman points out, is the lack of an unambiguous governmental mandate to regulate the economy for the common good. It was the accomplishment of the New Deal to establish mechanisms for maintaining private-sector prosperity while regulating economic behaviour and extracting the cost of a welfare apparatus. Democratic capitalists claim the New Deal, too. It is instructive that the extreme socialists of the time blamed Roosevelt for "saving capitalism."

Do the New Deal reforms lead to a social market economy, as democratic capitalists argue, or are they a form of latent socialism which cannot continue to coexist with the for-profit sector? Clarity on these matters could well erase the differences between many of the theological combatants in the capitalism-socialism debate. Wogaman notes that "there may well be a need for private centres of economic power." What is important, he argues, is whether the private sector will be "subordinate to governmental power" and "accountable to society through law and government." Wogaman and a democratic capitalist like Michael Novak would obviously concur on this point, if the terms were carefully defined. After all, Jacques Maritain, whom Novak praises, made the same case for corporate accountability while arguing *for* the legitimacy of private-sector enterprise as one component of a democratic pluralist society. Maritain's *Reflections on America* is a classic in the literature of the emerging discipline of "democratic capitalist" theological reflection; he preferred the term "economic humanism."

The "democratic capitalist" alternative

The kind of society imagined by Maritain and Novak may well be, in the final analysis, the fulfillment of the current theological longing for discernment in matters of economic justice. A summary outline of this "American vision" — as Novak calls it, without engaging in the sacralization of America — is required to counterpoise Wogaman's democratic socialism. Novak's complete expression of this vision is found in his *The Spirit of Democratic Capitalism.*

The democratic capitalist society is a pluralistic society, it is three-in-one: the political, economic, and moral-cultural sectors coexist in a relationship of *relative autonomy.* The democratic constitution of a nation defines a limited sphere of primary governmental concerns: national defense, maintenance of a strong currency, financing of social welfare services. The production and distribution of most kinds of goods and services is the province of the economic sector, which is relatively autonomous in relation to the political sector. Government may undertake certain forms of productive activity, such as building roads, or may even compete in the marketplace alongside private firms. Nevertheless, the spheres of operations for business and for government remain distinct, although they overlap at points.

One of the most important events in the history of economic philosophy has occurred in the last few decades, primarily in the U.S. and Great Britain. The welfare state, first of all, is now seen as a permanent feature of Western democratic societies and, secondly, it is obvious that the welfare state is dependent upon transfers of surplus wealth created in the private sector. Every society hopes that it will remain prosperous enough to take care of its disabled and unfortunate few; every society must find a scheme for financing the ministrations of social insurance.

The third sector

A third and final sector, the moral-cultural sector, is the last of the "societies within a society." It is the idea sector, consisting of the information professionals: clerics, teachers, experts, consultants, analysts of all kinds. And when the critical insights of so many intelligent people are collected and winnowed in the public media, they operate as a check-and-balance mechanism vis-à-vis the political and economic spheres. The moral-cultural elite may criticize the business elite for their avarice, and the government elite for corruption or some other weakness. The government may put checks on the actions of business, and frequently does, but businesses may also demand before the law that government refrain from abridging economic liberties, just as the idea sector demands and receives from the state the right of free speech.

Checks and balances

This three-in-one society, this democratic pluralism, is a vast system of checks and balances between the political, economic, and moral-cultural sectors. The complexity and adaptability of this kind of social organization make it preferable to a system in which the three sectors are controlled by a single elite, frequently accompanied by a one-party political system. When politicians make all decisions and control all aspects of human life, they establish totalitarian states, they become modern tyrants. The three sectors are collapsed into a system of revolutionary committees with a single politbureau controlling the committees. The apex of this pyramidal social organization is a single individual, the president or party chief. It is no accident that Stalin's "dictatorship of the one" dominated the twentieth-century communist movement. Stalinism is the inevitable result of such a monolithic and cumbersome governing apparatus.

It seems clear that the democratic capitalist nations, including the social democracies of Western Europe, will continue to practice and defend the pluralist way of ordering society: limited government, an affordable welfare state, a prosperous private sector, and a vigorous and responsible moral-cultural sector. The totalitarian nations will continue to advertise their model of political organization. Assuming there is no nuclear conflagration, we are likely to live in a turbulent and dangerous international order for some decades to come. There are great dramas being played out in the Third World as nations choose between the totalitarian and pluralistic models. It is in the best interest of the democratic pluralist nations to foster democratic pluralism in every nation on earth.

Attitudes to political alternatives

Wogaman urges us to be sympathetic towards experiments with democratic socialism in the Third World. And well we should. Some nations which call themselves socialist have thriving market economies and are likely to evolve further in the direction of democratic pluralism. We may acknowledge with Wogaman that socialists have had some successful experiments in governance, such as in the communist cities of Italy or the socialist government of France. But Wogaman urges even more sympathy than that. "Above all," he states, "we need to be cautious in the use of military power and covert activities to curb socialism. It is, in fact, in the deeper interest of the capitalist democracies that there *be* successful experiments with democratic socialism in various parts of the world—for that would greatly enhance the attractiveness of democracy in the more oppressive socialist countries." This sounds like making democracy attractive to oppressors by making it more authoritarian. Democratic socialism is *not* the answer to the world's economic problems, and the "democratization" of the marketplace is *not* a desirable goal, except in some limited, exceptional cases. In the real world, "democratization" too frequently becomes a smoke screen for totalitarianism. Wogaman's allocation economy *is* an alternative to our market economy, it is *not* a preferable alternative. And theological ethics does not unanimously point to the command economy as a vehicle for justice.

Wogaman does a service, however, by highlighting some important themes for consideration in any theology of economics. He calls these themes "six theological entry points": creation, grace before works, relational wholeness, vocation, and stewardship. One could imagine a trinity of virtues in matters economic—stewardship (The Way of Co-creation), vocation (The Way Out of Fallenness), charity (The Way of

Community). This trinity of economic virtues is parallel to the creation-fall-redemption motif.

An alternative theology of economics

By way of conclusion, we might compare another alternative theology of economics, one which can serve as a statement of general principles. The well-known Muslim theologian, Muhammad Abdul-Rauf has written an essay entitled *The Islamic Doctrine of Economics and Contemporary Economic Thought.* I have adapted his language to some degree and added the fourth point.

1. God's creation is the source of life and wealth.
2. Wealth is for human survival; it is potentially abundant but relatively inaccessible.
3. Honest work is a virtue and is worthy of respect.
4. Technology has creative and destructive potentialities which require social control.
5. All persons are equal and responsible before God and the law.
6. All persons have rights and liberties in personal and economic matters (including the rights to life, bodily dignity, lawful enterprise, ownership, labour organization, and equality of opportunity).
7. All persons have duties and responsibilities in the production and distribution of wealth (including the duties of work, stewardship of public and private wealth, charity and public assistance, and the dispersal of inheritance).

Abdul-Rauf's theology of economics is not Wogaman's, although there are many points of agreement between them. This set of principles is much more compatible with a free, democratic capitalist society. The mechanisms of the economy, its structure, and its practical effects are based on how one decides the matter of theological first principles. Thus, the debate currently going on among theologians has a deep and longstanding significance.

The mechanism of democratic capitalism

What are the practical mechanisms and economic policies of a democratic capitalist society? As I see it, the main outlines are as follows:

1. Incentives: real rewards are offered to all participants in an enterprise, harnessing self-interest for the common good.
2. Mixed economy: democratically-mandated monopolization of limited public concerns, but *contra* dominant public sector (provision for the health of the economy through the maintenance of a vibrant private sector).
3. Liberty: freedom of economic initiative in both labour and enterprise, with the right to proportional compensation, under social restraints (e.g. graduated income taxes).
4. Equality: equal opportunity and fair markets in both labour and enterprise (*contra* "equality of result" and *contra* monopolization of private markets).
5. Fraternity: programmatic provision for social welfare (within affordable limits and according to the principle of personal dignity and the ideal of economic self-sufficiency).
6. Balance of social forces: shared power among various sectors of society, each making indispensable contributions (e.g. business and labour, agriculture and industry).

This is the democratic capitalist alternative to Wogaman's plan. Neither side of the theological debate should be ignored, both have valuable contributions to make. However, in the final analysis Christianity will be better served if the institutions of pluralism prevail over the tendencies toward collectivization.

NOTE

See also John W. Cooper, "Elements for a Christian Theology of Economics," *Homiletic and Pastoral Review* (July 1982), "Self-Reliance and Solidarity: The Democratic Capitalist Model of Development," in *The Effect of Technological Advance on the Future of the Nation State,* Institute for Theological Encounter with Science and Technology, 1982, "Islamic Economic Justice," *Harvard International Review* (December-January 1979), and "The Cuban Revolution and Liberation Theology," *Christianity and Crisis* (July 21, 1980).

Comment

Walter Block

Both economics and theology, as well as the interdisciplinary field of economic theology (or theological economics) owe a great debt of gratitude to J. Philip Wogaman for his "Theological Perspective on Economics."

The clarity of Dr. Wogaman's exposition enables us to focus on agreements and disagreements without fear of misunderstanding. In the spirit of promoting dialogue I shall take up several points of disagreement, roughly in the order presented in his paper.

Small is beautiful

One of the beauties of the decentralized market economy is that we are each "free to choose"[1] whether to involve ourselves in large or small organizations. We can take "small is beautiful" to its logical end point and become economic hermits: this includes individual farms, shops and proprietorships, and in the extreme case, living alone on a remote farm or forest.

Under a centrally planned socialist economy, this range of individual choice simply does not exist. Arrangements, whether small or large, are mandated by the authorities. This is the case even in the more decentralized socialist economies such as Yugoslavia and Czechoslovakia: an *individual* may not sell "his" share of any enterprise, whether or not in conjunction with other like-minded individuals, and set up another, more in accordance with his vision of the "small is beautiful" philosophy.

Grace and works

Philip Wogaman states: "But if justice is patterned in accordance with the priority of grace, then economic goods should be distributed in such a way as to enhance human well-being and self-acceptance and communal fellow-feeling without asking first whether people have deserved what they receive."

One might indeed argue that: (1) if justice is equivalent to grace, and (2) grace is irrelevant to desert then (3) justice is irrelevant to desert and so, (4) economic goods should be distributed disregarding desert. (3) follows tautologically from (1) and (2); the conclusion follows inescapably from the mere definitions of the terms. (4) however, is an entirely different matter. It would appear to be a conclusion of a logical argument, but "economic goods" nowhere appear in the premises.

Perhaps we can make this point more clearly by substituting (5) for (4). According to (5), punishment for crimes should be determined disregarding desert. Now (5) has as little (or as much) to do with (1), (2) and (3) as does (4). (5) is thus as logically valid a conclusion to this argument as is (4). If economic goods should be distributed disregarding desert because of the dictates of justice, then so should punishment be determined regardless of the crime committed. Yet we know that a punishment unrelated to a crime is an obvious perversion of justice. We must therefore conclude that whatever the case for distributing economic goods without regard to desert, this case cannot be made on the basis of justice.

Moreover, we can and must challenge premise (1). This would appear to be a rather eccentric use of the term "justice." One could, with equal merit, argue that justice is equivalent to love or to charity. Justice is, however, neither love, nor charity—nor grace. Justice is justice.

There are further difficulties with Wogaman's position. Let us suppose, for argument's sake, the validity of (1) and (2) (therefore of (3)) and (4). Even given this, it still needs to be shown that distributing economic goods without giving any consideration to desert, or to productivity, or to ability to produce that which consumers desire, will "enhance human well-being and self-acceptance and communal fellow-feeling." Might not so arbitrary a distribution of income rather create resentment and ill-feeling? Might not the recipients of such ill-gotten gains feel guilty, and appropriately so, about receiving property they had no hand in producing? We must also ask, of a given policy which enhances well-being, self-acceptance and fellow-feeling, is it necessarily just? One can think of counter examples. The whipping, castrating or hanging of an innocent black man might well enhance the well-being, self-acceptance and communal fellow-feeling of white bigots. Enhancing these human qualities is thus certainly no guarantee of justice.

Then there is also difficulty with the phrase "should be distributed in such a way as to. . . . " Who is to do the actual distributing? And will not any such attempt have to confront the fact that all economic goods are *owned?* There are not two completely separate phenomena: production and distribution. Rather, people produce, and their incomes are a result of the voluntary interactions of millions of people.[2] Social scientists can describe the ensuing pattern as a "distribution," but this terminological procedure does not justify the imposition of an arbitrary *re*distribution on the economy.

A similar analysis can be applied to "see(ing) and treat(ing) poor people as less fortunate sisters and brothers." Dr. Wogaman implies that if we do so, we will necessarily increase the scope of welfare. But do we really want to teach our sisters and brothers that their income levels should be unrelated to their economic productivity, and instead based "upon God's free gift of love?" (Is income equality logically implied by "God's free gift of love" to an undeserving humanity?) One fears that there may be no better way of increasing resentment and of sapping the desire to improve one's lot in life than to tell people that since God gave them a free gift of love, other people owe them a living.

The cause of economic success

According to Dr. Wogaman, "Economically successful people need to be especially on guard lest they attribute their success to their own goodness while blaming poverty on the character deficiencies of poor people." It is of course true that we are all imperfect human beings, at least on this side of the Garden of Eden. We must *all* be on our guard against self-righteousness.

But why single out economically successful people? We have all heard that "It is easier for a camel to pass through the eye of a needle than for a rich man to get into heaven." However, the proper interpretation of this statement is not that wealth consigns one to the depths, but just that it does not furnish a shorter or guaranteed path to heaven; that all of us, rich and poor, will be judged, on our final day, on matters other than economic productivity.[3]

Private property

After very accurately describing Locke's theory of the genesis of private property rights, Dr. Wogaman criticizes it on the grounds that it is "in serious tension with the theological conception of stewardship," and is "a thoroughly self-centred view. In its individualism it is neglectful of the grand design."

Wherein lies the incompatibility with stewardship and private property rights? Based on Dr. Wogaman's treatment of stewardship, it would appear that "the grand design" and "the purposes of the Creator" in this regard, are to maintain property in good repair, so that "posterity" may enjoy it too.

But where is the evidence that the "loving purposes" of presumably social ownership are better suited to this task than the "selfishness" of a private property system? On the contrary, the economic evidence available indicates precisely the opposite.

One indictment of communal land ownership is the Soviet system of farm collectivization.[4] We may perhaps pass over the historic fact that it took the murder of some ten million kulaks to inaugurate this system. Instead, simply consider the sorrowful economic record of the enterprise. Nor is this an accident,[5] as shown by the startling differentials in productivity levels between those attained on the vast collectivized and mechanized farms, and on the tiny plots of land surrounding their homes that individual farmers are allowed to own.[6] The explanation for these startling divergences seems clear: the sheer incentive differences. On their private plots of land, the farmers are working for *themselves,* and for their loved ones; on the collectives, they work for bureaucrats representing faceless others. This is one reason why people the world over work from dawn to dusk on their own accounts—and leave expensive tractors out in the collectivized fields to rust.

Paradoxically enough, Dr. Wogaman cites one of the crucial concepts needed to make this point. I refer to his treatment of Garrett Hardin's "The Tragedy of the Commons," "Where a number of sheepherders are using the same grazing land, it may be in the interest of each to increase the number of animals in his/her flock. But if all the sheepherders increase the size of their flocks, the result may be the over-grazing of the commons, thereby undermining its value to each one. Only when a common decision is made to regulate the number of sheep can a rational decision be made that is in the interest of all."

But this is the tragedy of the *commons;* i.e., communal ownership and socialized ownership. The solution is thus to convert the commons into private ownership status, where the beneficence of private and individualistic "selfishness" can effectively be brought to bear. The reason each sheepherder over-grazes on the commons, is that while he receives the benefits of grazing, he pays none of the costs of over-utilization. He does not own the land, so he cannot lose, financially, from over-grazing. When the grass is eaten down in any one place, he just moves elsewhere. *Nor can he capture the benefits of a more rational program of optimal grazing.* For if he moves his herd away from grassland in danger of being over used, his lack of private property rights precludes him from seeing to it that no one else grazes there either! Moreover, if the grass grows back because of his non-indulgence, this gives him no more right to benefit from later use than anyone else.

Law of the Sea

As a result of his analysis of the commons, Dr. Wogaman urges as a substitute for private property "Governmental decisions, taken in behalf of the whole community.... " He then applies this conclusion to the oceans, Antarctica and even to the moon, calling for an international public ownership of these "common heritages of mankind."

In other words, he is advocating the same type of system for these new frontiers as are responsible for ecological disasters and the failure of Russian agriculture. The seabed authority, moreover, would be based along much the same lines as the Third World-dominated U.N. General Assembly. If given the mandate to " ... do some deep-seabed mining and (organize) a franchise system to regulate and tax the mining endeavours of private corporations," this would mean that the economic development of the seas and oceans — perhaps the last best hope for the economic future of millions of poor people — would be left to the tender mercies of the rulers of the undeveloped countries in the Third World, who have so egregiously mismanaged their own economies.

Why should central economic planning work any better on the seas than it has on the land? To be sure, the workings of the marketplace might appear to be no better than chaos and "anarchy," from the viewpoint which sees collectivized control as the only system with any semblance of order or rationality. But the free market system is the one responsible for the magnificent standards of living the advanced industrialized Western nations have managed to wrest from the land. Where is the evidence that this cannot be applied to the seas? The establishment of an international bureaucracy to interfere with the orderly development of the ocean's resources is what the philosophy of the "seas as the common heritage of mankind" translates into, in practice. This policy is not required by any theological argument presented by Dr. Wogaman, and would do immense harm to the world economy.

Business motivations

Dr. Wogaman is highly suspicious of the motivations of businessmen. But, determining people's motives is a complex and risky affair, for they usually range from one extreme to the other. Our author is quite correct, however, in resisting Gilder's description of selfless altruism as the ultimate motivating force behind all of business. He is also correct in allowing that "No doubt, there are numbers of businesspeople whose motives include loving kindness and concern for others."

I think Dr. Wogaman is on more shaky ground in his criticism of Michael Novak's characterization. Businessmen are subjected to a stream of abuse and invective, on a day-in/day-out basis, such that were it applied to almost any other profession, it would soon provoke a call for a halt on the part of men of good will. This denigration emanates from the pulpit, from the editorial office, from the classroom. So pervasive is this phenomenon that even children's cartoons are affected.[7]

And yet businessmen persevere in the face of this abuse. They may be in philosophical disarray; they may be guilty, in many cases, of not knowing where their own true long-run interests lie — of "selling rope to their hangman"; but they do go on producing.[8]

Dr. Wogaman is again correct in insisting that this type of nobility certainly does not apply to *all* businessmen. However, one might take exception to his characterization: "Is there no hint of desire for reward to *cloud* their motives?" (emphasis added). Why should a desire for reward "cloud" the motives of the "suffering servant" in Novak's account? Cannot a person be a suffering servant and also desire a reward? Is this not a most unrealistic standard to which Dr. Wogaman holds the businessmen? Are employee's motives "clouded" by a desire for their work to be financially rewarded? Is not the businessman, as well as the labourer "worthy of his hire?"

Dr. Wogaman charges that the market system's "very great focus upon material incentives may lead to the enthronement of materialistic greed" and that "the free enterprise system has appeared to spawn a good deal of plain, old-fashioned greed."[9]

However, the individualism spawned by the marketplace allows for very great variation in this phenomenon. Under free enterprise, the impoverished beatnik poet coexists with the wealthy rock star; the ascetic can live next to the materialist; the monastery dedicated to poverty may be located cheek-by-jowl with an opulent opera house, university or cathedral. In any case, some perspective might be useful here. Capitalism has indeed coexisted with greed, acquisitiveness and materialism; those who regard these as necessarily negative motivations may take comfort from the fact that the marketplace gives vent to these human feelings, and turns them to good account. For it is only by supplying the needs of others, that one can acquire material goods; it is only through voluntary trade that one can assuage one's greed.[10]

In contrast, where such human motivations appear under socialism, they are not readily sublimated into socially productive avenues. Nor is there any evidence that I know of (and Wogaman cites none) showing materialism and greed to be any less prevalent under socialism than under capitalism.[11]

Low wage exploitation

Dr. Wogaman begins this section by acknowledging the benefits of the cost-reducing qualities of capitalism, but objecting to the fact that the "market . . . is largely blind to the ways in which enterprises manage to cut their costs."[12] To wit: "firms are . . . rewarded by the market for keeping wages as low as possible, avoiding unnecessary costs to improve employee working conditions." As an example, he uses the plight of well-intentioned Christian growers in Central California arrayed against the farm labour movement of Cesar Chavez.

In order to do justice to this example, we must first take a slight detour, and consider how wages[13] are determined in a free market.

Suppose that a worker's marginal revenue product (MRP)[14] is equal to $2.00 per hour. What would the profit maximizing employer *like* to pay him? Let us assume that 1¢ per hour is the first offer.[15] Now this is pretty cushy for the employer, if he can get away with it, for he can earn a pure profit of $1.99 per hour on this worker (and presumably on every other one as well). However, this marvelous profit opportunity will attract other employers (and those on the margin between employee status, self-employment and the employment of others). How will they horn in on this bonanza? By offering a higher wage, so as to attract the 1¢ per hour workers away from the first employer. We may assume that the second wage offer is at 2¢ per hour because the motivations of the other employers: they want to pay more than the first employer, because they must do so in order to attract away his workers, but not to pay so much as to threaten their own profits.

At 2¢ per hour, however, the situation that prevailed at the 1¢ level will obtain again: massive profits will be earned by those fortunate enough to employ a $2 worker for 2¢; other will be still mightily attracted to make counter offers. The wage will be bid up to 5¢, 10¢, 50¢, $1.25, $1.75.[16]

Where will this process end? At no less than $2.00 per hour (when due allowance is taken of all costs involved in searching for workers whose pay is below their marginal revenue productivity levels, of inducing them to come to the employers' place of business, of transporting them there, of feeding, clothing and sheltering them, if these costs are higher than those which would prevail at home).[17] For at any lower wage, there would still be extra profits to be earned through upward bidding.[18]

This process is a very robust one indeed. Just as nature abhors a vacuum, the profit maximizing employer (in effect) abhors a worker paid significantly below his MRP level. Actually, he may not give a fig for the worker's plight, but he certainly *acts as if* he does, in the most demonstrative way possible: by going out, seeking after such a worker, *offering him a higher wage* and transporting him thousands of miles away, if need be. He "exploits" such a situation, and raises his own profits. In doing so, he increases the wage levels of the most downtrodden workers.

We are now ready to return to Dr. Wogaman's analysis of low wages, California growers and Cesar Chavez.

Yes, "firms are rewarded by the market for keeping wages as low as possible." But this process tends to insure wage levels commensurate with productivity; and if they were higher, unemployment would be the result.

Yes, thousands of well-meaning do-gooders have objected to what they were pleased to interpret as low wages and squalid working and housing conditions paid to Mexicans in the California orchards. (Moral outrage can be a heady and enjoyable feeling, and the Jane Fondas, the Tom Haydens, the Ed Asners and the other trendies have partaken to the fullest.) But from the viewpoint of the workers themselves, these conditions are seen as a vast improvement over the alternatives open to them in Mexico. How else can we explain their willingness to come back to work in central California, year after year?

As to the plight of the "good Christian growers," economically, they are in the same position as all other growers of whatever religious or moral persuasion: the marketplace forces them to pay wages commensurate with productivity. If they pay less, they will tend to lose their employees; if they pay more, they will tend to bankrupt themselves.

There are, however, two supererogatory actions that the particularly moral person could undertake to distinguish himself from all other growers: 1) he could increase his charitable contributions, but if he does so on the basis of combatting poverty, there are people on this globe in far worse conditions than the employees of the California growers; 2) he could be clear as to the economics of the situation, so that he will refrain from supporting those such as Cesar Chavez and his ilk, whose policies will *worsen* the plight of the farm workers.

Now let us consider the role of Cesar Chavez and his farm labour movement. The goal is to raise the wages of the farm workers. His main impediment to this end are the workers from Mexico—the wetbacks, or braceros—who are more than happy to take jobs at a fraction of the pay commanded by Chavez's United Farm Workers' Union. (These wages might be considered low by UFWU standards, but they are princely compared to opportunities available at home in Mexico.) They are a thorn in his side because if he can eliminate Mexican labour from competing with his own Mexican-American workers, Chavez can raise pay scales, to a certain degree, *without* creating unemployment within his union.

And what is the Chavez response? *To urge that immigration restrictions be tightened,* making it more difficult for the growers to "exploit" Mexican labour (i.e., making it more difficult for the Mexicans to flood fervently into the U.S. in the hope of being exploited by the California growers, who will raise their wages up toward their productivity levels). Chavez, in other words, is attempting to use a completely non-market sanction (the violence of the immigration authorities) to sacrifice the welfare of the truly downtrodden Mexican workers, to benefit himself and his more affluent Mexican-American UFWU. He is in effect a Robin Hood in reverse. He robs from the poor and gives to the (relatively) rich.

Public services

Dr. Wogaman objects to "exclusive reliance upon the free market" with regard to the provision of services such as "police and military and fire protection, education, transportation, parks, museums, and public works projects." But his account is somewhat unsatisfactory. First, he does not clearly distinguish between two separate schools of thought which both advocate the market system. One is the classical liberal school, or democratic capitalism, which advocates the free market-*limited government* philosophy. In this view, there *is* a role for government. And it is to function in precisely those areas that Dr. Wogaman himself mentions in the above quote. The other is the school of free market anarchism, which holds that the marketplace can be entrusted with *all* roles traditionally assigned to government, even including defense, security, provision of a law code, etc.

Secondly, he mislabels Milton Friedman as an advocate of free market anarchism. But as his book *Capitalism and Freedom* makes clear, Milton Friedman sees a strong, although limited role for government.[19]

It therefore follows, as far as Dr. Wogaman's subsequent questions are concerned, that he, along with Milton Friedman (and Friedrich Hayek, and Ludwig von Mises and David Hume, and Adam Smith and John Stuart Mill) would *all* be in accord—at least insofar as government's appropriate role is concerned. Yes, "... there (are) some kinds of consumption where it is better not to try to assess consumers precisely the costs of their consumption." And yes, "some forms of economic decision-making for society (should) be on the basis of one-person/one-vote rather than one-dollar/one-vote."

This role for government is, however, related to the provision of specific goods and services—those that exhibit certain technical properties, characteristic of so-called "public goods." The argument does not encompass "generalized social planning" through political arrangements, as Wogaman seems to imply. Nor does the argument rest at all on considerations of income or wealth inequality. The classical liberal school assigns a *limited* role to government. And although there is a strong conviction in the superiority of democratic over other forms of political arrangements, democratic institutions are not taken as an unqualified ideal, as they seem to be for Wogaman. "Democratic capitalism"[20] acknowledges objections to "exclusive reliance on free markets" but at the same time emphatically rejects "exclusive reliance on political arrangements."

Democratic socialism

While democratic capitalism and Dr. Wogaman's brand of democratic socialism have one thing in common — a belief in the superiority of the democratic political process over other forms of collective decision-making — the former allows this process far less scope than the latter, preferring the marketplace as the organizing tool for the provision of most economic goods and services.

This is why the democratic capitalist would be in profound disagreement with the sort of central economic planning through-the-political-process advocated in his paper. Let us consider some of the specifics.

"While even a democratic government can make mistakes, its actions will be based upon a publicly argued-out conception of the kind of community the majority of the people want it to be." This might perhaps appropriately describe an eighteenth century New England town meeting of several dozen people, but when is the last time any nation-wide decision was based on "publicly argued-out conceptions?"[21] The dwindling percentage of people who can even be bothered to vote is one bit of counter-evidence to this vision. Then, too, there is the point that *direct* democracy is now possible — given the revolution in computer technology, and the fact that nearly everyone now boasts of a telephone or television. Should we therefore disband parliaments and congresses and let the people "debate the serious issues" of legislation, and then vote on them? There is at least one good argument against this social-democratic vision — if inaugurated, and acted upon, most people would have very little time to work for a living.

It is crucial to consider Milton Friedman's explanation of why the political process so often fails to work in the interests of the average person. At the core of his analysis is the fact that we are relatively more concentrated as producers than as consumers.[22] We each consume literally thousands of different goods and services each year, but ourselves produce only one, or at most, a few items. Suppose a scheme is put forward in the legislature — a tariff protection, a licensing arrangement, or any other type of special subsidy to one particular industry — for example, toothbrushes. This scheme may not cost each individual more than a dollar or two per year, if only becuse of the limited role (in the financial sense) that toothbrushes commonly play in our lives. However, because of the sheer numbers of an entire national population, the total cost may be in the hundreds of millions. The benefits to the "toothbrush interests" may only be in the tens of millions, because of economic inefficiency, economic leakage, red tape, bureaucratic sloth, etc., *and yet the scheme may well obtain the approval of the constitutionally derived democratic process.* (Indeed, the cynic would claim that our legislatures are choked with enactments which do little else than raid the purses of the poor and middle class for the benefit of the well-to-do.) Why is this so?

The "toothbrush interests" eat, sleep, live and breathe toothbrushes. Their children are taught "toothbrush theory" from the very cradle. They know their entire fortunes may be predicated upon favourable legislative treatment. At any slight threat to these prerogatives, they are ready to mobilize — with every ounce of strength of their combined forces.[23]

And what of their opponents? The typical consumer couldn't care less. (And if, in the odd case, there were an eccentric consumer who cared, and cared deeply, about toothbrushes, how would he have time as well to combat the raids on the public purse of the widget industries, the steel interests, the auto protectionists, and other "robber barons" seeking after special government privileges?) He spends so little on toothbrushes in total, and the additional cost to him of the latest depredation will add so little; he certainly has not the time, inclination or ability to testify before a legislative committee, organize a protest or petition, or defend the public interest in any other meaningful way.[24]

Is it any wonder that our democratic system — when allowed to operate as a replacement for the marketplace, rather than a support for it — has degenerated into a type of Hobbesian war of all against all — where the better organized special interest groups are all too often able to prevail? Is it really in the consumer interest that this system be extended to cover more and more of our economy? Surely the necessarily disorganized and unconcentrated consumer would be better served by *restricting* the political sphere as much as possible, and allowing competitive market forces to better protect his interests.

Another consideration: when government's role is limited, it is at least theoretically possible for the direct representatives of the people — the elected officials — to make most of the decisions, and to stand or fall on this basis. As the scope of the public sector expands, this task becomes more and more burdensome and complex. It is soon impossible for a mere handful of elected officials to run virtually an entire economy.[25] Technicians, scientists, economists, lawyers, social workers and other bureaucrats must be brought in—by the thousands—to make the actual day-to-day decisions.

But these people are almost completely insulated from the democratic process. And a welter of civil service regulations makes it virtually impossible to fire them, except for the most egregious of violations. Most of the actual decision-makers in a democratic socialist economy thus come to be unresponsive to the desires and needs of the populace.[26]

Further, in the political process, the majority wins, and the losing minority often resents this. In the market, in contrast, each opinion can be satisfied. For example, with public education, whether or not sex education is taught in the schools, one group or another is outraged. If education were privatized, each faction would be free to patronize schools which catered to its wishes. Thus the private alternative, in eschewing the imposition of majority wishes on unwilling minorities, is less a threat to the spirit of co-operation and peaceful relations in society. The more we extend the role of the state, the more we risk tearing the social fabric.

Inequality

Scattered throughout this paper are several allusions to income and wealth disparities. We learn that "The poorest members of a community may be well enough off economically that they are not suffering physically while, at the same time, they are so much poorer than others that it is nearly impossible to relate as brother and sister to the affluent"; that free enterprise ". . . may lead to too great inequalities"; that ". . . *lassez-faire* economic policies . . . have perpetuated vast disparities of income and wealth in American society."

I am tempted to begin my reply to these charges by saying that the inequality is not as great as Dr. Wogaman thinks it is. But I cannot, since Dr. Wogaman does not vouchsafe us any measurements,[27] and contents himself with the assertion that whatever it is, it is too great.

Instead, let us consider several factors which may convince Dr. Wogaman that the kind of inequality he sees in Western democracies is not quite as serious or objectionable as it might appear at first blush. For example, it is well known that earnings vary with age: the income of the average 18-year-old cannot be expected to match that of an average 46-year-old. But this is a prime determinant of income inequality between the various American ethnic groups. Consider the following:[28]

Ethnicity	Median Age	Median Family Income as a % of National Average
Jewish	46	172
Polish	40	115
Irish	37	102
Italian	36	112
German	36	107
Japanese	32	132
National Average	28	100
Chinese	27	112
Black	22	62
Indian	20	60
Puerto Rican	18	63
Mexican	18	76

While there is no perfect (negative) correlation between age and income, there can be no doubt that age is an important part of the explanation of why Jews, Poles and Japanese, for instance, are on average far richer than blacks, Indians and Puerto Ricans. Would Dr. Wogaman, or any other concerned person, really wish to set aside such "vast disparities" which spring from a source like this?

But age is not the only such explanatory variable. Others include geographical distribution (people who remain in economically disadvantaged but beautiful rural surroundings earn less than those who move to where new jobs open up; wages are higher in Alberta than Newfoundland; higher in California than Arkansas; "blacks in Mississippi earn less than half the income of blacks in New York state");[29] cultural differences (attitudes, traditions and values about hard work and productivity); educational attainments; gender (the greater involvement in non-market activities on the part of married women explains virtually all of the male/female earnings differential).[30]

There is also the point that "inequality of income" is usually interpreted so as to include only *money* income (or wealth). But surely,

what the economist calls psychic income is ever so much more important, encompassing as it does money, or physical property, as well as
all other things which can create utility. We have already alluded to
the choice of a home in a pleasant rural setting where there are very
few well paying jobs or economic opportunities. There is also entry
into such (psychically) enjoyable, but usually low paying professions
as poet, sculptor, musician, artist, marathon runner or swimmer.
Then there is the leisure/labour choice. Some people work 60 hours a
week, 52 weeks a year, for 60 or more years. Others do as little as
possible. As a result, their incomes and wealth are far lower. But why
should people not bear the financial consequences of such decisions?

Perhaps the most important point is that forced equality of retro-
spective results (as opposed to equality of prospective opportunity) is
incompatible with human freedom. Consider people such as Muhammad Ali, Pinchas Zuckerman, Woody Allen, and Dolly Parton. If
economic freedom is allowed, people of such productive talents and
abilities will necessarily end up with more money than their fellows.

This holds true even if we began with identically equal wealth and incomes for all. For no sooner than we begin, but one of these people
will want to give an exhibition or a concert;[31] other people will be de-
liriously happy to part with some of their money in order to attend.
But on the assumption that the doings of these four people will be
more heavily subscribed to than on average, allowing such voluntary
interaction will create (horrors!) inequality. The choice is simple: if we
want to maintain equality, we will have to deny people the freedom to
interact with each other in this voluntary, peaceful and mutually beneficial way.

Another problem with Dr. Wogaman's analysis is that it fails to
compare the amount of inequality achieved under democratic capitalism with that attained under other political economic systems. As disparate as are wealth and incomes (in the sense which includes the psychic as well as the monetary aspect) in a free enterprise system, it is
even more so in a nation which relies on central planning and forced
income transfers rather than free markets. And there is a reason for
this. The marketplace is a "positive sum game." The only way to become fabulously wealthy is to enrich many other people as well. Henry
Ford, for example, made millions by manufacturing an automobile
the middle class could afford. In so doing, he enriched the lives (and
wealth) of all those who, but for his efforts, would not have been able

to purchase an automobile. Henry Ford gained, but so did almost everyone else. In that sense, Ford gained only a proportion of the total benefits his actions generated.

In contrast, Stalin too was a fabulously wealthy man (even more so than Ford, even only in terms of his strictly economic powers). But his wealth did not come to him through a process which created riches for everyone else as well. Rather, it came to him as a result of massive and forced income transfers. This was a process, then, which enriched him, and impoverished others. Stalin and Ford both gained absolutely; but whereas Ford only gained a percentage of what his activities generated, Stalin gained *all* of what *his* activities generated (or more than all, since he destroyed net wealth in the process).

Socialism

Dr. Wogaman advocates socialism in numerous places without ever coming to grips with what this term really means.

The way I see it, there are two kinds of socialism: voluntary socialism, and coercive socialism.[32] What do the two have in common? An allegiance to a certain kind of income distribution, some variant of the Marxian aphorism "From each according to his abilities, to each according to his needs."

And what are the differences? As the names imply, voluntary socialism establishes this doctrine on a voluntary basis, and coercive socialism does it coercively.

The family, the kibbutz, the monastery, the urban or rural commune, the experimental utopias which flourished in the past century; they are all examples of voluntary socialism. They each live according to this socialistic axiom.

Let us consider the typical family, which consists of a working father, a stay-at-home mother, and several children. The father produces in accordance with his ability; he creates, we may assume, 100 per cent of the family's entire money income. But he consumes based on his needs, which are, of course, far less than 100 per cent of total family income. The mother produces no money income, but not only does she consume based on her needs, she typically has the largest say in determining which needs of each other family members shall be respected. And the children, who earn no money at all, nevertheless usually are first accommodated, when it comes to parcelling out economic goods. (A similar economic pattern applies to all other above-mentioned examples of voluntary communalism.) But entrance to, and exit from, such voluntary socialist institutions is completely free; one is not forced to join, nor is one compelled to remain. In contrast, under coercive socialism, which ideally works in the same internal manner, *one must join the collective whether or not one wishes to; nor may one resign at one's own option!* This would appear to be the meaning of "central economic planning" or "democratic socialism" or "socialist democracy" or "economic decision-making for society on the basis of one-person/one-vote" or "social control over resources," or "permitting the community as a whole to determine priorities and assemble the resources needed to accomplish social objectives."

But perhaps not. Perhaps Dr. Wogaman is really an advocate of voluntary socialism (which, of course, is completely compatible with classical liberalism). So let me pose the following question to Dr. Wogaman, and to "the Socialists of All Parties" (to whom Hayek dedicated his book, *The Road to Serfdom*): are you now, or have you ever been, an advocate of *coercive* socialism? If you had your way, would you *force* recalcitrant people to join your One Big National Commune? Or would you leave them free to trade among themselves, unmolested on the property they own? If not, how can you reconcile your brand of socialism with an adherence to morality?

Breast milk substitutes

According to the Infant Formula Action Coalition (INFACT), several multinational corporations have been guilty of launching an aggressive advertising campaign, aimed at selling breast milk substitutes to Third World mothers. This had led to an outbreak of infant death, or "baby bottle disease," because, while the product may be perfectly acceptable in Europe and North America, this does not hold for the Third World. The reasons:

1. the water supply there is usually polluted, so the infant formula is mixed with impure water, with deleterious effects;
2. severe poverty makes it difficult to buy the fuel necessary to boil and sterilize the water;
3. Third World mothers cannot afford to buy sufficient amounts of formula to replace their own milk; they must therefore dilute the

formula well beyond the point called for in the written instructions;

4. they are often illiterate, and cannot read the instructions;
5. they do not refrigerate the milk, also contrary to instructions, since very few own refrigerators; and
6. by the time the mother realizes that infant formula leads to a sickly, malnourished baby, her own milk has dried up and she has no alternative to continued formula usage.

Although not spelled out in his paper, it is presumably for these or similar reasons that Dr. Wogaman approves of Third World or international (U.N.) efforts to better "govern the practices of transnational pharmaceutical companies."

The implicit premise of the argument is that bad as these practices of the multinationals are, the effort of the various U.N. organizations would not be worse. But, when looked at in this way, such a claim is very difficult to sustain.

For it is conceded by INFACT and other opponents of the multinationals that there is nothing wrong with the baby formula *per se.* The difficulty concerns only the economic situation in the Third World with which the formula must interact: the poverty, the impure water, the illiteracy, the lack of refrigeration, etc.

But which organizations are responsible for this sad state of affairs in the first place? The collectivist economic planning of the Third World socialist governments (and the U.N.) is itself responsible for the poverty, the impure water, the illiteracy, the lack of refrigeration, etc., which are the root causes of the infant formula tragedy.[33] Asking the Third World governments, or the U.N., to take charge and improve matters, is thus like asking the arsonist to put out the fire.

Let us now consider a second argument against government control of pharmaceutical multinationals, again on the assumption that the scenario as given by INFACT is accurate.

We live in a sea of ignorance. On this side of the Garden of Eden, even with the best of intentions, men are likely to err. Their mistakes, moreover, are liable to be serious, upon occasion, even causing the deaths of numerous people. There is nothing that can be done to alter this unfortunate situation; it follows directly from man's imperfection.

There is, however, one (admittedly imperfect) remedy: if we cannot eliminate this error, let us *at least* resolve to adopt a system which automatically and quickly rewards people who are less liable to such mistakes, and discourages people who are more prone. As discussed above, under Democratic Socialism, the marketplace is far preferrable in this regard than the regulatory bureaus which are very indirectly controlled through the political process. In order to further cement this insight, let us consider yet another multinational pharmaceutical tragedy which rivals even the milk substitute horror: the thalidomide case.

Thalidomide was produced by a private company, and approved for use by the West German regulatory bureau concerned with pharmaceuticals. Given this horrendous mistake, how have the two fared? Which one was more heavily discouraged: the private company, by the marketplace, or the regulatory bureau, through the political process?[34] Obviously, the former; the latter remained unscathed.

Having assumed the accuracy of the INFACT story, it is now time to challenge it. According to the infant formula protestors, manufacturers' advertising is responsible for the adoption of breast milk alternatives. Yet there is little statistical correlation between advertising efforts and infant formula use. "In the Philippines, there is intensive advertising and frequent gifts of milk samples to mothers who deliver in the hospital. And sure enough, only 69 per cent of economically advantaged mothers ever breast-feed. Yet Nigeria has similar advertising and milk-sample practices, and 100 per cent of such mothers breast-feed. With little advertising, only 32 per cent of rural Chilean mothers are still breast-feeding at 18 months; with intensive mass advertising 82 per cent of Nigerian rural mothers are. Hungary, which has no advertising, and Sweden, where advertising is limited by law to professional journals, have the lowest figures of all for breast-feeding at one month and beyond. Such statistics do not a correlation make."[35]

Further, in a six-country study undertaken by the World Health Organization in 1981, only in Hungary (not usually considered a Third World country) and in Guatemala, is there any significant possibility that people might feel formula is preferrable to breast milk.[36] In all nine countries, the overwhelming reason given for not breast feeding is "little or no milk" on the part of the mother; the second most typical is illness, either the mother's or the child's. Are such people to be cut off from breast milk substitutes?[37]

Then there is the widely touted claim that "up to one million infant deaths per year are attributable to infant formula," made by James Grant, executive director of UNICEF.[38] However, as it turns out, the "evidence" for this claim, reports *Newsweek,* is a "symbolic figure"; i.e., made up out of the whole cloth by an anti-infant formula activist.[39]

As Dr. Wogaman points out, WHO and UNICEF developed "a marketing code to correct abuses," which was adopted by the World Health Assembly, with only the U.S. voting against it. Since he does not give the reason behind this decision, we will supply it:

> . . . But the United States cannot support the proposed Code because it would be, if enacted into national legislation, an unwarranted invasion of the freedom of men and women to engage in peaceful exchange of goods and services and a denial of the rights of consumers to make informed choices about products which appear to them to best meet their needs.
>
> Freedom is important to Americans. Our political, economic, legal and social systems are based on the idea of maximizing individual freedom. We believe it is not an accident that our country has achieved its present degree of prosperity, for prosperity is the result of the labor, the investment, and the confidence of free men and women in a society founded upon the ideal of freedom.
>
> Freedom, in the economic sphere, must admittedly be regulated to some extent. Laws against fraud and misrepresentation must be enforced, so that consumers can make informed choices about the products they buy. Products potentially dangerous to human health can be restricted or banned. But if a product can be lawfully sold in the marketplace, then it is essential that those who offer the product have the right to announce its availability to customers, and to describe its merits without misrepresentation. It is essential that the sellers have the freedom to promote their product through sales incentives. And it is essential that consumers have the opportunity to exercise free and informed choice in the selection of products and services.
>
> The proposed Code does not claim that breastmilk substitutes are harmful to infant health. They are not, unless consumers make them harmful by ignoring the instructions and adding polluted water to the powder. But the Code would deny to sellers of this non-harmful product the freedom to advertise its merits, and to make voluntary contractual arrangements for its marketing. The United States believes that these proscriptions strike at the heart of an economic system built upon free choice and voluntary exchange in the marketplace. Believing as we do that such a system offers the best hope for the increased prosperity and well-being of mankind, and recognizing the privation and grief endured by so many millions of people

in countries which prohibit free choice and voluntary exchange, we are compelled to vote against the recommendation of this Code for adoption by member governments.[40]

Based on this reasoning, analysis and evidence, Hickel asks:

What motivates the antiformula forces? If the concern is for Third World families, why haven't their efforts been directed toward convincing appropriate organizations of the need for an educational campaign to make both health care professionals and mothers more aware of the positive case for breast milk and of the proper use of formula when it is used? Why, instead, have they devoted themselves to reducing the choices open to mothers? Why have they not sounded the alarm about the health hazard of using natural supplemental foods that are mixed with often impure water, instead of singling out manufactured formula as a danger?

Why is there no concern about the costs to Third World governments — that is, to their citizens — of implementing the WHO code? And why is there no acknowledgement of the fact that the code may well foster interference with those mothers who are unable or simply do not wish to breast-feed and could use infant formula to enable their children to survive?[41]

Dr. Wogaman tells us that "Many companies resist such regulation (the infant formula companies did so quite vigorously)." But at least with regard to Nestle, one of the main participants, this is disputable. Childs points to "... the craven actions of Nestle, which, instead of taking the claims of the boycotters seriously, and moving to address them in a way which maximizes the positive, constructive use of its products in the Third World, has instead caved into a crazed list of 'recommendations' made by the WHO/UNICEF meeting last month."[42]

One last view of Dr. Wogaman on this episode is worthy of comment. According to our author, "The code was adopted purely as a recommendation for national law and company policy, but its adoption by the international body gave it considerable moral weight, ..." Now this is the U.N. we are talking about, an organization which has distinguished itself by issuing hundreds of arbitrary, capricious and immoral resolutions. Surely we must therefore question whether its adoption of any particular code adds "considerable moral weight" — or the very opposite? Either that, or we must note that the term "moral" is being used here in a stipulative, not a reportive, sense.

Conclusion

The first half of "Theological Perspective on Economics" is devoted mainly to theology; the second, mainly to economics. The basic premise of this paper is that theology commits a religious person to a particular economic philosophy: as it happens, democratic socialism. Although this premise is never stated in these exact words, Dr. Wogaman does come close: "From a theological perspective, it seems clear that it is easier for more people to be what God has intended them to be as participants in the life of community because of active interventions by government; Theology has an important, even indispensable, role to play in contributing perspective to economic life."

Dr. Wogaman makes a valiant attempt to put forth this thesis, but I think, ultimately, that he fails.[43] I do not believe that his theology is either a necessary nor sufficient condition for his economic opinions. One could agree almost entirely with his theological perspective and yet still take a *laissez-faire* position. Nor does Dr. Wogaman's variant of Galbraithian economics need his theological viewpoint as a precondition; many social democrats are complete atheists. One is not guilty of internal self-contradiction for adopting Dr. Wogaman's theology without his economics, or his economics without his theology.

Paradoxically, it was Dr. Wogaman himself, at the very beginning of his essay, who warned against the facile deduction of economic conclusions from theological premises. He showed that any attempt to directly apply theology to specific contemporary problems is fraught with danger: how to reconcile the Parable of the Talents and St. Paul's "If anyone will not work let him not eat" with the numerous biblical passages condemning wealth. And does not Christianity justify "slavery in our own time," based on some passages of St. Paul's? Had Dr. Wogaman taken his own warning more seriously, he might not have so directly deduced his economics from his theology.

NOTES

1. The title of the book, and film series of the same name, by Milton and Rose Friedman, *Free to Choose,* New York: Harcourt Brace Jovanovich, 1980.

2. Says Robert Nozick "There is no more a distributing or distribution of shares than there is a distributing of mates in a society in which persons choose whom they shall marry." *Anarchy, State and Utopia,* New York: Basic Books, 1974, p. 150.

3. I owe this explanation to Father James Sadowsky, S.J.

4. For statistics on Soviet grain production, see Roger A. Clark, *Soviet Economic Facts: 1917-1970,* London: MacMillan, 1972, pp. 110-113; on imports, The Economist, *The World in Figures,* London: Economist Newspaper, Ltd., second edition, 1978, p. 28; "Russian Agriculture: the Good Earth Stubbornly Refuses to Deliver the Goods," *The Economist,* November 15, 1980, pp. 19-22; Carlo M. Cipolla, ed., *The Fontana Economic History of Europe,* vol. IV, The Emergence of Industrial Societies, Part II, Glasglow: William Collins Sons & Co., 1973, Statistical Appendix, pp. 752, 753.

5. As one wag put it, there has been bad weather in the Soviet Union every year since 1971.

6. The 97 per cent of the collectivized farm land accounts for less than two-thirds of total farm produce; the 3 per cent of the land where the rights of private property still prevail accounts for over one-third of the produce. *The Economist,* November 15, 1980, op.cit., p. 21.

7. Cf. *The Christmas Chipmunks,* National Film Board of Canada.

8. For a novel which explores the theme of businessmen on strike, see Ayn Rand, *Atlas Shrugged,* New York: New American Library, 1952.

9. I have yet to see a satisfactory definition of greed that would account for the loathsomeness with which this concept is applied. Webster's Seventh New Collegiate Dictionary defines it as "inordinate or reprehensible acquisitiveness." But this is of little help. For this definition would appear to concede that mere acquisitiveness is not evil (thank goodness; without acquisitiveness, the human race would never have gotten past its hunting and gathering stage), but only when carried forth to an inordinate or reprehensible degree. The same treatment, however, could be accorded to almost any human characteristic. Faith, logic, love or charity would also presumably be evils, if carried forward to "an inordinate or reprehensible degree." But no one is ever moved to refer *derisively* to "a good deal of plain old-fashioned charity." So perhaps what is really being objected to is simple acquisitiveness — whether or not carried to "an inordinate degree."

Paul Heyne defines greed as "claiming for the self more than is due." (See his "The Concept of Economic Justice in Religious Discussion," in this volume.) As such, greed is practically a synonym for cheating, stealing, or fraud. But this is surely an eccentric definition.

10. Says Adam Smith, *Wealth of Nations,* "It is not from the benevolence of the butcher, the brewer or the baker that we expect our dinner, but from their regard to their own interests..."

11. I cannot leave this section devoted to motivations without at least noticing a brief critique of the capitalist system offered by Dr. Wogaman. "The competitive character of economic life may lead to divisive individualism, particularly evident during times of economic crisis and unemployment .... The system may be too vulnerable to the contrasting problems of inflation and recession." I am not sure what *divisive* individualism is, but there is a well-entrenched economic literature showing the link between government fiscal and macro-money mismanagement, on the one hand, and "economic crisis and unemployment" on the other. See in this regard: Milton Friedman and Anna Schwartz, *The Great Contraction 1929-1933,* New York: National Bureau of Economic Research, 1965; Henry Hazlitt, *The Failure of the New Economics,* New Rochelle, N.Y.: Arlington House, 1973; Constantino Bresciani-Turroni, *The Economics of Inflation,* New York: Augustus Kelley, 1968; F. A. Hayek, *Prices and Production,* London: Routledge, 1931; F. A. Hayek, *Monetary Theory and the Trade Cycle,* New York: Kelley, 1966; *Studies in the Quantity Theory of Money,* ed. by Milton Friedman, Chicago: University of Chicago Press, 1956; Murray Rothbard, *America's Great Depression,* Kansas City: Sheed and Ward, 1975.

These readings will also serve as a useful antidote to Dr. Wogaman's view that "The *laissez-faire* assumptions that guided economic policy before 1933 were impotent to prevent or deal with the greatest economic catastrophe in American history."

12. The marketplace itself *is* blind to the ways in which entrepreneurs can act; but the advocates of classical liberalism never meant the market to operate in a vacuum. On the contrary, they have always insisted that it be embedded in a legal framework. As Dr. Wogaman himself states "Where the free market is dominant ... the role of government in economics is limited to the protection of property and the maintenance of agreed rules of the game." Thus, entrepreneurs cannot act as they want; they are bound by the "rules of the game." Broadly stated, these rules mandate that no one should be allowed to initiate force or fraud upon innocent persons (people who have not themselves initiated force or fraud). Thus, given an appropriate legal code, firms would not be allowed to indiscriminately dump

wastes into rivers. In this regard, see Edwin G. Dolan, *TANSTAAFL: The Economic Strategy for Environmental Crisis,* New York: Holt, Rinehart, 1971.

Nor would entrepreneurs be allowed to do "*anything* else that will lower the costs of doing business" (emphasis added), as claimed by our author. This sounds as if Dr. Wogaman has murder or theft in mind; but clearly anything of this sort would be strictly forbidden, as it is now. This holds for product misrepresentation as well. For a treatment of the rules appropriate to a free society, see Bruno Leoni, *Freedom and the Law,* Los Angeles: Nash, 1972; F. A. Hayek, *The Constitution of Liberty,* Chicago: Regnery, 1960; F. A. Hayek, "The Principles of a Liberal Social Order" in *Studies in Philosophy, Politics and Economics,* New York: Simon and Schuster, 1969.

These remarks apply, as well, to Dr. Wogaman's statement that "The real question is whether private centres of economic power will be kept subordinate to governmental power, which alone can uphold the order of justice." This is not the real question at all, since the democratic capitalist philosophy stipulates that economic power shall be subordinate to the "rules of the game."

13. I refer, here, to total wages, which would include money wages plus the quality of working conditions, fringe benefits, etc., and all other elements which comprise the entire wage "package."

14. Marginal Physical Product (MPP) is defined as the extra amount of physical product that will be created by one additional worker, with all other factors such as land, capital, other employees, held constant. Let us assume an MPP of 10 widgets per hour; this means that for every hour of labour, the employer will have 10 more widgets than if this worker had not been employed.

Marginal Revenue (MR) is defined as the additional revenue which will accrue to the widget manufacturer, for each extra widget he can sell. For simplicity's sake, we assume he can gain 10¢ for each and every extra widget he can produce. Thus:

$$MRP = MPP \times MR = 20 \times 10¢ = \$2.00 \text{ per hour}$$

15. The technical answer to this question is "minus infinity." If the profit maximizer were true to his calling, he would prefer that the employee pay *him* an infinite amount of money for the privilege of being employed.

Needless to say, the identical analysis applies to the question asked from the other side of the bargaining table. What would the profit-maximizing employee like to be paid for his labours? Also an infinite amount of money.

16. It is extremely unlikely that a wage of 1¢ per hour could ever have been paid in a real world situation. The competitive process between employers would have made this impossible. We mention this contra-factual scenario only in order to highlight the underlying process which renders such a result impossible.

17. There is also the technical matter that productivity levels (and indeed, everything else in the marketplace) are continually changing. The $2.00 MRP is likely to change long before this process would arrive at a wage of exactly $2.00. MRP may rise, say, to $2.25, whereupon the process of upward wage bidding must begin again. For an analysis which focuses on the continually changing character of the market process, see Israel Kirzner, *Competition and Entrepreneurship,* Chicago: University of Chicago Press, 1973. In addition, for the assumption that wage and MRP will come to exact equality, we must make the assumption that no monopsony power exists, or rather that if it does, it will not be supported by legislation.

18. What would happen if a union were to enter this happy pastoral economic idyll, and somehow raise wages to $3.00 (without, of course, raising productivity levels)? Well, the employer would now be in a position of paying $3.00 per hour for workers who add to his receipts at a rate of only $2.00 per hour. He would lose $1.00 every hour he was open for business, multiplied by the size of his payroll. Such a union would have killed the goose that lays the golden eggs, and created unemployment at $3.00 per hour where employment at $2.00 per hour had previously existed.

19. Perhaps Dr. Wogaman is confusing the little-known Milton Friedman with his more eminent son, David, who *is* an advocate of free market or philosophical anarchism. For an explanation of this position, see David Friedman *The Machinery of Freedom,* op.cit., part III; also Murray N. Rothbard, *For a New Liberty,* New York: Macmillan, 1973; William Woodridge, *Uncle Sam, Monopoly Man,* New Rochelle, N.Y.: Arlington House, 1970.

20. See Robert Benne, *The Ethic of Democratic Capitalism,* Philadelphia: Fortress Press, 1981; Michael Novak, *The Spirit of Democratic Capitalism,* New York: Basic Books, 1982.

21. In Canada, although every public opinion poll taken on the subject indicates that an overwhelming majority consistently favours the death penalty for first degree murder, Parliament has not only refused to enact this into law, it even refuses to consider it. In the U.S., a similar pattern emerges regarding school busing and prayer in the public schools. Can anyone imagine a similar disregard for consumer desires on the part of merchants and entrepreneurs, who fall over themselves to please their customers?

22. Milton Friedman, *Capitalism and Freedom,* Chicago: University of Chicago Press, 1962, p. 143. People who are familiar with Friedman's contribution will appreciate my debt to him in the following paragraphs.

23. As should be clear from this account, the classical liberal philosophy is by no means necessarily "pro business," at least not in the extreme short-sighted and short-run sense in which businessmen themselves all too often favour. It favours markets, but not specific businesses—a vital distinction.

24. The same applies to public interest groups such as Consumers Union, National Taxpayers Union, Good Housekeeping, Common Cause, and the various Naderite groups. Apart from their fatal adherence to democratic socialism as a means of promoting consumer interest (in the case of the latter two), the plain fact is that these "consumerist" organizations have but a small fraction of the power or wealth of those who are organized on the production side.

25. Even were this somehow possible, the elected official is *still* far less responsive to the political voters than is the entrepreneur to the dollar voters. Consider the fact that while an unhappy electorate may have to wait four or five years to "turn out the rascals," (this was of particular relevance in Canada in the summer of 1982), the unhappy consumer is able to register his dissatisfaction *immediately:* by simply refusing to purchase any more of the offending goods and services.

    Then, too, there is the point that in the political arena, we can only vote on a package deal basis: we have no way of expressing approval of the government's handling of any one specific program. We may take this ability for granted in the economic arena, but there is no doubt that we can make very fine distinctions between goods and services provided by particular individuals. For further reading in this subject, see James M. Buchanan, *The Demand and Supply of Public Goods,* Chicago: Rand McNally, 1968; James M. Buchanan and Gordon Tullock, *The Calculus of Consent,* Ann Arbor: University of Michigan Press, 1962; James M. Buchanan, *Fiscal Theory and Political Economy,* Chapel Hill: University of North Carolina Press, 1960; James M. Buchanan and Robert D. Tollison, *Theory of Public Choice,* Ann Arbor: University of Michigan Press, 1972; Anthony Downs, *An Economic Theory of Democracy,* New York: Harper, 1957.

26. See Friedrich A. Hayek, *Road to Serfdom,* Chicago: University of Chicago Press, 1944, for an insightful description of this phenomenon.

27. For several studies on income and wealth inequality, see Donald Armstrong, Peter H. Friesen, and Danny Miller, "The Measurement of Income Institutions in Canada: Some Problems and Some Tentative Data," *Canadian Public Policy,* vol. III, no. 4, 1977; Morton Paglin, "The

Measurement and Trend of Inequality: A Basic Revision," *American Economic Review,* September 1975; Morton Paglin, "Response and Reply," *American Economic Review,* vol. 67, no. 3; Gian Singh Sahota, "Theories of Personal Income Distribution: A Survey," *Journal of Economic Literature XVI,* March 1978; Donald Armstrong, "Executive Incomes, Myth and Reality," *Chimo,* December 1979.

28. Source: Thomas Sowell, "The Presuppositions of Affirmative Action," in *Discrimination, Affirmative Action, and Equal Opportunity,* ed. by Walter Block and Michael Walker, Vancouver: The Fraser Institute, 1982, pp. 42, 46.

29. Sowell, *ibid.,* p. 44. Those familiar with Sowell's work will see my great reliance on it here.

30. See Walter Block, "Economic Intervention, Discrimination and Unforeseen Consequences," *ibid.,* pp. 105–113.

31. See Robert Nozick, *Anarchy, State and Utopia,* New York: Basic Books, 1974, pp. 160–164, for a discussion of "How Liberty Upsets (Income Distributional) Patterns." Asks Nozick: "If D was a just (income) distribution, and people voluntarily moved from it to D₂, transferring parts of their shares they were given under D, (what was it for if not to do something with ?), isn't D₂ also just?" (p. 161).

32. This distinction is akin to that made by Benne between "hard" and "soft" utopianism. In the soft utopian scenario, "The Kingdom of God would come through the long march of persuasive love through institutional life." Continues Benne: "Other types of utopianism are not so soft. When Christians grew self-righteous in their assessment of their own virtue and overly confident in their vision of the good society, they did not hesitate to impose that virtue and vision on society. They even used violent means to achieve what they knew was right and good. This is 'hard' utopianism. . . . What makes this viewpoint 'hard' is that it is willing to use coercive power to press its vision onto a reluctant society." Robert Benne, *The Ethic of Democratic Capitalism,* p. 42.

33. To be sure, one cannot claim that there are no other causes for Third World poverty besides government mismanagement. There are overpopulation and lack of resources — although rich and relatively free market Hong Kong is subject to these difficulties. For a thorough critique of Third World central planning, see: P. T. Bauer, *Dissent on Development,* London: Weidenfeld and Nicolson, 1971; Peter T. Bauer and Basil Yamey, *The Economics of Under-developed Countries,* Chicago: University of Chicago Press, 1957; P. T. Bauer, *West African Trade,* London: Cambridge University Press, 1954; Bauer and Yamey, "Competition and Prices: a Study of Groundnut Buying in Nigeria," *Economica,* February

1952; P. T. Bauer, "The Economics of Marketing Reform," *Journal of Political Economy,* June 1954; P. T. Bauer, *The Public Industry,* London, 1948; P. T. Bauer and F. W. Paish, "The Reduction of Fluctuations in the Incomes of Primary Producers," *Economic Journal,* December 1952; P. N. Rosenstein-Rodan, "Problems of Industrialization," in *The Economics of Underdevelopment,* ed. by A. N. Agarwala and S. P. Singh, London: Oxford University Press, 1969; P. T. Bauer, "Ecclesiastical Economics is Envy Exalted," *This World,* Winter 1982, no. 1, pp. 56–69. For a defense of the view that the multinational corporations have acted so as to *alleviate* these problems, see Robert C. Brown, "U.S. International Firms Create Jobs, Goods, Profits, Tax Revenues," *Tax Review,* vol. XXXVI, no. 10, October 1975.

34. A similar point can be made for the Vischyssoise soup company, which quickly went out of business after causing several deaths due to poisoning, and the U.S. Food and Drug Administration, (under whose guidance all such companies must operate) which is still doing business at the same old stand quite nicely thank you.

35. James Hickel, "Infant Formula: WHO Mixes It Up," *Reason,* December 1981, p. 42.

36. Source: *Contemporary Patterns of Breast Feeding,* New York: World Health Organization, 1981, Table A.

37. According to INFACT, "the Nestle boycott 'must continue until the companies make direct and enforceable commitments to halting all formula promotion.'" See Roy A. Childs, "The Nestle boycott: the unsettled issues," *The Libertarian Review,* vol. 8, no. 10, December 1979, p. 8. But without advertising, sickly mothers and mothers unable to breast-feed may never come to know of this life-saving alternative.

38. Reported in the *New York Times.* See Hickel, op. cit., p. 43. The problem with an "up to" claim is that it is true even if zero, one, two or three deaths occurred as a result. If John ate one pickle, it is *true* that John ate "up to" 1,000,000 pickles. This is demagoguery. (I owe this point to John Chant.)

39. Ibid., p. 43.

40. Ibid., p. 45. This principled and ringing statement was from a May 13, 1981 U.S. government draft. Unfortunately, only a watered-down version was officially released.

41. Ibid., pp. 44, 45.

42. Childs, op. cit., p. 8.

43. For two other attempts, see Michael Novak, *The Spirit of Democratic Capitalism,* op. cit., especially p. 39; Robert Benne, *The Ethic of Democratic Capitalism,* op. cit.

TABLE A

Reasons given for not breast-feeding (percentage distribution of answers)*

Country	Group[a]	Child			Mother							Medical advice	Other
		Number re-sponding	in hospital, ill	does not suck, "dislikes"	no milk insuffi-cient milk	breast and nipple problems	ill	emotional problems, beliefs	work "too busy"	does not want to			
			%	%	%	%	%	%	%	%	%	%	
Chile	A	25	16	12	28	16	12	0	0	4	4	8
	C	27	15	11	52	7	15	0	0	0	0	0
	R	21	43	14	29	10	5	0	0	0	0	0
Guatemala	A	69	6	6	43	9	4	13	0	13	0	7
	C	59	20	10	37	3	2	2	0	3	0	22
India	A	37	8	0	59	0	16	0	0	16	0	2
	B	37	3	3	51	0	38	0	0	0	0	5
Philippines	A	190	8	4	37	13	6	3	15	6	0	7
	C	131	5	8	50	12	6	8	8	2	0	2
	R	51	0	12	39	18	8	12	4	8	0	0
Hungary	all	251	0	0	45	0	14	0	0	0	0	41
Sweden	all	47	17	6	23	23	11	13	0	6	0	0

* "Child in hospital or ill" includes some infants hospitalized because of prematurity. No explanation is available for the high proportion of "other" reasons in the returns from Hungary.

* See footnote to Table 1

A = economically advantaged   C = urban poor
B = urban middle income   R = rural

Reply

J. Philip Wogaman

Mindful of P. T. Barnum's dictum that one should not fear criticism as long as one's name is spelled correctly, I am grateful for the attention given my work by both Walter Block and John W. Cooper. The former has examined my paper, "Theological Perspective on Economics," in voluminous detail, and the latter has sought to deal with its essential theme, though with greater parsimony of words. I am likewise grateful to the editors of this volume for offering the opportunity to reply to these friendly critics, although I hasten to assure the reader that I shall not go at this by attempting to reply to every single point.

The primacy of theological commitments

The paper's main commitments are theological, and economic ideologies and policies are therefore subordinated to deeper-level value commitments. Neither critic appears to question that ordering of relationships, although Block questions whether I have drawn the right conclusions from my own theological premises. He is particularly troubled by the way in which I relate the theological doctrine of "grace" to the concept of justice. It is clear that my way of relating the two terms to each other is foreign to him, and I suspect it would take a considerably longer essay to elaborate the connection to his satisfaction (if not to his agreement). He appears to find it especially difficult to think of justice in any way other than that of apportioning benefits (or punishments) in accordance with deserving — in what I have elsewhere called a compensatory view of justice. Clearly that is a part of the meaning of justice, and it is the part that large numbers of people think of when they think of "justice." But I believe there is a deeper way of grounding our understanding of justice, namely by speaking of it as the ordering of society in such a way as to protect everybody's opportunity to participate fully as a member of the community. Supporting this conception there are two important assumptions: first that every human being matters very much and second that we realize our full worth as human beings in society. Both of these assumptions have powerful theological undergirding in the Hebrew-Christian affirmation that we all have our being in and from God. Because God cares for each of us, we are important as individuals – and no individual can be disregarded nor oppressed without violating the relationship we all have with our creator. But God's love for each of us also constitutes the meaning of community: ultimately, humanity is God's family and all questions of human relationship are, finally, family questions. People who are used to thinking of human nature as a purely individual matter and of human freedom as the highest norm must stretch a bit to grasp this understanding of human nature and human value, and I suspect that is the root of Block's difficulty with my paper. I do not wish to put words in his mouth or pen, but I suspect his view of human nature rather sees each of us as individuals, finally responsible for our own value-creation, whose relationships with and within society are based upon exchange for mutual benefit at best and personal self-interest at least. That more individualistic understanding of humanity does not comprehend how profoundly we belong to one another and how inextricable our humanity is from that of our sisters and brothers.

Justice as grace

My point is that to be treated justly is to be treated as a brother or sister. Rewards and punishments (which concern Block very much) may be a very important part of the ordering of the good society, just as they are in the confines of the typical ordinary human family. But the ordering of the family is ultimately predicated upon that more organic sense of oneness than it is upon a nice calculation of how much reward or punishment has been earned. The reader will note the section of my paper devoted to the importance of sin. The reality of sin means that a proper or just ordering of society must indeed come to terms with the need for positive and negative incentives – rewards and punishments. But these things are for the sake of the deeper reality.

Block correctly perceives that the implication of this understanding of God's caring love (or grace) would be, *ceteris paribus,* that economic goods would be available to all regardless of their contribution. But in the real world things are not that simple – *ceteris* rarely is *paribus!* There is enough selfishness and indolence to make it necessary to use incentives to assure the production of an adequate supply of goods, and it is necessary to counter anti-social tendencies in many people by having a criminal law code. The direct implication of grace must be supplemented by institutions and practices that correct for what a theologian might call the "fallen" aspect of human nature. But one does not begin to understand what justice is all about unless one first sees the ultimate context in God's intended community of love. Justice is first of all the ordering of society so that all can participate in that community.

The doctrine of grace is a reminder of yet another important point, however, namely that it is easy for us to overestimate what we have personally earned and to underestimate the degree to which we are the beneficiaries of unearned gifts from others (and ultimately from God). That point is underscored in the parables and sayings of Jesus, where the sharpest criticism is reserved for those who are most self-righteous about their own accomplishments and how much they have earned all the good things they have. In that perspective, the self-righteous attitude of many prosperous people toward the poor people of the world is positively wicked! At the very least, we should all acknowledge that most poor people have had few opportunities to compete successfully in a competitive economy. Those who do make it in Horatio Alger fashion should not assume that if they could do it everybody can — for there are many reasons why that is often not the case. But in any event, the deeper theological perspective is that human beings are not ultimately competitors. Ultimately they are brothers and sisters.

Socialism — a correction of the record

I must comment on a curious error in both of my critics' responses to my paper. Both treat my paper as a socialist writing. I do indeed believe that socialism, particularly democratic socialism, needs to be taken seriously. I do indeed believe that its criticisms of existing economic systems need to be listened to thoughtfully. I do indeed think it possible that humanity may one day turn to this way of organizing economic life. But my paper stops very far short of advocating this alternative, and I clearly and specifically do not consider Christian theology to lead *necessarily* to democratic socialism. A careful re-reading of my paper should make it clear that the paper is not a defence of democratic socialism.

It may, however, be instructive to ask why Block and Cooper were predisposed to interpret the paper in that way. I am prepared to offer a theory: I think it may be because both critics have so negative a view of the economic role of government that anything that contemplates a positive, even necessary place for government in economic life appears socialistic. As I read them, that is more true of Block than Cooper. The latter does speak positively of the New Deal, and my differences with him may come down to the details of *how much* government is desirable rather than *whether* government has an important economic role to play. In the case of Block, however, I rather have the impression that he is suspicious of all government. Where Cooper joins me in rejecting extreme forms of *laissez-faire* capitalism, I believe Block embraces those forms. If everything to the left of *laissez-faire* is socialism then I am, of course, socialist! But if we mean by socialism the government's ownership of all the means of production, then I have issued a number of cautions about that throughout my paper and, in the final analysis, I just don't believe we yet know enough to make a choice between some form of mixed economy capitalism and some form of democratic socialism.

Democratic governance

But the real point I sought to make in the paper about the economic role of government is that we *must* have democratic government, and democratic government must be strong enough to regulate economic life for the sake of the common good. Block is much more skeptical than I about the possibilities of democratic government. He is so eager to avoid the coercive aspects of all government that he (in my opinion) overlooks the even more coercive realities of life without government. The genius of democratic government is its making the coercive aspects of life accountable to a civilized process of decision-making in which the right of every citizen to participate is respected and protected. Without that, society disintegrates into the brutish conflict of "each against all" which characterizes the Hobbesian society and, like Hobbes, we are reduced to yearning for a single strong authority that can at least bring order. Hobbes, too, was skeptical about democracy. But I suspect that most people, if faced with only the alternatives of strong authoritarian rule or the anarchistic tendencies of a purely libertarian state, would join Hobbes in preferring the former to the latter. But I believe — as do most North Americans — that democratic society can provide a vastly superior third possibility that avoids the unacceptable aspects of either of the Hobbesian extremes.

Applied to the economic sphere, I have argued that the market, left entirely alone, simply will not suffice in creating and undergirding the just society. It must be supplemented by and regulated by democratic government. The sum total of private economic decisions may (and I think, will) yield unsatisfactory results for society as a whole if not corrected by government. Those who do not believe in public highways and schools and parks and welfare programs may not be impressed by that argument, but such people have already gone far too far in the direction of individualism, and their model of the good society may be very remote from the one advanced here. I am prepared to concede the utility of the market system as a device for allocating many of the goods and services we all need, and I find it interesting that even many socialists are willing to concede that up to a certain point. But whether we finally opt for some form of democratic socialism or some form of mixed economy capitalism, economic life must ultimately be accountable to the will of the people as expressed through democratic government.

Discussion

Edited by: Kenneth G. Elzinga

John Cooper: I have two main points to make about Phil Wogaman's paper: one on economics, and one on theology. Because I suspect that many of the points he makes on economics will be debated, I've placed a little more emphasis on theology.

I've tried to make the simple point in my comment that there are about as many varieties of theologies of economics as there are people trying to construct them. Phil puts himself, I think, in a large group of democratic socialist theologians. Another identifiable group would be the democratic capitalists, like Michael Novak, Richard John Neuhaus, and Robert Benne.

Now, if Wogaman's democratic socialism suggests in our minds and in his mind the kind of reality we see in Western Europe—mixed economies which call themselves "socialist," but which in fact are based on substantial private sectors and various schemes for the transference of wealth, or even production from the private sector to the public sector—then as I said in my comment, we could all be democratic socialists.

On the other hand, if Phil is saying something more than that, that there should be a revolutionary socialist transformation, as is the case, for example with some radical groups in Canada, then that is another thing altogether. The worst case, I take it, in the world today of coercive socialism, indeed religious socialism, is what we see in Iran. And examples of totalitarian socialism abound.

On the economy, although Phil doesn't use these terms, the basic issue he wishes to discuss is "markets versus planning." Or, I would say, "markets versus government allocation of production and distribution."

Finally, then, turning to the theological side of the theology of economics, I would suggest that Phil Wogaman's paper does us a great service in talking about questions like stewardship, grace versus works, and so forth—issues we may all want to explore in greater detail. But I would make only one comment in this regard. I think there are three economic virtues, if you will, which parallel the traditional theological triad of creation, fall and redemption. These can be paralleled with three economic virtues: stewardship, vocation and charity. Perhaps this last theme, the notion of redemption or charity in Christianity is something we might find at this conference to be quite an issue.

Does the whole question of the relationship between justice and love suggest to us a progressive social ethic, to use Reinhold Niebuhr's term? I think it does. I think a progressive social ethic is crucial to a Christian theology of economics. Otherwise, how would we ever be able to agree that the abolition of slavery, for example, or the emergence of the labour movement, or the development of legal structures which make possible collective bargaining, were steps of progress? Perhaps we don't agree, but I would suggest that a Christian theology of economics includes as well this redemptive notion. And I'd like to redeem that particular theme from Phil's paper.

Walter Block: I find that I'm in virtually full agreement with the goals and the ends that are expressed in Phil's paper. And I find that I'm in virtually full disagreement with the means by which he proposes to attain these goals. I think that if he agreed with me that my means were correct, he would agree with me fully as to what the policy prescriptions are. And I also think that if I agreed with his implicit views of what the best means are, and what the explanatory theories are, I would fully agree with his policy prescriptions. So I think that while there might be some slight differences in goals between us, the differences in goals between us are not very much. They're not really worth talking about. Whereas the differences in means are quite substantial.

Let me go over some of the high points – for example, stewardship. I think that we have a rational means of making sure that we don't have wastage, or pollution, or what have you. I happen to believe that a system where there is a clear definition of private property rights is a much, much preferable means to this end than a system where property rights are very vague and amorphous.

One instance I might give is the difference between how we as a society have treated cows and buffalo. As far as I'm concerned, cows and buffalo look alike. They are probably part of the same genus or species. Yet the private property right systems with which we human beings dealt with these animals are as different as night and day. With the buffalo, in the 1800s, there were no clearly demarcated private property rights. You shot one and you owned it; and if you didn't shoot one, you couldn't have it. You had no incentive to preserve them on the range. The range was open and was communally owned. If you didn't shoot a particular buffalo, it got away, and you had no claim to it later.

As a result, thousands – millions of them – were shot; and buffalo practically became an extinct species. And I claim, it's not because of greed or anything else like that. We treat cows very differently – solely I would contend, because of the private property rights arrangements that we have with regard to them; namely, cows are fully privately owned. If you don't shoot it, it stays there the next day, and you can milk it or farm it for later sale.

With regard to business motivation, it's my feeling that while some businessmen are motivated by greed, by the lust for the buck or what have you, others are motivated by altruistic purposes. And people's motives are as varied as they are. They're very heterogeneous. But I don't see any great difficulty with greed as a motivating force; because I think that Adam Smith really put his finger on this—that the marketplace has an ability to turn private greed into public good. Said Adam Smith, "It's not out of benevolence that the butcher, and the baker, and the candlestick maker provide us with the goods that they do. It's rather out of an attempt to maximize profits, or to increase revenues, or what have you." And in that, they act as if by an invisible hand, to promote an end that wasn't theirs, namely the reasonable allocation of goods for the satisfaction of human desires, which I take to be the goal that Phil Wogaman and I both favour.

Let's consider the question of democratic socialism, or voting for things. Now as I tried to express in my paper, I don't think this is an issue between the democratic capitalists and the democratic socialists, because both do agree that we ought to have a democratic political system for certain things. So, it's not a difference *per se*. The difference concerns what things ought to be amenable to democratic political voting, and what things ought to be amenable to the market or dollar voting.

And here, the classical liberals in the nineteenth century sense would say that government ought to be limited. The government ought to have some very important functions, but nevertheless limited functions. The usual things are defense, or contracts, or law, legislation, roads, things like that—the command points of the economy. But, much else ought to be left to the individual market participants.

As consumers, we consume literally hundreds, if not thousands, if not tens of thousands of items. As producers, we produce one, two, three at most. Thus, when it comes to a tariff, or a bailout, or a subsidy, or some scheme by which a few people can benefit at the expense of many, the producers are much better organized. So again we have the point that while Phil and I might agree as to the goals, we have very different means as a way of reaching them.

Another point is one that Hayek makes in his *Road to Serfdom:* when you have political voting for many, many things (pretty much for running the entire economy), the tasks become insurmountable. It becomes impossible for a parliament, or a senate, or a house of representatives to run the whole economy. They must of necessity call in reams of bureaucrats and so-called experts; and thus it isn't really that democratic. We have rule by expert, not rule by democratic vote.

In conclusion, let me sum up by saying that I cannot see my way to agreeing with Phil's view that he is deducing the economics from the theology. I think that there is no logical implication of the one to the other. I think a person of his theological views could be an advocate of classical liberalism, in the nineteenth century sense, or an advocate of social democracy, as Phil is.

And on the other hand, I think that an alternative theological vision, or even an atheistic one, could reach either of these two political propositions. So, I don't think that the theology is necessary, nor sufficient, for the political views. And I think that the political views are unsatisfactory in various ways — not again, let me emphasize, because of the goals, or the aims, or the purposes which I see as the highest and most benevolent, but rather of the means. I don't think they'll reach the ends that Phil wants them to.

Philip Wogaman: First, dealing with Cooper's response, I can't very well be both Galbraithian and democratic socialist in a thorough sense, I think. And I want to say flatly that this paper is not a democratic socialist paper. I will simply read again what I said toward the end of the paper:

> Perhaps what is needed in the world today is a healthier sense of economic pluralism. Neither socialism nor capitalism has yet provided humanity with conclusive evidence that it alone best serves the cause of economic justice and human well being. Our basic commitments should be deeper than any economic system, and then we can be free to evaluate various economic practices and experiments more lucidly. We may see that socialists have managed to solve some kinds of problems more successfully than capitalists; and vice versa.

I think that paragraph summarizes points that are made throughout the paper. I don't want that to be understood as a fundamental rejection of democratic socialism, either. But I've tried with some nuance and, I hope, balance to first deal with the theological perspective and then come down to some remarks about the issue of market economics, which is the subject matter of this conference, and apropos of that make some comments about both the socialist broad alternative, and the capitalist broad alternative.

In my book, *The Great Economic Debate,* I've attempted to do that with a longer discussion, examining several fundamental positions, and finding at the conclusion of that study that both democratic socialism and mixed economy capitalism can be weighed and balanced by persons of faith, without anybody attempting a definitive conclusion, at least at this point in history.

I have problems with pure *laissez-faire* capitalism, and I gather you do too. Perhaps our differences then, Walter, are not as fundamental as you suggest (at least at certain points), but come down to the question: What works best in different kinds of arenas? I have remarked in the paper that I think there will be some divergence of opinion at various points. Some might say there ought to be more of a planning function in basic economic allocation. Others would say there ought more to be a market function. My quarrel would be with those who would say, "only the market." And I guess I would have a quarrel too with those who would say, "only planning."

I do want to be clear that my paper is not read through the lens of a democratic socialist. It is socialist only in the sense of those who characterize F.D.R. as being a dangerous communist or a socialist. There are people whose views of socialism are so undifferentiated, that anything to the left of Adam Smith is, by definition, socialist. But I think we need to do our thinking with a little more refinement about that.

Now, regarding the question of the uniqueness of theology, and does theology have anything particular to say. That's going to be a theme that's going to run through our discussions, I feel. We got into it in the last hour. We're into it in this hour. We will return to it.

My own judgement of that is sort of "yes" and "no" to it. I suspect my reason for arriving at a particular economic judgement, insofar as it is basically a theological reason, would have to do with (in my mind), what is the ultimate meaning of this practice, or this institution? I might agree with any range of other people that a particular practice or institution is desirable. But at least I find myself, in talking with humanist friends who agree with me on certain issues of ethics, that the character of that agreement is a little bit different.

Ultimately, I believe that every human being is valued boundlessly by God. Now an out-and-out atheist who treats the human adventure as being a transitory thing, may still take the view that we should treat all human lives as of supreme importance. And yet I suspect there is something of a difference of quality in the ways in which we relate to human beings, and policies that affect individual human beings.

To me it is a decisively important question whether we view all humanity as being essentially a family. Now, I know people who don't take that view; and who take the view that there are some people who are literally expendable, and whose lives and views do not really matter. Well, at the same time there are non-Christians who would take the view that all humanity is one moral community. But that is a very important watershed issue. It may not tell us what is the correct economic policy. It does tell us that we can disregard the economic distress of any human being. It seems to me, it also would tell us (and this goes a bit beyond the paper) that economic policy should be seen first through the plight of those who are least well served by a particular economy. That is, the decisive question, or certainly a crucial one, facing us in economic analysis must always be: What is the effect of this upon the most underprivileged members of the community?

The issues of vocation and stewardship have been cited already. The question of the priority of grace to works has a number of interesting points to it. We're going to get to that in a couple of the other papers. To me, one very important implication of a Christian understanding of grace is that we ought to avoid self-righteousness. An awful lot of the discussion of poverty, especially, is predicated upon the self-righteousness of people who consider poverty to be the fault of the poor, as in some cases it may be and in other cases not. But self-righteousness as a general attitude would be precluded.

I would want to emphasize the doctrine of original sin as being very important. By the way, that doctrine is my reason, ultimately, for not wanting to accept classical Marxism. I think classical Marxism has a utopian understanding of human nature at its root, which to me is inconsistent finally with Christian faith.

Milton Friedman: When I read the paper by Philip Wogaman, what it reminded me of was a comment by a nineteenth century American humorist, Josh Billings, when he said, "The trouble with this world ain't ignorance. It's what we know that ain't so." The problem I find with this paper is that what are stated to be unquestionable and unexceptionable facts, simply are not. I call your attention, to begin with, to this statement: "If we have learned anything over the past, it is that unrestrained, *laissez-faire* market economics is what does not work." Now, the closest approach we have had to unrestrained market economics was in the nineteenth century in North America, U.S. and Canada. It would be very hard for anybody who compared the experience of the North American continent of the nineteenth century, with that of other parts of the globe, then or any other time, and especially for people who were concerned with the conditions of the most disadvantaged, to say on that experience that unrestrained market capitalism did not work. It was during that period that millions of the most disadvantaged people in the world were able to come to this country, and find a new home, and build a life for themselves and their children. Most of us here are beneficiaries of that period of the closest approach to unrestrained market competition.

The Mexicans, the Haitians, the Cubans, who are trying to come to this country, would be far better off today and would have a far better future in my opinion, if we had something more nearly approximating what existed in the nineteenth century in the form of governmental organization.

Let me go on to another specific comment: "The *laissez-faire* assumptions regarding economic policy before 1933 were impotent to prevent or deal with the greatest economic catastrophe in American history." I would like to recommend to Mr. Wogaman, a book that Anna Schwartz and I wrote on the monetary history of the United States, which I think demonstrates rather conclusively that the Great Depression was produced not by unrestrained, *laissez-faire* economics, but by government intervention in monetary arrangements. It was the federal reserve system, and not the market system that produced that collapse.

That may be wrong. But it is not a remark that is made without examining the evidence. As to the particular remark here, I challenge Mr. Wogaman to find any appreciable body of evidence which will support his view.

I continue: "Even if *laissez-faire* economic policies had not brought a massive breakdown of the system, they would have perpetuated vast disparities of income and wealth in the American society"—wholly undocumented and the facts are quite the contrary. Again, the nineteenth and the twentieth century is a period when economic disparities of income and wealth were being *narrowed*. The widest disparities in income and wealth are in the collectivist societies. The difference between the economic position and condition of the top people in the Soviet Union and bottom people is far wider than it is in Western capitalist countries.

The comments I've just been making are about what everybody would call fact. Maybe I'm wrong. But these are statements about the *facts* of what produced the Great Depression: The *facts* of what the experience of unrestrained, or nearly unrestrained market capitalism was in the nineteenth century; the *facts* of what's happened to the distribution of income and wealth—things we can research and investigate.

You go on to say, "The competitive character of economic life may lead to divisive individualism." Now this is a very common misconception about the word "competition." Because the word competition in economics, as we use it, has a very different meaning from its ordinary meaning of rivalry. Economic competition is not rivalry. In a case of perfect competition: one wheat farmer doesn't feel that he's competing with his neighbouring wheat farmer. There's an impersonal market in which both are operating. And again, the great virtue of a competitive market is that it eliminates the kind of personal rivalry which becomes dominant in the politically organized society.

Now I spoke too long, so I only want to make one point which is rather of a more humorous character. I believe your footnote 18, in which you refer to my book, *Capitalism and Freedom,* refers to the wrong Friedman and the wrong book. I believe the right reference there should have been to David's book, *The Machinery of Freedom,* because by the standards of David and some of his friends, I am far from stating an extreme view. On the contrary, I am an extreme interventionist. (laughter) I hope your reference to the wrong book does not mean that you haven't read either of them. (laughter)

Philip Wogaman: It doesn't. Now I haven't read his; I have read yours.

Arthur Shenfield: As Milton Friedman has pointed out, in all human history there has never been so powerful an uplifting force for the poor taken as a group, taken as a class, as through the free market economy. However, and I'm sure Milton will agree with this, although from the point of view of the poor as a group or a class, nothing in all human history has surpassed this, any particular individual poor man may well not be protected by the free market.

Any individual poor man may suffer from unforeseen or unforeseeable calamity. And the champions of the free market have never claimed, therefore, that it is necessarily an uplifting force for every, single individual poor man. But something, very, very vital follows from this. It follows that the measures that ought to be taken to deal with the poverty of any particular poor man should primarily be private charity, because private charity is more likely to see to the individual needs of individual poor men. And secondly, that insofar as we bring the state into the picture, everything we do should be designed so as to interfere with the free market, minimally.

So that, even if we say charity, Christian charity is not enough, and we need the state to do something because there will be some individual poor men, who will suffer from some calamity, everything we do should be so designed as not to interfere, except minimally, with the marvelous uplifting force which the free market is for the group as a whole.

And that's the reason, for example, why Milton has proposed the negative income tax, which doesn't necessarily mean that he's right on that. But if we keep our eyes on that, anything we do devise should be and would be of that character.

Geoffrey Brennan: Several people have attempted to justify the free market system in terms of the results it generates. In contrast, I want to pose a question about the ethics, or the theology if you like, of the use of political power. And then to consider the use of political power potentially to secure ends that we might regard as being good. I think it would be very difficult not to acknowledge an obligation to or concern or compassion for the needy and the poor. That seems to me to be unexceptionable. I don't know whether people here would dispute that. But it seems to me that it is one of a number of obligations which Christians have.

But it is only one of a number of obligations. There are others that we might freely acknowledge that Christians have — to say prayers, or go to church, or a large number of other things. Yet typically, the ecclesiastical establishment is reluctant to legislate these particular obligations. And I think that there is underlying this a recognition that the use of political power to legislate obligations of various sorts is illegitimate.

Now, if that's true, unless one is prepared to draw a distinction between the obligation to be compassionate, and the obligation to say one's prayers, or to read the Bible, or whatever else it happens to be, I don't see how one can develop a completely coherent argument for political intervention to insist that the obligation to compassion be undertaken, without an appeal to rights.

The Marxist and Lockean positions are in some sense basically coherent in a way that the argument from obligation is not. And I think most of us would recognize that obligations don't imply rights. It's certainly right to say, or correct to say, that the Good Samaritan and indeed for that matter, the priest or the Levite, have an obligation to help the man who falls amongst thieves. I think it's a much more problematic thing to say that the man who fell among thieves has a right to be helped. So it just seems to me that all this discussion about justice, rights, entitlements, deserts, doesn't come to the heart of the question, which is: What is a legitimate use of political power, if all that is at stake is an obligation? In other words, is there any case to be made on the basis of Christian understanding for a genuine liberal policy for anything other than a theocracy?

David Friedman: I wanted to talk on three different points, and I want to start with a point where I agree with Mr. Wogaman. And that is, it does seem to me that the religious position undercuts one of the moral arguments in favour of capitalism. That is, I think that some, especially the more extreme supporters of capitalism (myself among them), are inclined to support it partly because they feel it is somehow unjust to take away from a producer what he has produced. This is essentially the Lockean argument. And it does seem to me that if you take the position that God really created everything, including us, that seriously undercuts the moral force of that kind of an argument.

There are two points where I would want to disagree. The first is the initial comment that economics has to involve theology because after all, how can you talk about problem solving without values to tell you what are or are not problems. That, it seems to me, is wholly wrong. Physics does not require theology, although it is true that one of the reasons we wish to study physics is in order that we can get to the moon, or blow up our enemies, or save people's lives in some way, or whatever. And similarly, it seems to me that the only sense in which economics is about problem solving, is that it is about understanding how people solve the problems they happen to have, without making any judgement about whether they are correct in wanting the things they want.

The third point is, I suppose, in some part theological, and that is that it seems to me his deduction from grace is wrong. And it's wrong in the following sense. As I understand the Christian position, what God did was not to go to one man and say, "I will make you give an unearned gift to someone else." Rather God, of His own free will as it were, gave of His own an unearned gift.

It would seem to me that the implication, if you believe you should pattern man's acts after God, is charity, not welfare. They are two wholly different things. The welfare state involves using force as a result of a political decision to redistribute, whereas charity involves my saying, "Here is something which I could choose to spend on myself and which I choose to give someone else."

Walter Block: In my commentary, I pose a question for us to consider. And that is, I try to define socialism in two different ways. One I call "coercive socialism," and one I call "voluntary socialism." What they have in common is an allegiance to the Marxian kind of income distribution device, which would be "from each according to his ability, to each according to his need." That's what I say defines socialism. And I add that under that rubric the distribution could be done on a voluntary basis, or on a coercive basis. Examples of voluntarism would be a commune, or a kibbutz, or a monastery, or even the average Canadian family. In most families, consisting of say a father and a mother and a child, the father produces according to his ability and gets according to his needs, which is a lot less than the total family income, which is his ability; and the child and mother usually get in accordance with their need, not in accordance with their ability to produce.

So, on the one hand we have this Marxian income distribution device done on a voluntary basis, within a family, or a kibbutz, or a commune, or a monastery, or what have you. On the other hand, we have what I call coercive socialism, which would seek to instill this discipline upon people whether they wanted to join it or not, whether they were willing or not.

I think to talk about socialism versus capitalism is inexact, and will really get us nowhere. I think that a similar distinction, by the way, has to be made on the capitalist side. Do you believe in a free market system where the income is distributed according to entitlements, namely property rights, and voluntary agreements, capitalist acts between consenting adults? Or, do you believe in, let's call it, corporate state capitalism, where the income distribution is marked by a large share of government largess — namely, socialism for the right, or taking money from the poor and giving it to General Motors, or something like that? The way I see it the real choice is between voluntary socialism and classical liberal capitalism on the one hand, versus both corporate state capitalism and central socialism on the other.

Walter Berns: I'd like to ask Anthony Waterman a few questions about the Law of the Sea negotiations; and the thrust of my question is whether your position there with respect to the Law of the Sea rests on an economic or a theological judgement? The United States has been much criticized, of course, because of all the nations in the world, it alone voted against the Law of the Sea treaty. I happen to agree with that decision on the part of the United States. And it indicates to me that the United States is right to have voted against this. In part, I would make a defense of the United States by saying that it was relatively easy for Canada, for example, to vote for it because under the treaty, Canadian minerals will be amply protected in terms of their price and so forth. They will not be undersold by anything that's dredged from the bottom of the sea. I could also say that if the Prime Minister of Canada wants to be the leader of the Third World, one way of accomplishing that is to drive his country into the position where, economically, it qualifies for that status, (laughter) and he seems to be well on the way to that goal.*

But to get back to the principal point: Is it a theological judgement that "the common heritage of mankind" means that everyone in the world has a property right to an underwater mineral, or (since it is a Lockean phrase) does it mean that no one has property in it until he adds his labour to it and makes it his own by appropriating it?

My judgement is that economically, if one wants to help the people of the disadvantaged countries, the Law of the Sea treaty is not the way to do it. Because I am told (and have reason to believe) that in fact, if this treaty is adopted, there will be no minerals scraped from the bottom of the sea. There will be a monstrous bureaucracy located in Jamaica; and of course the people in the U.N. are all for this. (Having served my country in the U.N. on one occasion, I understand what these people are after.) They would rather be in Jamaica in this new plush setting, supported by the United States incidentally, than go back to some of their wretched capitals (just as they'd rather be in New York than go back to their wretched capitals).

So, to get back to the first question: Is it an economic judgement that makes you in favour of the Law of the Sea treaty? Does it flow from your notion that these minerals down there are given by God, and all mankind has a property right in them? Or, is it simply an economic judgement?

Anthony Waterman: I want to make a doctrinal history point. Three people now have mentioned John Locke. Now they may all be, in fact, correct in saying that what confers property rights is the mixture of one's labour with the gift of nature. But they mustn't claim Locke's

---

*Pierre Trudeau was the Prime Minister of Canada in 1982. — eds.

authority for that, at all. That's a theory of the way in which, in the state of nature, appropriation takes place.

What Locke actually said, as Locke begins his argument in the second treatise, is the classical Christian view that creation is God's gift to the whole of the human race; and those who want to invoke Locke have got to start there.

Roger Shinn: I keep trying to find out where some of our apparent arguments and agreements are real, and where they are just verbal. And in the earlier session, I concentrated on a seeming argument. This time I'm going to concentrate on what might be a seeming agreement.

John Cooper made a valiant effort to sketch out a common ground that we might all share. I don't think it quite works, but I'd like to know more, not just from John, but from everybody here. He said, "If democratic socialism includes Western Europe and Israel, we could all be democratic socialists." And he said, "Democratic capitalists claim the New Deal." He said, "The welfare state is now seen as a permanent feature of Western democratic societies." Now, if this is true, then we still have a lot of disagreements, but they're all negotiable, relatively minor. However, I suspect as I read the papers and listen to the discussion that there's a more dogmatic edge to the argument than that sketched out by John Cooper. I'm not asking for him to answer on this, but let me keep listening for the next couple of days.

Aaron Levine: I think the issue that we're dealing with is "Will the market system produce the highest level of morality that we adopt as our goal?" If we take an ideal model of the free enterprise system, it does force ethical conduct on market participants.

But the market's morality is one based on fear of detection. If a person is fearful, knowing that perfect knowledge permeates the marketplace, he's not going to introduce shoddiness in his goods or charge a higher price than someone else. He won't do it, because he knows that he will be punished. The market system will punish him. But what about a higher morality system that's not based on fear of detection? Is it possible for a free enterprise system, if we don't allow any type of intervention at all, to promote a higher morality?

Where do we have a morality that is based on a higher level than simply detection, human detection? That is, a divine morality based on absolute norms? That's one problem, I think, with the market system that can be perfected.

Another problem with unbridled capitalism is the income distribution pattern that develops. The market system is very cruel and cold. Someone could have an esoteric skill that took him many many years to cultivate, for example, in space technology, and then there is a precipitous drop in demand for that service. And this person is left helpless. The question is, what will a system of voluntarism produce for this type of person that is hurt when changes in supply and demand occur in a very sudden manner?

Of course, in the long run, things work out as people realize they should not train for space technology; but in terms of the short-term effects it could be traumatic. Of course there is a day of reckoning for the dishonest. But what about all the people that are harmed in the short term?

Richard Baepler: I think that my brotherhood of theologians, broadly speaking, has probably not done too fine a job in offering prescriptions for solutions to social/economic problems in society. I think they've done a better job at producing critiques. As we all know, it's easier to spot things that are problematical or wrong, rather than to produce constructive solutions—even assuming you have the expertise to do so.

I'm fascinated by the passionate proposals concerning the way in which the free market system does produce, not only abundance, but also the charitable impulses, presumably, which have bettered the lot of mankind. And I am attracted by that argument, and think that it needs to be made over and over again. But, as a theologian, I would be very interested in learning whether or not within the community of experts in the free market system, there is also a spirit of self-criticism, whether or not the sort of common goals I think we mostly share— broadly humanistic and religious—are criteria by which the free market people can also criticize their own work.

From a theological standpoint this has got to be done because the doctrine of original sin means, among other things, that we have an enormous capacity of self-deception, and of rationalization.

I would like to learn, perhaps not immediately, but in the course of the discussions, from the free market experts here, whether or not the functioning of the free market does, or does not, lead to enormous concentrations of wealth, and therefore of power. And if it does, then the Christian perspective, which is put by Lord Acton about power corrupting, absolute power corrupting absolutely, (which I believe is a statement of the doctrine of original sin), has got to be dealt with.

Philip Wogaman: I don't think the discussion here is representative of the broader discussions of economics, much less theology, in North America or the world today. And in some respects, issues that are raised are a function of who's there to raise them. But having said that, let me cite two or three issues that I think may be fairly important.

First the issues which Professor Friedman, the elder, has raised concerning the track record of *laissez-faire* capitalism. I am not surprised by the reaction which he's given to that, having read with profit much of his work.

I think the historical memory of much of this country would be a little bit more paradoxical than his remarks here were. First of all, there's memory of very great suffering attached to the nineteenth century, which would suggest that not everything was working perfectly in the economic system. Secondly, that more was happening than *laissez-faire* capitalism in the nineteenth century. We were exploring a vast new continent rich in resources; and that's an important variable in all economics. What is there to be worked with? Well, we could pursue that matter further, but that's a point where I am not yet personally persuaded.

The matter of the farm workers, the illustration which Professor Friedman, the younger, posed is interesting. I wonder whether you, and others, would be satisfied with the actual operation of the market system in farm labour, as it worked prior to the unionization movement?

David Friedman: Yes.

Philip Wogaman: If so, then let me say, having experienced the human suffering, at first hand and pastorally, I simply cannot buy that.

Also the question of the character of rights, which I believe Geoff Brennan made, is fundamental. Are we dealing here with using the state to enforce a particular morality, in the manner of what some of us would consider the track record of some religious groups today, and maybe some of us? I think what many of us Protestants did, or our forebearers did in imposing prohibition upon the United States, would be a good illustration of using the state to promote a particular morality, in a misguided way. It seems to me that a right is an understanding of a claim that human beings have against the community, which the community recognizes and is willing to enforce.

Now religious perspectives can contribute to an understanding of what rights ought to be defined in the pursuit of the kind of community that we want to have. And I believe all of us have to contribute to that enterprise. What is the character of the community that we want? Theology, when it deals with economics, always must be asking that question. What kind of community do we want the economy to undergird? Now, I will, with that, rest what may be a very imperfect case here, and we'll enter into many more discussions later.

Chapter 3

The Christian Century on Religion and Society

Edmund A. Opitz

I. INTRODUCTION: THE ROLE OF IDEAS

It is my persuasion that the strongest social force in any society is public opinion or public sentiment. David Hume, in one of his essays, wonders at "The easiness with which the many are governed by the few." Hume continues, "When we inquire by what means this wonder is effected, we shall find that, as force is always on the side of the governed, the governors have nothing to support them but opinion."

Abraham Lincoln raised the same question in one of his debates with Stephen Douglas. He observed that "In this and like communities, public sentiment is everything. With public sentiment, nothing can fail; without it nothing can succeed; consequently, he who molds public sentiment goes deeper than he who enacts statutes or pronounces decisions. He makes statutes and decisions possible or impossible to be executed." This is another way of saying that ideas rule the world. Force is governed by ideas. The ways in which force is organized and used is decided by the beliefs of those who constitute the consensus.

The clergy is one group in our society among several other groups, which exerts a continuing influence on public opinion, or public sentiment. The clergy does not now exercise so powerful a hold over the American mind as was the case during the colonial period, or even a hundred years ago. The church was then a shaping force by the indirect influence it exerted over society, government, and the economy. As Tocqueville observed: "In the United States religion exercises but little direct influence upon the laws and upon the details of public opinion; but it directs the customs of the community, and by regulating every day life it regulates the state." Organized religion today applies direct pressure on officials in the form of the lobbying efforts of the several denominations, as well as by interdenominational agencies such as The National Council of Churches and The World Council of Churches. Ad hoc groups such as Clergy and Laity Concerned take out ads in the *Times* and also employ charades such as sit-ins and pray-ins.

II. *THE CHRISTIAN CENTURY:* **THE HISTORICAL BACKDROP**

The printed word has long been a powerful shaper of opinion within Protestantism, and our task in this paper is to assess the influence of the weekly journal, *The Christian Century,* founded in 1908 and still widely read by clergy and laity alike. I began to read *The Christian Century* during my school years, was a subscriber for more than twenty years, and continued as a reader after that. The Fundamentalists had their own magazines, and I suspect that the typical graduate of a bible college, or the sect type of preacher would not be appealed to by *The Century.* The typical clergyman attracted to *The Christian Century* would likely be a well-schooled graduate of a good college, who later received his theological degree from one of the better seminaries, before being called to preach in a church belonging to one of the so-called mainline denominations, or as a college chaplain and/or professor of religion. *The Century* supplied indispensible intellectual and religious nourishment week after week for tens of thousands of such ministers.

Sometime during the 1950s the Opinion Research Corporation of Princeton, New Jersey, polled clergymen to determine what magazines and journals they read. Of the ministers polled 74 per cent said they read *The Christian Century* regularly; 43 per cent subscribed. This compares with 48 per cent who read *Christianity and Crisis* and 54 per cent who read *The Christian Herald,* a family magazine with little intellectual content.

When clergymen were asked to list the publications which they "rely on most heavily for guidance in social, political, and economic problems," *The Christian Century* headed the list with 14 per cent, *Time* was second with 10 per cent; then came *Reader's Digest* with 8 per cent, *Newsweek* with 4 per cent, *New York Times* with 3 percent, *U.S. News and World Report* with 2 per cent. In other words, of all publications, religious and secular, read by ministers, *The Christian Century* is far and away the most influential reading matter for clergymen who are trying to make up their minds about social, political, and economic problems.

Liberalism vs. Fundamentalism

The religious outlook of *The Christian Century* might be roughly labelled "Liberal." Liberalism in this context is contrasted with Fundamentalism. There are shades of difference within Fundamentalism, but Fundamentalists typically believe in an infallible Bible, committing themselves to a literal acceptance of the Genesis account of Creation, the fall of man in the Garden of Eden, man's redemption achieved by Christ's atoning death on the Cross, and so on. The Liberal in theology seeks to apply the same canons of critical scholarship to the biblical record as to other literatures, and concludes that the Bible, as we know it, is largely the work of later editors piecing together older manuscripts. Thus he finds two accounts of Creation in Genesis and puts a poetic, rather than a literal or scientific interpretation, on each. The historical books of the Bible must be validated by the same tests applied to other works of history. And so on throughout the Old and New Testaments. Liberal theologians also try to come to terms with developments in the several sciences, especially as relating to the size of the universe, the age of the earth, the place of life, and biological evolution. The serious study of the other world religions convinces many scholars that non-Christian faiths also give evidence of the workings out of the Divine Purpose to enoble character and produce sanctity. The evidence that God is not without witnesses in non-Western cultures laid the groundwork for the ecumenical developments of the twentieth century.

The Fundamentalist is secure in his belief that he has the key to salvation, that there is but one path to God, as revealed in his Bible. The Liberal has no such assurance. The Liberal theologian and minister no longer has a monopoly product to offer, and his job is consequently that much more difficult. Squaring biblical insights with modern knowledge and applying spiritual truths to contemporary issues, personal and social, is uphill work. The Liberal was fortified in his struggle by the weekly ventilation of these difficulties on a high philosophical plane in *The Century*.

Early history of *The Christian Century*

The Christian Century was launched in 1908 with Charles Clayton Morrison as editor, a post he held with distinction for the better part of the next half century. Morrison was reared in the old time religion of the nineteenth century, from which he gained the piety that endured a lifetime. But contact with modern knowledge broke the old shell, as he relates in an autobiographical fragment. Wrestling with the disturbing idea of biological evolution he read *The Ascent of Man* by Henry Drummond, a book which portrayed scientific evolution as God's way of working in the world. The result, as Morrison put it, was "a new faith, deeper and firmer, as it was richer, for having found God in his work and world without losing him from his word." This is a good enough statement of the confident Liberal theology of many other early twentieth century theologians. Neo-orthodoxy was yet to come, and come it did from the Continent, with a mighty surge, in the decade after World War I; it is still a force in both Europe and America. Fundamentalism persisted, and a sophisticated development of it led to the emergence of those who called themselves Evangelicals, organizing their churches into the National Association of Evangelicals. An Evangelical voice, *Christianity Today,* was launched in 1956, brilliantly edited by the redoubtable theologian, Carl F. H. Henry.

A fourth R emerged in the 1930s, Humanism. The traditional three R's were Protestantism, Catholicism, and Judaism, but modern secularism produced a document in 1933, *The Humanist Manifesto,* and organized a religion without God. A generation later a few wayward theologians intercepted a revelation and proclaimed "God is dead!" These and other vagaries, in church and in society, came under Morrison's scrutiny, and were suitably analysed and criticized by the able contributors to *The Century*.

The legacy of the Enlightenment

It is a matter of some interest that in the same year, 1908, that *The Christian Century* began publishing, The Federal Council of Churches was established. The two enterprises were ideologically connected, sharing basic outlooks and similar goals. And neither *The Century* nor The Federal Council would be explicable, appearing when they did, without some understanding of the social movements that agitated churchmen, as well as their secular counterparts, during the preceding sixty years. These movements, in turn, are rooted in the new mood that seized Europe during the late eighteenth century. Somewhere around this period — The Enlightenment — the Kingdom of God came down to earth with a thud; the dimension of transcendence receded from the consciousness of Western man, as confidence in his own powers increased. Science and technology enhanced man's understanding of the way the physical universe works, and this new knowledge gave man power over nature, enabling him to use natural forces to serve his own ends. The democratic revolutions of the time deposed the kings and assured that man's new found knowledge and power would redound to the benefit of the people. Later, with Darwin, the transcendent idea disappeared altogether. Now, not only was man's body merely one item in nature's catalogue, but so was his mind; "his origin, his growth, his hopes and fears, his loves and his beliefs, are but the end result of accidental collocations of atoms" — as Bertrand Russell was to say some years later. There may be a God, or there may not be a God; it matters not. The several sciences give us sound knowledge and unassailable truths about the only world that matters, the world we are living in now. And science further promises unimaginable progress — mankind onward and upward forever. If there is a realm beyond nature, science can tell us nothing about it; it is the unknowable and, by the same token, it is the unnecessary.

The church's response

How shall the churches respond to this radically new climate of opinion and the expectations generated by it? Here is an institution teaching that God created all things, especially man, whose soul is precious in God's sight. But man is estranged from his Maker, and in his aloneness and lostness needs personal salvation — uniquely available through the church — in order to "get right with God." To save his soul man was to conduct himself in accordance with the will of God as set forth in the Bible, be redeemed by faith, refine and elevate his character by persistence in good works, and aim at that alternation of consciousness from self-will to God's will defined by the Greek word *metanoia*. But all this is foolishness, in the light of the new *Weltanschauung,* which discounts or denies the dimension of transcendence.

Was there anything in the church's program salvageable, once the idea of the holy vanished? Yes, there was the church's concern for justice and mercy; its humanitarian solicitude for the poor and lowly; its preachment of love for the neighbour, the person in need. Society might be restructured and the Kingdom of God realized on earth, if the church gave guidance to the newly released social forces. No longer can salvation be regarded as an individual matter only, a question of "winning souls for Christ." Salvation must be social. Moral exhortations are not enough — as witness our desparate condition now after nineteen centuries of preaching and good works designed to convict men of their sins and appeal to the better sides of human nature. The object of moral obligation must be social progress, and the engine of social change is the democratically controlled political process.

The Christian Socialist movement

It is not surprising, therefore, that in 1848 a movement called Christian Socialism should be launched by two able Church of England clerics, Charles Kingsley and F. D. Maurice. These were deeply spiritual men and they infused socialism with a religious passion. It was the aim of Christian Socialism to vindicate for "the Kingdom of Christ" its "true authority over the realms of industry and trade." No one who believes that God is the Lord of all life — as the church had always taught — could possibly object to these stated goals. It is the means employed to achieve these goals that is objectionable, or at least questionable, for Kingsley and Maurice viewed "socialism (in) its true character as the great Christian revolution of the nineteenth century." A couple of decades later a popular slogan in English clerical circles was: "Christianity is the religion of which socialism is the practice."

The Communist Manifesto also appeared in 1848, and in it Marx has a sneering reference to Christian Socialism: "As the parson has ever gone hand in hand with the landlord, so has Clerical Socialism with Feudal Socialism. Nothing is easier than to give Christian asceticism a Socialist tinge ... Christian Socialism is but the Holy water with which the priest consecrates the heartburnings of the aristocrat."

The Social Gospel movement

The same constellation of ideas and social forces which produced Christian Socialism in England resulted in a counterpart movement in this country, the Social Gospel. A sympathetic historian of this movement, C. H. Hopkins, declared that the Social Gospel "was called into being by the impact of modern industrial society and scientific thought upon the Protestantism of the United States during the half century following the Civil War." One of the movement's later leaders, Dean Shailer Matthews, of Chicago Divinity School, defined the Social Gospel as "the application of the teaching of Jesus and the total message of the Christian salvation to society, the economic life, and social institutions . . . as well as to individuals." "The social expectations of the Social Gospel leaders were not untypical of the age," wrote Dean Liston Pope of Yale Divinity School. "The organization of the Methodist Federation for Social Service in 1907 reflected these purposes and gave institutional forms to efforts for their realization." And C. H. Hopkins, in *The Rise of the Social Gospel in American Protestantism,* wrote, "The climax of official recognition of Social Christianity was attained in the organization of the Federal Council of Churches of Christ in America in 1908. The significance was two-fold. Not only was the Social Gospel acknowledged in an impressive manner by this most representative body in American Protestant history but social action itself was one of the important factors that brought the Federal Council into being."

In 1912 the Federal Council published its social platform in a little volume entitled *Social Creed of the Churches,* largely written by Harry F. Ward. An anecdote related many years later by Bishop G. Bromley Oxnam unwittingly revealed how deeply enmeshed was ecclesiastical social action with the mainstream progressive ideology in the secular realm. Bishop Oxnam tells about a discussion he had with the then Governor Thomas Dewey of New York. "Bishop," said the Governor to me, "you churchmen are awfully good when you stick to your own field of theology and things spiritual. But when you dabble in economic and political matters, you are quite wide of the mark." "That may be so Governor," I replied, "but I notice that your Republican Party has adopted into its platform every point we made in 1912 in the *Social Creed of the Churches.*"

In England, during the 1930s, there flourished an organization called simply The Christian Left, under the leadership of John Mac-

Murray and others. The Christian Left believed in "the religious mission of the working class to achieve socialism." This group sponsored an influential book, a symposium entitled *Christianity and the Social Revolution,* edited by Lewis, Polanyi, and Kitchin, which advanced communism as the heir to the Christian tradition.

Niebuhr and the Fellowship of Socialist Christians

In 1932 in America a group whose prime mover was Reinhold Niebuhr launched the Fellowship of Socialist Christians. The name is significant. They disliked the term "Christian Socialism," reads their statement, because this label makes "Christian" the adjective and "Socialism" the noun. Their desire was to restore the word "Christian" to a substantive, indicating their primary loyalty to their religious faith. "Socialist" is now reduced to a modifier to denote its role as a means to an end. But it is amusing to note that when this same group — Reinhold Niebuhr, John C. Bennett, Liston Pope and others — launched Christian Action in 1950, they once again reduced "Christian" to adjectival status. Niebuhr, by this time, had quit the Socialist Party, declaring that the remedy of total Socialism would be worse than the liberal errors it sought to correct. He embraced instead a pragmatic, piecemeal, New Dealish approach to political change and hoped to move the newly formed National Council of Churches in the same direction.

The World Council of Churches, launched at Amsterdam in 1948, was two years old when the Federal Council of Churches and several kindred organizations united to form The National Council of Churches of Christ in the United States of America. This was a multipurpose organization, but its Department of Church and Economic Life was so deeply committed to propagandize and lobby for further socialization of the American nation that Christian Action disbanded in 1956, its services no longer required.

Summary

Let me try to restate the point I have been sketching in broad outline: The great social drift discernible in nation after nation during the past hundred and fifty years or so has resulted in the collectivist organization of society, with governments playing a more active role to control and regulate the economic and social activities of the citizens. The most dynamic movement within this drift is Marxian Communism. The total Communist package holds little appeal for citizens of those nations which have come under the influence of the Classical and Christian heritage of individual worth, the higher law, free political institutions, and our birthright of individual liberty. Such people are repelled by the totalitarian nature of Communism, its philosophical materialism, its phoney utopianism, its "ends justify the means" excuse for terrorism and torture. But there are many able and dedicated people who dismiss these repellent features of Communism as mere superstructure, having no intrinsic connection with Marxist economic analysis and the Marxist recipe for organizing business and industry. Reinhold Niebuhr has drawn the distinction: "Whatever the defects of Marxism as a philosophy and as a religion, and even as a political strategy, its analysis of the technical aspects of the problem of justice have not been successfully challenged, and every event in contemporary history seems to multiply the proofs of its validity. . . . The program of the Marxian will not create the millenium for which he hopes. It merely will provide the only possible property system compatible with the necessities of a technical age." (*Interpretation of Christian Ethics,* page 184)

Many of those in mid-twentieth century America who accept Niebuhr's truncated Marxism would call themselves Liberals. I cite Reinhold Niebuhr once again: "Liberalism connotes a desire to use all the instruments and authority of the political state for the attainment of justice. This means the welfare state, the politics of the New Deal, and the Kennedy Administration's current integration progam. . . . " (*The New Leader,* 7/22/63)

Referring to the principal thesis of the New Deal, Niebuhr describes it as the idea "that it is within the power and competence of the state to direct the political and economic life of a technical society for the purpose of assuring the general welfare and guaranteeing at least minimal securities of the people most exposed to the hazards of the complex machinery of a technical age." (*The New Leader,* 12/56, page 11)

III. NIEBUHR IN *THE CHRISTIAN CENTURY*

I am putting Niebuhr's views on record because his theology of society so powerfully swayed the minds of a generation of opinion moulders in church circles and beyond. Niebuhr was far and away the most influential American theologian of his time, and the most prolific. His

Gifford Lectures for 1939, published in two volumes as *The Nature and Destiny of Man,* are brilliant. He wrote regularly for *The Christian Century,* and published in numerous secular periodicals as well. His books dealing with religion and society were widely read by churchmen and non-churchmen alike. During the 1940s there was a semi-serious coterie of intellectuals who referred to themselves as "Atheists for Niebuhr."

Niebuhr directly influenced his students at Union Theological Seminary, and by participating in a variety of social activist organizations he created Niebuhrians among professors of religion in colleges and seminaries, as well as among thought leaders in the pulpit, in denominational agencies, and in councils of churches.

Niebuhr on Marxian economics

Niebuhr dismissed Marxist metaphysics and politics, but embraced Marxist economics, which he declared had never been successfully challenged. This astonishing confession is analagous to a contemporary physicist in our age of Einstein declaring that Newtonian Mechanics had never been successfully challenged! While Niebuhr was writing the words quoted above, the monumental work entitled *Socialism* by Ludwig von Mises became available in English. As far as Niebuhr and *The Century* was concerned, Mises did not exist. There's no evidence that Niebuhr allowed himself any exposure to such contemporary economists as Frank R. Knight of Chicago, or Frank Fetter and Edwin Kemmerer of Princeton, or Fred Fairchild of Yale, or Lionel Robbins of London. Devastating critiques of *Socialism* appeared around the turn of the century by Max Hirsch of Australia and Robert Flint of England. Alfred Marshall of Cambridge launched a school of Marshallian economics. In Austria, a younger contemporary of Marx, Carl Menger, founded the Austrian School of marginal utility analysis; and his associate, Eugen von Böhm-Bawerk demolished Marx's exploitation theory in a book published the year after Marx died. In England there was Stanley Jevons; David Ricardo before him; and Adam Smith, the fountainhead. Adam Smith wrote his masterpiece in opposition to mercantilism, the planned economy of the period, referring to his own philosphy of the free economy as "the liberal plan of equality, liberty and justice."

None of this affected the thought of those who sought to advance the collectivist organization of society under Christian auspices by means of the Social Gospel through such agencies as the Federal and National Councils of Churches, and various periodicals. Niebuhr was a seminal figure in this movement, so let us examine the message he projected through the pages of *The Century.*

Niebuhr on the political demands of discipleship

In *The Christian Century* of August 8, 1924, Niebuhr contrasted European and American reform, lamenting that our churches lack the "willingness or capacity to think honestly and kindly upon the implications of the Christian gospel for the reconstruction of human society, which has become such a marked characteristic of the British churches." He continues:

> American idealism is narrowly individualistic, partly because of the very protestantism which produced it and which is older than the wealth of America. Puritanism is constitutionally individualistic. It was no accident that it came to power in England in the very days when the middle classes began to challenge the aristocracy. Their motto was 'liberty' and they had a passion for the individual. Religiously this passion produced the high type of personal morality which has since been associated with puritanism. Economically it expressed itself in the immoral doctrine of *laissez faire.* Curiously, or perhaps naturally, this type of protestantism has ever since associated a very sensitive personal conscience with a complete indifference to the problems of social life. It has placed very definite and sometimes very irksome restraint upon personal conduct but has insisted that the social processes shall be without restraint. In the intricacies of the soul it felt at home and spoke with authority but the complexities of economics were beyond it so it was pleased to regard the economic life as a mystery in which 'by the providence of God each man seeking his own could serve the common weal.'

In an earlier issue (April 17, 1924) Niebuhr observed that "Among Western nations, England alone gives promise of developing a political party which approximates the Christian ideal in both aim and method. The British Labour Party is both radical and democratic. It is the first party to elevate men to power who were suspicious of economic factors in the last war." He "wonders what kind of a Christian political party could be created if the church took the social invitations of its gospel seriously and became the trusted champion of every cause which seeks to free man from the forces which enslave his life and debase his world."

"Is not the doctrine of progress little more than a dogma?" he writes in the issue of December 13, 1928. "Is it not true that history is a sorry tale of new imperialisms displacing old ones; of man's inhumanity to man, checked in one area or relationship expressing itself in new and more terrible forms in other areas and relationships? Is it not a monstrous egotism and foolish blindness which we betray when we imagine that this civilization in which commercialism has corrupted every ideal value is in any sense superior to the middle ages, or that the status of the industrial worker differs greatly from that of the feudal slave?"

Niebuhr on the Social Gospel in America

Writing in 1930 (*The Christian Century,* 7/23/30) Niebuhr discusses contemporary German theology and then reflects ruefully on the Social Gospel in America.

> Another consideration must occupy the American thinker on religious and ethical themes as he surveys German theology. 'The social gospel' he may be convinced, forms the heart of American Christianity. It represents no merely theological speculation, it is not the religion of mere assent to traditional confessions; it represents a conception of Christianity, which has grown out of the very life of American Christianity, out of its needs, out of its whole history, out of its struggle to understand its Bible in a new world and in the face of new world problems. And yet, the social gospel which in Walter Rauschenbush and Washington Gladden had its anchorage in an inclusive phase, whose center was God in Jesus Christ and which in them was mated with a piety that did not ignore the peculiar needs of a man's standing and solitariness before the final facts of life—this gospel has today often cut adrift from all God-centered religion. It seems at times to be a program of action only, lacking the support of the faith, of the complete philosophy or theology.

Niebuhr on communism

Niebuhr was never really taken in by communism, nor did he ever regard Russia as a workers' paradise. In *The Century* for September 30, 1930, he declared that Russia had "destroyed wealth without abolishing poverty. . . . The passion of Russia today is not so much socialization as industrialization." He sees a nation

> enduring the privations caused by its economy partly through an iron discipline which makes disaffection dangerous and partly through a boundless enthusiasm among the people which transmutes the necessities of the situation into voluntarily accepted sacrifices. 'What,' said one of our young Communist guides, 'do I care if I haven't a good pair of shoes to wear, if it helps my country to buy more machines?' A nation cast loose from its moorings and free of all the cultural, religious and moral traditions which once disciplined its life has, after several years of chaos and a few more years of indecision, suddenly found the channel into which it is willing to pour its vitality.

Returning to this theme (10/15/30) Niebuhr speaks of "The tremendous energy which the new Russia is unfolding is, in one of its aspects at least, not the product of communism at all, but simply the vigor of an emancipated people who are standing upright for the first time in the dignity of a new freedom. It is the same kind of vigor which American free men unfolded on our shores after they had escaped the various tyrannies of Europe."

I note, in passing, that Niebuhr does not mention the kulaks, who were being liquidated during this period — some 5 million of them.

Niebuhr and the 1932 socialist campaign

Niebuhr involved himself in the 1932 socialist campaign to put Norman Thomas in the White House, as Chairman of the Organization Committee of Five Thousand, which he hoped would change its name as it grew to twenty, fifty, or a hundred thousand. He addressed an impassioned plea to the readers of *The Century* (8/3/32) not "to be neutral in this crisis."

Some months earlier (11/4/32), Norman Thomas had contributed a long article to *The Century* examining "the problem of Christianity and the churches in relation to the social order." It appears to Thomas that "If a man does accept in any sincerity a faith in Jesus and Jesus' God, whether he calls himself orthodox or modernist, it is impossible to see how he can be at peace with the present social order whose god is profit and whose largest social loyalty is the inadequate and divisive loyalty of nationalism." Thomas believes that "our present social order is a denial of Christianity," and that the churches might still redeem themselves "by inspiring clergy and laity to seek a human meaning for their vision of the kingdom of heaven on earth."

Niebuhr's plea that we might "have the social imagination to bring the economic intricacies of our common life under the control of reason and conscience" (3/25/31) went unheeded. Thomas received just under 885,000 votes in 1932 to Roosevelt's nearly 23 million. But twenty years later Norman Thomas would take satisfaction in pointing out that both major parties had constructed their platforms with planks appropriated from the Socialist Party. Thus, no matter which major candidate won, socialism couldn't lose!

IV. JOHN BENNETT IN *THE CENTURY*

Another frequent contributor to *The Century* was John C. Bennett, long associated with Union Theological Seminary, as professor and later as its president. Writing in the issue of February 8, 1939, Dr. Bennett says: "A few years ago I was an active member of the Socialist Party and of various Christian Socialist groups. I still believe that the private ownership of the means of production is without moral justification, and that only by changing capitalism beyond recognition will it be possible to distribute the goods which the machine is capable of producing for the benefit of all classes. But, today, I am as much concerned to avoid totalitarianism in all forms, and the danger of civil war, as I am to end capitalism."

Three years later (2/19/42) he urges the churches to accept two revvolutionary demands; the first is for a world political organization.

> The second kind of revolutionary demand that the church can prepare the mind of the nation to meet is the demand for economic justice, not only between nations but also within each nation, and most of all within America. It is difficult to disentangle the political, the ideological and the economic causes of this War, but it is safe to say that the failure to deal successfully with the problems of the world depression did much to discourage men's faith in

political democracy and gave support to both Communist and Fascist ideologies. The truth in the idea of 'the wave of the future' is that the future does set for us a new and drastic choice, the choice between totalitarian and democratic planning of economic life for the benefit of all people. No people who have discovered that they can use the instruments of government to provide economic security for themselves are going to be the sport of unregulated markets or privately owned monopolies. If democracy means that, then they will choose totalitarianism.

In 1948 at the formative meeting of the World Council of Churches, Dr. Bennett chaired the commission which proclaimed that "The Christian church should reject the ideologies of both communism and *laissez-faire* capitalism, and should seek to draw men away from the false assumption that these extremes are the only alternatives." Dr. Bennett's commission condemns a "capitalism" that no defender of the free market economy has ever endorsed. The thing condemned is an economic order that enthrones greed, rewards the powerful, condemns the masses to periodic unemployment, produces inequalities, and holds out the vain promise "that justice will follow as a by-product of free enterprise."

In 1944 F. A. Hayek produced a stunning little book entitled *Road to Serfdom*. Its main thesis was that central economic planning, even with the best of intentions, leads away from the free society and gives the state inordinate power over the day-to-day life of the citizens. Inspired in large part by Hayek, Paul Hutchinson, associate editor of *The Century* wrote a fine little book in 1946 entitled *The New Leviathan*. At Amsterdam in 1948 Emil Brunner gave an impassioned speech warning the delegates against our "crazy faith in the state." The warning went unheeded.

V. EMIL BRUNNER IN *THE CENTURY*

Writing in *The Century* several years later (7/11/51), Brunner drew some important distinctions. "We today have come to understand again that the gospel of Jesus Christ is not a program of world betterment and social reform. Modern times have coined the phrase 'social salvation.' There is immense confusion in that phrase. . . . Our time has forced us to consider again to whom the gospel is really addressed — the individual human being, the individual soul. It has also made us realize that the real theme of the gospel is eternal salvation, eternal life in Christ — not 'social salvation.'"

"The word that goes with 'social' — an abstract term — is not 'salvation,' but 'improvement,' 'reform' and so on. That too is important — a word about it farther on — but it is certainly not the theme of the gospel."

"That must be said today, because not only the world in general but the church too is infected by the spirit of collectivism. Many Christians, preachers and theologians among them, are caught by the spirit of abstraction and think that social salvation is after all 'more' than 'mere individual salvation.'" Brunner changed few minds.

VI. THE CHURCH AND POLITICS

The decades under review in this survey reveal the infatuation of highly placed churchmen with political power; their failure to grasp the meaning of the free society and their efforts to enlist the church in programs hostile to it; their ambiguity toward communism.

Insinuations about communists among the clergy were met by vehement denials, as for instance a sweeping denial, widely publicized by Bishop G. Bromley Oxnam. This occasioned a *Century* article by Reinhold Niebuhr (8/19/53) entitled "Communism and the Clergy." Referring to Oxnam, Niebuhr wrote, "Such a statement causes difficulties, because there are in fact communist sympathizers and fellow travelers in the Church. I wonder whether Bishop Oxnam ought not to have admitted this more freely...."

Niebuhr goes on to assert that "it must be affirmed that there have never been many explicit Stalinists in the churches.... Nevertheless, there are a few and we ought to admit it." How does this seemingly incongruous union between Stalinism and Christianity occur, we ask, and Niebuhr answers, "The pathetic clerical Stalinism could not have developed except against the background of a very considerable Marxist dogmatism in the 'liberal' wing of Protestant Churches."

From time to time *The Century* sought to lay the spectre of communism in ecclesiastical circles. For instance, it declared correctly (11/15/61) that "If some Christians were temporarily deceived into believing that theoretical communism and Christianity sought the same earthly goals, the deception was brief and the deceived few." But the question is why *any* were deceived, and why the few were treated so deferentially.

The Hromadka case

Take the case of the Czech theologian, Joseph L. Hromadka. Hromadka taught at Princeton Theological Seminary during the 1940s, then returned to his native land and became an outspoken apologist for the communist regime of that country. He was a delegate to the Evanston meeting of the World Council in 1954, where his presence caused some tension. It was broken when he began his speech with these words: "I come from the other side of the iron curtain, but not from the other side of the Church." Hromadka continued in the good graces of American churchmen and was addressed in generous terms by *Century* editor, Theodore Gill, (12/23/59) who speaks of " . . . those of us who knew your passionately conscientious commitment to Marxist analyses and prescriptions and who knew you well enough never to question your Christian integrity in these commitments." The same generous tolerance is rarely if ever extended to those who approach political and economic questions from the standpoint of Classical Liberalism and the free market economy.

The Cuba case

A second case in point is *The Century*'s early response to the 1959 Castro take-over of Cuba. About a year after the Castro coup *The Century* carried an article entitled "Cuba in Revolution" by the veteran, leftist journalist, Carleton Beals. The editorial lead reads: "Cuba's regime is showing great restraint in dealing with Batista criminals. Let the U.S. beware of turning that restraint into violence!" Beals does not deny that hundreds of people have been disposed of before firing squads, but in extenuation of this horror he refers to the United States "where the legal processes have become so complicated and devious that a poor man is lucky if he secures justice." Furthermore, concludes Beals, if Castro falters in his executions "then the Cuban people, at present showing such remarkable restraint, will act, and their action will not be pretty." The politicized religious mind, responding to such sentiments as these, has lost whatever title it may have had to speak to or for the conscience of our time.

Every issue of *The Century* contains material of general religious interest and of high quality; but when the editors of the journal, or writers for it, address political and economic issues they speak with virtually one voice—against the free economy and for government controls. As John Bennett puts it: "The leadership and many strategic centers such as theological seminaries and church boards and periodicals in most of the denominations are committed to the position that Christianity demands drastic changes in the structure of social life. The policies of the Federal Council of Churches are based on this assumption." Speaking from within this group, one churchman declares that we few are called upon to "witness to the convictions of an advanced minority . . . without being chained to any majority or consensus; . . . (for we have) a broader perspective than the average layman can hope to have." The executive secretary of Christian Action observed that "All of us are in a position, and all of us can get ourselves into a better position, to advance our common convictions through the religious institutions to which we have direct access."

The response

Such sentiments as these, and the programs designed to carry them out, have generated opposition among clergy and laity alike. The objections are several. Socialism, the planned economy, the welfare state — however one labels the "drastic changes" Dr. Bennett has in mind — have been subjected to devastating analysis and criticism; the planned economy is rejected by many honest and able scholars as bad politics, unsound economics, and dubious morality. But even if socialism — such as the program championed by the late Norman Thomas — were one hundred per cent sound, it would further be argued that the Church should not commit itself to a specific program of political and economic action. Let the churchman who finds socialism persuasive seek to advance it in his own way, as an individual, not as the self-appointed spokesman for the Church. When a Norman Thomas collects money from true believers to crusade for socialism everything is open and above board, however misguided we may deem his cause. But it smacks of dishonesty for an ecclesiastical official to use money dropped into the collection plate by parishioners for purposes they would oppose if they knew, and then to allow the press and public to falsely believe that he is speaking for X million American Protestants. This impropriety is compounded by the pretense that the only objections to such conduct come from the lunatic fringe.

The counter-attack

Here, for example, is an article entitled "The Attack on the Churches," by James W. Wine, of the National Council of Churches (7/6/60). Wine declares that "our position as churchmen should be one which encourages free and honest appraisal of all that we do." But how can we expect honest appraisal from those who engage "in a deliberate effort to distort the truth for self-serving purposes, to release pent-up hostilities. . . . " He speaks of "a severe, almost continuous and sometimes sinister attack on Protestant churches and clergymen," conveying the impression that there are no measured, thoughtful treatments of the proper relation of the churches to social issues. In the eyes of Wine, the attacks are the work of "professional detractors," a term he repeats eight times in the course of his 2,100 word article. Our opponents are "Purveyors of half-truths, perverters of fact, willing tools of any person or group that will pick up the tab for their activities." They are opportunists; one is "a well known apostle of discord."

"The untutored egotist merely wants what he wants," writes Aldous Huxley. "Give him a religious education, and it becomes obvious to him, it becomes axiomatic, that whatever *he* wants is what God wants, that *his* cause is the cause of whatever he may happen to regard as the True Church and that any compromise is a metaphysical Munich, an appeasement of Radical Evil."

An article entitled "The Myth of the 'American Way'" appeared in *The Century* for March 13, 1963. The writer alleges that there are "those who attempt continually and methodically to identify the Christian religion with the economic ideology of Adam Smith, and to call the product of this spurious wedding the "'American Way'. . . . And the theme has been developed in detail in three recently published books; *God, Gold and Government,* by Howard Kershner; *The Powers That Be,* by Edmund A. Opitz; and *The Kingdom Without God* by Edmund A. Opitz, Gerald Heard and others."

The author of the article refers to these three books as "recently published." They appeared in 1957, 1956, and 1956 respectively, six and seven years before *The Century* article, which leads one to suspect that the allegations about them are based on hearsay. Is the hearsay based on anything substantial enough to justify the charge? I think not. The thesis of the two books with which my name is associated has been summarized in my 1961 pamphlet, "Problems of Church and Society," which speaks directly to the point at issue:

> It is the aim of many Protestant churchmen to put the Church officially on record as sponsor for the movement which, in this country, has produced the welfare state. To the extent that any Church puts most of its eggs into a collectivist basket, it absolutizes the relative and temporary. It impairs the primary responsibility of high religion, which is to recall men to a proper sense of their creaturehood and destiny that they may order their souls aright. Civilization is a happy byproduct of spiritual activity but cannot be its direct goal, and because the Kingdom of God is beyond history, the true Church must expect to forever confront political and social institutions in an atmosphere of encounter and tension. "If the Church marries the spirit of this age," wrote Dean Inge, "she will be a widow in the next."

The author of *The Century* article is the director of the Religion and Labor Council of America. He speaks, therefore, from within the broadly collectivist tradition; and his fire is directed at those within the conservative-libertarian tradition. But is not this a case of seeing the speck in another's eye and ignoring the plank in one's own? The author's thesis doubles back on itself when we reflect on the implications of the fact that there is nothing in America remotely resembling a Religion and *Management* Council to counter his own organization. A Fellowship of Socialist Christians was founded here in 1930; but who would think of starting a Fellowship of Capitalist Christians? We have heard the terms "Christian Socialism" and "Religious Socialism" so much that they have ceased to grate on our nerves, as they should. In earlier days the members of these groups were accurately skewered by one of England's greatest churchmen as "black-coated advocates of spoliation." No one has ever had the effrontery to draft such a slogan as "Christianity is the religion of which capitalism is the practice!" It is the Left, and not the Right, which for a century and more has sought to promote the social revolution by putting religion and the churches behind it.

VII.   THE MARKET AND CHRISTIANITY

There are theologians who occupy strategic positions in seminaries, in councils of churches, in editorial offices, in influential pulpits, and in denominational structures, who have repeatedly and officially placed "The Church" on record as favouring drastic changes in the thing they think "Capitalism" to be. If these theologians who opt for socialism have had any contact with the great names in economics, from Smith to Mises, they give no evidence of it. Nor do they seem to be aware of the political tradition associated with *The Federalist*. They speak with authority in their own field, and they assume that this expertise lends authenticity to their opinions in a different field. Every intellectual is in danger of being ambushed by this temptation, including economists. Economists pull as many boners in theology as theologians do in economics! But little harm is done when an economist commits a *faux pas* in theology; we pick him up, dust him off and send him on his way. But a theologian's mistaken economics has unfortunate consequences, for he is able to enlist a powerful institution and a mystique in support of his errors. The Truth will have its way eventually, but what people believe to be true is the immediate spur to their actions. Economic and political error, given theological support, has immense consequences in a society.

Does the free market make profit a god?

It is the mistaken opinion of the theologians we have quoted that the free market economy, or capitalism, "denies Christianity and makes profit its god." In their view, capitalism means that "social processes operate without restraint and that markets go unregulated." They tell us that "private ownership of the means of production is immoral." "Privately owned monopolies" reduce industrial workers to a status comparable to that of feudal slaves. The "immoral doctrine of *laissez-faire*" leads to a "narrow individualism" which puts "economic processes beyond the control of reason and conscience." We have the technical capacity to produce abundance for all, but only government ownership will release the machine's potential.

The wilful ignorance embodied in the preceding paragraph is monumental, and the smugness imposes a formidable barrier to any effort at clarifiction. It is common knowledge that the anti-capitalistic ideologues of twentieth century totalitarianisms exalt the state into Hobbes' "mortal god." They do not acknowledge a Law above the laws; they deny the idea of an order of majesty overarching the state; they have no place in their theory for the moral law, right and wrong being whatever the party decrees them to be. It is a theoretical necessity for collectivists of every hue to deny transcendence in order to enthrone an *ersatz* religion which is secular and political.

The theological neutrality of the market

The free economy makes no theological statement one way or another; it's absurd to say that it denies Christianity. Some economists may be atheists, but their atheism has nothing to do with their economics. However, the free economy, or capitalism, is involved with religion and it is significant that capitalism emerged in the culture whose world-view derives from Christianity. Among the relevant ingredients of the *Weltanschauung* of Christendom are the elements of a free society. There is the belief that man partakes of the divine creativity, which means that he has free will, plus a sacredness at the core of his being which translates politically as his inherent rights. Government, then, is structured so as to protect the private domain of each person and provide each with equal security for the peaceful exercise of his prerogatives. This created being is placed in a world where everything, himself included, is unfinished. The material world is good because God made it, and man is challenged to work in it towards its, and his own, completion, using his reason to figure out what he must do and his conscience to determine what he ought to do; working, as Francis Bacon put it, "for the glory of God and the improvement of man's estate."

If profit is a dirty word, what shall we say of loss? When the scarce factors of production — land, labour and capital — are misallocated or used wastefully and inefficiently, people and planet are poorer; there is loss. The appearance of profit simply means that the scarce factors of production are being intelligently combined so as to satisfy urgent human wants in the order of their urgency, as the people themselves decide.

Theologians are not the only ones who talk nonsense about "the profit motive," as if approval of the profit motive is equivalent to endorsing the shallow view that the goal of life is to make money; but theologians have less excuse than others because they have, presumably, been exposed to Max Weber's book, *The Protestant Ethic and the Spirit of Capitalism*. This work appeared in Germany around the turn of the century and has been available in English since 1930. A few sentences are worth quoting at this point: "The impulse to acquisition, pursuit of gain, of money, of the greatest possible amount of money, has in itself nothing to do with capitalism. This impulse exists and has existed among waiters, physicians, coachmen, artists, prostitutes, dishonest officials, soldiers, nobles, crusaders, gamblers, and beggars. . . . It should be taught in the kindergarten of cultural history that this naive idea of capitalism must be given up once and for all. Unlimited greed for gain is not the least identical with capitalism, and is still less its spirit." (*The Protestant Ethic,* page 17)

Market institutions and economic freedom

John Bennett is exercised by the thought that capitalistic society resembles a free for all where anything goes, even "privately owned monopolies." A moment's thought should convince any rational person that such could not be the case. Nobel Prize winner, Milton Friedman, puts the matter thus: "Economic progress is not possible anywhere in the world, or at any time, unless there is some relatively stable structure of law and rules and regulations, some security of person and property." (Speech at Texas A & M 3/25/80) Capitalism did, in fact, come into being in the West among a people schooled for centuries in the practice of the traditional moral code; don't murder, don't assault, don't steal, don't covet, keep your word, deal justly, fulfill your contracts. These are the main ingredients in Adam Smith's "liberal plan of equality, liberty and justice." (*Wealth of Nations,* page 628) Smith is not here discussing economic processes; he is discussing the framework of rules which make the free economic order possible. Operating within these rules, free people with a diversity of talents and skills contribute their respective specialties, and the multiple exchanges that ensue "as if guided by an invisible hand," give each person a return commensurate with his contribution, as that contribution is judged by his peers. It is hardly the fault of the economy if the value framework on which it depends decays; the blame lies elsewhere, with the institutions of society charged with maintaining religious and moral values.

The point is important enough to warrant the inclusion of some words by another Nobel Prize winner, F. A. Hayek: "The classical argument for freedom in economic affairs rests on the tacit postulate that the rule of law should govern policy in this as in all other spheres. We cannot understand the nature of the opposition of men like Adam Smith or John Stuart Mill to government "intervention" unless we see it against this background. Their position was therefore often misunderstood by those who were not familiar with that basic conception; and confusion arose in England and America as soon as the conception of the rule of law ceased to be assumed by every reader. Freedom of economic activity had meant freedom under the law, not the absence of all government action. The "interference" or "intervention" of government which those writers oppose as a matter of principle therefore meant only the infringement of that private sphere which the general rules of law were intended to protect. (*The Constitution of Liberty,* page 200)

VIII. SUMMARY AND CONCLUSION

Churchmen in every age are tempted to adopt the protective coloration of their time; as intellectuals they are swayed by whatever currents of opinion exert the strongest pull. The gravitational tug of environmental determinism exerts a powerful attraction today on men of all creeds or none; this is the belief of Marxists and non-Marxists alike that it is possible to construct an improved society out of unimproved people.

The writer of Proverbs was confident that it was from the heart of man that the issues of life proceeded; a good society could come only from a people who had learned to order their lives aright. If there is disorder in the soul, that is, in people's faulty thinking and erroneous beliefs, in their misplaced loyalties and misguided affections, there would be friction and conflict in the relations of persons to one another in society. So religion traditionally focused on the inward and the spiritual, on the mind and conscience, as a way of elevating character and thus improving the tone of society.

But in the modern world it is assumed that man is mainly a product of environmental forces, that his character is made for him not by him. It is only necessary, then, to correct the external structures by which people are moulded and the result will be correct behaviour. Transform society and it matters little if men remain unregenerate! This is the modern heresy.

Influential segments of the church have been deeply influenced by this set of ideas, though not necessarily converted wholly to them. The result is the Christian Socialist movement, walking in lock step with its secular counterparts. *The Christian Century* is one of the agencies generated by this movement and, in turn, *The Century* has powerfully shaped the thinking of two generations of churchmen to regard support of the welfare state as a religious imperative.

Comment

James M. Wall

My role is to speak as editor of *The Christian Century* magazine in response to Edmund Opitz's paper. I should say first that it is a honour to participate and I am happy to acknowledge that this meeting takes seriously the contribution *The Christian Century* has made to American thought over the past hundred years. In reading Dr. Opitz's paper, I am moved first to express appreciation to him for the gracious manner in which he places the magazine at the forefront of publications that address themselves to thoughtful citizens, particularly those of the Protestant persuasion and especially those who profess to examine issues from a theological and intellectual viewpoint.

The Opitz straw man: Niebuhr and *The Christian Century*

In attempting to respond to this paper, I have run into some problems as it is apparent to me that Dr. Opitz is setting up a straw man which he plans to link to the magazine's editorial policy. As he summarizes it, "The great social drift discernible in nation after nation during the past hundred and fifty years or so has resulted in the collectivist organization of society, with governments playing a more active role to control and regulate the economic and social activities of the citizens. The most dynamic movement within this drift is Marxian Communism."

Collectivism, then, is the evil centre of his plot. And he quickly identifies theologian and social activist Reinhold Niebuhr as the carrier of this evil into the intellectual circles of American life during the period 1920–1960. The problem these two assumptions pose for me, in the first place, is that they are both wrong. I do not think he makes the case that societies have drifted into collectivism, and certainly, with a Ronald Reagan in the White House, and his potential democratic challengers scrambling to be more conservative than one another, I don't find collectivism taking over in the United States. Reinhold Niebuhr's Marxist phase, which he outlived and built upon to develop his brilliant understanding of Christian realism, is hardly sufficient historical data to label Niebuhr as the carrier of Marxism.

But in the second place, neither of these assumptions need detailed refutation by me in this response for I do not think Dr. Opitz has succeeded in linking his definitions of collectivism with Niebuhr as the evil bearer of bad news with *The Christian Century* magazine. To accomplish this, he would have to prove that Niebuhr was a pervasive and constant influence in the pages of the magazine. He does not do this, and indeed, makes no specific effort to do so. He merely wants us to assume that Niebuhr and the *Century* are identical: "Niebuhr was a seminal figure in this (collectivist organization of society) movement, so let us examine the messages he projected through the pages of the *Century*." He then cites pieces that Niebuhr wrote for the magazine in 1924, 1928 and 1930.

As Opitz points out, Niebuhr was an active supporter of Norman Thomas's socialist campaign for the presidency in 1932, and in a piece published in August, 1932 before the fall election, he wrote in the *Century* that the magazine's readers should "not be neutral in this crisis."

Morrison and the *Century*

Unfortunately, for Opitz's thesis, as one contributor among many to the pages of the magazine, Niebuhr's contributions are not nearly as significant in ascertaining how the publication stood on "religion and society" as were the writings in the editorial columns, especially those of its editor, Charles Clayton Morrison. It was Morrison, the Disciples of Christ minister, who took the magazine in 1908 and shaped it as a major influence on American thought from that year until his retirement in 1947. To ascertain how *The Christian Century* thought on most any subject through those years, one must look not to Niebuhr, but to Charles Clayton Morrison. And it is no small matter that the two men had a public falling-out over the issue of Morrison's near pacifism in 1940. It was at that time that Niebuhr, by now pushing hard for Christian realism, wanted the United States to take an active role against facism in Germany and Italy. Morrison, a strong peace activist, was writing editorials urging that the U.S. stay out of the war up until Pearl Harbor Day. Indeed, the first editorial he published after war was declared was called, "an unnecessary necessity."

But to return for the moment to Opitz's argument that Niebuhr plus Thomas plus *The Christian Century* equals three peas in a pod, let me cite Donald B. Meyer's 1961 book, "The Protestant Search for Political Realism, 1919–41." Meyer makes frequent references to the *Century* in tracing the interaction between religion and politics in that period, calling its editors "the keenest and most persistent of political observers."[1] Morrison's *Century* was too much concerned with culture-religion, that is, the identification with what is best for the nation, to have pursued the ideology involved in a hopeless third-party effort.

Speaking, for example, of Calvin Coolidge's inaugural in March, 1924, the *Century* commented:

> [It had been] as near being a national sacrament as any political
> event in the remembrance of our generation . . . [There was] some-
> thing almost high-priestly in the way he lifted the whole nation up
> to God in an eloquent and understanding commitment of himself
> and the state to high sovereignty. No statesman in our history has
> uttered words of moral interpretation which surpass those with
> which the President closed his inaugural address.[2]

This is no radical collectivist publication speaking. It is rather, a magazine editor expressing emotional commitment to the high ideals of the culture of the United States, which Morrison saw lifted to a high level in the Coolidge address. Of course, Morrison's real concerns were high ideals and a commitment to a society that cared for all its people, including those who could not care for themselves.

Morrison's politics and editorial policy

It was in the 1928 presidential election that Morrison's strongest convictions came into play. There were two issues that were to plague him in that campaign, Catholicism and prohibition; he opposed what he felt was the danger of Roman Catholic "control" of society and he was opposed to alcohol. It was natural therefore that he gave his specific endorsement in the 1928 election, to the Republican candidate, Herbert Hoover, over the Catholic-wet Democratic choice of Al Smith. Those two issues, plus his constant concern with peace and disarmament, dominated Morrison, and the *Century,* during the period 1920–1940. What he felt about, and what we know about, issues of economic structure in American society must be gleaned more from the attitude of his writings than from many direct editorial comments.

Morrison was no radical and he was certainly no Marxist. Nor was he, to use Opitz's term, a "collectivist." He was rather, a culture-Christian. Morrison's opposition to Catholicism revealed a conviction that this country would be better off if every one would be like "us," which is to say, Protestant, white, Anglo-Saxon.

To Morrison, and to the liberal church leaders of his day, "democracy meant a state of being even more than a process; it referred to a type of character more than to a pattern of outward relationships. It meant a type of man. Politics was not seen as in its nature a realm of power, nor political democracy as a particular arrangement or distribution of power."[3]

It was this commitment to democracy as a "state of being" rather than a "process" that made it possible for Morrison to endorse Hoover again over Franklin D. Roosevelt in 1932. The magazine saw in Hoover someone who would preserve the ideals of middle America, which is to say, the mainline liberal communities with Protestant churches as the bearers of the virtue and morals of the community. Even so, Morrison and the *Century* editorial stance were not enthusiastic about a Hooverism that did not plan carefully enough to insure adequate care for all people. In keeping with the principles of the social gospel – the conviction that the Christian faith required concern for society's inequities – Morrison felt deeply that the free enterprise system did not concern itself enough with the care of the needy and the larger community.

Bennett and the *Century*

In his examination of the *Century*'s social views, Opitz turns from Niebuhr to John C. Bennett, another frequent contributor to the magazine, but again, not a major voice in the shaping of *Century* editorial policy. It is important, in this connection, to make the point that *The Christian Century* has enjoyed a virtual monopoly in the field of mainline serious journalism, and as such, has served more as a forum for major thinkers in Protestantism than as a single-minded advocacy publication for one narrow perspective. Morrison's pet causes – peace and disarmament being major – did get a strong emphasis, but the intellectual ferment within mainline Protestanism found in *Century* pages an opportunity to be heard.

Opitz cites Bennett's role in the formation meeting of the World Council of Churches in 1948, where he chaired a commission that issued a statement rejecting the "ideologies of both communism and *laissez-faire* capitalism," and objecting to the "false assumption that these extremes are the only alternatives." This is finally the mature position of Niebuhr's realism as well. He has observed various forms of political ideologies and he concludes that none are worthy of baptism as the official religious answer. Both Niebuhr and Bennett, and the evidence is clear that the *Century*'s Morrison agreed, preferred democracy over any other form of government. They never felt that any economic system was superior enough to replace the system we have in the U.S. and Canada. But in no instance did they feel that these systems deserved to be called superior for "religious" reasons.

Is the *Century* pro-communist?

This leads me to take strong exception to various comments that Opitz makes toward the end of his paper. For example, he charges that during the "decades under review", his survey has revealed "the infatuation of highly placed churchmen with political power; their failure to grasp the meaning of the free society and their efforts to enlist the church in programs hostile to it; their ambiguity toward communism." He has not successfully proven that these highly placed churchmen do not grasp the meaning of a free society, unless he is proposing that their "ambiguity" toward communism, whatever that is supposed to mean, is in itself a rejection of "freedom." And since this paper is supposed to focus on *The Christian Century*—and not on Bennett and Niebuhr—I quite simply assert that no magazine edited by Charles Clayton Morrison, who endorsed Herbert Hoover in both his elections, could be termed "ambiguous" toward communism and unable to grasp the meaning of a "free society." On the contrary, it would be easier to accuse Morrison's culture-Christianity of being too enamoured of American culture, and too willing to accept a national status quo.

Opitz appears to resort to some vague charges that at one time we called "red-baiting." He wonders why "any [Christians] were deceived [regarding communism] and why the few [who did] were treated so deferentially." He is referring to a *Century* editorial of 1961 that said some Christians were temporarily persuaded that communism and Christianity shared the same goals, but that the deception was "brief." The implication here is that if *anyone* fails to absolutely condemn all forms or expressions of communism, he is guilty and deserves severe condemnation. There is no room, in Opitz's world-view, for anyone living in a communist country to profess belief in Christ, nor should people living in a "free" society fail to condemn such people.

Opitz makes an unsubstantiated observation that "when the editors of the [*Century*], or writers for it, address political and economic issues they speak with virtually one voice — against the free economy and for government controls." What can this possibly mean? Has Opitz determined that what is wrong with society is that we don't have enough free economy and too much government control, and therefore unless people agree with him absolutely, they are to be condemned? Even if this dubious extreme position were granted for the sake of argument, Opitz fails to indicate just how it is that the *Century* speaks with one voice on these two topics.

In truth, the assertion that the *Century* "has powerfully shaped the thinking of two generations of churchmen to regard support of the welfare state as a religious imperative" is simply not true. What I find in Opitz is a position on modern life that objects strongly to certain emotional terms like "welfare state," whatever that means any more, and a desire by him to find that evil posture within the official position of *The Christian Century*. It is not there. It is not there in Opitz's paper because he did not examine the *Century*'s editorial policy; he took two major figures of American thought — Bennett and Niebuhr — and identified them as the *Century* in that period. They wrote for the *Century,* along with many other writers, and both strongly disagreed with the editors on several occasions. They simply did not represent the Century in the 1920–1950 period. Who did? We do not discover in Opitz's paper.

The crucial role of editorial writings

But I can say that the way to find the *Century*'s attitude toward economic issues in particular and religion and society in general during the period of 1908 to the present — it is not not clear to me why Opitz chose to stop in the 1960s with his analysis unless it was because Niebuhr became less active by then — is to examine the editorial writings of the various editors of the publication. This would not exhaust the topic, for editorials constitute perhaps less than twenty per cent of each issue, and a wide spectrum of mainline Protestant thinkers and church people were writing for the magazine in that period.

But the six editors who have served at the head of the publication since 1908 would provide an overview of the attitude of the magazine toward economic and societal issues. I have already suggested that Morrison was very much a Republican, celebrating the virtues of mid-America during his long tenure (1908–1946). His successors, Paul Hutchinson, Harold Fey, Kyle Haselden, Alan Geyer and myself, are considered in mainline Protestantism, leaning to liberal, especially among the latter three. None could be considered radical, and indeed I am willing to suggest that almost without exception, they were editors (including the present incumbent) who considered themselves patriotic Americans who very much wanted this nation to live up to its highest ideals of freedom and concern for those in need.

It would take a closer study of each editor's tenure to make a specific analysis, but in general, *The Christian Century* has known nothing of the love for "collectivism" and the "welfare state" that Opitz professes to find in its pages. The editors have been critical of "greed" in capitalism; of the absence of freedom in socialism; and of the failure of all systems to inspire citizens to higher ideals. The magazine has blessed no single system. It has been consistent in a commitment to the Christian faith, a faith, I should add, that does *not* "deny transcendence" as Opitz seems to imply, as he suggests that "collectivists of every hue," must do. He has not clarified what he means by collectivists; he does not connect the *Century* to collectivists; and he does not say why it is that a collectivist "must deny transcendence." As one who believes strongly in a transcendent God – and who has edited the *Century* for ten years – I find that implication strange and finally a little disconcerting.

A closer examination of each editor's tenure – in Morrison's case, a breakdown by decades – would reveal a fascinating evolution of styles and attitudes toward social issues in the United States and Canada. Morrison, for example, wrote many editorials that sought to deal with labour unrest in the 1930s. The Social Gospel inspired Morrison to champion programs that would put people to work, and reduce poverty. He abhorred violence but he finally supported strikes as a way of forcing employers to give basic rights and fair wages to employees. But just what this meant would have to be seen in the context of the period in which he was writing his editorials. In the same manner, an observer studying the editorials of the decade 1972–1982, during the period I have edited the magazine, might come across an evolution in the editor's thought, from naive hope to realistic expectations. Someday I might contribute to that research with an autobiography. But for the next decade or so, I intend to contribute weekly editorials, worked out in the crucible of the events of that week, against the background of the *Century*'s tradition and the faith of the community which follows a transcendent God.

NOTES

1. Meyer, Donald B. *Protestant Search for Political Realism, 1919-41.* Berkeley: University of California Press, 1960, p. 120.

2. ibid.

3. ibid. p. 125.

Reply

Edmund A. Opitz

Mr. Wall's response to my paper does not attempt a critical assessment of the points I tried to make. He objects to my paper because it is not the paper he would have written, given my assignment — which was to sample the ideological flavour of *The Christian Century* in the context of the social creed of the churches during this century's middle third. In staking out the parameters of my topic I first assayed my own memories as a reader of the journal for more than two decades — from the late thirties to the early sixties. The *Century*, when it dealt with the political and economic issues took the "liberal" position, as that label is customarily used in contemporary discourse. The word "liberal" in our time evokes such labels as New Deal, Fair Deal, New Frontier, Great Society, the welfare state. I understand that labels may be libels, as Dean Inge used to say, but what is one to do? The great social drift of the twentieth century in both the secular and the sacred realms is in the direction of more extensive and more centralized political planning of the nation's economy, with the purported end of providing cradle to grave security for the nation's citizens. The impression left upon me by my reading is that *Century* articles and editorials which dealt with economic and political issues were in the vein of New Deal liberalism, somewhat sermonized.

The Christian Century Reader as source-book

I checked my personal impressions against the *Century*'s own assessment of what it considered important by consulting *The Christian Century Reader,* a 447 page anthology of fifty years of religious journalism. This grab bag volume contains a variety of editorials, articles, reportage, and poetry. Some is human interest material, some scolds Americans for moral failure, some deals with the social order. There are nineteen entries, amounting to 76 pages, which deal with economic and political issues. The viewpoint of the authors spans the spectrum from the Social Gospel to Christian Socialism, from the outlook associated with Walter Rauschenbusch to the more sophisticated approach of Reinhold Niebuhr and Norman Thomas.

In addition to the 76 pages of social action advocacy there are 50 pages devoted to the ecumenical movement. Everyone agrees that it is well for the brethren to dwell together in peace and harmony, and virtually everyone favours Christian unity in theory; but there have always been differences of opinion as to the nature of the foundation on which that unity shall be based. The twentieth century has virtually reached a consensus in the matter; the ecumenical movement in our time is founded on the idea of "seeking together as Christians ways of meeting the challenge of human social disorder," as a 1954 World Council of Churches document puts it. The resolution of social disorder is to be sought in a middle ground somewhere between "communism and *laissez-faire* capitalism," according to the famous Amsterdam pronouncement. The author of these words identified his middle ground with British Trades Union socialism. Neither he nor any other ecclesiastical expert on the economy published in the *Century* exhibits the slightest understanding of market theory, the free economy, or the political and legal philosophy of the free society. Nor do they display any awareness of the operational imperatives of the socialistic ordering of society.

Mr. Wall feels that I set up a straw man, which I call "collectivism," and he accuses me of making this "the evil centre of his plot" — which is to say, *my* plot. He declares that I identify "Niebuhr as the carrier of this evil..." and "as the evil bearer of bad news with *The Christian Century*..." and that I want the reader to assume that "Niebuhr and the *Century* are identical."

Niebuhr — error vs. evil

Mr. Wall amazes me! Niebuhr was America's most influential theologian for several decades. He was neither an evil man nor an evil influence; but even if I believed he was I would not feel called upon to press that kind of judgement. I make a distinction between evil and error, and I do believe that Niebuhr purveyed some egregious errors — as he himself would be forced to acknowledge. During the twenties and thirties Niebuhr was a pacifist and a scourge to those who were not. With World War II in the offing he renounced pacifism and became a devout anti-pacifist and a zealous advocate of America's entry into World War II. Niebuhr can't have it both ways; if his belligerency was correct his pacifism was in error.

Around 1950 he renounced his life-long socialism, declaring that he now believed that the socialist remedy would create more problems than the ills it sought to cure. I agree with Niebuhr that much of his life's energy had been devoted to the promotion of erroneous notions in economics and politics, and that bad consequences resulted, even if his intentions were good. *The Christian Century* was one platform from which Niebuhr's errors were transmitted to American churchmen.

Similar considerations apply to another influential theologian and familiar name to readers of the *Century,* John C. Bennett, at a time when he and Niebuhr were members of Norman Thomas' Socialist Party, and when both men were the most powerful theological spokesmen for America's armed intervention in the war then raging.

This belligerent position was staunchly opposed by Charles Clayton Morrison, whose *Christian Century* editorials made a brilliant case for

American non-intervention. The distinction between non-intervention and pacifism eludes Mr. Wall. Morrison was peace-loving but not a pacifist, and anyone who reads these editorials (collected in book form as *The Christian and the War,* 1942) can satisfy himself on that point.

The consistency of Christianity and communism

Mr. Wall reads page 135 of my paper and finds "some vague charges that at one time we called 'red baiting.'" There are no "charges"—in the sense of accusations—on page 135; but I do speak of Hromadka as an apologist for the communist regime of Czecho-Slovakia. This is to speak mildly of Hromadka compared to the fulsome praise bestowed upon the man precisely because of this Marxism by *Century* editor Theodore Gill. Addressing Hromadka, Gill speaks of "... your passionately conscientious commitment to Marxist analyses and prescriptions..." Gill paints Hromadka a darker red than I, but where he praises Hromadka's integrity I question Hromadka's rationality—as I question the rationality of any theologian who believes that the earthly goals of communism and Christianity are the same, or even compatible. It is the Christian vision that man is made to serve a transcendent end, that the Kingdom of God is beyond history. It is, therefore, an earthly goal of Christianity to school man for life eternal. Communist theory, on the other hand, makes the State all-powerful in preparation for its withering away, its demise designed to leave the classless society depicted by the fevered imaginations of Marx and Trotsky. First Marx: "Communist society... by regulating the common production makes it possible for me to do this today and that tomorrow, to hunt in the morning, to fish in the afternoon, to carry on cattle-breeding in the evening, also to criticize the food—just as I please—without becoming either hunter, fisherman, shepherd or critic."

Trotsky is even more lyrical: "Man will become incomparably stronger, wiser, finer. His body more harmonious, his movements more rhythmical, his voice more musical... The human average will rise to the level of an Aristotle, a Goethe, a Marx. Above these heights new peaks will arise."

However, the classless society is a long way off. Meanwhile, as Bertrand Russell observed, there is "poverty, slavery, hatred, spying, forced labor, extinction of independent thought, and refusal to cooperate in any way with nations that have heretical governments."

A Christian society is inspired by the vision of justice voiced by the Old Testament prophets and finds its ground for individual freedom in the conviction that there is a sacredness in the person, an inviolable soul, which the law should respect. Communism, by contrast, regards people as objects who are used and used up as required for achieving its earthly utopia. Christian ethical theory tries to relate to God's will, whereas right and wrong in communist theory are whatever the Party decrees. It is a sad fact that communism has practiced its deadly principles, whereas Christianity perennially betrays the ideals it professes. Similar earthly goals? Indeed not!

Mr. Wall really goes off the deep end in his wild allegation that "There is no room, in Opitz' world view, for anyone living in a communist country to profess belief in Christ, nor should people living in a 'free' society fail to condemn such people." This is a misrepresentation too gross to be dignified by a rebuttal.

The meaning of collectivism

Mr. Wall appears to be disconcerted by the term "collectivism." I use the word according to the accepted and familiar dictionary definition: "The socialist principle of control by the state of all means of production of economic activity," and I am critical of those churchmen who try to identify Christianity with collectivism. The great modern Swiss theologian, Emil Brunner, observed that "not only the world in general but the church too is infected with collectivism." I couldn't agree more. Paul Tillich remarked, as if to illustrate Brunner's point, "Any serious Christian must be a socialist." Let the late Dean Inge have the last word on this point: "I do not like to see the clergy, who are monarchists under a strong monarchy, and oligarchs under the oligarchy, tumbling over each other in their eagerness to become court chaplains to King Demos. The blackcoated advocates of spoliation are not a nice lot."

Mr. Wall misreads the paragraph at the bottom of page 32 of my paper. I declared that "the anti-capitalistic ideologues of twentieth century totalitarianism exalt the state into Hobbes' 'mortal god.'" It should be obvious that the reference here is to the red, black, and brown shirted True Believers of Communist, Fascist and Nazi nations. These are the people who have embraced an *ersatz* religion which is secular and political, and who persecute faithful Jews, Christians and Moslems. The "mortal god" state cannot allow the loyalty of its minions to be divided between itself and the true God. Those who acknowledge the claims of the transcendent over their lives and try to live by its mandates are a constant threat to the collectivist state, and must be subdued, body, mind and soul.

Two religions are here in contention. The secular religions of collectivism is driven by its internal logic to deny God and the moral law as being subversive of a state demanding total loyalty from its subjects. The historic faiths are barely tolerated—if they survive at all.

Mr. Wall feels that "welfare state" is an emotional term. I am opposed to the welfare state, although some of my best friends are welfare staters! I don't use the term pejoratively, but try rather to translate the "welfare state" idea into its practices. Apparently the term means little or nothing to Mr. Wall, who speaks of the "'welfare state;' whatever that means any more." The term does mean something, and I assume that it meant a great deal to Mr. Justice Douglas, otherwise he would not have referred to it as "the greatest political invention of the twentieth century."

The politics of power and the politics of freedom

Politics under the Old Regime involved the unabashed use of political power for the economic benefit of the kings and nobles who wielded it. There were other elements in it as well, but the economic role of the state loomed large. Royalty and nobility neither toiled nor spun; they lived off the labour of peasants and serfs. Those who wielded power got something for nothing; those who actually produced the goods and services got nothing for something. Within this arrangement, into which virtually all states fall, there has to be a body of subjects whose interests are sacrificed to the advantage of those who rule.

Whig political theory broke with this pattern. Constitutional government and the Rule of Law would assure an evenhanded justice leaving men and women free in their productive pursuits and in the enjoyment of the results of their labour.

The welfare state reestablished the political pattern of the Old Regime; those who rule exercise their power for the economic advantage of themselves and friends at the expense of productive citizens. But there is a new twist; ideologists for the welfare state have convinced the public that this new system of compassionate rule is exercised for the benefit of "the poor." The welfare state does not in fact operate this way, and contemplating the nature of power we may come to understand why it does not and cannot. When political power allocates economic rewards, the lion's share of the rewards will inevitably go to those who are shrewd, farsighted, and best organized to lobby government for subventions and subsidies of one kind or another. And these will not be the poor. In such a contest the poor serve as a stalking horse for those best able to manipulate the political process for economic gain. Thomas Sowell, the economist who has done meticulous work in this area concludes: "To be blunt, the poor are a gold mine. By the time they are studied, advised, experimented with and administered, the poor have helped many a middle class liberal to achieve affluence with government money. The total amount of money the government spends on its "anti-poverty" efforts is three times what would be required to lift every man, woman, and child in America above the poverty line by simply sending money to the poor."

The time-span

Mr. Wall wonders why I did not carry my study beyond the early 1960s. For several reasons. My paper was already overlong; I had used up by allotted space. Secondly, the agenda of the welfare state was well fixed in place by the sixties. We had the New Frontier followed by the Great Society. But meanwhile the country was turning its attention to the spread of overt social unrest — turbulence on college campuses, street demonstrations, "participatory democracy," the Vietnam War. I found the *Century* less and less helpful during this period, its tone crankier, its partisanship more blatant. So I gave up on it, and found this a sufficient reason to close my paper at this point.

Discussion

Edited by: Kenneth G. Elzinga

James Wall: I am certainly grateful to Dr. Opitz for introducing Reinhold Niebuhr into the discussion this morning even though if you've read my paper you are aware that I believe that the Niebuhr he describes is simply not the full-blooded Christian realist who shaped my own thought in religion and politics.

In addition, in linking Niebuhr to *The Christian Century,* the magazine that I have edited now for ten years, and which has been for mainline Protestantism a major avenue of communication for this century, I think Dr. Opitz gives far too much credit to one man's ability to shape a magazine's viewpoint. Certainly during the period of time that his paper cites, essentially the beginning of the 1920s and coming up to the end of the 1950s, the magazine's outlook was shaped more by its editors in that period of time. This was primarily a man named Charles Clayton Morrison, who was a fairly well-known Republican with a strong affinity for American culture as well as a pietistic bias regarding such matters as alcohol, and similar concerns, and whose politics permitted him to endorse Herbert Hoover, in both of his campaigns for the Presidency.

But certainly in one sense, Ed Opitz is correct. Reinhold Niebuhr, and he also cites John Bennett, influence the editorial policy of this magazine in that they do influence its current editor, and in that they do shape, to a large extent, much of the thinking in American theology regarding the inner connection between religion and politics. And this, of course, involves religion and economics. Just as many of you around this table have reached the point in your thinking regarding economics with considerable input from the work of Milton Friedman, senior, and I suspect have already and will in the future be influenced by Friedman the junior, Reinhold Niebuhr is essential to how we view religion with politics and economics.

I cannot have Niebuhr around the table, because he is not with us anymore. (You are blessed with having Dr. Milton Friedman with you.) I do, however, have around the table the Reinhold Niebuhr professor of Christian social ethics, Roger Shinn who will, I hope, be able to say more for us regarding Niebuhr.

But I think more really is at stake in Dr. Opitz's paper than how *The Christian Century* magazine views economics and theology. As much as I might enjoy indulging myself, and having the conference focus on my editorial policy, there's simply a larger question here at stake.

For I take it that what his paper wishes primarily to do, is to point to what he feels is a socialist bias in mainline Protestantism. And he, I think correctly, has pointed to a major publication to see if he can find, in that publication, evidence of this bias: what he calls the "collectivist organization of society," with government playing a more active role to control and regulate the economic and social activities of its citizens. So really, the larger question his paper raises is, of course, 'What economic bias is operative in today's religious community?' And it is to that question I would like to address a few remarks.

I can indulge myself a little about *The Christian Century*, because that is the subject of his paper. We have, in this magazine, sought to identify various manifestations of economic bias in contemporary Protestantism. And I think I can testify that there is no monolithic viewpoint.

Rather, present day Protestantism is influenced in part by Liberation Theology of Latin America; in part, by the neo-conservative persuasion of the likes of Michael Novak; and in part, by a continuation of the moralistic, prophetic voice of certain liberal, democratic oriented thinkers.

Liberation Theology is a contextual theology. It grows out of a deep concern that in Latin America, and certainly in other parts of the world, there is a form of capitalism (if we may call it that) that clearly is oppressing the poor, and which calls for something to be done. This isn't so much a theological support of socialism, as it is an analysis of a particular situation critiquing what is wrong with a particular setting. And certainly the World Council of Churches, and to some extent the National Council of Churches which only represents some elected representatives, have argued that there are emerging nations, and emerging churches in those emerging nations, for whom the planned economy and a socialist setting appear to be the better option. Programs through the World Council and the National Council do speak on occasion with the rhetoric of socialism, and they do show a preference for certain systems of a planned economy. But there are also strong voices in *The Christian Century* magazine—the editorials that I write are among them—which reject this rhetoric, and reject this preference, asking instead, "What is the context, what is the system that will best enhance all of society?"

Now in the U.S., as I indicated, Michael Novak and Richard John Neuhaus have themselves embraced a particular political and economic ideology: democratic capitalism. They, I think, (and we've been critical of them) have elevated this to a point of theological supremacy. They share Dr. Opitz's conviction that collectivism and government control are not only bad economics, but bad theology as well.

The liberation and neo-conservative brethren are functioning contextually; they are not following Niebuhr. Nor are those Protestants following Niebuhr who continue to insist that political and economic solutions, as opposed to systems, may somehow be blessed as God's precise will.

In *The Christian Century,* we've called these groups (at least I have in various things I've written), by shorthand terms (and journalists can use shorthand terms and get away with it, because we're not fair basically in such matters) (laughter); we call them "liberationists," "patriots," and "prophetic moralists."

But what the real thrust of mainline Protestantism is, is none of these (although we are influenced by all). Rather, it is a "politicist" thrust. It much more partakes of Niebuhr's influence, which refused to baptize any single economic or political ideology as theologically superior. Dr. Opitz's paper is valuable to us, then, in that he has introduced Niebuhr in our discussions, and he has properly identified Niebuhr as a shaper of *Christian Century,* though I do not believe in the way he identifies it.

And I will close by giving you a quote you perhaps know very well from Niebuhr, but it certainly sums up what he sees in religion, politics, and economic thinking. Niebuhr said:

> In moral man and immoral society, politics will, to the end of history, be an area where conscience and power meet, where the ethical and coercive factors of human life will inter-penetrate and work out their tentative and uneasy compromises.

This is not the voice of an ideologue.

Edmund Opitz: When I was asked to do a paper on *The Christian*

Century, it wasn't the kind of thing I went into eagerly; but I felt I had done a sufficient number of things, anyone of which would be cause for doing penance, (laughter) so I plunged into re-reading a lot of material that resulted in the paper under consideration. First there was the question of how to go about this thing, or where to focus it. I had been a reader of *The Christian Century* for many years, a subscriber for most of those years; so I had my own recollections of what was in it and what its major thrust was which is reflected in my paper.

Secondly, I consulted *The Christian Century Reader,* a thing put together in 1962 by Harold Fey, one of the editors, and Margaret Frakes, another editor. I quote from the preface:

> Here is recorded... the swing from the concern of the social gospel with the outward structure of justice, to the inwardness of an ethic of culture.... The movement in Europe from Ritschl to Barth has been paralleled in America by the swing from Rauschenbusch to Reinhold Niebuhr.

This gave me a second clue that Niebuhr certainly was, and is, a key figure in this thing. In *The Christian Century Reader,* there is a potpourri of material—poetry, human interest stories, things of interest to anyone in the Christian world. But there are nineteen entries—articles and editorials—76 pages in all, roughly about twenty per cent of the total book, (and this has been selected, you recall, by the editors of *The Christian Century* as representing the main thrust of the magazine) which deal with Christian attitude toward the current social disorder. And the term "social disorder" reflects the failures of something that they would regard as capitalism and an absence of warranted government regulation. And it seems to me, from a lot of reading over the years, that official and unofficial church documents intend by reconstruction something along the lines of further intervention by government over economic life.

Furthermore, the *Century* has been dedicated to the ecumenical movement. This was a major interest and concern of Charles Clayton Morrison, one of whose books deals with the sins of denominationalism, and whose whole life was devoted to the advocacy of Christian unity, which the *Reader* says "animated the *Century*'s pages from the start."

Now Christian unity and the ecumenical movement are certainly not things that any one of us would say are unimportant. The unity of Christians living together in love and harmony is certainly a desideratum. But this particular move for Christian unity, the one that culminated in the World Council of Churches formed in 1948, has been built around the common concern, not for unity or harmony in theology, so much as in economic and political matters.

A 1954 publication, entitled "Ecumenical Documents on Church and Society," says that "A very large part of the energy of the movement has in turn been directed towards seeking together, as Christians, ways of meeting the challenge of human social disorder." And again, "social disorder" refers to the disorder of what is rather crudely labelled "capitalism."

I shall append a number of comments on Jim Wall's critique of my paper. At the outset, he says I set up a "straw man" which is collectivism. Well, it seems to me that in our circles, the definition of "collectivism" is fairly well understood. There are always dictionaries, and I consulted Webster's large one before I left. It does say that this is a word virtually synonymous with "socialism."

I'm not saying that socialism is evil. In my paper I didn't say that anything or anyone was evil, and yet I'm charged with identifying Reinhold Niebuhr as the carrier of this evil, collectivism. I prefer to describe collectivism, to say what its implications are, and what it does to people, on principle, rather than simply label it as evil.

I did not attempt to make the case that societies have in our period drifted into collectivism, because the case has been made far better than I could make it by, among others, F. A. Hayek in *The Road to Serfdom*. I did not label Niebuhr as a carrier of Marxism. I simply quoted him.

I made no attempt to link my definition of "collectivism" with Niebuhr. I have no particular, peculiar, individual, unique definition of collectivism. I refer simply to the ordering of society from the top down, the political ordering of society, a theory common in official church documents.

As well, I mentioned Niebuhr's brilliant Gifford Lectures. The Gifford Lectures, as some of you know, are the most prestigious lectures in the Protestant world, given successively at the four Scottish universities. I happen to be a fan of those lectures. Niebuhr's Gifford Lectures of 1939, "Human Nature and Destiny," are brilliant.

I am content to sit back and wait for posterity to judge Reinhold Niebuhr in terms of the Gifford Lectures, not in terms of his shifting position on a variety of social issues. His revelation back in the 1920s was pacifism. There was yet a new revelation in the 1930s that pacifism had some inadequacies, and he became, along with his colleague

John Bennett (my former teacher), one of the chief American theologians urging other Americans to enter World War II. Niebuhr's other revelation during this period was socialism. He was a member of Norman Thomas's party, along with John Bennett. He received a new revelation in about 1950, and he decided that socialism, if it were to replace liberal errors, would replace them with evils even greater. So, I'm not going to judge Niebuhr on the basis of his ephemeral positions, but on the basis of his real contribution.

Now again, how do we measure the social impact of *The Christian Century,* or its political bias? You do it by: (a) the editorial contributions; and (b) the articles the editor puts in the magazine. Obviously, I was not attempting to assess the whole of *The Christian Century,* but only its political bias: the impact *The Christian Century* had upon the kind of readers it attracted.

I voiced my opinion that this journal, edited by Morrison and by his successors achieved a high level of journalistic excellence in American thought, particularly with liberal churchmen, people interested in news of the Protestant world, or the religious world. I would give it high marks for excellence. It certainly was not a radical journal. If it had been, its impact on its readers would have been far less. It was its general excellence that made the articles it carried advocating further collectivism carry the weight they did with its readers.

Incidentally, Charles Clayton Morrison was not a pacifist. I recall vividly his essay, entitled "The Unnecessary Necessity." Here Morrison describes his position:

> Now that war has been declared, it is necessary, but it was unnecessary prior to this. Now that we are in total war, there is no general oasis for a pacifist to occupy. You add your weight to the war effort, or you subtract it from our war effort, which in effect adds it to the other side. A pacifist who chooses to go to jail, ties up his jailer from doing adequate work for the war effort. He then coerces the taxpayer to support him.

Morrison was not a pacifist, but he opposed U.S. entry into the Second World War. Niebuhr had been a pacifist, but became very belligerent shortly before Pearl Harbor. Niebuhr also fell out with Norman Thomas on this issue, and Thomas fell out with the war party of some of his fellow socialists, who formed the Social Democratic Federation which published "The New Leader" during the war.

To say it again, *The Christian Century* is no radical, collectivist publication. I certainly did not charge that. Part of its impact results from the very fact that it was not. Morrison was no radical; he was certainly no Marxist. Who said he was? This reminds me of an article in *The Christian Century* back in about 1964 which began, "Goldwater is no Hitler, but...." (laughter) That type of article has no place in a magazine of the stature of *The Christian Century*.

Roger Shinn: I guess that it was about thirty-five years ago, I did a considerable study of the editorial policy of *The Christian Century* under Morrison. And it is certainly not at the tip of my tongue today, but I remember a few things from it that I think might contribute to the present conversation. Morrison was a good journalist who cultivated controversies within the pages of the magazine. I remember a particular series prior to World War II, of maybe twenty articles in which individuals were asked to write on the question, "What I will do if the United States gets involved in war?" (or approximately that question). And these ranged from pacifists to very militant types. Morrison knew what *his* position was; but he did cultivate that kind of controversy. And therefore in assessing the magazine, one must look at the distribution of articles and, then, above all, editorial policy. Now, here I would agree with Ed Opitz on one detail. Morrison, I think, was not quite a pacifist. He had a very general, Christian preference for peace, combined with a kind of isolationism, that in some ways ran close to the *Chicago Tribune*. And sometimes he particularly couched things in terms of geographical differences between east coast and the midwest. I would call him a "quasi-pacifist, isolationist."

Harold Fey, a later editor, came directly from the Fellowship of Reconciliation, which was a pacifist organization. And that is a different position.

Now I think the interesting theological issue that concerns us in so many of the debates, and so many of the papers here, is what Jim Wall refers to as the "culture religion" characteristic of Morrison. Morrison tended to merge ultimate religious ethics with political policies in a rather close way. Consider an example I'll pull out of memory (but I'm pretty sure I'm right). At one point he hailed Senator Borah, an isolationist of the time opposed to the League of Nations and so on, and said Senator Borah, "puts the day of the Lord's return close at hand."

Now he did not mean that Borah does this in the way that Hal Lindsay does: By merging a desired foreign policy to the eschatological imagery of the Bible. Morrison was almost ecstatic about the signing and ratification of the Kellogg peace pact. The nations agreed to renounce war as an instrument of national policy, which of course had nothing to do with the congressional appropriations for increased armaments that were passed in just about the same year.

Now that was a particular problem in Morrison's thought, as I would see it. And it is perhaps best illustrated by the fact that when he took this magazine, once a small denominational journal, bought it, and turned it into an ecumenical journal, he gave it the name, *The Christian Century,* in the quite literal sense that he expected the twentieth century to be, in human history, the Christian century—a little analogous to Charles Luce's later description of the twentieth century as "the American century." I have no idea how the thirtieth century, if the civilization survives, will characterize the twentieth century; but I'm about as sure as I am of anything human, it will not call it either the "Christian century" or the "American century." It is that quality of Morrison's thought that I always found particularly perplexing.

But the real issue that's involved here for all of us is: How do we relate our most exalted ideals to political realities? How do we relate the voluntarism of love to the elements of coercion in every political system? What is the role in society of what Seymour Siegel's paper calls "enforced philanthropy?" Should there be any such thing, or shouldn't there be?

Now a word on the relation of Reinhold Niebuhr to all this. Niebuhr's disagreements with *The Christian Century* were so great that in about 1941 he founded *Christianity and Crisis* as a kind of counter-journal, a counter-voice in Christian ethical thinking. And I should think the contribution of Niebuhr to *The Christian Century* editorial policy was not the articles he wrote, but (as Jim Wall has already heeded) his general influence on theological ethics. This is so great that later editors, particularly Haselden, Geyer, and Wall, have a sense of the moral ambiguities in political and economic ethics; but I think Morrison did not have this. That is, rarely, if ever, do they identify faith directly with a particular political and economic position; though they do assert a constant relevance of faith to such issues.

John Cooper: I am glad Roger Shinn mentioned *Christianity and Crisis* because I think that Ed Opitz's paper would have been perhaps more appropriate had he focused on this journal. I just finished, in the last year, a dissertation on Niebuhr and Maritain. And one of the key findings of that dissertation is that Marxism played a key role in their development. It was in responding to Marxism, first calling themselves Marxist, and later understanding in what ways Marxism was inadequate to their vision of society, that both Niebuhr and Maritain came to their mature positions. So, it's not inappropriate to talk about their particular stand on an issue at a point in time even though it did change later. But I think it does require some attention to what I would call "the mature Niebuhr" or "the mature Maritain." And there has been, in fact, something of a debate on this issue in *Christianity and Crisis,* among other places, in recent months.

It is my feeling that we have to do a lot more thinking about our history. It's a history that's a little too close to us to really understand. But the way I would characterize it, as it comes down to us through magazines like *Christian Century* and *Christianity and Crisis,* is that American Protestantism and in an occasional place American Catholicism had a good deal of consensus about democratic pluralism throughout the 1950s.

But somewhere along the way, a shift of tide occurred which split the leadership of American Christianity in two. And for handy shorthand, although it's inadequate, I call them "democratic capitalist theologians" and "democratic socialist theologians." If you wanted to find a democratic socialist, that is a truly "collectivist" ideology, in American theology, I think the only place you will find it is in the last decade or so. Up until that time, theologians were really pretty much in the mainstream of American ideological thought. Some were patriotic, some were critical, but not anywhere near the fringes. In more recent times, I would suggest that some people have gone further toward the fringe. And it parallels the secular political world—the transformation of liberalism into the "New Left." The collectivists are John Bennett, Robert McAfee Brown, Robert Bellah, William Sloan Coffin, Jr., M. Douglas Meeks, Gibson Winter, Tom Driver. Phil Wogaman can tell us whether he wants to be included in this list or not. And there are feminist theologians and black theologians, as well, who heap a great deal of praise on socialism.

In fact, you will find in the American Academy of Religion, a study group on religious socialism, another group on social justice, and a third group on economic justice. You would find that about two-thirds of the people have a bias towards socialism, and away from capitalism.

And that is the state, it seems to me, of theology today. It is worthwhile to study this phenomenon, because it's one of the most exciting debates going on among theologians. I think it's one of the most interesting topics at the American Academy of Religion.

But to return, finally, to Niebuhr and Maritain: they came to the conclusion that some of the things they learned from Marxism were important — the competition between classes, or between any groups within society, and the balance of forces in society — for instance, between industry and agriculture, between business and labour.

And they came to the conclusion that for all its faults, the American version of democratic capitalism has managed to create the greatest number of checks and balances of any of the western democracies. America was the kind of society which was not perfect, which indeed had a lot of disorders, but which was much better in every respect than collectivism — politically, economically, and spiritually. But if you want to find in theology democratic socialism, even collectivism of the most extreme type, you'll find it. And you will find its proponents will be claiming Niebuhr too.

Ronald Preston: When I first got to know Niebuhr, the thing that remained in my mind was his *extremely* critical attitude to *The Christian Century*.

I had not, when I first met Reinhold, (I was then an undergraduate), heard of or read *The Christian Century;* but later I did. But *The Christian Century* came into my life as the magazine that Niebuhr was always criticizing.

I think I was the second person in Great Britain to read a book by Niebuhr. It was introduced to me by the first person, who'd read it. (laughter) He has had an enormous influence on me. But in Britain, the interesting thing is that the politicians who've been most influenced by Niebuhr are, on the whole, conservatives. Hardly anybody on the left has been influenced by him. Tony Benn *claims* to have been influenced by Reinhold, but I have not been able to detect one single explicit influence in anything I've heard Tony Benn say. And he's almost the only politician on the Left that I've ever heard claim to be influenced by him. All the others are conservative. David Martin, whom we are going to come to later, has also been extremely influenced by Niebuhr's thinking; but not, again, very much on a left-wing side.

I think Roger Shinn is perfectly correct in saying that the important thing that comes out of Niebuhr is that religion must not be tied up with the cultural situation; and in particular, the ambiguities of cultural Protestantism. Now this speaks really powerfully to Britain where there is a traditional Anglican establishment which, of course, we'll be discussing later. So he has very important things to say to Britain.

The sad thing is that in my experience Niebuhr is hardly read by students today. This is why I'm extremely interested in finding how often he's coming into the discussion here. I have introduced people continually to him, in the last few years, and found at least half of them getting very excited, because they've never read anything like it before. This element of Niebuhr's thinking is very largely missing in the different constituencies of the churches who now make up the World Council of Churches. And this results in a great loss of theological perception in many areas of the world where other theologians, who are less perceptive in these matters, are much more widely heard.

Philip Wogaman: I have been a reader of *The Christian Century* since early childhood. That was in my parsonage home, with my father as a minister. It was a standard feature and, I think, in a way that helps underscore the point that Mr. Opitz was making about pervasiveness, in some circles at least, of *The Century*'s influence.

In the main, I don't find the Opitz paper terribly balanced, or a careful study of *The Century*. And, I think it might have been interesting to have placed *The Century* in relation to other journals. It's singled out in this setting as one very important formative journal. Perhaps it could rightly be viewed as the most important Protestant journal in the United States, at least.

But, I think to get a rounded picture of the influences bearing upon church leadership on economic questions, one would have to mention those other journals as well.

I would like to add two footnotes to the paper in areas where I know something a little more directly about the persons involved. One of them is Joseph Hromadka who was roundly criticized, in some respects justly, for being too uncritical of Marxism. At the time of the 1954 assembly of the World Council of Churches, he had a very difficult time getting into the United States. He was tailed by the FBI everywhere he went. As a historical footnote, it's worth noting that back in Czechoslovakia, Joseph Hromadka was the leading figure and creative force behind the emerging Christian-Marxist dialogue. And the Christian-Marxist dialogue was one of the formative influences in the development of the Prague spring—that is the reform movement in Czechoslovakia. Now one might view that still as dangerously left-ish, but certainly that was a very redemptive kind of thing, viewed in the context of Czechoslovakian Stalinism. And Hromadka's role certainly was not as an uncritical communist. It was to be a Christian, to have a transcendent view of Christian faith, transcending economic matters; and to bring this to bear in the cultural arena.

The second footnote is a little more minor, but reference is made to James W. Wine and his 1960 article which one must see in context. Jim Wine was a fascinating character. He was the associate general secretary of the National Council of Churches, a very stormy person in many respects. The flavour of his personality is caught a little bit here in the reference made to him in Ed Opitz's paper.

But the strong reactions of Wine in that article were severely critical of the churches as being pro-communist. This appeared in an official United States Air Force training manual used to train officers, which was brought out that spring. At that time I happened to have completed my graduate studies and was working briefly with the National Council of Churches in researching the background of those attacks; and during that period, I worked to some extent, with Jim Wine. Seen out of context, this might appear to be an irresponsible defensive charge on his part. Seen in context, it was in response to what was an absolutely outrageous use of military training procedures to castigate large numbers of American churches.

Seymour Siegel: I just want to make a few general comments. First of all, it's strange, although now I think when Mr. Opitz spoke orally we know the explanation, that almost all the references to *The Christian Century* stop at 1962 or 1963. We are now in 1982 — some twenty years later — and I think that that is of some significance, especially since it is in the 1960s, or the late 1960s and the 1970s, that conservative political and economic thought has gained currency in wide intellectual circles in the country, in the academy, and in the pulpit, and in the seminaries. And I think, therefore, any survey of anything that ends in the early '60s, as changeable and dynamic as these things were, leaves something to be desired.

Secondly, I think it's also interesting to note the influence of periodicals on the formation of thought, in political and economic spheres, especially. And I think that that is a very good place to begin, because religious practitioners, especially who are harried and don't have much time, do rely a lot on periodicals. And therefore both in analyzing the formation of their ideas and in projecting how to modify them, the periodical is a very good way to operate. As a matter of fact (if I can just put in a little plug) that is the reason why some of us founded the new journal, *This World.* It was projected to create a periodical literature which would promote a more conservative political and economic program amongst those who teach and preach religion, as well as practice it. As a matter of fact, *This World* magazine had its genesis in a conference something like this one, in which people who taught theology and social ethics in some of the leading seminaries of the United States, at least, said (with the exception of the Jewish seminaries, which are not infected and affected by this) that Marxism was one of the main economic and political ideologies that was being taught there. Now I don't know whether that's true or not, but that was asserted by the people who, themselves, were involved in this; and that is why we thought that it would be a good idea to launch this project in order to mitigate this, what I think is a lamentable fact, if indeed it is true.

Then, I just want to follow up on what Mr. Preston said, in regard to Reinhold Niebuhr, who has been one of the two foci of our discussion this morning. Almost everybody that I know in the Jewish community who claims to be and indeed is a Niebuhrian is always on the conservative political and economic side. The most famous one is Will Herberg, who claims in the introduction to his book, *Judaism and Modern Man,* to state Judaism in Niebuhrian terms.

So, I found it really strange that we should think that, if we had only Ed Opitz's paper, of the legacy of Reinhold Niebuhr as contributing to the promotion of collectivism.

Anthony Waterman: I want to come back to one feature of the paper which has been neglected in the discussion so far. And that is the attempt, or rather the assumption I suppose, that there is some connection between Marxian communism or, in general, Marxian ideology on the one hand, and the trend toward collectivist organization and government action on the other.

There's virtually no connection whatsoever, in my opinion, between the drift towards collectivism on the one hand, and Marxian ideology on the other. It began, as everybody knows, in Britain before Marx was ever heard of, in the 1840s and 1850s. And it began in response to some pressing social needs, which occurred in what economists call disequilibrium situations, as a result of very rapid industrialization.

And the people who first began to formulate what eventually became programs of government regulation and intervention were without exception people who professed to believe, and actually did believe in *laissez-faire* capitalism in its purest form. And bit by bit, they said, "Well, this is an exception. And here we absolutely have to intervene to regulate some particular abuse in the factories" or something of this kind.

The ideology of those who initiated this kind of process was entirely innocent of any kind of Marxism; and had they been aware of Marxism, they would have utterly repudiated it.

It seems to me that throughout the nineteenth century, the sorts of things which, in Britain at any rate, brought about the trend to greater government participation were if anything more a result of industrialization.

Example: Nowadays, in all countries, governments exercise some control over monetary conditions. How did that start in Britain? Essentially because in response to the requirements of the city of London for there to be a more or less stable pound exchange rate, the Bank of England almost accidentally discovered that by manipulation of interest rates, it could maintain the exchange value of the pound.

Example: Because of the rapid industrialization of Britain throughout the nineteenth century, there was a great need for social overhead capital. More roads had to be built. More schools had to be built. Harbours. Docks. Things which, by and large, the market isn't going to supply, at least not under those circumstances at that time. So, it seems to me that a lot of this drift toward collectivization is entirely unrelated to ideology. It is simply a function of industrialization. And I think that insofar as that's true, it's almost an irrelevance to invoke Marx.

Milton Friedman: I just want to make a comment on your comment, and raise one other question. I agree with you that so far as Britain is concerned, it was not Marxism that was responsible. But I don't agree with you that it was believers in *laissez-faire* capitalism that were responsible.

I recall that it was the aristocrats, the people from the aristocratic structure of Britain, who had the "noblesse oblige" notion, who did not really believe in *laissez-faire* capitalism at all, who were leading the movement in the ten hour day. And they were not believers in *laissez-faire* capitalism.

One other point. What you say about Britain is true. But I think what you say about the rest of the world leaves much to be desired. It was not industrialization that produced communism in Russia. Not in the slightest. And, in general, if you take the really collectivist movement in the twentieth century, Russia and China are two examples where you cannot attribute these developments to industrialization.

Now, while I have the floor, may I make one other comment? I just want to ask Roger Shinn a question. He referred to a Christian preference for peace. I would like him to explain to me how that differs from a non-Christian preference for peace.

Anthony Waterman: I'm responding to the second part, because I agree that Russia and China don't fit my model at all. But as far as the first point is concerned, I entirely agree, of course, that many of the proponents of these reforms were members of the aristocracy who had no love for capitalism at all. But it is also the fact that the most influential (may I call them) "ideologues" of the time, were people like Thomas Chalmers, (roundly abused by Marx for that role) Archbishop Sumner, author of *Treatise on the Records of Creation,* which was the major contribution in the 1820s and 1830s towards the *laissez-faire* ideology. Both those men, and their lesser colleagues on the episcopal bench who in those days sat on the House of Lords and had a large part to play in legislation, always supported intervention and always justified their support by saying that it was an exception.

Paul Heyne: We all know that the political character of a religious magazine, or of a denomination's social statements, or of the statements of a prophetic moralist, are going to be very difficult to describe in a way that is satisfactory, both to the people making the statements and to the critics who feel themselves somehow alienated by those statements. I think we all recognize how difficult it is to characterize *The Christian Century*'s political stance in a way that both Jim Wall and Ed Opitz will accept.

Why do we try? I think it's important to recognize that we try in these cases, with religious magazines, denominational statements, and prophetic moralist assertions, because none of us likes to be criticized from a transcendent perspective. And it is terribly easy to adopt a transcendent perspective, or to take for yourself a transcendent perspective, and not even recognize that you're doing it.

But the people who feel themselves excluded — who feel that the positions that they have arrived at on the basis of their own faith, reason, and evidence, are somehow being condemned as out of step with God — these people understandably are sensitive to such nuances.

I have no solution to this problem, but I do believe it is at the root of much of what bubbled into this conference. It is at the root of much of the concern of active, religious lay people with church activism in the social area.

Now, to finish up and tie it to Marx. In my judgement (I think I could support this with a considerable body of evidence) one role of Marxism is to supply a transcendent perspective for some people who want one but are unable, in a religiously pluralist society, to find one that is satisfactory. Marxism provides a transcendent perspective from which certain propositions are defended.

Roger Shinn: This is in response to Milton Friedman's question. I am very grateful if what I called a "Christian disposition towards peace" is quite widely shared. I've got no desire to make exclusive claims here.

But I'd like to refer to a course that Seymour Siegel and I co-teach, in both the Jewish and the Union Theological Seminaries. Here, when we come to the issue of peace, he points out that Judaism has never been a pacifist faith. There might be rare, individual exceptions, and so on. And I accept his word for that. But I would say that from the beginning, there has been a pacifist strain in Christianity, from Constantine on not dominant, but frequently recurring. Usually it takes a pretty big leap from the transcendent to the particular, very often sloppy — a few quotations from the Sermon on the Mount, and Isaiah, and so on, to conclude "we ought to be pro-peace," and maybe, therefore, you ought to be in favour of this particular government policy, and so on.

But I use the words in relation to Morrison, because I think that's exactly what he did. He took this legacy, this "pro-peace legacy," and he made it a quasi-pacifist sort of thing. That's all I meant.

Kenneth Boulding: In relation to that, I always regarded Niebuhr as a Judas. I mean for changing his previous vision about pacifism. I once had a row with him about this. It's published in the little book I wrote for the National Council of Churches, *The Organizational Revolution*. Niebuhr went after me in a whole essay, criticizing it, and I wrote an essay about him. He thought I believed in anarchy, and I thought he believed in tyranny! (laughter)

I do agree with Professor Wogaman that the movement for reform in Catholicism has very little to do with Marxism. The point is that something can go wrong with anything and everything. As you've seen it this morning, what went wrong with Christianity? I regard myself as sort of a Christian, in a sense, at least as a camp-follower of Jesus. That makes me at least 80 per cent Jewish and maybe 20 per cent Greek or something, I don't know. (laughter)

Marxism is a red herring, I think, in a great deal of this. One of my heroes is John R. Commons, who wanted to save capitalism by making it good. And that's what the reform movement is all about. It's a movement of saving capitalism, and in this sense, the saving of the market, by correcting its defects.

If you pretend the market has no defects, you are its principal enemy because every system has defects.

Edmund Opitz: Regarding the cutoff date of my survey of the *Century,* by the time I got to page 37, I was still twenty years behind the times, and I was kind of tired. (laughter) I rationalized my stopping then for four reasons. One, I thought most of you here would have had your own exposure to *The Christian Century* over the past two decades if you'd wanted it. Secondly, I did not want this thing to become a personal confrontation between myself and the present editor.

Third, I felt that I could sort of draw upon my own well-springs from personal exposure to it as a regular reader over a long period — in the period I covered — in a way I could not do for the past twenty years or so. And fourth, I surmised that the past twenty years have been shaped by the previous twenty years!

It does seem to me that the argument as to whether or not there has been a lineup between official church pronouncements, and a particular form of ideology, is perfectly clear. I have a little note from Tillich, an article that appeared on the 15th of June, 1949, which speaks of the central importance of social ethics. And social ethics, again, in this context means to get government to correct the evils of capitalism; this is the central importance social ethics has in American theology.

Mr. Preston quotes from William Temple, and Temple again is someone whom I greatly admire. I am now going through his great Gifford Lectures "Nature, Man and God" for the umpteenth time. But Temple identified socialism with the Christian gospel, with slogans such as, "Christianity is the religion of which socialism is the practice." For an organization that Niebuhr formed called "Fellowship of Socialist Christians" seems to imply that the men who belonged were socialist because they were Christians.

The identification to me is perfectly clear. And I am not criticizing them. There are lots of ways of being wrong besides being a socialist. I would criticize them for not boning up on the literature of the other side, and for selecting the particular opponents they choose to rebut.

Now there have been opportunities, presumably, for writers for *The Christian Century* or other journals, to pick a staunch opponent, and a serious opponent of socialization, and show what's wrong with this position, but to pick on the Air Force manual, or a Carl MacIntire, or whatever. If we talk about picking a straw man, these are the kinds of straw men one would pick — the most extreme irrational examples of opposition to what the church is doing.

If I had some confidence that Niebuhr exposed himself properly to any one of a number of books on economics, such as Hayek's *Constitution of Liberty,* or whatever (which I do recall was reviewed in *The Christian Century* by Gibson Winter; and reviewed, I thought, very very poorly) I'd feel more confidence in these men when it comes to this area. I have more things to say about Jim Wall's rebuttal, but I will refrain.

Chapter 4

From Theology to Social Decisions — and Return

Roger L. Shinn

I. INTRODUCTION

The roadway between theology and the social sciences, though bumpy and filled with pot-holes, is well travelled in both directions. But since the legitimacy of such travel is controversial, I shall start on a more fundamental level.

Long before there was any formal discipline of theology, there was religious belief and practice. And long before there were any social sciences, there were societies with organizations and institutions. So far back as we can go in human history, we find the interaction between faith and organized social activity. Each acts upon the other.

Thus Moses told a reluctant people that their God called them to move out of slavery into a promised land of freedom; faith required social decision and action. To this day Judaism commemorates the Exodus and the Passover; the social decision and the social history shape the religious cult and belief. Similarly the resurrection faith of the early Christian community led to actions that offended civil authorities, and the social history of martyrdom influenced and still influences the worship and doctrine of the church.

Eventually there came the intellectual disciplines of theology and the social sciences. Inevitably they interacted. Contemporary society is a scene of raging debates on how they ought, or ought not, to interact.

I begin with theology. It certainly intends to have an impact on social decisions and on the social sciences. The social sciences may resist, but they recognize the intention. The impact may be overt or subtle. "Every philosophy," wrote Alfred North Whitehead, "is tinged with the colouring of some secret imaginative background, which never emerges explicitly into its trains of reasoning."[1] Part of the business of theology is to explore imaginative backgrounds, to move them from secrecy to visibility, to criticize or cultivate them, to rationalize some of them into doctrines. Theology finds those imaginative backgrounds colouring the social sciences no less, or almost no less, than philosophy. It therefore claims to see the sometimes hidden meanings and motivations of social sciences. And it frequently tries to direct the social sciences toward the solving of human problems and the improvement of human life — goals that some social scientists accept and others reject.

Theology also recognizes a need for social sciences and a desire to learn from them. Motivated by historic faith, theology may ask: how in our world do we love the neighbour and show concern for the poor? We shall do these ineptly, especially in our highly organized society, unless we understand the social institutions and mechanisms that help or hurt the neighbour. It is common in our time to talk of the need for counter-intuitive behaviour. The impulse to do good may spend itself in futility or actually result in harm unless informed by a knowledge of social techniques and systems. So churches draw social scientists into their processes of decision-making.

As churches reach toward the social sciences, either seeking to influence them or asking their help, they find the social sciences reaching back in ways sometimes threatening and sometimes encouraging. The sociology of religion, for example, helps religious communities understand themselves. It shows churches, to their pain and illumination, that they often function to legitimate practices that are actually alien to their faith. The great debates about "the Protestant ethic," provoked by writings of Max Weber and R. H. Tawney and a host of their successors, are good examples of the issue. Did Protestant Christian belief nurture capitalism or did capitalism capture and corrupt Protestant Christianity? There are many answers to that question, but none of them derive from doctrine alone; the social sciences are needed to interpret the history and to throw light on some of the doctrines.

One definition of theology, much quoted in our time, comes from Gustavo Gutierrez, the Latin American Roman Catholic "liberation theologian": theology "is a critical reflection—in the light of the Word accepted in faith—on historical praxis and therefore on the presence of Christians in the world."[2] In so describing theology, he places himself in a tradition as old as St. Augustine.[3] But he says, as Augustine could not have said in his time or place, "The social sciences ... are extremely important for theological reflection in Latin America."[4] Not all theologians agree with Gutierrez on the importance of the social sciences or on his extensive appropriation of Marxist themes, but a sampling of theological literature will show a widespread awareness of the social sciences, as prominent in our time as the awareness of the physical sciences in the eighteenth century.

II. A PERPETUAL DEBATE ON "LINKAGE"

From faith to action in world religions

To understand the relation between theology and the social sciences it is necessary to return again to the prior issue: the relation of faith to action. That some relation exists is hardly debatable. It is impossible that any widely shared religious faith *not* influence the surrounding society and respond to the influence of society on it. But there are major debates on the nature of the "linkage," to adapt a term from contemporary controversies about foreign policy. The debate goes on in many religions all over the world.

The Ayatollah Khomeini, for example, has impressed the world with his fervent desire to build an Islamic society, in which the most detailed political decisions get the direct sanction of ultimate religious authority. His position has roots in traditional Muslim faith; it is in part a direct reaction against modern secularization of society. Yet other Muslims, while recognizing that their faith calls for action in the world, prefer that government have freedom for some pragmatic experimentation, some negotiation of conflicting interests, a step or two removed from the direct mandates of religion.

Hinduism, with its classic doctrine of Nirvana, might seem to remove the ultimate concerns of faith from the work-a-day world of *Maya* (appearance, perhaps even illusion). Yet Hindu religion has historically prescribed the minute details of the caste-structure of society.

Buddhism's disciplined path to Enlightenment appears at first to be as little concerned as Hinduism with political and economic controversies. Yet saffron-robed Buddhist monks were conspicuous in protests against the war in Vietnam and are today prominent in the opposition to nuclear armaments, both in Asia and in the United States.

Chinese Confucianism was for centuries deliberately related to political wisdom and the arts of government. Taoism, although far less directly concerned with government, produced characteristic styles of leadership in government and even of generalship in war.

Faith and action in the Judeo-Christian tradition

In short, the great world religions have always responded to social-historical situations and have exercised influence on society. And that double interaction has been especially evident in the religious heritage most influential in Western history — that of Judaism and Christianity. The Hebrew Scriptures give great attention to political and economic history. The writings of law and prophecy are filled with moral declarations directed to rulers, to controllers of economic power, and to the people in their social and economic relations. The Talmud and the rabbinic tradition carry on this concern, working out its details in a great variety of historical situations. Sometimes the Jewish people are in charge of their own societies, and sometimes they are scattered in diaspora under alien rulers; such differences determine their opportunity to shape society and therefore influence the ethical teaching. But in either case the concerns of faith touch all of social and personal life.

The Christian New Testament, in contrast to the Hebrew Bible, was written within about a century and its immediate purview covers little more than that. Furthermore, its writers were part of a minority community, and they expected an early end of history. So they rarely addressed themselves to the big issues of statecraft and organization of economies. But they too insisted that faith influenced all of life. They adopted the Hebrew Scriptures as their own Scriptures. And when in later years they came close to or even occupied the seats of secular power, they sought to influence political and economic life — most obviously in the Roman Catholic, the Calvinist, and the Social Gospel traditions. Yet there were always — or nearly always — some distinctions between theological and political judgements. The mystery and transcendence of God impose some reservations upon those who seek to declare the divine will. Those who are too sure they know God's will and too quick to condemn all who disagree with them are in greatest danger of the pride that is the central sin.

So the church struggled through the centuries with the relation between the certitudes of faith and the ambiguities of social ethics, with the connection between uncompromising religious commitments and the compromises that constitute political processes, with the meaning of the perfection of God's kingdom and the imperfections of all human kingdoms.

The contemporary picture

Today the American church, as it looks back on its history, wonders why it was sometimes so sure of ethical judgements that now seem so fallible. Equally often, it wonders why it was so reticent on ethical issues that now appear clear and important. Church people may look with an ironic smile on past confident attempts to legislate sabbath observance, outlaw contraceptives, and prohibit alcoholic drinks; but these same church people may painfully wonder why churches were so slow to speak out against slavery, against race prejudice, against imperialism and the economic abuses of the robber barons of the gilded age.

The debate about linkage between faith and social involvement is as confusing now as it has ever been. "Conservative" preachers a few years ago were criticizing "liberals" for mixing religion and politics in protests against the war in Vietnam; some of those same conservatives are now crusading for legislation and constitutional amendments against abortion, and they are studying "hit lists" of senators and representatives whom they want to defeat in the next election. "Liberals" have made careers of pleading for involvement of church people in political issues; now they are telling self-proclaimed "moral majorities" to be less sure of their own righteousness and to recognize that doctrine does not entail uniformity of political opinion.

If this situation makes for some confusion, it is also a good learning situation. Knee-jerk reactions, whether conservative or liberal, to issues of faith and social life are not adequate. Ad hoc responses, shifting from issue to issue, lack integrity. Religious communities and societies must rethink the linkage between theology and political life.

III. WHERE DOCTRINE MAKES A DIFFERENCE

The unintended consequence of religious views

An exploration of the "secret imaginative background" of philosophies and cultures discovers many themes that influence political and social systems. The important issues are not always the ones most obviously verbalized in propositions. They may appear in cult and myth more vividly than in doctrine. They include some sense of the relation of time and eternity, of matter and spirit, of humanity and nature (often of human law and natural law), of freedom and determinism, of political order and cosmic order, of religious commitment and pluralism. Convictions on such themes influence history and social problems, even though the makers of history may not articulate them or deliberately try to apply them to social problems. Historian Herbert Butterfield observes:

> Those who preached the Gospel for the sake of the Gospel, leaving the further consequences of their action to Providence, have always served the world better than they knew, better than those who worked with mundane purposes in mind—sometimes they served the world better even than they would have liked if they could have foreseen the consequences.[5]

To that I would add that unconscious or barely conscious religious apprehensions may also do harm in the world, far beyond the intentions of their holders. For better or worse, the traffic between religious and political-economic institutions makes a difference, beyond the deliberate plans and purposes of the people involved.

The Benedictine monks are an example of an influence, largely unintended, on economic history. Economist Kenneth Boulding writes:

> If one is looking for the beginning of a continuous process of scientific and technological development this might be traced to the monastic movement in the West of the sixth century A.D., especially the Benedictines. Here for almost the first time in history we had intellectuals who worked with their hands, and who belonged to a religion which regarded the physical world as in some sense sacred and capable of enshrining goodness.[6]

Similarly, historian Lynn White, Jr. says: "St. Benedict of Nursia, the founder of the Benedictine Order, is probably the pivotal figure in the history of labor." The Benedictine monk, he adds, "was the first intellectual to get dirt under his fingernails."[7] The historical influence extends to millions of people who know nothing about the Benedictines.

Explicit implications for social order

However, in other cases religious doctrine and ethics leads to deliberate efforts to shape society. If there are beliefs that have little direct effect upon social activity, there are others that require efforts to shape the social order. Two examples are conspicuous in contemporary Western theology: (1) the ethical values that guide conduct, and (2) the doctrine of human nature and history.

As to the central religious value in the biblical tradition, the emphasis is on a love that seeks justice. Jesus, asked what is the greatest commandment, selects two commandments from the Hebrew Bible: love of God and love of neighbour. An apostolic writing says, "he who does not love his brother whom he has seen, cannot love God whom he has not seen" (1 John 4:20). Love is not a mere disposition or emotion; it is active concern for the well-being of the neighbour. And the neighbour is anyone in need, including the stranger who is alienated by religious and ethnic conflicts (Luke 10:29–37).

In biblical ethics love is enacted in just human relations and institutions. It is hypocritical to claim to love while hurting other people. There are no formal definitions of justice in the Bible. But, in contrast to the Platonic and Aristotelian traditions in which justice is hierarchical, biblical justice moves in the direction of equality. There is an upsetting of hierarchies in the repeated expression of concern for common people against unjust demands of kings, in the attention to the needs of widows and orphans, the poor and the weak. The prophets and Jesus find themselves frequently in conflict with the wielders of power, whether the power be political, economic, or religious.

The Bible does not define an ideal political structure or economic system. But love enacted in justice clearly has significance for the distribution of power and of wealth. A biblically-based justice protests against destitution in the midst of affluence, against impotence in the midst of power.

Eschatology and ethics

Turning to the doctrine of history and human nature, we find repeatedly in the Bible the expectation of a messianic age or a coming Kingdom of God in which the poor will be blessed and the meek will inherit the earth. Much of Scripture communicates the mood of prophetic expectation. Particularly in the New Testament, people are called to live in the spirit of the coming age. Christ's beatitudes declare the reversal of values and of position in the coming Kingdom. Paul calls on Christians, "Do not be conformed to this world" – the Greek text says to this "age" – "but be transformed by the renewal of your mind, that you may prove what is the will of God, what is good and acceptable and perfect" (Romans 12:2).

Yet with this recognition of a coming era and a transformation of history, there is a recognition of the stubbornness of the old age and the necessity for institutions that take account of it. In the chapter immediately following his call for transformation, Paul – in a passage with a fateful later history – acknowledges the importance under God's sovereignty of the political institutions of the Roman Empire. The central problem bestowed by the New Testament on the ethics of the later church is the relation between eschatology and ethics, between the ultimate promises and demands of the Kingdom of God and the necessities of a functioning worldly society.

William Temple, a famous Archbishop of Canterbury, stated the issue in pointed terms:

> [I]t is sometimes supposed that what the Church has to do is to sketch a perfect social order and urge men to establish it. But it is very difficult to know what a "perfect social order" means. Is it the order that would work best if we were all perfect? Or is it the order that would work best in a world of men and women such as we actually are? If it is the former, it certainly ought not to be established; we should wreck it in a fortnight.[8]

That did not leave Temple complacent about the injustices in society. He was a foremost advocate of economic change in Britain, a representative of liberal leftist programs. The statement just quoted appeared in the context of a double-pronged ethical argument: that the church should exercise itself forcefully for the increase of social justice, but that the church simultaneously should practice some restraint in prescribing the details of a just social order.

An example of the tension between eschatology and ethics is the issue of motivations and incentives for action. Biblical faith seeks a world in which concern for the common good is as powerful an incentive as concern for self. It elevates love above personal ambition, cooperation above competition. But it knows very well that any political-economic order must take account of self-interest. If cooperation is ethically better than competition, still competition is better than collusion in restraint of trade. And an open appeal to self-interest is better than authoritarian compulsion in getting the world's work done.

Thus, to continue with the reasoning of William Temple:

> a statesman who supposes that a mass of citizens can be governed without appeal to their self-interest is living in a dreamland and is a public menace. The art of government in fact is the art of so ordering life that self-interest prompts what justice demands.[9]

An ethical politics and economics must constantly ask how to use the self-regarding motives of people without enhancing them and crushing the equally fundamental human concern for others. The *homo economicus* of traditional economic theory is as far from reality as the idealized *homo benignus* of utopian economic dreams.

Historically the biblical prophets and ethically sensitive leaders of the churches have been more effective in pointing out the wrongs in society and in calling on society to face issues of justice than in prescribing in any detail the methods and systems that love might employ in seeking justice. If that is clearly true in the biblical situation, it is even more evident in the modern world. One of the reasons is the emergence of the social sciences.

IV.   THE RISE OF THE SOCIAL SCIENCES

The social sciences — principally political science, economics, and sociology — provide new powers for understanding and guiding social processes. Yet their history is one of controversy, not only about specifics but about their definition and aim: are they normative enterprises, or are they solely descriptive and analytical? The debate arises in comparable form in all the social sciences, but their histories are different enough to justify a brief look at each in turn.

Political science

The oldest of the social sciences is political science. In Plato and Aristotle political thought was inseparable from philosophy: the love of wisdom and quest for the good life. Yet there was an empirical component in it. Aristotle's *Politics,* for example, began with an examination of both the idealized governments in Greek literature and the actual states that he knew. Both Plato and Aristotle assumed a hierarchical order of society, analogous to the metaphysical hierarchy of being, as they understood it. Yet both protested against tyranny.

Augustine was the father of political philosophy in the Christian West. His thought shows the tension, which I have already mentioned, between eschatology and political ethics. On his radical side, he desacralizes the Roman empire, stripping it of the divinity ascribed to it by pagan religions and some of his Christian predecessors. He declares that a state without justice is no better than a robber band. He refuses to absolutize any specific political system, tolerating and even encouraging diversity of customs and practices. He condemns the traditional Roman law for denying rights of inheritance to women. He insists that the separation of good and evil people must await God's final judgement, not be imposed now by church or state — although he wavers and makes an exception in the case of the schismatic and unruly Donatists.

On the conservative side, Augustine accepts the imperfections of the world. He longs for a better society, but does not expect it or urge radical reforms. Given the disruptive power of sin, he puts high value on order. His acceptance of slavery, unlike Aristotle's, is not based on the natural order; slavery is a consequence of sin, to be removed in the End but not yet.

With the Renaissance political thinking took a new turn. Machiavelli sets out to describe politics as it really is, not as it ought to be. He shows that things happen by manipulation, deceit, intrigue, violence, the use of power, the ambition of despots. But he does not formulate a value-free theory of politics. In *The Prince* he gives advice to a ruler who might unify Italy and restore something of its ancient glory. Since Machiavelli, Western political thought has exemplified a mixture of ethics and tactics, of idealism and realism or cynicism.

It is only since the Enlightenment that social scientists have developed the analytical tools that constitute a modern political science. But political science, more than the other social sciences, is rooted in a long tradition. And the issues discussed by a modern Hans Morgenthau or Henry Kissinger are analogous to issues debated through centuries of history.

The same issues appear in theological efforts to develop a political ethic. Repeatedly the hopes for an ideal society are shipwrecked in the squalls of conflicts of power; yet every lapse into despair is disturbed by new aspirations. In the famous words of Reinhold Niebuhr, "Politics will, to the end of history, be an area where conscience and power meet, where the ethical and coercive factors of human life will interpenetrate and work out their tentative and uneasy compromises."[10]

Economics

The origin of economics is much more recent than the origin of political theory. Although all societies have economic practices and beliefs about them, it is only in modern times that an intellectual discipline called economics has appeared. Even more recently has it been called a social science.

As Robert Heilbroner puts it, a "separate, self-contained economic world" did not "lift itself from its social context"[11] until the sixteenth or seventeenth century. The concepts of markets in land, labour, and capital are modern. So is the notion of economic "laws" (of supply and demand; of money supply, goods, and inflation), sometimes deliberately modelled on the laws of physics.

The ambivalence about the relation of ethics to objective analysis, which we have already noticed in political theory, persists in economics. One of the motivations of modern economics was to liberate economic activity from the stifling moral constraints of medieval Christendom. The most important of early economists, Adam Smith, in his most famous passage wrote:

> [The individual] is led by an invisible hand to promote an end which was no part of his intention. Nor is it always the worse for the society that it was no part of it. By pursuing his own interest he frequently promotes that of the society more effectually than when he really intends to promote it. I have never known much good done by those who affected to trade for the public good.[12]

Yet there is no denying a moral concern in this recognition of a-moral forces in the market. Adam Smith made his reputation as a moral philosopher before his great work in political economy. (I realize that there is a lively argument about the extent of continuity and discontinuity between *A Theory of Moral Sentiments* and *The Wealth of Nations.* Like Fred Hirsch,[13] I am persuaded by the sources that the continuity is real.) Smith assumes some basic human decencies and some restraints on predatory competition (even as he remains suspicious of the monopolistic scheming of producers and merchants). In the passage just quoted he acknowledges the interest "of society" and the "public good." He puts a value on personal freedom, on mobility, on decentralization of decision-making, on initiative and self-reliance.

Certainly the history of economics is well sprinkled with ethical discussion. John Maynard Keynes, the most celebrated economist of his time, made the point in a letter to William Temple. I have already referred to the book, *Christianity and Social Order,* in which Temple upheld the right of the church to "interfere" in the economic sphere, while recommending restraint in religious endorsements of specific economic measures. When Temple sent proofs of the book to Keynes, Keynes responded by saying that Temple had *understated* the case for the church's intervention in issues of economics. Keynes then continued:

> Along one line of origin at least, economics more properly called political economy, is a side of ethics. Marshall used always to insist that it was through ethics he arrived at political economy and I would claim myself in this, as in other respects, to be a pupil of his. I should have thought that nearly all English economists in the tradition, apart from Ricardo, reached economics that way. There are practically no issues of policy as distinct from technique which do not involve ethical considerations.[14]

In that respect the Keynesian tradition, although under criticism on many fronts, persists. When James Tobin won the Nobel Prize in economics for 1981, a former student recalled a course in theory that he had taken with Tobin: "It was abstract, but Jim never let you lose sight that the ultimate reason for studying theory was to make the world a better place. To him, the ultimate justification for economics and social science was to benefit people."[15]

Obviously not all economists agree. A school of contemporary economic thought, prominent some years ago and still persisting, maintains that the function of economics is to build models, independent of values and of policy recommendations. But when economists recommend public policies, as many of them frequently do, they inevitably enter into debates about ethical values as well as economic techniques. To point to an example, ethical language is conspicuous in the regular columns of Milton Friedman and Lester Thurow in *Newsweek*.

Sociology

The third of the major social sciences, sociology, has the shortest history. (I need not here enter into the argument as to whether anthropology is a sub-set of sociology or an independent social science.) Auguste Comte invented the word and the concept in the nineteenth century. It has become the most familiar of the social sciences, because everybody claims some first-hand knowledge about society.

Comte shared the ambivalence about science and value, fact and purpose that has haunted the history of all the social sciences. His positivism was certainly not identical with the logical positivism of more recent fame, but the common terminology is more than coincidental. In his version of the nineteenth century faith in progress, he divided history into three ages: the theological (the most primitive), the metaphysical, and the dawning positivist age, when science could become truly factual and abandon all mythology and speculation. He also ranked the sciences in order of development and maturity: mathematics (the only truly "ripe" science), astronomy, physics, chemistry, biology (including psychology), and the newly emergent sociology. His hope was that the science of society would develop in the direction of mathematics, astronomy, and physics.

Nevertheless Comte was a crusader. He wanted to rebuild society on a more scientific and "spiritual" basis. He established a Religion of Humanity, a sort of church without any God or metaphysical beliefs but with ritual, festivals, and sacraments. Scoiology has left behind that particular form of cultism. But the tension between the two aspects of Comte persists. People half expect sociologists to be objective, value-free and "scientific," while half expecting them to be liberal, enlightened, and reformist. And sociologists themselves contribute to these contradictory expectations.

These brief historical observations on the rise of the social sciences point to the perplexity that surrounds interactions between theologians and social scientists. Sometimes the two meet on a common turf of shared concern with social values. Sometimes the work of theologians seems totally irrelevant to the work of social scientists, except as an idiosyncracy of human behaviour that may, like any other aspect of behaviour, be studied scientifically. History helps to illuminate these differing situations. But their importance becomes more clear as we investigate what goes on in the decision-making processes of a society.

V. THE CONTRIBUTION OF THEOLOGY AND THE SOCIAL SCIENCES TO SOCIAL DECISIONS[16]

We approach the nub of the issue in two questions directed to me in the invitation to write this paper: What right does theology have to address questions of social organization? What qualifications and what limitations does it bring to this task?

I shall try to answer both questions. In doing so, I shall direct the same questions to the social sciences.

I begin by stating a few assumptions. (1) Neither theologians nor social scientists are an elite privileged to make decisions for societies. (2) Societies make their own decisions, intentionally or accidentally, partly by political processes and partly by thousands of personal and group decisions that result in an impact upon the total society. (3) Religious leaders and theologians have a right to participate in those decisions, just as social scientists do. (4) Both theological and social scientific insight have a contribution to make to the social process. (5) Religious communities and social scientific communities alike sometimes avoid their social responsibilities, sometimes out of timidity and sometimes out of indifference. (6) Both communities sometimes exaggerate their competence and their authority to influence decisions.

Rather than defend these assumptions, I shall show how they become operative in society. My continuing argument will illustrate the effect of assumptions.

Commitment and knowledge in social ethics

One proposition is essential to all that follows: *Social policies take shape at the convergence of two kinds of human experience that are distinguishable although not absolutely separable.* The first involves human commitments, loyalties, purposes, a sense of the meaning of life, a belief about the qualities of a good life and good society, and re-

flection on priorities and conflicts of values. The second involves a
body of information about the world and analytical skills for organizing that information, for understanding the physical universe and social process, and for maintaining or changing a society.

Every human being, starting from infancy, enters into both kinds of
experience. It is not the case that some people generate the first kind
of experience while others generate the second. But the first set of experiences is characteristic of the arts, of ethical insight, of religious
sensitivity and commitment. It is a central concern of religious communities, although certainly not of them alone. Its intellectual analysis
is a subject for some types of philosophy and for all theology. The second set of experiences is characteristic of every effort to survive and
function in the world. It is a professional concern of physical scientists, who investigate nature, and of social scientists, who investigate
societies.

It is easy and important to make some distinctions between the two
kinds of experience and to see the necessity for both. For the sake of
brevity, I shall identify the first kind of experience as commitment,
recognizing that it includes a wide variety of esthetic, ethical, human,
and religious responses to life. I shall identify the second as informational analysis, recognizing that it includes knowledge from everyday
experience, from the physical sciences, and from the social sciences.

The importance of distinction

Commitments are involved in any social policy, but commitments
without informational analysis can never prescribe an effective policy.
If I am committed to helping people in need, I cannot do much until I
know what the needs of people are. If they are hungry, if they are
drowning, if they are bored, if they are illiterate, if they are infected
with lethal viruses, if they are being invaded by enemy troops, these
different needs call for different responses. I cannot learn the needs of
people by steeping myself in religious tradition or by practicing mystical meditation *apart from* informational analysis. Even if I focus on a
single need — say, malnutrition and starvation — I cannot contribute to
an effective policy without learning something about calories and vitamins, climate and weather, economic pressures that help or hinder
producers of crops and their customers, international relations that
subject some societies to decisions made in other societies.

Equally important, no quantity of informational analysis adds up to a social policy apart from the commitments that are joined to it. Occasionally a commitment is so widely shared (or at least tolerated) that information leads almost inevitably to policy. When informational analysis showed the possibility of eliminating smallpox at a modest cost, there were no prolonged debates or power conflicts about the desirability of doing so. But most commitments are more controversial. Information about the destructive power of nuclear weapons for example, leads some people to work for higher defense appropriations, others to work for disarmament. Information about energy shortages leads some to calculate ways of protecting their privileges, others to search for ways of sharing limited supplies. Information about projected inflation leads some to call for policies to stop inflation, others to figure how to make money out of inflation.

Because social life is extremely complex, these illustrations are all too simple. For example, information is fairly clear — with many genuine controversies about quite extensive agreement — about the destructive capacity of nuclear weapons; it is not nearly so clear on what policies increase or decrease the likelihood of nuclear war. Opinions on that subject require informational analysis of weaponry, international relations, human motivations, and much more. Equally, informational analysis may show that some policies designed to stop inflation are ineffective or counter-productive, while other effective policies have serious side-effects. But at almost every stage of the decision-making process, there is some interaction of ethical purpose with physical and social scientific information, and neither alone produces a policy.

In a world of diverse specializations of knowledge and insight, it is easy — and sometimes valid — to criticize false uses of authority. If a famous athlete earns more money endorsing miscellaneous consumer products than knocking baseballs out of parks, anybody might ask why the athlete's real or pretended preference for a soft drink or an automobile should carry any weight with the public. But when a society enters into discussion of public policy, everybody must think beyond the confines of narrow professional competence. When religious communities try to influence public economic policy, the question invariably arises: what do those people know about what is *economically* good for society? The question is legitimate — just as legitimate as the counter question: what do economists and financiers know about what is economically *good* for society? In both cases a sound opinion requires some entry into a domain outside professional expertise, or at least some sustained conversations with people in other domains. The presupposition of a democratic society is that such entries and such conversations are possible. Without that possibility, expressions of commitment degenerate into ineffectual platitudes and informational analysis becomes so technically trivial as to be useless to the body politic.

The convergence of the two

I have been emphasizing the *difference* between commitments and informational analysis, and I have been insisting on the necessity of *both* for policy decisions. I have accorded to each a relative autonomy, arguing that commitments cannot dictate informational analysis and that informational analysis cannot dictate commitments. But now I must carry the argument another step. The difference between the two kinds of experience that enter into decisions, though important, is not total.

As an example of the issue, I refer to a recent article by economist Lester Thurow, "Why Do Economists Disagree?" With an admirable ability to smile at his own profession, he acknowledges that they do disagree. One reason is that economics is not a laboratory science in which investigators can run repeatable experiments isolated from all extraneous influence. Then he offers another reason, still more important for our present subject:

> There are no public policies so good that everyone's income goes up; there are no public policies so bad that everyone's income goes down. Every policy has income distribution effects. As a consequence economic recommendations contain two major elements. First, there must be some hard economic information as to whose income will go up, whose income will go down, and what is the net result of those gains and losses. This is the scientific part of every economic problem. Second, however, there is an ethical value judgment as to whose income "ought" to go up or down. This ethical value judgment has nothing to do with technical economics, but is usually at the heart of differences between liberal and conservative economists.
>
> .   .   .   .
>
> By the very fact that we use the words "liberal or conservative" with respect to economists, we are saying that the discipline is somehow different. No one talks about liberal or conservative

chemists. There are only chemists who in the rest of their lives
happen to be liberals or conservatives.[17]

The further significance of Thurow's theme is that people see in a
social situation what their desires, their commitments, and their social
location enable them to see. It is not as though the world offers a
knowable body of information and scientific principles waiting to be
discovered. At best, only some aspects of a total situation are apprehended; and among them, some one or few aspects become centres
about which observer-participants organize the rest into a meaningful
pattern.

"Facts" are not simply made to order — even though such may seem
to be the case in many public arguments. Facts, to be sure, have an
"objectivity" beyond wishful thinking. As Gunnar Myrdal puts it,
"Facts kick."[18] Wishes are not horses or houses or meals. Turnips are
not watches or good jobs or gold bars. But facts never come naked;
they come clothed in, imbedded in meaning. As Myrdal again says,
both "ignorance and knowledge are generally not simple and hap-
hazard but are opportunistic."[19]

The importance of social location

One major determiner of meaning and of the facts that fit meanings is
social location. A mountain looks different from various points of the
compass, from its peak, and from an airplane above it. Society offers
even more diverse perspectives. To say that a military objective is
worth ten per cent casualties means one thing to the general planning a
campaign and something else to the soldiers attacking. Unemployment has quite different meanings in the Federal Reserve Board Room
and among the unemployed.

That is why the making of policy requires participation not only of
experts with different skills but of people with different social locations.
Because people with access to power have more influence than others,
the process, even in a society intended to be democratic, is skewed.
Churches in our own society characteristically represent the more
stable and at least the moderately privileged social groups; but when
they remember their historic faith, they feel a responsibility to represent the less privileged. Usually they lack the imagination or will to do
so very well; but it is interesting that when churches take formal steps
to influence social policy, their positions are somewhat different from
the positions that come from an undifferentiated poll of the members.

Ideology

A second major determiner of meaning, almost as important as the first, is ideology. Since ideology is a word of many meanings, I shall say that I am here using the term in a non-pejorative sense to stand for any set of conceptions or any picture of society and the world that helps to guide action. It is not quite identical with a worldview, because a worldview may include speculations irrelevant to action. But in the sense that I use the word, everybody has an ideology, and the ideology influences decisions. It may often be that ideology, as Karl Marx and Karl Mannheim proposed, is a distortion of reality in the interests of protecting a privileged position. If so, the honest person will try to cleanse ideology and correct the distortions. But some ideology is necessary to guide effective action.

An ideology, as I am using the term, is neither sheer commitment nor sheer informational analysis, although it incorporates both — along with a lot of experience and common sense. It is an amalgam — powerful though usually imprecise — of information, ideas, purposes, emotional tones, hopes and fears, folk attitudes, and conventional wisdom of the dominant reference group for any individual.

Honest and rigorous thinkers and doers are uneasy about ideology. They try to whittle down its scope by identifying within it their considered commitments and their informational analysis. But they never eliminate it. The reason is that ideology is not simply a synthesis of values and facts; it is the framework into which people fit their values and facts; or it is the skeleton around which they arrange values and facts. Ideology determines what purposes and information, among infinite possibilities, will become the centre of organization for remaining purposes and information. It is both a magnifying glass and a filter for emphasizing and excluding perceptions in that opportunistic mix of knowledge and ignorance that Myrdal describes.

That is why a social-political process, designed to serve the needs of a society, will aim to secure the most complete and accurate informational analysis available, will relate this to the most carefully considered values of the society, and will incorporate in the process people from a variety of social situations and ideologies.

Social controversy, in fact, is largely ideological controversy. Such controversy is messy; it constantly argues values under the guise of facts and facts under the guise of values. It abounds in arguments hard to verify or criticize. We might wish for something better. But it is very hard to sort out the real issues and state them with precision.

Furthermore, none of us is expert on all the controversial issues that we are called to think and decide about. We listen to the experts and find them disagreeing. So we usually choose our experts on the basis of their ideological affinities with ourselves. And given the way experts make up their minds, we are not entirely mistaken in using that method of choice.

VI. CONCLUSIONS

I started with the title, "From Theology to Social Decisions — and Return." My position is that any serious theology drives the believer to make social decisions and contributes to those decisions because it articulates the commitments incorporated in those decisions. But rarely if ever does theology alone determine the decision. It must be joined with informational analysis, for which theology needs the help of other disciplines, particularly the social sciences. Decisions take place at the convergence of commitments and informational analysis. They take place in a social location — preferable one broad enough to include many sublocations — and within an ideological setting.

A reverse process is going on. As theology contributes to social decisions, those social decisions are contributing to theology. It is in making decisions and acting on commitments that persons and communities expose themselves to new social locations and insights that enlarge and deepen perceptions and thereby influence theology. Nobody completes a theology, then acts on it. It is in activity, as truly as in reflection, that people and churches discover their theologies.

"What right does theology have to address questions of social organizations?" It has every right to address such questions, not to dictate the answers, but to exercise whatever persuasion it can. It has no right to avoid addressing such questions.

"What qualifications and what limitations does it bring to this task?" It has the qualifications and limitations of all human activity, which is never omniscient or infallible. It has the particular limitation that it depends upon informational analysis that is not derived from theology as such, but that depends on contemporary experience and the skills of many disciplines, especially (in our time) the physical and social sciences. In the interaction of the most basic human commitments with a variety of professional skills, social locations, and ideological perspectives lies the possibility that a democratic society can cope with urgent decisions in this precarious age of history. To participate in the process is the right and responsibility of theologians.

NOTES

1. Alfred North Whitehead, *Science and the Modern World* (New York: Macmillan, 1925), p. 11.

2. Gustavo Gutierrez, *A Theology of Liberation* (Maryknoll, N.Y.: Orbis Books, 1973), p. 145.

3. Ibid., p. 6.

4. Ibid., p. 5.

5. Herbert Butterfield, *Christianity in European History* (London: Collins, 1952), p. 25.

6. Kenneth E. Boulding, *The Meaning of the 20th Century* (New York: Harper & Row, Colophon edition), pp. 6–7.

7. Lynn White, Jr., *Machina ex Deo* (Cambridge, Mass.: MIT Press, 1968), pp. 63, 65. Cf. Rene Dubos, *A God Within* (New York: Charles Scribner's Sons, 1972), Ch. 8.

8. William Temple, *Christianity and Social Order* (New York: Penguin Books, 1942), p. 37.

9. Ibid., p. 43.

10. Reinhold Niebuhr, *Moral Man and Immoral Society* (New York: Charles Scribner's Sons, 1932) p. 4.

11. Robert L. Heilbroner, *The Worldly Philosophers* (New York: Simon and Schuster, 1953), p. 15.

12. Adam Smith, *The Wealth of Nations* (Chicago: University of Chicago Press, 1976), Vol I, pp. 477–478.

13. Fred Hirsch, *Social Limits to Growth* (London: Routledge & Kegan Paul, 1977), pp. 65–66, 137.

14. F. A. Iremonger, *William Temple, Archbishop of Canterbury: His Life and Letters* (London: Oxford University Press, 1948), pp. 438–439.

15. William Brainard, professor of economics and provost at Yale University, quoted in the *New York Times,* Oct. 14, 1981, p. D1.

16. The argument of the following section is developed at greater length in my book, *Forced Options: Social Decisions for the 21st Century* (San Francisco: Harper & Row, 1982), Ch. 12.

17. Lester Thurow, "Why Do Economists Disagree?," *Dissent* 29:176–77 (Spring 1982).

18. Gunnar Myrdal, *Objectivity in Social Research* (New York: Pantheon Books, 1969), p. 40.

19. Ibid., p. 29.

Comment

Arthur A. Shenfield

Shinn in general

This is an essay on the interrelations between theology and the social sciences. With cogent argument Dr. Shinn upholds the claim of theology to pronounce upon the problems of society. At the same time he recognizes the right of the social scientist to face the theologian with the lessons of his information on social phenomena and his analysis of them, and to require him to take account of them in reaching his conclusions. The theologian and the social scientist, he tells us, must not only respect each other's standing and competence; they need each other. Each can help the other to follow his own discipline with greater success, to grasp its truths and elude its errors with greater certainty.

Thus, for example, on the theologian. "The mystery and transcendence of God impose some reservations upon those who seek to declare the divine will. Those who are too sure they know God's will and too quick to condemn all who disagree with them are likely to be in greatest danger of the pride that is the central sin." On the social scientist, for example, he gives us various references to eminent practitioners (Smith, Comte, Keynes, Tobin, Friedman, Thurow) who have recognized the importance, perhaps the primacy, of moral considerations in the study of their disciplines. There are numerous other statements, often pithy and to the point, which in Dr. Shinn's view describe a variety of aspects of the interaction or interface of theology and the social sciences.

The heart of the matter is described as follows. "Social policies take shape at the convergence of two kinds of human experience that are distinguishable though not absolutely separable. The first involves human commitments, loyalties, purposes, a sense of the meaning of life, a belief about the qualities of a good life and good society, and reflection on priorities and conflicts of values. The second involves a body of information about the world and analytical skills for organizing that information, for understanding the physical universe and social process, and for maintaining or changing a society." Thus commitments are basic to social policy, but they cannot be effective without informational analysis. Correspondingly "no quantity of informational analysis adds up to a social policy apart from the commitments that are joined to it."

In their essentials Dr. Shinn's propositions on the interface between theology and the social sciences are unexceptionable; and his exposition of them is admirably fair, judicious and well-rounded, with a clear intention to recognize impartially the proper functions and claims peering at each other across the interface. Hence it is regrettable that his essential argument is considerably vitiated when he descends to the consideration of particulars. Consider the following.

Shinn in particular

First, the most important. Dr. Shinn's concept of the informational analysis necessary to mesh with commitments is defective. He describes it as follows. "If I am committed to helping people in need, I cannot do much until I know what the needs of people are. If they are hungry, if they are drowning, if they are bored, if they are illiterate, if they are infected with lethal viruses, if they are being invaded by enemy troops, these different needs call for different responses. I cannot learn the needs of people by steeping myself in religious tradition or by practicing mystical meditation apart from informational analysis. Even if I focus on a single need — say, malnutrition and starvation — I cannot contribute to an effective policy without learning something about calories and vitamins, climate and weather, economic pressures that help or hinder producers of crops and their customers, international relations that subject some societies to decisions made in other societies." All this is entirely correct, but it misses what is by far the most important informational analysis necessary to balance, and to give a correct thrust to, the commitments prescribed by the theologian. What is sure to lead the theologian into grave error is ignorance not just of the fact of scarcity, as the economist defines it, but of the economist's analysis of the consequences of scarcity. Allied with this, and equally damaging, is ignorance of the nature of market order and of the consequences of governmental intervention into its operation. Secondly, less important but still serious, the essay contains numerous observations which are rooted in popular myth and superstition, though fortunately Dr. Shinn does not descend to the levels deplorably common among theologians and religious spokesmen. Here are examples.

i. "Did Protestant Christian belief nurture capitalism or did capitalism capture corrupt Protestant Christianity?" In the second part of this question capitalism is ignorantly convicted of evil, while this is by no means balanced in the first part because if one merely says that Protestantism nurtured capitalism, one may mean, as millions have been taught to believe, that it nurtured a viper in its bosom. Either way capitalism is assumed to be evil.

ii. "Not all theologians agree with Gutierrez... on his extensive appropriation of Marxist themes." This is like saying that not all theologians are prepared to accept the goodness of sin. It implies that Marxism, though disputable and contestable, is one social theory amongst others which a theologian might possibly accept or respect.

iii. "... these same church people may painfully wonder: why were churches so slow to speak out against slavery, against race prejudice, against imperialism and the abuses of the robber barons of the gilded age?" The list illustrates the confusions which buzz in the liberal (meaning, of course, illiberal) American mind. The listing of the last two with the first two is as odious as it is popular. There are imperialisms and imperialisms. No doubt Dr. Shinn has in mind, *inter alia,* the British, French, Dutch and Belgian empires which gave peace, law and liberty to hundreds of millions, and the dismantling of which may cogently be argued to have been one of the great disasters of the human race in this century. As for the alleged robber barons, Dr. Shinn has no doubt read the old muckrakers and Matthew Josephson, and imagines that they gave him gospel truth.

iv. "A biblically-based justice protests against destitution in the midst of affluence." Correct, and yet commonly the cause of pestilential error. First, it is vital to ask if the affluence is the cause of the destitution or not. In pre-capitalist societies it largely was; in capitalism it is emphatically not, *pace* the critics of capitalism. In fact capitalism is the most powerful engine for the relief of destitution ever known to the human race. Secondly, is the relief of destitution to be by private action or benevolence or by the pseudo-benevolence of the State's fist? One has the uneasy feeling that Dr. Shinn's unstated assumptions are on the side of the latter.

v. "That did not leave Temple complacent about the injustices in society. He was a foremost advocate of economic change in Britain, a representative of liberal leftist programs." Obviously Temple is here presented not just as a champion of justice, which according to his dim lights he certainly was, but without question as an intelligent champion of justice. In fact Temple had nothing to offer the British people other than the fly-blown nostrums of the supposedly moderate political Left.

vi. "... that the church should exercise itself forcefully for the increase of social justice." What nonsense, indeed evil, is perpetrated in the name of social justice! Dr. Shinn, and others, should read Hayek, *viz.* "What I hope to have made clear is that the phrase 'social justice' is not an innocent expression of goodwill towards the less fortunate, it has become a dishonest insinuation that one ought to agree to a demand of some special interest. If political discussion is to become honest it is necessary to recognize that the term is intellectually disreputable, the mark of demagogy or cheap journalism which responsible thinkers ought to be ashamed to use because once its vacuity is recognized, its use is dishonest. I may, as a result of long endeavours to trace the destructive effect which the invocation of 'social justice' has had on our moral sensitivity, and of again and again finding even eminent thinkers thoughtlessly using the phrase, have become unduly allergic to it, but I have come to feel strongly that the greatest service that I can still render to my fellow men would be that I could make the speakers and writers among them thoroughly ashamed ever again to use the term 'social justice.'" (Law, Legislation and Liberty, Vol. 2, page 97).

vii. "It elevates... cooperation above competition.... If cooperation is ethically better than competition...." Here is the familiar failure to grasp the fact that competition in a free economy involves cooperation, though not the form of cooperation which many have been taught to believe is the only ethical one.

viii. "The *homo economicus* of traditional economic theory is as far from reality as the idealized *homo benignus* of utopian economic dreams". Shades of Carlyle, Ruskin and all the other part-knaves-part-fools who denounced classical economics! Here is the old illusion that the *homo economicus* was the very picture of selfish man. It is utterly deplorable that after countless exposures of its error (eg. by, amongst others, Wicksteed, who was a man of the cloth) this hoary old misunderstanding keeps rearing its head. Economics deals with the implications of purposive action, but the purposes may be selfish or unselfish, egoistic or altruistic.

ix. "A school of contemporary economic thought . . . maintains that the function of economics is to build models, independent of values and of policy recommendations." Dr. Shinn does not understand the difference between positive and normative economics, still less why positive economics is as important as it is. He would have understood it if he had thought through his observations about the importance of informational analysis.

x. The passages on Comte — anyone who holds up Comte as any kind of scholarly thinker should know that his social "science" was about as scientific as the "science which Gulliver met in Laputa (see Hayek in "The Counter-Revolution of Science").

xi. *Pace* Lester Thurow, "liberal" and "conservative" economists do not disagree because they favour raising or depressing the incomes of different people. Economists of the classical, neo-classical and Austrian traditions favour policies which accord with the rights of *all* people, including those whose incomes may fall as the result of correct policy.

It is a pity that so intelligent and fair-minded a scholar as Dr. Shinn has not taken the trouble to clear his thought of the errors which commonly infest the public mind.

Comment

Murdith R. McLean

The risk of being wrong

I'm reminded of an occasion when several of us in the Philosophy Department with graduate students were meeting to decide on the distribution of graduate scholarships. One beleaguered colleague felt that in our deliberations the merits of one of his students were being quite ignored. After listening for a few moments to a resumé of alleged shortcomings in the written work of this student, our colleague drew himself up and exclaimed, "But at least what he says is *false!'*

Some of you will not be surprised to hear that among philosophers it is sometimes counted an achievement to say something false. Not that they admire falsehood above all else; given the choice, philosophers at least claim to prefer the truth. But it is — or at least has been — widely held among philosophers that on subjects of fundamental importance, people are more apt to utter profound-sounding nonsense than they are to say things which are even candidates for truth-value. Thus they avoid the sin of making false claims, by making claims which couldn't be true either; which really means not making claims at all.

I wouldn't want to suggest for an instant that Professor Shinn has avoided the risk of falsehood by uttering what is cognitively meaningless. In fact, if he is saying what I understand him to be saying, almost everything he says seems to me to be true. But I do think that Professor Shinn has paid an unduly high price — though not the price of meaninglessness — for avoiding falsehood. The price I believe he has paid is that of keeping the discussion at a level of generalization where there is little chance of disagreement — or of falsehood — but where genuine and important controversies are obscured or avoided.

That Professor Shinn carries on this discussion at an abstract level is in a way not surprising, for he takes on a daunting number of topics.

He begins with a discussion of some of the ways in which theology and the social sciences interact. He moves then to a consideration of the complex connections between faith (not just Christian faith) and action. Following that there is a capsule account of the emergence in recent years of the various social sciences. And, finally, Professor Shinn devotes some space to a consideration of the right possessed by theology and by the social sciences to address questions of social organization, as well as the qualifications and limitations each of them brings to that undertaking. Perhaps others more competent than I am in these subject areas will find bones to pick in the fairly general assertions Professor Shinn makes on these topics. My own reservations, as I have already indicated, have more to do with what surrounds and underlies Professor Shinn's comments. While he alludes at several points to the rockiness of the road between theology and social decisions, one is left, I think, with only the occasional sense of exactly what the impediments are like on this highway, and why any regular traveller should be obliged to put up with them. The result, I think, is just a general impression that there are rough spots in the relations between theology and the social sciences, and in their joint attempts to address matters of social concern; but on the whole the trip is managed by many without intolerable shocks to their intellectual suspension systems. I believe the road is and ought to be travelled, but there is need to be clearer about the location and dimensions of impediments. Part of the result may be that we come to see the road as even rougher than Professor Shinn suggests. But another part may be that we make better progress with serious road repair, and in the end more vehicles will get through reasonably intact.

The theologian's "rights"

Let me illustrate my point by considering the last topic discussed by Professor Shinn: "The Contribution of Theology and the Social Sciences to Social Decisions."[1] He takes direction for his enquiry from a pair of questions asked first about theology and second about social sciences. He asks what right theology/social science has to address questions of social organization, and then what qualifications and limitations each brings to that task. Professor Shinn prepares the ground by explicating six "assumptions":

1. Neither theologians nor social scientists are an elite privileged to make decisions for societies;

2. Societies make their own decisions, intentionally or accidentally, partly by political processes and partly by thousands of personal and group decisions that result in an impact upon total society;
3. Religious leaders and theologians have a right to participate in those decisions, just as social scientists do;
4. Both theological and social scientific insight have a contribution to make to the social process;
5. Religious communities and social scientific communities alike sometimes avoid their social responsibilities, sometimes out of timidity and sometimes out of indifference;
6. Both communities sometimes exaggerate their competence and their authority to influence decisions.

Having recorded his assumption that (among other things) theology and the social sciences have the right in question, Shinn expands somewhat on the familiar reminder that social policies result from the interaction of two elements: "commitment," and "information analysis." He emphasizes that these elements are distinct, at least to the extent that social policy cannot properly arise from either one on its own. But he insists also that they are not absolutely separable. Social scientists' commitments, he contends, are not clearly detachable from their practice as social scientists. Moreover, he holds, it is true for all of us that such things as social location and ideological perspective play a part in determining the size and shape of "the facts."

Professor Shinn concludes that theology and the social sciences interact in social decision-making; and that in the case of theology at least, there is a reciprocal effect, in that the process of translating theology into social choices does not leave theology unchanged. On the central question of what right theology has to address social questions, he concludes simply, "It has every right to address such questions." Concerning qualifications and limitations, he is equally plain-spoken. "It has the qualifications and limitations of all human activity, which is never omniscient or infallible. It has the particular limitation that it depends upon informational analysis that is not derived from theology as such. . . ."

Now even if one agrees with these conclusions—and I will be surprised if there are many that find them controversial—there is surely something unsatisfying about the way that they are expressed and the route by which they are arrived at. Start with the question of theology's right to address social questions. Surely to begin by simply assuming, as Shinn does, that theology has such a right is to ignore a set of quite fundamental issues. It is not clear that all thoughtful people will so willingly concede such a right to the theologian; and many of those that do would at least require that some argument be forthcoming in support of that claim.

It is instructive, I think, to begin by being as clear as we can about what it is to *have* a right of this kind, and what it is that such a right would entitle one to do. That way of putting things already brings out something of what a right is; it is some kind of *entitlement*. It is a moral or legal possession which may be thought of as something like a license. To say that I have a right to defend myself against injury, or to paint my garage whatever colour I choose, is to say that I have some form of permission (moral, legal or both) to do those things. It follows that my rights bear with them restraints on others. To say that I have a right to do a given thing is to say that it is in some way wrong for others to prevent or interfere with my doing that thing. My rights, so far as they are honoured, bring me freedom from hindrance.

Given this very sketchy notion of what rights are, it is hard to see how anyone could deny to theologians the right to "address questions of social organization." How could anyone deny that theologians are entitled to discuss such questions; and that if they wish to preach sermons on social topics, or write articles on such subjects for church papers and theological journals, it would be wrong to prevent them? This right seems but an instance of the more general right, given at least a good deal of lip service in our society, to freedom of speech. Perhaps this explains why Professor Shinn simply assumes the entitlement of the theologian to speak about social issues, and why he links it with the assumption that societies make their decisions about these issues as a result of the interplay of contributions from countless groups and individuals. And perhaps this explains as well his very modest account of the qualifications possessed by theology for this task, which are merely the qualifications "of all human activity." No more qualification than this is needed, if it is just the right to freedom of speech that is being defended.

The right to be taken seriously

But this just isn't the way the debate actually goes on. More is demanded of theologians by way of qualifications than just their membership in another human activity, and surely most theologians believe they can meet the demand. The reason that more is required—and that theologians at least attempt to meet the requirement—is that more is at stake than just the freedom of speech. The right that the theologian is interested in defending, and that is surely under discussion in Professor Shinn's paper, is not just the right to discuss social questions within the household of faith. There are those—some from within the household!—who would deny even this domestic right to theologians; but I shall (at the risk of overlooking some genuine obstacles myself) ignore that extreme position for now. Theologians are concerned to earn more than the right to speak amongst believers on these issues. They want the right to speak to the community *at large,* believers and non-believers. And more than that. What is at issue here is not just the right to speak about these issues, but to be *listened to* and *taken seriously.* So, the question is whether theologians have a right to expect a hearing, for their utterances to be taken account of, in those councils where decisions about social concerns are taken.

I've had to use vague expressions like "being taken seriously," "given a hearing" and "be taken account of," for there is no very precise way of describing the kind of influence the church ought to have on these matters; nor is there unanimity among church people as to its proper authority. Professor Shinn is surely correct to remind us that theologians ought not to expect to be treated as sole and infallible sources of social decisions. But surely he is, with that very reminder, recognizing implicitly that *some* form of influence is being sought; and that the right in question is more than just a "Hyde Park" right to speak our piece, however inane, without interference.

If *that* is the right which the theologian seeks, then it can be seen why it is not immediately granted by all parties. And we can see, too, why the accompanying question about qualifications and rights is not only appropriate but unavoidable. If theologians want not just to be tolerated, but listened to with some attention, then they must be prepared to answer the question "why?" And I believe it is worth recognizing the sort of demand this places on theology. Obviously it will not suffice to rest theology's claim on the modest proposal that Christianity is composed in part by a world view, which includes an account of the nature of humans and society, and that such views would be relevant to social decision-making. There are many world views, and to support its entitlement to be taken seriously Christian theology must establish more than its membership in the menagerie. Some theologians, or at least church members, who recognize this have elevated this form of justification one notch by adding the claim that Chris-

tianity is, as a matter of social fact, a prominent if not dominant outlook among citizens of Western societies. On those grounds, it is
claimed, Christian theology earns a right at least to an attentive hearing. Those with a taste for what are sometimes called "political
realities" may find themselves attracted by this argument. It has the
great advantage of proceeding from premises which require no religious commitment in order to be granted. But in the end it is unsatisfactory.

It cannot be satisfying to the theologian, or convincing to the pol-
icy-maker, to rest with a claim to be heard that is based on what can
only be viewed from outside the faith as a historical accident. If the
theologian is to exhibit qualifications which can be expected to earn a
hearing, they must have to do with the possession of insights relevant
to the making of social decisions. Professor Shinn recognizes this
when he includes in his assumptions the assertion that both "theological and social scientific insight have a contribution to make to the
social process." But to make this an *assumption* is to ignore a crater-
sized hole in the road to social decision-making. Earlier in his paper,
Professor Shinn rightly identifies two areas within theology that bear
especially upon the social order: Christian ethics; and doctrines concerning human nature and history. But to have these resources taken
seriously in the process of social decision-making, the theologian must
be willing to develop the relevant theological positions *clearly,* and
compellingly (Each of those adverbs invites considerable elaboration.)
Theologians *believe* they have insights to contribute to the process,
but they will have to make this evident to others than themselves. And
one of the ironies here is that it is not just non-believers who require
convincing.

Limitations on the right to be taken seriously

I have been talking about the theologian's qualifications to speak out
and be heard on social issues. I have touched upon what many theologians would regard as a qualification they hold; the possession of insights relevant to the discussion of these issues. But I have found myself drawn beyond that point to a reminder about another qualification which religious thinkers *ought* to possess; the ability to establish
in that forum where they hope to be heard, the fact that they *do* have
insights. With that reminder I believe we come to a point which has to
be recognized as a limitation in the approach of theologians to matters
of social importance.

One chronic difficulty faced by theologians when they attempt to win a hearing on social matters is that they do not speak with one voice. It may well be that the results of theological reflection on the raw material of the faith is rich with insights concerning human nature, society and history. But even the person who is anxious to bring these insights to bear upon social concerns will be struck at the diversity, and—what is worse—inconsistency, of what respected theologians have to say on these matters. Of course any intellectual discipline will be characterized in part by disagreement among its practitioners, sometimes on quite fundamental matters. Recent discussions about the logic of scientific enquiry, stimulated in part by Thomas Kuhn's *The Structure of Scientific Revolutions,* have spilled over into debates concerning the methods of the social sciences, and even theology.[2] One result has been a striking reminder of the extent to which intellectual disciplines may unite under one subject-title, thinkers who differ not just about the outcomes of any enquiry but about the very rules by which enquiry should be pursued. Perhaps theology is no worse off in this respect than its neighbours in the intellectual disciplines. But there are times when it *appears* worse off; when theologians appear to be starting from such disparate views concerning those insights which are supposed to inform our deliberations on social issues, that confidence in their utterances must be shaken. Indeed, the very questions of whether the churches should, as churches, address social issues, and whether other action on the part of the churches is permitted or required, are questions on which there is fundamental and chronic disagreement.[3] It is in the nature of theology that it begins with a form of experience which is rich, varied and related in complex ways with every aspect of individual and collective life. And theology must attempt to precipitate from this experience words; words which will guide action as well as further experience. The sheer extent of this realm of experience, and the way in which it is interwoven through so much of human life, make it understandable that theology has even less by way of an approved method than other disciplines. This is what makes the diversity and incompatibility of theological opinion a limitation of theology, and not just of theologians.

Professor Shinn quite rightly draws attention to the incompleteness of the theological contribution to discussion of social concerns, and its need for the "information analysis" provided by the social sciences among others. And he draws attention to the way in which ideological controversy—and theologies presumably at least resemble ideologies—typically blurs our view of the issues by mingling facts with values.

The limitation to which I am now drawing attention is no doubt connected with those identified by Shinn. But in the context of theology's right to address social issues, and its need to establish the credentials to do this, the limitation in theology's method assumes special importance.

Summary

I have made a few remarks about the right of theology to address matters of social concern and some of the qualifications and limitations it brings to that activity. I've made a suggestion about what right is actually being discussed here, and the way in which that requires certain qualifications. That, in turn, has led to an observation about one significant limitation in the theological enterprise: the uncertainty of its method, and resulting diversity in pronouncement. I have not touched on the rights and qualifications of the social sciences; but then Professor Shinn gave most of his attentions to theology also.

My complaint that Professor Shinn's discussion was too general may now be thought to be an instance of one with a plank in his eye drawing attention to the speck in someone else's. All I seem to have managed is a death grip on the obvious. My defense is that we sometimes need reminders of the obvious. It is my view that theology will have the impact on social policy that it wants to have, and arguably deserves, only if theologians are willing and able to *win* that right. And that, I think, will require not just an enlargement but some redirection of our theological energies.

NOTES

1. Professor Shinn points out in a footnote that his discussion is an abridgement of a chapter in a recent book. I have not read the book; but in any case assume it is fair to consider his argument in the paper on its own merits.

2. See Basil Mitchell's, *The Justification of Religious Belief* (London, New York: MacMillan; 1973.)

3. See, for instance, John C. Bennett, "Two Christianities"; Howard E. Kerschner, "What Should the Churches Do About Social Problems?"; and John Howard Yoder, "The Biblical Mandate"; all reprinted in Paul T. Jersild and Dale A. Johnson (ed.), *Moral Issues and Christian Response* (New York: Holt, Rinehart and Winston; 1976).

Discussion

Edited by: Kenneth G. Elzinga

Arthur Shenfield: I believe that in the form in which they are stated, and as far as they go, Roger Shinn's propositions on the interface between theology and the social sciences are correct, and indeed unexceptionable. Furthermore, it's clear that he seeks to distribute the rights and duties, respectively, of theologians and social scientists, with a most scrupulous and admirable fairness.

The question, however, is, "What happens as a result of grasping these propositions, when one gets down to brass tacks? How helpful are they in practice?" There, I fear, it is possible to grasp these unexceptionable propositions, and yet still be influenced by egregious errors.

I ventured to list a few of what I perceived to be such errors in Roger Shinn's paper. I don't propose to rehearse them, but it is very very important, it seems, to me, that one can have a very enlightened view, an intelligent view, of the interface between theology and economics, or the other social sciences, and still believe in some egregious errors about the social sciences.

I fear that it may well happen that some theologians sin against the light. They are, or ought to be, experts in theological propositions; but they do not hesitate to harbour in their minds propositions about economics, or other social sciences, without ever seriously seeking to study them. Thus, they become slaves of the popular notions which happen to be floating around amongst the general public. They have a duty not to do that; nevertheless, I fear that they too often do.

The only point in my comment that I would like to say a few more words about, concerns the quotation from Hayek on the emptiness, indeed the evil, of the concept of social justice. The concept of social justice leads people into terrible error, indeed often evil, because first it's an empty concept, and secondly the pursuit of an empty concept in itself is likely to produce evil. Or perhaps, using very old fashioned language, it could be that, as we know, the Devil is most effective when he mimics the voice of God.

So, if you have a concept which looks as if it's a divine concept, but in fact is empty, you are then the prey to the devil's machinations. The concept of social justice is empty because it implies that the Great Society in which we live can be just. And the whole point of Hayek's exposition is that it cannot. People can be just; individuals can be just; groups of individuals acting as groups purposefully can be just; clubs, corporations, governments, even mobs can be just or unjust because they act purposefully. But a society, that is to say the Great Society in which we live, cannot be just or unjust because it isn't something that acts purposefully. It is a network of people.

Secondly, the pursuit of this empty concept of social justice leads to a terribly dangerous atavistic notion or feeling which is clearly extremely prominent amongst the theologians who criticize the free society and the free economy. This atavistic feeling takes us back to the time when we humans lived in families or small clans. There, of course, you could have social justice because the family, or the small clan, wasn't just a network but a group with a collective will.

The principles on which the paterfamilias was able to dispense justice among his children were, of course, principles which enabled him to take account of the individual worth, deserts, or morality of each child, or each member of the family.

But when we come to the Great Society, the only thing which enables people to be just, not the society, is the establishment and maintenance of impersonal rules (Paul Heyne develops this in his paper) — impersonal rules of justice. Justice then has to be blind and must not be a respecter of persons. The individual moral worth of the plaintiff must not override the legal rights of the defendant, who may be a scoundrel, and so on.

Similarly, in the disposition of power by government, governments must not seek to do good according to their own lights. They may only seek to do good according to rules of law to which they are subject — impersonal rules of law; and so above all in the market.

What too many theologians see when they look at the market, and look at the free society, and what really irks them is the impersonal feature of it. So that what results is not what would result in a family, or a small clan. And, indeed, very often they talk in terms of the "family of man"; and all of us having a duty to our brothers, who are all mankind. They fail to see that if you try to pursue justice in that way, in the Great Society, you end up by undermining the impersonal rules which *alone* enable people in that Society to act justly as individuals, or as groups.

That, I believe, is the essence of this matter. And I hope we'll see more about it when we come to Paul Heyne's paper.

Murdith McLean: Well, my contribution, I think, is quite different from Arthur Shenfield's. First of all, I don't share his view that social justice is an empty concept. And neither do I detect, as I think Arthur does, all sorts of evidences of dangerous flirtation with left leaning views in Roger Shinn's paper.

Where I think I disagree with him most, though, is in the second sentence in his paper (that is Arthur's paper). He says, "With cogent argument, Dr. Shinn upholds the claim of theology to pronounce upon the problems of society." And that's my complaint: I don't believe Roger does uphold that with cogent argument.

And let me take out of the number of topics that Roger chose to deal with, the last one, the question: What right does theology have to address matters of social concern? And, what qualifications and what limitations does it bring to that task?

Now first of all, Roger lists in the assumptions that occur immediately after the posing of that question, the assumption that theology does have such a right. And he concludes at the end that it has the qualifications, and by the way the limitations too, of any kind of human activity, plus the particular limitation that it requires the supplement of factual judgements that the social sciences often are asked to provide.

But when you ask the question, commonly: What right has person A to do B?, very often what's built into that question is: What right, *if any?* In other words, it's not open to the person who's answering that question just to assume that you have a right, and just say the right is whatever people usually have when they engage in this activity.

I should have thought the normal thing contained in that question, at least the normal thing that ought to be contained in the question in this context, is: Does theology have any right, at all? I don't think that we can get away with simply assuming that theology does have a right. And I think part, also, of asking that question: what right does theology have, is then going on to say: If you think it has a right, you must be prepared to argue for it by showing what qualifications it has. And you must have the decency to show the humility of being aware of the limitations it brings.

I don't think that just being another human activity, when you put things into this context, provides anything like enough by way of qualifications. Especially, I think, when it's recognized that the right that's being sought here is not simply the right to be able to stand up on our soap box and talk to one another in whatever sort of terms we like. Rather, it is to speak out in public in the councils where these decisions are being made, with the expectation that they will be given an attentive hearing.

I think that this is one of the most evident limitations of theology. Very often, too often, it assumes it has the qualifications to speak out on social issues. And that's an assumption I think that not everyone is willing to grant, and that theology is going to have to establish.

Behind this, I think, lies another limitation. It is the notable disparity, indeed very often the utter conflict and incompatibility of pronouncements, that theologians make with equal emphasis and equal applause from their constituencies, on matters of very fundamental importance to these social issues. I know that theology is not alone in speaking with a mixture of voices on these issues.

But, it's particularly vulnerable; and especially when it's got to win a right, which not everyone is going to concede, to speak on these issues. I think we have to get our act together a bit better. Now I know, again, that that's not going to come about speedily. It's going to be expected of any discipline that's doing any sort of work on anything, that there is going to be fundamental disagreement. But I think we are too patient of it in theology. And we live with it far too easily.

Shinn didn't say much, and neither did I, about the other part of that question—the right of social sciences to speak out on social issues. And I think that would be a very interesting question. And perhaps a good commentator would have spoken about that. I didn't, but maybe we should in our discussion. What right, indeed, have the social sciences? God knows, if the voices of theology are mixed on these issues, I don't think the social sciences are noted for their unanimity either. The qualifications and limitations of social sciences, I think, would come in for some exploration.

One other thing. An intriguing question, that I don't think Roger raised, and I cannot blame him for not raising more questions when I registered a bit of a complaint that he dealt with as many as he did, but it would be interesting to ask: What right, if any, do the social sciences have to comment upon, not social questions, but theology itself? I'd love to have a go at that one, too. And what qualifications and limitations would the social sciences bring to their critique, if they ought to make it, of theology?

Roger Shinn: Mr. Chairman, my critics have shown a friendliness that does not hide the barbs in their comments. (laughter) And I'm not sure whether it's more bruising to a writer's vanity to be told by Murdith McLean that an essay says things so obvious they can't be controversial. Or to be told, as Arthur Shenfield does, that the essay is filled with egregious errors which commonly infest the public mind. Since both criticisms can hardly be valid, I'd like to think that neither is. (laughter) But I'd like to say to Murdith that I think I am more controversial than you think. And to Arthur, that I think I am more intelligent than you think. (laughter)

Now, I will start by referring to the question I was assigned to address. Though I was told from the beginning that the conference was on "the morality of the market, and its religious implications," that was not the topic I was assigned. I was almost sorry, because I lecture on that subject every year in the New York University Graduate School of Business Administration, where I co-teach a course with a professional economist; and I like lectures to do double duty.

But I was requested to write on the more theoretical question: the relevance of theology to social science and social thought. And that's what I set out to do. And that's why I took a look at the three major social sciences — not to do capsule histories, but to inquire into each of them as to the controversy within each, about the relation of values and ethical commitments to the rationale of each, and its empirical aspect.

Now in building my case, I opposed at least three positions fairly prominent in contemporary society. And maybe I should have made this more pointed. First, I am critical of those social teachings and activities of the churches. — about half of what they do in this area — that fail to take account of what I call the "relative autonomy" of the social sciences. Those guilty of this offer pretentious moralisms in answer to questions they've not studied adequately in their empirical and secular dimensions. Or they make the easy movements from the certitudes of faith to the complexities of the social process (for which I criticized Charles Clayton Morrison earlier this morning).

Second, I am equally critical of the widespread assumptions of secular culture that religious communities have no business intruding in social controversies. Now this assumption is partly supported by the ineptitude of much religious ethics. But I think it is totally mistaken in its understanding of religion.

And third, I am rejecting the positivistic strain of the social sciences, which assumes that they deliver authoritative judgements independent of the social location and ideology of their practitioners. And in answer to that I propose the outlines of an epistemology. This epistemology owes something to the Hebrew prophets. It owes something to Karl Marx, Max Weber, and Karl Mannheim, something to Gunnar Myrdal and Peter Berger, while disagreeing in part with all of these. And if it seems obvious and uncontroversial, this is the first gathering of scholars where I found that response. And actually, as I read the symposium papers, I think I have a lot of work to do in making converts of some of you.

Now, on this point as a matter of detail, I'd like to say to Arthur Shenfield that I do not at all disdain the importance of building models. It was one thing I referred to. I have some slight reputation as an advocate of models. My quarrel is with those scholars who say that building models is the sole task of the social sciences; and who are often oblivious to the epistemological and ethical assumptions that enter into their models.

I think Murdith McLean has asked a very important question, when he asked, "What entitlement does a theologian claim in addressing issues of social organization, beyond the bare rights of freedom of speech?" In my paper I said, "Part of the business of theology is to explore what Whitehead calls those secret, imaginative backgrounds present but not explicit in most human thinking." I am glad Murdith invites me to say a word more on that.

A theologian usually addresses, first of all, a community of faith. Theologians try to show the meaning of the beliefs, the rituals, the symbolisms, of the community for its intellectual life and activity in the world. And their right to be taken seriously depends upon how well they articulate those meanings, and relate them to the culture in which they live. Some do it well, some badly.

When theologians address social issues, their right to an attentive hearing depends on their ability to drive the meanings of their tradition to the point of intersection with the processes of social analysis, coming out of secular disciplines of political science, economics and sociology.

Next, a theologian may also address the wider community—the society in general. Some don't, but most do. Then they try, as theology has often done through the centuries, to relate the convictions of the religious community to the insights and secret imaginative backgrounds that pervade the society at large. And then, they usually discover convergences and clashes—as in the Hebrew Bible and the New Testament. The history of synagogue and church are full of examples of this.

Now turning to Arthur Shenfield's comments, I'd enjoy replying to each of his eleven specific criticisms, if there were time. I think I could please him on some of them; but here I'll pick only one where I am sure I shall displease him. I do think that Marxism is one social theory, among others, from which theologians may appropriate some themes.

No theologian gulps Marx down whole. But Gustavo Gutierrez (to take the example I mention) maintains he draws upon Marx in the way that St. Thomas drew upon Aristotle. Now I see more problems in Aristotle than St. Thomas did and I see more problems in Marx than Gutierrez does.

Each effort at first seems highly improbable, and at second and third glance, each involves problems. But I see no reason to refuse to learn from Aristotle or Marx.

Now perhaps my stance will be clear if I comment on a topic that I was not invited to write upon, but that enters into most of the papers (and Arthur thinks colours mine—probably it does). I personally am not much interested in arguments about the abstractions—capitalism and socialism. Neither exists in pure form, and as ideal types both are pretty remote from reality.

I prefer Charles Lindblom's approach in his book, *Politics and Markets,* in which he says all societies have markets, and all societies have political processes and decisions. And the real issues are how societies operate and relate the two. I find the same thing quite explic-

itly in Hayek. I find a little bit different wording in Milton Friedman.
Now, just to be candid, I'll say I am more persuaded by Lindblom's
way of doing it, than by Milton's. But that sort of thing we can talk
about.

I think the debates about how we mix the processes are very important, and much more useful than the debates about the abstractions. I
rather like the pragmatism of the Chinese official who told Fox Butterfield, "We're having trouble defining what our system is. We are
trying a number of experiments. Those that work, we will call socialism. Those that don't work, we will call capitalism."

In the United States, we tend to do it the other way around. I also
like the old, old Polish joke, "capitalism is the oppression of man by
man; socialism is exactly the opposite." (laughter) In reference to John
Bennett, who is mentioned frequently in the papers for this symposium, in his latest book, *The Radical Imperative,* he urges this generation, "to press the socialistic questions, even though they do not accept
ready-made socialistic answers."

Then he adds,

> Those of us who spent ten years resisting the state in connection
> with the war in Vietnam, should not now choose economic insti-
> tutions that have as their chief characteristic, the extension of the
> power of the state.

I think that perhaps the great social problem of our time is to discover
ways, because our present ways are not adequate, of keeping powerful
institutions—economic and political—somehow accountable to the
people who constitute societies. I know of no nation that does this
adequately. I do not expect or advocate utopia. I have theological and
pragmatic reasons to resist it, but I do advocate improvement.

Walter Berns: I would like to pick up a new question that Murdith
McLean gave us, and then reply to Roger Shinn in the form of a question. I will reverse the order of his questions. He asks, "What right has
social science to speak on social issues?" And as a political scientist, I
am struck by the muted quality of the voices of at least political science with respect to social issues.

It's not so true now as it was, and had been for a long time within
my own discipline, but ten to fifteen years ago it was a matter of almost faith that political scientists adopt the position of saying, "We

have nothing whatever to contribute to social issues." We, as scientists, insist upon this sharp division between facts and values, and we contribute only facts; and it was at that time that I gave up reading the *American Political Science Review*. Any large numbers of my colleagues gave up reading the *American Political Science Review*. And what characterizes that review is the absence of any counsel from political scientists on issues.

Now, I'll let the economists speak here as to their right to speak on social issues, and turn to the second question: "What right has theology to speak on social issues?" We must question the authority claimed by theology to speak on social issues. To exaggerate a bit, although not too much I think, theology claims to speak in the voice of God. And that raises a problem, because at its extreme, this takes on a revolutionary form. *One* famous archbishop, geographically not so far from here, *is* claiming the right to decide for himself and for those who listen to his voice what taxes should be paid by a citizen of his particular faith to the federal government. This is only one step before the extreme, and it is happening right now.

And in Texas, another bishop has adopted the position that to be a faithful Roman Catholic, one must not work in a nuclear bomb assembly plant. This sort of thing is frequent in the history of the clashes between theology and law. In extreme cases, it led to revolution and civil war. Liberal democracy can be said to have begun when Hobbes argued that no one, and especially no theologian, was entitled to exercise "private judgment" with respect to matters of law and justice.

Now I don't find that in Roger Shinn's paper. In fact, I was struck by the absence of it in his paper. Earlier today, in his comments on the first paper, I thought I heard him use that term "ideology" in attributing it to Christianity, as well as to other systems of thought. And if that is so, that's a very modest claim, indeed, he's making on behalf of Christian theologians. In fact, one could even conclude that if Christianity is an ideology, and an ideology is as he defines it, then theology has nothing whatever to contribute to the discussion of social issues.

James Wall: To Walter Berns' point: consider a man, such as Archbishop Hunthausen of Seattle, who considers himself as a religious speaker (and obviously he is an ordained priest and has been elected to be a church leader, and therefore is to be considered religious). If he speaks out on a social issue, I do not think we can say he is claiming to speak for God. I think, rather, he is speaking as he understands what is correct. And the influences on his life certainly include God. All of us do that. There is not a person around this table who does not speak with a certain amount of certainty. We don't claim to speak for God, or for whatever motivates us. But we are motivated by something. There is not a soul here who is not motivated by something.

And therefore I have real trouble with criticism aimed at people like Hunthausen who speaks on a subject in a way I wouldn't speak. I would not choose to withhold my taxes for the war effort, or a defense effort. But that's his way of doing it. I don't think we can ever say that Hunthausen has said, "God directed me to say this, and therefore I am directing you in the name of God to do it."

He is doing nothing more than any one of us would do when we say, "Here is where I stand. I happen also to be standing within a context of religion. Take it for what it is worth."

Walter Berns: I suspect that this subject will be discussed at some length tomorrow. And I would confine my rejoinder here to a very brief remark, indeed. Hunthausen is not simply speaking; he is acting. And that you know, then allows me to formulate what he's now doing in Jeffersonian terms. He is commiting an "act of the body." And Jefferson would say, "We have the right to put him in jail."

Philip Wogaman: I want to pose a question to Roger Shinn that, in a sense, was posed by Walter Berns, but I'd like to sharpen it and see if he could respond. I assure him that it's in the context of an overall very great appreciation for the paper. I think that it is a very solid, helpful piece of work. But on the matter of ideology: You remarked, Roger, a moment ago, that you didn't find the debate between capitalism and socialism a helpful exercise; and that the real issues came down to the more detailed questions of how government should relate to the economy, and the market. But then in your paper, as Walter Berns has pointed out, you have that statement "social controversy is largely ideological controversy," and so on.

On the next page, "we usually listen . . . we usually choose our experts on the basis of their ideological affinities with ourselves." And you indicate that's perhaps the way it should be. So the natural question that's left is: When you do your ideological thinking, and organize your ideological thinking, what do you find most helpful? Have you stated a different kind of ideology?

Roger Shinn: That is a very helpful question. Now, I am not happy about the fact that we choose our experts by their ideology. I say this is not totally erroneous. I would always, in a debate, prefer to get back to the evidentiary claims that support a particular position, and check it out that way.

Now because I cannot do this on every subject, on which as a citizen I have got to make up my mind, I am put in positions sometimes: am I going to take Milton Friedman's word, or John Kenneth Galbraith's word for something? So far as I can check it out, I ought to do that. Where I can't I will take the one who is more ideologically akin to me, because I will assume that that person has sifted out the evidence in the light of ideological criteria a bit like my own.

And I think you point to a real flaw in the paper, that on the one hand I seem to dismiss the argument between the great abstractions — capitalism and socialism. But insofar as these become ideologies, I do return and pay some attention to them. And I've got to think that one through a little further. Thank you.

Ezra Mishan: I want to address my comment to a question raised by Walter Berns. He spoke of the "right" of the church or theology to speak on certain questions. Well, the title of the conference was "Religion and Political Bias" with the subtitle, perhaps, "Why do Christians Tend Toward Socialism?" And yet, now we're talking of a "right" to pronounce on certain issues, to put it more strongly, in the name of God. Perhaps we ought to talk a little about the competence of an institution, such as the church, to pronounce on issues.

Now I can think of issues where it would seem to me that a Christian has an obligation to take up the particular position. Just to give an example, abortion on demand, or the persecution of a minority. This would seem to flow from the ideas of a Christian. But I will distinguish that from a competence to determine in advance which particular economic system would more tend to realize the aims and ideals of a Christian.

Milton Friedman: While I agree with many of the sentiments that Roger Shinn expresses in this paper, I think he has been led astray by asking the wrong question. He asked, "What is the 'right' of a theologian, or the 'right' of an economist (this ties in with what Walter Berns has raised) to speak on social issues?" And the answer is that an economist has no right to speak on any social issues as an economist; a theologian has no right to speak on social issues as a theologian. Roger correctly points out in his paper that any position on a social issue involves values plus information. This involves a view of what ought to be, plus a view of what is.

A theologian may be an expert, we hope, on what ought to be. Though there are differences about that too. An economist may be an expert on what is; but *qua*-economist, he has no right to speak on what ought to be. And *qua*-theologian, a theologian has no right to speak on what is.

It seems to me, we all of us have a right as citizens, as members of a community, every one of us has a right to speak on social issues. And in doing that, we ought to be careful to try to avoid speaking as if our discipline gave us that right. What gives us that right is our role as a citizen.

And I wanted to make this remark earlier by way of, in particular, one of Roger's comments to me, and his statement in his paper. He says: "A school of contemporary economic thought maintains that the function of economics is to build models independent of values and of policy recommendations." But he argues that when economists recommend public policies, as they frequently do, they inevitably enter into debates about ethical values. To point to an example, he quotes a *Newsweek* column of myself and Lester Thurow.

Now, of course when we discuss public issues, we do enter into debates about ethical values as citizens. But that is in no way in contradiction to the view which I hold very strongly, that economics as economics has the role of trying to find out what is, independently of values and of policy recommendations.

The wide scale misconception about economics on the part of the public, I believe, is because they judge economics from what we write as citizens and not what we write as economists. I would suggest that if Roger were to read my book on *A Theory of the Consumption Function,* he would find it very hard from page one to page end to find any implication about values. And the same thing is true of any of my other scientific writings.

I don't know Lester Thurow's bibliography as well, but I suspect that if you look at his scientific writings, you would say the same thing. If I may take a different example, which brings out my point very sharply: Oppenheimer and Teller had an enormous difference on the public issue of whether a hydrogen bomb ought to be built. But that's not evidence that physics is about values. Both Oppenheimer and Teller agreed on physics, on the basic scientific content of that discipline.

So I believe that the question of whether theologians have a right as theologians, or economists have a right as economists, to speak on public issues leads the discussion in the wrong direction. The really hard question is how do I avoid when I write a *Newsweek* column appearing to speak from my authority as an economist, instead of trying to combine my role as a concerned citizen with the information and expertise which I happen to have because I spent my life as an economist?

Ezra Mishan: A very brief comment on what Milton Friedman said about economists eschewing expertise in normative economics. And I don't think I'm contradicting him here. You see Milton Friedman is my old tutor. And I am always very careful of saying anything that would go counter to his views; so I put it in this form as a kind of qualified footnote (laughter): that there does exist a body of literature on economics — what we call "allocative techniques," cost/benefit analysis, linear programming — in which we come out with the conclusions that we ought to do this, and we ought to do that.

Now these things do depend upon values; if you like, ethics. Personally, writing in this area, I like to believe that the values we use spring from an ethical consensus.

James Wall: I am fascinated by Milton Friedman's assertion that he is seeking to speak as a citizen, not as an economist. I simply cannot comprehend, how you could, Milton, ever speak in any way other than as an economist, because you *are;* that is your life, that is who you are, that's the way you view the world. You simply cannot address any issue without the economic commitment that you clearly have. The second question would be, I cannot imagine it being value free.

So I have two concerns with your comment. I cannot imagine there being any value free economist; and I cannot imagine you ever speaking other than as an economist.

Geoffrey Brennan: My point is a semantic, terminological point. I think that it's unfortunate we've chosen to talk about all this in terms of "rights." You know, the "right" to speak. I just think that's terribly, terribly misleading. I think the question that we are interested in is the "nature of authority," which I think is a different question. We can all agree that people have rights to free speech. I think Murdith McLean made that point very well. The issue is whether what is being said is worth listening to or more broadly, it's a question of what the nature of the authority is, and where that authority comes from, and what authority means in these various domains. That seems to me to be crucial.

I could go on and say that I feel a little bit uncomfortable about Roger Shinn's talking about theology as a sort of exploration of this "secret imaginative background,' because I don't quite know what that means. I want to set against it something that seems to me to be fundamental to the Christian's self understanding, and I would have thought to the Jews and everybody elses — namely, that in some ultimate sense, what we are about is bearing witness to the truth. And that the nature of some claim to a true spiritual reality is fundamental to the whole exercise. And so "secretive imaginative backgrounds" seem a strange way of putting it. What I want to say is, I want to hear talk in the language of authority, and then I want to know what "authority" a "secret, imaginative background" really brings to bear, if any.

Milton Friedman: Just a brief point. Oppenheimer was speaking as a physicist when he was against the hydrogen bomb. That doesn't mean that physics isn't value free. I am speaking as an economist, because I am an economist, when I recommend social policies. But, that doesn't mean that economics isn't value free. I am using economics to try to infer what the consequences of policies are. Then, in judging whether I like those policies or not, I am not speaking as an economist. I'm introducing my personal value judgements, as a citizen. And I try, when I'm systematic about this, to do what Ed Mishan suggests, to separate the value judgements from economics.

But the notion that economics cannot be value free is, I think, a very serious mistake. That doesn't mean that the kind of topics an economist may choose to study may not depend on his values. Just as a physicist may choose to study nuclear physics, because of his values about nuclear energy. But that doesn't make his study of nuclear physics non-value free.

Aaron Levine: I would like to address myself to a point that Murdith McLean raised regarding the qualifications of theologians who enter into social issues. I think that each theologian can interpret his respective religion, and identify certain goals; and also, constraints regarding the attainment of those goals; and beyond that he would abrogate expertise as far as the means to achieve those goals. For example, Judaism espouses a social welfare function. And, of course, all religions do. And in Judaism the highest ideal of charity consists of preventing someone from falling into the throes of poverty, rather than extricating him once he has already fallen into that status. And this translates, for the government, into the role of pursuing economic policies that create a favourable economic environment. Now, that clearly is a goal that we can identify: creating a favourable economic environment. But the Jewish theologian certainly does not have the expertise to recommend what particular policies the government should pursue in order that this favourable economic environment would be promoted. This has to be left for experts.

But the goal can be identified. Now in relation to this particular goal, a constraint also can be identified. If, according to Jewish theological thought, we don't leave charity to voluntarism, but rather that we have a coercive tax — that is a constraint. A solution that economists and other social thinkers would come up with, which is really a means to an end, would have to take into account that constraint.

Paul Heyne: I have often claimed that theologians and church leaders and denominational committees ought not to speak out on social issues. And people have been horrified to hear me argue that.

My arguments all boil down to this: I claim such statements are counterproductive. Given the goals of the person to whom I am speaking, I argue those goals are not well accomplished through pronouncements on social issues by theologians, church bodies, and so on.

But then comes this response: "you're saying religion has nothing to do with everyday life"; or "you're claiming religion is only about some world beyond this"; or "you're claiming that religious people do not have to care about social concerns." The number of entailments that supposedly follow from the acceptance of the position that it is counter-productive for theologians to do social analysis in public seems to be infinite; and you can't refute an infinite number of wrong propositions. But I maintain that there are a lot of alternatives that are completely acceptable. If we bar theologians (not by force, but by persuasion) from making social statements, there are many desirable alternatives that these theologians themselves will welcome and will find more productive than what they are now doing. By the way, I want to say that this applies, not only to Roger Shinn, but also applies to Dick Neuhaus and Michael Novak.

Murdith McLean: I think Paul Heyne's intervention reflects a tendency that started off as soon as Walter Berns made his point about speaking out. I think we are really falling into a great unclarity about what "right" it is we are talking about here, or what "authority." What is it we are talking about the right to do, or the authority to do? Is it, as some of us are starting to suggest, to pronounce upon — that is, to make a public declaration as to what the right thing to do is?

Or is it, to use the words that Roger used in his paper, to "address?" There's a hell of a difference between those. I think theologians do have a right, (and ought to exercise it) to address social issues and can do it as theologians, or as social scientists, to make points that they think are relevant to the policy judgement, which is going to be made later. I think that's different from claiming that theologians, or social scientists, have a right or have the authority to *pronounce* upon social questions.

Now, I think just in terms of our continued discussion, it is crucial that we keep it as clear as we can: What the right is, that we are discussing. Is it to "address"? That is to make what we think are relevant points. Or is it to "pronounce upon"? That is to give what we think is the final truth, or maybe back it up with the force of law.

John Cooper: I am surprised that we've spent so much time on what seems to me to be a rather elementary point; but, as a theologian, I'd like to affirm Milton Friedman's simple point that we all speak with two voices, that we wear different hats. And the distinction between values and facts is an important one, although we could continue to argue about whether there can be a value-free social science. One almost hopes that there could be, but perhaps only in a theoretical sense.

I think that we could avoid a lot of problems if we took a look at the papal approach to this problem, which has a long history now — a hundred years, or so. In the social encyclicals, the popes are always calling for lay expertise. They are calling upon the Catholic parishes for laymen to emerge with a particular expertise in economics to help the church collectively choose the right policies in many different societies. After all, the Catholic church is a universal organization.

The popes make it very clear that their authority is to speak on general principles and goals, and that as respresentatives of the church,

they refrain from speaking on specific policies. They ask for lay expertise; in a sense they trust in God—rather than adding the church's
weight to a particular policy.

For example, consider the popes' view that all human life is sacred.
We need the popes and others, to say this, particularly if no one else
will. But what does the sacredness of human life mean when you come
to a specific policy—like abortion on demand? Or war? Or, the question of economic justice? Then we've got to make a distinction between general goals and principles, and specific policies.

And, frankly, I think the church—both Catholic and Protestant—
has worked out this problem fairly well. It should be a fairly elementary point; although for non-theologians it may seem that it isn't.

I would think, finally, that a deeper point of issue arises: whether
ethics is personal, individualistic, or social—an issue that I have heard
raised around the table quite a few times today?

The present pope, doing exactly what his predecessors have done—
that is, speaking on principles and not on specifics—has begun to
elaborate a theology of economics, which I think is based on two
notions—self-reliance and solidarity.

That is a way of saying that an individualistic ideology and a collec-
tivistic ideology are two extremes, which perhaps have something to
say but which, when isolated, are great distortions of reality.

So you always hear the papal social teachings trying to establish a
"third way." Now, perhaps that's a pipe dream; but it serves a purpose
intellectually. It is as a way of saying that the church stands outside of
ideology, affirms the right, and rejects the wrong in whatever ideologies the world may have to offer.

And in a specific case, it affirms not only all of the basic free market
notions of incentives and self-reliance and freedom, but also the notion of community, solidarity, political supremacy over economic decisions. After all, even the business corporation is one of the great car-
riers of community—its focus is not individualism, but community.

Edmund Opitz: The phrase "economic power" has been raised, and
one hears it frequently. Niebuhr uses the phrase and I quoted him. He
said even something beyond that, that a giant corporation is really a
part of government. It seems to me this is an error, and easily discernible as an error. Every one of us here remembers the Chrysler Corporation of, say, ten years ago. It existed then in a relatively more free
economy.

What power did the Chrysler Corporation have when it was part of the private sector? Did it have the power to persuade or force Americans to buy its products? No. So what did Chrysler do? It turned to the power structure in this society, and now it does have the power to make those of us who didn't want to consume its products contribute by our taxes for those who are now buying Chrysler products. This is not an unusual situation in American economic life. Americans have always, from the beginning, from the very first law passed by the very first Congress, Americans have used, or at least sought to use, the public power for private advantage. This is not capitalism. This is not the market economy. It's an abrogation of the market economy. It's the use of the power structure, which is government, to gain economic advantage for some at the expense of others.

Government is *the* power structure of a society. The phrase "economic power" is a metaphor, not a very good metaphor, because in the economic sphere the business man has no "power" over anyone except the quality of his product and his persuasiveness in telling us of its virtues. However, there is a power structure in the society. The "power structure" is the government. It possesses a one-of-a-kind power in a society, unless the society is indulging itself in a civil war. So the term "economic power," I believe, should not be used.

Richard Baepler: One person who has not been much discussed who I think is crucial in many respects to the questions being raised here, is the preacher — who is neither a theologian nor an expert social scientist, and is, however, called upon every Sunday to speak out. The poor person has to work under very difficult circumstances, being neither expert in those areas that we mentioned, plus he is so very much beholden to the congregation. In a voluntary system such as ours, he is paid not by the state but by the congregation. And it's very difficult to be a prophetic figure, staring down at the faces of the people who are paying your salary, particularly if there are two or three major benefactors who will assure the success or failure of your next big building project.

Thus I think that typically, in this country, the clergy, and therefore the Christian church, has been a very conservative force. Rather recently the habit of public pronouncements by theologians and committees in the church on social matters has tended to make some people think of the church as a more radical force. I think it continues to be a very conservative force, precisely because the preacher finds himself in this situation.

Seymour Siegel: One of Mr. Heyne's comments struck me very negatively, especially his last sentence because I had always thought that people, ever since Amos, said to religious spokesmen on social issues, "Go away. Go do something else," because they didn't like their message. And I presume that this conference would not have been called if the National Council of Churches, and the bishops, and everybody had strongly supported the market economy.

Ronald Preston: One comment — the welcome calling for lay expertise in the papal teaching is relatively new. That point, I think, is important and very encouraging.

But, more important is that it seems to me that when we are talking about these pronouncements and edicts, if theologians and church-leaders are going to produce them, they have to do it with group work behind them. They cannot sit in their studies evolving pronouncements about the modern world by themselves.

Good statements come from working with groups of people of relevant but different experience, and of sometimes conflicting views and seeing if out of this kind of work, you get some broad judgement as to what are the really significant things going on in the world to which we need to give attention.

Sometimes, you get a fair consensus about all this, and even about some broad directions you think people ought to go. Often you don't, and you get agreement only part of the way. What you are doing is sorting out for your constituency among the great confusions and voices in the world, a way of coming to grips with things that are happening.

David Friedman: A long time ago, somebody told me a story about James Mill and John Stuart Mill, according to which the latter, in his innocent youth, once remarked that something was true in theory but false in practice. His father made him sit in a chair in a corner until he could justify that statement. As far as I could tell, the point of the story was that he is still there. (laughter) At the risk of suffering the same fate, I would like to say that Roger Shinn's thesis seems to me to be true in theory, but false in practice. That is to say, I agree that in order to reach conclusions about what should be done in the world, one needs both values and facts.

The practical question however, is, is it our opinion about values or our opinion about facts, or perhaps both, that actually determines which conclusion we reach? And so I was moved to ask the following two questions. The first question is: Given the views I have about economics, if I were converted to the theological views of Philip Wogaman, would my political opinions change? And the answer is "No." Given the factual views I happen to have, any variation, any change in my values within the actual observed range of values that people hold (say, around this table), wouldn't substantially affect my opinion that the unionization of the American farm workers meant that desperately poor people in Mexico stayed in Mexico instead of finding what they regard as well paid jobs in America. And, by Philip Wogaman's principles, if that belief is true, it is an argument against the unionization of the farm workers.

On the other hand, I asked myself: If I were Philip Wogaman with Philip Wogaman's ideological and philosophical views, and were convinced of my, or even my father's more moderate economic views, would my social policies change? The answer is "Yes."

And therefore, as I say, it seems to me that Roger's thesis is unobjectionable *a priori* (we need both facts and values), but that in fact, it is the disagreement over facts, and not the disagreement over the values, that is the main reason for our disagreements on policy.

Roger Shinn: Both John Cooper and Arthur Shenfield have raised the point of whether justice applies to societies, or simply to individuals. And while I would agree there has never been a perfectly just society, I would insist that justice does apply to institutions as well as persons. Slavery is an unjust institution, even if a particular slave owner happens to be of a benevolent, ethical sensitivity. That totalitarianism is unjust, even if the ruler's a nice guy, and so on. But, trial by jury and freedom of press, with all their imperfections are efforts to incorporate justice in institutions. I could talk a long time about that, but I won't.

I come back to another point of Murdith McLean's that I did not answer earlier — the immense disagreement among theologians. Partly this troubles me, although since I dislike monopolies, partly I welcome it. I just say this is characteristic of our world.

My daughter happened to major in psychology at Harvard, at the time when the two most famous characters in the department were Skinner and Erikson. Well, they could hardly have a conversation. Bill Coffin and Jerry Falwell did a little better (laughter) on television conversing than Erikson and Skinner. This is a fact of our world. The theologians disagree, economists disagree, psychologists disagree, and so on. And that does not discredit the disciplines, it poses a problem.

Now the question of authority was raised by many people, initially by Walter Berns. I would say at this point, a theologian never claims to speak for God (well, that could be refuted empirically; some have). (laughter) So I'll say normatively, no . . . the prophet, who says, "Thus saith the Lord," is either inspired or the ultimate blasphemer; and history makes judgements on that.

Theologians say, "Given a certain tradition, revelation, whatever, we interpret it to mean thus, and so." I would think a Catholic bishop is doing what bishops are supposed to do when he says, "To be a faithful Roman Catholic, one must do so and so," which is a little bit different from saying, "Thus saith the Lord."

Now, it is the business of other Catholic bishops who differ from him to say so, and then they thrash this out. As a Protestant, I have a somewhat different idea of authority. But I think it's quite appropriate for a bishop to say, "To belong to this community, requires a such and such," and then the discussion goes on.

I am most grateful to Milton Friedman for helping me persuade Murdith McLean that my statements are not so obvious as to be uncontroversial. (laughter) And I half share what he says: I accept the tentative — what I call the relative autonomy, in the social sciences — a sort of a working distinction between facts and values, as being quite useful. If you push it to the ultimate point, I think it has roots in the Kantian dichotomy between the theoretical and the practical reason, which I think is wrong, epistemologically, psychologically, logically, and in every other way.

And I come closer here to Gunnar Myrdal and John Dewey who would insist that in the whole problem of learning, commitments and values have much to do with our sensitivities in apprehending information, and organizing it, and presenting it.

PART THREE

INTERNALIST EXPLANATIONS: ECONOMIC ISSUES

Chapter 5

Markets and Majorities, Morals and Madness: An Essay on Religion and Institutional Choice

H. Geoffrey Brennan

I. INTRODUCTION

As I understand it, the central thrust of this conference is to wrestle with the following question: is the observed (or allegedly observable) predilection for an anti-market political position within the religious establishment attributable to 'internalist' or 'externalist' causes? That is, can one justify that anti-market position on purely theological grounds (internalist) — or is its predominance attributable in some manner to causes unrelated to any theological position (externalist).

My particular assigned task in dealing with this question is to provide an account of the "merely economic" case for the market. I was explicitly asked *not* to attempt a *theological* defense of the market — a task that seems to me to be intrinsically much more interesting and much more in need of being done.

But this presents me with a major difficulty. While it is true that any ethical evaluation of the market (theologically grounded or otherwise) requires some analysis of how the market works, it is equally true that no account of how the market works can, on its own,[1] constitute "a case" either for or against the market. Of what, then, does the "purely economic" case for the market consist?

There is, to be sure, a "defense" of the market offered in most undergraduate textbooks, but it depends on certain quasi-utilitarian foundations the precise theological authority of which can hardly be accepted without question. Perhaps it would be sufficient to rehearse that familiar "defense," and let it rest secure in the knowledge that utilitarianism is not, after all, a totally outrageous ethical position and that some overlap with many theologically sound positions may be expected. Or perhaps I ought to seize the opportunity to do what I think ought to be done—to provide my own theological defense of the market, notwithstanding my instructions to the contrary. This latter task is, however, so large that I could, in any event, only offer a small piece of it here. Besides, this would leave me with an entirely implicit position on the central question of the conference, whereas I would like to speak to that question directly.

Internalist, externalist explanations

Accordingly, and, in obedience to Martin Luther's admonition to "sin, and sin boldly," I intend to focus on the central question, and to deal with my assigned brief somewhat *en passant*. Specifically, I want to offer an explanation for why the religious establishment (and indeed 'moral authorities' of all persuasions) might have a preference for decisions being taken in political rather than market contexts—an explanation that is "economic" in the sense that it makes appeal to the *language* of relative prices. This explanation depends on a difference between political and market processes that is, I believe, also crucially relevant to any proper evaluation of the market as an institution. As it happens, much that I will say will not be about the market *at all* but about majoritarian electoral politics. I make no apology for this; but, because it is an important aspect of my method, I do want to stress, before I do what I do, why I am doing it in the way that I am. To do so, I want to lodge my discussion in a general theological context (section II), which I hope will indicate my views on the status of my own remarks, and of the subject-matter of this conference (and perhaps incidentally all my own professional subject-matter). I also wish to emphasize one crucial aspect of the method of enquiry I shall use here (which will occupy section III).

From there, I shall proceed to lay out my central proposition (section IV) and then go on to examine what flows from it, both in terms of explaining what we observe (section V) and in terms of evaluating the market as an institution (section VI). I shall offer some brief concluding remarks in section VII.

II. THE THEOLOGICAL FOUNDATIONS

The Christian lives in a perpetual tension between the claims of *this* world and the claims of the next. He sees himself to be surrounded by a hopelessly imperfect natural order — of which he himself is an inextricable part — and yet he stakes his life on the conviction that the redemption of that world is already secured and that this redemption is something in which he already participates. This tension naturally colours his attitude to the present reality. That reality is partial, incomplete, unconsummated, a "shadow of things to come"; and the Christian must always in dealing with the current *partial* reality, carry the marks of his citizenship in the *celestial* city. Yet this reality is the only stuff he has; it is necessarily the context in which he must seek out his salvation; and, yet more compellingly, it is the substance in terms of which his salvation is actually secured. ("Since by man came death, by man came also the resurrection of the dead").

Within this tension, there is considerable scope for the individual to locate his particular attitude to the world he finds himself in. Some Christians will naturally take a strongly "incarnationist" position: "if God saw fit to commit Himself totally to the human predicament, how can the conscientious Christian refuse to do likewise?" Others will naturally be more overtly "spiritual," setting their hearts and minds on that place where "true joy is to be found."

However, although much variety can be expected (and, one might add, rejoiced in) there seems to be certain "immutable" theological principles ("relatively absolute absolutes") that set limits on a recognizably genuine Christian position.

For our purposes, one of the major such limits is set by the proposition that there is no salvation to be found in politics. No political system, however apparently good, can make an *ultimate* claim on the Christian's loyalty. There is *no* uniquely "right" system that can be given cosmic sanction in the sense that it is the single manifestation of God's kingdom on earth: "My kindom is *not* of this world." Political orders may be better or worse, more or less just, more or less peaceable, more or less human — but none is the source of our hope. "Some put their trust in horses, and some in chariots; but we will remember the name of the Lord, our God."

Politics imperfect

Relatedly, *all* political arrangements, like all aspects of the affairs of men, are imperfect. Men will still sin, still exploit others, still covet—even under the best of human institutions. (No one who is a practising churchman will deny the relevance of this among the body of the faithful, for example.) Nor is the Christian called to a heroic view of man. The strength of the promise that calls us into what we are *to be,* depends on our seeing ourselves as we currently are. We are under no obligation, or so it seems to me, to try to design human institutions that take no account of human reality—which means, in particular, the reality of human moral frailty. Indeed, the Christian is in some ways much better equipped to come to terms with the wickedness of men than are others (say humanists): the Christian expects nothing else. In other words, the Christian is denied the pietistic escapism of the utopian—he must deal with the world *as it is,* as best he may.

It follows from this that no decisive case *against* a human institution can be made solely on the grounds that it is imperfect. Specifically, no criticism of the market order (or any other), however telling, is sufficient in itself to enable us to conclude that that order may not be the best available (whatever 'best' may be construed to mean). We would have to argue, in addition, that there exists some alternative institutional arrangement that is *not* susceptible (or less so) to the criticism made, and is in addition not unacceptable on some other grounds.

To put the point in language more congenial to the economist, the domain of practical ethics is the set of *feasible* alternatives and no ultimately satisfactory ethical judgement can be made without an examination of the entire set.

Perfection denied government

It seems to me important to be very clear about all this, because popular discussion of social issues is often extremely sloppy on precisely this point and the sloppiness has implications for the sort of political position that seems to emerge. In particular, it is commonly remarked, when something is observed to be "wrong" in human affairs, that "the government" ought to do something to improve things. And such a remark is entirely understandable. As a disembodied moral injunction, it is in fact, quite unexceptionable — if something is wrong, someone ought indeed do something to correct it, and since the government is typically the institution which *could* act appropriately if the relevant power were assigned, then to say that "the government" should do something becomes just another way of saying that something is wrong.

But somehow there seems to have slipped into the remark an altogether gratuitous assumption that, if the "government" *were* to be assigned the power to correct things, it would act in the morally desired direction. No such assumption seems warranted. At the same time, those who query the virtues of government intervention are often enough seen to be querying the desirability of morally appropriate action, when all they may be doing is querying the presumption that governments will *in fact* act morally.

Accordingly, the general case for the market is as much the case against its alternatives as it is an extolling of the market's peculiar virtues. And in this paper, I shall have as much to say about those alternatives as about the market itself. To this point, the thrust of my remarks has been that the Christian proponent of the market can embrace the object of his advocacy with at best "*modified* rapture," and all that I say here should be interpreted with this in mind.

In this connection, I am reminded of a well-known remark by Maurice Chevalier, who was once asked how he was enjoying old age. "It's not so bad," he remarked "when you contemplate the alternative!"

My defense of the market system is rather along the same lines.

III. THE METHOD

If proper evaluation of the market depends on setting it against its alternatives, what *are* the alternatives? Or better put, if the market is one of the variety of things of a kind, what is the "kind" in question and what others of this kind might there be?

It is important to answer this question explicitly if we are not to talk endlessly at cross-purposes. So let me try to set out briefly what I am taking "the market" to be, before I become involved in the evaluation exercise.

In the social sciences, as I conceive them, the subject matter for analysis is the *interaction* of individual persons within the framework of a social order. Observed patterns of outcomes are observed as the result of separate actions taken by many independently operating agents. Outcomes are not *chosen* or *constructed;* they simply *emerge.* What outcomes happen to emerge from a particular set of individual actions, and how the independent actors are influenced by the actions of all the others in deciding how they themselves will act, are dependent upon the particular social *order* within which they all operate. The market is one such social order. It represents a set of "rules of the game" which defines how and in what ways individuals may interact; and given the set of rules, there will be a specific relation between the actions of the individuals and the emergent outcomes.

To take a simple analogy consider the notion of an ecological "system." Within such a system, particular species interact in particular ways, each species pursuing the objective of its own survival let us say, yet all species mutually co-operating to the survival of one another. This "co-operation" is not necessarily an intended thing: it may simply be a characteristic of the equilibrium outcome. But there is a network of relations between the various species, and this network constitutes the defining character of the system.

Invisible hand

Unlike the ecological system which is simply "observed," the human "system" (the particular framework of social order) can itself be the subject of choice. We can, in principle, *decide* the rules by which our social game is to be played. It is therefore necessary to evaluate alternative sets of rules with an eye to their properties; and it is more or less in such terms that economists since Adam Smith have examined the market order and found it to have properties that seemed to them to be highly attractive — at least over a very wide range of activities. Individual agents operating independently within the market order were seen to be led, as if by the famous "invisible hand," to operate in one another's interests so that the spectacular gains available from co-operation in human affairs could be maximized.

The prime alternative to the market order, with its reliance on the role of prices to co-ordinate the actions of individual actors, seems to be some form of political decision-making — involving explicitly collective and simultaneous decision on the part of all (or some subset of all) the relevant persons. For example, if the decision as to how many oranges should be consumed in the U.S. in 1982 is not simply to emerge as the result of a whole set of decentralized decisions taken by individuals responding to the relative price of oranges to other things, then it must be taken collectively under some other process whereby the differing views of all enfranchised individuals are amalgamated into some "social decision." Some such outcome must finally emerge: it is merely a question of how the decisions of all the individuals whose actions contribute to that outcome are to be co-ordinated.

Majority rule

The most common alternative to the decentralized market as a decision-making mechanism is majority rule. And by and large, when church dignitaries and others criticize the market, it can I think be presumed that they believe that certain decisions, hitherto emergent from the decentralized market, ought to be taken collectively under majority rule.[2] We ought then to ask what the properties of majority rule as a decision-making device are, and how the 'social order' of majoritarian politics compares with the social order of the free market. It seems to me that this is the sort of question that we must wrestle with, equipped with our theological perceptions and our spiritual sensibilities, if we are to make a proper, conscientious attempt to provide a Christian evaluation of the market.

Now, certain things about the operation of majority rule are clear. One—an important one undoubtedly—is that majority rule can, except under extraordinary restrictive assumptions about individuals' preferences, get us into situations that nobody wants. A simple example illustrates this point. Suppose there are three voters, and that the value each places on a particular outcome can be expressed in some numerical form (dollars possibly, though only an ordinal ranking is required). Consider the policies listed in Table 1. Clearly, policy B defeats policy A: voters 1 and 2 both prefer B. Likewise, C defeats B (voters 1 and 3 prefer C) and D defeats C (voters 2 and 3 prefer D). Yet *everyone* would rather have A.

This example obviously generalizes to large numbers of voters and large numbers of policies. The general result is that for *any* starting point in policy space there exists a finite sequence of moves to any other point in policy space such that each move in the sequence satisfies majority rule: one can, in principle, end up *anywhere!* This result means not only that any outcome is possible under majority rule. It

TABLE 1

Policy	Voter 1	Voter 2	Voter 3	Total Value
A	1000	1000	1000	3000
B	1200	1200	0	2400
C	1400	0	200	1600
D	0	200	400	600
		etcetera		

also means that by strategic manipulation of the agenda, an agenda-setter can secure any outcome he chooses, provided he knows the preferences of individual voters well enough.

But although such things are important, they are not what I wish to focus on here. I wish to draw attention to a different property of majority rule, one that is generally less remarked upon but bears importantly on the central question of this conference (and may help to explain the eccentricity of my title).

IV.   MAJORITY RULE AND VOTER PREFERENCES

When I was an undergraduate at university, the philosophy department used to run a course entitled "Ethics and Politics." Even at that early stage, the juxtaposition bothered me. Why was politics an ethical matter? Were there no purely personal ethics? Why not a course on "Morals and Markets?" As I saw it, the study of alternative political systems was a matter for the social scientist, and the role that ethics could play, or should attempt to play, in that was minimal. However, being a shy young economist, totally daunted by those who I saw to be the real intellectuals, I simply held my peace.

Now that I have myself become a "professional thinker" (and hence a philosopher by the Kantian definition), I see that I was wrong. There *is* a sense, and an important one,[3] in which ethics enters politics in a way quite different from the way it enters as a consideration in markets: ethical considerations *are,* I now believe, much more significant in political contexts than in market contexts — but for what are *externalist* reasons which I shall hope here to set out.

These reasons can be collapsed in a single simple proposition — which is that it is "cheaper" to behave morally in political than in market contexts.[4]

By "moral behaviour" in this setting, I shall mean behaviour in accordance with what the actor believes he "ought" to do. Such action is, I assert, often distinct from the way in which the actor "desires" to act, as evidenced by the way he actually behaves. To take a very simple example, a person may recognize that he ought to give some of his wealth to the poor, but he desires to spend it on himself (and will often do so). The behaviour we observe, then, is the result of a tension between desires and morals, and it makes some sense to say that the *cost* to the individual agent of acting morally is the *desired* action forgone.[5] The agent is then conceived as having two objects in acting: to satisfy his *desires;* and to obey his moral *convictions*. These two objects are taken to conflict over some range.

Two settings

I seek here to draw a distinction between the *terms* of that conflict in two different settings. In the first, the individual is choosing between alternative bundles of goods in the marketplace. I shall term these possible bundles A and B. In the second, he is choosing which of two policy packages to vote for in a simple election under majority rule: the policy packages may be associated with different parties or candidates, or be voted on directly. But let us take it that the bundles of goods that the two policy packages imply for the individual are A and B, just as in the market case. This assumption helps us to focus on the difference in the *nature of choice* in the marketplace and the voting booth, rather than any difference in the domain of choice.[6]

When the individual chooses A over B in the marketplace, the "opportunity cost" of choosing A is the B forgone. The action of the individual in choosing A is said by economists to "reveal a *preference*" for A over B. The preference for A is not merely hypothetical: the agent is not merely *saying* he prefers A to B, he is rather *acting* to indicate his preference. He may, of course, believe that he *ought* to take B rather than A, and the guilt he feels when he chooses A (in spite of this moral belief) is a cost that he will properly reckon with when he actually exercises his choice. But, by assumption, any such guilt is not sufficient to induce him to change his action — his desire for A is just too strong.

The ballot box

Now consider the identical choice presented to him at the ballot box under a majority election with a large number of voters. In terms of the individual's values, we have hypothesized:

(i) that he desires A rather than B, and if faced with a direct choice between the two would choose A;

(ii) that he recognizes that he "ought" to choose B rather than A, and suffers some measure of guilt if he does not obey his moral convictions.

In his choice of how to vote at the ballot-box, it is clear that the individual does *not* exercise a choice between A and B, but rather between a vote cast for A and a vote cast for B; and it is clear that the object and a vote cast for it are *not at all the same thing*. Specifically, a vote for A is equivalent to choosing A over B if and only if the individual's vote is decisive — that is, if and only if there is a tie among all the other voters. In large number elections, this probability is remarkably small. To cite an instance, in a presidential election where the expected majority is around one vote in a thousand, the probability of a tie is less than one in 10^{20} (i.e., negligibly small). In this sense, whether the individual votes for A or B exercises negligible influence on whether he actually *gets* A. In other words, the opportunity cost of voting for B is *not* the A forgone (except in a hopelessly remote case) but rather a *vote for A* forgone. Given the deontological claim that the individual should act morally, he will rationally vote for B, experience no sense of guilt for having done the wrong thing (rather a moral glow from having done the *right* thing) all the time knowing that this has negligible effect on the outcome, and hence on the object of his desires. Accordingly, his moral beliefs are rather more relevant than in the market context.

Aid to the poor

Perhaps a simple example might help here. Suppose that a moral norm that the individual acknowledges is that he ought to give to the poor. Faced as a "market choice," the cost to him of a dollar given to the poor is one dollar of own consumption forgone. It is a high price, and feeling a little sheepish, he spends his dollar on himself (or his own wife or children). At the ballot box, however, the same individual may well vote for a party that promises to give money to the poor, recognizing that his vote exercises negligible influence on the actual outcome but wanting to act in the proper way. A dollar given away costs a dollar: a vote cast for a party that will tax me a dollar to give it away costs me next to nothing in expected dollars of own consumption forgone![7] Accordingly, we might predict, in the light of our example, that many individuals who would not directly make transfers to the poor (or would do so in an entirely "token" fashion) might vote for a party that will redistribute to the poor, even though the cost to them if the party is elected is very considerable.

To restate the central point in the terms I orginally indicated—the cost of acting morally is lower at the ballot box than in the marketplace.

V. THE POSITIVE IMPLICATIONS

If the central proposition here is accepted as valid, what flows from it?

The first is that, whereas competition in the market will be oriented towards satisfying individuals' desires (or what economists might refer to as individuals' "interests"), competition in the political process (in majoritarian elections specifically) will be oriented much more towards satisfying individuals' moral convictions. Consider for example the nature of the "talk" (the rhetoric, the advertising etc.) that goes on in the two contexts. Market advertising—whether it purports genuinely to provide information about alternative products or simply to persuade —is directed towards indicating that the product in question will best satisfy individuals' wants or desires. Political advertising is typically oriented towards persuading voters that voting for the candidate in question is the "right" thing to do.

An institution, such as the established churches, which believes itself to be the repository of "moral truth," will therefore predictably address its attentions to that decision making arena in which moral arguments are likely to carry more weight. The church will therefore direct its preaching to players in political rather than market games. If the Church holds a vision of what ought to be, it will naturally seek to secure that vision by political means—not because political *implementation* is necessarily required, but because moral authority has rather more clout in the political setting.

Drug prohibition

A simple example may illustrate. Suppose the church holds the view that by and large a particular society would be a better society without extensive use of a particular drug (alcohol or marijuana are suitable examples). It could in principle attempt to achieve the objective of reduced use *either* by attempting to persuade individuals not to use the drug in question in their private capacities as consumers *or* by attempting to persuade those same individuals to vote in majoritarian elections for the regulation or prohibition of that drug. Of course, the alternatives are not *logically* contradictory — on the contrary. But they become competitive in the sense that the church has to choose how to direct its resources. And, more relevant here, they become competitive once the church has to grapple with the question: should a particular issue (alcohol prohibition, gun control or whatever) be a matter for political decision-making or not.

My claim here is that the church — and indeed any institution that exercises, or sees itself as exercising *moral* authority (or more generally of having a comparative advantage in moral matters as opposed to interests) — has a natural predilection towards reliance on the political arena. And this is because there is greater scope for the play of moral considerations in that setting. Or more precisely, if somewhat crassly, because there is greater demand for what seems to be one of the church's main products.

In other words, the church is likely to favour the assignment of matters of concern about the world to the domain of political decision-making because in this arena it has greater power. And this can be the result of a natural desire to increase its capacity for doing good rather than any desire to have power and influence for its own sake.

VI. THE NORMATIVE IMPLICATIONS

This provides us with what I have presented as an *externalist* explanation for the establishment church's predilection towards the political decision-making proces (and hence a predilection against the market as a decision-making process). But does it not constitute an *internalist* explanation as well? Once we have recognized that the cost to the individual of expressing a moral preference is lower in the political process than in the market does it not follow that we have a persuasive moral and theological case for the political as opposed to market regime? After all, the use of markets could be described as making it more difficult for agents to express their moral convictions in action — an inducement to sin, if you will — and on such grounds the ethical superiority of political processes as a decision-making device may seem to be established.

This attraction of the political mechanism is, however, only superficial. It is in particular important to recognize that the reduction in the cost to the individual of expressing a moral 'preference' arises because of *a detachment of actions from consequences.* In that sense, a vote is an inherently inconsequential act. If the cost of voting "morally" is low, this is so only because the cost of voting *irresponsibly* is also low.

One could, I think, construe this as a moral argument. Acknowledging that "actions speak louder than words," we could class voting as a form of *speech* rather than *action* in that dichotomy, and we could talk of moral voting as a form of public hypocrisy — as "cheap" morality, with all the negative connotations that "cheapness" entails. But such a construction is not too persuasive, and I for my part find it unconvincing.

My anxiety is rather a prudential one. It is that when people can act inconsequentially, they can also act irresponsibly. It is that, all too easily, a kind of "madness" can infect political action. It is that, in a sort of symbolic fervour, an electorate can cheerfully vote for outcomes that no single voter wants or would choose if he were confronted with a simple choice between alternatives.

Again, an example may help. And to make the point starkly, let me phrase the example in the same terms as the one involving giving to the poor, set out in section IV. Consider an individual who, for some reason, dislikes a particular class of citizens (the blacks, Jews, Catholics, non-Catholics, Christians, whatever — "the task of filling up the blanks, I'd rather leave to you," to quote Ko-Ko). To inflict damage on these individuals as a personal act is, however, a costly business. To punch the object of one's dislike (any member of the class in question) in the nose is to invite retaliation. Even to be rude, presuming that rudeness inflicts some harm on the person one is rude to, invites similar harm inflicted on oneself. And to inflict harm through the marketplace — for example, not to employ a Catholic when she is far and away the best candidate for the job, or not to use the cheapest and/or most convenient shop because it is run by Greeks — is to forgo profit or to reduce one's own effective income: individuals seem typically reluctant to do either, at least in well-established market orders.

Cut-rate bigotry

Specifically let us suppose that the individual in question would *not* pay one dollar to inflict a dollar's worth of harm on the object of his dislike, even though his dislike is genuine. Consider now his decision as to which political party to vote for. One of the parties has as a platform a specific program of causing harm to those he dislikes. Then the individual can act symbolically to express his dislike, by voting for the relevant party, knowing that his vote does not influence the outcome and hence that the expected cost of his voting in this way (including the resources used up in inflicting the harm) is negligible. It is as if, in voting this way, the individual is sticking pins into a voodoo doll. He obtains the satisfaction from acting in this way, but is not responsible for the consequence of doing so.

In another context, I have argued that there is a close analogy between the decision as to how to vote and the decision as to which team to support in a sporting contest; and, concomitantly, almost no analogy at all between the decision as to how to vote and the decision as to which house or which car to buy. Whatever it is that motivates the curious passions of the avid spectator, it is not clear that one would want to consign the fate of society to those passions. So that whereas what emerges from majoritarian political process may be, on occasion, more moral than what emerges from the market, and though the rhetoric that surrounds the political process will be characteristically more "moral" in content, what emerges from that process in the way of social decision is more likely to have a quality of "madness" about it. It may only *incidentally* bear any relation to the preferences of those who act to generate the social decision.

As I see it, this is a crucially relevant attribute of majoritarian political processes to be reckoned with in any proper evaluation of how social decisions should be made.

VII. CONCLUDING REMARKS

I have not, here, provided a catalogue of the sorts of "arguments" for the market order usually offered by modern economists. Nor have I attempted a proper theological apologia for the market. The explanation for such failure is a simple one: one can only write what is in one at the time.

But I believe I have, at least, offered an explanation for why the established Church may have an anti-market bias, and I have also attempted to argue that that explanation in itself contains the seed of an argument as to why the market order is to be preferred.

Even those who find my reasoning here unpersuasive or too partial to be satisfactory grounds for any such presumption, will I hope accept the general premises on which my approach is founded — namely, that any criticisms of *any* institutional order must be set in the context of a comparison of all the alternative institutional orders, and that the workings of those institutional orders be congruent with our theologically based convictions about our own nature.

Without such premises, I do not see how an intelligent discussion may proceed.

NOTES

1. To invoke a well-known claim of David Hume's.

2. They may possibly have in mind the Pope for king or the World Council of Churches for world parliament or some other political arrangement unspecified. This represents the sort of difficulty I alluded to earlier — that is, a failure to specify the preferred alternative — under which such discussion often labours. Perhaps it is too much to ask that the "prophetic voice" speaks to such sordid details.

3. Though it is not, I am sure, the 'sense' that my Australian National University philosophy colleagues would have articulated — or at least, not in the terms that I shall.

4. The language in which I have couched this proposition may seem objectionable to some. It is, I think, meaningful and appropriately precise language for the economist, and that is why I find it useful to express myself this way. The meaning should become clear to the non-economist as the argument progresses.

5. I concede readily that this is not a particularly sophisticated rendering of moral psychology; but it is simple, I hope comprehensible, and more or less congruent with some aspects of the biblical account.

6. Although often there will, of course, be differences of the latter type as well, these are not relevant to the central point here.

7. Other explanations, based on the alleged 'public goods' nature of gifts to the poor are possible, and may be plausible. They are totally distinct from the point made here and in my view much less important.

Comment

David I. Meiselman

A summary of the Brennan position

I agree that my Virginia Tech colleague, Geoffrey Brennan, has a point in demonstrating that private voting and political behaviour may not be consistent, or, may not *appear* to be consistent, with private market behaviour or with apparent private interests. For example, we all know of individuals who never make charitable contributions to the poor and who consistently vote for candidates and political parties and policies to redistribute income to the poor, even when it appears to redistribute income away from themselves. Also, there is the phenomenon, recognized even before Schumpeter, in which we observe support for anti-market, anti-capitalist measures by large numbers of individuals who benefit greatly from free markets, private property and limited government. The apparent paradox is, of course, especially troublesome to many economists who like to believe the utility maximizing axioms that people are rational, or at least consistent, that individuals generally know best what is in their best interests and that people act to further their own interests.

Brennan tries to resolve the apparent paradox. He seems to believe that there is generally a sizable difference between *actions* as revealed by private market decisions and voting decisions. As he says, "It is cheaper to behave morally in political than in market contexts."

It is less costly to act morally in making political choices because opportunity costs differ. In private markets, individuals come closer to bearing the full costs and reaping the full returns of their private acts. By contrast, in political choice, no individual is the decisive voter. Therefore, people can more readily vote their consciences or their morals, their loves or their hates, rather than their pocketbooks or their private interests. Moreover, people may vote for programs precisely because they do not believe the programs they vote for will be enacted or implemented. In other words, the act of voting is a force of empty talk or a costless gesture, like inviting to lunch a person who will never come to town.

Along these lines, I recall a conversation I had with my father some years ago in which I asked my father about his recollections about the adoption at the end of World War I of the eighteenth amendment to the U.S. Constitution which instituted the "noble experiment" of the prohibition of alcoholic beverages in the United States. My father said people in our home state of Massachusetts voted in favour of prohibition even though they were against the measure. Many people, and he included himself, wanted to do something to express concern about using grain to make beer and whiskey instead of feeding the hungry in the starving war-torn world. I recall my father saying that hardly anybody believed that the saloons would or could be closed. People who voted for prohibition wanted to make a statement; they didn't want to give up alcohol. They were surprised and dismayed that what they had voted for actually came to pass.

Although I agree with Brennan that it is easier for myopia to persist in voter behaviour than in market behaviour, partly because there is no efficient mechanism for driving people into bankruptcy who systematically make inefficient political choices, there are several points where I have some questions and reservations about Brennan's analysis. Some of these questions mainly touch on the empirical relevance of his analysis and the implications of his main analytical point. In a positive or predictive sense, what can Brennan's hypothesis explain? Brennan seems to agree that individuals believe they are not likely to be the decisive voter. He and Gordon Tullock believe that because their own votes matter so little, or not at all, they themselves do not vote or take their own voting seriously. However, it seems to me that voting must be more than an empty gesture or the salve of one's conscience. Otherwise, how explain why so many people vote, even granted that no single person's vote matters.

Some queries of the Brennan thesis

Moreover, it seems to me that people vote more than on a once for all basis. Is there no learning by voting when policies don't work, or work badly? In other words, political voting, or majority rule, does not separate what Brennan calls "desires" from so-called "moral acts," except as there is some kind of myopia, ignorance or schizophrenia at work. Although I agree with Brennan that political decision-making may, perhaps does, change the cost of choice, I do wish that Brennan had gone further in several directions. First, I wish Brennan had given more rigour and empirical content to those very general and somewhat vague propositions. Second, I wish Brennan had gone on to compare his own hypothesis with alternative hypotheses which seek to explain political choice of alternative sets of economic arrangements. I would also include an examination of alternative hypotheses regarding the apparent bias of religious institutions against free markets, private property and capitalism. For example, given what seems to me to be a decline in religious sentiment and religious authority in the Western world in the past century, if church teachings and activities are important sources of an anti-capitalist ethic and anti-capitalist voting behaviour, how do we explain why there has not been a parallel decline of the anti-capitalist ethic instead of the opposite?

In other words, on superficial reading, I do not see much connection between either the rise or the fall of capitalism in the past several centuries and the working of the Brennan thesis.

Finally, Brennan and others at this conference seem to view religious teachings, or The Church, as both monolithic and as altruistic and beneficent, which is to say, that religious institutions seek only the good or the true for the benefit of others. Political voting and political institutions are means to achieve the good and the true.

I have my own doubts about that. Religious teachings and religious belief often exhibit more certainty and are often intolerant of differences or deviations from revealed or achieved truth. Indeed it seems to me that one reason religious institutions may emphasize political choice is precisely to gain political power, both to use the coercive power of the government for higher, nobler ends, and perhaps also to gain power for its own sake, to gain wealth, and so forth—like other institutions. Indeed the very decline of authority and power by religious institutions in the past century may be the reason the same institutions have increasingly sought political power to substitute for their diminished spiritual authority. Certainly, the logic of Public Choice would lead us to believe that, like politicians and so-called public servants in the civil service, men of the cloth are also maximizers.

Yesterday, Brennan raised the question, aptly I believe, about the ethics of the use of political power. I wish he had considered the political power and coercion motive in evaluating and enriching his interesting thesis, or in considering it as an alternative hypothesis.

Comment

Kenneth E. Boulding

What are we about?

As all the papers reveal, the impact of the religious experience of the human race on its political and economic behaviour, institutions, and ideologies is extremely complex, and yet very important in the ongoing evolutionary pattern of human history. I sense an underlying theme which is: Why does the market and indeed the exchange relationship, when it has so many virtues, ethical as well as economic, have such a bad press among the moralists and religious thinkers? This is a problem which has been around for a long time. We see it, for instance, in ethical concerns over payment of interest and the burden of debt— clearly, a market phenomenon. Such concerns are evident both in the

Old Testament, and more particularly in Islam, where the prohibition of interest is very rigid. We find that same concern among Medieval scholastics and the Jesuit casuists. We find also a very ancient worry about the tendency of the distribution of property to concentrate in a few hands, going right back to the Hebrew prophets. The modern worry, however, does not appear before Karl Marx. Perhaps, then, the real topic is this: Why has Marxism, which clearly has so many defects, both as a religion and as a social science, been such an extraordinarily successful competitor both of the old established world religions and of capitalism, which it could be argued is, like science, a cultural mutation out of Christian-European culture? It can hardly be denied that both capitalism, in the modern sense, and science, originated in the extraordinary triangle with its apexes in Ireland, Poland, and Italy. Perhaps the first social thinker to wrestle with this problem was my old teacher, Joseph Schumpeter, in his book on *Capitalism, Socialism, and Democracy.* In that work, Schumpeter argued for both the virtues and the vulnerability of capitalism. The vulnerability arises because capitalism rests on what I would call an integrative structure of Christian culture which preceded capitalism, and yet which capitalism itself could not generate. Banks may be enormously useful and productive, but very few people love them. Governments are destructive and morally outrageous, yet they command remarkable amounts of human loyalty and affection. If, as I have argued, it is the integrative system, involving such things as loyalty, legitimacy, love, identity, and so on, which really dominates the other two major systems (which I have called the exchange system and threat system), then the future of capitalism, and with it perhaps the future of democracy, looks rather bleak.

The incarnationist foundations of science and capitalism

Geoffrey Brennan, in whose paper I detect a certain spicy odor of Lutheranism, calls attention to two very important points: One is the tension within Christian culture between this world and the next. Adopting a phrase from my biographer, Cynthia Kerman, we could certainly call this a "creative tension," and it goes right back to the origins of Christianity. The historical record, imperfect as it no doubt is, presents overwhelming evidence at least for the existence of an extraordinary community in the Early Church. There was a group of people transformed by the belief that another world in another dimension had indeed penetrated this one—a penetration that was evidenced in some very extraordinary events experienced by some very ordinary people—fishermen, tax collectors, tent makers, and so on. If we look at the New Testament as a kind of oyster shell secreted by the living organism of the Early Church, we can deduce a good deal about that community. The evidence is very strong that this was a body of people united by the belief that someone had risen from the dead, and that a new order of being had broken into the world of ordinary life. We can think of the Resurrection perhaps as a kind of Michelson-Morley experiment, an unplanned experiment perhaps, which revealed to those who experienced it, whether in the flesh or by communication, the overwhelming evidence of a transcendent order. The history of the Christian church is the history of the acceptance of that evidence. Christianity is not a "spiritual" religion. It is not just images in the human mind. It is Saint Thomas reaching out his fingers, touching the flesh. I, and many others indeed, have argued that it was no accident that the scientific subculture came as a mutation out of Christianity, not out of Hinduism or Confucianism, though it might have come out of Islam had it not been for some very bad luck. As my wife once said very profoundly, "The difference between Buddhism and Christianity is that Buddha was a prince and Jesus was a carpenter." Science could only have come out of a culture founded by a carpenter or a like artisan.

The case for the Christian origins of capitalism is seldom made, but I think it is almost as strong. Capitalism could not come out of a spiritual culture, or even a gentlemanly culture, like Confucianism. It could only come out of a culture for which the material world is not only real and important, but is the way in which the transcendent world is made manifest. Strangely enough, both science and capitalism came out of an incarnationist culture. Perhaps this is not so strange after all. This seems to me the implication of what Geoffrey Brennan is saying in the first part of his paper, and I am in entire agreement with it.

Brennan on voting

In the second part of the paper we reach daily life with quite a bump. His "modified rapture" (I detect a fellow Gilbert and Sullivan fan) about the market is certainly something which I share. It is not only Christian doctrine but good common sense to point out that it proves nothing to show that something is bad; you always have to show that something else is better. The case for the market is certainly the moral and economic inadequacy of its alternatives. Brennan shows very clearly that voting is a much less attractive occupation for the individual than buying and selling. Exchange, as economists have always said, is a positive-sum game in which both parties benefit. When we buy something we know what we are getting, more or less. When we vote we do not know what we are getting. The impact of a vote is so small that it is a wonder that anybody does it. This is the reason, he argues, that ethics is more significant in politics than in markets, simply because morality in politics is cheap. It is easy to advocate voting a certain way when you know that it makes no difference whether you do. Voting, therefore, costs the individual voter nothing morally, whereas when he buys something he may get a lemon. Hence, I think, perhaps a little cynically, he attributes the church's interest in politics to the fact that this is very cheap morality. It is easier to vote for a nasty party than to do a nasty thing.

All this, however, strikes me as being less than a half-truth about politics, although being a frustrated anarchist myself I do have a sneaking sympathy with this view. However, I have never quite been able to make the grade as an anarchist because I can never get rid of the idea that there are public goods and public bads which cannot be dealt with by the market. For this reason, there has to be something like a legitimated threat system; otherwise we run into tragedies of the commons, as Garrett Hardin has pointed out so eloquently. It seems to me, therefore, that Brennan has made a serious mistake in identifying voting with politics, or in regarding voting as an alternative to the market. Even though the individual voter has very little impact on the system through his vote, an individual can have a considerable impact through other forms of political activity, like running for office, being a member of a party, knocking on doors, and all the other things that constitute political activity.

Indeed, the principle that the individual voter does not affect the outcome could equally be applied to the market, where the individual buyer or even seller does not affect the social outcome. If he does, there is something wrong with the market in terms of monopoly or monopsony. The market is a means of coordinating a very large number of individual valuations. Indeed, as Mancur Olson pointed out, it has the great virtue of economizing agreement; and agreement is something that we very much need to economize because it is very costly. The political structure is certainly much more of a threat system (you do something I want, or I will do something you do not want) than the market, but it also has quite strong elements of exchange in it in terms of log-rolling, political trade-offs. There is also the very important principle that in a two-party democracy, especially, each party has to slide towards the middle in order to be elected. The individual vote is at least as important in this process as is the individual purchase in the market. Nevertheless, it is true that voting has to be what might almost be described as a quasi-religious act — that is, an act of ritual — and, indeed, the atmosphere at the polls is remarkably like that of a church. People come out of the voting booth with the same rather smug expression on their faces that they have coming out of a church, as if they feel themselves to have done their moral duty. (Still, I confess I detect a slightly similar expression on the face of house spouses coming out of a supermarket, of having done their duty to society and to the family by earning money and spending it.)

It is quite true, as Brennan suggests, that voting is a form of speech. But one should not underestimate the power of speech, for speech is a very important instrument of human learning. Human learning is what changes the content of human minds and what changes the "noosphere," to use Teilhard de Chardin's concept. Human learning, in this way, changes both the economy and the polity. Being a social ecologist, I am not sure that anything rules the world ecosystem, but if anything does it is probably gossip. We gossip about markets just as we do about politics — that car is no good, that store gives you good service, and so on; likewise, I do not trust this candidate, I think we ought to advocate this policy, and so on. The parallels are very close.

The importance of system pathologies

It is not my task in this comment to discuss all the papers, but perhaps like Brennan I can sin boldly in this regard. I do find the whole symposium very deficient in one very important regard. None of the papers really discusses the potential pathologies of systems of different kinds, yet this seems to me the fundamental problem at the heart of ethics and ideology. Just as salvation in some sense is at the core of the human religious experience, pathology involves both the dynamics of systems and the evaluation of these dynamic movements in terms of some kind of human values. There are two problems here which several of the papers, and particularly that by Roger Shinn, brought out:

One is the problem of the accuracy of our perception of the nature of system change, particularly the impact of our own decisions on this. This is the problem of "facts" or realism. If our images of the future are unrealistic, then no matter how exalted our valuations, we are almost certain to make bad decisions. It is true that all decisions are made about imaginary worlds, for a decision is a choice among different images of the future. But there almost certainly is a real world and some images are closer to it than others.

Even with realistic images of the world, however, we can make bad decisions if there is something wrong with our valuations. This is a trickier problem, but we cannot put it aside. There is a constant evolutionary process at work in society which changes the structure of human valuations, just as it changes the structure of our images of the world. I am enough of an optimist to believe that error is a little less stable than truth, in that error is at an evolutionary disadvantage in human history — error can be found out and truth cannot. In the same sense there is an evolutionary critique of our valuations. This certainly takes place in subcultures, where individuals either conform to the values of subcultures or get out of them, or are thrown out. I have a lively faith, however, that this is also true of the large processes of human history. And that while, like the Jews of the Old Testament, I hesitate to give this process a name, something certainly "moves in a mysterious way its wonders to perform."

However, back to pathology. One of the great problems of society is that individual human valuations are different. A person who has just won an election no doubt thinks the world has gone from bad to better, while the one who has lost the election thinks it has gone from bad to worse. We do, however, coordinate these different valuations, as I have suggested elsewhere, by three major processes. I describe them as the three P's: prices, policemen (or politics), and preachments. Coordination does not mean agreement, but there are valuations about which there is very wide agreement. These are what I call "cliffs." Any system of valuation implies what I have called a "goodness function," which is really very similar to the economist's welfare or utility function; goodness being simply what goes up when we evaluate a change as for the better and down when we evaluate a change as for the worse. Economists rather tend to think of the goodness function as having a peak. This is why they worry about optimization.

My own view is that the goodness function is a mesa. This indeed is suggested by the concept of the Paretian optimum, which is defined as a tableland rather than the top of the mountain. The mesa, however, is surrounded by cliffs. There is a large area over which it does not matter very much what we do; then there are some points at which it matters very much. This is the concept of catastrophe, over which there is fairly wide agreement, although it does present some difficulties. Thus, in medicine, pathology is a movement of a system towards the cliff of death, and it is a great object of the medical profession to reverse that movement. Health, again, is a great plateau. In many different places it really does not matter very much where we are on it. But it is surrounded by cliffs and we move towards these as our temperature fails to be regulated, or if the innumerable homeostatic mechanisms of the body get out of order, and so on. That is, homeostasis is a device to turn us around when we are moving toward the cliff. There is a problem here that, when looked at in terms of ecology and evolution, death is a good. So is aging, the process from which there is no return and which will carry us all over the cliff. Without death, however, there could be no evolution. Evolution is mainly a property of ecosystems, not of organisms. It would certainly console some of those here to reflect that an ecosystem is free private enterprise beyond the dreams of my friend, Milton Friedman. And it is an absurd metaphor of biologists to call the forest a community when it does not even have a mayor. On the other hand, the organism is a planned economy and does have a mayor — in fact, a dictator — in the shape of the genes.

Destruction and evolution

These considerations are of great importance in evaluating social systems. I suspect that it is a universal principle that every system is capable of pathological movements, particularly towards its own destruction. Movements towards destruction might be described as the "ultimate pathology." I suspect, though I am not sure, that the more complex a system is, the more it contains within itself the potential and the probability for its own destruction. A gold nugget will stay around forever until the temperature of its external environment rises above its melting point, which will happen pretty soon if it is found by a human being. With DNA, however, the fruit of the Tree of Knowledge entered this planet and, according to Mishan, by knowledge came to sin, and, according to Saint Paul, by sin came death. For the gene is a plan. Even the amoeba is a planned economy. And part of the plan is aging and death, for without aging and death biological evolution could not have taken place. With Adam and Eve—whatever their names were—evolution went into a new gear. The apple of the Tree of Knowledge was a gene that mutated into a plan to form the human brain with its extraordinary capacity for images of the world and for the knowledge of good and evil—that is, for evaluation. It was that mutation that destroyed Eden and there is no way back to it, not even through a *"mishanary!"* We can only go on to Zion or to an Apocalypse in nuclear war and the setting back of evolution, perhaps by a billion years.

In the light of the present situation and the enormous threat which the institution of national defense presents to this whole planet, the ideological debate between communism and capitalism takes on the air of a student bull session. I myself am a considerable believer in the virtues of the market. However, I do think that my friend, Milton Friedman, has a distinctly unrealistic view of the nature of the social and economic system, in that he believes in the existence of a spiritual entity called money instead of a vast ecosystem of financial instruments. I would also probably shift the line between public and private goods to include a rather larger area of public goods than he does. On the other hand, I think Wogaman's faith in socialism is naive and a complete failure to understand the enormous diseconomies of scale of collective action. The popularity of socialism, especially among Christian church people and intellectuals, can be traced mainly, I think, to a false analogy with the family, and a failure to understand what I have called the "principle of moral perspective"—that is, that the near tend to be dear. An attempt to run a whole society on familistic principles can only result in terror and in the use of threat. The substitute for the market is not love, but fear. So I think socialism is a fraud that cannot generate societies in which individual beings can flourish. Furthermore it seems to me clear that our experience with socialism should shatter all faith in it.

The institutional foundations of the market

Nevertheless, although I think, yes, Virginia, there is an invisible hand, it has to be created by political and property institutions. The market itself does not create these institutions, but assumes them. Capitalism, also, therefore, is capable of very deep pathologies, as, for instance, in the Great Depression, when it almost went over a cliff.

It could do so again. Exchange *assumes* property rights in the things exchanged; otherwise exchange cannot take place. Property is a creation of politics, not of the market itself. I like very much the quotation from Archbishop William Temple in Roger Shinn's paper: "The art of government in fact is the art of so ordering life that self-interest prompts what justice demands." I have myself described government, indeed, as "social agriculture." Just as the farmer distorts the "natural" — that is, inhuman — ecosystem in favour of human valuations, so government distorts the social ecosystem to diminish the weeds — criminality, folly, and ignorance — and to plant the seeds that lead to the fulfillment of human potential for good.

I believe myself that the Achilles' heel of capitalism is the financial system, which permits interest under some circumstances to exceed profits. This, to my mind, is the primary cause of "unemployment," by which I mean the failure of the private labour market. Anyone in the private labour market who hires somebody sacrifices the interest on the wage paid in the hope of profit on the product of the work. The "social gospel" made a tragic mistake in attacking profit rather than the classic attack on usury. Profit is the reward of the productive use of capital and property, whereas interest is the reward for the abandonment of this productive use and redirection of funds to those who could use them better. As such interest is not wholly illegitimate, but its cost should be as low as possible to be consistent with the operation of the system. This is something that economists as well as social gospelers have forgotten. Figure 1, showing the proportion of national income going to profit and interest over the last fifty years, illustrates this dramatically in the Great Depression. Anybody who hired anybody in 1932–33 was either a philanthropist or a fool. The diagram, incidentally, also indicates how close we are to the cliff now, and how totally inadequate our economic policy is.

Another responsibility which the political system cannot escape is that of the definition of property. This is a problem of great complexity and involves many difficult ethical questions about the legitimacy of the threat system on which the defense of property rests. The problem of the realism of our images of the system itself is a very difficult one. All social systems are "ecosystems." This means, as I have said elsewhere, that they are "echo systems," in which any single act echoes and re-echoes all over the system, so that its ultimate results are extremely hard to assess. I have even postulated a "law of political irony" — that everything that we do to help people hurts them and

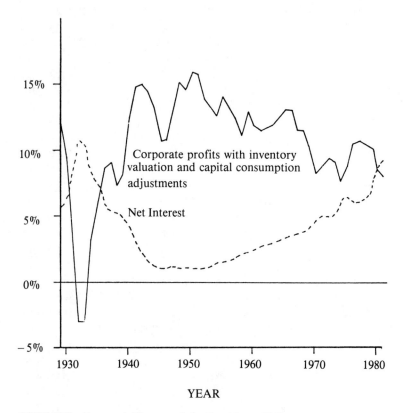

CORPORATE PROFITS AND NET INTEREST AS A
PERCENTAGE OF NATIONAL INCOME
U.S.A., 1929–1981

YEAR

SOURCES: *Economic Report of the President, 1969*
Economic Report of the President, 1982

everything that we do to hurt people helps them. While there are some
exceptions to this law, there are also some very notable examples of it.
It is at least reasonable to suppose, though we cannot be sure of this,
that within a given legal framework in a given political order, the distribution of property and of power (of which property is only one
form) may move towards some sort of equilibrium distribution. But
we have to be careful even here because the statistical distribution
hides the life patterns and distributions among different individuals of
different generations. For example, we can imagine a society in which

all the young people are poor and all the old people are rich. Since all young people live to be old, lifetime incomes would be quite equal; but the Gini index of inequality at any moment would be simply horrifying.

One does worry about what has been called the "Matthew principle"—to him that hath shall be given—which suggests that beyond a certain point equality is unstable. The critical question is: How do we create a legal framework that produces or moves towards an equilibrium distribution that is tolerable in terms of our perceptions of justice? Justice is an almost impossible concept. Even injustice, which may be more definable, is still highly multidimensional. We must face, for instance, the fact of uncertainty in the system—the ubiquity of lotteries. How is such uncertainty to be evaluated? I guess that there is a strong demand for random inequality which cannot wholly be brushed aside. What "lottery of life" are people willing to accept?

All these questions, however, have quite minor significance as compared with the overwhelming problem which is put to us by the breakdown of national defense and the enormous threat which the institution of national defense presents to us. It is astonishing to me that only one paper, that of Mishan, even mentioned this, and I would hope that we could devote considerable time to it in the actual discussions.

Discussion

Edited by: Kenneth G. Elzinga

Kenneth Boulding: I do think the market has a very high moral value, mainly because it economizes agreement, as my friend Mancur Olson says; and agreement is a very scarce commodity indeed, and nearly always leads to some kind of trouble. I have often quoted the old nursery rhyme about, "She liked coffee and I liked tea, and that was the reason we couldn't agree." And yet, if you have a market, you don't have to agree. In fact I have tea for breakfast, and my wife has coffee, and there is no problem at all. And there is a moral value in this which is overlooked by the critics of the market. On the other hand, as I have been saying, one of my fundamental principles is that everything has its pathologies.

And you always have to worry about this, that certainly the market has its pathologies, like anything else, and it has its instabilities, and we certainly saw this in the Great Depression, which you can hardly blame on Mr. Hoover's socialist government.

But still, that wasn't the whole story by any means; any system can get into unfamiliar regions, as we did in the Great Depression. And if you look at Figure 1, you see that in 1932 and 1933, interest was 11 per cent of the national income, and profit was 3 per cent. And in those years, anybody who hired anybody was either a philanthropist or a fool. And the really surprising thing is that unemployment was only 25 per cent. Why wasn't it 75 per cent? Why didn't the whole thing collapse? There is a potentiality here of a market system getting into what I call the Three Mile Island syndrome, where you get into regions of the system that are so unfamiliar that you don't know what to do. You don't know what buttons to press. In such cases the "invisible hand" slaps you in the face. And I believe in the "invisible hand," you know, "Yes Virginia, there is an 'invisible hand.'" But it doesn't always shake yours with its. Sometimes it hits you, and it can.

The "invisible hand" has to be tamed and trained. That's the point, really. That is, it depends on the institutions of the society, its capacity for what you might call social cybernetics. If you are heading to a cliff, how do you turn back? That's the great question. It is quite easy for societies to go over cliffs — as we very nearly did, economically, in the Great Depression.

And you have the same thing in the socialist countries: socialism is no answer to this problem whatever. I think that socialism is a total fraud. It promises things it just cannot achieve. Centrally planned economies are almost certain to fall into tyranny. Nevertheless people survive.

I must say, the most extraordinary religious experience I ever had in my life was going to the Baptist church in Moscow. I have never seen, or experienced anything like the intensity, the joy of these people. And when they go out of the church, a wave of joy goes down the street. I thought Russia was going to be Baptist by the year 2000, after all these dreary communists! (laughter)

After all Marx was a great Victorian, wasn't he? And all the socialist countries impressed me with their Victorian charm. They are just left behind by the twentieth century, in a way. How long can this last? I don't know. How long can the Soviet Union last? I don't know.

But of course you've got the ethical skeleton in the closet of the market because the market depends on the existence of property. Property goes back somewhat into the threat system, doesn't it? I like to tell a story about my good Methodist, blacksmith grandfather who used to tell a story about how a friend of his got into an argument with a local squire, as to why he had all these broad acres while he didn't have anything. And the squire drew himself up and said, "Well, my ancestors fought for it." So my grandfather's friend said, "O.K., I'll fight you for it now." (laughter)

But that's what the Indians are saying, isn't it? Underlying the system of exchange, with all its value, and validity, and ethical business, is this skeleton in the closet of property which may well have originated in theft.

I produced two limericks about the buffalo and the cow, by the way, which you might as well have.

> The buffalo, nobody's property
> Went o'er the plains Clippity, Cloppity

In thunderous herds where now only birds
Fly and rabbits go Hippity Hoppity. (laughter)

The cow, now, is kept on the farm
And flourished and came to no harm,
For its owners to thrive
Had to keep it alive
So property worked like a charm. (laughter and applause)

Well that's it. There is a magic in property. There really is. We even see this in the socialist countries, where if it wasn't for the private plots of land the whole thing would fall apart.

I think, just to get back to the paper, that it underestimates the complexity of politics. Politics isn't just voting. And voting is a religious act. There are no other words to describe it, otherwise you wouldn't do it. I always think when I go to the polls, everybody looks as though they have just come out of church (laughter) — smug look, you know, that they are doing their civic duty. Because everybody knows it isn't going to make any difference who you vote for.

But you do it; and maybe it doesn't make any difference whether you go to church, either, but you do, you know. Then you've not got a total political system, when you look at Ralph Nader and *The Fraser Institute,* and all these things, which have influence. And of course influence is a very large part of the political system. This has its ethical problems, too, for if power corrupts, influence corrupts more absolutely. Because after all, power has responsibility, influence has none. I've been a totally irresponsible person. I never had to pay for any of it. I never had to pay for any of the mistakes that my influence may have created. So this worries me about the virtuous, because the virtuous tend to have influence; and I have a sneaking sympathy with the people who are idiots enough to want power. (laughter)

David Meiselman: Thank you. At the outset, let me say that I agree that my colleague, Geoffrey Brennan, has a point in demonstrating that private voting and political behaviour may not be consistent, or may not appear to be consistent, with private market behaviour, or apparent private interests. For example, we all know of individuals who never make charitable contributions to the poor, but who consistently vote for candidates, political parties, and policies to redistribute income, even when it appears to redistribute income away from themselves. Then there is the phenomenon, recognized even before

Schumpeter, regarding support for anti-market, anti-capitalist measures by those individuals who have benefited from markets, private property and limited government. The apparent paradox is, of course, especially troublesome to many economists who would like to believe that people are rational, or at least consistent; that individuals generally know best, what is in their own interests, and that people act to further their interests.

Brennan tries to resolve the apparent paradox. He seems to believe that there is generally a sizeable difference between actions, as revealed by private market decisions, and voting decisions. As he says, "It is cheaper to behave morally in political than in market contexts."

This is so primarily because opportunity costs differ. In private markets, individuals come closer to bearing the costs and the consequences of their private acts. Whereas in voting, no individual is the decisive voter. Therefore, individuals can vote their consciences, their morals, or their hates, rather than their pocketbooks on their private interests.

Moreover, people may vote for programs, precisely because they don't believe the programs will be enacted. They want to make a statement.

I am reminded of a discussion I had with my father many years ago, when I was curious about what went on in the United States, or at least in his own immediate experience, when the 18th amendment requiring prohibition was passed. And he said at the time, that even he was in favour of it. And he said that people didn't know what they were doing. But more than that, nobody really believed it would ever come into effect.

Now there are several points where I have some questions and reservations about the Brennan analysis. These questions mainly touch on the empirical and positive relevance of his analysis, and the implication of his main analytical point. In a positive or a predictive sense, what can Brennan's hypothesis explain?

Now Geoff seems to believe that individuals believe, as he and our colleague Gordon Tullock seem to believe, that their votes matter so little, or not at all, that they don't vote or take it all that seriously. But it seems to me that voting has to be more than an empty gesture, or the salve for one's conscience.

I know that I, individually, am not the crucial voter. But I do vote. In addition to that, millions of other people vote. And if, in fact, people don't take their vote that seriously, how can we explain why so many people vote, even granted that no single person's vote matters? Moreover, we vote more than on a once-for-all basis. If I vote for policies that hurt my interests, is there no learning here? In other words, political voting (majority rule) does not clearly separate what Brennan calls desires from so-called moral acts, except as there is some kind of myopia, ignorance, or schizophrenia at work.

Now, again, I agree with Brennan that political decisions perhaps do change the costs of choice. However, I wish that Geoff had gone further, first to give more rigour and empirical content to this general proposition, and second to compare his hypothesis with some alternative hypothesis, which seeks to explain political choice regarding alternative sets of economic arrangements; or alternate hypotheses regarding the apparent bias of religious institutions, against free markets and against capitalism.

For example, given what seemed to me to be a decline in religious sentiment and in religious authority in the Western world in the past century, if church teachings and activities are important sources of an anti-capitalist ethic, and anti-capitalist voting behaviour, how can we explain why there is not a parallel decline in the anti-capitalist ethic, but precisely the opposite.

In other words, in a superficial reading, I don't see much connection between either the rise or the fall of capitalism in the past several centuries, and the working of the Brennan thesis. Along the same lines, I don't see any clear relationship in any cross-section comparisons of capitalism and the Brennan thesis, either.

Finally, Brennan, and others at this conference, seem to view religious teaching, or the church, as both monolithic in its altruism and beneficence, which is to say, that the church seeks only the good, or the true, for others. Acting as the devil's advocate, I have my doubts about that. Indeed, it seems to me, that one reason for emphasizing political choice is primarily to gain political power—both to use the coercive power of government for a higher good, perhaps also, to gain power for its own sake, to gain wealth, and so forth, just as other institutions and interest groups do. Now yesterday, Geoff raised the question, aptly I think, about the ethics of the use of political power; and I think it would be interesting to apply that to the use of political power by religious institutions, as well.

Geoffrey Brennan: I certainly don't claim (and I try to make this clear in my paper) that the operation of individuals in majoritarian electoral contexts is all that one would want to say about majority rule. I do think it's something that's important, and I think it's an idea worth thinking through. What astounded me, in Ken Boulding's remarks, was the very free acknowledgement that basically voting is a religious activity.

Now if one accepts the idea that what people do in majoritarian elections is behave in some sense symbolically or representationally or religiously—that this is something like a liturgical activity—then that is indeed something very close to what I want to say. And it is thinking through the implications of this that I am concerned about. I think that's a very important exercise. It seems to me to be a fundamentally important exercise in the current context, because when Professor Boulding, or indeed anybody else, talks about the taming of the invisible hand, then the obvious question to ask is, "Well, who is to do the taming?" What institutional structure do we presuppose in which this taming is possible?

The answer most of us would give is that it's going to be tamed by political processes. But in political processes what happens is that precisely the same individuals who act in market contexts, precisely the same sorts of people with precisely the same sorts of interests and moral sensibilities that act in market contexts, act in political settings as well.

And the question is in what way will what emerges be different? There are a large number of possible answers to be given to that question. But I think it's worth focusing on the difference that the institution makes. I mean, if we lift these individuals out of the market setting and put them into the political process, what will be different in what emerges?

Now, I think Ken Boulding is right when he talks about public goods and public bads. I hold myself back from total anarchy on more or less essentially the same grounds. But I think there is a profound non sequitur here. Just because the market doesn't work perfectly, as with public goods, does not mean that the political process must work better.

There is an analytic issue to be addressed here. What is the nature of the equilibrium that emerges from the political process? Consider the centrality of voting in our understanding of democratic institutions. It does seem to me very difficult to argue that the idea of electoral constraints, in some sense analogous to the constraints that operate through the market, influencing the behaviour of individuals in the pursuit of their self-interest, isn't fundamental to an understanding of the way in which democratic processes work. And if we were to abolish electoral competition and the majority rule, I don't know what we would call what we had, but I doubt whether we would be inclined to call it "democracy."

So it does seem to me that, in some sense, majoritarian elections are central; and what emerges from majoritarian elections is a very important ingredient in understanding the whole operation of the political process.

And then, having disposed of majoritarian elections, we come to the following proposition — that in a two-party democracy, especially, each party has to slide towards the middle in order to be elected. There is a substantial body of evidence to indicate that that's true only under extraordinarily special circumstances. But in general the principle is false — false in an important way, and a way which I, in a very imprecise manner, try to indicate in my paper.

But suppose the circumstances in a two-party democracy that are necessary to ensure a tendency to move towards the middle, are in fact obtained. Is this centrist sort of outcome in any sense a true representation of the interests of the electorate, even broadly conceived?

Let us suppose that you are in front of a Coke machine. If you push the left button, you get Mountain Dew (as they call it where I come from), and on the right you get Coke. It is reasonable to say that in that context that the thing that weighs in my decision is essentially which of the two I prefer. And, in some sense, when I press the Mountain Dew button, I can say, "Well the action that I've undertaken reveals something about my preferences, about my interests."

Now, I want to contrast that with the following situation, in which I come to the machine, and I can press one or the other button as before, but in the back of the machine is an enormous revolving wheel. And it's only one case in a million, let's say, that the button that I press will determine what emerges in the bottom of the machine. In all other cases, it will simply emerge from the machine itself. The machine has a will of its own.

Now my mother has always told me that I should stick to the left. O.K., if I go to the machine in the ordinary market context, of course I weigh that in my calculus. Mom always told me to sort of stick to the left, so I have a predilection to push this left-hand button, but actually I prefer Coke; and that's a preference that I weigh, and so I exercise my preference for Coke.

But in the case where the machine has a will of its own, the analogue I am arguing of the majoritarian elections, then the sorts of things that Mom says go to make my choice between these two buttons a very incidental choice because what I really care about is what I get at the end, presumptively.

What emerges from the political process is, in a sense, only incidentally related to the preferences of individuals, as those of us who study market processes are inclined to attribute essentially one-to-one relationship between action and purpose, behaviour and mental state. That central connection, it seems to me, is severed, or at least is given a great hack, in the political process.

Now it's that fact, which seems to me to be a very important attribute of majoritarian politics that I am trying to trace through. If we acknowledge that what's at stake here is a sort of representation or liturgical or ceremonial activity, then maybe this does have something to do with the predilection for ecclesiastical institutions, perhaps more than most, to think in terms of political processes to achieve desired outcomes.

There are two aspects of this that are very important for our inquiry. One is the normative exercise of the evalution of what emerges from majoritarian politics in the light of recognizing this. And the second is whether this has anything to do at all with the church's attitudes toward political solutions. I think both questions are interesting and worth talking about.

Murdith McLean: I think I must be missing something in Geoff Brennan's paper because there is one gap that I cannot quite fill. I take it that one of the things he's trying to do is to give an account of such anti-market views as exist in the church. And I guess we haven't yet established exactly what the extent of those are. But assuming that this is true, he is just attempting to give an externalist (although he contends at some point that it becomes internalist) account of what that anti-market prejudice is.

But of the account that he gives, in terms of the lower cost to people of political action, surely the most that it could explain is why the church, in its attempt to make an impact on social issues, might ignore the marketplace, or might not waste a lot of its time getting people to put their energies into the market. What it wouldn't account for is the extent to which some church people, anyway, actually disapprove of the market. They don't just ignore it; they disapprove of it. So I wouldn't have thought that what you've given us there, even if it's so, would give us an account of that anti-market view, that disapproval; but perhaps I misunderstood you there.

What I think I want to contest, also, is the truth of the premises of the argument. I think you might have given us an account of the view people ought to take of their voting — its uselessness, its randomness, its miniscule contribution to any outcome. But I really dispute whether that's an accurate picture of what most people do, in fact, think about their voting.

I can think of grandmothers in my family who would be led to the gallows before they would vote other than Conservative, or Social Credit, or whatever it was. And out of all proportions to what, I suppose, any unbiased onlooker could think that his or her vote is going to have to do with an outcome.

Walter Berns: My comment is a political comment. It seems to me that what Geoff Brennan is talking about are the "diseases of majoritarian democracy." But, of course, the Constitution of the United States most emphatically is not intended to be, and is not, a "majoritarian document." All those institutional devices that one has in the Constitution are an attempt to oppose obstacles to these "diseases." Then indeed (and I'll conclude on this note), in the most famous of the Federalist Papers, "Number Ten," James Madison concludes by saying (with reference to all that he said in that most famous of the Papers), "What we have here, in these various institutional devices, constitutes a 'Republican remedy for the diseases most incident to Republican government.'" So, you have not sustained your argument (it seems to me) with respect to American politics, because American politics is not, as you describe, "political choice."

Kenneth Elzinga: I have a concern that there is another flaw in Geoff Brennan's paper. His "public choice" model argues ingeniously, I think, (although it may be empirically inaccurate) that the church has a preference to exercise moral authority through the government. Now if by the "church" he means denominational professionals who work in denominational offices in New York, or Philadelphia, perhaps I would agree with his proposition. But if by the "church" he means (at least speaking within the Protestant church) pastors and clergymen with local congregations, then that just doesn't fit, at least in my judgement.

I don't know how to test this rigorously. But at least in my own experience, having listened to hundreds and hundreds of sermons, I can recall only *one* where a Protestant clergyman has urged or exhorted me to vote in a particular way, or to support a particular governmental program.

Over and over again, I'm exhorted to behave in a certain way with regard to chaste relationships, if I am single, or with regard to unadulterous relationships, if I am married. I am encouraged to, if I drink, to drink in a prudent fashion. I am encouraged to be a good steward over my income, and instructed on how I am to use it voluntarily with regard to tithes and offerings. Only once have I recalled the church speaking to me politically, in the common parlance of that word.

Now, maybe Geoff isn't the person to raise this with, but perhaps people close to denominational headquarters, like Roger Shinn or Jim Wall, could speak as to whether there is this bifurcation between denominational professionals and the clergy.

But I was reminded of what Dick Baepler said earlier when we speak of the church. People, like the professional theologians here, are perhaps only the tip of the iceberg. There is this enormous body of individuals who can lay claim to being called the church, as well, who work in the trenches, so to speak, as priests and pastors. And I am not certain that Geoff's model really tells us very much about their behaviour — at least as I have experienced it.

Walter Block: I wanted to make a different point. But let me just try to answer the last question very vaguely — not from my own knowledge. In the magazine, *This World,* the Summer 1982 issue, there was a survey of quite a few clergymen. And I don't know whether it focused on the people in Philadelphia or in New York but I suspect it did, rather than those on the periphery. The findings however were pretty clear that the ecclesiastical people are quite a bit more liberal, in the American sense of that word, than the American public.

Kenneth Elzinga: They may be more liberal; but is that reflected in the sermons that are given on Sunday morning?

Walter Block: I don't know. But the point I wanted to address myself to was one that Ken Boulding raises. He says, "None of the papers really discuss the potential pathologies of systems of different kinds, yet this seems to me the fundamental problem at the heart of ethics and ideology." I wish that we had more time to tease out the implications of that. But I would like to take it upon myself to take one implication of this possible pathology. And that is where he says,

> Ideally, indeed the principle that the individual voter does not affect the outcome, could equally be applied to the market — where the individual buyer or even the seller does not affect the social outcome. If he does, there is something wrong with the market in terms of monopoly or monopsony.

I would not like to concede that something is an imperfection just because in reality it does not measure up to the perfectly competitive model. I think it's a methodological mistake to put the argument in these terms. I see monopoly and monopsony in a very different way. I think we must make the crucial distinction: is the monopoly a product of government grants of privilege on the one hand (like the Post Office); or is it based on the fact that when you have a competitive scheme, or a competitive system, sometimes some people win the competition?

This latter kind of monopoly is not only not harmful, but it is positively beneficent. IBM or Alcoa Aluminum are cases in point. To my mind they are examples of success — of satisfaction of consumer desires — even though, according to the perfectly competitive model, there are certain dead weight losses. I think the analysis put forth by Israel Kirzner regarding competition and entrepreneurship, and the analysis of Schumpeter (to go to the source of this), or Von Mises would show that if we look at it in a static sense, then perhaps there is some sense to it. But the market is not a static place. It's a continuing, unfolding, changing kind of operation. So these would be my remarks about one possible pathology as it was seen by Ken Boulding.

Aaron Levine: It is well known that a basic reason for government intervention in the marketplace is the elimination of the free-rider motive. For the benefit of non-economists, let me give a very brief example of this: the famous example of the lighthouse. It was used by Henry Sidgwick to show how the free market breaks down and produces a paradox. Ship owners see the value of the lighthouse in terms of reduction of cargo loss. Yet no ship owner would want to contribute towards the construction of the lighthouse, knowing full well that the idea is such a fabulous one that someone else will want to do it. Once the lighthouse is constructed and the light is shining brightly, everyone in the vicinity will benefit from it, gratis.

So there is a paradox. Here is an economic good. The presumption is that people would want to spend money for it. Yet it will not be constructed, because people will be exercising a free-rider motive.

There was a very famous article in the *American Economic Review* in 1967 written by Hochman and Rodgers that provoked responses for about six years. I think that Professor Mishan wrote one of the responses to that article. Its thesis was that economists ought to look upon philanthropy as something that might fit the free-rider motive. We can presume that people would like to eliminate misery and poverty in the world. But they feel that this is a social evil that can be eliminated through other people's actions, so they don't have to really do anything about it themselves. And, in fact, they feel a distance, in terms of elimination of this problem; they do not feel it personally. Therefore, they would experience just as much satisfaction if its elimination came through other people's efforts, as opposed to their own.

This is certainly possible in a very impersonal society. People do look upon social problems in that manner. If you leave the elimination of these problems—such as poverty, and the associated problems—to a system of voluntarism, let's say through a market system, then possibly there would be a very substantial under-allocation of resources.

The political process may be a more potent mechanism to bring about virtuous behavior than the market system.

I think, in this particular area, that the political process would be a much more potent mechanism. In the political system, people feel that somehow the cost is being spread out to others. It's being shared by others; and the cost to oneself is minimal.

Milton Friedman: Unfortunately, Aaron Levine chose a very unfelicitous example with the lighthouse because it turns out that Ronald Coase has investigated, very carefully, actual experience with lighthouses. And it turns out that lighthouses were provided by private organizations, without any governmental intervention, entirely through free market arrangements. It's like the fable of bees that Steve Cheung demonstrated to be wrong. The fable that somehow lighthouses are an example of governmental externalities to correct a market failure turns out to be wrong.

Now in response to what Walter Block was saying, I believe there are two very separate issues. We want to define "monopoly," "competition," and so on, for different purposes. And for the purpose of market failure, I agree with him, the crucial question is one of free entry—and not one of power to control the price, or anything else.

From other points of view of examining what the consequences will be in different markets and of different measures, I believe that the concepts of competition, and monopoly, and monopsony have to be interpreted differently. They have different effects.

But, I want to go one step farther. There is a reason, based on political, and not economic grounds, for being concerned not about monopoly, but about large aggregations of wealth. And that is the fact that they represent a way of buying a congressman, or buying political power. And the only reason why I, as an economist and citizen, would be concerned with the problem of whether the system is leading to an undue concentration of economic wealth is because experience suggests that under those circumstances, the wealth is likely to be used to purchase political power — which political power will then be used in a coercive fashion.

Walter Block: I couldn't agree with you more that that is the danger, practically the only danger really, to the free market system — namely, businessmen buying it out, and controlling it. I think that's a crucial point. The question, though, is how best to deal with aggregations of economic power. And I think the best way to deal with this is to do nothing about it. Any attempt to do anything with it, I think, will be worse than leaving it alone. For the only way that you can deal with it is through the political system. And to deal with it through the political system, is to allow that which we don't want — namely, business control over the political system in the first place. But I don't think that we need be pushed into the position of saying, "Well, since there are only three or four entrants into the market, or even one, that somehow there is something suspicious or wrong about it."

Ezra Mishan: Aaron Levine had chosen the case of what is sometimes called "the public good." I think that's misleading, because it compounds the issue, and a good deal of debate among economists has arisen because of using the terminology of "public good." Whereas, the concept of "a collective good" might be better, because that would be a functional definition suggesting that it's a good which simultaneously confers benefits upon a large number of people.

Now the question of a lighthouse is interesting, in that the number of beneficiaries is limited; and therefore the internalization which Milton Friedman suggested becomes feasible. Here the costs of the arrangements are probably small. But I think Milton might agree that as the numbers become larger, it becomes less likely or less feasible that a private company would do it; and in the limiting case, possibly only government action could undertake it.

And that leads me to the initial example used in this paper by Geoff Brennan of giving charity. Here it's not only the free-rider case. Here is a person who wants really to do good. But if he is sensible, he might think, "Well, if I just do good alone, it's not very much." Really to do good effectively, we should have all of the community contribute. And therefore, he says, by casting his vote in this way, that he will do good *on the condition* that all other people have to do good in the same way. So the argument is slightly different, I think; but possibly quite telling.

Walter Berns: Many times during the course of our conversations we have used the word "compassion"; and it occurs usually in the following context. The religious oriented person is "compassionate," and he makes the charge against the "market" for its lack of "compassion." I would merely like to remind everybody here, and I am sure everybody would agree with me, that compassion, like love, like hate, like anger can be blind. One can love the wrong things; hate the wrong things; be angry at the wrong things; and exercise compassion on objects that don't deserve it.

David Friedman: I had two comments. The first was a response to some of Ken Boulding's remarks; and, I am afraid, it took awhile, but that's because I wanted to follow his form.

> An economist known as Ken
> Fears that we imperfect men
> Will fall into a land
> That we can't understand
> Again, and again, and again.

> But it seems there's a way we can hedge
> Since Boulding is willing to pledge
> That if *he* can command
> The Invisible Hand
> It will push us all back from the edge. (laughter and applause)

My second comment was on the public good problem. While I agree with both Ken Boulding and with Ed Mishan that there are such things as public or collective goods and that they do provide problems, I also believe that there may be situations in which there are no satisfactory solutions and one has to take the least unsatisfactory one.

And there are two points, which I think are usually missed in discussions with the public good problem: the first is that it's not an all-or-nothing kind of problem. That is, the fact that something is a public good means you can expect it to be underproduced, but not necessarily not to be produced at all. And in the particular case of charity that was discussed a moment ago, there are various clever private ways of helping to get around that, of which the one that I happen to be familiar with (and everybody who reads *New Yorker* ads is familiar with) is the idea of connecting a particular donor to a particular recipient, of saying, "There is a starving child in Lebanon. You can be this child's sponsor." And once that situation is set up, if you don't feed her, she goes hungry. And so there is not the question of, "If I don't, somebody else will." Someone else is responsible for a different starving child. So that in general, I think you ought to expect that people trying to solve public good problems will provide imperfect but existing solutions. And that therefore what you have is an imperfection, not necessarily a catastrophic one.

The other mistake people make, continually, is forgetting that the public good problem is also the reason why governments cannot work. That is to say that producing good laws, or producing good government, involves me as an individual producing something, whose benefits are shared with two hundred million other people. I have enormous underincentives to do that, so to speak, since I get a small part of the benefit. Consequently, governments work catastrophically badly. Therefore, we cannot confidently expect that this badly run government, providing a public good, will do any better than the imperfect market providing the public good. So that is essentially why I am an anarchist in spite of believing there is a public good problem; because I think it may well be that living with underproduction of some public goods is a less bad solution than creating a government to produce them, and having that poorly controlled government do a lot of undesirable things.

Philip Wogaman: I'm sure this opens up a whole new "can of worms" or "throws gasoline on fire" or something of the sort, but I am still going to voice it in relation to this topic. It makes a good deal of difference how one sees fundamental human nature. Much of our discussion has been predicated on fairly individualistic assumptions. I am reminded of Aristotle's understanding that man is, by nature, a social or a political animal. But I think even that is susceptible to distortion if one thinks of society as being monolithic. And I find myself as an ethicist grappling with the polar character of human nature — both individual and social. Which leads me to the observation that in some of our decision-making, it's a question of "How do we enhance the sense of 'we'ness about society?" That is, society as a whole is 'we,' and we can act as a whole in some particulars. In others, probably to enhance the individual side, it's very important to have zones of individual freedom and action. And consequently, I am always looking for those difficult ways of balancing, rather than, what may be the simple matter of constructing a model based entirely on individualism, entirely on a market; or on the other hand, entirely on a collective model.

Geoffrey Brennan: It seems to me, we are still left with the question, "Why do people actually go to the polls?" I think that I have to take some of the blame for some of the misconceptions about this, because I think to use the word "moral" and perhaps the way in which I have set up the problem, is a misconstruction. To describe the behaviour in question as liturgical or religious, in Ken Boulding's terms, is probably more apt.

People often talk as if the world were divided into two mutually exclusive domains — a political mechanism, in which people search for goodness and truth; and a market, in which they all indulge self-interest. But the political mechanism is an institution in which individuals pursue self-interest. It's a machine for the pursuit of self-interest. And the question at issue is: Why do we believe that that machine for self-interest will, as if by an invisible hand, generate public goods, for example, justice?

In my paper, I wanted to be able to explain why that might be a legitimate view — that there might be something about the way in which political processes work that somehow means that the political process isn't so much a machine for self-interest; that in some important fashion, the way in which people act in markets, and the way in which people act in political mechanisms, is different.

That's what I was concerned about; and I feel it's been difficult to stake out that middle ground for three reasons:

1. because the economists have been reluctant to accept it;

2. because non-economists have been reluctant to accept it; and
3. because people didn't want to talk about that particular issue of the paper.

Now that may be my fault, and I may have misjudged what was appropriate.

Chapter 6

Religion, Culture, and Technology

Ezra J. Mishan

Summary

Some religions, like the Anglican Church, are light on faith. Others, like the Church of Rome, are more doctrinaire. All traditional religions, however, are losing ground. The growth of religious pluralism in the post-war period, especially in North America, does not represent any resurgence of faith. It is indicative rather of division and despair.

There may well be among orthodox churchmen a bias against the operation of unchecked markets and an adherence to an "adversary culture" that is antagonistic to our "bourgeois" civilization. But it is doubtful whether there is a political trend in the churches toward socialism conceived as collectivist economic planning under direction of the state.

Bourgeois capitalism is not, in any case, repressive of church doctrine or activity—as, for instance, is the socialism of the Eastern bloc. The arch enemy of traditional ecumenical religion is the scientific establishment. Nor, again, is bourgeois capitalism directly responsible for the disillusion expressed by intellectuals and many of the young. The abrasive and despicable features of modern life may be attributed rather to the sort of technological progress made since the turn of the century or earlier, though more particularly since the second world war.

The ordinary individual today finds himself in a dilemma. He has faith in the manifest powers of science to which he owes his present standard of living with all its material comforts. But it is dawning on him that faith in science and faith in religion are mutually incompatible. It is also dawning on him that without faith in the divine, his life is without purpose or dignity.

I. PROLOGUE

The current state of religious faith in the West

Although there exists today a greater variety of religious denominations than ever before, the view that there has been a continuous decline of religious faith in the West, at least since the Enlightenment of the second half of the eighteenth century, is common enough. The post-war proliferation especially in North America, of new movements, denominations, orders, factions, and cults, both domestic and imported, is best interpreted as a manifestation of religious faith in the throes of disintegration.

True, some religious organizations have never been strong on faith. While it continued to be a pillar of the Establishment from the Restoration of 1660 onward, the Church of England grew in the regard of the public more as a peculiarly British institution than as a branch of ecumenical Christendom — rather like the game of cricket, in which any show of passion would be deemed unseemly.

A cynic might well say that to ask a Church of England cleric what his beliefs are would be considered bad form. A sporting interest in the contents of the Bible might reasonably be expected of a vicar. But one could hardly aspire to the mitre without having also established a reputation as a liberal agnostic.

If Trollope's novels are any guide, this doctrinal urbanity is not a recent development. The younger sons of country squires would customarily have to make a choice between entering the legal profession, embarking on a military career, or taking holy orders, weighing up the net social advantage with the help of friends and relations.[1] With the possible exception, in the Barsetshire novels, of the curate Mr. Crawley, all of Trollope's prelates, from the most humble prebendary to the Bishop — agreeable men for the most part, though often eccentric — were invariably quite busy with the things of this world and conscious always of the importance of a good domestic and social life in spreading the influence of the Anglican Church.

The modern Church of England

Today, the Church of England clergy has progressed only in enjoying life less and in involving itself more with man's welfare here on earth than with his immortal soul. The institution has, indeed, begun to look very much like an extension of the social services of the modern state. Many a local church, like the local YMCA, offers amenities to the young, and practical advice to unwed mothers and Borstal boys. Your average Church divine prides himself on being a practical man. He is not likely to be caught offguard thumbing his Bible. More often than not, his breezy affability conveys the impression that he has a far livelier interest in the affairs of this world than of the next and, moreover, that there is very little about this wicked modern world that he is not comfortably familiar with. Church-of-England sermons, over BBC radio, begin to sound each year more like editorials from *Modern Living* magazine—although, in deference to tradition, served up with a light sacramental garnishing.

Lest I be accused of exaggerating the cultivated worldliness of the servants of the Anglican Church, let me remind you that Bishop Robinson's "Honest to God" monograph gently chided those gullible churchgoers who, as he puts it, pictured God as "an old man in the sky" or—not to put too fine a point on it—as a personal God rather than as a pantheistic force. His worldliness was further manifested in a *Sunday Times* article (1969) in which he welcomed the permissive society and the pleasures it afforded of gazing at nude bodies—while covering his flanks from attack by men of smaller vision by contriving a distinction between erotica (good) and pornography (bad).[2] With examples such as this to draw upon, it is not surprising that churchmen, increasingly concerned to "do good" here on earth—and at a time when economic and political judgements are increasingly difficult to make—are losing influence and respect.

The nadir was reached (or was it?) when the World Council of Churches found itself making financial contributions to South African terrorists—invariably represented by that newspeak term "liberation fighter." In newspaper articles and letters (in the British press) its spokesmen sought to vindicate such action by *realpolitik* considerations, among which was included the argument that the ends (liberation from the yoke of white rule) justifies the means (the use of bullets and bombs to maim and murder innocent people).

If we exclude a dwindling minority of true believers to be found more often among the older generation, members of the Anglican Church are unlikely to find in their religion any impediment to their worldly ambitions. Indeed, it can well serve to extend them. On both sides of the Atlantic, although more so in North America, the considerations that enter into the choice of a particular church or chapel bears comparison with those that enter into the choice of a social club. And it may be more important to a business or professional man to belong to a Masonic lodge or to a Rotary club than to a church.

By far the greater proportion of the Roman Catholic Church is no less worldly, although it is a good deal more superstitious. Generally, Catholics are dimly but uneasily aware that the Holy See is fighting a rearguard action for survival against the sweep of world fashion (the ordination of women priests), against global imperatives (reducing the growth of world population) and, more particularly, against the more recent findings of secular disciplines and the immense and increasing prestige of science. In the meantime, the mass of Catholics prefer to confess their sins than to curb them, to hedge their bets by offering incense to a variety of saints, acting as if an all-knowing God is yet too foolish or too busy to remark their blatant hypocrisies.

The religious "resurgence"?

Turning now to the so-called resurgence of religion, or rather religions, in the post-war period, more counterfeit than current is to be found in it. Much that looks at first glance like reversion to an older tradition, such as the "moral majority" movement in the U.S., is best understood as, in large part, a recoil from the excesses of post-war "permissiveness," which permissiveness itself is both a response to historically unprecedented mass affluence and a reaction to the psychic stress of modern living. Much like the earlier movement for Prohibition in America, which gathered its strength from Puritan clements and the more conservative small towns, it cannot prevail against the psychological drive and institutional innovations impelled by modern economic growth.

New fundamentalist movements, like the older Jehovah's Witnesses, appeal to those who want "to come out of the cold," to struggle out of the spiritual void that is the legacy of the Scientific Enlightenment. Fundamentalism in varying degrees is characteristic also of an assortment of evangelical movements of mixed provenance. Watching the faces of soul-starved audiences transfixed by the pugnacious rhetoric of Bible-thumping ranters of the Billy Swagger variety — reminiscent of Sinclair Lewis' Elmer Gantry — one is momentarily reminded of the faces of concentration-camp inmates at the sight of food they despaired of ever tasting.

In all age-groups we shall find those who seek wistfully for signs and for wonders, turning in their anxiety to astrology, to pagan rites, or to Oriental gurus. Others there are — denizens of Jacque Ellul's *Technological Society* — who conceive of religion as offering techniques for achieving tranquility (TM) or for releasing "potential." Scientology, blending ancient myth with modern superstition, offers its initiates a *scientific* religion putatively designed to enable them to cope successfully with the body and pressure of the times. Yet others, taking their cue from the more wanton features of post-war permissiveness, seek to found Dionysian cults, or to transform aspects of Christianity into pop or freak religions, or jazzy ones, like the "swinging Jesus" movement, or else to seek thrills and perhaps secret power in pursuit of the occult, in witchcraft or in Satan-worship.

From Christendom to religious "pluralism"

One might want to continue sorting out, identifying, and interpreting, the variety of shrill noise emanating from this post-war Babel of "irrationalist" recidivism. But such a fascinating exercise is best reserved for another occasion. Instead, as historians, let us mark the stages in the spiritual journey made from the ecumenical Christendom of the Middle Ages, through Reformation and Counter-Reformation in the Western world, down to what we might euphemistically call the religious "pluralism" of the last quarter of the twentieth century. Is it possible so to deceive oneself as to associate this phenomenon with a revival or resurgence of religious faith — approving of it with cynical detachment as offering to the individual "an increase in the area of choice," to use the economist's jargon? Does it really amount to more than a medley of frantic cries lost in a spiritual tundra? Certainly very little of this post-war religious renaissance has struck root and taken blossom in the Western world in the form of a resurgence of rectitude and virtuous conduct, the essential products of a serene faith and trust in the Divine.

Far removed we are today from the religious climate of the early Middle Ages. Over all the hardships, cruelties, and other deficiencies of that time, a sacramental religion suffused life, lending to even the ordinary events of the week, the season, the year, a dignity and transcendent purpose. In an age such as ours, abounding with technical vitality, all the events in an ordinary person's life shrink into insignificance. Religious organizations have need, themselves, to employ *technical innovations* in order to be heard above the ignoble clamour, and even the more respectable denominations of Christian and Jewish religions are not above borrowing the *resources of science and salesmanship* in bids to attract a wider membership; not above veering with the winds of political fashion—twisting doctrine a little in response to feminist and other liberation movements; not above revamping ritual, litany, scriptual interpretation, as better to accommodate the tastes and style of the modern disoriented mind.

In sum, if a sceptical interpretation of the recent course of religious activity in the West is accepted, it will be seen as evidence not of a growth in religious faith but of a decline—an anguish of religion in its death throes. Explanations of this impending collapse are not hard to come by. My own explanation, possibly very imperfect and (if plausible) possibly not altogether novel, follows.

II. INTRODUCTION

The modern anomie

De Grazia's *Political Community* argues cogently that in any society ordinary men have a deep-seated need for leadership and authority. It is painful for them to live without firm beliefs—beliefs not only in their origins or their destiny or in their institutions, but beliefs also in persons, in heroes, in myths, in gods. And, I may add, the pain of unbelief can be aggravated by other factors inseparable from a high technology civilization; in particular by a welter of innovations that have incidentally produced a style of living that is responsible for the anomie peculiar to the modern age. The elements comprising this anomie include mutual estrangement in urban areas, family disintegration, growing apprehension of the hazards of new technologies, a sense of loss of control—attributes I shall touch upon later.

But whether this anomie or despair—that which technocrats scorn as "loss of nerve"—has in fact been active in moving the Church, or some churches, towards socialism (as vaguely comprehended) is an auxiliary question, one of secondary importance and, in any case, one that cannot be answered with any great confidence.

Unless one has some particular church or faction of a church in mind, the belief that there is a movement of ecclesiastic opinion favouring socialism, at least when understood as collectivist economic planning, is far from evident. Fundamentalist religions certainly have no truck with that kind of socialism. It is circumspect to place the world "socialism" in quotation marks since like so many ideological terms — liberty, equality, fascism, democracy, anarchy, imperialism — it is encumbered by a weight of emotive associations and means very different things to different people.

What does "socialism" entail?

At one end of the spectrum we may identify the term with what Lionel Trilling called the "adversary culture" of a bourgeois society, a phenomenon recently illustrated and deplored by Irving Kristol (*Encounter*, 1980). If all that is meant by "socialism" is this sort of antagonism to, and distrust of, "the system," and of the mass culture and commercial ethos it produces, it has been all too common a reaction since the Second World War, and indeed is familar to the social historian as a reaction to contemporary life that can be traced back to the beginning of the nineteenth century. If Christian churches, and Christians themselves, are believed to be moving toward "socialism" in this sense, then it is an unremarkable tendency, one shared in some degree by the greater part of modern societies, although more especially by the "educated classes" to be found in academia, in the professions, and in many departments of government.

If at the other extreme, however, we use the term in its more precise economic meaning, as a form of social organization in which the "instruments of production" are collectively owned, and are directed by the state to fulfil a succession of economic plans then, as indicated above, the proposition that the Church, or the churches of the Western world, have been moving toward "socialism" is doubtful.

I might add, as a gratuitous footnote, however, that even if it were a true proposition it could easily be explained. After all, those who are repelled by the unrepressed manifestations of corruption and social injustice in the "bourgeois" or "capitalist" society in which they are immersed are sorely tempted to repose their hopes for social justice, for personal dignity, for human fulfilment, in that as-yet unrealized ideal socialist dispensation that will spring up joyously, after the successful revolution, from the ashes of the old order. Yet it is a temptation that cannot easily withstand sustained reflection. For even a casual romp through the pages of modern history would be enough to convince an open-minded thinker that the wanton enthusiasm that sweeps a revolution to its crest is soon transformed into alarm and dismay as "enemies of the people" are discovered by the legion, as the blood-letting begins, as the struggle for power culminates in an unprecedented tyranny — and as veteran idealists in the West bewail once more "a revolution betrayed." At any rate, having left behind me the reckless revolutionary fervour of my early youth, and advanced toward the outskirts of maturity, I am content to endorse the epitomized judgement of Dr. Johnson that "the remedies for the ills of society are palliative, not radical."

In the circumstances, I shall not dwell upon the evidence of the existing antagonism to "bourgeois culture" in the West, or upon the disillusion with so many aspects of our post-industrial civilization. These widespread attitudes have been chronicled by many historians and sociologists. Instead, I shall argue that such a development is all but inevitable in a technically dynamic society; I shall further argue that such antagonism and disillusion are themselves linked to the decline in religious faith; and that the religious decline is itself an unavoidable consequence of the secularization of thought and feeling in a civilization shaped and controlled by the expanding powers of a Scientific Establishment for which, seemingly, no achievement is impossible.

To endure, a civilization requires a certain moral consensus. For a person like myself who believes that any such moral consensus has to be grounded upon religious foundations — upon an acceptance of the great myths from which humanity in all ages has drawn its spiritual sustenance — the prospect before us is not only surpassingly sad, it is also surpassingly grim. For it follows, as I indicate later, that the chance of our Western-type civilization holding together much longer in the absence of a wide extension in the coercive powers of the state is negligible.

III. CAPITALISM AND FREEDOM

Why the malaise?

To represent the adversary culture today (as does Irving Kristol) as a form of ideological rejection by the intellectual and middle classes of the values of a "bourgeois" society is to underrate the strength and sweep of the current of discontent that courses through our society.

Intellectuals or would-be intellectuals are, of course, more vociferous than others, more articulate in their protest, and more habituated to attributing causes and, occasionally, to proposing solutions. But the dissatisfaction with the over-all dimensions — the style, pace, pressure, artifice — of modern living takes many forms and, in different ways and different degrees, affects the greater part of all Western communities. I begin, therefore, by putting the rhetorical question: why, despite the exultant claims of technocrats, despite the excitement of political events, despite the pervasive sales euphoria and the unprecedented popularity among the masses of the get-away package tour, is there so persistent a sense of malaise? Is it just possible that people have begun to detect beneath the shiny synthetic skin of our affluent civilization something that feels like a malign growth?

Allowing this impression to be true, the explanations I offer for it have little direct connection with capitalism or, more generally, with the institution of private property, private enterprise, and the operation of free markets. It seems proper, therefore, before attempting to explain the prevailing discontent and the adversary culture it produces, to prepare the way by indicating briefly the position I take in the eternal debate about the relative economic and political merits of market (or "mixed") economies on the one hand, and of socialist (or collectivist) economies on the other.

Socialism vs. market order: A preparatory clarification

I confess at the start that I have a strong predilection for the former. I am persuaded of both the historical and logical connections between capitalism and freedom, both political and personal — a theme propounded over the years by writers in a variety of disciplines, and more recently argued with lucidity and conviction in the more popular works of two distinguished Nobel prize-winning economists, Friedrich Hayek and Milton Friedman. I am in no doubt that the extending power of the state, even in the most democratic country, diminishes choice and weakens the power of the individual *vis à vis* the bureaucracy, enmeshes him further in detailed legislation that, incidentally, endangers the rule of law. The growth of the state's "citizen-protecting" functions, especially its mass welfare services, entails tax rates that encourage tax evasion and so, also, contempt for the law, at the same time as it acts to undermine the independence and character of individuals, many of whom become adept at "milking" the welfare services as a way of life. To boot, the modern state undertakes enterprises that can be more efficiently performed by private industry. It introduces a welter of regulations that almost invariably strengthen the monopoly practices of the industries putatively being regulated. Worse, in the attempt to gain electoral support, big government has become economically so powerful, that today members of new ethnic groups, as well as highly organized industries, repose their hopes for material advance more on the prospect of government economic aid or privileges than on individual effort and enterprise.

Indeed, governments beyond a certain size and economic power will convert libertarian democracy into populist democracy. They offer prizes to everybody, the executive power appeals in the main directly to the electorate, making ample use of the media, keeps its eye on public opinion polls, and surrenders to the temptation to bend principle in order to maintain popularity. It talks perpetually of "the national interest" while appraising almost every measure in the light of its effect on the next election.

No one more than I would welcome a contraction of government to a fraction of its current size. Yet I am certain that, however cogent are the reasons for constricting and contracting modern governments, they will expand in size and power over the foreseeable future—for which belief I give reasons below.

Why the adversary culture?

Returning to the need to explain the popularity of the adversary culture mentioned above, I shall first consider some of the features of the operation of existing economic systems, both market (or "mixed" capitalist) and collectivist, that may be thought vulnerable to criticism, and attempt also to assess their importance. I shall then move on to those factors, associated with technological progress, which I hold to be crucial to any understanding of the spirit or, rather, the dispiritedness of the times.

In ascending order of importance—and perhaps also in descending order of detachment—the subjects I discuss will be grouped under four headings:

1. Some inadequacies of economic systems with respect to consumer or producer bias, stability, choice, and risk.
2. The failure of economic systems to cope with spillovers, with some emphasis on post-war hazards resulting from the pace of innovation.

3. Broader connections between technological progress and the quality of life — consideration of which takes us to

4. The economic rationale, the nature, and the consequences of the "new permissiveness."

I end the essay with reflections on the basic incompatibility of science and religion, and on the incidental inhumanity of science.

IV. INADEQUACIES OF EXISTING ECONOMIC SYSTEMS

A preliminary — some familiar "inadequacies"

Unemployment and inflation are topics that are too controversial to be broached in this essay. They are less disturbing and not nearly so unnerving as are the other phenomena we shall discuss in the last two sections. During the interwar period, unemployment was undoubtedly one of the considerations, if not the chief consideration, that disposed people in the West to favour the idea of socialism and economic planning. Since the war, however, increasing disenchantment with Soviet-type utopias, and widespread scepticism about their economic and social claims, have reconciled populations in the West to being more tolerant of their own economic ills. Moreover, the experience in the West of near-full employment for about thirty years after the Second World War has left the impression that unemployment is not, as Marxists would have it, an inevitable feature of a capitalist system. It is regarded, rather, as a "recession" through which we are passing in a bid to reduce inflation rates to more tolerable levels. There is concern, but not despair.

Again, I shall say very little here about fears of an impending shortage of natural resources; no more than to voice my opinion that the reasons some economists give for their optimism are ill-founded: the classic (Hotelling) optimal depletion path is vulnerable (the discount rate in an intergeneration context does not, in any case, meet the conventional economic criterion). A quite unwarranted confidence is placed on the price trends of raw materials over the last fifty or a hundred years, and, in general, there are too many "ifs" and "buts" lurking behind the facade of confidence.

As for the current concern at the continuing global destruction of vast ecological reservoirs and of areas of natural beauty, or at the rapid extinction over the past thirty years of species of flora or fauna, it is one that I share. And I can conceive no system of enforceable property rights that would effectively reverse these world trends. I am resigned to the near-certainty that my great grandchildren will come to inherit a world of dwindling wild life and few accessible retreats of unsullied natural beauty. Theirs will be a more desolate, uniform, and monotonous planet. For this dismal consummation I do not blame the market, but the growth of technology and population that, as argued by Richard Wilkinson in his *Poverty and Progress* (1974), are mutually reinforcing.

Environmental problems are as bad or worse in existing Soviet economies. More benign forms of socialism are, of course, readily conceivable (as are more benign forms of capitalism). But they are not emerging. Environmental concern is certainly not high on the list of priorities for the kind of socialist state as envisaged, say, by the British Labour party's Tony Benn.

Consumer vs. producer orientation in the market

Turning to the consumer bias of the market, I have no criticism of those instances in which workers are attracted to moving into new areas or industries by the prospect of material gain or net advantage. The more troublesome case, however, is that in which, following a shift of consumer expenditure, capital and labour are subject to the "discipline of the market." In this connection one thinks in particular of workers who are laid off by declining industries and who, in addition to enduring anxiety and perhaps some hardship until re-employed, are impelled to incur search costs and later on possibly moving costs, retraining costs, and also those "psychic costs" associated with leaving a familiar neighbourhood and settling the family in a new one.

It is not easy to devise quantitative criterion that would compare an increase in consumer satisfaction from maintaining freedom of choice over market goods with the consequent increase in hardship suffered by workers. Even if it could be demonstrated that in almost all important cases the losses suffered by members of the community in their capacity as workers or resource-owners exceeded the gains conferred on members of that community in their capacity as consumers, economists could always fall back on the long-term advantages of having a more flexible and dynamic economy. Without drawing any firm conclusions, however, it is reasonable to conjecture that, as the vicissitudes of consumer demand grow in the affluent economy, the entailed trade-off of consumer satisfaction for worker dissatisfaction, resulting from the unchecked operation of competitive markets, becomes less beneficial: in high consumption societies, increments to existing consumer choice become less valuable whereas "increments" of worker readjustment become more irksome.

Technical advance and individual uncertainty

Expectations of increasing versatility of consumer demand arise chiefly from technical advance. In the first place, the mass affluence in Western countries produced by technical progress leaves a greater margin for "impulse buying" in contrast to those countries where the bulk of consumption expenditure is restricted to staple items (even the demand for luxury items by the wealthy in such countries is relatively stable). This "fickleness" of consumer demand, especially within broad categories of goods, is aggravated by competitive advertising and by international competition. Looked at *ex post,* then, the value to society of consumer freedom under prevailing conditions in the West is easy to overestimate.

In the second place, and associated with the decline in freight costs over the last hundred years or so, the greater part of the goods currently being traded between industrial countries are close substitutes for one another, thereby conferring only limited benefit — as compared, say, with the benefits from international trade between countries producing goods that are complementary to each other's economy. The fierce international competition today in autos, stereos, television sets, cameras, watches, computors, cassettes, and a host of other modern devices and accessories, if allowed to prevail without hindrance, could be vastly disruptive of the domestic economy and could inflict anxieties and hardships out of all proportion to any sober estimate of the consumer gain to be derived from the often-bewildering assortment of hardware in the stores. The tariff and trade controls despised by economists are, of course, the means by which producers and workers seek to protect themselves from loss and hardship.

In the third place, continuing innovation entails not only new goods but new technologies, the adoption of which can overnight make hardearned skills virtually obsolete. In these circumstances, it is easy to understand the obstinate resistance of workers to the introduction of more efficient technologies, and also to understand the growing concern of labour unions not merely with real wages but with maintaining the actual employment level of their members and ensuring large compensatory sums in the event of dismissals arising from "reorganizations." If such trends continue—and there is no reason to believe otherwise—the problem will become more acute since market mechanisms of themselves can do little to resolve it. Through its political decisions, then, society as a whole may be seen as being more willing to sacrifice some consumer choice in order to reduce the strain on domestic producers and workers. Independent of union action, international trade and domestic industry are likely to be subject to more government control, not less.

State controlled economies, such as those within the Soviet bloc, are not so wealthy as those of the West and the scope for "impulse buying" is therefore correspondingly smaller. But even were they as wealthy, consumer demand would almost certainly not be allowed to disturb the detailed pattern of industrial production planned for the period. Job security therefore might well be greater.

To sum up, the consequences of the consumer bias of competitive markets in conditions of affluence and rapid technical change—in particular, apprehension among workers of their skills becoming obsolete, and of their becoming technologically unemployable—are among the secular problems that I believe will grow in importance. But they are not, just now, among the most vital.

Pollution and disamenity

We turn next, in this section, to the growing attention paid in Western countries to the many forms of pollution and disamenity that are subsumed under the umbrella term "spillover effects"—those incidental effects and products of legitimate economic activity. Over the last two decades the economic literature on this topic has swollen to astonishing dimensions, a significant part of the resulting controversies being of a doctrinal nature. At one extreme, within orthodox economics, there is the Chicago School holding to the belief that with more carefully delineated systems of property rights the unfettered market can cope comfortably with spillover problems. At the other extreme perhaps are those economists who, like myself, are churlish enough to dismiss this believe as a doctrinal delusion: indeed, to maintain that, given any realistic extension of property rights, the contribution that can be made by markets, no matter how flexible and competitive, to resolving the allocative problems presented by the sort of spillovers being generated in the present state of technology is miniscule. I give reasons for this pessimistic view in the following section. In the present section I wish only to touch upon one aspect of the spillover problem: that implied, engagingly enough, by the title of the recent popular book written by Professor and Mrs. Friedman, *Free to Choose.*

As the Friedmans convincingly argue and illustrate, the more the public sector takes over from the private sector of the economy, the less the choice remaining for the individual: his money is used by the government to produce goods he may have no interest in consuming or in amounts he may not wish for. But expansion of government in displacing private enterprise is not the only phenomenon that effectively reduces individual choice. The expansion of the incidence of spillovers is another source of choice-reduction, one that is certainly no less potent. For irrespective of the allocative efficacy of property rights — irrespective, that is, of whether the operation of the market in any particular instance is able or not to generate an optimal level of pollution as commonly conceived — individual choice necessarily declines as the extent and variety of spillovers expand.

Pollution and freedom of choice

If the keen environmentalist deplores the increase in smog or the increase in aircraft noise within his vicinity, it affords him no consolation to be assured by the economist that, bearing in mind transactions costs, etc., the disamenities he deplores are being produced at optimal levels. He may himself have no use for the goods produced by the smog-creating activity or for air travel services. And even if he did have some use for them, he still has no choice but to bear with the incidence of disamenities being generated. He cannot, so to speak, decompose these packages of goods-cum-bads (any more than can the recipient of government largesse): he cannot, that is, at market prices choose *both* the amounts of the market goods in question — autos, industrial products, air services — at market prices, and *also* the amounts of the "bads" he is willing to absorb. Under these conditions he is worse off than he would be with a tied sale, since he can always refuse the tied-sale package if on balance it will make him worse off. He cannot, in contrast, refuse the market-goods-cum-environmental-bads package, no matter how much it offends him. He has no choice but to bear with the environmental bads — or strive to reduce them in some degree by incurring costs — as and when they appear.

Thus in an area of great sensitivity having occasionally far-reaching effects on society's welfare, the operation of competitive markets — even where property rights are such as to issue in optimal outputs — can offer no protection to the individual. If it is believed that spillovers as a whole will grow over the future, then whatever gains may be made from the exercise of individual choice arising from a hoped-for expansion of the private sector of the economy, and from the production of new goods, will have to be offset by losses of individual choice in respect of environmental goods. And there can be no certainty that the balance will be favourable.

I need hardly add that I do not see a centrally-planned economy, in the same stage of development, dealing any more successfully with the problem.

V. THE PROBLEM OF THE NEW SPILLOVERS

Technology and the nightmare prospect

Difficulties of dealing satisfactorily with environmental spillovers extend to a new dimension once we move from the familiar instances of smoke, noise, effluent, and mutual interference, that are popular in the conventional economic model, toward a veritable epidemic of new spillovers that have descended upon the globe since the Second World War — fears about which are a part of the incipient nightmare about the future that has come to blight the American dream.

These new spillovers spring chiefly from two sorts of technologies that carry a risk of local or global disasters. The first involves the spread of virtually invisible industrial wastes that if allowed to accumulate beyond critical levels could destroy man's habitat, or destroy man himself. The second arises from the manufacture and use of new synthetics, chemicals, food-additives, drugs, fertilizers, and pesticides. The long-term health and ecological effects about which, singly or in combination, we as yet know precious little.

The almost daily discovery of new hazards,[3] and the media publicity accorded them, has begun to effect a fundamental change in people's attitude toward science and technology. They have begun to see themselves not only as beneficiaries of technological progess but also as its victims. Public alarm and the consequent opposition to certain technologies have occasionally thwarted the plans of governments and planning agencies who, in their turn, believe that the safety assurances being demanded by vociferous segments of the public threaten the nation's economic future.

Safety and the demand for government

Explicit forms of safety assurance are, of course, also being demanded in the U.S. by other government agencies. Risk assessment has been a major component in their decisions. The recent Toxic Substances Control Act mandates that all chemicals (more than 3,000) be tested for carcinogenicity, mutagenicity, teratogenicity, and other effects. The difficulties are immense. Extension of results from animal experiments to humans introduces a high level of uncertainty.[4]

Clearly, vital public decisions are being made under conditions in which analysis, dominated as it often is by a large element of uncertainty, cannot be rational. In some instances it is hardly a question of setting confidence intervals, for virtually nothing is known of a new substance or technology except the fears of some scientists of the possibility of a variety of calamities.[5] What, for example, is the risk that some malignant man-made bacterium will escape from a micro-genetic engineering laboratory and spread a disease against which men and animals have no natural defences, and against which modern medicine— within the relevant time span—would be powerless? Perhaps not too great just at present. But as the number of even very small risks of precipitating an irreversible or earth-crippling catastrophe continue to accumulate year by year—and some risks are far from small—the passage of time brings us closer to a near certainty of some such catastrophe.

Obviously there can be very little individual choice with respect to the many new hazards of this sort arising from post-war innovations. Nor is there the remotest prospect of the market transmuting these collective choices—whether they are made explicitly or (in default of an explicit decision) implicitly—into individual choices. Whatever the nature and extent of the risk in question, such a risk is involuntary for the individual.

It may be argued that even where the degree of risk is known, and it is clearly explained to the public, people perceive the danger to be larger than it actually is; worse, that when the degree of risk is not known, or when the public disbelieves the estimates of scientists, the risk may be exaggerated out of all proportion. Yet the economist, sticking to his last, is constrained by his evaluative criterion to accept as the only relevant data the valuation that each individual taken singly places on each good or bad including, of course, involuntary risk.

From this brief consideration of the public's growing awareness of the proliferation of hazards, large and small, local and global, that has taken place since the Second World War, two main conclusions follow. First and more obvious, the degree of public anxiety has increased, is increasing, and will almost certainly continue to increase. In the circumstances, one should hesitate to accept the affirmation of growthmen that, over the post-war period, technological advance has on balance improved the human condition; that simply because of the availability of more market goods the general sense of well-being has grown in spite of public anxiety and trepidation.

The second conclusion emerges from the first and also from the fact that spillovers, old and new, produce conflicts of interests within the community as between beneficiaries and "maleficiaries" — as between government and industry, as between consumers of polluting goods and the victims of such pollution, as between particular industries (sometimes supported by governments) and segments of the public, as between ecologists and technocrats, as between environmentalists and blue-collar workers.

Both these facts — the public's growing unease at the expanding horizon of hazard, and the inevitable conflicts engendered by the hazards in question — tend to activate public demand for more government control and more detailed legislation, so diminishing further the prospect of a reduction in the power of government and an increase in individual freedom.

VI.   TECHNOLOGICAL PROGRESS AND THE QUALITY OF LIFE

Some preliminary clarification

Turning to the all-important connections between modern technology and the experience of living (other than the effects mentioned in the preceding sections), let me concede at the outset an adherence to the following propositions in order to avoid unnecessary and often trivial controversy:

1. That acting within his budget and within existing legal constraints a person choosing among market goods old and new places a value on them that reflects his anticipation of benefit. Indeed, economists such as I, employing evaluative techniques, seek to estimate *anticipated* benefits of communities of individuals at different points of time — *not* their subsequent or *ex post* assessments.

2. That the progress of science and technology over the last two centuries has made available to ordinary people living in the richer countries of the world a range of goods producing comforts, conveniences, experiences, and entertainment, that could not even be imagined by earlier generations.
3. That there have been many instances of scientific discoveries and technical innovations that have conferred seemingly unambiguous benefits on society, and that there may well be others potentially able to do so.
4. That modern medicine and hygiene has reduced infant mortality, contributed to the prolongation of expected life, and eased physical suffering.

In return for these handsome concessions, growth-minded economists who also recognize the notion of optimality might concede the *possibility* at least that the optimal level of technology — optimal with respect to human well-being — was reached at an earlier period in Western civilization than the last half of the twentieth century. So much by way of civil interchange and ground-clearing before giving utterance to scepticism.

I hope we can all agree also that the existence of consumer freedom of choice with respect to market goods along with freedom of choice of occupation and enterprise, though undoubtedly good in themselves, provide no assurances for the quality of life; that such coveted freedoms are altogether compatible with a decline in the quality of life and, indeed, with a civilization that is sinking into cultural barbarity. Thus, when the evaluating economist says that he will equate an increase in social welfare with an increase in the area of (market) choice for individuals, he is — or he should be — aware of the weight being borne by the *ceteris paribus* clause.

The capacity for enjoyment as endogenous

It is not simply the fact that there can well be too much choice — an array of brands or models that bewilders more than it delights the consumer — nor simply the fact that what is actually offered by the market is determined also by law and custom, facts that have to be disregarded in the above definition of social welfare. Far more significant is the implied holding constant of tastes and of capacity for enjoyment which vary over time in a modern economy with the continuing advance of material progress. Inasmuch as technology and its products can alter radically within a person's lifetime, and today do so with incredible rapidity, the physical environment — the size, shape, architecture and traffic of towns and cities, their atmosphere, their impact on the senses — along with the style of living alter rapidly, and in doing so alter for better or worse the attributes, beliefs, and aspirations of the members of society. These are among the vital aspects that enter into the welfare of society, and they do not easily, if at all, lend themselves to measurement. But they can be observed, interpreted, pondered upon — and debated, if not perceptively at least intelligently. Surely we get closer to an understanding of American life in the 1820s from an acute observer such as de Tocqueville than from any pile of econometric studies directed to estimating per capita real income or indices of trade and production.

From glancing through the pages of a large number of erotic and sex magazines, along with numberless manuals on sexual techniques, available on the shelves and in the windows of ordinary bookshops in large cities (also in the campus bookshop of many a North American university), one discovers that many pages are devoted to advertising vibrators and other electric gadgetry for women. The impression that a majority of American women over sixteen today possess one or more of these obliging instruments is borne out by private inquiries. Here, indeed, is a prime example of an expansion in the area of choice, which the orthodox economist must unquestioningly translate into an increase in social welfare, that has taken place within a decade or so. Over the same period the bounty of technology has also provided us with an astonishing range of chemical poisons and quite a cornucopia of offensive-defensive small weaponry, from silent submachine rifles to letter bombs, from spring-blades to mace sprays.

The necessity of moral aesthetic criteria

These outlandish examples are chosen to persuade us that even with due regard to the *ceteris paribus* clause, an expansion of consumer choice may not always conform with our notions of an increase in welfare. Granted this much, we can open up with a weightier generalization: within a social order premised on insatiability, where perforce the tenth commandment is more honoured in the breach, and where it may be cynically affirmed that life has become a progress from discontent to discontent, any assessment of the value of the goods that people come to choose, and therefore the sort of life they come to lead, has to be referred to other than economic criteria. If the currents of modern life are to be judged by reference to criteria of taste and propriety, to artistic and cultural criteria, to moral criteria, we must be prepared for discouraging conclusions. If we are concerned, again, with such attributes as social felicity and cohesion, or with the integrity and character of individuals, we must be prepared to be saddened by the course of events. If we wonder seriously whether the post-war period has witnessed a growth in serenity of spirit; whether there has been a growth in courtesy, tolerance, mutual trust; whether there has been an improvement in family life, we are impelled to answer in the negative.

With the advantages of hindsight one may conclude that these and other untoward developments are not really so surprising. Indeed, I hope to convince some of you that worse is yet in store. Yet to earlier economists, reformers, humanists, and historians who wrote during the eighteenth and nineteenth centuries, such developments would appear not merely as aberrant but as monstrous. Macaulay, the great Whig historian of the first half of the nineteenth century, the apostle of progress, representing the spirit of mid-Victorian England in all its brash overconfidence, and certain that material progress would be followed by cultural and moral progress, would be horrified at the tasteless vulgarity of modern life and appalled at the eruption of urban violence that disfigures the "post-industrial" society of the West. For he shared with John Stuart Mill and others the belief that that growth and diffusion of wealth would act both to elevate taste and enhance morality. Among the later Victorians, we may pick out Matthew Arnold as one among many who agitated for the spread of education in the serene belief that in the fullness of time, and with the growth in the nation's prosperity, the cultural treasures of the world would be available to all classes, affording "sweetness and light" and edification to ordinary men.

The culture of modern society

Alas for those far-off innocent days. Matthew Arnold has been spared a visit to the modern mega-university where young philistines stalk the campus, pocket computers at the ready, where the bulk of the student body come to have their plastic minds pounded into a shape necessary to cope with the electronic machinery of a high-technology economy. In these sprawling knowledge-factories humming with technical equipment, where the young seem to have lost the art of linguistic expression, the traditional notion of the university as a community of

scholars and the notion of higher education as classical education—education in the humanities, education as a civilizing process—have a distinctly nostalgic air. Our Victorian reformer has
thankfully also been spared those breathless spectacles appearing on
the modern television screen, on which, it has been calculated, the
average American youngster will have taken in, some 6,000 scenes of
mayhem and murder before reaching the age of fourteen. The amount
of "high culture," even where it is readily available, that the ordinary
man willingly imbibes is apparently very limited. In contrast, the
amount of unadulterated bilge (judged by any reasonable artistic standards) he can stomach is apparently unlimited. Since the high hopes
once entertained by our distinguished forbears have been rudely shat-
tered, the modern humanist or liberal is left with a lot of explaining to
do. In the meantime he may dredge some comfort from the thought
that if, in existing socialist countries, mass entertainment is not so sick
and vulgar as it is in the West, it is still heavily larded with party prop-
aganda.

Notwithstanding the disillusions mentioned above, I believe that
there is an irrepressible propensity for the modern mind—the mind of
the ordinary citizen and even the mind of the thinking man in the last
half of the twentieth century—to overvalue the benefits conferred on
the human race by science and technology and to under-rate and ex-
tenuate their destructive power. This is partly because in a society of
relative abundance, the ubiquity of advertising media acts to direct
men's thoughts of what constitutes self-betterment toward worldly
things, toward material achievement, status, and toward the things
that money can buy. Consequently they attach disproportionate value
to these components of well-being. Indeed, in making invidious comparisons between past and present, neither is the journalistic historian
free from this bias. How often are we exhorted to imagine what life
would be like without electricity, or without all those modern conveniences that make life so comfortable! "Just picture how dull and con-
fining life would be without modern means of travel and communication!"

The transcience of novelty

But if we are to exercise our imaginations in making invidious comparisons between past and present, there are some additional facts of
life to be borne in mind. The pleasure afforded by novelty—the theme
on which so much advertising turns—is necessarily ephemeral. It

would not be too harsh a judgement to say that the morale of the citizen of post-war affluence is coming to depend upon a succession of novelties—upon "new experiences," "new sensations," "new thrills"—as a drug-addict comes to depend for his self-assurance on a succession of shots. And frequent fashion changes help to maintain the illusion of continuous novelty; not only fashion changes in clothes but in cars and furniture. In fact every conceivable device or toy is remodelled every year or so by hard-working design departments. Yet even when the novelty is quite genuine, even when it is regarded as a miracle of technology, it does not live up to the anticipations of pleasure. As Roszack remarks somewhere in his *Where the Wasteland Ends* (1978), a century ago people would have thrilled to the idea of travelling in a flying machine from one country to another. Today air travel is regarded by many as an ordeal, and by most as a continuous struggle against boredom—in which struggle we are fitfully assisted by liquor, magazines, taped music, films, and plastic-tasting tid-bits. The delight once generated by the introduction of the "gramophone," the stereo, the transistor, the cassette, the television, has given way to a routine and listless submission. I cannot believe that a future in which we hurtle through space in rockets will provide any more enduring entertainment than travelling by air does today: at all events the view from the rocket windows—black space punctuated by distant glimmers—is not likely to fascinate us long. Those whose hopes for a joyous life are premised on excitements and novelties yet to come will eventually find themselves fighting tedium in order to escape despair.

The costs of ease

Two other facts of life are no less telling to this connection. First, the successful pursuit of a life of physical ease, realized through a succession of labour-saving innovations, which appears to be shunting our civilization toward a push-button utopia, is not merely self-defeating, it is subversive of human well-being. Put aside the ill effects on our health from leading lives far more sedentary than nature ever intended us to do, and bear with the thought that life cannot be fully enjoyed save through contrasts. Central-heating, for instance, passes for a convenience that is now available to almost everyone in the West. But gone is the joy of warming to the blaze of a log fire, especially after having been out in the cold cutting up the wood and while so occupied cheerful in anticipation of the crackle and glow of the fire to come. As the historian Huizinga writes of the Middle Ages: "We, at the present day, can hardly understand the keenness with which a fur coat, a good fire on the hearth, a soft bed, a glass of wine, were formerly enjoyed." There can be no real gratification without prior effort of frustration. True friendships, comradeship, spring up between men sharing common dangers or facing hardships together: they are not formed on package tours.

Recall that only in Aldous Huxley's *Brave New World* were all sources of hardship and frustration removed. And the outcome was a population of emotional cretins. Since there was no sublimation of the sex drive in the Brave New World, there was no romance either. Since all conflicts were removed neither was there any human drama. Since there was no danger, neither were there any heroes. There was no occasion for discipline, and no occasion for sacrifice. And consequently there was no poetry, and no aspiration to the good and the beautiful.

The modern "independence"

The second fact of modern life is that labour-saving and other innovations distance us from our fellows. The automobile, the stereo, the radio, the television, the home computer, are also the elegant instruments of our mutual self-estrangement. Thus we have come to depend since the turn of the century both for our needs and entertainment increasingly more upon the products of technology and increasingly less upon the direct help and the company of friends and neighbours. In consequence, the direct flow of feeling and sympathy between people that enriches life becomes thinner.

What is more, these innovations that keep us to ourselves, that keep us indoors and in our automobiles, also keep people off the streets and so encourage street crime. The nuclear family, which better serves the industrial need for a highly mobile labour force, is also a family that fails to strike roots. The individual can no longer count upon the support of an extended family group and upon a community or a neighbourhood in which he is known, in which his parents and grandparents were reared. As Vance Packard observes in his *Nation of Strangers* (1972), the chances today are that in the larger cities a person does not know the names even of his immediate neighbours.

Since the foot-loose city dweller has no commitment to the vicinity in which he takes up abode, and being unable to depend upon the help, support, and loyalty of neighbours, it is not surprising that he does not wish "to become involved." He sees a crime committed on the streets, and he quickly turns the other way. He hesitates even to inform the police lest he or a member of his nuclear family be victimized. In this and in other ways to be mentioned, the unprecedented rise in street crime and violence over the last thirty years can be traced back to technological innovation.

VII. THE PERMISSIVE SOCIETY

Permissiveness defined

Let us now turn to a phenomenon that looks like the combustible product generated by high technology and affluence when combined with the commerical ethos – the so-called permissive society of the last quarter of a century. It is sometimes misleadingly regarded as an extension of "the open society" or as a manifestation of a "pluralist" society, whereas its significance is better appreciated by referring to it as the *amoral* society. Certainly the term "permissiveness" as currently used has no necessary affinity with the Western-type liberal democracy that is characterized by freedom of political debate and dissent. Instead, it is characterized by three interrelated developments:

a) most obviously, by a suspension of traditional norms of propriety and etiquette that is making the question of what is proper or improper, decent or indecent, especially with respect to sexual behaviour and to licentious entertainment and literature, increasingly a matter of individual taste and discretion;

b) by a decline in the respect for long-standing political procedures upon which all forms of self-governing societies have depended (occasionally expressed in open defiance of new legislation by interested segments of the public, and by attempts to obstruct its implementation through direct action or "confrontation"); and

c) by the fragmenting of the moral consensus.

This last development is indeed portentous. For whatever our conflicts of interest, or our political differences about ideal or better arrangements for society, effective argument is stultified if there is no longer a common set of ultimate values or beliefs to which appeal can be made in the endeavour to persuade others. I doubt whether so fragile a social artifice as a liberal democratic society can continue to endure if each individual or, rather, if each of a small proportion of the individuals comprising a society, is to be his own ultimate authority in all that touches on propriety, legitimacy, and morality.

Decadence as economic necessity

On reflection, however, this permissive society may also be viewed as a providential development by means of which a technically sophisticated economy, under institutional compulsion to expand, may continue to do so in an already affluent society. For in these circumstances, the continuous expansion of industry depends directly upon its success in whetting and enlarging the appetite of the consuming public as to enable it to engorge a burgeoning variety of new goods. A consuming public that looks as if it might eventually become satisfied with what it has, or a consuming public whose demand is restrained by traditional notions of good taste and propriety, or by firm ideas of what is right and wrong, will not serve. The required insatiability even in an age of reckless abundance can be ensured only by undermining traditional restraints, by subverting cultural norms, and by encouraging promiscuity. In all the large cities of the West, increasing numbers from all sections and classes of society, following the lead of artists, filmmakers, publishers, impresarios, free-booting "intellectuals," in their clamorous rejection of any limits to sensate experience — sometimes rationalized as joyous rejection of "Victorian guilt" — are coming to believe that "life enrichment" is to be attained simply by dedication to hedonistic pursuits.

Bear in mind that we are not talking of "decadence" as commonly understood and often associated with an effete aristocracy or pseudo-sophisticated coteries. For modern industry to continue to expand, the decadence of a minority would not suffice. Nothing less than the decadence of the consuming masses themselves is necessary. And this spreading decadence of the masses — especially the younger masses — has in it little relish of refinement or epicureanism. Nurtured on the spicey pap of television entertainment their tastes are becoming increasingly vulgar and visceral, moving toward the sadistic. True, many continue to go to church, but they act as if God is not. If they turn for guidance at all, it is not to precepts based on traditional ethics but to what they choose to call an "own ethic" — a congenial ethic to those in pursuit of "autonomous self-fulfilment." Whenever they have to justify their conduct, whether inspired by impulse or calculation, it is by reference to the strength and depth of their own private convictions. The moral touchstone in effect has become their "absolute sincerity." Alas, the appeal to "sincerity" has always been the readiest excuse for iniquity. No historian can doubt the intensity of Hitler's incandescent sincerity. And, as we know, Charles Manson killed other men because he knew "in his heart" that he was right.

Conscience vs. convictions

Convictions are one thing. Conscience is another. A conscience is moulded within an ethical matrix—in this context, an ethical matrix common to the great ecumenical religions. And it evolves through effort, through the pain of repression, through fear, through love, through example, through hope, beckoned by awakening aspiration to the good, and, perhaps, by a need to feel worthy of the grace of God. The individual conscience is not, then, an autonomous creation. It is the manifestation of man's spiritual heritage and, in settled conditions, forms part of the moral consensus by which a social order survives.

I have stated elsewhere (*The Economic Growth Debate,* 1977), as a judgement of fact, that a moral consensus that is to be enduring and effective is the product only of a general acceptance in its divine origin. A moral order, that is, can rest secure only on religious foundations. It cannot be raised on humanist principles, or on enlightened sweet reason—at all events, not so long as society continues in that corrupt state in which sinners outnumber saints, in which human weakness is more evident than human strength, and in which temptations abound.[6]

The decline of moral order and the growth of the state

The preceding two sections of this essay argued that recent technological innovation in the West has created unprecedented ecological hazards and social conflict, and that the resulting rise in public apprehension has acted to invoke increased government intervention taking form as detailed legislation and an expansion of bureaucratic power. I am now suggesting that this trend toward larger government and, therefore, less personal freedom, is sure to be reinforced by the perils attendant upon our new permissive society. Not only does the popularity of the "own ethic" concept undermine the traditional pride taken in personal rectitude, so threatening the efficient operation of industry and government. More importantly, it poses a threat to civility and order. In a society in which ideas of right and wrong become ephemeral and self-serving—in a society in which a growing number of people feel free to act on their own privately reconstituted consciences—the resulting climate of unease, edginess, anxiety, along with the community's fear of anarchy, will eventually sanction surrender to the police, and other internal security organizations, increased powers of surveillance and control.

Thus as the moral order upon which any viable civilization has to be founded is eroded in the name of personal emancipation so, in the name of security, must the state expand its powers. In effect, as repressive mechanisms internal to the individual are scrapped, repressive mechanisms external to him have to be forged. The permissive society, it may be inferred, is precursor to the totalitarian state.

VIII. EPILOGUE: THE CURSE OF PROMETHEUS

The non-neutrality of science

I end these reflections with what will doubtless pass muster for a reactionary view of scientific progress. Certainly, I maintain that science, or at any rate the spirit animating scientific enquiry, is inherently incompatible with any traditional conception of religion. I maintain further that this science has underwritten a technology that wrecks any prospect of the good life, and has capped this achievement by placing the survival of man, indeed of the planet itself, in imminent danger.

I brush aside impatiently the standard pretext that science itself is neutral; that it is left to man himself to decide whether to use the discoveries of science for benevolent or malevolent purposes. One reason for my impatience is that the products of scientific research, even when they are believed put to good uses, often result in damage or disaster, and sometimes in irremediable disaster, simply because unsuspected, perhaps unforeseeable, adverse consequences also arise from their use. As mentioned earlier, scientists just do not know the range of consequences of a growing number of new drugs, additives, synthetics, pesticides, etc. In all innocence we sprayed large parts of the earth with DDT. Later on, and notwithstanding works like Rachel Carson's *Silent Spring,* agribusiness began to use more deadly pesticides. Again, physicians in Europe took to sedating pregnant women with the new wonder drug Thalidomide, as a result of which many thousands of families are now condemned to suffer the prolonged anguish of having to rear deformed children.

Another reason for my scorn of such pretexts is that scientists also, and quite knowingly, seek to produce innovations that are unambiguously destructive. They dedicate their talents to discovering more effective means of bacteriological warfare, more paralysing gases, more powerful nuclear warheads and neutron bombs, etc. And even where there is clear choice in the use of a new method or product — as dynamite, for example, useful for blasting rock in building a highway can also be used for blowing up people, or the laser beam which can be used in industry to cut through the hardest metals can be used also as a death ray by the military or by criminals and terrorists — one can be sure that, in a world erupting with fanaticism and violence, the uses to which it will be put will often enough be largely destructive.

The spirit of science and the death of religion

I assert, finally, that the spirit of science is antithetical to, indeed subversive of, the spirit of religion. For we either believe our religion to be true, or we believe nothing. And how can we believe in God today! Once the ethos of science comes to dominate the human mind; once, that is, people come to accept that every phenomenon has a "natural" cause; that it is the duty and the destiny of science to uncover all nature's secrets; that "free inquiry" is sacred; and that all statements or beliefs, whatever their character or provenance, must yield to the test of a scientifically approved methodology — why then, all the great myths that for millennia have sustained the human spirit are effectively undermined.

In short, the sacralization of life cannot go hand-in-hand with its secularization. God becomes expendable in a science-based civilization; becomes transmuted into a metaphor — encouraged by churchmen such as Bishop Robinson. There may be exultation among humanists, among technocrats, and among the scientists themselves (apparently always on the verge of a new "break-through"). But for the ordinary mortal who prefers to believe, nay who needs to believe, but is no longer able to, the loss is irreparable. Today, the ordinary man, the man-in-the-automobile, the insatiate creature of a hyper-commercial civilization, garlanded with gadgetry, festooned with technological frou frou, is now also prone to glimpses of despair. Bereft of a sustaining faith, he struggles to repress the prospect of his journey toward the dread moment of his final and total extinction.

As Kierkegard has written: "If there were no eternal consciousness in a man, if at the foundation of all there lay only a wild seething power which, writhing with obscure passions, produced everything that is great and everything that is insignificant; if a bottomless void never satiated lay hidden beneath all — what then would life be but despair."

Science as a competitive religion

Despite its triumphs, some of us see science today in a light quite different from that in which it is wont to bask, and to discover in its monstrous proportions a character and a purpose scarcely suspected. Just how much of its self-assessment is hypocrisy and how much self-deception is difficult to determine.

Ice-cool, dispassionate, all-penetrating, all controlled, and with pious whisperings of the common good, of its ordained mission that must be fulfilled. With overspread hands, beneath the jet of holy waters, intoning its sacred right to uncover all of every stitch of nature, to chart every breathing pulse in the living universe, to capture every fluttering beat that else might escape. To expose every particle and cell to the pitiless glare of its great cormorant eye — an eye like Lucifer's possessed of a raging unquenchable lust for knowledge. And even now, heedless, it quests on "with compulsion and laborious flight" to its own destruction.

This raging spirit of science has ripped the warm mysterious darkness from the soul of the earth. It has spun its computerized web and has mantled the globe with a myriad flickering lights, electronic bleeps, battalions of grinning symbols, slowly strangling the throb of the human voice. It freezes resistance on the instant with the promise of glinting power. For this satanic science is determined to leave nothing unslit; not a sliver of flesh, nothing. Its jaws are set to crunch and to burst open every close secret of nature, every once-wondrous mystery; to scotch every flight of fancy, every source of myth and magical belief that for so long inspired hope and rejoicing in the heart of our forbears. All has now to be prised open, the temple treasures ransacked, the juice of life spilt, the earth's fragrance dispersed, and the last veils of mystery and wonder cut through, chewed to tatters, until naught remains to discover and destroy — naught but to weep alone in the cold of annihilation's waste.

It is not, then, the noble Prometheus, the darling of science, that is the hero of human adventure on earth. That legend is man's flattering unction of himself, his cosetted self-image, a legend he clings to so that he may, when the day of reckoning comes, whisper cringingly that "Oh, he did it all for the best, to ease the lot and to relieve the suffering of his fellow men." In all the tortuous record of human self-deception, there can hardly be a more superb instance — Faustian lust masquerading as dedication to the altar of truth.

Science, technology and malaise

To conclude, there is no doubt that something like alarm and dismay have begun to creep over our Western civilization. The mood of the public fluctuates, but the whiff of foreboding persists. Something serious seems to be going awry, something that transcends our current economic difficulties.

I suggest that we should be wrong to seek explanations for this malaise in capitalism *per se,* much less in the operation of the market. Explanations are to be sought, instead, in the unfolding consequences of science and technology over the last century and more especially since the end of the Second World War.

There is no need today to remind people that humanity lives precariously, close to the brink of a nuclear Armageddon. For we have, finally, learned to think of the unthinkable. The so-called balance of terror hardly looks like a stable equilibrium at this point in time. One false step, one too hasty reaction to a reckless threat, could start the conflagration. And in a world where smaller countries, currently ruled by tyrants and fanatics, will soon come to possess the means of atomic destruction, that one false step looks frighteningly close.

But even if our civilization should survive such imminent physical perils, the prospects for humanity are far from promising. Mounting public anxiety in all the countries of the Western bloc about the dangers of new technologies and their products, and about the associated upsurge of crime, is sure to augment the size and power of governments, and so reduce our personal freedoms.

For the rest, we pay dearly for our technological toys. The centrifugal forces of technical progress have sundered the filaments of the once-intricate web of custom. The pervasive sense of kinship and loyalty, of pride and propriety, the unquestioned acceptance of duties and privileges, of those mutual obligations that marked the more traditional and hierarchical society, have all but vanished. In its place we find the virtues attributable to modern economic man—the motivated man, the insatiate man, the uprooted man, the hedonistic man, the godless man, the man who acts on the principle of net advantages. What human warmth remains is generated in the main through inter-group hostilities, through perpetual political jostling, through the claims and recriminations of new ethnic minorities and self-styled liberation movements.

Thus personal relations once rooted in mutual trust are everywhere giving way today to formal contracts that render mutual trust obsolete. Even within families, just and proper treatment can no longer rely on accepted obligations or be referred to immemorial custom. Recourse is had to litigation and enforcement agencies.

As morality shrinks, legislation expands, and as the peripheral support system of formalities, courtesies and conventions – uncongenial to the pace and turnover of modern life – atrophies, whatever is needed to prevent minor frictions and conflicts is done by state regulation and central direction. Indeed, in modern Western communities, the emerging population of self-seeking atomistic units, highly mobile, highly motivated, increasingly conscience-free, can be held together as a people, as a nation, only through an expanding bureaucracy, its rulings enforced through the ultimate agency of an increasingly powerful police.

Knowledge and the fall of man

A final reflection. The human adventure just might have turned out otherwise. If one speculates, as does Lynn White, on the connection between the Judaeo-Christian religious tradition (which confers on man, as God's supreme creature, dominion over all other forms of life) and the subsequent exploratory and exploitive nature of his activity (which has extended his power over nature to an awesome degree) another route is imaginable, one that does not lead to the present impasse.

Pagan and tribal religions did not, for the most part, envisage man as the paragon of the universe, but as no more than a component part of nature, one creature among an uncountable number of different creatures, one form of life among a limitless variety. As such, the savage had a reverence not only for all life, but also for all things in nature. A tree, a spring, a rock, was not to him an inanimate object. It had a spirit of its own, a place in the universe. What a man needed from the earth for his own survival had to be taken with care, with respect, sometimes with conciliatory prayer or ceremony.[7] One had to placate the spirit within all things to ensure that one's own spirit should not be violated.

Had such an attitude toward life prevailed throughout the world, civilizations or organized communities would not have advanced very far by the lights of modern achievement. We should be inclined to refer to such communities as "static" or, worse, as "stagnant." But it would be parochial to dismiss the idea that a necessary condition for global survival is that the civilizations that emerge remain static — after advancing to some level of technology, that is, remaining in a steady state. A dynamic civilization — dynamic in the technological sense, that is — looks to be inherently unstable. It is impelled ever onward to a stage where eventually it cannot draw back from the precipice — even, as now, when the precipice comes into view.

We are told in the Scriptures that "the love of money is the root of all evil." And this is surely so in the diurnal drama of human affairs. But, in today's global context, and thinking poignantly of the small planet earth that is man's heritage, and his only refuge in a dark, cold, and inhospitable universe, it is surely the love of *knowledge,* of scientific knowledge, that is the root of all evil — and the seed of his self-destruction.

NOTES

1. The Reverend Sidney Smith, one of the founders and editors of the *Edinburgh Review,* whose satirical pen advanced the cause of reform in Britain, was also something of a *bon vivant* and one of the most celebrated wits of his day. A frequent visitor at the sumptuous gatherings of the great Whig houses, he was a particular friend of Lord and Lady Holland.

   Although Sidney was ordained deacon in 1794, he felt at the time no calling for the Church. Indeed, he wished to follow his elder brother in a career at the bar, but his father refused to finance his legal training.

2. See the article, "Obscenity and Maturity" in *The Sunday Times* (December 14, 1969) by Dr. John Robinson (formerly Bishop of Woolwich) which by any standards is a model of vacuity, ambiguity, and inconclusiveness.

3. The damage wont to be associated with the exposure of workers to a contaminating atmosphere is now held to be undervalued as evidence accumulates to show that exposure can result not only from inhalation but also from absorption through the skin and the digestive organs.

4. Food is the most complex part of the environment to which the individual is exposed. We are discovering that, in addition to nutrients, foods contain a large number of trace elements supplemented today by chemical additives, contaminants, and other substances arising from the application of modern technology such as pesticides, animal drug residues, and

migrants from packaging. In recent years, the FDA has begun to adopt methods designed to incorporate risk-assessment into decisions for certain classes of food, and additional legislation may be anticipated.

5. The cumulative effect of fluorocarbons (from spray cans) and nitrogen oxide gases in dissipating the earth's protective ozone mantel would be one of such instances — except that few scientists today would dismiss this possibility as negligible.

6. There is, of course, no lack of instances in the records of history of religious corruption, religious fanaticism, and religious persecution. Yet it should not be necessary to remark in such an essay that the value of religion to humanity cannot be dismissed merely because of the abuses to which it has frequently been put.

Perspective requires that a distinction be drawn between the inspiring spirit and purpose of an institution, and the improper uses to which it invariably lends itself; a distinction between the office and what it stands for on the one hand, and on the other, the behaviour of the incumbent himself.

No man was more acutely aware of ecclesiastic intrigue, bigotry, and corruption, than was Lord Acton, the great Roman Catholic historian of liberty. But he ever kept in mind the distinction between the church authorities and the Authority of the Church.

As I remarked in my *Costs of Economic Growth* (1967), an institution disposing of the enormous wealth, power, and patronage, of the Church, is a magnet for opportunism, attracting to its service men of worldly ambition. It is no cause for wonder, that good men could be inflamed to battle under the banner of God when, in fact, the stakes were in the main temporal and material.

Who can say whether more crimes against humanity have been committed in the name of God (so breaking the Third Commandment), in the name of liberty, in the name of fraternity, in the name of justice — or in the name of any other virtuous attribute when it is tied to a slogan and brandished by a revolutionary movement inspired by an all-sweeping ideology!

For all the dark pages in the history of religion, I affirm my statement in the text that faith in a benevolent Diety is a necessary condition for the good life inasmuch as — for ordinary mortals at least — such a faith is the ultimate source of legitimacy for a society's morality and sense of right without which it loses its identity and cohesion.

7. In Carlos Castaneda's *Journey to Ixtlan,* Don Juan who lays a net to trap birds for a meal succeeds in catching six of them. To the consternation of the author, however, he lets four birds free, since the two remaining would suffice to remove their hunger: one does not take the life of a creature simply to gorge oneself.

Comment

David Friedman

I. MINOR DISAGREEMENTS: A BRIEF CATALOGUE

I disagree with many of the details of Professor Mishan's paper. One important example is his refusal to accept, as a working approximation, Marshall's rule for welfare comparisons (compare net advantage measured by money equivalent unless you have good reason to believe that you know whose marginal utility for income is higher[1]). Mishan writes as if we have no grounds for an opinion as to whether the injury to consumers produced by tariffs and other forms of protection outweighs the advantage to producers. Marshall's rule combined with the conventional assumption of stable utility functions implies that tariffs have a net welfare cost. The conclusion may be wrong, but it has some basis; Mishan's grounds for believing the opposite conclusion seem to be nothing more than an attempt to guess the utility functions of a hundred million strangers, few of them much like him.

Another and less important point I would disagree with is his description of the problems associated with ignorance about private goods (drugs, food additives) as a spillover effect. If, of course, utility functions are strongly interdependent, so that you are made miserable by side-effects experienced by other people, *that* is a spillover, but such spillovers have no particular connection with modern technology; people have been claiming a benevolent interest in others as a justification for making their decisions for them for some millenia now.

Finally, to end the (partial) catalogue of inessential disagreements, I find Mishan's suggestion that permissiveness is necessary to provide markets for "a technically sophisticated economy, under institutional compulsion to expand" not merely misguided but silly; pornography is not a major component of the GNP and the traditionally religious are not, so far as I know, any more inclined to live far below their income than the rest of us. An expanding economy can expand by producing safer cars, better schooling, or improved videotapes of sermons or "Hamlet"; insofar as it produces vibrators and video games instead that reflects a divergence between Mishan's tastes (with regard at least to what he wants others to consume) and those of the market, not some inevitable logic of growth.

While I disagree with Mishan on all of these points, none of them is essential to his argument. Given the existence of spillovers and the possibility of changing tastes, spontaneous change, even in a market society, is not necessarily improvement. That is his essential point, and I agree with it. The opinion that human welfare in the technologically advanced societies is declining and can be expected to continue to do so is defensible; I will devote the first section of this comment to some of my reasons for believing it false. The second section will consider Mishan's thesis that the essential problem is the conflict between religion and science, and the third an alternative view of what is going on.

II.   ARE WE GOING TO HELL IN A HANDBASKET?

> The annual produce of the land and labour of England, for example, is certainly much greater than it was, a little more than a century ago, at the restoration of Charles II. Though, at present, few people, I believe, doubt of this, yet during this period, five years have seldom passed away in which some book or pamphlet has not been published, written too with such abilities as to gain some authority with the public, and pretending to demonstrate that the wealth of the nation was fast declining, that the country was depopulated, agriculture neglected, manufactures decaying, and trade undone. Nor have these publications been all party pamphlets, the wretched offspring of falsehood and venality. Many have been written by very candid and very intelligent people; who wrote nothing but what they believed and for no other reason but because they believed it.[2]
>
> Adam Smith

Is the gloomy view that Mishan (and others) hold of the present state of the world merely the current version of the phenomenon mentioned by Smith, updated to explain away statistics of real income by arguing that only the *unmeasurable* components of welfare are declining, or is it an accurate perception of reality? While I believe there are serious problems with the modern world, I incline to the former conjecture. Given the nature of Mishan's argument, statistics about improved consumption bundles and the like are obviously ruled out of court. My evidence is instead the observed behaviour of people with regard to their choices of where and how to live. While we cannot each independently choose a separate preferred bundle of environmental and private goods, we can and do choose among a considerable variety of alternative bundles. If Mishan is correct, we would expect people living in those areas of the country least affected by urban sprawl, pollution, and the manifold ills of modern life to stay there, and others to try to emulate their good fortune by abandoning the "reckless abundance" in which they live and returning to the farms and small towns of the recent past. This is precisely the doctrine preached in the pages of "Mother Earth"; my impression is that while a few follow it (and many more subscribe in order to combine the pleasures of Sodom and Gomorrah with the vicarious enjoyment of a more bucolic sort of paradise), they continue to be enormously outnumbered by those moving the other way. The same seems to be true in the developing countries, where a sizable fraction of the rural population has moved into urban slums, apparently because, however bad they may be, they are better than the countryside.

It is, of course, possible to argue that all of this is experimental error. The peasants pour into the city because they have been misled by tales of golden sidewalks (tales told, presumably, by relatives who migrated the year before) or because, in each case, some special circumstance of demography or land tenure has recently ruined the countryside. The inhabitants of American cities have been permanently ruined, their taste buds made incapable of appreciating the simple life and their minds habituated to a diet of vicarious violence (unlike, one presumes, the pacific audiences who put the *Iliad* and the *Chanson de Roland* at the top of contemporary Neilson ratings); they can no longer return to their paradise forever lost.

It may also, and more plausibly, be argued that while change has until recently been improvement, the trend has now reversed and migration patterns will soon begin to reflect the change. To make this case, however, one must argue that the decline so far has been small, which is hardly consistent with the tone of Mishan's article. I prefer to accept the revealed preference of those best able to compare alternative sorts of life, and to suspect that the popularity of the simple and the past reflects the combined effect of the attractions of distance and the superiority of remembered youth to actual age.

III. IN THIS CORNER SCIENCE...

In Mishan's view, the essential source of the problems of our society is the conflict between Science, with its insatiable pursuit of truth, and Religion. This raises at the outset an interesting question; does Mishan believe that Religion (or at least some religion) is true? If so then Science can be expected (save for occasional mistakes) to provide confirmation, supporting rather than threatening the myths on which a society is built. I conclude that Mishan regards Religion as a useful lie, and I will discuss his position on that assumption.

I agree with Mishan that both private virtue and a considerable degree of moral consensus are useful and may be essential. I disagree with his (apparent) belief that both must depend on false beliefs about physical reality—such as the belief that the Bible is literal truth. Societies have existed for long periods of time without such support. Consider Confucianism, a "religion" named, appropriately, after a moral philosopher rather than a god, or classical paganism which, as Chesterton persuasively argued,[3] was regarded by its adherents as an edifying and aesthetic myth, not a description of the real world.

There are three sorts of explanations for why people believe normative propositions—sociological (they have been trained to do so), socio-biological (ethical behaviour proved reproductively useful and was therefore selected for) or metaphysical (because normative propositions are true). None of the three seems to require that the normative propositions have positive support. As a matter of simple logic, the existence of an omnipotent creator does not imply that we should do what he wants; he might (as has occasionally been asserted) be the Devil. If one is able to take it on faith that certain acts are virtuous because God wills them, why should not another one be equally able to take it on faith that the acts are virtuous whether or not there is a God to will them? If one believes that acts are virtuous because mommy and daddy and all the neighbours say so, surely that is a Nash equilibrium whether or not all concerned also believe in Noah's flood.

IV. BUT IT MIGHT BE A LONG TUNNEL

The incidental consequences of "progress"

The reader, and even more the subject of these comments, may by now have concluded that I believe everything is for the best in this best of all possible worlds. If so he is mistaken. The modern world suffers from serious problems, some of which may prove fatal. What I disagree with is Mishan's vision of a world driven to destruction by the inevitable implications of scientific and technological progress. The modern world suffers from (at least) three sorts of problems. First, there are those problems which happen to occur here and now but might happen, and have happened, in other times and places. An obvious example is the decline of *laissez-faire* and the growth of the centralized state. Henri Pirenne argues somewhere that there is an alternation between strong and weak government going back to about the eleventh century, with the cycle taking about two hundred years to complete itself. Whether or not this is the case, one can observe major changes towards and then away from individual freedom in recent centuries, hence it seems unreasonable to regard state power as an essentially modern problem.

It is, however, a problem that explains many of the problems of the modern world, in particular militarism, crime, and poor education. Schooling and law enforcement are virtual government monopolies, hence it is not surprising that both are done badly. Furthermore, the ideological trends that have accompanied and supported the drift towards socialism undercut the legitimacy of private property; if poverty is the fault of the rich, and if "making it" by hard work is an impossible and unworthy goal, then why not a little private redistribution in one's own direction?

The second category of modern problems consists of those which result from particular—one might almost say accidental—features of modern technology. The obvious example is the enormous power of offensive weapons, both absolutely and in comparison to defensive weapons. This poses a very real risk, but one which, large though it is, can be and frequently is exaggerated. While it is now technically possible to annihilate the human race, it is not clear to what extent that is a new development; it has been possible to kill everyone, one at a time, for some thousands of years. More realistically, the consequences of a thermonuclear war fought with the objective (achievable or not) of victory rather than mutual annihilation would be grim, but not unprecedented; the death toll in the belligerent nations would presumably be comparable to that resulting from the great plague or the thirty years war (about half the population); the most obvious difference is that it would take a few days instead of a few decades, which some might consider an improvement.

Another consequence of modern technology (and population) is the increased scale of human activity and its effects; while current warnings of imminent catastrophe do not seem solidly based, the size of what we can now do does imply potential threats. It also implies potential solutions; if our technology is advanced enough to heat the earth, it is also advanced enough to deliberately raise the earth's albedo and cool it. While we may be depleting low cost sources of raw materials, we are also becoming rich enough to mine lower quality ores and skillful enough to bring minerals in from the asteroid belt. Similarly with energy. The most serious problem with such developments, and one which Mishan quite properly emphasizes, is that increasing scale tends to lead to increasing problems of interdependence. Even if we are capable of raising the earth's albedo, who would pay for it, given the wide dispersion of benefits?

Other problems in the same general category involve the effects of modern technology on the balance of power between state and individual. Here the effects go in both directions, so that it is hard to estimate the net result. The development of computers makes it easier for a government to keep track of its citizens, but it also greatly improves the possibilities for decentralized forms of organization, competing information nets, etc. — especially now that a good small computer costs considerably less than a car. Developments in military technology are equally ambiguous; weapons of mass destruction in the hands of central governments might prove useful for suppressing secessionist movements but are not of much use to the police. At the same time, increasing wealth and developments such as hand held anti-tank weapons, combined with the difficulty of preventing arms smuggling in a world with extensive trade, seem to have reduced some of the advantages that governments traditionally have over their citizens. Trade and interdependence also, and perhaps more significantly, make it more difficult than it used to be for a government to control the movements and information sources of its citizens.

So far, the sorts of problems I have discussed (save perhaps for increased interdependence) are accidental, not essential, consequences of progress. The final set of problems are of a different sort; they are the problems associated not with a particular sort of technology but with change.

The costs of change

In any society, a great deal of capital exists in the form of information about how to live. Much of it involves private decisions — at what age to marry, how to spread income earning and child bearing decisions across a lifetime, and the like. Some of it involves interactions among many people, and consists in sets of mutual expectations, Nash equilibria, elaborate dances depending on each person knowing his place and his steps. As a society changes, much of that information becomes obsolete. To the extent that people have the option of "staying in the boondocks" where the old expectations are still valid, or doing without the new technological improvements that make old patterns of life obsolete, their observed failure to do so implies that the changes bring net advantage, even if we take account of the cost of learning to live with them. To the extent that individuals cannot opt out no such conclusion holds; an obvious example is the producer whose customers no longer want to buy what he wants to sell. Even in this case, it is worth remembering that the producer's desire to continue in his old path will be reflected in his willingness to do his sort of work for a lower income than he requires to change over to something else; it is only if, after allowing for that, consumers still prefer the new product, that he will choose to "scrap" his informational capital.

It seems to me that the problems which Mishan attributes to the inevitable march of scientific progress are mostly of this sort. Informational capital of many different sorts has been rendered obsolete. Both producers and consumers are inclined to believe that what was done last decade cannot be done this decade. If the myths of the past were based on religions whose factual assertions have been refuted by modern science, then modern science is the implacable enemy of myth, and hence of mankind. If the family structure of the recent past depended on a technology of household production which is now obsolete, then the family is done forever.

I see little basis for this pessimistic view. When Aquinas incorporated Aristotelian physics into Catholicism, Aristotelian physics really was the latest thing going, and similarly with Ptolemaic astronomy. Both, as it happens, are false, along with traditional views about the origin of mankind and the creation of the earth. Sects which fail to acknowledge that are likely to have a hard time. There is no obvious reason why religions cannot adapt their doctrines to modern ideas, nor why, if they fail to do so, new religions cannot develop to replace them.[4] I find it hard to see any necessary connection between inspiring myths and false facts.

Similarly for the "breakdown" of the family. The pattern we have come to consider normal depended on a society where being a housewife was a full-time job. Falling infant mortality, improved technology in household production, and the increased division of labour, which moved a lot of production out of the household, has made that particular specialization obsolete, save for the minority of mothers who wish to produce a large number of children. Other developments have undercut the foundations of the "extended" family: alternative forms of old age insurance, the development of ownership patterns not linked to kinship, increased mobility, and the like. These changes have not eliminated wants, they have merely made obsolete certain ways of satisfying them. People still want affection, stability, company, help in child rearing, and the like. My impression is that new ways of providing for these wants are developing, or perhaps that technologies which coexisted with the traditional family are now in part replacing it. The example which comes immediately to mind is the way in which the extended family is replaced by, at the small end, "artificial families," groups of friends who interact as if they were relatives, and at the large end by groups of people united by common interests—bridge players, science-fiction fans, libertarians, creative anachronists, to take only those groups with which I have had some contact. These provide an effective substitute for the very extended family; instead of locating a distant relative in the city you have just moved to, you get in touch with a fellow member of such an interest group, a friend or a friend of a friend, and are provided with a place to stay while you find yourself an apartment and a connection to some part of the local society.

How fast such institutions will develop, and how successfully they will replace traditional forms, I do not know. There are good reasons to believe that information is produced suboptimally, given the difficulty of enforcing property rights in it. On the other hand, it is produced; human institutions have adapted to changing circumstances in the past, and can be expected to continue to do so. The problem is especially difficult when what is to be produced is a pattern of mutual expectations; it is simplified by the existence of numerous subsocieties, geographical and otherwise, within which such patterns can evolve before trying out for the big time.

V. CONCLUSION

Mishan's paper paints a colourful picture of a world rolling rapidly towards the precipice, driven by the inevitable consequences of the scientist's thirst for knowledge. It is a moving and paradoxical vision. I think the truth is more complicated and less grim. There are a number of things wrong with modern society. Some, I believe, are consequences of political facts which could be changed; some are consequences of the particular nature of modern technology. Many of the problems are consequences of changes to which social institutions have not yet adjusted. It is quite likely that some of these problems will kill large numbers of people, as such problems have in the past; it is certain that some of them will make — indeed are making — many human lives less happy and less productive than they might have been.

Perhaps we will wipe ourselves out in spasm war or ecological catastrophe; perhaps, as a character in one of Heinlein's novels suggests, the rats are the second team, kept around in case mankind blows the game. All that is possible, but there is little reason to think it inevitable. What Mishan has really demonstrated is not our condition but his talent — as a myth maker. It is a scarce talent, and one which could prove useful in the next few decades. Unfortunately, the particular myth he has created, while effective as a work of art, seems to have limited potential as a way of making life more meaningful or providing an imaginative foundation for moral philosophy.

NOTES

1. Alfred Marshall, *The Principles of Economics,* (fourth edition: 1898) Book III, Chapter VI 4.

2. Adam Smith, *An Inquiry Into the Nature and Causes of the Wealth of Nations.* Book II, chapter 3. 1937.

3. G. K. Chesterton, *The Everlasting Man.* 1925.

4. One interesting place to look for the birth of new myths is in science fiction, an art form which requires for its success the portrayal of lives of purpose and dignity within the context of a scientific worldview.

Comment

Kenneth G. Elzinga

Getting a grip on Professor Mishan

In reading Professor Ezra Mishan's paper, "Religion, Culture and Technology," I was reminded both of an event at a country fair and a famous economist.

The country fair event is the greased pig contest, where a young swine is coated with a harmless lubricant, such as vaseline or lard, and set loose among a group of eager contestants who must catch and hold the beast in order to win the prize. The combination of the pig's slipperiness and its unexpected strength and speed make the assignment a difficult one.

Professor Mishan's paper, like the greased pig, is difficult to get a handle on. Its contents slip quickly from criticizing theological liberalism in the Church of England to decrying consumer fickleness to expressions of shock at today's standards of sexual morality to grave concerns about the negative externalities of modern corporations, and much more.

The economist that came to mind in reading the Mishan paper is John Kenneth Galbraith. The more I read, the more I saw a similarity between the two gentlemen — except Mishan, as I shall explain more fully, has a far different prognosis of the future. The formula for concocting Mishan's paper is simple enough: you begin by mixing one part Galbraith with one part eschatological despair. This formula is a useful one for understanding writings of Professor Mishan other than this one; but, of course, he is much more than this simple formula.

Those of us who have read portions of Professor Mishan's output know that his technical credentials as an economic theorist are very solid. We do not look to Professor Galbraith, whose intellectual roots are sunk deep in Veblen, Berle and Means, for technical contributions to economic theory. But from Mishan, who has roots in Marshall and Pigou, we expect and benefit from work such as his essays on welfare economics. Perhaps because of his technical skills, his work, unlike doomsday writers of a journalistic stripe, is read seriously. But while I find this paper engaging, I also find it slippery and at times misdirected.

Mishan and the dependence effect

What is the Galbraith element in Mishan? Narrowly speaking, it is his adoption of Galbraith's dependence effect.[1] Broadly speaking, it is their shared antimarket mentality. Let me take each up in turn.

Central to Mishan's paper is his reliance on the dependence effect. Mishan's reference to consumer fickleness and the impulse buying that unsatisfactorily ministers to inconsequential wants is straight Galbraith. A current example of this phenomenon is the extraordinary growth in demand for a branded product of the Hershey Company. Stocks of this candy, called Reese's Pieces, cannot be maintained because it was the candy of choice of the space creature E.T. in the contemporary and immensely popular movie of that name (that brand having been selected for E.T.'s diet because it was the favorite candy of the son of Universal executive Steven Adler). Mishan, like Galbraith, would see this craze as episodic of the free enterprise system regularly moving scarce resources into particular markets not because their use there is superior or important in any intrinsic manner (the way a sturdy hoe is superior to a plastic rake for weeding a garden) but rather as the result of unthinking responses by consumers to corporate and media stimuli over which they, the consumers, have little control.

Mishan as a Galbraithian

This, as I say, is straight Galbraith. But it is not pure Galbraith. In this paper, as he has elsewhere, Mishan describes an additional implication of the anticonsumer-sovereignty doctrine, one not contained in the Galbraith litany. Mishan argues that the costs to workers and their families who are dislocated by shifts in consumer's preferences (of the Reese's Pieces sort) should be weighed in balancing the benefits to consumers of unfettered markets. But who does this balancing? Thorstein Veblen drew a sharp distinction between what he called the technological and the ceremonial, and would have argued, with Mishan, that imposing dislocation costs upon workers so that additional ceremonial goods could be produced was poor public policy—but to produce more technological goods was a social benefit. The market system, Veblen claimed (and Mishan would agree) produced too many ceremonial goods.

Frank Knight dismissed this dichotomy, in a review of Veblen, arguing that if Veblen could inform us how to distinguish unambiguously between ceremonial and technological activities, then his contribution would indeed have constituted a *tour de force*. Short of this, it comes to a value judgement about which no man's voice should be loud.

In addition to the specifics of the dependence effect, Mishan adopts Galbraith's more general antimarket mentality. Surely it is with tongue in cheek that Mishan writes that no one more than he would welcome a contraction of government. Galbraith and Mishan perceive enormous efficiency and equity faults in the market system; both can restrain their enthusiasm for the tastes expressed in the marketplace; the two are equally disconcerted by the negative externalities of modern industry; each sees government as necessary to restrain and correct in these areas. But whereas Galbraith welcomes the intrusion of the state, Mishan broods over it, predicting that the expanded role for the state will not produce economic salvation.

Mishan's eschatological despair

This brooding brings us to the second element in my formula: Mishan's eschatological despair. With government-as-redeemer a delusion, and the market-as-redeemer argued to be deficient, Mishan (unlike Galbraith) perceives himself as without a satisfactory social mechanism to adopt or propose (except for a veiled reference to pantheism at the end of his paper). And this produces the eschatological despair, the doomsday scenario, that is so different from conventional liberal dogma about the merits of state versus market.

What is the core of this paper's theme of despair? If I have caught the thesis of the paper, it is that modern technology (the byproduct of modern science) deleteriously, even tragically, alters our economic lifestyles by changing the "attributes, beliefs, and aspirations of the members of society."[2] The title of Mishan's paper is worth recalling at this point: it is Religion, Culture and Technology. The three nouns in the title can be rearranged to depict the sequence of Mishan's thesis as follows: technology determines (adversely) our culture, and religion is too anemic to prevent the deterioration. It too has been swamped by the onslaught of technology/science.

Let us all concede at the outset that many technological inventions have caused and will cause great social mischief and exacerbate the negative consequences of immoral behaviour. But the effects manifested in the breakdown in Western society are more complex in their causes than simply applied science. For example, the published and manufactured pornographic materials that Mishan condemns and uses to illustrate his thesis were technologically available well before the current level of supply. The printing technology and publishing technology that are predicates to the books and magazines he decries have long been known (and used for other purposes). The level of engineering competence to produce and manufacture vibrators has, I assert, also been long known. Nothing is more destructive of the health and vitality of young people today than drug abuse and addiction. Yet the technology to produce destructive drugs has been in existence for centuries. But there was not at an earlier time the demand for these products now extant. We must look elsewhere than science and technology as the cause of their demand. Professor Mishan's sequence must be revised.

Science and religion

Mishan claims specifically that science has been the undoing of religion. If all Mishan means is that advances in science have made belief in God more difficult, this is no doubt true for some. But the claim could also be made with great force that advances in literature or the arts or music, (not to mention the social science of psychology) have made belief in God more difficult for others.[3] Mishan's assertion that "science is incompatible with religion" is simply incorrect and represents a truncated view of science. Science is arguably based upon and dependent upon the view of God's character that is Judeo-Christian. In the Western world, pioneers in science saw a distinction between their creator and the created order. It was fundamental to them that God made the earth and all that is within it, but his Being stood apart from his creation. Because God is not creation, man can examine creation: indeed there is a biblical mandate to do so. The fall not only breached man's relationship with God but also man's relationship with nature, because nature also became fallen. The Genesis mandate is to subdue and redeem a fallen nature. Science lagged in the East partly because an investigation into nature would be construed as looking into God himself, and Eastern religions give no mandate to do this.

If science stands counter to all religion, how can Professor Mishan explain the deep religious convictions held by many who were instrumental in the formation of modern science? How would he account for the profound religious beliefs held by Pascal, Maxwell, Newton and Faraday? And this is not only a phenomenon of the past. At major universities and research centres today, in searching for believers in God, one is better advised to visit the engineering schools and departments of natural science than departments in the humanities and social sciences. A chemist is more likely to have and practice a religious faith in God than a sociologist.

Mishan diminishes and underestimates the benefits of modern science. Most of us, or at least a goodly proportion of us, would not be present even to address the subject of this conference had medical science remained at its turn-of-the-century level.[4] As for the non-medical benefits that the technology of market economies have made possible, Mishan, as academician, may be unaware of the mechanical devices that have freed women from chores that once took up most of their day, and have freed workers from types of labour that were both dangerous and extraordinarily arduous. Indeed, as Mishan reminisces about the joys of gathering wood and warming to a log fire, I wonder if he is unaware of the recent emergence of what is now a semi-major industry in the United States. Almost half of the families I know have wood stoves, as supplements to central heating systems, and regularly engage in the task, with varying degrees of enthusiasm to be sure, of splitting or stacking wood, and are warmed by the operation of this old but now contemporary device.

Prospects for hope

I share three convictions with Mishan. The first is that a market system will function far more efficiently and beneficently if those transacting in it have firmly entrenched Judeo-Christian norms. As my colleague Roland McKean has explained, if individuals are not respecters of property and practitioners of courtesy, the delineation of property rights and the voluntary exchange of property is hindered significantly.[5] Secondly (and with somewhat less confidence) I believe that Mishan is correct when he states that a moral order can rest only on the acceptance of divine origins, i.e. religious foundations. And I concur in his prediction that moral decline will only increase society's demand for greater powers of the state over economic affairs. But I do not concur in the determinism of his counsel of despair. He overlooks the evidence of the redeeming work of the church in the economic fabric of society. And more fundamentally, he does not understand that there is nothing in the warp and woof of technological advance that must ineluctably deter a religious revival. The great awakening in the United States did not, after all, occur at a time of technological retreat, nor was it scientific advances that quenched it.

Mishan cannot anticipate religious revival, as much as he would welcome and benefit from it, because, if I read him correctly, religion is myth and myths cannot succeed in the face of modern science. But believers in divine providence are not constrained to despair in this manner. They believe that God, the creator and sustainer of the universe, may act, as they believe He has done in the past, to prosper a land spiritually and economically. As the Scriptures promise:

> If my people, which are called by my name, shall
> humble themselves, and pray, and seek my face,
> and turn from their wicked ways; then will I hear
> from heaven, and will forgive their sin, and will
> heal their land. (II Chronicles 7:14)

Within the Christian church today, there is a remnant of people who endeavour to lean against modern culture, seeking to be *in* the world but not *of* the world. To Mishan, they may appear as ordinary people—dentists, masons, schoolteachers, housewives, clerks, and attorneys—but they endeavour to take their signals from biblical norms and not modern culture. Such individuals, in their family and charitable and ministerial patterns, are not the subject of media focus and consequently the attention they receive (and seek, for that matter) is small.[6] Their choice of religious fellowship is not akin to the choice of a social club and they do not dislocate themselves and their families in response to the wealth maximizing dictates of a free market— though they rejoice in the religious liberties afforded them by the free market.

Professor Mishan portrays science as the "arch enemy of religion." Note that practitioners of what was once called "vital religion" do not share his fear of science (except, in some circles, with regard to the Darwinian strain of evolution theory), but, if they fear the academy at all, are more afraid of the teachings of the softer disciplines.

The capacity for redemption

I can speak with most familiarity of evangelical Christianity. And where evangelicals would part company with Mishan is his implicit denial for the potential redemption for all areas of human expression, scientific and non-scientific. Mishan implies that our knowledge of the material precludes our belief in the religious. Evangelicals believe that man was not created with the design of living on two inseparable levels: the religious and the material. What man does with art, literature, music and science was intended to be exercised under an understanding of God's sovereignty that stretched beyond just worship and morals, narrowly defined. As Saint Paul instructed followers of Christ:

> And whatever you do by word or deed, do it all in
> the name of the Lord Jesus, through whom you are
> offering thanks to God the Father. (Colossians,
> 3:17)

The theme of this conference is the morality of the market. Mishan concludes that moralists who criticize capitalism for the malaise in the West are misdirected. With this I agree.[7] But he, in my judgement, underestimates the extent to which professionals in the Protestant, Catholic and Jewish faiths are hostile to capitalism and sympathetic to socialism (in both senses that he uses the term socialism). Even among evangelical Christians, where free enterprise leanings have historically been very strong, there is a public questioning and reexamination of the merits of the market economy.

That the malaise in the West is explained by "the unfolding consequences of science and technology over the last century" is an assertion of Mishan's I greet skeptically. The malaise is much more complex in its origins than "science and technology" and has been led by developments in philosophy, literature and the arts, as well as the social sciences. Surely moral relativism, and the abandonment of absolutes in the realm of ethics, have done more to promote libertine and covetous behaviour than the invention of the airplane or the electric razor.[8] At very root, and at a time before today's scientific and technological attainments could ever have been anticipated, this hypothesis for the malaise Mishan eloquently describes was offered by the prophet Jeremiah:

The heart is deceitful above all things, and desperately wicked:
who can know it? (17:9)

NOTES

1. As Galbraith perceives most consumer preferences, "wants are increasingly created by the process by which they are satisfied." See *The Affluent Society,* 1958, p. 158. For a concise summary and critique of the dependence effect, see William Breit and Roger L. Ransom, *The Academic Scribblers* (2nd. ed. 1982) pp. 169–176 and the references therein.

2. There is a technological determinism in Mishan's thesis that is, of course, very different from that of the Marxists and American Institutionalists, both of whom studied technology in far more detail than neoclassical economists (and welcomed its advance).

3. See Francis A. Schaeffer, *The God Who Is There* (1968) Sections I and II on this point.

4. Sir James Simpson, whose scientific research on anesthetics, has helped relieve immeasurable amounts of pain, was asked which of his discoveries he ranked as most important. Never perceiving a contradiction or tension between his chemistry and his theology, he responded, "The greatest discovery I have ever made is that I am a sinner, and that Jesus is Savior."

5. See his "Some Economic Aspects of Ethical-Behavioural Codes," 27 *Political Studies* 251 (1979).

6. Even the Church of England, which receives a scathing attack from Mishan in his prologue, is not the caricature of theological liberalism and pastoral anemia that he describes. Donald Coggan, Archbishop of Cantebury from 1974–1980, was in that role evangelical in doctrine with orthodox beliefs about the inspiration of the Bible and the centrality of preaching. In his book *On Preaching,* he claimed that for fifty years he was "under the joyful tyranny of being a minister of the Word."

7. See my "The Demise of Capitalism and the Christian's Response," *Christianity Today,* July 7, 1972.

8. Although the inventor of the electric toothbrush may have much to answer for.

Reply

Ezra J. Mishan

The pig triumphant

Although Ken Elzinga finds that attempts to grasp the import of my paper are rather like trying to catch a greasy pig, I have the impression that he thinks he has, after all, managed to catch the beast by the ears while his co-critic appears to have enjoyed himself by vigorously tweaking the pig's tail.[1] With all respect to their efforts, however, I do not think the pig has suffered much discomfort.

Admittedly, mine was a long paper, and as Ken Elzinga truly reports, I "underestimate the benefits of modern science." This however is to be regarded as my considered opinion and not, as implied in his context, the error of a cloistered academic who has not yet noticed the existence of such modern conveniences as the washing machine and the bulldozer, to say nothing of medical advances. I did, after all, make handsome concessions to the marvels of technology in my propositions 2 to 4.

Let me now address myself, first, to five strictures on my paper common to both my critics, following which I deal briefly with three issues raised by David Friedman.

Sexual gadgetry and popular taste

Not surprisingly, both have siezed on my mention of the space devoted to advertising sexual gadgetry. Elzinga assumes I was shocked. I assure him that I am beyond being shocked by anything today — though I might, momentarily, lose my balance if I overheard a Chicago economist voicing dissatisfaction with competitive market mechanisms. Elzinga informs me that vibrator-technology has long been known. But the productive technology that makes these "goods," and others, available to the mass market today was *not* my point. The example is used to illustrate a more general point: that it is through technological advance that mass affluence is created, and to maintain that advance the minds of the mass of people need to be disoriented (with the help of the mass media). A discriminating and fastidious public would threaten an economy that expands by trivial and tasteless innovation.

David Friedman, on the other hand, interprets my remarks as reflecting a divergence between my tastes and those of the market. While this is true, it is not enough to score with, for two reasons: (a) because a misleading impression might be conveyed that I am overruled by the "evidence" and ought rightly to hold my peace and (b) more important, because as an aspect of the new permissiveness, the implications for freedom have to be taken very seriously. Let me elaborate each in turn:

(a) To use an analogy, his illustrious father, Milton Friedman, believes in Western democracy. It does not follow, however, that he also approves of all political decisions—else he would approve of tariffs, farm price supports, government regulatory agencies, and so on. Milton Friedman continually opposes such democratically-enacted legislation because he believes that voters are ill-informed and do not foresee the range of consequences entailed by such legislation.

If I believe in competitive markets but, at the same time, I do not approve of all outcomes, it is for much the same reason: consumers are often ill-informed also and cannot always be expected to foresee the consequences of their purchases on their own lives, much less on the character and welfare of society as a whole.

I will go further. After Hitler had been democratically voted into office in 1933, he would almost certainly have won election in any subsequent year up to 1944. Bearing this in mind, Milton Friedman might well agree that, as a judgement of fact, in addition to the ill-informed, there were many Germans during those years ready to vote for Hitler and the regime who could foresee the immediate consequences such as the persecution of Jewish citizens, the conquering of other nations and enslaving their populations. Yet their characters being corrupted by the regime, they rejoiced in the prospect.

Surely, then, there is nothing presumptuous about a man who takes issue sometimes with the changing character and morals not only of voters but of consumers also—and, of course, seeks to discover the factors operating to promote their promiscuity.

As for (b) the issue is not that of Mishan versus the libertines. It is the perils of permissiveness, perils that arise not merely from an *erosion* of the ethical consensus (in particular, the cult of the "own ethic" with its concomitant contempt of conventional morality and the rule of law) but also from a *fragmentation* of that consensus — worse, a fragmentation into mutually antagonistic and fanatical groupings which can be contained only by increased political repression.[2]

The spirit of science vs. the spirit of religion

Both my critics take me to task for arguing that science is irreconcilable with the traditional world religions. Elzinga maintains stoutly that I am wrong and mentions a number of great men (between the seventeenth and nineteenth centuries) who could be fairly described as believers. If I thought it relevant, I could produce a list of prominent personalities who were or are agnostics and atheists, including a few Anglican prelates.

We can agree that, as a matter of historical fact, the Church has absorbed many of the findings of science. As David Friedman says "Aquinas incorporated Aristotelian physics into Catholicism." For that matter, the Church might have stomached Newton also. But certainly the Catholic church did not rejoice at the discoveries of Copernicus and Galileo. Nor did the Church of England in the nineteenth century evince any enthusiasm for *The Origin of Species,* or the *Descent of Man.*

Religious explanations of the physical universe that were almost universally accepted in the Middle Ages have gradually been abandoned, in contrast to the explanations offered by science which have continued to gain ground. According to the Bible, the creation of the world took place about 6,000 years ago. According to science, the earth was born about 10 billion years ago. True, there are some churches who still stand by the literal story of the Bible. Others, including the Church of England, may be considered as "moving with the times" inasmuch as they refrain from publicly challenging findings of science that can reasonably be held to conflict with the Scriptures or the religious beliefs derived therefrom. In sum, the authority of science never surrenders an inch to the authority of the Church whereas the Church has surrendered much to the authority of science.

In general, the growth of silence over the last few hundred years has acted to produce a secular world in which the causes of events and phenomena are held to be "natural"; not supernatural or Divinely ordained. Moreover, science seeks to explain *everything* — including, of course, the growth of religions itself. For science, nothing is sacred. Everything is open to enquiry.

Thus my reply to Elzinga is that I am not contesting the proposition that a person can believe in both science and religion or, for that matter, science and astrology. My contention is that the spirit of religion — expressed in the idea of faith in a benevolent Diety and in a Divine Lawgiver whose precepts are morally binding — is incompatible with the spirit or ethos of Science, which is essentially sceptical (even of its own theories), which questions everything, and which accepts nothing on faith.

Turning to Friedman who, in contrast to Elzinga, apparently does not lay much store by traditional religion, and is quite ready to fabricate new religions, including secular ones, as and when required, I did in fact point out that humanistic or secular religions (Confucianism, for example) may serve for the saintly few. But for ordinary folk, a religion must comprehend the Divine and must be regarded as absolute and eternal if it is to be morally effective. Ready as he is to improvise (secular) religions to meet all future contingencies, nothing of this sort can provide men with the spiritual nourishment that they crave.[3]

As an afterthought, I might add that not only will "secular religions" and purpose-built religions (Friedman's "new religions" developed to "replace . . . religions that cannot adapt to modern ideas") be out of tune with the psychic needs of men, they may prove to be morally objectionable, as indeed are some of the proposals in Garrett Hardin's *New Ethics for Survival.* Perceiving world overpopulation as an immediate threat to Western civilization, Hardin favours the growth of homosexuality and also abortion on demand. I see no reason why, without inconsistency, he should not also favour infanticide or, for that matter, geriatricide — so affronting further the traditional belief in the sanctity of life. Clearly all such purpose-built "ethical systems" or "religions" are explicitly relativistic and are designed to meet the imperative needs of technocrats, the fevered cults of the media-dominated societies of the West, or the exigencies of totalitarian regimes. There can, therefore, be no assurance that the goals acclaimed and the means employed may not be increasingly abhorrent by traditional moral standards.

Survival vs. flourishing

There is a methodological point to be stressed in any debate about the course of the future: we should be able to agree that arguments turning on man's (infinite!) adaptability be discounted. Man has indeed the capacity to adjust to trying and tortuous conditions. He has survived extreme hardship and persecution. He has survived brutality and the sadistic savagery of Nazi concentration camps. I choose extreme cases to make it evident that the relevant question is whether the entailed adaptation in question is one that can be depended upon to improve his well-being. And if we accept the conservative (Burkean) view, the burden of proof ought properly to fall on the person who asserts that the proposed change, and its effect on man's well-being, are improvements in comparison with those conventions and institutions with which we have long been familiar.

To illustrate, if it is recognized that continued technological progress looks to be making the role of the mother-in-the-home obsolete, and that this is a factor (I would say a powerful factor) in the rising post-war trend of family breakdown, it is not enough to speculate — as David Friedman does — on the future possibility of "artificial families" interacting "as if they were relatives" or the wonderful new connections to be made through participating (perhaps by satellite communication) in transnational bridge-parties or through weekly chit-chats with other enthusiastic bird-lovers in Hong Kong.[4]

Bearing in mind that the human family, whether nuclear or extended, has been the basic cell upon which all human societies, tribal or state, have evolved since man appeared on earth, anyone contemplating its disintegration with equanimity should have at his disposal powerful arguments and evidence.

The costs of change once more

My remarks on the burden borne by workers in affluent societies in consequence of rapid and frivolous shifts in consumer demand have attracted the attention of both my critics who, incidentally, attribute to me an arrogance I rather wish I possessed. Ken Elzinga asks: who balances one against the other, and bids me mute my voice. But in fact I do so. I mildly draw attention to a possible outcome — gains of consumers falling short of losses to workers — of a perfectly functioning market. I did not propose to resolve the problem.

David Friedman goes further and takes the liberty of referring me to the literature (quoting Marshall's rule for welfare comparisons). As it happens I do not draw upon interpersonal utility comparisons "of a hundred million strangers, few of them much like him." I believe he is under the impression that economists do have grounds for their presumption in favour of a removal of tariffs, which impression is erroneous.[5]

Even were we able to discover the ideal utilometer, the problem cannot be solved by maximizing utility. The sadistic pleasure experienced by a million voyeurs at watching a man flogged to death might well exceed in total utility the disutility of the victim: yet, in its ethical capacity, the community would discountenance it.

The fact is that remaining without the prospect of employment in one's trade, feeling obsolete, unwanted, rejected, day by day, week by week, month by month, is among the most painful experiences a person can suffer. And if this happens to be an unavoidable consequence of an otherwise well-functioning market in an affluent society, we should at least have the grace to recognize it. A sensitive critic might agree to one of the ethical rules proposed by Karl Popper; that it is more important to prevent avoidable suffering than to provide further opportunities for pleasure and profit.

Spillovers, side-effects and intervention

I turn finally to three minor points raised by David Friedman alone since they may be of passing interest to the economics fraternity.

Apropos my so-called "New Spillovers" of the last thirty years or so which carry some risk of local or global disaster, David Friedman elects to deal with this new and terrifying phenomenon by (quite arbitrarily) *defining* spillover in terms of the utility functions of individuals that are "strongly interdependent, so that you are made miserable by the side-effects experienced by other people." He then dismisses my arguments by the irrelevant and seemingly derogatory remark that "people have been claiming a benevolent interest in others as a justification for making their decisions for them for some millennia now."

As an aside I venture to point out that had he troubled himself to read any of my work on spillovers (or externalities) he would have discovered that there can be many examples of this definition of his—though not of the conventional and widely accepted definition

—that would have to be excluded from the calculus of welfare economies inasmuch as they do not comport with the ethical consensus of the community for which the economist is prescribing.

The conventional and widely accepted definition of an externality has regard to the incidental (that is, unintentional) effects on the welfare of others arising from the legitimate economic activities of persons or entities, say industries A and B. Therefore my "New Spillovers" that are indeed the unanticipated consequences inflicted on the health and, more generally, the welfare of members of the public by the new manufacturing processes, or by the distribution of new synthetics of industries A and B . . ., fit quite properly into the definition. A well-known instance is the effect on the happiness of many European families of the hideous — though unanticipated — mutagenic consequences of the manufacture and distribution of the drug Thalidomide.

Moreover, as I indicated in my paper, the importance of these "New Spillovers" resides not only in the risk of fearsome side-effects arising, singly or in combination, of the many thousands of new drugs, synthetics, pesticides, etc. now being put on the market each year, but also in the consequent unease and edginess of the public which has, over the last fifteen years or so, been demanding increased government investigation, regulation, and controls — so augmenting the size and power of government bureaucracy.

The income statistics and flight to the farm

In his first paragraph David Friedman enquires whether my "gloomy view" is "an accurate perception of reality" or merely an attempt to explain away "statistics of real income by arguing that only the *unmeasurable* components of welfare are declining." Not surprisingly he assumes the latter explanation and, in an attempt at refutation, offers what he believes to be "evidence" grounded on "the observed behaviour of people with regard to their choices of where and how to live."

Two small comments should suffice to deal with his paragraph:

a) It is not hard to generate scepticism about the significance of "real income" statistics by reference not only to the less measurable components of welfare, but also by reference to many of the more measurable items in the conventional GNP calculations. For example, most of the expenditure in adult education (investment in human capital), the services of banks and innumerable other agencies, the expenditure on government's infra-structure and its military expenditures, to mention those that come readily to mind, enter the estimates of net national income as *final outputs* whereas they are more reasonably interpreted as intermediate goods, or *inputs* into the economy. (If readers wish, I can expand on this).

b) Incredible though it may seem, David Friedman argues that if my belief that social welfare is declining were correct, one should expect to observe people moving from areas of urban sprawl, where pollution and disamenity are rife, to farms and small towns. Yet, on balance, the reverse is the case.[6]

The first thing to say about this canny observation is the obvious one: choice is *not* welfare. If everybody in the United States moved over time into the cities, it would tell us nothing about the course of their welfare. When it comes to the larger decisions, few people can be counted on to know where their net advantages lie. A good deal of people's time is spent unwishing the decisions they had made years before — notwithstanding which they would, quite rightly, be outraged if they were to be subject to greater constraint in implementing their own decisions.

The second thing to say is that, independent of the course of their welfare, a number of seemingly rational factors can explain the trend toward the city.

i) In terms of relative economic opportunity population in the agricultural areas is under pressure. In the West, over the last two centuries, capital innovation and investment in agriculture and, therefore, rising labour productivity, creates surplus farm labour. In Asia and Africa, the growth of village population cannot be sustained on the limited land, and the young flock to the cities where, in the last resort, they can beg or steal.

ii) The post-war immigrant flow into the Western democracies — the so-called South-to-North movement — especially the illegal part of it has strong incentives to settle in the large towns and cities.

iii) We need hardly mention the affluent foot-loose young anxious to move from small towns to the big cities "where the action is."

iv) Finally in terms of relative amenity, the attraction of the farming life and the countryside has declined markedly over the last three or four decades. We expect today to be assaulted by perpetual engine noises in the city, but it is now no longer easy to escape them in the country either. Agriculture has become agri-industry, machine-intensive; the once-quiet skies torn with the whine of helicopters, once-quiet valleys echoing to the snarl of chain-saws. And every acre of parkland or garden roaring with motorized implements. The bucolic joys of farming are memories only. The farming scene today, where it is not one of unrelieved furrows or crops, is a complex of animal barracks — animal factories, battery hens, pig dungeons, calf pits, an imprisoned mass of tormented creatures processed and deformed to meet the carnivorous appetites of growing city populations.

David Friedman may continue to believe "in his heart" that happiness increases decade by decade (at least in America), but the belief can salvage nothing from the movement of population from farm and small town toward the sprawling conurbations all over the world.

Technology and tyranny — public and private

A last point, David Friedman wants to qualify my argument that technology acts to strengthen the hand of government in a number of ways by attention to the particular case of computer development. While apparently agreeing that the incredible capacity of modern computers facilitate central control of citizens, he states that computers also provide greater opportunities "for decentralized forms of organization, competing information nets, etc. — especially now that a good small computer costs considerably less than a car."

Granted, but in just what ways do the data banks kept by private corporations, or state or local governments, act as *countervailing* power, so increasing individual freedom, is not made clear. I fail to see any reason why the spread of computers among private firms, among states, or among individuals, should act to safeguard individual freedom or weaken the control of the central government.

His similar assertions about weapons innovation are also a puzzle. I cannot believe that improvement in small arms, and their diffusion through smuggling, adds anything to the sense of safety or freedom of the law-abiding citizen. The contrary surely is more plausible, for it is not unreasonable to relate innovations in small weapons and communications to the increase in crime and terrorism — as a result of which again, alas, the public becomes that much more ready to cede increased powers of surveillance and control to the state's internal security agencies.[7]

NOTES

1. David Friedman's untempered exuberance is such that in the space available to me I shall have to ignore some of his more wanton assertions — for example that my talent is really that of a myth-maker whereas I could justly retort that I am a myth-destroyer (especially the myth of progress) — and occasional remarks calculated to expose my wondrous innocence.

2. For example, we already have, on the one hand, "liberationists" — homosexual, feminist, and others — and those self-styled progressivists who believe in abortion on demand, avant-garde pornography, ultra-bohemian life-styles, and untrammelled hedonistic pursuits. On the other, we have the "new traditionalists," including the "Moonies," the fundamentalists in religion such as the Creationists and Jehovah's Witnesses, and the so-called "moral majority." Each of these broad groupings loathes the other, and it will need increasingly strong police controls to prevent demonstrations from spilling over into violence and possibly internecine warfare. Consider also conservationists versus developers.

3. Secular "religions" or ideologies (communisms, feminisms, . . .) not only lack the magic, the otherworldliness that men seek, they cannot in a rapidly changing world command a loving allegiance for long: the "religion," not being Divine in origin, is always open to dispute and reinterpretation. Disillusion grows as the leaders of the movement are seen bending maxims and slogans to expedience, revising doctrine to meet current exigencies, explaining manifest failures as the result of conspiracies by "enemies of the people."

4. The charitable reader will prefer to think of Friedman's complacent remarks about the disintegration of the family as a momentary surrender to his customary forensic abandon rather than to suspect that he suffers so pernicious a form of emotional anaemia as seriously to regard activities promoting common interests and hobbies, or organizing science fiction fans, as a substitute for the warmth and closeness, the joys, the pangs, and the poignancy of traditional family life.

5. Among other things my 1957 *Economica* paper made it clear that Samuelson's 1939 *Canadian Journal* article, purporting to prove (using index numbers) that trade is better than autarky for a single country, was invalid—as also, incidentally, was a later attempt by Kemp, 1964, to demonstrate that some trade is better than none. *Economic Journal.*

6. I am tempted to refer him to a passage in my "Dr. Pangloss on Pollution" (1973) where Dr. Pangloss explains that "pollution" is an elitist fad; the poor certainly have no interest in reducing it: quite the contrary in fact. Drawing on the empirical evidence, Dr. Pangloss goes on to say, "In my close reading of social history, and in all my experience over the years, I have observed that the poor invariably choose to take up residence in the most polluted, noisiest, and dirtiest parts of the city" (or words to that effect).

7. In passing, I cited as a prime instance of the imminent and ghastly peril in which we stand today, by grace of the technological establishment, the incredible ease and swiftness by which the nuclear destruction of our planet can be accomplished. It needs but a few men siezed by a moment of folly, fanatacism, panic, raging vengeance, insane ambition, or paranoia, and within hours the world could be transformed into a dead and poisoned planet.

I cannot but marvel at David Friedman's almost-truculent optimism, even in the face of this balance-of-terror mischance, contrived by means of a quibble with my use of the adjective "unprecedented." He concedes (with what reluctance, I can imagine), that the consequences of a thermonuclear war would (at least when fought "with the objective of victory") be "grim but not unprecedented," an opinion which rests on his use of words to exclude the possibility of "mutual annihilation." In evidence thereof he reminds us of "the great plague" (in fact there were several before that of 1665) and the Thirty-Years' war which destroyed a sizable proportion of the population of Europe.

If I interpret him aright, he may be quite unique in being able to dispel anxiety about living today on the brink of a nuclear conflagration and to distil his complacency from a recitation of the chronicle of major disasters that, in the event, did not succeed at the time in wholly destroying the human race.

Discussion

Edited by: Kenneth G. Elzinga

Kenneth Elzinga: Professor Mishan's paper is entitled, "Religion, Culture and Technology," and to oversimplify its thesis, it is that technology determines our culture. It determines it adversely. And poor old religion, in a post-Enlightenment age, is too feeble to offset the effects of technology and modern science.

I would like to note at the outset that there is a peculiar type of supply-side economics being posited here. Technology, which is essentially the assembly of factors of production, or inputs, in new ways, determines, as Professor Mishan puts it, "our attributes, beliefs, and aspirations." And technology determines them, he argues, in such a way as to cause the malaise in the West that he describes.

Now, in my judgement, all this is too great a cross for technology to be asked to bear. The technology, for much of what Mishan and I both find unpalatable in the West today, existed long before the demand for these goods and services on a large scale was evident. The technology of printing versus the current quantity of pornography is one case in point.

I would suggest that it is no historical aberration that Guttenberg chose to print Bibles, instead of lascivious stories, though this was a technological option open to him. The drug abuse that my own generation narrowly avoided was technologically an option; that is, the technology was known to produce and distribute mind-altering drugs. When people my age were in high school and college, the demand wasn't there. So I suggest we have to look elsewhere than technology to locate the root causes of the West's malaise.

Also in this paper, as in other of his writings, Professor Mishan decries the absence of the simpler lifestyle that technology allegedly takes from us. And I must confess that I have never fully understood him on this point. In most cases, it seems to me, technology increases our range of alternatives; and if we're fortunate enough to be in market economies, it keeps the earlier vintage alternatives open to us.

In coming to this conference, I chose to drive part way across southern Canada. I suspect most of you took a technologically more advanced alternative mode of travel — an airplane. Some of you may have taken a less advanced one — the railroad. While driving, I saw some people hiking, others bicycling, across southern Canada for what seemed, to me, to be enormous distances, but nevertheless they had adopted that mode of transportation. I don't know for certain, but presumably horseback riding was an option to us in coming here. When Professor Mishan was a visiting professor at the University of Virginia, he could have chosen to live just a short distance from Charlottesville on a small farm, raised vegetables, pumped his own water, stoked his own woodstoves, as some of us on the faculty do. Or he could decide to live in the city, for that matter in the country, and surround himself with electronic and electric gadgets. All I am saying is that a simple lifestyle is still an alternative in a market economy.

As to technology and religious belief: Here Professor Mishan and I appear to be quite far apart. It has not been my experience, nor my understanding, that science and religion are opposed. Indeed, as I argue in my paper, it is the Judeo-Christian world view that caused science to prosper. I'm not just saying "allowed," but *caused* science to prosper in the West; but not in the East, which did not adopt this worldview. Men like Pascal, Newton, Maxwell, and Faraday, — these were not only renowned scientists, — they were very devout and pious men.

As to the proposition that modern science, today, has made faith in God untenable, or extraordinarily difficult, all I can say is that if I were a parent sending a son or a daughter off to college, and being concerned that my son or daughter's religious faith would survive the four or eight years at the university, my concern would be the greatest when they went to their classes in modern literature, or psychology, or in the case of my own university, religious studies. (laughter and applause) I would have very little concern about the sustaining of their religious faith when they picked up their physics or their calculus book. Within medicine, I am told, it is much more trying to be a believer in God when studying psychiatry, which is certainly the most unscientific of the medical rotations, than when doing surgery, which is the most precise.

Let me close by noting only that I have focused in these remarks on my disagreements with Professor Mishan. It would be inaccurate if I left the impression that I didn't learn from the paper, or agree with many parts of it. For example, I am very much drawn to the "small is beautiful" tilt of the paper. Although I am also mindful of what Robert Nisbet said, that, "Today we can afford to take a sentimental view of nature, because science has done so much to ameliorate it."

I agree with much of Professor Mishan's factual portrayal of the malaise in the West. We disagree on causes, to be sure. And I concur with his very grim concern that the declining moral standards in the West are ultimately going to lessen the scope for market forces, and probably will provoke greater measures for state control over individual behaviour.

David Friedman: As some of you know, I am an enthusiastic reader of science fiction; and I accordingly felt grateful to the organizers of this conference for giving me Ed Mishan's paper to discuss. The essential stylistic approach seemed to derive from Stapleton, who, as some of you know, was fond of vast canvasses in which civilizations rose and fell, new breeds of man replaced old breeds, and so forth. It seemed to me that although Mishan's piece was entertaining, considered as a portrayal of the real world it was implausible. I discuss a good many of my reasons for thinking this in the written form of my comment. Let me concentrate merely on his vision of history.

As some of you may also know, my hobbies include cooking from thirteenth century cookbooks, making Anglo-Saxon jewellery, and reading Icelandic sagas. So I'm not entirely unsympathetic to the Middle Ages. But even so, I find it a little hard to stomach his somewhat utopian vision of the world informed by the rituals of the Catholic church, and all the rest of it.

I also find that in his description of the Catholic church at present, he talks as though Catholics preferring to confess their sins rather than stopping sinning was a new development. My understanding is that one of the strengths of the Catholic church for a very long time has been its realistic attitude towards sin.

And, again, he comments that the Church nowadays uses all the devices of modern science and technology to try to attract followers. As was pointed out by Ken Elzinga, "Who was it who first used printing?," which was, after all, a new technology being used for the Church's purpose.

In any case, my reasons for disagreeing with his description of the modern world are, in some detail, in my written notes; and I see no point in repeating them. I would like, therefore, to start by talking about what I think is the very interesting issue he raises, of the relation between science, myth, and the survival of a civilized society. I have a good deal of sympathy with the idea that myth, broadly conceived, is an important and perhaps essential part of a social order. People want to have some kind of a perception of a moral pattern in the universe they live in, and the lives they are living. Without that it becomes very difficult to survive, at least to be happy and to fit into the world.

What disturbs me is his belief that there is some necessary conflict between truth and myth. That is to say, that in order for a myth to be effective, it must first be a lie, and second be a lie which gains its strength from people believing that it's true.

In fact there are two other kinds of myths. On the one hand, there is the kind of myth which is perceived as a fiction. The obvious example nowadays would be the works of J. R. R. Tolkien. Tolkien wrote immensely moving and, I should say, as literature, very sophisticated works of art. A lot of the reason people like them is that the reader is introduced to a world which makes moral sense — not, as critics sometimes say, a world of black and white, by any means, but a world where black and white have meaning. People like to feel that. They like to feel they are in an ordered world. And I believe that having read them, and having made them a part of your imaginative universe, you're affected forever after — in spite of the fact that you know perfectly well that the history in those books is fictitious, and that the author knew it was fictitious.

One could give other examples; but it seems to me that myths, in order to inform people, do not have to be believed to be literally true. Furthermore, I see no reason why myths have to be false — why one cannot have a set of inspiring myths which are consistent with the world as we know it and consistent with things that we will discover in the near future. The one example which comes immediately to mind is the set of science fiction novels written by C. S. Lewis, of which the first was *Out of the Silent Planet,* in which his science fiction assumption is that the Christian religion is literally true; and he works that out in three quite interesting, and effective novels.

I see no reason why existing religions cannot adopt the views of Newton, and Einstein, and other such people; and thus adapt themselves to the modern world.

So, it seems to me that Mishan is right, that there is a problem with people needing myths. He may well be right that some of the problems of the modern world have to do with the fact that the firms which are producing myths are producing an obsolete product, and that causes serious difficulties. But I don't see that there is any essential, as opposed to accidental, reason why one cannot have myths that are consistent with science.

Now, let me go on to make a somewhat different point. And that is that the thrust of Mishan's answer to the question, Is religion anti-capitalist? is: Religion is not anti-capitalist. It is critical of the modern world; and the reason it's critical of the modern world is that the modern world deserves to be criticized.

I think he may well be wrong. I think he is right in saying that the criticism of the modern world is much wider than religion. And that part of what we are observing is something in common between religious intellectuals and atheist or agnostic intellectuals.

I agree that the fact that intellectuals in general are critical of the modern world is a fact to be explained. On the other hand, I think it is at least a possible explanation that intellectuals have always been critical of the contemporary world. And I would refer to that passage of Adam Smith's that I quote in my piece, where he remarks that:

> During this period, five years have seldom passed away, in which some book or pamphlet has not been published. Written, too, with such abilities as to gain some authority with the public, and pretending to demonstrate that the wealth of the nation was fast declining, that the country was depopulated, agriculture neglected, manufacturers decaying, and trade undone.
>
> Nor have these publications been all party pamphlets—the wretched offspring of falsehood and venality. Many have been written by very candid and very intelligent people, who wrote nothing but what they believed, and for no other reason but because they believed it.

That is, I think there is a tendency (which I am not sure I entirely understand), for professional intellectuals to view themselves as adversaries of their culture, whatever and whenever that culture is; and that we now have a society in which the percentage of the population who are professional intellectuals is very much higher than probably any society in the past.

There is one more comment I would like to make. When I objected to his objection to vibrators and pornography, the point I was making was not that there was any reason why he shouldn't object to market outcomes but rather that he seemed to be claiming in that passage that those outcomes were a necessary result of a technologically expanding market. It seemed to me a silly argument. The fact that in an expanding economy people choose to buy vibrators and pornography rather than videotapes of famous sermons is a result of their tastes (or the fact their tastes differed from his). I didn't see any reason why permissiveness was a necessary part of a technologically developing and expanding market.

The second point I want to make is that I don't think that mass permissiveness really requires modern technology. I would cite the Albigensians — not the Perfecti, the few holy men, but the rest of the population — as one counter example, at least from what I understand of their views and practices.

Finally, I notice that Ed Mishan keeps speaking about religion, where I keep speaking about myth. In his initial argument, he talked about the necessity for a myth (which is what I agree with). One form myths may take is to be enshrined in a set of beliefs about a Supreme Being which people really believe in. As I suggested in my paper, historically they've taken other forms. I think it very dubious that Confucianism can be described as a set of beliefs about a Supreme Being. Confucius, whenever anybody asked him about spiritual things, essentially said, "I don't want to talk about that." And I was suggesting that the same objective of organizing, making sense out of the world around you in a moral, meaningful way, could be provided in several other ways, where I include in that both myths that are perceived as fictions and myths that are not religions because they don't involve a Supreme Being. It may be that somebody could either make one of the present religions consistent with what we are going to learn for the next hundred years, or create a new such religion. I don't know. The opinion I was expressing was merely that there was no reason why you couldn't have myths, just because some of the things that were believed by the existing religions turned out to be false.

Seymour Siegel: I have a certain fuzziness about what we're supposed to be very certain about — namely a set of empirical facts. We assume in the discussion that almost every theologian, or theological group, is anti-market, when the fact of the matter is, it's the reverse. The growing religions in North America or even in Europe, are the ones who are pro-market, for example the evangelical, right-wing, "moral majority" people, whom you are supposed to sneer at (which I think is wrong to do). And that is not taken into consideration in any of our discussions here. The same is true about an assumption, which we heard in the previous discussion, that religion — both in its organized form and in its more internal form—is declining. The fact of the matter is that the United States of America (and, I presume, Canada—since our brothers or sisters share the same phenomena), which is the most technologically advanced society in the globe and in the history of the world, is probably the most religious one, measured in any way that you want to measure it.

Andrew Greely pointed out a very interesting fact, in one of his recent books, that more people attend religious services, on the average, in this country, than vote in elections. Notwithstanding what we've discussed, we assume that politics is a concern that everybody shares. That's a most popular sport in the United States. And yet, less people participate, even in the most rudimentary expression of politics—like voting—than they do in religion. Therefore, the notion that everything is decaying, and that has something to do with technology, is not borne out by any empirical investigation of technological societies, especially the ones north of the Rio Grande.

The other thing is that non-technological societies are more materialistic than our societies are, and more Victorian in their morality as well. Examples include the leftists, the communists, the socialist blocs, and China.

I also think that David Friedman, regardless of the brilliance of his remarks, just lost track of the whole history of religion in the modern age, beginning with the Enlightenment. There's been enormous efforts, and stacks and libraries of books, on integrating traditional religions—Judaism, Christianity, Islam—(Islam less, because Islam resists modernization for some reasons that we can discuss a little later on but certainly Judaism and Christianity) with the discoveries of science, technology, even social science, psychology, and so forth.

But there's one point which I think is very important to stress, which David made before; and I want to repeat it again, because it's extremely crucial. I know from long experience in speaking to various audiences around the country, and even beyond, that the worst thing you can do to an audience is to say that things are pretty good. (laughter) People rebel at that. You have to tell them that things are bad; if you say things are going pretty well, they'll boo you off the stage—at least the audiences that I have an opportunity to speak to. Maybe other speakers here are more fortunate in their invitations. (laughter) The past is good. The present is lousy. The future may be better, depending what your formula is; but it probably will be even worse.

Somebody made a study, just very parochial—a study of Hebrew literature over a thousand years—in which they pointed out writers who, in the eighteenth century, would always say, "In the seventeenth century things were wonderful. In the eighteenth century, they're terrible." And the same people in the seventeenth century were saying that in the seventeenth century, it's terrible. It's the sixteenth century which was the flowering of culture, or piety, or whatnot. I think this has a good function because it destroys smugness, which is important; but it also has a corrosive influence which makes people so despair of their current condition, that they feel there is no way out except revolution, which turns out to be worse, or some retreat to privatism, which makes it worse for them and for the whole society.

John Cooper: In support of what Seymour Siegel has just said, I would suggest a comparison between two oil rich nations, Saudi Arabia and Libya, for example. In my reading of the situation, the Saudis are putting a lot more money into building up a productive capacity that will sustain them over the long run. And it looks like Libya is a classic case of sudden wealth harming a society, because it is being spent primarily for consumption, and the social and religious fabric of Libyan society is getting rather frayed. So technology has its blessings and its curses. They usually come hand in hand.

I wonder if Ed Mishan would accept this if I substituted for the notion of science or technology, the word "scientism." If we imagine Enlightenment, progress and reason multiplied to the nth power, amplified to the level of an ideology—as in the thought of Francis Bacon, for example—then I think there is a very strong case that all religions have a fundamental disagreement with such a scientism—but not with science itself.

Edmund Opitz: Ed Mishan's paper provoked two of the most interesting commentaries. When I first read the paper, I thought of that old Puritan of several centuries ago from the Boston area who said, "My heart leaps for joy every time I hear the good news of eternal damnation." (laughter)

It seems to me that there is a great deal of truth in what Mishan has said; economics and politics, by themselves, have usurped a position in our lives which their intrinsic merit does not deserve. But once they are in their proper role, and functioning well, they are like our digestion or our breathing. We can sort of forget about them, not entirely;

but we keep them in reasonably good working order, and then tend to the more important things.

I thought also when I read Ed Mishan's paper that we have about four and a half billion people on the planet; and that without science, technology, and large-scale production, a lot of them could not stay alive. But there is food for thought in the non-academic portions of his paper as well. People need to find meaning in the universe, and purpose for their lives in a religious sense. They must develop some life-enhancing myths (in the sense in which David Friedman used the term); and on top of that, we need the kind of sensory experiences that, in a world emphasizing more comfort, we have lacked. And so people are climbing mountains. They're jogging. They're working up terrific sweats in all kinds of strenuous exercise. They're seeking danger. I think we have gone through a period — maybe we're getting out of it — where the educational system has not done much to give people, young people, means of expressing themselves. They cannot get out what is within them by speaking it, whistling it, singing it, dancing it, or acting it out; and so they tend to take it out on other people in murderous rages, and crime, or driving suicidally, and so on.

It seems to me that our culture, as Matthew Arnold pointed out, has suffered certain deprivations because the whole of our nature has not been expressed in it. Arnold said that there were five social instincts. They come in pairs. The first instinct which alone has been given full and free expression, is the instinct for *accumulation and expansion*. Accumulation means making money; expansion means gaining power or influence; making our mark on other people.

But four other facets of our nature have not been given full expression, or have been perverted. There is the instinct for *intellect and knowledge*. Once it was knowledge for the sheer joy of knowing, or the sheer delight in learning, but now it is knowledge for power, or to change things, "to alter this universe in one way or another."

Then there is an instinct for *beauty and poetry*. Beauty is in the eye of the beholder, we are told; and so painting is simply the more or less extravagant expression of more or less interesting personalities. The old artist thought he did something on canvas for which there was an answering echo in the nature of things. And the modern poet, if you tell him that you understand his poetry, is insulted.

Fourth is the instinct for *social life and manners*. The attitude towards people which is a lubricant of intercourse in society. This is not "natural"; it is learned.

And the final one, the instinct for *religion and morals.* We have been getting into those areas here. I think Arnold's criticism as to what religion has become, on the one hand push button salvationism, and on the other, social action, is an indictment in some degree of what religion has become in the modern world.

PART FOUR

EXTERNALIST EXPLANATIONS: SOCIOLOGICAL ISSUES

Chapter 7

THE CLERGY, SECULARIZATION AND POLITICS

David Martin

I. THE CONVENTIONAL SOCIOLOGICAL WISDOM

The initial object of this essay is to state the conventional sociological wisdom with regard to the contemporary situation of the clergy. Then I want to sketch idealized portraits of the views of two kinds of clergymen, one who embraces a "realistic" view, consonant with the old state/church position, but not necessarily linked to it, and one who inhabits the ill-defined terrain between liberality and liberation. I hope the connection between the two parts of the argument will be sufficiently clear. The link is that the sociological changes here described make possible, indeed make much more likely, the emergence of the kind of clergyman who is located between liberality and liberation.

In restating the conventional wisdom, I shall rely on the concluding chapters of Canon A. J. Russell's excellent book "The Clerical Profession," which deals in particular with the Church of England. It is helpful to use the Church of England as a vantage point because it provides a traditional yardstick by which to measure the extent of contemporary transitions. The Anglican Church has been deeply embedded in English social structure and the Anglican ecclesiastical elite has, in the past, been closely interwoven with the social and political elite. Moreover, it seems to me arguable that not only does the Anglican Church provide a historical yardstick of tradition but also provides an index of extensive radicalization. The old fashioned liberalism which once permeated the free churches is now rather conservative by comparison. The sometime upholders of law and order, social and personal discipline, tradition and national identity, now make the running in the field of radical causes. This is particularly the case in the specialized agencies of the Church.

The changing social role of the clergy

So what then is the contemporary situation of the clergyman? Canon Russell sets out the background of a traditional paternalistic society where the cleric was usually the most educated man and where his views were woven into the whole fabric of the social worldview. The Church then became one element in a differentiated society, offering one option amongst several competing viewpoints. The teacher, in particular, emerged as the local rival of the clergyman, and he might even promote some version of radical politics or of idiosyncratic religion or of humanism. The marginality of the Church was exemplified in the way the clergy became bearers of a home-centred rather than a work-centred culture, and that meant that their sphere became increasingly comprised of the women and children. Their role was also more and more identified with devising entertainment, or running uniformed organizations. In short, clergy belonged to a part not the whole, and that part was "passive" rather than implicated in the active agencies of social reality.

Many of the clergy probably retained elements of an older anti-industrial and anti-urban approach, which might be conservative, but could also be utilized against capitalist civilization. Traditional conservatism, which was shared by the clergy with part of academia, contained an anti-capitalist fuse which could one day be lighted. It was, of course, stronger in countries like England than in the U.S. where "conservatism" lacked the traditional Burkean approach. Seminaries and seminars alike contained seeds of anti-capitalist ideology. This is an important point, because part of the radicalization of the clergy has to be related to the downward mobility of a key sector of traditional social structure.

The clergyman was once aligned with "the professions," above all the law and medicine, but also the military. That meant that he exemplified gentlemanly culture and technical expertise combined. However, in today's world, the professions have vastly expanded, and expertise has fragmented into a myriad specialisms. The old individualistic, personalized approach has been eroded in many professions in favour of the collective exercise of a limited, impersonal competence. Teams of experts or groups of officials are more and more characteristic of contemporary professional life and the clergy are no exception. They are exceptions only in that they find it less easy to define their expertise, or its appropriate area of activity. To be generally "cultured" or even caring is not an avocation in itself.

Perhaps it is important here that professional men when organized in teams tend to treat each other as their primary reference group rather than their clients. If this happens among clergy, it can lead to a form of neo-clericalism. Neo-clericalism is interesting because it is in conflict with the attempt to de-clericalize the Church and assert that the "laos" is the active centre of what is meant by the Church. Thus the new style clergyman may be emphasizing the importance of the laity or of "the people of God" and at the same time referring to and deferring to his colleagues. This has a further important consequence. He may with his outward lips be speaking of a *rapprochment* with the world and of being "open" to the secular reality, but his social point of reference may make more for closure than for openness.

Forces towards political activism

We have already noticed one or two aspects which may have a bearing on the way in which the clergy have become politically activated in recent years. One has been the relegation of the clergyman to the sphere of leisure rather than work. Another has been the anti-industrial "charge" still lodged to some extent on the clerical worldview. We now come to a further pressure, which derives from a query about the relevance of the skills possessed by the clergyman. For complex reasons which cannot be gone into here, the whole activity of ritual performance, whether it be secular or religious, has been downgraded in the view of many people. The cult of authenticity, however socially unrealistic, has thrown doubt on any avocation which is centred on the constant repetition of rituals. A man whose whole social being is based on the role of religious "master of ceremonies" is felt to be play-acting rather than acting in earnest. This prejudice against ritual and repetition extends to the wearing of uniforms, or in the case of the clergy, the collar.

The result is that just at the time when there is a kind of collectivist ethos growing up based on team work, and associated with a form of neo-clericalism, there is also a tendency to dissociate the self from the clerical role. The clergyman is peculiarly sensitive to the charge of marginality and irrelevance and feels compelled to divest himself – and the word divest retains its sartorial reference – of the specific clerical character. He is not exclusively a man of the cloth, a designated preacher or sacrificing priest, but a man among men. How then is he to free himself from the constricting collar? Well, of course, he can take it off. Many do. But the act of removing a collar symbolizes far more than sartorial divestment. It signifies an attempt to leave the world of ritual and leisure pursuits and find an active role in "the world."

The clergyman, then, is somewhat shut off in a professional reference group, but he has designs on mundane activity. He no longer fears the enticements of the world, or for that matter perhaps the seductions of the flesh and the devil, but is anxious to be where the action is. Indeed he has a rather exaggerated notion of the degree of "action" enjoyed by those outside his own order. The cleric does not compare himself with a clerk, whose office after all, is hardly more active or "political" than his own, but with some exemplary figure of heroic proletarian proportions. Or else he compares himself enviously with the committed intellectual, whose role appears to consist in researching the contours of the real world and proposing how it may be reformed.

Some clergy do attempt to enter the world of blue-collar work, but as hinted above, the blue-collar image is increasingly unrelated to today's work force. In any case, the natural skills of the clergyman are more closely allied to those of the teacher or academic. To put it rather harshly, the clergyman finds himself in the proletariat of the intelligentsia. This is not a particularly pleasant place for him to be. It represents a form of downward mobility from the time when he was *the* man who knew. But at the same time, he is also a person – or parson – with a commitment. He has not entered on holy orders just to be a minor member in the lower reaches of teaching. He has a vision and a mission. The only way in which that vision and mission can be actively followed is by a form of politics.

It is not easy to be a political vicar or minister in the parish or in the local chapel. The exigencies of running and administering the hundred-and-one minor tasks of a local church are a massive constraint.

The expectations of the congregation are also constraining. The world of family, of ritual and leisure pursuits, does not open easily onto the world of politics. The parson can, of course, convert his vision and his mission into a form of social work. His caring is then validated by what claims to be a certificated expertise. But what beckons more seductively is a specialized ministry either in the central agencies of the Church or in the world of communications. He can leave the closed circle of communicants and enter the wide-open arena of communications. That, after all, presents a chance to make an impact and allows for a redeployment of his original skills: talking, "acting." Indeed, it is another form of liturgical drama. This is how the central agencies of the Church and the communications outlets associated with them often become filled with refugees from the constraints of the local ministry. Thus the voice of the Churches becomes in many ways divorced from the local constituency.

However, this is not universally the case. The voice of the "electronic Church" is not notable for radicalism, though it has acquired a vigorous political resonance. Here we must distinguish between types of motivation to the sacred ministry and notice the conflict now developing between those political in a radical or liberal direction and those who have emerged even more recently and are politicized in the direction of the so-called moral majority. To make that distinction, I propose deploying a rather simple bi-polar model of clergy viewpoints put forward by Professor A. P. M. Coxon and Dr. R. Towler. They acknowledge that many clergy cross their bi-polar divide.

The Puritan/anti-Puritan distinction

In their researches among Anglican ordinands, they distinguished Puritans from anti-Puritans. The Puritan type is characterized by a high degree of religious interest and a lack of flexibility. His faith is clearly defined and rigidly maintained. He feels himself clearly "called" to a definite role. Furthermore, his interests are somewhat constricted, particularly in the aesthetic direction. He maintains a distinct withdrawal from the world. The anti-Puritan, of course, displays the reverse of these characteristics. The distinction here is not between old and young, or between sacerdotalist and evangelical. Indeed, the sacerdotalist may, and often, does, belong to the Puritan type.

The re-emergence of the "Puritan" type in the form of a politicized commitment to conservative morals expounded through the new forms of communications technology has been sufficently commented on. In the United States it amounts to a major conflict between the politicized liberal clergy and the politicized clerical partisans of the "moral majority." Elsewhere one may say that the radical dominance is still maintained, though increasingly challenged. However, our concern in this paper is primarily with the radical versions of politicized clerical Christianity, and in that respect one further element has to be noted.

The 1960s saw the emergence of a strongly anti-elitist movement. The attack on ritual was also an attack on elites. This combination of anti-elitism and anti-ritual had a peculiarly strong impact on the declining and marginalized elite of ritual practitioners i.e., the clergy. By virtue of living next door socially to the knowledge class, reach-me-down versions of anti-elitist sentiment constantly seeped through into the clerical mind. Clergymen, in order to achieve some kind of edge and social coloration, are often seen to adopt the more extreme versions of the anti-elitist tags and slogans that are available. It is as if their relatively recent departure from the conventional social structure and from the role of guardians of "civil religion" has given an added animus to their repudiation of the past.

The vigorous repudiation of the role of guardian of civil religion and the espousal of anti-elitist positions has various consequences. These can perhaps best be noted by way of the two portraits which are to follow of "idealist" and "realist" clergymen respectively. However, before we proceed to that, it is important to stress that nothing follows from what has been said concerning the "truth" or otherwise of the positions taken up. The positions espoused by the radical clergyman are not invalidated by the recent social history of his role any more than the position of the guardian of civil religion is invalidated by his particular place in traditional social structure. Nor, of course, are the positions mutually exclusive. There are clergy who maintain traditional civil roles and also utilize them to make radical or liberal pronouncements. Indeed, for some there is considerable *frisson* to be derived from combining all the appurtenances of priesthood with a startling deployment of revolutionary views.

II. THE "REALIST" CLERGYMAN

How then may we proceed to construct an "ideal-type" of the "realist" clergyman? I intend to begin by stressing certain role-performances within the context of civil religion, or, as it would be in England, *the* National Church. I do this because it seems to me that the first step in a realist position involves a recognition of the tension between particularity and universality. The realist is critically tender towards the particularity of human attachments. These include the locality and the nation. Nothing so distinguishes the "realist" from the liberal "idealist" as this tenderness towards the sense of being located and defined by territorial loyalties. It is interesting to notice that liturgical reformers are particularly ambivalent towards state prayers and those petitions which speak of "the maintenance of thy true religion and virtue."

The affection for particularity

"Civil religion" is of importance to the realist precisely because it stands in contrast with two forms of universality: the generalizing, abstract loyalty to humanity preached by the liberal, and the international fellowship created by the Church Catholic. It is no part of a realistic approach to deny overarching loyalties to humanity at large or to ignore the fact that people are people whatever their nationality. Nor is part of such an approach to ignore the international scope of Christian fellowship. What is at issue is the sense of being rooted in a place and in a sense of continuity. Time and place are not abstract qualities but means whereby people locate themselves in a sequence and a context.

You have only to consider the role of the Church in Poland or in the Basque country to see how closely the Roman Church is bound up in the affirmation of a continuing culture and in the integrity of a people. "Nationalism" is a bad word, and one which the right-minded shun as connected with every form of national and xenophobic prejudice, and with collective self-glorification. Rightly so, but the consciousness of being a people, united by a common past and by a deposit or inheritance carried lovingly into the present, is supremely important for identity and for identification. The realist accepts this identification, with its particular contingent loyalties, and he tries to cherish the best elements in it. The special character of things is to be nourished, whether it is the specialness of a people or a church. The identity of persons grows in the soil of what is distinctive. So the realist does not attempt to eliminate the character of a tradition in favour either of liberal cosmopolitanism or ecumenical union. Everything has its place. This matters precisely because the radical tendency tends to pluck up roots as barriers to wider loyalties and broader sympathies.

The realist also accepts the social necessity of roles and institutions. The relevance of this lies in the way that many radicals identify social structure as a problem in itself. Of course, in reality nothing is achievable without such structure, but many liberals carry their dislike of institutions to the point of aiming for chaos. No sooner is a convenient mould established than they try to break it up. This is one of the sources of confusion in the contemporary churches, whether it is constant new services or new versions of scripture or exercises in renaming things. Dynamism is identified with changefulness. This means that faith cannot be "the still centre in a turning world." Clearly times *do* change and much is relative, but the realist recognizes that people need familiar points of reference and that flexibility *depends on fixity*. Of course, there is a problem here as between two kinds of conservatism. A capitalist conservatism actually thrusts in the direction of continuous change and creates a *laissez-faire* in the psyche parallel to *laissez-faire* in the economy. An older more organic conservatism checks and qualifies this by seeking out and establishing points of reference. People need markers: places, names, standards, formulae. One of the great disservices offered by some contemporary churchmen has been the dissolution of place and name and formula. This means that people do not know where they are going to or where they are coming from. They cannot conceive of a trajectory, and find themselves dimly and dumbly searching for one. The realist tries to offer shape and definition, without rigidity and stasis.

The political mind of the realist

Realism also involves a particular approach to political options and exigencies. A realist assumes that political action is a very exacting discipline and that moral choices are hedged about by very rigorous conditions. To choose politically is *not* to think up the most attractive package of current rostrums. It is not to assemble all the available forms of approved niceness. Rather it involves a careful weighing of options which exclude other options in terms of what can actually be pursued and carried through given the disposition of forces and influences currently at work. Of course, one may attempt to modify or deflect such forces, but political life is a balancing of pressures into which one inserts an option or choice. The defiles through the barriers are narrow ones. All kinds of Draconian measures may have to be taken en route — some short, sharp and painful. Indeed an unjustifiable act may be necessary within a wider context which is justifiable. Policy is an ensemble which on the whole points in the right direction but which may logically imply actions of doubtful morality.

This is not to say that the ends justify the means. Quite the contrary. But there has to be a realistic assessment of how ends and means are related, and how political consistency may require actions of a hurtful kind. Once this is recognized the realist will not seek to cover up such actions as part of a crusade. They are and remain part of unfortunate necessity. It is precisely this unfortunate necessity that a great deal of sentimental Christian politics seeks to avoid. The crusading mentality forgets what most historic crusades have been like. It was the crusaders, after all, who ruined Byzantium. In short, given the disposition of men and their likely proclivities the realist assumes that setting off for the Holy Land is a dangerous enterprise which may end in sordid self-advancement. Heaven on earth turns out to be hell on earth.

The realist and awareness of evil

So, the final aspect of realism concerns some proper estimate of evil. Here again one may observe at least two kinds of conservatism. There is an optimistic conservatism, well represented in the U.S., which hears no evil and sees no evil. Many progressive educators in liberal democracies assume that the appetites will be benign given appropriate environments. Realism assumes no such happy likelihoods. It is not awaiting the paradise which is just around the corner if only this or that is undertaken, or a particular circumstantial barrier removed. Again, of course, some things *do* have to be removed, but the snake still roams in the garden. Even the poor, once given power, will misuse it in their own interests. Political life is essentially *interested*. On that, its predictability depends, and it will never be otherwise. There will be no change of era in which mankind emerges into a new apolitical, disinterested age.

III. THE "IDEALIST" CLERGYMAN

However, clergy are especially likely to succumb to such a notion, particularly once deprived of the notion of original sin and endemic evil. So it is now important to turn to an idealist Christian view to see how that works out and how it is linked with various forms of secular Utopianism. The groundwork of Christian theology, once the sense of endemic sin is removed, becomes very well adapted to secular idealism. Indeed, Christianity is a powerful originating source of such idealism. Loosed from social structural constraints, and from the doctrines of creatureliness and sin, Christianity itself participates in Promethean illusions. The simplified tags of individualistic morality become simplified political slogans.

Individuality vs. communality

In what way? I begin by summarizing certain contrasting attitudes to individuality and to communal consciousness. I want to lay as much stress on this now as I did earlier in the contrast between national or local belonging and loyalty to abstract humanity. Over recent years contemporary clerics have shared the usual lust of the intelligentsia for *true gemeinschaft*. Given that Christianity has spent a large part of its history embedded in communal types of social organization and took off from sect-like beginnings, this has a historic appeal. Clergymen today seek to create cells resistant to secular corrosions, even as they abandon the larger, looser, almost shambling, structures which used to relate the Church to the wider society. No matter that this is at odds with the prejudice against structures and roles *as such*. There is a quest for the in-group and within that in-group the clergyman orchestrates communal consciousness.

He wants to be close and to eliminate the area of defensible private and individual space. A great deal of liturgical reform, so-called, drums up a kind of raucous participation intended to overrun the boundaries of individuality. Conscience, defiantly individual, is overwhelmed in consciousness. The point can be overstated. A great deal of contemporary radicalization makes people aware of the range of injustice in the world. It is, in my view, to be welcomed. Nevertheless, there is a communal emphasis which runs dangerously parallel to collectivism. The communal and the collective stand adjacent to each other. The end result is quite paradoxical since one finds the ideal of spontaneous authenticity yoked to an admiration for collective belonging. What is *not* admired, however, is individual striving and achievement. To strive and achieve is adjusted very anti-social and definitely non-Christian. Games are to be played but no goals are to be scored. Excellence is a crime against equality.

I have underlined a contradiction between the search for spontaneous authenticity and the setting-up of cell-like structures in which to nourish communal consciousness. This contradiction is, as I have argued elsewhere, quite central; and it distinguishes those who are basically oriented in a radical liberal direction from those whose end is total, collective liberation. But both liberals and liberators are inimical to what they regard as capitalist individuality and also to the kind of individuality nourished in organic conservative structures. Go-getting initiative belongs to capitalist notions of individualism and sets itself non-Christian goals of accumulating wealth. Roles and modes, restraints and manners govern the other kind of individuality and maintain private controls and standards resistant to popular invasions. To put it in a nutshell, the liberal contemporary clergyman is opposed first to the idea that man maketh money, and second, to the idea that (in the words of the motto of Winchester School) "manners maketh man." They are against money and manners. This relates to what I said earlier concerning the prejudice against ritual performance.

Communal redemption and the new society

However, one difficulty which emerges is that individual redemption becomes almost meaningless as compared with the construction of a new society. It seems useless to preach for the conversion of individual souls just as it seems odd to say "I believe" rather than "we believe." So that remarkable discovery of selfhood and individual conscience associated with Protestantism begins once more to recede. The bourgeois invention of privacy is to be subject to systematic disruption in the interests of communal control. Here we can see the way in which Catholic communalism and contemporary collectivism can overlap and, in some circumstances, actually merge.

The gospels do, of course, warn expressly against perverse individualism, egocentricity and the pursuit of wordly goods. So there is a point of contact between the contemporary search for communal consciousness or the condemnation of capitalist striving and the original deposit of faith. This is part indeed of the morphological resemblance between Christian theology and Marxist doctrine, which has often been remarked upon. What is at stake, however, is the extent to which individual economic initiative is linked to the expression of individual selfhood *as such*. None of the societies which have banned individual economic activity, have succeeded in nourishing individual selfhood and the rights of conscience. Even Yugoslavia, which is the least oppressive of Marxist societies in this respect, is far behind most developed capitalist societies.[1] Capitalist societies have generated checks against their own worst tendencies; Marxist societies (so-called) have accelerated their own worst tendencies and exalted them as virtues.

Finally then, what attitudes follow from liberal-cum-liberationist politics in that interim that remains before the contradiction between them is apparent? Let me take an admirable Catholic Canadian theologian, Gregory Baum, as my example. Since my "realist" was sympathetically portrayed, it seems only fair to have an equally sympathetic portrayal of an idealist. Professor Baum also offers an example of a man who is steeped in a sociological understanding. I take a small article by him entitled "Moral People, Immoral Society" as my point of reference.[2]

Baum as characteristic idealist

Professor Baum begins by saying "Christians often lament the breakdown of values in our society. They tell us we no longer share a common vision, that each person promotes his or her own career, that selfishness and apathy have become dominant characteristics, and that the social intercourse between persons at work and in the neighbourhood is defined by impersonal, purely contractual relations. We become isolated, preoccupied exclusively with our own affairs, we lose the sense of solidarity, and even the intimate ties of marriage and friendship are easily undermined by the pressure of social life."

Baum then goes on to make his crucial point which is that Christian values can never be introduced by individual conversion or by personal dedication. This is because the logic of the market determines public values. Whatever you consider, whether it be housing or the production of food, is based on the principle of profit, and above all dominated by the power of giant corporations. These corporations are concerned to garnish their image and so they may support reforms as the best way of assuring social stability. When we participate in the life of these corporations, we absorb their understanding of life by seeking to compete, promote our careers, have a pleasant private existence, remain free of obligations, and — above all — neglect the common good. To preach the importance of *individual conversion* is to pull the wool over people's eyes, when in truth they ought to become *critics of the system.*

Given that the *system* is responsible for the "emergence of universal selfishness," there are two critical strategies available: radical and reformist. Reformists argue that the logic of existing institutions, though it does not offer real democracy, equality and participation, nevertheless generates the desire for these things. This democratic thrust, which at the moment is at odds with the inherently hierarchical nature of capitalism, will in the end, produce a new community-oriented ethos and a vision of life beyond egotism.

Radicals disagree. They do not see democracy as a counter-balance to capitalism, but rather as infected by capitalism. The owners will only allow reforms which also happen to benefit them. Preaching justice and love remains "ideological" unless part of the practice of criticism and revolutionary engagement. This, says Professor Baum, is not some maverick intellectual view but the basic stance of the major Canadian churches. The Labor Day Statement of the Roman Catholic Church in 1976 said that the present system produces a gap between rich and poor people and rich and poor nations, and concentrates the control of the world's resources in the hands of a small elite. Christians must, therefore, listen to the victims of the system, and thereby achieve their own self-knowledge. The answer lies in working for co-ownership, solidarity and sharing. Professor Baum adds, and this again is crucial, that all this has nothing whatever to do with the extant revolutionary regimes, since they have created a form of bureaucratic centralism "closer to state capitalism than to socialism."

An English verison of the same basic argument can be found in "Poverty, Revolution and the Church" by Michael Paget-Wilkes.[3] He argues that the poor reject the Church because the Church rejects them, and excludes them from its machinery of decision-making. The Church should comprehensively dissociate itself from present values and structures and develop a participatory structure, aligning itself with community experiments and minority protest movements. Disestablishment is a natural concomitant of this strategy.

The political mind of the idealist

The themes, then, are clear enough: the promotion of community and participation, identification with the underprivileged, the evening up of disparities between nations, and the impossibility of effective democratic action or individual conversion. The list of aims seems admirable, indeed *is* admirable. But it rests on the following approach. First, that political action is arrived at by assembling a list of approved *desiderata*—what, in short, would be nice. Second, that pessimism about the present set-up is compatible with optimism about the future. Third, that the observed consequences of the proposed structural changes elsewhere are irrelevant. If they turn out even more inimical to participation and solidarity than capitalism, they are to be labelled just another version of capitalism. Indeed, capitalism is the term for what is regarded as evil. Fourth, that no rigorous examination of exactly what would be implied by rule by the poor or by processes of participation is called for. The invocation of nice-sounding terms is adequate. Yet participation can be extremely oppressive. It can be everyone's right to be continuously oppressed by his or her fellows. The real problems of decentralization and the state are never faced, especially the fact that decentralization is bound to lead to an increase in the inequality and local concentrations of power. Fifth, the interested character of all political action is ignored. Once the poor nations acquire wealth, as they have done in the Middle East, they act in an almost entirely interested manner. The substitution of governments deriving their mandate from the masses rather than elites, will make no difference. Indeed, oppression is even easier when carried out in the name of the masses. People can then be oppressed in the name of *The* People. The realities of power are never analysed directly or in terms of real options.

Nevertheless, it is policies of this kind which are embraced by idealist clergy, reading off the requirements of policy from lists of approved values. This is not to say, of course, that justice and peace are not central to human aspirations, or that nothing can be done. But the problems are immensely complex, and every political choice involves severe losses and implication in evil happenings and consequences. Democracy is indeed "a damn bad system," but it is probably the best we can hope for. The limiting of evil is difficult enough, let alone the institution of *the* good.

NOTES

1. Michael Novak (ed.) *Capitalism and Socialism,* Washington, D.C.: American Enterprise Institute for Public Policy Research, 1979.
2. Gregory Baum, "Moral People, Immoral Society" *The Witness* Vol. 63, No. 10, October 1980.
3. Michael Paget-Wilkes, *Poverty, Revolution and the Church,* Exeter, Devon: Paternoster Press, 1981.

Comment

Lance Roberts

The historical frame of reference

Professor Martin has confronted a wide range of issues in choosing to explore how secularization has affected the role of the clergy, especially with respect to their views on the market economy. I admire his tackling this task, agree with much of what he says, and was provoked to ponder various issues. In the short space alloted me, I have chosen to outline my thoughts on but a few of the issues raised by his paper.

First, I think Dr. Martin has correctly identified the historical frame of reference that can be used to place the clergy's present situation in proper sociological perspective, although I would have preferred he elaborate on the nature of that situation. It seems to me that the pre-secularized situation can be described as "structurally tight"; that is, a social world in which there is a broad consensus on basic norms and values and where these expectations can be imposed upon people in a relatively effective manner. This contrasts with a structurally loose situation, like the present ones in modern societies, where expectations are more likely to be proposed by authorities and interpreted by recipients. In this structurally tight system the Church, of course, held a very influential position and members of the clergy were of high status.

As Professor Martin points out, the nature of this social structure was radically transformed after the two great revolutions stirred the forces of modernity. A fundamental feature of this process was that of secularization which brought a progressive withdrawal of religious institutions and symbols from sectors over which they had previously held sway (Berger, 1971:274). In this sense the Western world did disintegrate from a condition of relative institutional and ideological unity. Modern societies became progressively more socially differentiated and with this increased division of labour and institutional multiplication (due in large part to the operation of industrial capitalism) came a diversification of viewpoints often labelled as "ideational pluralism."

Such radical transformation in both the structural and cultural arrangements had understandably disorienting consequences. With the shuffling of traditional benchmarks, the clergy and laymen alike were left without a well-defined set of institutions or ideas on which to peg their identities. As Professor Martin notes, the Church and its normative network was moved from the centre to the periphery; they became one "amongst several competing viewpoints" and within the new marketplace of ideas the Church was less able to sustain its form as a "greedy institution" (Coser, 1974).

Role ambiguity among the clergy

It is important to remember that such broad social changes influenced both church leaders and followers. In sociological terms the new position of the clergy can be identified as one of role strain due to role ambiguity. We know that strong identities are nourished under social conditions characterized by a high degree of stability among role partners regarding the expected obligations and privileges of each status. Where such mutual expectations are poorly defined or unrealistic (the situation called "role ambiguity") then occupants of positions and their relationships to others are strained, largely because they have difficulty articulating and meeting the demands of their roles. Such strain is well documented in the social psychological literature as prevalent when social change is extensive (Vander Zanden, 1979), as has been the case of the clergy over the past century. One consequence of such a structurally ambiguous situation is that it is considerably more difficult for holders of relatively high status, like clergymen, to maintain their credibility and authority; after all, they are forced to act in a poorly defined situation. As a result, we have the situation Professor Martin describes: at the very time when laymen most need a steady, guiding institution to help them cope with the dislocations of modernity, the clergy are unable to fulfill this need reliably because they themselves are wrestling with the disrupting effects of the same social forces. In short, both modern clergy and laymen suffer from estrangement and alienation. Reactions to this condition are to be expected. In general, these reactions are usefully characterized as a "quest for community" (Nisbet, 1953).

The clerical response

Professor Martin informs us by cataloguing several of the responses the clergy use to clarify their new situation, to resolve their condition of role ambiguity, and to find a new form of community. One is to denigrate the capitalistic market ideology since this is identified as largely responsible for the spread of ideational pluralism and the subsequent loss of the clergy's ideological monopoly. Another form of role articulation involves a strategy of clerical specialization and bureaucratization as "professionals," with a consequent divorce from the concerns of the people and concentration on the narrower interests of the "neoclerical" reference group. A third approach involves an attempt by the clergy to align themselves with the supposed interests of laymen by becoming "relevant," which centres on discarding the core of ritual performance and becoming increasingly politicized. In a modern society such strategies can be expected to take several forms and Professor Martin acknowledges this in his characterization of Puritan and anti-Puritan types and, by extension, in his discussion of the idealist and realist types.

There are two central questions that focus all of this discussion. First, have the recent manoeuvers by the clergy succeeded in providing them with an articulated and credible status and set of functions? Second, how have their various attempts in this regard affected their views on the market? Regarding the issue of credibility one has to be at least skeptical. It seems to me that the plethora of activities that clergy engage in, both wide in range and often shallow, suggests that there is not a great deal of consensus about the social roles, purpose, and utility of the clergy. At the same time, the decline in attendance at orthodox churches and the level of commitment of those attending suggest that the people, in general, are not finding what they seek in the present structure of religious institutions (Bibby, 1980).

What might the churches do?

Granting such scepticism, one might speculate on the sociological form and function religious institutions might take on were they to define themselves more appropriately to the context of modern society. In my judgement such redefinition might begin with a realistic appeciation of what modernity has done to the social position of the Church and, moreover, what distinct needs are left for it to fulfill. On the first account it is essential to appreciate that "regardless of their theologically absolute self-interpretations, religious groups become *voluntary associations* . . . in the last resort no one is *compelled* to adhere to any religious group" (Berger, 1971:278, emphasis added). In other words, modern society is not structurally tight; it is loose in the sense that most institutions can only propose (rather than impose) a set of values, norms, and beliefs. Consequently, potential participants may choose among competing interpretations those which they find most credible. This state of affairs, in my judgement, places the clergy in a much more advantageous position than Professor Martin suggests when he reports their dissatisfaction with the fact that they "became bearers of a home-centred rather than a work-centred culture." As various observers have noted, one consequence of modernity has been a separation of individual's lives into public and private spheres where their public existence is most closely associated with highly bureaucratized forms of work. Generally, such work is perceived both as alienating and as permitting little autonomous action and potential for self-development. As a result, people have turned to the private sphere, to their home-centred lives, to pursue those voluntary activities which they find most fulfilling. Appreciating this social fact, the Church should see its opportunity. Surely there is little hope of the Church ever reachieving its presecularized influence. The fact remains, however, that if churches offer a meaningful product in the pluralistic marketplace of ideas and action they increase their chances of attracting a strongly committed membership, though perhaps not as broad a membership as they might wish.

Just how broadly based under such circumstances participation may be is an open question. Much depends on the specific social and psychological purposes on which the churches choose to focus their attention. As Professor Martin notes, clergymen, somewhat justifiably, view one of their strong suits as existing in the realm of ideas since, as Nisbet notes (1977:161), religion is among the oldest sources of thought. Clergymen of many persuasions presently use their positions to market their ideas on all sorts of social, political, and economic issues. One problem with this strategy, from the viewpoint of authority maintenance, is that by commenting on such an array of subject matters depth of insight probably suffers and, additionally, distinctiveness is also lessened. It would seem that precisely the opposite (namely, distinctive, informed, and in-depth commentaries) are what the Church should be aiming for if it is to establish itself as a credible voluntary institution in the modern world.

Ecclesial expertise

One could reasonably ask what distinctive area of expertise the Church might focus on. In my opinion it is that ancient function of "theodicity" that Berger *et al.,* (1973:185) describe as "any explanation of human events that bestows meaning upon the experiences of suffering and evil." No matter what changes the forces of modernity may have brought to our social structures, there has been no change in the fragility and mortality of the human condition. The "crises of existence" still remain and, as others have argued, the segmentation and deterioration of forms of community associated with complex societies may well have reduced our ability to cope with these crises. The provision of a coherent set of ideas that allow people to define and rationalize the basic facts of life and death is an ancient and important function of religious institutions.

There can be little doubt about the continuing demand members of all societies have for such services. If the churches do not provide such symbolic "solutions" to the great problems of meaning then people will turn to other sources for fulfillment, as they appear to be doing. At this point we must not neglect one further and important advantage religious institutions have in this regard. Under conditions of ideational pluralism, religious worldviews have to exist and compete with various secular ideologies for the minds of men. Religion has, however, a crucial advantage which stems from its sacred status, should that be invoked. Sacred judgements, of course, have the capability of being much more compelling than merely mortal, secular evaluations and rationalizations, because sacred statements transcend individual consciousness and are, as Durkheim tells us, preeminently social in nature. The very idea of morality connotes a force beyond the individual, "a force which makes demands and punishes transgressions" (Collins, 1982:38). People adhere to moral precepts because the group to which they belong demands it. This proposition is so fundamental that the idea of a moral existence without the backing of a strong social structure can be thought of as, in John Scott's words, "a sociological anomaly." Without going into detail, it can be said that the advantage that religious institutions have in marketing their ideas and ideals is directly related to their ability to establish sound religious organizations. Through participation in a religious community, assembled members become capable of generating energy and confidence, and ultimately of transforming the ideas of mortal men into sacred statements—statements that are continuously appealing by virtue of their ability to provide ultimate answers and purpose to our lives.

The role of ritualized activity

At this juncture we can underline the significance of a point Dr. Martin makes about the decline of emphasis the modern clergy give to the place of ritualized activity. To the extent that this occurs it would seem that the clergy are giving up a crucial organizational advantage. We know from several sociological studies that a fundamental requirement in the transformation of secular, individual notions into sacred, collective ones is that, in addition to assembly, members must participate in a ritualized set of actions. There must be a common coordinated pattern as they focus on the symbols that identify the group. Only through ritualized action can persons come to share the same emotions and become conscious that others feel the same way. It seems ironic, as Professor Martin notes, that modern men, in an attempt to cope with the alienation and estrangement so prevalent in complex societies, turn inward in an attempt to "find" their true, authentic selves. The irony stems from our appreciation of what social psychologists have long been telling us: that we are *social* products. It follows, then, that if we have lost our direction amid the complexity of our society and wish to "find ourselves," then we would do well to look for ways to connect ourselves meaningfully to others through communal action. In this regard the clergy, in their role as "the masters of religious ceremonies," could prove most functional.

My position concerning how the clergy might work toward resolution of their role ambiguity is essentially pluralistic in nature. It emphasizes the need for them to legitimize their role through definition of a distinctive function that recognizes the voluntary nature of their institution. To the extent that clergy use their resources to compete with other belief systems in areas that are not distinct, as they do when they comment on economic matters, I would anticipate a continued dilution of their authority. Many of the characteristics of what Professor Martin labels the "realist" position support this pluralistic outlook. In stressing the importance of tradition, hierarchy, autonomy, and decentralization Martin outlines the form of a religious institution that might be able to establish itself as a credible and independent source of authority in the lives of ordinary men and women. However, if we turn to Dr. Martin's central thesis, it would appear that the present configuration of social forces is more conducive to the adoption of what he calls the "idealist position." I would like to conclude my remarks by emphasizing what is probably the prime structural reason why this path has been, and will likely continue as, the predominant route.

Why the idealist position will predominate

Whereas the realistic portrait of clergymen might be thought of as based on a pluralistic form of organization, the idealist position stresses a system based more on unity. Throughout Professor Martin's portrayal of this type there is an emphasis on communal consciousness, collective liberation, and common vision. From a sociological point of view, this idealist vision can, like the realist position, be conceived as a response to the dislocations concurrent with modernity; it seeks to establish a renewed sense of community by using the oldest form of integration, mechanical solidarity, based on similarity. The extensive social differentiation of modernity, with its emphasis on specialization, individualization, and atomism, has proceeded so extensively in many places that the result is egoism and alienation of considerable consequence. The pluralistic solution to this disintegrated state is to seek the reestablishment of meaningful, intermediate scale institutions and communities to which individuals can voluntarily commit themselves. Following this course, the present strain experienced by the clergy would be resolved by the identification and establishment of religious institutions that would have a distinctive focus and to which the clergy's status would be attached and confined. This idea of a religious community existing among other forms of community, as Professor Martin notes, does not appear to be dominant. I believe the reason for this outcome is that it runs against a predominant social fact in this century; namely, that society is becoming increasingly politicized. As Robert Nisbet notes: "What we have witnessed, however, in every Western country... is the almost incessant growth in power over the lives of human beings — power that is basically the result of the gradual disappearance of all the intermediate institutions which, coming from the predemocratic past, served for a long time to check the kind of authority that almost from the beginning sprang from the new legislative bodies and executives in the modern democracies" (Nisbet,1977:170). Without going into detail, it would seem that those clergy adopting the idealist view have recognized the salience of this fact, and rather than work toward reestablishing their position as a legitimate mediating institution, have chosen to politicize the Church. The idea appears to be that if power is becoming concentrated in the society then the Church needs to become active in this manner in order to maintain, and possibly expand, its own influence. The attractiveness of this model lies not only in its congruence with recent social facts but with its potential for increasing the status of the clergy. After all, if power becomes concentrated and the Church can manage to affiliate itself with the sources of such power, then the clergy, as official church representatives, can only better their position.

If these structural analyses appear plausible then it becomes comprehensible why clergymen of all persuasions are not keen on the ideas that govern the market. The realists, with their pluralistic orientation, view the market emphases on individualism and competition as a pervasive levelling force that threatens so to absorb participants that little time, energy, and commitment are left for the maintenance of other mediating institutions. By contrast, the idealists with their more unified vision see the diversity encouraged by the marketplace as one of the last major forces which disrupt the steady monopolization of power that is necessary if they are to participate in the reconstruction of society in their own image.

REFERENCES

Berger, Brigitte (1971) *Societies in Change.* New York: Basic Books Inc.

Berger, P., B. Berger, and H. Keller (1973) *The Homeless Mind: Modernization and Consciousness.* New York: Random House.

Bibby, Reginald (1980) "Religion" in Robert Hagedorn (ed.) *Sociology.* Toronto: Holt, Rinehart and Winston.

Collins, Randall (1982) *Sociological Insight: An Inquiry Into Nonobvious Sociology.* New York: Oxford University Press.

Coser, Lewis (1974) *Greedy Institutions: Patterns of Undivided Commitment.* New York: The Free Press.

Nisbet, Robert (1953) *The Quest for Community.* New York: Oxford University Press.

——— (1977) "The New Despotism" in *The Politicization of Society.* Kenneth S. Templeton (ed.) Indianapolis: Liberty Press.

——— (1978) *The Social Philosophers: Community and Conflict in Western Thought.* New York: Thomas Y. Crowell Company.

Vander Zanden, James W. 1979 *Sociology.* New York: John Wiley and Sons.

Comment

Ronald Preston

Some relevant background

The Martin paper does not spell out the connection between its subject and that of the conference as a whole, "The Morality of the Market: Its Religious Implications." Nor shall I. I shall stick closely to the paper. Martin is both a distinguished sociologist and a competent theologian. Originally a Methodist, he has recently been ordained to the non-stipendiary ministry in the Church of England while continuing in his Chair in Sociology at the London School of Economics. Since his paper is illustrated by a number of broadly liturgical references it is relevant to note that he has become widely known as a leader of the opposition to the revised services of the Church. It is necessary to say something about the present position of the Church in this respect, for those not familiar with the English situation.

On November 1, 1980 the *Alternative Services Book* was published. As its name implies it is an alternative to the *Book of Common Prayer* 1662, which was hitherto the only legal prayer book of the Church. *The Alternative Services Book* contains a complete series of revised services, which had been through a period of experiment and revision, before being finally accepted by the General Synod of the Church. As an established Church parliament remains the ultimate legal authority but, suffice it to say that, in practice, nearly everything is left to the Church to decide, including the revision of its liturgies.

The *Alternative Services Book* is widely used, but it has to be with the consent of the parochial Church councils; no one is obliged to use it. The opposition, of which Martin is a leader, is largely made up of those concerned with the cultural life of the country, particularly professors of English literature. Many are not regular church-goers. They raise a problem which faces a church which was in a "Christendom" situation and is now no longer. In 1662, and still more in 1549, when the *Book of Common Prayer* originated, Church, State and Culture were one; and the Church had the good fortune, largely through Thomas Cranmers' linguistic skills, to possess a prayer book whose language deeply embedded itself in the culture of the country, so that a dictionary of quotations has as its three biggest single sources the Authorized Version of the Bible (King James), Shakespeare and the *Book of Common Prayer*. The Authorized Version can still be read by those who love it whenever they like, but a liturgy not used is dead. And yet the *Book of Common Prayer* has long been inadequate to the needs of the modern church. The church clearly has a cultural responsibility here which it is not easy to discharge. But instead of illuminating this problem Martin has persisted in maintaining that the whole process leading to the production and use of alternative services has largely been due to "trendy" clergy, discountenanced by their changing sociological status, and bringing about neo-clerical liturgical changes against the wishes of the faithful laity. Anyone who had known the Church of England would know that this is far from the case. Ever since the Oxford Movement (the High Church or Anglo-Catholic

Movement) of the last century the Church has had clergy who came into parishes and altered services on their own authority – illegally in most cases – without reference to the wishes of the congregation. In this case they cannot do so without consent. Of course they are often active persuaders – the full-time trained "professional" usually is the one to advance ideas – but that is a different matter – and in this case he must persuade.

This misunderstanding by Martin may seem far away from the theme of this present paper, but it does illuminate nuances in it, for the paper is about the clergy, their role and attitudes. Indeed Martin is a "nuanced" writer. It is not always easy to tell exactly what he is saying. One of the problems with his paper is that it is unclear that he is relying on sociology as much as he claims. His aim as he states it is to show how sociological changes have made more likely the emergence of a new type of clergyman with attitudes characterized by variations on the term "liberals" or "liberation" (neither of which has a self-evident meaning). Yet one cannot help raising the question whether he is not weaving a case against recent movements in the Church, and in favour of a conservative-organic attitude, which is less connected with academic sociology than he indicates. In theory Martin accepts "methodological agnosticism" in sociological studies of religion. I am not sure about the practice in this case.

It should be noted that the paper is confined to the U.K., to England in fact, and to the Church of England. This is legitimate. England was the first industrialized country and has had the longest experience of the quite new kind of society which industrialization produces. And the Church of England, as an established Church, is an excellent example of a Church formed in an archetypal "Christendom" situation having to deal with its disintegration in the pluralism of the twentieth century. So it is a good example to take.

The three terms in Martin's title

a) The Clergy.
As soon as a church can afford a "professional" ministry, that is to say people who earn their living as "professional Christians," it is in great danger of being clericalized. When the roots of the doctrine of ordination are examined, it is clear that whether the priest or minister is paid or not, and whether he operates on a full-time basis or not, is entirely irrelevant. If the Church had no paid clergy, it would still ordain

clergy. In the course of Christian history almost all traditions have been clericalized, including those traditions which do not have a very strong doctrine of ordination. Such clericalization is nicely expressed by the remark, often made by lay folk, about someone who is offering for ordination that he is "going into Church." The result has been the downgrading of the role of all the rest of the church members — the laity in the modern sense of the term, not the New Testament sense. One of the healthy tendencies in the Church today is a widespread awareness of the distortions this has caused. At any rate the question arises as to whether it is wise to concentrate on the clergy as a useful guide to what is happening in the Church as a whole. With due caution, I think it is.

b) Secularization.

Secularization is not defined in Martin's paper. There has been an enormous discussion in recent years among sociologists of religion of the term, and the alleged process, usually in terms of the relation between Christianity and Western civilization. Martin himself has played a large part in this discussion. At one time he advocated dropping the term because of its many and contradictory meanings, but since then he has developed his own general theory of secularization. Attitudes among both sociologists and theologians to "secularization" vary. Some sociologists have seen it as a process leading to the inevitable collapse of religion, and some secular theologians have seen it as the way to maintain the reality of religion amid the characteristic outlook and structures to which advanced industrial societies lead. In this essay, Martin seems to mean by secularization the decline of ecclesiastical and clerical control over social institutions. Whether that means a decline in influence is part of the debate; the decline in control is indisputable.

c) Politics.

In his discussion of politics, Martin's main interest is in the adaption by what he calls "anti-Puritan" clergy of a different, and more critical, attitude to public and political affairs. Here it is important to note that the Church, the clergy, and theologians have always been political: the Church as an institution operates in a political milieu and theological thought goes on in a political context, because "man is a political animal." The central question is rather how far the Church, and the clergy in particular in the present discussion, have tended to be politically acceptive or critical of the *status quo*.

Traditional Christian theology, since the conversion of Constantine, has been overwhelmingly in support of the existing authorities, and of regarding the *status quo* as being divinely appointed. (This has become increasingly hard to maintain in a time of rapid social change, and is a source of many difficulties at the moment.) "Throne and altar" is a phrase often used to characterize this attitude. So is the assumption that any call to act "for Queen and country" is bound to have divine approval. The Christendom situation epitomized this political theology very clearly. The "political" theologians of today have pointed out that the decline of this Christendom situation has produced a "privatization" of religion, which professes to be a-political (separating religion from politics) when in fact, instead of expressly giving religious sanction to the *status quo* like the old political theology, it gives irresponsible sanction to it by simply acquiescing in it and concentrating on private virtues and individual "soul making." The result is that as long as the Church and the clergy explicitly, or tacitly, sanction the *status quo* they are thought to be non-political, whereas if they criticize it they are accused of being political in a pejorative sense. In the last few years, the term "politicized" has been used extensively in this pejorative sense. Martin is well aware of this situation, though the tone of his article at times suggests the pejorative use. The question then is not whether the Church and the clergy are political, but in what way they are: and how astute they are in understanding the problems of politics. Certainly a religious faith with a strong element of "prophecy" within it, like the Judaeo-Christian faith, cannot be content to be confined to a purely acquiescent political role, a fact which causes great difficulties when faced with totalitarian states of Right or Left.

Malaise among the clergy

To come at last to the substance of Martin's paper, I take first his contention that a malaise among the clergy has arisen because of their failure to keep up with the new and growing professions, or to define any professional expertise they claim to possess in a way accepted by the public. Martin claims that such malaise creates an ambivalence between a neo-clericalism (partly expressed in liturgical changes) and a new style of cleric who sinks himself in the laity and takes to a "form" of politics.

There has undoubtedly been a sense of malaise in parish work. About 10 percent of those ordained, in the only study made of it, dropped out of ministerial work subsequently. This was not due to loss of faith in most cases, but to marital difficulties or frustration with parish work. Objective causes appear more obvious than subjective professional malaise. In urban areas, much church property is too extensive and in the wrong place. With the decline in conventional church-going, there are fewer people to pay for church structures. Also there is still a lot of time taken up by the expression of residual conventional religion in *rites de passage* of those who have not had, or do not have, any intention of taking part in the life of the church. This element is declining fairly quickly, except for funerals. It is not easy to escape being buried by a parson. If concentration is turned to the faithful who do regularly attend, the result can be a neo-clericalism. At present in the General Synod, the House of Clergy is frequently blocking changes which have clear majorities in the House of Bishops and House of Laity (an indication that one must not attend exclusively to the clergy in analyzing what is going on in the church). But there are signs that a church less constrained by the conventional church-goer of the Christendom situation may be fitter for Christian life and witness. The abandonment of much clerical dress arises from the sense that the old style is not necessary, and indeed a barrier when the ordained person is seen as one with the people of God, except for symbolical use for liturgical purposes. Here Martin misunderstands the liturgical situation. If he means by his remark that ritual action has been downgraded in the view of many people to apply to regular church-goers, it is not true of them. His blindness to the Liturgical Movement is serious at this point. This has been steadily renewing the public worship of all the confessions, not least the Church of England and the Anglican communion, and not least in the establishment of the general communication of the people at the main service on Sundays. On the Catholic side, the non-communicating High Mass has almost gone; and on the Protestant side, the ideal of the Reformers has at last been realized after 400 years. At the time of the Reformation, they failed because of the unwillingness of the laity to communicate, a mediaeval corruption. The fact that traditional vestments, often in an improved style, are increasingly worn and are much less controversial than they once were (contrast Martin) is one outward sign of this. More significant is the much greater lay involvement, greater communal participation, and greater friendliness of Anglican worship. Martin thinks of this as "raucous participation" and what he regards as invasion of privacy seems to be what St. Paul was writing about in Ephesians chapter 4 as central to life together in the Church.

The reference to cells within parish life as further expressions of this invasion (compare the traditional Methodist class meeting) is puzzling. I see no contradiction at all between this and a Christian personal authenticity. Martin thinks this contradiction "quite central." I think so far from being that, it is what the New Testament is aiming at. One would need to know a lot more about the individuality which Martin thinks is being infringed, that which he says is nourished in "organic conservative structures." He does not amplify this.

The new "form" of clergy politics

So we come to the "form" of politics which the new style clergy are adopting. "Form" is a vague term. What could be meant? If it is meant that clergy are identifying the gospel with a particular political programme or with support of one particular party, this is true of such a tiny number as to be insignificant. Martin seems to include under the "form" of politics the growth in the number of clergy who abandon parochial work for the central agencies of the Church, where they are "refugees," and out of touch with the grassroots. This denigration is unjust both to the clergy involved and the work they have done. Most go back to parish work after a period of service. And the work of the Central Boards has been of very high quality. The Board of Social Responsibility in particular has produced a whole series of good quality reports, always taking care that they are backed by expert sifting of evidence. These reports have done a lot to educate members of the General Synod, fed the speeches of Bishops in the House of Lords, and much more slowly have percolated through Diocesan Boards of Social Responsibility to local areas. Some local Boards have also done good work in local terms. The upshot has been that there has come about a considerable change in the competence of the Church in the social field. Prior to 1914 it is difficult to exaggerate the incompetence and ineffectiveness of the Church in these matters. Its roots were rural and in a relatively stable society and it had never come to grips with the new dynamic, urban civilization which the technological developments of the Industrial Revolution brought into existence. The Church had an outlook that essentially thought of the present in terms of the past. Now the situation has changed. If one asks in this dynamic world, "What is going on?" the Church has the means to be up-to-date in analysis. The Ecumencial Movement has been a great stimulus here in widening the frame of reference within which a national church has been tempted to be restricted. What use is made of the up-to-date analysis is another matter. But ignorance can no longer be a plea.

Moreover, the Church has realized the inadvisability of having almost all its ministry related to the home, when the separation of work and home is so widespread. This is why the more traditional ministries to hospitals, prisons and residential schools have been extended beyond seamen and the theatre to local government, holiday camps, commerce and, above all, industry. It still remains true that nine out of ten ordained men are in the parochial ministry.

Perhaps by a "form" of politics, Martin means that the clergy are more critically engaged, and that this critical engagement has a Leftist orientation. It is possible to be critically engaged on the Right, as he points out, but in England we have scarcely anything to correspond with the "moral majority" in the U.S. The nearest equivalents are Mrs. Mary Whitehouse's National Viewers and Listeners Association and a body called The Festival of Light, but they are insignificant compared to the "moral majority" in the U.S. The very able layman who recently left the Secretaryship of the Board of Social Responsibility (to seek ordination) has analyzed the traditional attitude of the Church of England to public affairs down the centuries as one of "critical solidarity with the authorities in the State. I should say that in the past the emphasis has been more on the solidarity rather than an even balance between the two, and that now the balance is shifting more towards the critical. On economic issues, the General Synod still reflects the general attitudes of the middle and upper classes of which it is almost entirely composed. On social issues, it is much more "liberal" than the general population. A remarkable event occurred three years ago when the Synod condemned with only one dissentient vote details in clauses of the Thatcher government's Nationality Bill on the grounds that it was in effect white racism. Later all the churches maintained their point that the Falkland Islands service should not be nationalistic and jingoistic in tone. A conservative government can no longer count on the endorsement of the Church.

Ideal types in Martin's discussion

Martin then polarizes clerical attitudes on two "ideal types," on the lines of Max Weber's method, the realist and the idealist. I think this is quite in order for heuristic purposes. I have used it myself, in polarizing the demand or free market economy as opposed to the command or centralized one. It is quite a useful device. Martin makes the appropriate remarks about it having no reference to truth claims, and that one does not expect ever to see an ideal type in its pure form. People and societies exhibit various shades of both. I am certainly a realist as between his two types, but I am not happy with some of his detailed analysis of the idealist.

The objection to the State prayers of the *Book of Common Prayer* is that they teach the Divine Right of Kings (Tudor monarchs) and pray only for Christian rulers, assuming that we live in a cosy Christendom. The objection to the phrase "maintenance of Thy true religion and virtue" (and I have not heard of many objectors) is that in its context it referred to the State support for the Anglican Settlement and proscription of others. (It can now be used without that mental association.) All the revised services give ample scope for prayers for the State.

It is too easy to point to the dangers of an "abstract loyalty to humanity." We are painfully grasping the necessity to reach out to the oneness of mankind if the world is not to destroy itself, and are aware that nationalism, originating in "Christian" Europe, and backed by the churches in different countries has plunged the world into two wars in this century. Moreover these national churches have often imposed adventitious Western cultural values on new churches in other areas of the world as if such cultural values were identical with the Christian faith. We are now learning from the backlash against this, and the Ecumenical Movement has helped a lot in this task. The churches have had no problem in being rooted in the culture of the West, the problem is how to be rooted in it and at the same time transcend it with the necessary universalism of the gospel.

Martin on the church and politics

Martin seems to me good on the necessity of structures and roles, and the dangers of atomistic conservative capitalism. What he might have pointed out is that conservatism must know when to change, otherwise a backlog of protest builds up which leads to pressure for radical, and perhaps violent, changes which are hard to control, and end up not where the instigators intended. They are not appropriate for the delicately interconnected structures of an advanced industrial society. I think Martin is also good on the "interested" nature of political activity. The doctrine of human imperfectibility is brought in, or original sin (an unfortunate term). But it must be remembered that the Christian faith is a gospel of good news, and that (to use this terminology) original righteousness is also part of the Christian faith. In other words while a Christian does not expect Utopia (or the Kingdom of God in its fullness) on this earth, he does have terrestrial hopes of how men and women may live together in a more humane and just society, and not just celestial hopes beyond the grave.

Martin indicates that there is in the end a contradiction between liberals and liberators. I am not clear where the relative virtue of the liberal lies in his view, though I share his disapproval of liberators who in fact collectively suppress persons in the name of "The People." But we must continue to wrestle with the problems of participation, in spite of their frequent over-simple presentation, else we shall abandon one of the greatest problems of industrial society, which pre-occupation with the market does not face.

The essential point is that persons mould structures, so there is point in individual conversion, but also that structures mould persons from infancy upwards, and therefore salvation must be thought of also in corporate terms. So to his five points related to Gregory Baum, I would say,

1. Usually we begin to be aroused by a critical judgement on some aspect or aspects of the *status quo*. It is not so much that we have an ideal picture of a just social order in mind, but that features of the present one strike us as unjust.
2. We are not Utopian about the future, but we do have hope.
3. We do need to take warnings from present experience; I think those who do not are in fact few.
4. Greater participation in decision-making is indeed important; it presents many difficulties, and much of the talk about it at present is over-simple. There is a lot of work to be done here; but it cannot be avoided.
5. If the interested character of all political action is ignored, this is indeed foolish.

This century has seen a tremendous movement towards the unity and renewal of the churches; we call it the Ecumenical Movement. It has proved searching and creative, but has still a long way to go. Martin has not paid much attention to it; his passing reference to "unprincipled unions" is a travesty of what the Faith and Order side of the

Ecumenical Movement has been about, or indeed the Church of England in its own small corner. If he had he might have seen more signs of hope.

NOTE

In a book *The Testing of the Churches 1932–82* (Epworth Press, London, 1983) which deals with the main churches in England, I have covered the Church of England, and have provided evidence for the general references made in this paper.

Discussion

Edited by Kenneth G. Elzinga

Ronald Preston: Much of the nostalgia for the 1662 Prayer Book comes from those who are only occasional church-goers. Until recently in the Church of England you would have a fair number of people who came to non-sacramental services especially on more public occasions, but who never went to communion at all. They regarded the Church of England as rather a good thing, to which in general one should give respect. But they wouldn't take it seriously as far as any personal time and commitment went. This is what a friend of mine used to call a "Duke of Wellington-type of Christian."

Now, in the course of my lifetime, there has been a collapse of this. So, if you go to church on Easter Sunday, there certainly will be more communicants than usual; but that is because everybody who is still a regular attender will make an effort to be there that Sunday. But there will be very few people whom you don't see at other times of the year. And the decay of occasional attendance at non-sacramental services has been very marked indeed. So it now comes mostly to attendance by such people at funerals of public figures, and things of that sort. The people who only come occasionally rather like to think of the church as going on as it always has. And if they do attend and find it different from when they were last there four or five years ago, they tend to get upset. And this lies behind some of the comments in David Martin's paper. It is the objective decay of a Christendom situation, which has gone very rapidly, in my lifetime, as far as the Church of England is concerned. Many things will pass with it.

It is true, for example, that the language of the *Book of Common Prayer* in a sense is magic. I quote one Collect from this book to do justice to Martin:

> Oh, Almighty God who alone canst order the unruly wills and affections of sinful men; grant unto thy people that they may love the thing which Thou commandest, and desire that which Thou dost promise; that so, among the sundry and manifold changes of the world, our hearts may surely there be fixed where true joys are to be found; through Jesus Christ, our Lord.

This is what moves David Martin. And it moves me. This is what he wants to defend. But when you look at it in the widest sense, you can see that the Prayer Book is wholly unsuited to the modern church situation. I've tried to illustrate that in my paper, and I say no more.

As to the politicization issue, I thought I had gone into that fairly closely, and I think I've shown that people in Britain only talk about politicization if the clergy or the church make political remarks *against* what is going on. If they support the *status quo,* that is not thought to be political. But David Martin ignores that altogether.

Then there is the question of the typology between the realist and the idealist clergy. Here I am with Martin, in a sense. His typology owes an enormous lot to Reinhold Niebuhr who influenced me as well.

So if I am going to class myself according to this typology, I am a realist clergyman. But I am very dissatisfied with Martin's picture of the idealist clergyman. It isn't only that those of us who are realists have to realize that Original Sin is not the only or, indeed, the essential element in the Christian gospel. It is a misleading term. Niebuhr ceased to use it in the end, because he felt that it was so misunderstood that he could never convey what he meant by using it. But if you are going to use it, you have to also bring in original righteousness, as well, as a source of not merely pessimistic thoughts about the problems of human life, but of hopes about human life as well.

It seems to me that persons need saving, if you like, or liberating, if you like, because they mould institutions. But institutions need changing because they mould persons from infancy upwards. There are those who say "either you change persons, or you change institutions," but this seems to me a false alternative. You have to do both.

Now the free market is a human institution; and it therefore has to be evaluated as a human institution. And I ask myself, "What virtues does the free market presuppose? Is it clear what it presupposes? Does it foster them? Does it ignore them? Does it undermine them?" These are all relevant questions about the human institution of the free market. And finally, since it's only one institution among others — what other virtues are needed? And what institutional expressions do we need for these other virtues as well?

Paul Heyne: I hope we can all agree that sociological criticisms of ideas are both useful and dangerous. They are useful because ideas do have causes. And they are dangerous because such criticisms too easily degenerate into ignoring the validity of the ideas and concentrating on *ad hominem* attacks and assumed motives. I think this applies to both sides in the general discussion in which we are engaged. It's easy for defenders of capitalism, such as myself, to ignore the clerical critics, such as Gregory Baum, by claiming that everything they say is a result of status anxiety. And it's easy for the clerical critics of capitalism to dismiss, or heavily discount, the arguments of economists who are, I think the principal formulators of arguments to defend capitalism. It's much too easy for them to dismiss these arguments on the grounds that, well, all social scientists operate in some kind of value framework.

Now, having said that it's both useful and dangerous, what follows from it? I think one thing, maybe, follows from it. Sociological explanations should only be provided by people for those movements in which they, themselves, participate. Don't do it to your enemies. Do it to yourself.

Milton Friedman: May I just interject that I think that's utterly wrong. I don't want to be in the position where I say, "I only want a physician to advise me on cancer if he's had cancer." I think sociologists ought to study whatever sociologists study.

Paul Heyne: That's not quite what I am saying.

Milton Friedman: Why isn't it?

Paul Heyne: I think in practice, you'll find it isn't useful. Take your famous argument about the distinction between positive and normative economics. It's interesting how the people who agree with that are the people who also like your economics. But the people who don't like the economics of the Chicago School won't have anything to do with the "positive-normative distinction." They say it's a dodge. It's a "cop out."

Murdith McLean: I was, in fact, going to say something like what Paul said. I'm not sure I've got a really good grasp of the distinction; but I know I do have a methodological problem here. The distinction between internalist and externalist explanations is a slippery and a hard one. But I suppose it means something like this: If you give an externalist explanation of an event, or a belief, or a bit of behaviour, then you explain it in terms of social forces, or brain chemistry, or some other kind of causal phenomenon. If, on the other hand, you give an internalist explanation, I take it what you're giving is an account in terms of people's beliefs, rational preferences, or that kind of thing. If that's right, then something like the following kind of thing happens.

When we are accounting for some kind of activity, or belief, or whatever, that we don't approve of, we may give it either an internalist or an externalist account. We can give it an internalist account in terms of mistaken beliefs, and go on to expose the mistakes therein. Or — and this is probably more likely — we'll give an externalist account of it, in terms of the antecedent conditions, the rigorous toilet training to which this person was subjected, or something else.

If we given an externalist account of it, it's almost from the beginning bound to be at least somewhat dismissive. If I say to somebody, "Why do you believe in God?" and that person is a believer, the person is not likely to say, "Well, given the fact that I was born into a middle class family, this is the sort of thing that you can expect." I mean, that's not the sort of explanation a person is likely to give.

Nor is the person going to give it as an explanation of why somebody else believes in God, if they tend to approve of that kind of belief.

This is why I'm sympathetic to Paul's point about requiring it of social scientists when they are giving externalist accounts of anything, that it might be something for which they have at least a sympathetic regard. I am not sure they have to be adherents, but at least they should have a fairly sympathetic regard.

The trouble is—and this is just a methodological problem of mine—to know how each of you can even square an externalist account at all, with the sympathetic appreciation; because it almost seems, if I just think about it in the way we ordinarily treat explanations, that to give an externalist explanation is to dismiss the phenomenon.

Seymour Siegel: In the United States, we favour the more psychological or even psychiatric explanation as to why people do, say, or think, or act in certain ways. And of course the question is, Can you apply that to the psychiatrist himself? That is, consider the sociologist who accounts so neatly for clerical behaviour. Can, or will he subject himself to the same sociological analysis as to why he is a sociologist and why he has this view of the clergy?

Obviously he doesn't, because then it's an infinite regress and nobody will say anything—which may not be a bad thing. (laughter) But then we wouldn't have conferences here, except to discuss why we shouldn't say anything. (laughter) And I have attended many such conferences, especially theological ones, in which the main burden of the proof is that you cannot say anything real about God because he's beyond any conception. And then you spend a whole week, or a book, or a series of books explaining why that is so, which is good.

But the point, however, is that there is a question of authenticity here. That is, the sociologist, or the psychologist, or psychiatrist, or even the economist, or other people who have good explanations for why other people do what they do, perform a tremendously important service. And that is, tell the individual who is a subject of all this analysis, "You should look into yourself to find out authentically what it is that you believe, or what your faith principles are."

And I think, for example, psychiatrists have a tremendously important impact on people whose religion becomes refined, even more pure, because they understand that what they are saying or doing is not really out of an authentic relationship to what they consider to be God, or the absolute, or the ultimate concern but of some external reason. Taking that away, then opens the door to a more profound, and even a more religious religion, than the one that had been practiced previously, I think.

That, and the other thing I wanted to say (I don't know whether it's right on the same level here) is this, Is there a difference, do you think, between the situation in Great Britain, and the situation in the United States or Canada? I think of the movies, and of books, where the Anglican priest is either dowdy or a detective. (laughter) I don't recall now in the television, or movies, or even books, except the Victorian books, but I mean modern books, of the clergyman being depicted as some kind of dynamic individual who changes lives, who is a real force in the life of other individuals. Whereas, the picture of the clergyman in North America, or at least in the United States, is either some faker, like Sinclair Lewis's, or a very activist, dynamic kind of impactful person. And I'm just wondering whether all these reflections that Professor Martin and some of the commentators have made, might not be apt, as a reflection of the sociological and cultural situation of the clergy in the two different countries.

Philip Wogaman: Just to follow Seymour Siegel on the externalist and internalist business, I want to remark that an internalist theological approach could never allow itself to be reduced to the external, and would have to resist that in any kind of scientism, or whatever. At the same time, the externalist accounts, insofar as they are rigorously presenting aspects of reality, (and sociology, I think, frequently does that) can actually help the internalist enterprise, if it is taken seriously. For example, insofar as church behaviour is dependent upon external factors, the theologian had better know that; and had better be able to supply an internalist account or reason. To put this in more classical, Hebrew-Christian language, we may be dealing with sources of idolatry. And it's very important to identify the idols, and to be able to criticize them, and deal with them. And so I don't think an internalist, theological perspective ought ever to be lured into a defensive posture.

At the same time, it can scarcely surrender the terrain without abandoning its whole enterprise, as apparently this other chap at Oxford that Ronald Preston has mentioned.

Milton Friedman: I think we're confusing two very different sets of distinctions — methodological and substantive. Going back to Paul Heyne's original point, some of the people who disagree with me most sharply on methodology are the Misesians, Hayekians and so on with whom I agree most strongly on policy. And they disagree with me on methodology because they want an internalist methodology. That is to say, we know things about society because we are people and we look within ourselves. I argue that while introspection may be a source of insight, may be a source of hypotheses, in order to have an appropriate scientific methodology, it has to be externalist in the sense that you must make predictions, and check those predictions against what really happens. The real test of the validity of your theory is whether it works, and not whether it corresponds to your internal psyche. That has to do with methodology.

What most of the discussion has been about is something altogether different, namely whether the hypothesis with which you explain a class of events depends on relating external forces to individuals, or somehow or other is derived from internal attitudes and ideas; whether it has something to do with the internal utility function in terms of economic terminology, or something to do with the market opportunity set.

Now that's a wholly different distinction. But if you are going to test those hypotheses, the tests all have to be externalist, in my opinion. I don't think there are any internalist tests, except in the sense in which you depart from trying to explain the religious approach to trying to convert.

Anthony Waterman: I think I must apologize for introducing what seems to be a source of great confusion here. As I understood the use of the terms in the discourse of philosophy of science, the distinction means something quite different from what Milton Friedman has just been using it to mean. It has nothing whatsoever to do with whether or not explanations come from subjective introspection on the one hand, or objective experimentation on the other. It's something quite different.

It arose out of the debate between Kuhn and Popper over the logic of scientific inquiry. The issue essentially was whether or not one could say that the transition from scientific theory A to scientific theory B occurred because the persons who made this claim followed the logic of scientific discovery. This would be said to be an internalist account. Or whether, because as Thomas Kuhn was suggesting, all the old scholars died out and new ones moved in. This would be an externalist account—an account which in no way guaranteed the truth claims of those who said that a scientific advance had been made.

Now, it's in this latter sense, I think, that we . . . or most of us, (and I think Milton Friedman is an exception) have been talking about this distinction. And I think it's the latter sense which is the relevant one for this particular discussion.

Roger Shinn: In general, I welcome this kind of sociological analysis, provided it doesn't claim to establish the final validity of things. Now, very often it makes the ritual claim to do so and in effect tries to (and you've got to watch out for that game). But the reason I would not accept Paul Heyne's limitation is that I owe too much, in my self-understanding, to my critics who have given me economic, sociological explanations of my conduct. Now, I may reject them, but I think I've got to think it through. At this point I think of Peter Berger describing one of the functions of sociology as a debunking. And I, for one, need the debunking. Now this can lead to a kind of nihilistic, total skepticism, relativism, and so on. And so I just repeat it. It doesn't establish the validity of the thing; but I generally welcome it.

I also want to say something about the way in which I think the situation in the United States may differ from that described in the paper and cited by Ronald Preston. It seemed to me that unlike the British Anglican state church situation, we had a kind of dualism in the United States from very early times, between what very loosely speaking I would call the Puritan and the Pietist approach to the church and world.

The Puritan, from Calvin through the British and on, is trying to shape society—trying very hard to shape society. The Pietist is trying to convert individuals and save their souls. And these often mingle, as in Jonathan Edwards, but they are two very different strains, and they just reflect in popular culture. You hear something is wrong. The Puritan answer is, "There ought to be a law about that." The Pietist answer "We ought to convert individuals."

There is a split psyche in America because of this. The Puritan got modified by separation of church and state, which initially did not apply to the United States. But, it had some influence from the beginning. Now, what I think is happening in our society is that the Puritan is getting modified by everybody's awareness of pluralism in society. You cannot make the old Puritan assumptions. You might still try to influence this society, but you've got to do it on grounds that make some kind of sense to people of diverse religious commitments.

The Pietist is getting modified by the entrance into the political arena of many groups with that tradition—on the right, the "moral majority" style; on the left, Sojourners, Ronald Sider, the organization of Evangelicals for Social Action. So the whole thing is getting much more mixed up. And, I think, this accounts for a lot of confusion, some of it a stimulating, healthy kind of confusion in our public debates.

One last incidental comment. I would be interested in a little more historical perspective. I don't know the English situation at all. But this secularization of the clergy was very prominent in the U.S. in the 1930s. At Union Theological Seminary where I teach, one of our illustrious graduates of that period (different ones sort of claim him with different degrees of enthusiasm) is Norman Thomas. The majority of the graduates of this theological seminary were then going on to political or social work, or the labour movement, and Reinhold Niebuhr used to tell of the time when Dietrich Bonhoeffer was a student at Union. He came up at the end of a class to complain, not about the lecture, but about students' questions, saying, "Is this place a theological seminary, or a school for labour leaders?" (laughter)

Now, nobody would be surprised at that sort of story in a seminary in the 1960s and early 1970s but there it was in the 1930s—which doesn't prove anything. It just says we've really got to think about this historically and not assume that something new is happening.

Arthur Shenfield: I find Ronald Preston's defense of the Anglican clergy against the allegation that they are politicized faulty—if not perhaps a little disingenuous. He tells us that when they criticize what is going on, they are accused of being politicized. But when they approve of what is going on, they are not so criticized. In my judgement, they are politicized in both cases, and politicized in the wrong way. When they criticize what is going on, they are politicized, and their criticisms are almost uniformly of what we would broadly call a "Left" character. In part that results from their misunderstanding of what they are talking about—they haven't read or digested Milton Friedman.

But more importantly, when they do not criticize what is going on, they are accepting the establishment in Britain. But that's not the old establishment. At the present time, by far the most important element in the British establishment is the trade union movement. There is nothing in the British establishment to compare with that in power, in authority, and in prestige. You will *never* hear a bishop, or a parson in Britain really criticize the trade union movement as such. You may hear him say some very mildly and apologetic words of criticism about some particular act of a particular union. But the idea that there is anything in trade unionism itself which is worthy of fundamental criticism, you will never hear expressed.

Here's an even better example. Britain has been plagued for nearly 70 years with rent controls. For the economist that is an obvious cause of terrible waste of capital, terrible misuse of resources, and so on. But what about the morality of it? Clearly, there is (at least one can argue) some element of legalized theft in it. You will *never* hear a bishop or a parson say that there's *any* element of theft that anybody could reasonably allege in the system of rent controls. Indeed, he will accept that system as having been established for a long time, and therefore it must be automatically good. You might say, "Well, this is wrong anyway. It's not theft. There isn't any element of theft in it."

Let me take an even better example. (Ronald Preston will be familiar with this.) A few years ago, the Labour government passed a *Leasehold Enfranchisement Act*. That was absolutely 100 per cent theft. That is to say, the law said that now the property of the freeholder will be taken away, and handed over holus bolus to the leaseholder. The purpose was obvious. The freeholders concerned don't vote Labour. And a fair number of the leaseholders concerned do vote, did vote, Labour.

You could not possibly describe that in any other terms than legalized theft, the clearest possible case. Yet you never heard any parson, or bishop, or anybody in the church (well, I didn't—I am open to correction on this) say anything about the morality of it. For these reasons, I think, David Martin's allegations are correct, although they are founded on some different considerations of fact than those that I have put forward.

Philip Wogaman: I want to come back to Lance Robert's paper a little bit and react to what I think was the general tendency of his proposal for a more modest role of the clergy, seeking to do those things which no other group can do (such as economists), finding its place in that market, defining its product and being then in a better position to sell it.

In a way, I think Lance has formulated what is causing some of the tension that may be running through our conference on the point of the proper role of religious leadership in relation to economics and other social issues. It seems to me that this would be exactly the wrong advice to give to religious leadership, even viewed in market terms, over the long haul, because a religious group ultimately is going to stand or fall on its capacity to organize the experience of people in its totality. Now, whether or not religious leaders are giving sound advice in the area of economics, or whether it's even their province to give advice in that area, it's terribly important to the church to be able to articulate the meaning of what's going on in the economic sphere, and do it intelligently.

It would be no secret to most of you that I am not a disciple of Milton Friedman's prescriptions in the area of economic policy. I have great respect for him. It's just not my view of things. Even if it were, I would still feel it terribly important to be able to give an account of its meaning in theological terms. Even if my reasons for adopting it were not initially theological, at some point I would have to be able to incorporate the meaning of that into theology, or my theology would be fragmented.

We live in a fragmented age, and the one thing that theology cannot surrender to, is becoming a fragment in that fragmented age. If it does that, it is dead. And it's only a question of how long it is going to take to bury the corpse.

Now, there is another aspect that I think we mustn't overlook. And that is (this, I guess, tags into Ronald Preston's point made toward the end of his intervention), theology must be especially careful in diagnosing those areas where people in their institutional living are committed to patterns of existence that are contrary to, or in tension with, their faith.

Walter Rauschenbusch, this great prophet figure of the social gospel, had a great definition of what he called a "Christianized social order." I think it is very suggestive. Said he, "An unChristian social order is one where good men are forced to do bad things." By contrast, a Christian social order is where bad men are forced to do good things. Now, I have a problem with that. But I think I would want to rephrase that slightly and say, "a just social order is one in which persons inclined to injustice may be required to behave justly."

I think we must constantly work at that kind of analysis. Those who are making the most penetrating case against capitalism in our age today, it seems to me, are raising the serious question, "Do capitalist institutions compel us to live life in such a way that it is contrary to our most fundamental values?" And, of course, the charge made against socialism would be of the same order.

What I am saying is, I think Christian leadership, Jewish leadership, the leadership of any religious faith that attempts to be serious about the whole world in its existence, may be grappling always with the question, "Is it possible for people to live in this world, in such a way that it does not commit them to life patterns that are fundamentally self-contradictory?"

Paul Heyne: Very briefly, I agree with Phil. I think this is a core issue in the religious dissatisfaction with capitalism. But I also think that the religious critics of capitalism have not understood capitalism correctly. And my rather quick way to respond is to recommend essays by Frank Knight written back in the 1920s. Whatever his religious views, he was always in dialogue with religion.

The first two essays in his book, *The Ethics of Competition, and Other Essays,* remain (I re-read them every two years or so) the most profound exploration of the complexities of this issue. Everybody could learn from them. And I heartily recommend to all religious critics of capitalism that they read those essays. Knight was not an ideologue. He was a man who refused to ignore any aspect of reality and who tied himself in knots in the process, to the benefit of all the rest of us, though he wrote badly.

Edmund Opitz: First I would like to say that I would second what Arthur Shenfield has said a moment ago. I think these are very pregnant observations, and similar ones could be made about the situation in the United States.

A matter of terminology now, "capitalism." I find myself over the years invariably getting into discussions, where the "capitalism" I am defending is not at all the same thing as the "capitalism" my opponent is attacking. If you go back to the old *Encyclopedia of the Social Sciences* — about 1934, that multi-volume thing — the editors looked around for someone who could write the entry on capitalism. Of course, they chose a Marxist, Werner Sombart — an opponent of capitalism. He points out that the word "capitalism" came into the vocabulary as part of "socialist polemics"; and said that he was the first one to use the term "capitalism" systematically in his analyses and criticisms published around the turn of the century. So he, himself an opponent of capitalism, was the one that began to systematically use the term.

I would ask, "At the present moment, right now, is Chrysler engaged in capitalistic actions?" And the answer of course is, "No. It is not." When it was in the private sector, Chrysler could not persuade us to buy its products. When it was part of business, it had no power, except power in the metaphoric sense, to persuade. Because Chrysler could not persuade us to buy its products, it turned to a friendly government which has people within it always eager to extend public sector tentacles over any part of the society that will yield to it.

So, Chrysler became "cartelized." Chrysler adopted a fascistic relationship to our government in Washington, which means that, although Chrysler did not before have the power to make anyone work for it, it now has the power to make every taxpayer work for it. Every taxpayer now works a fraction of his or her time to support Chrysler. Now, is this capitalism? And the answer, of course, is "No, it is not."

I have abandoned, as a rule, the practice of using the word "capitalism" and use instead the phrase the "free economy." The "free economy" is the free market institutionalized. The free market is simply a phrase to describe individual persons engaged in voluntary exchanges of goods and services. The free market existed at primitive levels. It exists in Russia. The free market is ubiquitous. The free market yesterday, today, and forever. But the "free economy" the free market institutionalized, came into being only after a certain legal, moral, framework was established. There is a sense in which the "free economy" is what happens when you have a political-legal structure which protects every person's private domain, and maximizes every person's opportunity to pursue his personal goals. And you get that political-legal structure when you have general acceptance of the idea of inherent rights — something we possess by virtue of being human beings. The idea that every person does have these inherent rights prevails only after you have a culture in which the idea has been drilled into people that each person possesses a portion of the sacred — that there was "that of God within us," as the Quakers would say.

Murdith McLean: I know that we spent some time on the distinction between external and internal, and have gone past that. But I really want to emphasize one thing I think that should follow from looking at that distinction. In attending, for instance, to the activities of clergy, or to fire a shot in advance to the apparently Left leaning views of Jewish leadership, we should attend not just to the causal factors in surrounding society, but to the reasons the people themselves give. And if we think they are defective, to show why. That might allow some of us on the theological side, or some of us who are on neither side, like me, to learn from the economist or from other people, in the way that we are being invited to.

Geoffrey Brennan: I want to make a comment about the Anglican church, generally, and the language of religious expression. Like David Martin, I am an Anglican. It seems to me that the Anglican church is a repository of certain cultural practices, which I find personally very attractive and endearing. Indeed these are terms in which, somehow, I understand things which are very, very important to me, at some subliminal level. And I think this is true, in fact, of most Anglicans. I think that it's also true that this is part of an important language in which we express spiritual sensibilities.

And, if it's insisted that we try to talk about that in other languages, such as in terms of ordinary verbal expression, then there are enormous difficulties. It is true to say, I think, that there is a problem of whether what one really loves is a particular cultic sort of experience, or Jesus Christ, or certain basic principles.

David Friedman: Two things I wanted to say. First, a little over 200 years ago, a prominent Scottish moral philosopher, well known as the author of *The Theory of Moral Sentiments,* wrote a book in which he argued at considerable length and ingenuity, that the market society tended to give bad men an incentive to do good things, with certain exceptions that he discussed.

It is my impression from quite a lot of unsystematic and promiscuous political argument with people over the last 20 years, that a negligible fraction of the people who are strongly opposed to capitalism have read that book, let alone anything written on the subject in the discipline of economics by people in that tradition since then. And, while it is no doubt true that there are difficult, and interesting, and subtle philosophical questions involved in what sense the market is or isn't moral, I don't think that those questions have anything to do with the observed opposition of the market. I think that if you just listen to what people write and say, they believe things about the market that most serious, competent economists don't believe. They simply don't know the arguments. And consequently, the problem is not that the defense hasn't been written, it is that it hasn't been read.

Now the second point I wanted to make, very very briefly, is a criticism of Ronald Preston's argument. He seems to claim that not taking a political position is the same as coming out in favour of the *status quo.* But not taking a political position is both not condemning the reformers and not condemning the people in the *status quo.* There is a neutral position. It is appropriate for an economist to be neutral on the question of whether or not we can travel faster than light. It may well be appropriate for an expert on moral philosophy to be neutral on those questions that really depend on economic issues.

And it seems to me that the justification of the Churches' involvement in social issues is the assumption, which I think arrogant but possibly true (I'm not sure), that the reason people don't do what you think they should do, is because they are wicked, rather than because they disagree with your facts, in which case the clergy have no expert advice to give.

Ronald Preston: There are just four things I would like to say, briefly. On the internalist and externalist discussion, I have nothing more to say except I ought to have made it clear that I am thoroughly in favour of sociological studies of religion. And I would not put any bounds upon them, and say anything was too sacred to be studied. I'd let the sociologists have a go at anything they like. If they wanted to investigate the sociological influence of prayer for instance, and thought they could, I would let them have a go, and see what they could make of it. I would not in this be defensive in any way about religious institutions, or religious persons, or anything of that sort. I'm entirely in favour of sociological studies of religion, carried out methodically in as pure a form as possible, and open to criticisms themselves.

Secondly, nobody took up Roger Shinn's illustrations of the difference between the U.S. situation and the British; but personally I found it very illuminating, and I would hope others might.

Thirdly, regarding the remarks of David Friedman, I didn't make myself clear to him. I didn't mean to say that it was illegitimate ever to take a neutral position, if one had thought it out, on some issue. What I meant to say was that, in general, people who say they are apolitical do not think about it at all. They imagine they're being apolitical, but in fact by tacit rather than explicit acceptance of things as they are, they are tolerating and supporting implicitly the *status quo,* without taking the responsibility of having seriously thought it out.

Lastly, I want to say a word about Arthur Shenfield's remark. The situation is that if you are talking about the individualized world at the moment, trade unions aren't as strong as they might appear by a long way. To a large extent, working people have not got a sufficient participatory place in industrial decision-making, but industry in the end cannot be run without their acceptance, but neither can they compel management to do what they want. We have got a new situation which makes advanced industrialized societies extremely difficult to govern.

Chapter 8

Capitalism and the Jews*

Milton Friedman

I. PARADOX EXPOSED

Post-war collectivism in the West

Immmediately after the Second World War, the prospects for freedom looked bleak. The war had produced an unprecedented centralization of economic controls in every belligerent country. The "socialists in all parties" to whom Hayek dedicated his brilliant polemic *The Road to Serfdom,* seemed well on their way to establishing central planning as the standard for peace as for war, pointing triumphantly to the full employment that had been produced by inflationary war finance as decisive evidence for the superiority of central planning over capitalist chaos. And, if that occurred, there seemed little hope of halting the slide toward full-fledged collectivism.

Fortunately, those fears have not been realized over the intervening 35 years. On the contrary, government inefficiency together with the clear conflict between central planning and individual freedom served to check the trend towards collectivism. In Britain, in France, in the U.S., war-time controls were dismantled and market mechanisms were given greater play. In West Germany, the courageous action of

---

*This paper was first given as the Presidential Address to the Mont Pèlerin Society at Montreux in 1972 — eds.

Ludwig Erhard in ending controls in the summer of 1948 triggered the so-called German economic miracle. Even behind the Iron Curtain, Yugoslavia broke with its Soviet masters, rejected detailed control of the economy, and treated us to the surprising vision of creeping capitalism in an avowedly communist society.

Unfortunately, these checks to collectivism did not check the growth of government. Rather, they diverted that growth from central direction of the economy to central control of the distribution of the product, to the wholesale transfer of income from some members of the community to others.

The collectivist trend in ideas

Much more important and much more relevant to our society, the favourable trends in the world of affairs were not paralleled in the world of ideas. For a time, there was an intellectual reaction against governmental intervention. Some of us optimistically envisioned a resurgence of liberal values, the emergence of a new trend of opinion favourable to a free society. But any such resurgence was spotty and short-lived. Intellectual opinion in the West has again started moving in a collectivist direction. Many of the slogans are individualist — participatory democracy, down with the establishment, "do your own thing," "power to the people." But the slogans are accompanied by attacks on private property and free enterprise — the only institutions capable of achieving the individualistic objectives. They are accompanied by a demand for centralized political power — but with "good" people instead of "bad" people exercising the power.

West Germany is perhaps the most striking example of the paradoxical developments in the world of affairs and the world of ideas. Who could ask for a better comparison of two sets of institutions than East and West Germany have provided in the past two decades? Here are people of the same blood, the same civilization, the same level of technical skill and knowledge, torn asunder by the accidents of warfare. The one adopts central direction; the other adopts a social market economy. Which has to build a wall to keep its citizens from leaving? On which side of the wall is there tyranny and misery; on which side, freedom and affluence? Yet despite this dramatic demonstration, despite the Nazi experience — which alone might be expected to immunize a society for a century against collectivism — the intellectual climate in Germany, I am told, is overwhelmingly collectivist — in the schools, the universities, the mass media alike.

This paradox is a major challenge to those of us who believe in freedom. Why have we been so unsuccessful in persuading intellectuals everywhere of our views? Our opponents would give the obvious answer: because we are wrong and they are right. Until we can answer them and ourselves in some other way, we cannot reject their answer, we cannot be sure we are right. And until we find a satisfactory answer, we are not likely to succeed in changing the climate of opinion.

The Jews as an example of the paradox

My aim here is not to give a ready answer — for I have none. My aim is rather to examine a particular case of the paradox — the attitude of Jews toward capitalism. Two propositions can be readily demonstrated: first, the Jews owe an enormous debt to free enterprise and competitive capitalism; second, for at least the past century the Jews have been consistently opposed to capitalism and have done much on an ideological level to undermine it. How can these propositions be reconciled?

I was led to examine this paradox partly for obvious personal reasons. Some of us are accustomed to being members of an intellectual minority, to being accused by fellow intellectuals of being reactionaries or apologists or just plain nuts. But those of us who are also Jewish are even more embattled, being regarded not only as intellectual deviants but also as traitors to a supposed cultural and national tradition.

This personal interest was reinforced by the hope that study of this special case might offer a clue to the general paradox — typified by West Germany where Jews play a minor role. Unfortunately, that hope has not been fulfilled. I believe that I can explain to a very large extent the anti-capitalist tendency among Jews, but the most important elements of the explanation are peculiar to the special case and cannot readily be generalized. I trust that others will be more successful.

II. THE BENEFIT JEWS HAVE DERIVED FROM CAPITALISM

An anecdote and some history

Let me start by briefly documenting the first proposition: that the Jews owe an enormous debt to capitalism. The feature of capitalism that has benefited the Jews has, of course, been competition.[1] Wherever there is a monopoly, whether it be private or governmental, there is room for the application of arbitrary criteria in the selection of the beneficiaries of the monopoly — whether these criteria be colour of skin, religion, national origin or what not. Where there is free competition, only performance counts. The market is colour blind. No one who goes to the market to buy bread knows or cares whether the wheat was grown by a Jew, Catholic, Protestant, Muslim, or atheist; by whites or blacks. Any miller who wishes to express his personal prejudices by buying only from preferred groups is at a competitive disadvantage, since he is keeping himself from buying from the cheapest source. He can express his prejudice, but he will have to do so at his own expense, accepting a lower monetary income than he could otherwise earn.

A recent personal experience illuminates sharply the importance of competition. Some years ago, I attended an International Monetary Conference held in Montreal. The persons there consisted, on the one hand, of members of the Conference, who include the two top executives of the major commercial banks throughout the world; on the other, of persons like myself invited as speakers or participants in panel discussions. A conversation with an American banker present who recounted a tale of anti-Semitism in American banking led me to estimate roughly the fraction of the two groups who were Jewish. Of the first group — the bankers proper — I estimated that about 1 percent were Jewish. Of the much smaller second group, the invited participants in the program, roughly 25 percent were Jewish.

Why the difference? Because banking today is everywhere monopolistic in the sense that there is not free entry. Government permission or a franchise is required. On the other hand, intellectual activity of the kind that would recommend persons for the program is a highly competitive industry with almost completely free entry.

This example is particularly striking because banking is hardly a field, like, say, iron and steel, in which Jews have never played an important role. On the contrary, for centuries Jews were a major if not dominant element in banking and particularly in international banking. But when that was true, banking was an industry with rather free entry. Jews prospered in it for that reason and also because they had a comparative advantage arising from the Church's views on usury, the dispersion of Jews throughout the world, and their usefulness to ruling monarchs precisely because of the isolation of the Jews from the rest of the community.[2]

This anecdote illuminates much history. Throughout the nearly two thousand years of the Diaspora, Jews were repeatedly discriminated against, restricted in the activities they could undertake, on occasion expelled *en masse,* as in 1492 from Spain, and often the object of the extreme hostility of the peoples among whom they lived. They were able nonetheless to exist because of the absence of a totalitarian state, so that there were always some market elements, some activities open to them to enter. In particular, the fragmented political structure and the numerous separate sovereignties meant that international trade and finance in particular escaped close control, which is why Jews were so prominent in this area. It is no accident that Nazi Germany and Soviet Russia, the two most totalitarian societies in the past two thousand years (modern China perhaps excepted), also offer the most extreme examples of official and effective anti-Semitism.

If we come to more recent time, Jews have flourished most in those countries in which competitive capitalism had the greatest scope: Holland in the sixteenth and seventeenth centuries, and Britain and the U.S. in the nineteenth and twentieth centuries, Germany in the late nineteenth and early twentieth century – a case that is particularly pertinent when that period is compared with the Hitler period.[3]

Freedom of entry and Jewish representation

Moreover, within those countries, Jews have flourished most in the sectors that have the freest entry and are in that sense most competitive. Compare the experience of the Jews in banking, that I have referred to, with their experience in retail trade, which has been almost a prototype of the textbook image of perfect competition and free entry. Or compare their minor role in large industry with their prominence in the professions such as law, medicine, accountancy and the like.[4] Though there are barriers to entry in the professions too, once past the initial barriers, there is a large measure of free competition for custom. Even the differences within the professions illustrate my theme. In the U.S., for which I know the details, there was for a long time a major difference between medicine and law in the extent to which state licensure was an effective bar to entry. For reasons that are not relevant here, there was significant restriction of entry in medicine, relatively little in law. And Jews were proportionately much more numerous in law than in medicine.

The movie industry in the U.S. was a new industry and for that reason open to all. Jews became a major factor and this carried over to radio and television when they came on the scene. But now that government control and regulation has become more and more important, I am under the impression that the Jewish role in radio and T.V. is declining.

Capitalism and Israel

A rather different example of the benefits Jews have derived from competitive capitalism is provided by Israel, and this in a dual sense.

First, Israel would hardly have been viable without the massive contributions that it received from world Jewry, primarily from the U.S., secondarily from Britain and other Western capitalist countries. Suppose these countries had been socialist. The hypothetical socialist countries might conceivably have contributed, but if so they would have done so for very different reasons and with very different conditions attached. Compare Soviet aid to Egypt or official U.S. aid to Israel with private contributions. In a capitalist system, any group, however small a minority, can use its own resources as it wishes, without seeking or getting the permission of the majority.

Second, within Israel, despite all the talk of central control, the reality is that rapid development has been primarily the product of private initiative. After my first extended visit to Israel two decades ago, I concluded that two traditions were at work in Israel: an ancient one, going back nearly two thousand years, of finding ways around governmental restrictions; a modern one, going back a century, of belief in "democratic socialism" and "central planning." Fortunately for Israel, the first tradition has proved far more potent than the second.

To summarize: Except for the sporadic protection of individual monarchs to whom they were useful, Jews have seldom benefited from governmental intervention on their behalf. They have flourished when and only when there has been a widespread acceptance by the public at large of the general doctrine of non-intervention, so that a large measure of competitive capitalism and of tolerance for all groups has prevailed. They have flourished then despite continued widespread anti-Semitic prejudice because the general belief in non-intervention was more powerful than the specific urge to discriminate against the Jews.

III. THE ANTI-CAPITALIST MENTALITY OF THE JEWS

Despite this record, for the past century, the Jews have been a stronghold of anti-capitalist sentiment. From Karl Marx through Leon Trotsky to Herbert Marcuse, a sizable fraction of the revolutionary anti-capitalist literature has been authored by Jews. Communist parties in all countries, including the party that achieved revolution in Russia but also present day Communist parties in Western countries, and especially in the U.S.,[5] have been run and manned to a disproportionate extent by Jews—though I hasten to add that only a tiny fraction of Jews have ever been members of the Communist party. Jews have been equally active in the less-revolutionary socialist movements in all countries, as intellectuals generating socialist literature, as active participants in leadership, and as members.

Coming still closer to the centre, in Britain the Jewish vote and participation is predominantly in the Labor party, in the U.S., in the left wing of the Democratic party. The party programs of the so-called right-wing parties in Israel would be regarded as "liberal," in the modern sense, almost everywhere else. These phenomena are so well known that they require little elaboration or documentation.[6]

IV. WHY THE ANTI-CAPITALIST MENTALITY?

How can we reconcile my two propositions? Why is it that despite the historical record of the benefits of competitive capitalism to the Jews, despite the intellectual explanation of this phenomenon that is implicit or explicit in all liberal literature from at least Adam Smith on, the Jews have been disproportionately anti-capitalist?

Fuchs, Sombart and Glazer: The Jewish history

We may start by considering some simple yet inadequate answers. Lawrence Fuchs, in a highly superficial analysis of *The Political*

Behavior of American Jews, argues that the anti-capitalism of the Jews is a direct reflection of values derived from the Jewish religion and culture. He goes so far as to say, "if the communist movement is in a sense a Christian heresy, it is also Jewish orthodoxy—not the totalitarian or revolutionary aspects of world communism, but the quest for social justice through social action."[7] Needless to say—a point I shall return to later in a different connection—Fuchs himself is a liberal in the American sense. He regards the political liberalism of the Jews in this sense as a virtue, and hence is quick to regard such liberalism as a legitimate offspring of the Jewish values of learning, charity, and concern with the pleasures of this world. He never even recognizes, let alone discusses, the key question whether the ethical end of "social justice through social action" is consistent with the political means of centralized government.

This explanation can be dismissed out-of-hand. Jewish religion and culture date back over two millennia; the Jewish opposition to capitalism and attachment to socialism, at the most, less than two centuries. Only after the Enlightenment, and then primarily among the Jews who were breaking away from the Jewish religion, did this political stance emerge. Werner Sombart, in his important and controversial book, *The Jews and Modern Capitalism,* first published in 1911, makes a far stronger case that Jewish religion and culture implied a capitalist outlook than Fuchs does that it implied a socialist outlook. Wrote Sombart, "throughout the centuries, the Jews championed the cause of individual liberty in economic activity against the dominating view of the time. The individual was not to be hampered by regulations of any sort. I think that the Jewish religion has the same leading ideas as capitalism. . . . The whole religious system is in reality nothing but a contract between Jehovah and his chosen people. . . . God promises something and gives something, and the righteous must give Him something in return. Indeed, there was no community of interest between God and man which could not be expressed in these terms—that man performs some duty enjoined by the Torah and receives from God a *quid pro quo.*"[8]

Sombart goes on to discuss the attitude toward riches and poverty in the Old and the New Testament. "You will find," he writes, "a few passages [in the Old Testament and the Talmud] wherein poverty is lauded as something nobler and higher than riches. But on the other hand you will come across hundreds of passages in which riches are called the blessing of the Lord, and only their misuse or their dangers

warned against." By contrast, Sombart refers to the famous passage in
the New Testament that "it is easier for a Camel to go through a
needle's eye than for a rich man to enter into the Kingdom of God"
and remarks, "as often as riches are lauded in the Old Testament, they
are damned in the New. . . . The religion of the Christians stands in the
way of their economic activities. . . . The Jews were never faced with
his hindrance." He concludes, "Free trade and industrial freedom were
in accordance with Jewish law, and therefore in accordance with
God's will."[9]

Sombart's book, I may say, has in general had a highly unfavourable reception among both economic historians in general and
Jewish intellectuals in particular, and indeed, something of an aura of
anti-Semitism has come to be attributed to it. Much of the criticism
seems valid but there is nothing in the book itself to justify any charge
of anti-Semitism though there certainly is in Sombart's behaviour and
writings several decades later. Indeed, if anything I interpret the book
as philo-Semitic. I regard the violence of the reaction of Jewish intellectuals to the book as itself a manifestation of the Jewish anti-capitalist mentality. I shall return to this point later.

A more balanced judgement than either Fuchs' or Sombart's with
which I am in full accord is rendered by Nathan Glazer, who writes,
"It is hard to see direct links with Jewish tradition in these
attitudes; . . . . One thing is sure: it is an enormous oversimplification
to say Jews in Eastern Europe became socialists and anarchists
because the Hebrew prophets had denounced injustice twenty-five
hundred years ago. . . . The Jewish religious tradition probably does
dispose Jews, in some subtle way, toward liberalism and radicalism,
but it is not easy to see in present-day Jewish social attitudes the
heritage of the Jewish religion."[10]

Jews, intellectualism and anti-capitalism

A second simple explanation is that the Jewish anti-capitalist mentality simply reflects the general tendency for intellectuals to be anti-
capitalist plus the disproportionate representation of Jews among intellectuals. For example, Nathan Glazer writes, "The general explanations for this phenomenon [the attachment of the major part of the
intelligentsia to the Left] are well known. Freed from the restraints of
conservative and traditional thinking, the intelligentsia finds it easier
to accept revolutionary thinking, which attacks the established order

of things in politics, religion, culture, and society. . . . Whatever it is that affected intellectuals, also affected Jews."[11] Glazer goes on, however, to qualify greatly this interpretation by citing some factors that affected Jews differently from other intellectuals. This explanation undoubtedly has more validity than Fuchs' simple-minded identification of anti-capitalism with Jewish religion and culture. As the West German example quoted earlier suggests, non-Jewish intellectuals are capable of becoming dominantly collectivist. And there is no doubt that the intellectual forces Glazer refers to affected Jewish intellectuals along with non-Jewish. However, the explanation seems highly incomplete in two respects. First, my impression is that a far larger percentage of Jewish intellectuals than of non-Jewish have been collectivist. Second, and more important, this explanation does not account for the different attitudes of the great mass of Jews and non-Jews who are not intellectual. To explain this difference we must dig deeper.

The moral ambiguity of the free order

A third simple explanation that doubtless has some validity is the natural tendency for all of us to take the good things that happen to us for granted but to attribute any bad things to evil men or an evil system. Competitive capitalism has permitted Jews to flourish economically and culturally because it has prevented anti-Semites from imposing their values on others, and from discriminating against Jews at other people's expense. But the other side of that coin is that it protects anti-Semites from having other people's values imposed on them. It protects them in the expression of their anti-Semitism in their personal behaviour so long as they do it at their own expense. Competitive capitalism has therefore not eliminated social anti-Semitism. The free competition of ideas that is the natural companion of competitive capitalism might in time lead to a change in tastes and values that would eliminate social anti-Semitism but there is no assurance that it will. As the New Testament put it, "In my Father's house are many mansions."

No doubt, Jews have reacted in part by attributing the residual discrimination to "the System." But that hardly explains why the part of the "system" to which the discrimination has been attributed is "capitalism." Why not, in nineteenth century Britain, to the established church and the aristocracy; in nineteenth and twentieth century

Germany, to the bureaucracy; and in twentieth century U.S., to the social rather than economic establishment. After all, Jewish history surely offers more than ample evidence that anti-Semitism has no special connection with a market economy. So this explanation, too, is unsatisfactory.

I come now to two explanations that seem to me much more fundamental.

Judaism and secularism

The first explanation, which has to do with the particular circumstances in Europe in the nineteenth century, I owe to the extremely perceptive analysis of Werner Cohn in his unpublished Ph.D. dissertation on the "Sources of American Jewish Liberalism." Cohn points out that:

> Beginning with the era of the French revolution, the European political spectrum became divided into a 'Left' and a 'Right' along an axis that involved the issue of secularism. The Right (conservative, Monarchical, 'clerical') maintained that there must be a place for the church in the public order; the Left (Democratic, Liberal, Radical) held that there can be no (public) Church at all. . . .
>
> The axis separating left from right also formed a natural boundary for the pale of Jewish political participation. It was the Left, with its new secular concept of citizenship, that had accomplished the Emancipation, and it was only the Left that could see a place for the Jews in public life. No Conservative party in Europe — from the bitterly hostile Monarchists in Russia through the strongly Christian "noines" in France to the amiable Tories in England — could reconcile itself to full Jewish political equality. Jews supported the Left, then, not only because they had become unshakeable partisans of the Emancipation, but also because they had no choice; as far as the internal life of the Right was concerned, the Emancipation had never taken place, and the Christian religion remained a prerequisite for political participation.

Note in this connection that the only major leaders of Conservative parties of Jewish origin — Benjamin Disraeli in England, Friedrich Julius Stahl in Germany were both professing Christians (Disraeli's father was converted, Stahl was baptized at age 19).

Cohn goes on to distinguish between two strands of Leftism: "rational" or "intellectual" and "radical." He remarks that "Radical leftism . . . was the only political movement since the days of the Roman empire in which Jews could become the intellectual brethren of non-Jews . . . while intellectual Leftism was Christian at least in the sense of recognizing the distinction between 'religious' and 'secular,' radical Leftism — eschatological socialism in particular — began to constitute itself as a new religious faith in which no separation between the sacred and the profane was tolerated . . . [Intellectual-Leftism] offered [the Jews] a wholly rational and superficial admission to the larger society, [radical Leftism], a measure of real spiritual community."

I share Glazer's comment on these passages: "I do not think anyone has come closer to the heart of the matter than has the author of these paragraphs."

Cohn's argument goes far to explain the important role that Jewish intellectuals played in the Marxist and socialist movement, the almost universal acceptance of "democratic socialism" by the European Jews in the Zionist movement, particularly those who emigrated to Palestine, and the socialist sentiment among the German Jewish immigrants to the United States of the mid-nineteenth century and the much larger flood of East European Jews at the turn of the century.

Yet by itself it is hard to accept Cohn's point as the whole explanation for the anti-capitalist mentality of the Jews. In the United States, from the very beginning, the separation of church and state was accepted constitutional doctrine. True, the initial upper class was Christian and Protestant, but that was true of the population as a whole. Indeed, the elite Puritan element was, if anything, pro-Semitic. As Sombart points out in reconciling his thesis about the role of Jews in capitalist development with Max Weber's about the role of the Protestant Ethic in capitalist development, the Protestants, and the Puritans especially, went back to the Old Testament for their religious inspiration and patterned themselves on the ancient Hebrews. Sombart asserts: "Puritanism *is* Judaism."[12] Cohn too emphasizes this phenomenon, pointing to Puritan tolerance toward Jews in the colonial era, despite their general intolerance toward other religious sects.[13]

To come down to more recent times in the United States, Theodore Roosevelt was highly popular among the Jews partly because of his willingness to object publicly to Russian pogroms. Outside of the closely knit socialist community in New York most Jews probably were Republicans rather than Democrats until the 1920s, when first Al Smith and then Franklin Delano Roosevelt produced a massive shift to the Democrats from both the Right and the Left. The shift from the

Left betokened a weakening of the European influence, rather than being a manifestation of it. Yet despite that weakening influence, the American Jewish community, which now consists largely of second and third and later generation Americans, retains its dominant leftish cast.

The Jewish reaction to the Jewish stereotype

The final explanation that suggests itself is complementary to Cohn's yet not at all identical with it. To justify itself by more than the reference to the alleged role of the Jews in Christ's crucifixion, anti-Semitism produced a stereotype of a Jew as primarily interested in money, as a merchant or money-lender who put commercial interests ahead of human values, who was money-grasping, cunning, selfish and greedy, who would "jew" you down and insist on his pound of flesh. Jews could have reacted to this stereotype in two ways: first, by accepting the description but rejecting the values that regarded these traits as blame-worthy; secondly, by accepting the values but rejecting the description. Had they adopted the first way, they could have stressed the benefits rendered by the merchant and by the money-lender — recalling perhaps Bentham's comment that "the business of a money-lender . . . has no where nor at any time been a popular one. Those who have the resolution to sacrifice the present to the future, are natural objects of envy to those who have sacrificed the future to the present. The children who have eaten their cake are the natural enemies of the children who have their's. While the money is hoped for, and for a short time after it has been received, he who lends it is a friend and benefactor: by the time the money is spent, and the evil hour of reckoning is come, the benefactor is found to have changed his nature, and to have put on the tyrant and the oppressor. It is oppression for a man to reclaim his own money; it is none to keep it from him."[14]

Similarly, Jews could have noted that one man's selfishness is another man's self reliance; one man's cunning, another's wisdom; one man's greed, another's prudence.

But this reaction was hardly to be expected. None of us can escape the intellectual air we breathe, can fail to be influenced by the values of the community in which we live. As Jews left their closed ghettoes and shtetls and came into contact with the rest of the world, they inevitably came to accept and share the values of that world, the values that looked down on the "merely" commercial, that regarded money-lenders with contempt. They were led to say to themselves: if Jews are like that, the anti-Semites are right.

The other possible reaction is to deny that Jews are like the stereotype, to set out to persuade oneself, and incidentally the anti-Semites, that far from being money-grabbing, selfish and heartless, Jews are really public-spirited, generous, and concerned with ideals rather than material goods. How better to do so than to attack the market with its reliance on monetary values and impersonal transactions and to glorify the political process, to take as an ideal a state run by well-meaning people for the benefit of their fellow men?

Israel as a Diasporal reaction

I was first led to this explanation of the anti-capitalist mentality of the Jews by my experience in Israel. After several months there, I came to the conclusion that the quickest way to reach a generalization in any area about values in Israel was to ask what was true of the Jews in the Diaspora and reverse it.

Jews in the Diaspora were urban dwellers engaged in commercial pursuits and almost never in agriculture; in Israel, agriculture has much higher prestige than commerce.

Jews in the Diaspora shunned every aspect of military service; Israelis value the military highly and have demonstrated extraordinary competence.

These two reversals are readily explained as the children of necessity, but let me continue.

Yiddish or Ladino was the language of the Jews in the Diaspora; both are looked down on in Israel, where Hebrew is the language.

Jews in the Diaspora stressed intellectual pursuits and rather looked down on athletics. There is tremendous emphasis on athletics in Israel.

And for what may seem like an irrelevant clincher: Jews in the Diaspora were reputed to be excellent cooks; cooking in Israel is generally terrible, in homes, hotels and restaurants.

Can this record not be interpreted as an attempt, no doubt wholly subconscious, to demonstrate to the world that the commonly accepted stereotype of the Jew is false?

I interpret in the same way the evidence assembled by Wilson and Banfield that Jews (and "Yankees") tend to adopt a "community-serving conception" of the public interest, and to vote against their own immediate self-interest, in larger proportions than most other groups.[15]

Fuchs and Sombart in this perspective

I interpret also in this way the attempt by Fuchs to trace Jewish "liberalism" to Jewish values and the negative reaction of Jewish critics to Sombart's book. If, like me, you regard competitive capitalism as the economic system that is most favourable to individual freedom, to creative accomplishments in technology and the arts, and to the widest possible opportunities for the ordinary man, then you will regard Sombart's assignment to the Jews of a key role in the development of capitalism as high praise. You will, as I do, regard his book as philo-Semitic. On the other hand, if you are trying your level best to demonstrate that Jews are dedicated to selfless public service in a socialist state, that commerce and money-lending were activities forced on them by their unfortunate circumstances and were wholly foreign to their natural bent, then you will regard Sombart as an anti-Semite simply reinforcing the stereotype against which you are battling. In this vein, the *Universal Jewish Encyclopaedia* says in its article on Sombart: "He *accused* the Jews of having created capitalism" (my italics).

The complementary character of the final two explanations is, I trust, clear. Whence comes the value structure that puts service to the general public above concern for oneself and one's close family; government employment above private business; political activity above commercial activity; love of mankind in general above concern for men in particular; social responsibility above individual responsibility? Very largely from the collectivist trend of thought to which Jews contributed so much for the reasons advanced by Cohn.

Consider, for a moment, the reaction to the anti-Semitic stereotype by a nineteenth century English Philosophical radical steeped in Benthamite utilitarianism — by a David Ricardo, James Mill, even Thomas Malthus. Could one of them ever have termed the allegation that Jews created capitalism an accusation? They would have termed it high praise. They would have regarded widespread emphasis on rational profit calculation as just what was needed to promote "the greatest good of the greatest number," emphasis on the individual rather than the society as a corollary of belief in freedom, and so on.

CONCLUSION

I conclude then, that the chief explanations for the anti-capitalist mentality of the Jews are the special circumstances of nineteenth century Europe which linked pro-market parties with established religions and so drove Jews to the Left, and the subconscious attempts by Jews to demonstrate to themselves and the world the fallacy of the anti-Semitic stereotype. No doubt these two main forces were reinforced, and the view of the Jews altered in detail, by their historical and cultural heritage, which made them specially sensitive to injustice and specially committed to charity. They were reinforced also by whatever the forces are that predispose intellectuals towards the Left.

Whether or not this explanation is a satisfactory resolution of the paradox which was my starting point, it remains true that the ideology of the Jews has been and still is opposed to their self-interest. Except behind the Iron Curtain, this conflict has been mostly potential rather than real. In the West, so long as a large measure of *laissez-faire* capitalism prevailed, the economic drive of the Jews to improve their lot, to move upward in the economic and social scale, was in no way hindered by the preaching of socialism as an ideal. They could enjoy the luxury of reacting against the anti-Semitic stereotype, yet benefit from the characteristics that that stereotype caricatured. On a much more subtle and sophisticated level, they were in the position of the rich parlor socialists — of all ethnic and religious backgrounds — who bask in self-righteous virtue by condemning capitalism while enjoying the luxuries paid for by their capitalist inheritance.

As the scope of government has grown, as the collectivist ideas have achieved acceptance and affected the structure of society, the conflict has become very real. I have already stressed the conflict in Israel that has led to giving a far greater role to market forces than the ideology of the early leaders envisioned. I have been struck in the United States with the emergence of the conflict in reaction to some of the proposals by Senator McGovern. His early proposal, later rescinded, to set a top limit on inheritances produced an immediate reaction from some of those who might have been expected to be and were his strongest supporters. It came home to them that his measures — completely consistent with their professed ideology — would greatly hamper the upward social and economic mobility of which they had been the beneficiaries.

Perhaps the reality of the conflict will end or at least weaken the paradox that has been the subject of my talk. If so, it will be a minor silver lining in the dark cloud of encroaching collectivism.

NOTES

1. The only other writer I have come across who explicity stresses the benefits Jews have derived from capitalism is Ellis Rivkin,* *The Shaping of Jewish History,* New York: Scribner's, 1971. Unfortunately, Rivkin's interesting analysis is marred by misconceptions about the nature and operation of capitalism. He takes the accumulation of capital rather than free entry as its distinguishing feature.

2. See for example Hannah Arendt, *The Origins of Totalitarianism,* New York: Harcourt, Brace & Co., 1951, on "court Jews," also Werner Sombart, *The Jews and Modern Capitalism,* London: T. Fisher Unwin, 1913 (translated from 1911 German original).

3. Sombart argues that the relation is the reverse: that capitalism flourished where it did because Jews were given a considerable measure of freedom. But he would not have denied that the relation is reciprocal. And his version has been seriously questioned by economic historians. See Introduction by Bert F. Hoselitz to the American edition of Sombart's book, *Jewish Contributions to Civilization,* 1919, chapter viia, pp. 247–267.

4. See Nathaniel Weyl, *The Creative Elite in America,* Washington, D.C.: Public Affairs Press 1966, particularly the tables in Appendix III giving results for different "elite rosters."

5. For the U.S., see Nathan Glazer, *The Social Basis of American Communism,* New York: Harcourt, Brace and World, Inc. 1961, pp. 85, 130, 132.

6. For the American record, see Werner Cohn, *Sources of American Jewish Liberation—A Study of the Political Alignments of American Jews,* unpublished Ph.D. thesis, New School for Social Research, June 1956; Lawrence Fuchs, *The Political Behavior of American Jews,* Glencoe, Ill.: Free Press, 1956; Nathan Glazer, *American Judaism,* Chicago: Univerity

---

*See Rivkin's contribution to the companion book to this volume, *Religion, Economics and Social Thought*—eds.

of Chicago Press, 1957; Nathan Glazer and Daniel Patrick Moynihan, *Beyond the Melting Pot,* Cambridge: MIT Press, 2nd ed. 1970.

7. *Op. cit.,* p. 197.

8. *Op. cit.,* pp. 153, 205, 209.

9. *Ibid.,* pp. 216, 221, 222, 248.

10. Nathan Glazer, *American Judaism,* pp. 135, 136, 139.

11. *The Social Basis of American Communism,* pp. 166–167.

12. *Op. cit.,* p. 249.

13. However, according to Abba Eban, "Jews were refused admittance into Massachusetts and Connecticut by the Puritans whose idea of religious liberty was linked to their own brand of faith. However, in liberal Maryland and in Rhode Island, where freedom of conscience was an unshakable principle, they found acceptance." *My People,* New York: Behrman House, Inc., 1968.

14. Jeremy Bentham, *In Defense of Usury* (1787).

15. James Q. Wilson and Edward C. Banfield, "Public-Regardingness as a Value Premise in Voting Behavior," *American Political Science Review,* LVIII, 4 (Dec., 1964), pp. 876–887; "Political Ethos Revisited," *American Political Science Review,* LXV, 4 (Dec., 1971), pp. 1048–1062. The similarity between the Jews and the Yankees in some of the characteristics examined by Wilson and Banfield is some evidence, if rather weak evidence, for the influence of religion and culture in view of the connection between Puritanism and Judaism.

Comment*

Aaron Levine

I. SOCIALISM AND CAPITALISM IN THE JEWISH TRADITION

Prior to introducing his own rationale for Jewish opposition to capitalism, Professor Friedman presents various other explanations. One of these explanations is the Fuchs thesis which views the Jewish anti-capitalist mentality as rooted in the Jewish religion. Friedman rejects this thesis out of hand on the ground that "Jewish opposition to capitalism and attachment to socialism is, at most, two centuries old, while the Jewish religion dates back more than two millennia." Moreover, Sombart, in Friedman's view, makes a far stronger case that Jewish religion and culture implies a capitalist outlook than Fuchs does that it implies a socialist outlook.

At the outset, let us point out that Jewish attachment to certain aspects of socialism goes much further back than two centuries. During the periods of Persian and Greco-Roman subjugation, the Jews enjoyed considerable self-government. Throughout the Middle Ages, when European society generally was constituted of distinct corporate groups each with its own way of life, the Jews were also governed by their own laws and institutions. The Christian authority granted them various privileges of self-rule. These dealt mainly with their rights of commerce, money-lending, or litigation with Gentiles. The internal political and social life of the Jews was left inviolate.

Jewish religious law heavily influenced the economic organization of these autonomous communities. The religious influence is particularly evident from the responsa literature of the Rishonic period

*This paper is based on my book *Free Enterprise and Jewish Law* (New York, Ktav, Yeshiva University, 1980)

(eleventh to the middle of the fifteenth centuries), which consisted of inquiries of the various Jewish communities to the leading religious authorities of the day on matters of economic organization. This source together with the earlier Talmudic (200 C.E. to end of fifth century) and Mishnaic (beginning of common era to 220 C.E.) literature combine to form the basis of determining what Jewish religious law regards as the ideal model of economic organization.

It will be our purpose here to delineate the model of economic order Jewish law espouses on a normative basis as well as to describe its conceptualization of the actual operation of the marketplace. We will demonstrate that the Jewish religion fosters an economic system based on freedom of entry and competition, but at the same time is decidedly opposed to unbridled capitalism. This portrait, bearing directly on the Sombart and Fuchs theses, we trust, will shed some light on the Friedman paradox as well.

Freedom of entry and Jewish law

The most salient feature of capitalism is free entry. Jewish law's favourable attitude toward freedom of entry is clearly evidenced by R. Huna b. R. Joshua's (fourth century, Babylonia) widely accepted[1] ruling regarding the protection a townsman is afforded against a potential new entrant. Enjoining a new entrant is legitimized only when the plaintiff is an out-of-town tradesman who does not pay taxes in the complainant's town.[2]

Jewish law's freedom of entry stance emerges even in connection with the out-of-town intrusion case. This is evidenced from the following considerations:

1. Protection against non-local competition is limited to the retail-trade level. The Jewish community may not, however, place any restrictions on foreign wholesale-trade activities.[3] Allowing the community to regulate foreign wholesale trade would, in effect, disrupt intercommunity trade.[4]
2. Should locally available merchandise be offered by out-of-town merchants at a lower price, the latter group, according to R. Joseph Ibn MiGash (1077–1141), Spain), may not be barred from competing for local patronage. Insofar as competition here decidedly benefits local consumers, protectionist pleas of local merchants must be resisted.[5] Nahmanides (1194–1270, Gerona),

however, disagrees with the above ruling of R. Joseph Ibn MiGash.[6]

Understanding the anti-protectionist stance of R. Joseph Ibn MiGash to refer only to the circumstance where the out-of-town merchants offer to undercut the local competition by a significant margin, R. Joseph Habib (fourteenth century, Spain) finds R. Joseph Ibn MiGash's view .to converge closely with Nahmanides' position.[7] Other commentators, however, find the two views diametrically opposed: Nahmanides' protectionist view is advanced even when the proposed price cut is significant, and R. Joseph Ibn MiGash's freedom of entry view is held even when the price cut involved is slight.[8]

The implication of the above conflicting views for Jewish law is that the Jewish court would not enjoin out-of-town merchants when they offer to undercut the local competition by a significant margin. Accordingly, R. Hiyya Abraham b. Aaron di Boton (ca. 1560–1609, Salonica) refused to issue an injunction against an out-of-town tailor who offered his services at 50 per cent of the local price.[9]

3. Restrictions against out-of-town merchants must be suspended on "market days" (yoma dishuka).[10] On these days the marketplace expands to include consumers from nearby towns as well as the local population. Given that foreign retail trade at this time cannot be said as a matter of certainty to attract local customers away from local merchants,[11] Tosafot (twelfth-fourteenth century French commentators) and R. Asher b. Jehiel (1250–1327, Germany) would allow the out-of-town merchants to cater to the non-local portion of the market on these days.[12] A still broader view of the trading rights of out-of-town merchants on market days is taken by R. Joshua ha-Kohen Falk of Lemberg (1555–1614). According to his view, out-of-town merchants on these days may sell their wares indiscriminately to local and non-local customers alike.[13] The presumptive claim of local merchants to the local market, according to R. Falk, is apparently lost entirely on market days.

Retail trading privileges on these days allow non-local merchants only to sell their wares in the marketplace. Peddling their merchandise from door to door in the local community is a privilege not extended to them even on market days.[14]

4. Debt or loan connections with members of the local community provide the non-local merchant with another legitimate basis for gaining business entry to a town. Until such time that the out-of-town merchant collects or pays off his debts, as the case may be, the community may not interfere with his subsistence-generating business activities.[15] Though not a bona fide member of the community, the out-of-town merchant must participate in some measure in the burden of local taxation for the duration of his stay. His tax liability is assessed proportional to his business profits.

Individuals forced to leave their own communities to avoid impending harm may enter another community on the same terms outlined above.[16]

5. By virtue of a special enactment of Ezra (fifth century B.C.E.), foreign cosmetic salesmen are conferred with special status. To afford women with easy access to beautification aids, the community must allow these salesmen to peddle their wares from door to door. These non-local peddlers may, however, be prevented from marketing their wares in a retail outlet. When the peddler is a rabbinical scholar, the latter privilege must be extended to him as well.[17]

6. Increasing the supply of substitute products represents another means of weakening a monopoly position. Should the out-of-town vendors offer for sale merchandise unobtainable locally, the community may not obstruct their entry. Heterogeneity of product, in R. Joseph Caro's (1488–1575, France) view, is what is crucial in generating free trading rights. Hence, should the out-of-town merchants offer to sell a product available locally, but superior or inferior in quality, the outsider's freedom of entry is vouchsafed.[18] Loss of local profits due to the substitution effect apparently provides no grounds for excluding the non-local merchants.

7. Primary-school religious teachers (melamdei tinokot) are offered access to any community they might desire to enter. The free movement of the primary-school teacher is guaranteed even when he desires to enter a town where a competitor is firmly entrenched. Competition in this profession is very favourably viewed. The Talmud's approving attitude toward rivalry here finds expression in the adage, kinat soferim tarbeh hokhmah ("jealousy among scholars increases wisdom").[19]

Other forms of economic freedom specifically endorsed by the Talmudic Sages include price competition and promotional activities.[20]

The interventionist tradition in Judaism

While Judaism essentially fosters an economic system of capitalism, the notion that perfect knowledge permeates the marketplace is rejected. In addition, intervention in the free interplay of market forces for the purpose of promoting its concept of social justice and to restrain undue leverage in the marketplace is called for.

1. Judaism's rejection of the notion that perfect knowledge permeates the marketplace clearly emerges from an analysis of the laws of ona'ah (price divergence).

   The ethics of the price terms of transactions concluded within the framework of a competitive norm are governed in Jewish law by the laws of ona'ah. These regulations provide a taxonomy of grounds for invalidating or otherwise modifying transactions concluded at a price that diverges from the prevailing norm. Analysis of the various details of the laws of ona'ah suggest that the basis of the price divergence claim is opportunity cost.[21]

   Further evidencing Judaism's attitude that the marketplace is not a self-regulating mechanism is its call for the appointment of market inspectors to insure honesty in the use of commercial weights and measures[22] and for the enforcement of a profit-rate constraint in the necessity sector.[23]

2. Intervention in the marketplace for the purpose of restraining the profit motive is called for by the Jewish law in the form of imposing a one-sixth profit rate constraint on sellers of essential foodstuff.

   The one-sixth profit rate constraint consists of the duty of the Jewish community to impose a price ceiling on essential foodstuff. Rather than imposing a restraint on individual vendors, the one-sixth profit level merely serves as a guidepost in the design of the price ceiling in the essential foodstuff sector.

   Analysis of the various details of the one-sixth profit rate constraint suggest that the constraint amounts to nothing more than a restraint on economic rent.[24]

3. Unrestrained rivalry in the marketplace in the form of competition for choice location, competitive price cutting, or aggressive salesmanship and advertising may result in the ruination of the less inventive and efficient firms. Talmudic decisors dispute whether Jewish law entitles an established firm to restrain its rival from a

competitive tactic that would ruin its livelihood.[25] Interestingly, Israeli courts today follow the anti-protectionist school.[26]

It should be noted that the insulation called for by the protectionist school is limited, as evidenced from the following considerations:

(a) To qualify for protection against a competitive tactic, a complainant must demonstrate to the court's satisfaction that it is not within his means to counter the tactic without falling below his opportunity cost earnings.

(b) The deprivation-generating criterion would not call for umbrella price protection when the competitors involved are geographically separated.[27]

4. Raising price on the basis of an upward shift of the demand curve is regarded in Jewish law as unethical when the shift is rooted in a changed circumstance, e.g. war, which makes the consumer's need for the product desperate.[28] Similarly unethical is the raising of price when the shift is due to an artificially created need by dint of religious law.[29]

Jewish law places in the realm of the Jewish community's public sector the following functions: (1) security measures; (2) water supply projects; (3) public road repairs; (4) a variety of projects of a religious character, including public education for the young and the establishment of charitable institutions for the poor.[30]

The "free rider" problem in Jewish law

Given that for the capitalist Pareto optimality forms the basis for assigning the role to the public sector, Judaism's call for a heavy social welfare role for government does not fit well into the capitalist ethic. It should be noted, however, that the Talmudic literature recognizes the "free rider" motive basis for government intervention in the marketplace.

The "free rider" phenomenon finds explicit expression in Jewish law in connection with laws dealing with zoning codes. In this regard, the Mishnah (Baba Batra II:8) relates that to preserve the aesthetic quality of a town, trees must be kept at a distance of at least 25 cubits from its limits. Violation of this zoning ordinance subjects the tree-owner to the penalty of having his tree cut down, with compensation for his loss not recognized. Deference to the amenity rights of the townpeople requires the tree-owner to cut down his tree even if its presence antedates the existence of the town. Nonetheless, in the latter instance, the community is required to indemnify the owner for his loss after removal of the tree is effected. Defending the procedure in the latter instance of first requiring the removal of the tree and only then allowing the owner to exact his compensation claim on the community, the Talmud asserts that reversing the procedure would effectively allow the tree to remain in place indefinitely since "a pot with two cooks is neither hot nor cold."[31] Elaborating on the intent of this analogy, R. Solomon b. Isaac (1040–1105, France) comments that given man's proclivity to avoid or delay payment as much as possible, each member of the community would refuse to inaugurate the collection with his share of the indemnity payment. With the collection process subject to snags, removal of the tree would not be accomplished unless the compensation obligation devolved upon the community only after the tree had already been removed.[32]

The relevance of the "free rider" motive for the problem of public taxation policy is explicitly found in the writings of R. Meir of Rothenburg (1215–1293). In a responsum dealing with the concept of unjust enrichment, R. Meir draws a distinction between a private and a communal expenditure. Hence, should A's private expenditure generate an external benefit to B, B bears no compensation responsibility to A, i.e., B's captured benefit is not regarded as unjust enrichment. Since A would, in any case, have undertaken his expenditure, and, in addition, B plays no role in making A's expenditure higher than otherwise would be, denying the latter his captured advantage on anything less than a gratis basis would be Sodomitic (i.e., denying someone a benefit when it involves no cost to oneself). In sharp contrast, should A's expenditure consist of an outlay for a communal project, B bears compensation responsibility for his advantage. Assimilating the latter case to the former, points out R. Meir, would effectively frustrate the emergence of any communal project. Each resident of the town would rely on the initiative of his neighbours to create the communal project. Once it was completed, the non-participating resident would claim exemption from his financial responsibility on the grounds that the sponsors' financial commitment would have taken place in any case and was not increased on account of him. Widespread maneuvering of this sort would obviously frustrate altogether the emergence of communal projects.[33]

Examination of the various details of the Jewish security tax levy, including its tax base, residency requirement and the variability of the tax formula highly suggest that elimination of the "free rider" motive forms the basic rationale for its inclusion in the purview of the public sector.[34]

The social philosophy of American Jewry

The aforementioned normative model Jewish religious thought calls for, can, in our view, go a long way in rationalizing the basic economic and political philosophy of American Jewry. Consistent with the normative model, Jews do not oppose the basic concept of capitalism, that is, an economic system based on free entry and competition. Indeed, as Professor Friedman has pointed out, Jews have flourished most under a system of competitive capitalism. What Jews are opposed to is unbridled capitalism. Jewish religious values of social justice and its presumption that perfect knowledge does not permeate the marketplace, lead American Jewry, it can be theorized, to support government regulations of the marketplace and income redistribution programs.

Let us now turn to Professor Friedman's own thesis that the Jews' anti-capitalist attitude reflects their reaction to the anti-Semitic stereotyping of them as being primarily interested in money, putting commercial interests ahead of human values. Injecting Jewish religious values and norms into the argument will, we submit, bolster the above thesis.

While Judaism takes a very positive attitude toward the pursuit of a livelihood,[35] excessive preoccupation with the acquisition of wealth is looked upon very dimly. Judaism teaches that man must give primacy to the spiritual domain. Wordly pursuits are permitted only a minor and subsidiary claim on man's time and energy.[36] Stereotyping the Jew as being extremely materialistic amounts to attacking him as having failed to live up to the ideals of his religion. What better defense mechanism can the Jew resort to than to become the champion of social welfare programs and other government measures designed to protect the disadvantaged. This social ethic assuages for the Jew his guilt feeling for having been excessively immersed in material pursuits and at the same time legitimizes him in the eye of the Gentile world.

NOTES

1. Free entry advocacy is espoused by the following Talmudic decisors: R. Isaac b. Jacob Alfasi (1012–1103, North Africa) *Rif, Bava Batra* 21b; *Tosafat* (twelfth century, France), *Bava Batra* 21b; Maimonides (1135–1204, Fez), *Yad,* Shekhenim VI:18; R. Asher b. Jehiel (1250–1327, Germany), *Rosh, Bava Batra* II:12; R. Jacob b. Asher (1270–ca.1343, Germany), *Tur, Hoshen Mishpat* 156:10; R. Joseph Caro (1488–1575, France), *Shulhan Arukh, Hoshen Mishpat* 156:5; R. Jehiel Michael Epstein (1829–1908, Belorussia) *Arukh ha-Shulhan, Hoshen Mishpat* 156:6.

2. *Bava Batra* 21b.

3. *Rosh, op.cit.* II:12; *Tur, op.cit.* 156:11; *Sh. Ar., op.cit.* 156:7; *Ar. hash., op.cit.* 156:10.

4. R. Joseph Caro, *Beit Yosef, Tur, Sh. Ar., op.cit.* 156:11.

5. *Ri MiGash, Bava Batra* 21b.

6. *Nahmanides, Ramban, Bava Batra* 21b.

7. R. Joseph Habib, *Nimmukei Yosef, Bava Batra* 21b.

8. *Beit Yosef, Tur, Sh.-Ar., op.cit.* 156, part 3; R. Mordechai *b. Hillel* on interpretation of R. Abraham Hiyya di Boton.

9. R. Abraham Hiyya di Boton, *Lehem Rav,* p. 216.

10. *Bava Batra* 22a; *Rosh, loc.cit.; Yad, op.cit.* VI:10; *Tur, loc.cit.; Sh.-Ar., op.cit.* 156:7; *Ar. hash; loc.cit.;* R. Joel Sirkes (1561–1640), *Bah, Tur loc.cit.* understands *yoma dishuka* to refer to the weekly market days and not to the elaborate annual fairs. R. Jehiel Michael Epstein (*loc.cit.*), however, understands *yoma dishuka* to refer to the annual fairs.

11. *Beit Yosef, Tur, Sh. Ar., loc.cit.*

12. *Tosafat, Bava Batra* 22a and *Roch loc.cit.,* both on the interpretation of R. Joseph Caro (*Beit Yosef, loc.cit.*).

13. R. Joshua ha-Kohen Falk, *Perishah, Tur, Sh.-Ar., op.cit.* 156 n.11; *Derishah* ad loc; *Sma, Sh.-Ar., op.cit.* n.20. R. Falk understands this to be the position of R. Jacob too.

14. *Bava Batra* 22a; *Rosh, loc.cit.; Yad, loc.cit.; Tur, loc.cit.; Sh-Ar., loc. cit.; Ar-hash., loc.cit.*

15. *Rif, Bava Batra* 22a; *Yad, op.cit., Rosh, op.cit.* II:12; *Tur, op.cit.* 156:11; *Sh-Ar., op.cit.* 156:6; *Ar-hash., loc.cit.*

16. *Beit Yosef, Tur, Sh-Ar., loc.cit; Rema, Sh-Ar., op.cit.* 156:6; *Ar-hash., op.cit.* 156:11.

17. *Bava Batra* 22a; *Rif* ad locum; *Yad, op.cit.* VI:9; *Tur., op.cit.* 156:12; *Sh-Ar., op.cit.; Ar-hash., op.cit.* 156:9.

18. *Beit Yosef, Tur, Sh-Ar., loc.cit.; Ar-hash., op.cit.* 156:11.

19. R. Eliezer b. Nathan of Mainz (ca.1090–1170), *Raavan Bava Batra* 21b; *Beit Yosef, loc.cit.; Derisha ad loc,* note 13. For a variant view, *see Tosafat,* Bava Batra 21b.

20. Majority view in opposition to R. Judah, *Mishnah* Bava Mezia 60b.

21. For a detailed discussion on the laws of *ona'ah* and the development of the opportunity cost theory as the basis of the claim, *see* Aaron Levine, *Free Enterprise and Jewish Law* (New York: Yeshiva University, Ktav, 1980) pp. 99–110.

22. *Bava Batra* 89a; *Rif ad. locum; Yad, op.cit.* VIII:20; *Rosh, op.cit.,* V:22; *Tur, op.cit.* 231:2; *Sh-Ar., op.cit.* 231:2; *Ar-hash, op.cit.* 231:3.

23. *Bava Batra* 9a; *Yoma* 9a; *Yad, op.cit.* XIV:1; *Tur, op.cit.* 231:26; *Sh-Ar., op.cit.* 231:20 *Ar-hash, op.cit.* 231:20.

24. *Ibid.,* p. 91–95.

25. Members of the protectionist school include R. Eliezer b. Joel ha-Levi of Bonn (1140–1225), quoted in *Mordekhai, Bava Batra* II:516, and in *Haggahot Maimuniyyot, Shekhenim* VI:8; R. Joseph Ibn MiGash (Ri Mi-Gash, *Bava Batra* 21b); R. Moshe Sofer (1768–1839, Hungary), Responsa *Hatam Sofer, Hoshen Mishpat* 38. Members of the free entry school of thought include R. Ephraim Zalman Margolioth (1762–1828), *Beit Ephraim, Hoshen Mishpat* 26; R. Mordechai Jacob Breisch (contemporary), *Helkat Yaakov,* Vol. 2, no.65; R. Isaac Arieli (contemporary), *Enayim le-Mishpat, Bava Batra* 21b.

26. See *Piskei Din shel Botei ha-Din Ha-Rabbaniyim bi-Yisrael,* vol. 4, p. 9; vol. 8, p. 82.

27. See, Levine, *op.cit.* p. 26–30.

28. *Bava Mezia* 58b; R. Hai b. Sherira (939–1038), *Sefer ha-Mikkah ve-ha-Mimkar; Rif,* Bava Mezia 58b.

29. *Samuel, Pesahim* 30a.

30. See Levine, *op.cit.* pp. 131–160.

31. *Bava Batra* 24b.

32. R. Solomon b. Isaac, *Rashi, Bava Batra* 24b.

33. R. Meir b. Baruch of Rothenburg, *Responsa Maharam,* no. 39.

34. See Levine, *op.cit.* pp. 136–142.

35. *Berakhat* 8a, 35b; *Avat* 11:2; *Kiddushin* 29a; R. Samuel Eliezer b. Judah

ha-Levi Edels (16th century), *Maharsha Berakhot* 35b and Kiddushin 82a.

36. R. Judah b. Ila'i, *Berakhat* 35b; R. Judah Loew b. Bezalel, (c.1525–1600, Worms), *N'tivat, Olam,* Vol. 2, *n'tiv h'Osher* chapters 1, 2.

Comment*

S. Herbert Frankel

I. SOMBART REVISITED

My point of departure in this comment is to take up Friedman's reference to the once classic, indeed notorious, book published in 1911 by Werner Sombart under the title *Die Jüdean und das Wirtschaftsleben.*[1]

Werner Sombart was born in Germany in 1863 and died there in 1941. He held the Chair of Economics at the University of Breslau from 1890–1906 and later at the Handelshochschule in Berlin. He aimed at making it his life-work to discover and to explain the rise and development of modern capitalism. In 1902 he published *Der Moderne Kapitalismus,*[2] which purportedly revealed the very essence and spirit of capitalism.

Sombart claimed that his book *Die Jüden und das Wirtschaftsleben* was written as a result of his accidental discovery of objective facts which showed him the importance of the role of the Jews in modern capitalism. Whether or not this was the origin of his views cannot be

---

*This paper is based on a monograph entitled "Modern Capitalism and the Jews" published by the Oxford Centre for Postgraduate Hebrew Studies, 1983 — eds.

proved. It has been suggested, rather unconvincingly, by Bert Hoselitz that it was an act of courage for Sombart to write the book at all "because in the Germany of his day, plagued as it was by a strong and increasing undercurrent of anti-Semitism, no matter what his conclusions were they were unlikely to please anyone and this was precisely what happened."[3] The book was, indeed, denounced both because it was seen as giving comfort to anti-Semites and "by Jew-baiters to support those who wanted confirmation of the viciousness, parasitism and moral depravity which they attributed to the Jews."[4]

It is just as fallacious to argue that a work must be impartial because it appears to rest on objective facts, as it is to assume that if an opinion is equally attacked from opposing sides it must be true. What motivates an author in his search for the "facts" and determines their alleged "discovery" often takes, as every historian knows, very peculiar twists and turns, as do the conclusions ultimately drawn from them.

Capitalism and the Jews: Sombart's thesis

Sombart asserted that the Jews had created modern capitalism. Indeed the term Jewish and capitalism were used synonymously by him, as was quite common at the time. Practically all early German (and French) socialists, as Edmund Silberner has shown,[5] decried Jewry for its putative predominance in trade and finance. Karl Marx's well-known but usually misunderstood epigram "The social emancipation of the Jews is the emancipation of society from Judaism," i.e., from commercial calculation, is based on this use of the words Jews and Judaism.

Sombart asserted that capitalism could be traced back to the quality of cold calculation and rationality of the desert nomad, quite foreign to the Nordic peasant. This intellectual disparagement of commercial calculation can still be found in unexpected quarters in the Western world. Sombart saw the "commercial spirit of the Jews" as having overwhelmed the utterly opposite nature of the Nordic. His thesis, although anti-Semitic only by implication, was taken up not only by socialists and anti-Jewish agitators but by conservatives in response to the development of the liberal economic order sponsored by Bismark. After the great crash of 1873, a spate of literature emanating mostly from reactionary quarters inundated Germany.[6]

Urbanism, commercialism, stock speculation, disgruntled industrial workers, economic crisis—in a word capitalism, was declared to be newly emancipated Jewry's ungrateful response.

Sombart's reception

Paul R. Mendes-Flohr, a Senior Lecturer at the Hebrew University, has pointed out that it is perhaps paradoxical that these notions of a particular Jewish aptitude for money-trade and commerce were granted academic respectability by philo-Semitic scholars eager to demonstrate that the Jews were deserving of emancipation and full participation in Germany's liberal economy. It is also significant that when Sombart first published *The Jews and Modern Capitalism* in a serialized form, he was asked to lecture before audiences "recruited mainly from the Jewish intelligentsia." This is astonishing for, as pointed out, the picture Sombart presents is so constructed that one senses the zealotry and compulsiveness that guided his pen. Indeed, the eminent economic historian Professor David S. Landes,[7] observed that it is difficult to understand why his book was not dismissed out of hand as pseudo-scholarly work. Be that as it may, the fact remains that for the most part Sombart's characterization of the economic ethos of the Jew was not radically questioned. This, suggests Mendes-Flohr, "is perhaps explained by the pervasive familiarity and *ergo* credibility of the motifs Sombart embroidered into his tapestry."[8] (Although Sombart had earlier embraced socialism, he finally became a staunch Nazi.) In *Deutscher Sozialismus* (1934) he justified the exclusion of Jews from the spiritual and economic life of Germany because he claimed "capitalism was the expression of the 'Hebraic spirit.'"

Sombart's ideas on the role of the Jews in the development of modern capitalism have been refuted by so many scholars both Jewish and non-Jewish that there would seem to be no purpose in again raising the issues involved. Oddly enough, however, the ghost of Werner Sombart has still not been laid to rest. Had it been otherwise I should not have ventured to add this little footnote to the long drawn-out discussion of his work.

II.   MILTON FRIEDMAN AND SOMBART'S GHOST

My renewed interest in the subject was the result of an unexpected experience. In 1972 I heard echoes of Sombart's thesis in a lecture by an economist who is, in our time, if anything even more distinguished than Sombart was in his. I refer to Milton Friedman's paper, now published in this volume.

Friedman's general question is this. How can one explain the movement of intellectual opinion within the West towards general collectivism? Friedman regards the current trend in this direction as a paradox, and its explanation as a major challenge "to those of us who believe in freedom." Why has there been this failure to persuade intellectuals of the virtues of freedom? Until we can find a satisfactory answer to this question, Friedman claims, protagonists of freedom are not likely to succeed in changing the climate of opinion.

Friedman has no answer, as he freely admits, to this general question. His focus is more narrow. He hopes to examine a particular case of the paradox—the attitude of the Jews towards capitalism. He asserts that it can be readily demonstrated both that the Jews owe an enormous debt to free enterprise and competitive capitalism and that, at least for the past century, the Jews have consistently opposed capitalism and have done much ideologically to undermine it. He asks how these propositions can be reconciled. Friedman believes that he can, to a large extent, explain the anti-capitalist tendency among the Jews, but points out that the most important elements of his explanation are peculiar to the special case and cannot readily be generalized. He nevertheless holds the hope that the study of this special case may offer a clue to the general paradox.

It is necessary first to understand what Friedman means by his contention that the Jews owe an enormous debt to capitalism. He means in fact that they owe an enormous debt to the free market. Where it has been free, enabling people generally to enter trades, occupations and professions according to their abilities, Jews have been able to prosper. There were in the past and still are many sectors in which Jews are discriminated against. In these, few Jews will be found and there will also be found privileged classes of persons protected by their relative monopoly position. The same phenomenon occurred in many countries. Where competition and the free market flourished so did the Jews, and Friedman stressed particularly that the record shows that Jews have rarely benefited from authoritarian regimes, except as selected individuals chosen by monarchs or the Church, as in the case of the Court Jews of the eighteenth-century.

Friedman's paradox is why, given the beneficent effects of the free market, did the Jews not support it? Why, on the contrary, and particularly for the past century, have the Jews been a stronghold of anti-capitalist sentiment? How, he asked, did it come about that in spite of the intellectual explanation, from Adam Smith to the present day, of why the free market was so beneficial have the Jews been so disproportionately anti-capitalist? In passing, it is worth stating that this question could, of course, logically speaking also be asked about innumerable other groups of individuals or sections of society. It could be asked about blacks, or Catholics, or about Asian immigrants or even about men or women as separate groups. Among all of these categories there must inevitably be some, or even a majority, who are socialist or anti-capitalist. Is the existence of these groups therefore also to be regarded as giving rise to a paradox?

Friedman on Sombart

Friedman considered the views of various writers to account for the alleged anti-capitalist mentality of the Jews. He dismissed out-of-hand the attempt to explain it as a direct reflection of values derived from the Jewish religion and culture because Jewish opposition to capitalism and attachment to socialism was a modern phenomenon. In his opinion it occurred only after the Enlightenment and then primarily only among Jews who were breaking away from the Jewish religion. It is curious that he then proceeded to argue that Sombart made out a far stronger case for the contrary view namely that Jewish religion and culture implied a capitalist outlook. He referred to Sombart's view that throughout the centuries the Jews championed the cause of individual liberty in economic activity and that the Jewish religion should have the same leading ideas as capitalism. He quoted Sombart that "The whole religious system is in reality nothing but a contract between Jehovah and his chosen people . . . . God promises something and gives something, and the righteous must give him something in return. Indeed there was no community of interest between God and man which could not be expressed in these terms — that man performs some duty enjoined by the Torah and receives from God a *quid pro quo."* "Free trade," Sombart concluded, "and industrial freedom were in accordance with Jewish law and therefore in accordance with God's will."

Friedman was aware of the generally unfavourable reception accorded to Sombart's book and referred to the fact that something of an aura of anti-Semitism had come to be attributed to it but he suggested that there is nothing in it to justify any charge of anti-Semitism. Indeed, he interpreted the book as philo-Semitic and stated categorically "I regard the violence of the reaction of Jewish intellectuals to the book as itself a manifestation of the Jewish anti-capitalist mentality." It is worth noting in passing that Friedman apparently did not realize that Sombart was using the Jews deliberately or unconsciously as a foil to promote socialist, and later national socialist ideas in the service of his fervent German patriotism.

Friedman expressed the view that it is hard to see direct links with Jewish tradition in these attitudes to capitalism, and he approved Nathan Glazer's view that "One thing is sure: it is an enormous simplification to say Jews in Eastern Europe became socialists and anarchists because the Hebrew prophets had denounced injustice twenty-five hundred years ago. . . . The Jewish religious tradition probably does dispose Jews, in some subtle way, toward liberalism (used in the American sense of the word) and radicalism, but it is not easy to see in present-day Jewish social attitudes the heritage of the Jewish religion."

Friedman also dismissed the view that the Jewish anti-capitalist mentality simply reflects the general tendency for intellectuals to be anti-capitalist, this accentuated here by the disproportionate representation of Jews among intellectuals. It was his impression that a disproportionately large number of Jewish intellectuals were "collectivists," and, moreover this explanation did not account for the attitudes of those Jews who were not intellectuals.

The Friedman theory

Friedman finally arrived at a theory of his own. Anti-Semitism produced the well-known stereotype of a Jew as primarily interested in money, who put commercial interests above human values and who was cunning, selfish, and greedy. To this stereotype, it was Friedman's thesis, Jews could have reacted either by accepting the description but at the same time rejecting the idea that the character-traits in the stereotype were really blameworthy or they could have accepted these traits and values as blameworthy but have rejected the stereotype which embodied them in the Jew. Friedman argued the Jews could have accepted their role in the capitalist world and openly defended the beneficence of the free market. Since few of us can escape the intellectual air we breathe, it was hardly to be expected that they would.

Indeed, they inevitably came to share the values and prejudices of the world which despised the "merely" commercial. They were led to say to and of themselves that if Jews are like that, the anti-Semites are right.

The other possible reaction concluded Friedman is to deny that the Jews are really like the stereotype and to do this by explicitly persuading oneself, and not only oneself but the anti-Semites also, that Jews contrary to the stereotype were not money-grabbing, selfish, and heartless but in fact public spirited and concerned with ideas. And, asked Friedman, how better could they do this than by denigrating the free market and glorifying the political process?

This impressionist view of the Jew who overreacts is, of course, whether Friedman realized it or not, the well-known stereotype of the *Salon Kommunist* (lounge-communist)—the rich man who hides his conscious or unconscious feelings of guilt for being rich by joining the communist cause or parading his communist sympathies for the sake of humanity. Friedman thus applied the guilt feelings of estranged individuals to a group on the basis of race. He explained that he was led to this, surely astonishing, solution of the paradox of the anti-capitalist mentality of the Jews by his experience in Israel, where "after several months" he came to the conclusion that the quickest way to generalize about values in any area in Israel was to ask what was true of the Jews in the Diaspora and reverse it: thus in the Diaspora Jews lived in towns and pursued commerce but in Israel agriculture had much higher prestige; in the Diaspora Jews shunned military service, while in Israel they had demonstrated extraordinary competence in it and so on—he even found that in the Diaspora Jews were excellent cooks while in Israel cooking was generally terrible. It is not astonishing that he reached the conclusion that the main explanations of the paradox of the anti-capitalist mentality of the Jews was to be found (1) in the special circumstances of nineteenth century Europe which linked pro-market parties with established religions and so drove Jews to the Left and (2) in their subconscious attempt to demonstrate to themselves and the world the fallacy of the anti-Semitic stereotype.

III. AN ANATOMY OF THE FRIEDMAN VIEW

Notwithstanding the fact that at certain times individual radical Jews or Jewish groups played an important role in political movements, I

regard Friedman's generalizations as a-historical and as indefensible. I
believe that the question posed by Friedman is actually a non-question
based on the mythology or fallacy that races and peoples can be regarded as having identifiable general social characteristics or attitudes
which determine their behaviour.

But there is an even deeper question. What, one must ask, could
have been the cause of Friedman's astonishing generalizations?

Let us turn once again to the case of Werner Sombart. The deeper
study of it, I suggest, provides a clue to finding the answer.

Four years after Friedman gave his address, Dr. Mendes-Flohr published his arresting analysis, to which I have already referred, of what
I would call the Sombart paradox. He unravelled what accounted for
Sombart's extra-ordinary coupling of the Jews with modern
capitalism. I say extra-ordinary advisedly — for it is not indeed extraordinary that a small and but recently emancipated minority in the
modern European nation states should be regarded as having been a
prime force behind the capitalist system? Looked at objectively, is not
this in itself a most peculiarily impressionistic view of history?

A relevant anecdote

I am reminded of a personal experience which I should like to share
with you to illustrate what I mean. About thirty years ago I was engaged in an official investigation in East Africa and was very friendly
with a high-ranking, and I should add, a most dedicated member of
the colonial government in Kenya. One day he fetched me for a lunch
engagement. His car was delayed at a road-junction because a large
number of Indian children were rushing out of school to a playground
across the road. At this my friend blurted out a highly uncomplimen-
tary epithet about all those children's parents who he said were responsible for the backwardness of the Africans. As it happened I had for
some time been examining the "Indian question." The facts bore no
relation whatever to this stereotype. The Indians were the visible
bearers of an emerging free market economy in so far as they were
permitted to operate in it by restrictive laws of the colonial government and by African custom which confined Indians mainly to
commercial occupations. Yet they were accused of being responsible
for the consequences of the economic changes that the developing free
market and capitalism were slowly creating. Similar to Sombart's
accusation against the Jews with which I will deal in a moment, they

were accused of being so poor that they could undercut both the Africans and whites and yet so rich, because of their alleged unduly high profits, that *obviously* they were freezing out everybody else because of the money they invested. Moreover it also was *obviously* clear that they were sending their money illegally to India at the same time! Actually they had by being largely confined to commerce developed the most efficient system of commodity distribution East Africa has known, ever, to the great advantage of the indigenous population. I think a study should be written to elucidate the official and unofficial anti-Indian feeling in the African colonial territories. It would, I believe, show that it originated in the realization that the outmoded and paternalistic economic attitudes in Africa were failing. That failure was unconsciously demonstrated daily by the growth of free market activities which government paternalism did not understand and of which, hitherto it had taken insufficient account. But let me return to Mendes-Flohr's analysis, with which my little historical anecdote is not as unconnected as may at first be thought.

The anatomy of Sombart's position

Sombart's *The Jews and Modern Capitalism* formally claimed, as Mendes-Flohr shows, to be a scholarly revaluation of Max Weber's study on Puritanism and modern economic behaviour. Sombart set out to demonstrate that Weber should really have localized the spirit of capitalism in Judaism because fundamentally "Puritanism is Judaism." It is Mendes-Flohr's thesis that Sombart's study of the Jews' economic life is not merely another Weberesque academic contribution in the debate on religion and economic behaviour or that it was his intention to pay a compliment to the Jews as the progenitors of capitalism but that it was an ideological exercise — in a sense even a personal psychological one. Sombart despised the capitalistic present in which he lived and identifying it as a product of *Judentum,* offered him the possibility of reconciliation with his overriding *Deutschtum.*

Sombart, as Mendes-Flohr notes, "began his scholarly career as a member of the *Verein für Sozialpolitik,* an association established in the wake of the social dislocations engendered by the liberal economic order sponsored by Bismarck's Second Reich. Although many of the businessmen, civil servants and academicians who founded the *Verein* in 1873 were liberals and proponents of *laissez-faire* and a United Germany they were still somewhat sentimentally attached to the 'idyllic life' of pre-industrial Germany" (p. 88). Their outlook was still predominantly paternalistic. "They expected from unification and economic progress a spiritual regeneration of their idealized Germany—the *Volksgemeinschaft*" (p. 88). Instead of this they perceived a growing division which they ascribed to the excesses of applied Manchesterism, i.e., those of the English *laissez-faire* liberal economists. Sombart's first studies showed a close identification with the ideas of the *Verein* and with his father who was one of its founders. Both father and son showed hostility to industrialism. But in the 1880s Sombart, increasingly aware of the rising standards of living of the peasantry and the proletariat resulting from the increased productivity of the modern economy, experienced a personal crisis and felt compelled to assert his identity in the *Verein* as distinct from that of his venerated father. He abandoned patriarchal ideals and embraced more "Leftist" views.

In Max Weber's view capitalism (i.e., the free market), if properly guided by a politically mature and responsible bourgeoisie, could lead Germany out of its social malaise. By contrast Sombart, in his early writings tried to square the circle dictated by his need to reconcile the obvious benefits of modern industrialism with the "spirit of the idealised past." He unequivocally rejected capitalism and plumped for socialism. But some ten years later he had developed doubts about the role of the trade unions and the proletariat in the spiritual regeneration of the *Volksgemeinschaft*. How then could the circle be squared now?

Entepreneurship vs. calculation in Sombart's capitalism

Over the ensuing years he formulated the ideas contained in *The Jews and Modern Capitalism*. Briefly what Sombart attempted was to split the capitalist spirit into the entrepreneurial on the one hand, and that of the commercial calculating bourgeoisie on the other. Real entrepreneurship, Sombart argued, in its fully adventurous disciplined amoral character and drive for power, had come to be fused in modern capitalism with the bourgeois spirit which he identified with the image of the stereotype of the Jew. As Mendes-Flohr sums up: "the many logical inconsistencies in *The Jews and Modern Capitalism* suggest a compulsive desire to demonstrate that the 'guilt' of capitalism, or rather its more deprecatory aspects viz., acquisitiveness, artificiality and practical rationality, lies with the Jews." It is difficult not to agree with Mendes-Flohr's conclusion that Sombart's cultural despair found expression in "The Jews and Modern Capitalism" whose basic contention was that not *Deutschtum* — not his idealized United Germany — but *Judentum* was responsible for bourgeois capitalism.

Sombart's evidence

Let me for a moment glance at the kind of historical facts which Sombart relied on and at the fallacious and logically inconsistent way he presented them. Such inconsistencies often betray one. For example Sombart, although admitting the paucity and inconclusiveness of the statistical data associating Jews and commerce nevertheless suggested that one should assume "that since many Jews converted or assimilated, they and their descendants who appear as Christians still retain Jewish characteristics," for "again and again men who contribute to the development of capitalism appear as Christians, who in reality are Jews." Many Huguenots, for instance, were probably Jews, especially "when we take into consideration the numerous Jewish names (i.e., biblical first names) found among (them)." *Post hoc ergo propter hoc.* Because of this "fact" "the contribution of the Jews to the fabric of modern economic life will, of necessity, appear smaller than it was in reality."[9]

With this perspective and alleged historical background Sombart wrote of the golden thread of Jewish wealth from King Solomon to Bismarck's banker, Bleichröder, as if it was one grand bank account handed down from generation to generation. Moreover since the Jew thus clearly had money he was able to lend it and this Sombart asserted paved the way for capitalism. The argument is circular. The "proof" that the Jews had money to lend was the inference that as they lent it they must have had it. As in the case of the Indians in Africa, to which I referred previously, Sombart explains the Jews' alleged ability to undersell by their extreme frugality — an argument which hardly tallies with his previous inference that the Jews had money because eye-witnesses related that the Jews made "ostentatious" and "conspicuous" displays of their wealth. Thus the circle was squared. *Deutschtum* — idealized unified Germany — can be saved by real heroic capitalism as long as it is cleansed of the bourgeois spirit — the spirit of Judaism. In contradistinction to the Jews, who constitute a *Händlervolk* the Germans, with their aptitude for bold enterprise, are in his view, at least politically a *Heldenvolk*. Only by reasserting its primal heroic spirit represented by the Prussian aristocracy, could Germany be preserved as "the last dyke against the muddy flood of commercialism."

In 1915 Sombart wrote a war tract in which it is perhaps not astonishing to find that there is a temporary transference of the guilt of bourgeois capitalism from the Jews to the English. In it Sombart, in rejecting the idea of a "European culture," asks "How could a European emerge from a mixture of a heroic German and a calculating Englishman?"[10]

IV. SOMBART AND FRIEDMAN

In conclusion, let me draw some threads together. I have attempted to focus attention on the ironical circumstance that some one-hundred years after Sombart accused the Jews of responsibility for modern capitalism, Milton Friedman accused them of disproportionate intellectual and political support for socialism.

It is astonishing to find that Friedman uses impressionistic evidence or forms of argument which have a striking resemblance to those used by Sombart. Even the thesis put forward by Friedman—that one way for Jews to counter the idea that they are like the popular caricatures or stereotypes of them is to persuade themselves and if possible the anti-Semites that far from being selfish and heartless, Jews are really public-spirited, generous and concerned with ideals rather than material goods—is directly paralleled by Sombart who wrote:[11]

> If we find so many Jews with just the opposite manner of thinking, with what one might almost call an extravagant altruistic sense, a rigorous selflessness and a zealousness against all selfishness, we may then deduce just from these reaction phenomena the existence of the indicated national characteristic.

Indeed, Friedman as well as Sombart, it may be argued, was seeking, in this way, simple explanations of political and economic circumstances which ideologically and emotionally deeply concerned them.

Sombart was concerned about what he saw as the threat to his ideal society by capitalism. Friedman was concerned by what he perceived as the renewed threat of socialism and collectivism. Neither Friedman nor Sombart were able to support their arguments by historical facts or by logical analysis. In this connection it is not only tragic but also

ironical that support for the free market and capitalism, which Friedman advocated as the obvious and certain way the Jews should have
chosen, was by Sombart and later by the Nazis the economic crime of
which they were accused and for which so many suffered martyrdom.
It is just as tragically ironic to find that those who remained for the
most part economically unemancipated in the ghettos of Eastern Europe and sought for new hope in socialist and political action finally
fared little better.

The significance of the question

But the fundamental issue with which this essay is concerned, is not
only that the answers we have examined were wrong but that so too
were the questions which gave rise to them. These questions posed
apparent dilemmas which were in reality false. As Gilbert Ryle has
shown,[12] often thinkers are at loggerheads with one another, not because their propositions do conflict but because they imagine that they
do. They find themselves at cross-purposes because they suppose
themselves to be giving rival answers to the same questions, when this
is not really the case. Such cross-purposes can be characterized by
saying that the two sides are hinging their arguments upon concepts
which really fall into different categories of thought but which they
suppose fall into the same category or vice versa.

Both Sombart and Friedman, as so many others do, used the words
"the Jews" and "Judaism" as distinct categories which depict attributes
by which Jews can be identified in their economic, political, or social
actions as if there were a world of the Jews – a Jewish world or, one
could add, a Protestant or Catholic world – as distinct from the real
world. I will not here attempt to unravel this philosophical problem.
Let me only assure you that there is no need to despair. There is no
contradiction between the real world and the apparently different
world of Jews or Catholics or what have you – these so-called different worlds are but particular aspects of the one real world – indeed
they are what constitutes it. The world of the banker who happens to
be a Jew is not a different banking world than that of the Protestant
or the Catholic. The physicist who is a black man is not engaged in a
different type of physics than one who is white. The world of Jews
who are capitalists or socialists does not differ from the world of capitalists or socialists who are Gentiles.

Adam Smith regarded the propensity to truck, barter and exchange
as common to all men. To attempt to categorize their economic, poli-

tical and social actions, as if they depend on different natural attributes, does violence not only to language and logical thought but contributes to human tragedy.

NOTES

1. Leipzig: Dunker und Humblot 1911. trans. by M. Epstein in London in 1913 as *The Jews and Modern Capitalism*. Introduction by Bert F. Hoselitz. The Free Press, Glencoe, Illinois 1951. I wish to thank Professor Uriel Tal for his helpful advice in the preparation of this paper.

2. 2 vols. Leipzig 1902.

3. Hoselitz. Introduction to *The Jews and Modern Capitalism*. p. xviii.

4. ibid.

5. Karl Marx, "On the Jewish Question," in *Early Writings,* trans. and ed. by T. B. Bottomore, New York 1964, p. 40. Quoted from Paul R. Mendes-Flohr, "Werner Sombart's: The Jews and Modern Capitalism." *Leo Baeck Institute Yearbook,* XXI. 1976. p. 87.

6. Uriel Tal discusses this literature in detail in his book *Christians and Jews in the Second Reich 1870–1914* (in Hebrew), Jerusalem 1969. (An English edition, *Christians and Jews in Germany. Religion, Politics and Ideology in the Second Reich, 1870–1914,* was published in 1975.)

7. David S. Landes, "The Jewish Merchant: Typology and Stereotypology in Germany," in *Leo Baeck Institute Yearbook,* XIX (1974), p. 22. Quoted by Mendes-Flohr ibid. p. 94.

8. Mendes-Flohr ibid. p. 94.

9. Quotations in this paragraph are from Mendes-Flohr ibid. p. 97.

10. Mendes-Flohr ibid. p. 106.

11. Quoted from Arthur Mitzman's analysis of Sombart's sociology. Mitzman added: "Sombart's evidence for the prominence of selfishness in the Jewish character is a good example of the Catch-22 logic usually in racist arguments." Arthur Mitzman, *Sociology and Estrangement.* Alfred A. Knopf, 1973.

12. Gilbert Ryle, *Dilemmas.* Cambridge University Press, 1957.

Reply

Milton Friedman

One quibble

I interpret Aaron Levine's comment as supporting my assertion that "Jewish . . . attachment to socialism is, at most, two centuries old." I welcome his extensive and authoritative documentation of that proposition—a documentation that I was and am incompetent to provide.

I have only one quibble with Dr. Levine's comment. He implies that the opposition of "the Jewish religion . . . to unbridled capitalism" is a qualification of the proposition that "Jewish religion and culture implies a capitalist outlook." It is not. Who is for "unbridled" anything—other than a wild horse? Would today's socialists say that they are for "unbridled" socialism? Nineteenth-century Britain and United States, and twentieth-century Hong Kong, are generally regarded as exemplifying free market capitalism—the "salient feature" of which, as Levine correctly notes, is "free entry." Yet in all three, government has been important and has assumed functions that, according to Levine, Jewish religion assigns to the community rather than the market, supposedly because of the Jewish religion's opposition to "unbridled capitalism."

This opposition could indeed have led "American Jewry . . . to support" some of the activities local and state governments undertook in the nineteenth century such as provision to help the poor. It stretches the principles Levine outlines beyond reason to regard them as justifying the kind of "government regulation of the marketplace and income distribution" that have been adopted in recent decades.

No effective criticism

My reaction to Herbert Frankel's comment is in one respect the same as my reaction to Aaron Levine's: it too strengthens my confidence in the thesis I expressed in my paper, though for wholly different reasons. It does so because so able, scholarly, and knowledgeable a person as Frankel has been able to come up with no effective criticism of the thesis, despite his long-time instinctive negative reaction to it. He has been reduced to attacking Sombart rather than me (every reference to Sombart could be expunged from my paper without affecting its main substance one iota), to using adjectives and assertions without citing any evidence to support them, and to ruling my thesis out of order on what are essentially metaphysical grounds.

To take the final point first, Frankel regards "the questions that gave rise to" my essay as "wrong," as posing "apparent dilemmas which were in reality false" because I "used the words 'the Jews' and 'Judaism' as distinct categories . . . as if there were . . . a Jewish world . . . distinct from the real world." I find this an extraordinary position. There is not "a Jewish world . . . distinct from the real world." But does Frankel deny that there is a Jewish world that is part of the real world? If so, how is it that he is chairman of the Board of Governors of the Oxford Centre for Postgraduate Hebrew Studies? (His attack on my paper was first delivered as a lecture at that Centre and published by it.) Is there any question at all that there is a Jewish culture, that there is a Jewish people — heterogeneous, diversified, differentiated into many separate groups, some with very different beliefs and culture (e.g., Ashkenazi versus Sephardic; European versus Oriental), but nonetheless with a single identifiable heritage that gives the Oxford Centre its reason for existence?

Common culture and heritage

Frankel states "that the question" I pose is "based on the . . . fallacy that races and peoples can be regarded as having identifiable general social characteristics or attitudes that determine their behaviour." The word "race" does not appear in my article. There is not a word in it which implies that I treat "a group on the basis of race," as Frankel asserts, if race is interpreted in a biological sense. I treat Jews as a group formed by a common culture and historical heritage. Is there any doubt that people who are regarded by themselves as Jews and who are classified by others as Jews have some characteristics in common that distinguish them from people who are classified by themselves and others as Lutherans or for that matter as vegetarians? Would it be "wrong" and "false" and a case of treating "a group on the basis of race" to discuss why it is that vegetarians have certain views in common, or to suggest that their being vegetarians leads them to behave in certain ways that distinguishes them from other people? Would using the words "the vegetarians" imply that there is a vegetarian "world . . . distinct from the real world"? Frankel's knee-jerk reaction against talking about "Jews" or "Judaism" as a distinct category is itself a phenomenon requiring explanation — which I believe my article in part provides.

As to Frankel's use of adjectives and assertions in place of evidence, at various points he refers to my argument or conclusions or generalizations as "curious," "impressionistic," "astonishing," "a-historical," "indefensible." In no case does he give any evidence to justify the adjectives. He asserts that I was not "able to support [my] arguments by historical facts or by logical analysis," but points out no errors in logic and refers to no historical facts that contradict anything I said. He claims that "Sombart's ideas on the role of Jews in the development of modern capitalism have been refuted by . . . many scholars both Jewish and non-Jewish" but gives no citations. The one analysis of Sombart's work he discusses in some detail, that by Dr. Mendes-Flohr, is, to judge from Frankel's account, concerned with the sociology of knowledge issue of why Sombart expressed the views he did rather than the substantive issue of whether Sombart's thesis is correct. After all, the validity of ideas cannot be determined simply from their provenance. Correct views may be expressed to promote objectionable ends.

Some paradoxes

Finally, a few details. I agree with Frankel that "it is . . . fallacious to argue that a work must be impartial because it appears to rest on objective facts." But it is equally fallacious to suppose that a statement is wrong because it is contained in a work that is not impartial. After all, a paranoiac may have real enemies.

Frankel regards it as "extra-ordinary that a small and recently emancipated minority in the modern European nation states should be regarded as having been a prime force behind the capitalist system." His comment refers to Sombart not to me, since I did not express this view or use Sombart as evidence for it. My reference to Sombart was solely with respect to his analysis of the compatibility between the Jewish religion and capitalism. However, to be the devil's advocate, is Sombart's view really more extraordinary than the idea expressed by

Eric Voeglin that "Israel has been an abiding, ever creative, and indispensable part of Western history" (*Public Interest,* Spring 1983, p. 115)?

Frankel notes that the contrast I stress between the debt of the Jews to capitalism and their opposition to capitalism may hold for other groups — "blacks, or Catholics, or... Asian immigrants or even... men or women as separate groups." He then asks, "Is the existence of these groups... also to be regarded as giving rise to a paradox?" It most certainly is — especially with respect to the blacks in the United States. It is encouraging that in the more than a decade since my article was written, some black scholars — notably Thomas Sowell and Walter Williams — have recognized the paradox and have explored it in detail. Their work has demonstrated how much minorities such as blacks and Jews can gain from fuller reliance on free markets and private enterprise; how much they have been harmed by governmental measures, even measures explicitly enacted for their benefit. Their work adds significantly to the evidence that has, I believe, encouraged a distinct change in the intellectual climate of opinion, if not toward whole-hearted acceptance of the virtues of competitive capitalism, at least toward far greater scepticism about the beneficence of governmental intervention.

Discussion

Edited by: Kenneth G. Elzinga

Aaron Levine: The central focus of Professor Friedman's paper concerns the paradox, as he calls it, of why Jews are opposed to capitalism, while they have materially benefited most from this type of economic organization compared to any other. The latter proposition, I agree wholeheartedly to; and it has been, of course, demonstrated very ably by Milton Friedman himself that it is correct; this goes as well for the general proposition that capitalism does maximize wealth compared to other types of organization.

However, I would like to take issue with the monolithic statement that Jews oppose capitalism. What I would like to show essentially is what the Jewish religious law type of economic organization would propose, and to show that there are only certain aspects of capitalism that would call for some type of correction. The essential feature of capitalism is of course, free entry and economic freedom. As I tried to show in my paper, going back to the fourth century, there is a very clear cut mainstream view in Jewish theological thought of the importance of free entry—even to the extent, according to one school of thought, where it would result in ruination of a competitor. This is the punishment of the marketplace, and the Jewish tradition would go along with that as well. But in terms of certain types of government intervention, which I think that a free enterprise economist could be comfortable with, I think we would find very much a kinship between what Judaism, as a religion, would call for and what the economists would be comfortable with.

Let me just take three main areas. One would be an enforced charity provision, where we don't rely upon charity as a form of voluntarism. As we discussed yesterday, this could be justified or rationalized on the basis of being a more efficient way of accomplishing charity, as it has some elements of a pure public good.

A second area in which Jewish law calls for an intervention is in areas of economic leverage. I would submit that when we look at the various cases that are involved, it does not really raise a concern for resource misallocation. Take a classical example of this particular phenomenon.

Suppose an individual found himself on an airplane, and the pilot announced that it was about to crash, and someone ran through the aisles selling parachutes. Judaism is concerned about the ethics of pricing in that particular situation. (laughter) And, I submit if we would impose some type of restraint on the pricing of the seller, that it would not really impose much of a problem in terms of resource misallocation.

There is a third type of intervention which Jewish law calls for, with which I again think the free enterprise economist could be comfortable. It occurs in instances where imperfect knowledge exists in the marketplace. And here, I think that Judaism adopts, not a naive view of model building, such as perfect competition where we assume perfect knowledge, but rather that people don't have perfect knowledge.

A very interesting type of intervention that is called for is called *ona'ah* in Hebrew. This involves price divergence — that if an individual would buy an article, or sell an article, and the terms of the agreement would diverge from the competitive norm, the individual that was victimized, whether it be the seller or the buyer, may have recourse to modifying the transactions, or, in some instances, nullifying it entirely.

The basis of the intervention here is the presumption that perfect knowledge does not permeate the marketplace. The whole basis of the claim is opportunity cost, that the individual could have bought the article and sold it at a higher or lower price, whatever the case may be, and therefore he's entitled to modify the transaction.

Now, why does Judism take the view that the marketplace is not permeated by perfect knowledge?

Very much rooted in Jewish religious thought is the notion that market activities could not claim the dominant portion of man's time — that there is the spiritual domain, to which an individual is obligated to devote himself in terms of the study of scripture, and the Talmud, and also the performance of good deeds. And, many of these activities are non-market activities. If there are other claims on his time, and the materialistic drive has to be subsidiary to these other claims, we cannot really expect the market participant to be sophisticated and knowledgeable. So he would be entitled to claim naiveté in dealing in the marketplace. I would suggest that this is the basis of the presumption that imperfect knowledge permeates the marketplace; so there are modifications that are in order.

One other intervention which would be, for the economist, I think the least comfortable of all, but must be mentioned, is that Judaism calls for a profit constraint in the necessity sector. In this respect the Talmud only mentions foodstuff.

However, an analysis of the various details of this law indicates that what it amounts to is really a restraint on economic rent, rather than interfering with the opportunity cost of the seller. The key biblical verse that is associated with this particular intervention is, "Let thy brother live together with you." This means that we expect that the market participant should forgo some of the profit he could earn from market transactions so that his brother can maintain a decent standard of living. I want to emphasize that it amounts to a control over economic rent, rather than opportunity cost interference.

And that brings me to the final point. Professor Friedman develops the idea of the opposition to capitalism, which I don't think is really monolithic. I think if we would take, for example, Nathan Glazer in his survey of liberalism among American Jews, that you would find that their concern is in those areas I mentioned. The Jews do not reject the essence of capitalism, in terms of free entry, economic freedom, which is the type of system Jews, and everyone else, would benefit from.

But I would just want to add this last factor that perhaps Jews feel a very great psychological need to respond to stereotyping, which we find quite a lot of in the literature. This need is reinforced by the fact that, given the obligations that religion imposes upon the Jew, in terms of what he should be doing, even in terms of allocating his time, that he might feel a little guilty if he was immersed in materialism. The theological outlet would be to put on a very strong image of public philanthropy, in terms of supporting different types of programs that tried to protect the disadvantaged and the poor. This would assuage his conscience, and would be in line, I think, with Professor Friedman's thesis itself.

Milton Friedman: I have really very little to say in response to what Aaron Levine has just said, except to say that, as I have observed the situation, I believe that the opposition to capitalism has arisen primarily among Jews who were emancipated from religion, not among those who retained the orthodox persuasion. Hence, I regard Aaron's remarks as fascinating, and as expanding, and providing in greater depth, support for my rejection of the thesis of Fuchs, that the reason why Jews have been so predominantly anti-market is because the Jewish religion requires them to be. I appreciate and welcome that support. I only want to say one more thing. That is, I am delighted to have discovered, from what Phil Wogaman said here before, that I can now say, "An unJewish order is one in which good men are forced to do bad things." (laughter)

Walter Berns: Jews have benefited in another respect; and that has to do of course, with the connection between liberal democracy and capitalism. And it's important I think for this conference to recognize, what is (by some of us) alleged to be the necessary connection between the free market and liberal democracy. In this connection, I would like to recount something that happened to me once. I was asked to go to Jerusalem and deliver a paper on "Religious Aspects in the United States"; and for that assignment, I went back and got George Washington's famous (at least in some circles) response to the Hebrew community of Newport, Rhode Island. And it's a perfect statement of the principles of liberal democracy, because Washington, in addressing this Hebrew community (which had addressed the statement to him, and he was responding) said essentially that, in the United States, the Jews could expect tolerance, not as an indulgence, but as a matter of right. And the Jews, like the Scottish covenanters, would not have to fear Archbishop Laud shoving the Prayer Book down their throats, and lopping off their heads if they refused to open their mouths. The Jews and the Scottish covenanters, and everybody else, could sit under their own fig tree and all that was required of them is that they obey the laws.

Now, that struck me to be a perfect statement of liberal democracy, and I made quite a bit of it in my paper, hoping to take this to Jerusalem. Well, as it turned out, it was like taking coals to Newcastle, because I arrived at the VanLeer Centre, in Jerusalem where the conference was to take place, and there in a great big display was George Washington's letter (laughter) . . . under a kind of plastic cover. It was almost the constitution of the State of Israel, you know.

But, the point I want to stress is that as liberal democracy started, its premises were developed to protect the Jews, and the Scottish covenanters, and the Roman Catholics, and so forth. And, there is, we insist, some of us, a connection between liberal democracy and a particular kind of economic order; and we would suggest that you can go around the world, and look to see whether this connection between these two things, is refuted by any evidence existing in the world.

So, what is important is not that Jews have prospered financially, but that Jews can exist as Jews, as a private group, because religion is no longer the basis of the civil society.

Seymour Siegel: I just wanted to make a few comments. One I wanted to make was made by Professor Friedman himself, orally, just now. But I think it's important to restate it. I think it's just a literary flaw to say "the Jews do this," "the Jews do that." That is wrong, because the Jews as a whole don't do anything, except suffer, I guess. (laughter)

And, it is important to realize, and I want to underscore it in this context, that *no religious Jew that I know of, that is loyal to his or her religious community, was ever a socialist.* And that all the great names, Jewish names, in the socialist movement had all broken with their religious community first.

The paradox, by the way, in your statement is that you don't want to give us credit for Disraeli being a conservative, because he was baptized, but you do give us credit for Marx being a socialist, who was also baptized. (laughter)

Now, the idea that Jewish voters always vote democratic has changed. In the 1980 election, in the United States, a minority of the Jewish voters voted democratic — that is voted for Carter. I count Anderson as non-democratic. The majority did not vote for the democratic candidate. About 45 per cent were for Reagan, about 10 per cent for Anderson, and the rest for Carter.

And the interesting thing about those voting patterns is that it's almost inversely proportional. It's related to, you might call, intensity of religious observance — that is, the neighbourhoods which are strongly orthodox, went for Reagan. But also coupled with that is the fact that the more affluent precincts went more for Carter, than the less affluent ones.

Also, I don't think knowing that people who vote Liberal in Canada or whatever the equivalent is, or Democratic in the United States, do it with the self-awareness that they are somehow casting a vote against the market or against capitalism or against a free economy. They don't see themselves as doing that. They see themselves as casting a vote for compassion — which is a word we should have a conference about, the "compassion monopoly" that some groups think they have.

And I think even deep down, people are aware of the point which has been now confirmed, that no Jewish community has flourished either economically, culturally, religiously, or in any other way, under a socialist economy. And that includes Israel, by the way, which is fortunately not as socialistic as it thinks it is.

And so when Allende came into power in Chile, one third of the Jewish community ran away the next day, or at least as soon as they could. The same was true of Castro's Cuba. Out of the twenty thousand people who lived in that Jewish community, there are only two hundred left, at the moment. Everybody else ran away. This was not for anti–Semitic reasons but rather because of the realization that a community, under a very tight, controlled economy (a community which is made up, in large measure, of people practising the free professions, or a business of some sort) just cannot function under those sorts of situations; and therefore, if there is an opportunity to get out, you get out.

Kenneth Elzinga: I was in the peculiar position of having read Aaron Levine's book before I read his comment on Milton Friedman's paper; and I found myself wondering if this was really the same Aaron Levine in both cases. The tenor of his paper, and his comment and remarks today, is that the free enterprise economist could be "very comfortable" with Jewish law. And yet, if you read his book, you find Jewish law is shot through with many more significant constraints on free markets than he mentions in his comment today. In addition to the one-sixth profit constraint on so-called essential commodities, he neglected to mention that the Jewish court would appoint a commission to supervise the prices to meet this profit constraint. Interest was prohibited within the Jewish community, so there could be no organized capital markets.

There were examples in his book of using temple funds to prop up agricultural prices. Middlemen under Jewish law were not entitled to a mark-up. I don't understand how they existed, given that restriction, but that was apparently the law. His chapter on labour markets indicates the vast interference of the Jewish courts in free, or voluntary, exchange for labour services. So, I would have expected, based on his book, that orthodox Jews, or at least those very close to the Talmudic and biblical sources, would have an anti-market tilt, because of this. And, as a free market economist, I would find myself quite uncomfortable with Jewish law.

Aaron Levine: I am glad that Ken Elzinga brought up these other types of interventions. My intent was merely to cite interventions having a major resource allocation impact.

Let me just talk about interest rate regulations and the effect this has on capital resource allocation. And it really has a very limited effect. For example, a view that is widely held is that, if an individual makes available capital to someone for the purpose of allowing him to maintain his job, or to avoid a forced sale of his home, that's regarded in a very broad sense as a business provision of capital, as opposed to a consumer provision of capital. In Jewish law, there is no restraint on the return that may be earned on this type of investment. It's just a matter of form. (We don't have time to go into all the details of how this is arranged so that it does not violate the interest prohibition.)

So, it really amounts to a prohibition when an individual is giving someone a loan that is defined in a very, very narrow sense as a consumer loan; and in this instance, there's absolutely no mechanism available to avoid making an interest-free-loan. But I would submit this applies to a very, very limited number of cases which are trivial in relation to the issue of resource allocation.

David Friedman: My initial reaction, or one of my initial reactions to Aaron Levine's paper, was that he made it sound as though these legal institutions were particularly Jewish. And I was wondering if he knew how much of it either prefigured or echoed medieval Catholic doctrine. In particular, the cancelling of a contract when the price was substantially different from the value of the good, was the doctrine called "Laes enormis" in medieval Catholic law.

On the other hand, in the particular case that he cites of auctioning parachutes, there is a passage in Aquinas — a rather interesting one — where he cites the case of the first grain cart to arrive in a famine stricken area. The grain merchant happens to know that there are other carts of grain behind him on the road. The question is, is he obliged to tell the purchasers. And Aquinas's answer is, "No." Aquinas says that indeed it would be a generous and virtuous act for him to tell them, but that it is not unjust for him to take advantage of the temporarily high value for grain without giving them this additional information.

The impression that I got from Aaron Levine's paper was that he is really not talking about things that are peculiarly Jewish, but about things that are peculiarly medieval. The same thing could be said about medieval Catholic law.

Now, I also wanted to say a couple of brief things about the Jews fleeing Cuba. There are two things going on that are special to the Jews. On the one hand, even if the dictator is not anti–Semitic, the population is overwhelmingly non-Jewish; and it seems to me plausible that in a command economy, being disliked by a majority of your neighbours is much more dangerous than in a market economy.

The other element, though, which I think you ought to note, is that in a sense Jews are more mobile — that is to say, they are part of a world-wide community. They can go to Israel. They can go to New York and, if they like, be part of a Jewish community there. And therefore the larger fraction of the Jewish middle class fleeing than of the Gentile middle class, might simply be due to better opportunities to leave.

Geoffrey Brennan: I want to talk about the other function that the market makes, in terms of the allocation, and this goes precisely to David Friedman's remark. Let's suppose that there are twenty people on the plane and there are only ten parachutes. Now it's true, some very difficult choices have to be made here. We have to allocate ten parachutes among twenty people. And let's suppose that each parachute can only carry one person. It's certainly true that we might be uncomfortable about the market result. We might feel it odious that only the richest people on the plane are the ones that get saved. On the other hand, it is true that some decision making has to be done here. And if we have a command economy, then it is rather more likely, I would have thought, that it might be Christians first and Jews afterwards; (laughter) or Jews first and Christians afterwards (laughter). And I think that's a very important point that we shouldn't lose sight of. There is a sense in which the market is blind precisely because it's an institutional structure which is independent of ethnic backgrounds.

Aaron Levine: I would like to comment on David Friedman's point, that many of the sources and the issues that I discuss here, and also in my book, predate the medieval era, considerably. They're Mishnaic and Talmudic sources, rather than in the Responsa literature. What one finds remarkable, I think, when one investigates these sources, is the degree of detail and nuances that are dealt with in regard to these various ethical issues of pricing in the marketplace.

Paul Heyne: One more point about the parachute before we bail out. I think it's very important to notice that in such a case neither the market nor government is likely to function effectively, because the basis for either kind of transaction will collapse. I cannot imagine people in such a plight agreeing to a rationing by price, or sitting down and forming a committee to allocate parachutes.

Now I think that's an important point, because it gets back to Geoff Brennan's essential point, that when market transactions don't work, don't immediately assume that there exists a can opener out there. It's quite possible that the same social disillusionment that makes the market not work, is going to keep the government from working, too.

Roger Shinn: Several years ago, I had a discussion with Arthur Hertzberg, a famous United States rabbi. He was president of the American Jewish Congress. And what we got together to discuss was the prominence of some Jewish leaders in the neo-conservative movement. I had been in the habit of finding the centre of gravity among Jewish intellectuals a little closer to my opinion, than among the Protestants. And I'd always ascribed this to a superior virtue of Jews. (laughter) I'm very glad that Milton Friedman has given me an alternative external explanation, so I don't have to make that kind of assessment. (laughter) But Arthur Hertzberg's answer was, "Why are you surprised that Jews are learning to do what you've done all the time — vote your interests?"

My real point is a question: I would appreciate it if Aaron Levine or Seymour Siegel would tell us a little bit more about how comprehensive a conception enforced charity was meant to be, and when it was invoked. It could be a very small thing to be used only in emergencies or it could be a universal principle of society. I'd like to know just a little more about that.

Milton Friedman: May I make a comment first on the neo-conservative aspect. I don't take that into account because it occurred since my paper was written. I may say that I hadn't read this paper for ten years, until I came up on the plane, yesterday. (some laughter) And I found very little in it that I would change. I would change something. I think it's probably no longer true that most of the prominent neo-conservatives have come to neo-conservatism from the Left, and from the rather far Left, either Trotskyite or Marxist.

But second, I do not regard the neo-conservatives as defenders of free markets. We must be very careful to distinguish foreign policy aspects from domestic policy aspects. That is, a position of defense of the free market, from a position in which people, who are seeking to achieve their same so-called socialist goals, have concluded that government doesn't work very well in pursuing those socialist goals; and so they are going to achieve those socialist goals by trying to get corporations to exercise the coercion on their behalf and for their goals, that they had earlier sought to get the government to exercise.

Just read what the neo-conservatives write about "corporate responsibility." That's the area in which they are trying to transfer non-market approaches from government to corporation. So I don't at the moment regard that group of Jewish intellectuals as being an exception to what I wrote in my paper.

Obviously, I don't mean to suggest, along Seymour Siegel's line, that all Jews have taken that position; on the contrary it's a very small minority of Jews that have. It's only that they bulk very large among the people who are of that political persuasion.

Murdith McLean: I would like to come to one of my many areas of complete ignorance. I'd like to ask a little bit about what kind of discussion and rhetoric surrounded, in the founding of Israel, their election of what, in these circles, would be regarded as largely collectivist approaches to these sorts of things.

Milton Friedman: I believe I know the answer to that. And it's very straight forward. There is a very interesting phenomenon. I gave a commencement talk at the Hebrew University when I got an honorary degree there, in which I said two things which are related to this paper.

The first was that Israel probably could never have been founded, except for the socialist ideals of some of its founders. And second, that Israel's faithfulness to those socialist ideas was likely to destroy it. And I think both propositions are true. There is no doubt that the socialist character of the ideals that founded Israel derived from the fact that the founders were mostly from the Jewish community in Eastern Europe. In the European Enlightenment period, the only place where there was a home for Jewish intellectuals was among the more radical left-wing parties, because they were anti-clerical, they were anti-establishment. Now, you realize that there was also anti-Semitism among them. Hannah Arendt documents the existence of socialist anti-Semitism — of Labour party anti-Semitism. But, nonetheless, that was the only place where they could find a home. The ruling parties were fundamentally pro-clerical, pro-established religion, anti-Jewish, anti-Semitic. And as a consequence, if you take the early people who started in Israel, they started with socialist ideals. That's what underlay the establishment of kibbutzim.

If you've ever been in the Israeli kibbutzim, it's a fascinating story. Some twenty years ago we spent a few days in a Jewish kibbutz. And we were fascinated by the contrast between some of the older and original members of that kibbutz, who were among the most idealistic, most admirable characters you could possibly imagine, and the attitudes of their children, and grandchildren, and the newer members of the kibbutz, who were primarily people who had a strong aversion to risk, and wanted to have a secure and sheltered life.

And there was all the difference in the world between these two groups. There were those animated by the religious ideals. But those who founded the state as a secular state were not those. They were the people who were animated by the socialist ideas and vision.

Seymour Siegel: Well, I think what Professor Friedman said is essentially correct. But again (and this is something that's not too well known), political Zionism, which was the first push towards the establishment of the Jewish state in Israel, was also secular. The great Zionists—like Ben-Gurion or Golda Meir or Weizmann—those were people who again had broken with the traditional Jewish community, which was more messianic in a sense that the re-establishment of a Jewish state should wait for the culmination of history, which is symbolized in the messianic idea—although there were a lot of religious elements who were interested in the holy land as a holy land.

But, as a political state, these were mostly (if not almost exclusively) secular people. That's why I think people are puzzled about the term Jewish, about when you say "the Jews" because you can be a Jew, from the point of view of Judaism, and never darken the door of a synagogue, or even open the Bible. I don't think that's true about being a Christian, and therefore one reason . . . one of the two reasons to have a Jewish state was to have a place where the Jews could function as Jews, independently, and where they could have a chance to found an ideal social order, which was, in those days, identical with socialism. And that viewpoint still persists somewhat.

I would also add that, regarding Israel, the only real supporters of Israel in political terms have been Christian nations. There isn't a non-Christian nation that I know of that is in any way supportive of Israel. I don't know whether that's an accident or not, but that is a fact.

I want to make just one last point here, which is very important. We are discussing two different things in this session and we get them mixed up. One is, "What are the teachings of Judaism concerning these economic questions?" And the other question is, "Why do Jews who either profess Judaism or have some formal tie with it, act politically in a certain way?"

Now, the first question is a very complicated issue, and this is not the place to solve it. A lot of these regulations, even the Bible or the Talmud, reflected different kinds of economies than we have now. They were very much simpler. Certainly the biblical economy was not commercial in the sense that credit was a foundation of the economy. That's why you could have a regulation not to have interest, because, if you have an agricultural economy, I come to you and say, I need a sack of wheat to plant the seeds this year, and the next year when you need

458   *Discussion*

it, I'll give you one too; and then it would be wrong at that point to say, "Pay for it. Give interest," or something of that sort. But as the economies developed into commercial economies, the laws were modified.

Now, the other question about why do Jews act in a certain way. Again, it is broken into two points. One is, how indeed do they act? And there (as I think Professor Friedman pointed out) all the studies that I know of are both either superficial or incorrect — basically because the U.S. Census Bureau is not permitted to ask questions about religion. And therefore there is no reliable statistic about Jews in the United States — either their number, their income, or even their voting patterns. It's all guesses.

And then the question is, why do they, at least empirically or intuitively, seem to act in a paradoxical manner that has been described so well by Professor Friedman? And I would say that he's right in the sense that this paradoxical behaviour partially is due to some ancient teachings, which are either misinterpreted or misapplied, and, I think more important (and I think he made that point very well), is who represents what. What persons, or images, or myths represent which people?

Kenneth Boulding: I am very much interested in the Judeo-Christian origins of Marxism. It is, one of the very fascinating questions that hasn't quite come up. Now, it is after all, sort of the apostolic succession because it was Hegel-Feuerbach-Marx, wasn't it? It is sometimes said that Marxism is the third great Jewish religion after Christianity and Islam. It has these very profound roots, even though, of course, Marx was raised a Lutheran, as you know. I think his first essay was on the doctrine of the Holy Spirit in the gospel of St. John, if I recall, in high school. You never quite recover from having gone to a Lutheran high school. (laughter)

The question I want to ask is about the year of Jubilee. I have always been very fascinated by this, because I have never found out whether it ever happened. There it is, in the Bible. you see. And if they didn't ever do it, fine, but if they did, the five years before must have been very interesting. (laughter)

This was the year in which you forgave all your debts. Well, this in a sense I feel is the origin of the ideology of revolution. Here the Jubilee is a revolution, isn't it? And I am very curious as to whether it ever happened, or whether this was just a sort of ideal that might have happened. I don't recall any record in the Bible of a description of it happening, so, I am really curious about this.

Milton Friedman: I have very little that I would sum up. I would only like to say that I should welcome any comments from those of you here who are more knowledgeable about the subject of this paper. I did not publish this paper at the time I wrote it because, talking with a number of people about it, some of whom are among the most prominent neo-conservatives I may say, they suggested that they were not persuaded by it; and so I decided I would have to do some more work; but I never did any more work, and I really don't know what more to do.

As I read my paper over on the plane coming up, I felt that I really didn't want to change very much in it. So I don't mind having The Fraser Institute publish it in this form. But I would appreciate very much, from those of you who are more knowledgeable, correction of errors which may be made in it. I do think that the distinction between those who have stuck with the religion, and those who have not, is an important one that I overlooked and should have included in here; and I will try to insert that somehow. But beyond that, I really have very little to add to what's in the original paper.

Part Five

RELIGIOUS IMPLICATIONS

Chapter 9

The Concept of Economic Justice in Religious Discussion

Paul Heyne

Identifying the problem

What is *economic justice?* The concept is clearly a central concern for those who believe that the salvation and the righteousness of which the Bible speaks are social and not merely individual.[1] Nonetheless, the concepts of economic justice commonly employed or assumed in theological essays and denominational statements do not seem to have been thought through with any care. A critical reader might wonder if those who use the phrase know themselves what they mean by it, and whether they could really intend what they seem to be asserting.

Justice is notoriously hard to define in any way that goes much beyond platitude and still commands wide assent. That probably explains, at least in part, why most people who use the term do so without defining it. They assume (or hope) that others will understand the word as they do. But by excusing themselves from the necessity of stating clearly what they mean, advocates of justice often fail to discover that what they are proposing has no defensible meaning at all.

The problem of talking clearly and sensibly about justice diminishes considerably, however, when we shift our focus and talk about *injustice*. "Injustice wears the trousers," as J. R. Lucas has put it.

> [I]t is when *in*justice is in danger of being done that we become agitated.... And therefore we should follow the example of Aristotle, and adopt a negative approach, discovering what justice is by considering on what occasions we protest at injustice or unfairness.[2]

What, then, do writers in the biblical tradition have in mind when they protest against economic injustice?

Unequal money incomes

They most commonly seem to be pointing to an objectionable *inequality of money incomes*. Since no one is willing to argue that *all* inequality is unjust, the question immediately arises: When and why is inequality of income unjust? When the question is seriously pursued, it proves extraordinarily difficult to answer satisfactorily.

A basic but generally neglected difficulty stems from the fact that inequality of current money income is not a reliable indicator of inequality in the power to acquire valued goods. There are many reasons for this. One important example is provided by the case of Americans over sixty-five. While their money incomes tend to be low, they often own capital goods (home, automobile, furniture, a lifetime's accumulation of household tools) and special entitlements (reduced fares, tax exemptions, medicare benefits) that make their money income a very poor gauge of their real income.

The situation of older persons raises the more general question of age. Since earnings typically change with age, it will always be misleading to compare the incomes of different groups without taking explicit account of their ages. The average income of U.S. families in which the principal earner is 45 to 54 is about twice the average of income of families in which the principal earner is under 25.[3] This is obviously an inequality, but it is not an injustice. On the contrary, it would be unjust to allow a medical student to qualify for welfare assistance, on the grounds of low current income, rather than having to borrow against expected future income.

Choices and incomes

Family size and composition also affect both money income and the welfare significance of that income. Other things being equal, people's incomes decline when they separate or divorce, or when they choose to live alone rather than with relatives. Inequalities resulting from such decisions are not injustices unless we believe that people have a right to make these decisions without experiencing any income change as a consequence.

People make many other decisions that cause their incomes to differ in ways that few who thought about it carefully would want to call unjust. Some families have a single earner, others have two adult members pursuing careers. Some people work a forty-hour week or less, while others seek overtime, moonlight, or take up a trade or profession that enables or requires them to work twice as long and hard as their neighbors work. Some devote their resources predominantly to current consumption, while others opt more heavily for investment activities: schooling, training, or the purchase of assets that will yield larger future returns. Some simply manage their resources more carefully than others. Everyone does not have an equal opportunity to make such choices, of course; but it is surely not unjust to let these choices have some effect on people's incomes. A quite substantial inequality of money incomes would seem to be compatible with even highly egalitarian concepts of economic justice.

But why do we focus so exclusively on money incomes and the goods that money will buy directly? Our society also displays a highly unequal distribution of power, prestige, challenging and satisfying work opportunities, as well as risks and uncertainties. At some level of income these other goods surely become more important than money income. Are we preoccupied with money incomes because we think we know how to redistribute them, whereas we don't know how to redistribute power, prestige, and "meaningful" work? Is this perhaps a form of "commodity fetishism," in which we transform the indexes of economic calculation into measures of welfare and even worth? If so, this would be an ironic ideological triumph of capitalism over its critics.

How much less inequality?

Those who infer economic injustice from income inequality are rarely willing to tell us how much inequality would be consistent with justice. "Less" is not an adequate answer.[4] Where is the limit? Many advocates of greater income equality have argued that the maximum inequality compatible with justice is the minimum inequality that will preserve incentives to work, risk, innovate, and perform competently and conscientiously. It is not obvious why this should be so. But in many areas of economic life, this limit has long since been passed. Incentives don't simply "disappear" at some point. They diminish, at different rates for different people under different circumstances. More importantly, they *change*. People *alter* their activities in response to high marginal tax rates; they don't simply retire.

The best evidence that the incentive criterion is not in fact being used by advocates of income redistribution is their widespread indifference to the readily demonstrable effects of high marginal tax rates, explicit on high incomes and implicit in current welfare programs. Imagine a situation in which acceptance of an $8,000 per year job entails a loss of $6,000 in cash and in-kind transfers such as Medicaid benefits and food stamps, plus payment of $2,000 in income and social security taxes and the acceptance of job-associated costs. That amounts to a 100 per cent *marginal* tax on earnings. The fact that our income redistribution system has created marginal tax rates of this magnitude and allowed them to persist is fairly good evidence that the preservation of work incentives is not an important criterion for those advocating further redistribution.[5]

The criterion of need

Equality (or less inequality) in the distribution of income does not seem, then, to be a workable criterion of economic justice. What about the criterion of *need?*

If we define need in terms of what is required to sustain life on an adequate level, we run into two problems. Most simply, the criterion of need is unrealistic in poor economies and irrelevant, at least for most of those who talk about economic justice, in affluent ones.

For the vast majority of the people who have ever lived or are living now, poverty is the consequence of low productivity, not of unequal distribution. No redistribution of income within the country would satisfy the "needs" of all the people currently living in Kampuchea, Bangladesh, or Ethiopia. There is simply not enough to distribute.[6]

At the other end of the income scale, people who speak of "needs" in Canada, Sweden, or the United States clearly do not have in mind anything even remotely close to subsistence incomes. "Need" in these countries is culturally defined. An American family today "needs," if it is to maintain a decent, socially acceptable level of living, enough income to secure housing, clothing, food, furniture, recreation, and medical services in a quantity and of a quality that *could not* have been provided to more than a small minority as recently as fifty years ago. By today's standards, then, a majority of Americans did not have enough income to meet their "needs" at a time when our incomes were the highest in the world and the object of widespread admiration and envy.[7]

The fact is that, in wealthy countries, "need" is continuously redefined to embrace whatever becomes widely available as a result of increased production. "Need" defined in absolute or physiological terms is accepted as a standard for economic justice only with reference to very poor countries, where low productivity makes the standard impossible to meet. In wealthy countries, "need" is relative. But as soon as we allow "need" to be determined by prevailing incomes, we have actually abandoned the criterion of need for the criterion of equality. And we are back to the question, When does inequality become injustice?

The notion that "need" or subsistence is more a sociological than a biological fact has a long and respectable lineage. Adam Smith, David Ricardo, and Karl Marx all defined subsistence at least partly in sociological terms;[8] the propensity to view poverty as a relative matter is therefore not simply the product of some modern rage to reduce income inequalities. However, neither Smith, Ricardo, nor Marx had any pressing reason to wonder about the ultimate implications of defining poverty in terms of *relative* deprivation. If it is the social significance of differences that matters, and if, as a great deal of evidence strongly suggests, the elimination of some differences increases the social significance of those that remain, then the pursuit of a just pattern of income distribution based on need could be the costly pursuit of a mirage. It might even be no more nor less than the sanctification of envy.

The criterion of merit

What about the criterion of merit or desert? This criterion has always figured prominently in formal discussions of justice.[9] It is therefore somewhat surprising to discover how rarely it is invoked in contemporary ecclesiastical statements on economic justice. Is that because theology, or at least the kind of theology dominant in contemporary economic discussions, has no place for the criterion of merit? If all that we possess, including our intelligence, aptitudes, and attitudes, is the gift of God, then claims of merit or special desert would indeed seem to be ruled out.

I believe that this is in fact the explanation for the puzzling absence of the merit criterion from so many theological discussions of justice. But that absence makes the discussions thoroughly unrealistic. All of us, including the most egalitarian theological ethicist, do in fact regard merit as relevant to the distribution of economic goods. We do not regard the parable of the employer who gave the same wage to all his employees,[10] regardless of how long they had worked, as normative for the employment relationship. Those who have borne the burden and heat of the day *deserve* more than those who started work just before quitting time. The employer may, if he wishes, pay the late arrivals as much as he is obligated to pay those who worked all day. But that would be a matter of benevolence, not justice. And it would surely be unjust for him to strike an average and pay five hours of wages to those who worked eight hours and to those who worked but two. Those who worked eight hours have a claim in justice to receive a reward proportioned to their merit, a merit acquired by their efforts. *In some contexts* it may be relevant to point out that they did nothing to earn their ability and willingness to work long hours at hard labor, or that they wouldn't have had the opportunity to work at all if they hadn't just happened to be standing in the hiring hall when the employer walked in. But no one will claim that these facts diminish their deserts in the case at hand or that it would therefore be perfectly just for the employer to pay them for fewer hours than they actually worked.

A theology of economic justice that neglects merit or desert is simply not addressed to the world of social decisions. What we deserve at the hands of God is not the same as what we deserve from one another.[11] To suppose that we can settle the one question by answering the other is to abandon the question of economic justice altogether.

Perhaps this is not always recognized in theological statements on economic justice because those statements are so frequently formulated as antitheses to a system which seems to exaggerate the role of merit or desert. Defenders of capitalism often claim that capitalism distributes economic goods justly because it distributes them on the basis of merit. Those who don't accept this claim and who believe that the distribution which occurs under capitalism is unjust may have responded by rejecting the merit criterion when they should have been criticizing its application.

Differing grounds for entitlement

There is an important difference between earning something and having a right to it. Neglect of this distinction generates confusion on the subject of merit as a criterion of economic justice. A teenager given the keys to the family car for the evening has a right to use it. The teenager would be unjustly deprived of a right if someone else — an older brother, perhaps — saw the car on a theater parking lot and appropriated it for his own use. This does not imply, however, that the teenager deserved the right to use the car that evening, or that he would have been treated unjustly if the keys had been denied. If he had been promised the use of the car in return for washing and waxing it, then he would indeed have earned its use, and failure to grant the use would have been unjust.

Defenders of capitalism sometimes seem to be assuming that all entitlements are earned entitlements and can therefore be credited to merit. This position cannot be defended without stretching the concept of earning past the point when it loses its ordinary meaning. People are sometimes lucky. They may well be entitled to what came to them as a result of luck, but they cannot properly say they earned it or that it has accrued to them as a result of their merit. Defenders of capitalism do their cause a disservice, I believe, when in their eagerness to establish the moral legitimacy of capitalism they undertake to argue that people deserve, as a consequence of their merit, whatever they receive in a competitive capitalist economy.

It is both interesting and of some theological significance to note the great difficulty that many of us have in accepting as ours what we aren't certain we have earned. Are we consequently tempted to fabricate merit for ourselves so that we may claim to deserve that to which we are merely entitled? It is not enough to possess; we want to possess in good conscience, which too often means that we want to deserve whatever we rightfully possess. Adam and Eve, it seems to me, did something very similar to this when the serpent raised its guileful questions.

The function of rules

The mishandling of the merit criterion, both by defenders and by religious critics of capitalism, points to what I believe is the gravest flaw in contemporary theological discussions of economic justice. That flaw is the general failure to perceive the role and importance of *rules*.

Since the position for which I am now going to contend strikes many religious people as fundamentally immoral, let me begin indirectly, with a question based on an everyday dilemma.

After the bus has pulled away from the designated transit zone, should the driver stop the bus and open the door for someone running to catch it?

Some passengers will pull the stop signal and call out to the driver when they see a tardy passenger running to catch the bus. If the driver ignores their signals and drives on, they may comment disapprovingly: "A *mean* driver this morning." If he does stop, open the door, and wait for the running passenger, he will, of course, earn the gratitude of the beneficiary; but he may also be the recipient of approving comments from other passengers: "Someone who likes people more than schedules."

My purpose in recounting this familiar scene is a simple one. Here is a politically uncharged illustration of the function that rules play in a society and of the common ethical confusion that results from ignoring that function.

We begin by noticing that the driver who stops in such a situation is not necessarily helping people more than the one who does not. He certainly helps this one passenger—assuming that the driver's action doesn't cause an accident! But in addition to increasing the probability of an accident, the decision to stop delays all the other passengers on the bus. If the next bus will be along in 15 minutes, there are 25 other passengers, and the driver's action delays them all by 30 seconds, some might argue that the driver's action produces a net social benefit of 2½ minutes.

But this is an unconvincing claim. We can't compare different people's minutes in this manner. The 30 second delay, multiplied by the number of times the driver acts in this way, could cause a dozen passengers to miss their transfer connections. Those dozen people might consequently be late for important meetings, so that eventually many hours of other people's time is lost in the process of saving 30 seconds for each of a handful of late-running bus passengers.

The rights of unknown persons

The argument still involves illegitimate comparisons, however. A minute of one person's time is *not* the moral equivalent of another person's minute.[12] The principal reason for rejecting such an equation is not that people in fact value time differently, although that is certainly true, but rather that punctual people have a right not to be delayed by tardy people, and the bus driver has an obligation to respect that right. The man who gets up late does not have a right to delay the people who arrived at their bus stop on time. He ought to pay the cost of his tardiness, and it is unfair of him to avoid that cost by shifting all or a part of it to others.

Suppose, however, that he overslept because he had been up most of the night tending a sick child, and now must catch this bus in order to keep a counselling appointment with a distraught alcoholic who's contemplating suicide. Would we want to say in such a case that he, rather than the punctual passengers, *ought* to bear the cost of his oversleeping? Doesn't he deserve commendation rather than blame? Moreover, it isn't he but rather the suicidal alcoholic who will bear the cost of his being late.

All of this is quite irrelevant, however. *The bus driver has no way of knowing* why his passengers are punctual or late, whether they're embarked on important errands or simply taking a trip for the fun of it. The driver's moral obligation is to provide safe transportation and stay on schedule; the passengers must assess their own individual circumstances and decide whether or not to be at the bus stop by the scheduled time. Adherence to these rules will sometimes produce results inferior to what an omniscient driver could achieve; but bus drivers are not omniscient.

Moreover, a driver who elects to disobey the rules is behaving unjustly. He is violating the rules of the game and benefiting some at the expense of others in an essentially capricious way. The passengers who applaud his behavior when he stops in the middle of the street fail to consider the harm he may be inflicting on others. They may also be quite wrong in assuming that he was motivated by kindness; he could well be trying to curry favor, secure praise for himself at the expense of others.[13]

Rule coordinated social interaction

Thinking through this trivial example helps us see why it will often be more ethical, more socially responsible, and even more humane to "go by the rules" than to violate the rules in order to serve the known interests of particular people. We have been conditioned to believe that it is morally wrong to adhere to rules in circumstances where we believe our doing so will harm particular people. We are not used to thinking about the broader consequences for others, or the long-term consequences for the system in which we're participating. Not only do bus drivers make punctual passengers late when they choose to violate the rules; they also begin to change the relative costs and benefits of adhering to the rules, which means that the rules start to break down. We would probably be less sanguine about this consequence if we more fully appreciated the extent of our dependence upon rule-coordinated social cooperation.

What we loosely call "the economy" is essentially a system of social cooperation overwhelmingly dependent for its functioning upon rule-coordinated behavior. If all the farmers in the United States, for example, decided to devote their time and other resources to producing what was specifically wanted by the most needy or otherwise most worthy people they knew, millions of people who are now well fed would soon starve to death. The production decisions of American farmers are in fact made for the most part according to a simple rule: choose the available option from which you expect the largest net revenue. Those who believe that production for profit is morally inferior to production for use have apparently never thought through the consequences of what they're recommending. They are ignoring the incredible complexity of the system of social cooperation by means of which we are fed, clothed, housed, warmed, healed, transported, comforted, entertained, challenged, inspired, educated, and generally served.[14]

We must accept and honor rule-coordinated behavior not only in order to maintain our level of wealth. Justice also demands it. A large society cannot be a just society unless most of its duties and benefits are allocated in accordance with established and accepted rules. This truth is in no way confined to the so-called economic system. A college professor teaching a class of 500 students must, if she wants to be just, clarify the rules in advance and then apply them impartially. If a student confronts her with circumstances that the rules had not contemplated and so do not cover, she must search for a response that can be generalized. She must not allow some students to take advantage of other students by securing unique advantages. Each of the 500 students, if pressed, could probably find an explanation, unrelated to what the student actually knew, for missing one or more items on the last test. It is fundamentally unfair to give extra credit exclusively to those students whose obsession with grades or personal belligerence prompts them to ask for it. If the same privilege is extended to every student in the class through a general announcement, it might seem at first that justice would be salvaged. But now the question arises as to whether the teacher can in fact adequately hear and evaluate the explanations of 500 students. Justice in large societies requires not only that general rules binding on all be promulgated, but also that they be applied in a non-arbitrary manner. The more likely outcomes of such an attempt to apply personal criteria in a large-society situation are capricious decisions and poorly-used time.

Knowledge and justice

What would we say about a judge who discovered that the defendant coming before him on a drunk-driving charge was his next-door neighbor and nonetheless decided to hear and dispose of the case? Justice requires that the judge disqualify himself and turn the case over to someone else. The reason is that he knows the defendant *too well.* The judge is consequently in a position to know far more about the special circumstances of this defendant than he can know in other cases brought before him. To know all is, in a very important sense, to forgive all. It is therefore the responsibility of a judge *not to know too much* about a particular defendant, so that he can save the lives of many unknown persons by applying impartially the rule against drunk driving.

A judge in a small village might be able to act simultaneously as a just judge *and* a just neighbor. Justice will sometimes demand that we go beyond impersonal criteria in allocating burdens and benefits. We are properly horrified by David's famous painting of Lucius Junius Brutus and his two sons whom he had ordered executed for treason; a father owes more than that to the members of his own family. And it is possible to supply something more than impersonal justice in a small society where people know one another well. The size of the society is the crucial issue, however.

It is hard to see, for example, how a law against loitering could be a just law in a city of any size. Its application would inevitably leave too much discretion to police officers who *could not know enough* to enforce the law fairly, and who would therefore necessarily enforce it unfairly. It is conceivable, for the same reason, that the personal discretion which has to be exercised in the enforcement of any anti-loitering ordinance could be exercised fairly in a small village. The essential point remains. Justice itself demands that we use impersonal criteria to allocate burdens and benefits in a large society, where inescapable limitations on our knowledge make it impossible to take personal considerations into account in any consistent way.

Justice, expectations, and promises

It seems to me that our reflections on economic justice would be far more satisfactory if we recognized the connection between justice and the keeping of promises. I have increasingly come to think of justice as basically *the fulfillment of legitimate expectations.*[15] This definition is faithful to our most fundamental moral perceptions, I believe, while illuminating a wide range of issues. Injustice is done, I suggest, when someone's legitimate expectations are not fulfilled because others broke their promises.

Sometimes promises are made explicitly by one person to another. The breaking of such promises, other than for reasons beyond the control of the promisor, is an injustice whenever the promisee's well-being is thereby lessened.

More often, however, our promises are implicit, part of the unarticulated compacts that we have with our families, our neighbors, members of our church, associates at work, plus millions of people whom we will never even meet. I commit an injustice when I fail to provide family members, friends, or associates with the assistance, support, or other cooperation that my previous actions have legitimately led them to expect. We won't always agree completely on which expectations are legitimate, because we will inevitably disagree to some extent about what has been implicitly promised. But we always promise more than what we spell out formally, because explicit promises entail prior commitment or tacit assent to a vast network of "background" agreements.[16]

In this approach to the question of justice, laws can be thought of as promises. They bind everyone within their jurisdiction to behave or refrain from behaving in specific ways, and thereby they create legitimate expectations. An unjust law would be a law that repudiated prior promises; because of the resulting inconsistency of promises, the expectations that such a law might create would be less legitimate than the expectations created by a law whose justice was undisputed.

Customs and traditions are also promises. Moreover, every society is grounded in some kind of moral consensus, and the basic principles of that consensus are the most fundamental promises that the members of the society make to one another. Because these principles are not fully articulated, they can become mutually inconsistent in the course of social evolution. This most commonly happens, I think, when new possibilities for behavior lead to situations in which basic principles start to yield conflicting promises. The development of such situations threatens the stability of a society, because it removes, at least temporarily, the common ground which must exist if disagreements about justice are to be resolved. At such moments in a society's history, it is especially difficult but also especially important for the members of the society to refrain from caricaturing the positions they are rejecting. The ultimate bond of any society is its members' commitment to their common humanity; so long as that can be preserved, we are not compelled to say "thy blood or mine" and to settle our disagreements about justice by the naked criterion of force. When we impute immoral motives to our opponents, we are in effect declaring war on them by expelling them from the community of moral discourse.[17]

Now it seems clear that if we make promises or otherwise create expectations that we cannot subsequently fulfill, we inflict harm on others. It is not true that they are neither better nor worse off as a result of our promising but not delivering; they are worse off. People build upon their expectations, and when those expectations turn out to be illusory, the structures erected on them collapse. This is a psychological and an economic truth. In both the realm of feeling and the realm of action, we make investments on the basis of our expectations. And we sustain a loss when those expectations turn out to have been overly optimistic. Not every unfulfilled expectation constitutes an injustice, of course. Some expectations are bound to prove mistaken in a world characterized by uncertainty. Injustice is done only to people whose expectations are disappointed by the failure of others to fulfill promises they were capable of keeping.

Promises and the size of the society

A satisfactory theory of economic justice must recognize not only the importance of honoring commitments, but also the crucial relationship between the size of the society and the kinds of promises that can be made and fulfilled within it. The members of a nuclear family can conscientiously promise to assign tasks among themselves on the basis of ability and to distribute benefits on the basis of need. In larger societies, such a promise is impossible. If it is made, it is made in ignorance. There is simply no way for even one-hundred people, much less 225 million, to acquire the knowledge that would be required in order to assign tasks on the basis of ability and benefits on the basis of need. We don't have to raise the question of whether people would be *willing* to make and keep such promises to one another. Incentive is a necessary but not a sufficient condition. Information is also necessary. This point is important because religious discussions of economic justice tend to focus on the incentive issue and to overlook the problem of information. They thereby hold out the false hope that a "change of heart" would enable us to get rid of capitalism, or at least of certain features of capitalism that they find morally objectionable.

The nature of "capitalism"

Let me say at this point what I mean by *capitalism*. I think of it as a social system in which individuals are free to choose what they will supply and demand, offer and bid, subject only to general rules known in advance. These rules will be both legal rules, externally enforced, and moral rules that are internally enforced. I call capitalism a social system because it is the social rules that determine whether the society will be capitalist, socialist, or something in between. Capitalism, in short, is a system of individual freedom under law, where law does not mean "legislation" but rather the whole body of established rules, agreements, and conventions by which the members of a society acknowledge themselves to be bound.[18]

The engine of the system is the individual's perception and pursuit of net advantage. Collective behavior is not excluded, but it must be the product of the voluntary choices of individuals. The pursuit of one's net advantage is not a synonym for greed, selfishness, or materialism. All purposeful human action is self-interested, in the crucial sense that it aims at goals accepted by the individual, using means evaluated by the individual. Greed or selfishness, by contrast, is a matter of claiming for the self more than is due. I would want to describe greed or selfishness in terms of a failure to fulfill obligations, and hence as injustice. But the point here is that greed is about as common under capitalism as it is under any other kind of political system, but no *more* common.

Capitalism is thus by definition an impersonal system. It is not altogether an impersonal system, because the individuals within it do participate in families and small, face-to-face associations, where they can know other persons well enough to be concerned with and to care for their unique qualities. But the distinguishing characteristic of capitalism is the impersonal nature of the social interactions that make it up. It can be described paradoxically as a social system in which people do not care about most of those for whom they care. The farmer who feeds me does not even know I exist, and while he wishes me no ill, he does not and cannot care *about* me in any subjective sense. Nonetheless, he cares *for* me, and very effectively, in an objective sense.

We are all dependent, throughout our lives, for our actual survival as well as our many comforts, upon the assistance and cooperation of millions of people whom we will never know and who do not know us. They help us to fulfill our aims in life not because they know or care what happens to us, but because this enables them to fulfill their own aims most effectively. They are *motivated* by their own interests, whatever these may be. They are *guided* by the rules of the society and their perception of the expected net advantages from alternative decisions. These net advantages, or structures of expected costs and benefits, are created by the similarly motivated and guided efforts of everyone else in the society.

The necessity of "commodity" production

Marx was thus correct. He saw more clearly than most of his procapitalist contemporaries that capitalism was a system based on commodity production. It had replaced (by supplementing, I would argue, more than by displacing) a system based on relations of personal dependence. Thereby, as Marx and Engels observed in the first part of *The Communist Manifesto,* capitalism had achieved productive wonders. Their mistake, and the mistake of so many who followed them, was in supposing that capitalism could be replaced in turn by a system of production based on "socialist relations," a system retaining the productive powers of capitalism while assigning tasks on the basis of ability and distributing the product according to need.

The roots of resistance

I suspect that the deepest root of this belief, a belief remarkably immune to either theory or evidence, is the conviction that an impersonal social system is morally unacceptable. I maintain that this is a tragically mistaken prejudice. Impersonal does not mean inhumane, as we sometimes carelessly assume. Nonetheless, our model for the good society seems to be the family, where production is from each according to ability and distribution is to each according to need and merit (though we tend to underestimate the actual importance of the merit criterion in thinking about family distribution decisions).

The religious heritage of Western thought pushes in the same direction. The Old Testament's criticism of economic behavior often presupposes a society small enough and sufficiently close-knit for its members to care *about* as well as *for* one another. A more prominent feature of this literature, in my judgement, is its emphasis on impartial administration of the rules; but this feature has rarely been noticed by those who turn to the Old Testament for passages with which to support their concern for economic justice. The New Testament emphasis upon love as the fulfilment of all law has further reinforced our inclination to suppose that impersonal relations are somehow morally deficient relations.

A false option

Our basic mistake may be the belief that we must choose between personal, face-to-face societies and impersonal societies. If we accept as fully legitimate the impersonal, rule-coordinated societies in which we participate, we are not repudiating or depreciating in any way marriage, the family, intimacy, I-thou relationships, the unique value of the individual, or the power and significance of personal caring and sacrifice. If we were in fact compelled to repudiate all of this in order to enjoy the benefits that only large and hence impersonal societies can provide, we would be foolish to opt for those benefits. In the long run that choice would deprive us of the advantages of both worlds, because the moral values essential to the successful operation of a rule-coordinated society can only be nurtured in personal societies.

But we are not *forced* to choose. We are tempted to choose, it is true, and from both directions. The expanding wealth of opportunities that the impersonal society lays before us makes us progressively less dependent (or so we believe) on particular other persons. As we enlarge our individual freedom and power, we simultaneously declare our continual independence. We view commitments as entanglements and we work toward fuller emancipation. That kind of freedom is really perpetual mobility, and I doubt that it is ultimately compatible with the institutions and virtues of personal community.

My primary concern in this paper, however, is the temptation coming from the other direction, a temptation whose appeal might be in large part a function of the anxiety that many of us feel about the decline of personal community in our own lives. Many of the "best people" in our society, including theologians, denominational leaders, and deeply religious people, sincerely believe that economic justice requires the destruction of rule-coordinated societies. Moreover, they are committed to the belief that they may legitimately use the coercive power of state legislation to accomplish this goal. They seem determined to do so, with little thought about what justice might actually entail and often the most superficial attention to what occurs in the democratic legislative process.

False promises and injustice

Legislation that aims at the achievement of economic justice cannot succeed in this purpose unless the promises that it offers are genuine, realistic, and not in themselves unjust. Legislators often hold out promises of benefits, for vote-gathering purposes, when they have no intention of enacting the enabling legislation which would impose the requisite costs on the public.[19] For very similar reasons legislators will sometimes refuse to consider the consequences of what they are doing; it is not in their interest to recognize, much less to admit, that a bill which offers electoral gains to those who support it cannot in fact achieve its stated purposes. Legislation of this kind is unjust legislation because it deliberately creates expectations that will not be fulfilled.

Particularly common and troubling is the tendency of democratically-controlled legislatures to defend special-interest legislation on the grounds that it secures economic justice for its beneficiaries, while ignoring the injustices that this legislation will impose on others. The most familiar and to my mind most disturbing contemporary example is the arbitrary expropriation, through legislated rent controls, of people who have invested in residential rental property.

Those who draft the "social concern" statements of church bodies too often endorse this kind of legislated injustice, apparently because they can think of no way to measure economic justice except by looking at the pattern of outcomes. They are not deterred by their inability to provide a coherent, applicable, and defensible definition of a just pattern of outcomes. Meanwhile they ignore or repudiate in their official pronouncements some of the most basic principles of justice that they themselves use in their everyday, "real world" activity. The fundamental dependence of justice in a large society upon adherence to general rules is almost totally overlooked.

What do religious pronouncements about economic justice really accomplish? What interests do they serve? Those are the pressing questions with which I find myself left. But they would be questions for some other study.

NOTES

1. If the Hebrew words *yeshuah* and *tsedeq* and the Greek words *soteria* and *dikaiosune* are translated as "deliverance" and "justice," the individualistic connotations of "salvation" and "righteousness" are diminished.

2. J. R. Lucas, *On Justice* (1980), p. 4. I am indebted to James Buchanan for urging me to read this book. The "negative" character of justice is a central point in F. A. Hayek's *Law, Legislation and Liberty,* where he also traces the long intellectual history of the insight that we can best approach an understanding of justice through our ability to recognize its absence. See especially *op. cit.,* Vol. II, pp. 35–48, 162–64. My indebtedness to Hayek in this essay will be obvious to anyone familiar with his more recent work.

3. Here are the mean incomes of families in the U.S. in 1978, by age of what the Census Bureau now calls the "householder": 14–24 years, $12,570; 25–34 years, $18,205; 35–44 years, $22,575; 45–54 years, $25,363; 55–64 years, $22,408; over 65 years, $13,754. Per capita income differences will be much less because of age-related differences in family size.

4. For a recent instance of this answer and a representative example of the reasoning that accompanies it, see Robert Lekachman, "Capitalism or Democracy," in Robert A. Goldwin and William A. Schambra, eds., *How Capitalistic Is the Constitution?* (1982), pp. 127–47, and especially p. 146.

5. An illuminating discussion of this issue, along with a presentation of the basic data, may be found in Edgar K. Browning, "How Much More Equality Can We Afford?" *The Public Interest* (Spring 1976), pp. 90–110.

6. Per capita gross national product in 1978 has been estimated by the World Bank at $120 in Ethiopia, $90 in Bangladesh, and less in Kampuchea. These data must be interpreted with great caution, since a much smaller

fraction of production enters GNP calculations in poor than in wealthy countries. Data were taken from *Poverty and Human Development* (1980), p. 68.

7. The disposable personal income (roughly income after taxes) of Americans per capita in 1929, in dollars of current (1982) purchasing power, was about $3,765. That's considerably less than half of current disposable income per capita, despite the fact that far more services now than then are financed through taxation and hence no longer have to be purchased out of disposable income.

8. Adam Smith, *The Wealth of Nations,* Book V, Chapter II, Article IV, discussing taxes upon consumable commodities; David Ricardo, *On The Principles of Political Economy and Taxation,* Chapter V (see pp. 96–97, 100–01 in the Sraffa edition); Karl Marx, *Wage-Labour and Capital,* Chapter VI.

9. J. R. Lucas offers a useful overview in *op. cit.,* Chapter 8; see especially the long footnote on pp. 164–65.

10. Matthew 20:1–16.

11. This criticism applies also to some of the core arguments advanced by John Rawls in his influential *A Theory of Justice* (1971). J. R. Lucas puts the problem concisely: "Rawls yearns for a theodicy. To be morally acceptable, a distribution must be justified completely." *Op. cit.,* p. 191. Robert Nozick has pointed out that Rawls' argument finally does not take individual persons seriously. *Anarchy, State and Utopia* (1974), p. 228.

12. Economists generally insist that they have no basis for making "interpersonal utility comparisons"; they rarely recognize that judgements about the relative efficiency of alternative resource allocations require either the making of such judgements or prior decisions on who possesses what property rights. What it all comes to is that judgements about efficiency in multi-person transactions presuppose judgements about the justice of people's exercising certain powers. For a concise presentation of the central issue, see John Egger, "Comment: Efficiency Is Not a Substitute for Ethics," in Mario J. Rizzo, ed., *Time, Uncertainty, and Disequilibrium* (1979), pp. 117–25.

13. Most of the contemporary literature advocating "corporate social responsibility" totally overlooks this point. Examples could be multiplied endlessly. Christopher Stone offers an excellent critical survey of the discussion about business social responsibility in *Where the Law Ends: The Social Control of Corporate Behavior* (1975).

14. The most serious single error committed by non-economists in their proposals for reform of the economic system is their neglect of *information problems.* I have often wished that I could persuade everyone interested in

social justice to begin with a careful reading of the classic essay by F. A. Hayek, "The Use of Knowledge in Society," originally published in the *American Economic Review* (September 1945), pp. 519-30, and frequently reprinted since. It is included in Hayek's 1948 collection of essays, *Individualism and Economic Order.*

15. This is the tradition first spelled out by David Hume in *A Treatise of Human Nature,* Book III, Part II, Sections I–VI. I do not think my argument here is vulnerable to the criticisms put forward by J. R. Lucas, *op. cit.,* in pp. 208 15, a chapter he entitles *"Pacta Sunt Servanda."*

16. Michael Polanyi, *Personal Knowledge: Towards a Post-Critical Philosophy* (1964; Harper Torchbook edition), especially Part II.

17. The controversy over abortion laws in the United States provides the most distressing example.

18. The conception of "freedom under law" that I am assuming here was thoughtfully spelled out by Bruno Leoni in *Freedom and the Law* (1961).

19. Neither the theoretical analyses nor the abundant empirical evidence put forward by public choice theorists in recent years seems to have influenced church pronouncements on political issues.

Comment

Richard Baepler

As I find myself basically sympathetic to the positions taken by Professor Heyne both in the realm of theology and economics, my comments will tend to be internal to the argument which he has developed rather than criticism taken from a quite different posture.

It was not Heyne's intention to develop and state a theological position in this paper. Rather he concentrates on demanding that moral judgements made by theologians and church leaders in ecclesiastical documents be based on sound reasoning and that they take into consideration both economic and political realities. Occasional references to theology, however, do appear and they may seem confusing to some readers.

He begins by references to biblical language about "salvation and righteousness" as "social and not merely individual" and then proceeds directly to comment on problems of economic justice. There should perhaps be more awareness of the quick leap from God's righteousness and salvation to man's efforts to effect these within history. This is not to forget the main point Heyne is making, that biblical language is social as well as individual in its various references to human affairs. Indeed, the biblical vision is broader than that: it is cosmic and historical as well.

A similar difficulty appears in the discussion concerning "merit" where the point is made that what we deserve at the hands of God is not the same as what we deserve from each other. He is dealing with a very basic problem, one which is beyond the purview of the paper, but it should be recognized. The problem is the question of the relationship between nature and grace.

Both in these explicit theological references and in his whole approach to the economic order, the author seems to reflect the Lutheran theological tradition out of which I do my own thinking and writing. This tradition makes a clear distinction between the order of creation (or nature) and the order of redemption (or grace).

The order of creation refers to the basic structure and processes of historical life with its institutions and dynamics available to empirical inspection and study. These institutions include, of course, the economic order as well as government, education, family and so on. Theologically viewed this order is God's continuing creation and preservation of the basically good world He created, and these processes are meant to convey His good gifts to people. In removing these institutions from the tutelage of the church the Lutheran reformers acknowledged that there is no normative, ecclesiastically sanctioned form of these institutions. Nor do Christians have special insight into their best development. Better a good Turk be governor than a foolish Christian, said Luther. For in the realm of the created order reason and experience are the masters and proximate justice the goal. God works in history through law and through mysterious masks, as when the pagan Cyrus was raised up to free Israel from the Babylonian captivity.

This view gives, then, a certain integrity and autonomy to the development of the secular realm. There is in brief no proper form of "Christian" economics, or government. There are various ways of ordering the economic and political realms and our evaluation of them depends on reason and experience. Thus the Lutheran tradition would expect there to be Christian capitalists and Christian socialists. This position is not totally free from problems as the appearance of Lutheran Nazis made quite clear. On the other hand, it frees religious discussion in this tradition to explore problems such as economic injustice on the basis not of biblical or theological authority, but on the analysis of the validity of moral reasoning, and especially in relation to the actual world of social and economic decisions, to which Professor Heyne's paper appeals at crucial points.

A second theological perspective from this tradition on the order of creation is the affirmation that this order is fallen and therefore corrupt, but so are our education, our government and our marriages. This anti-utopian theme in Lutheran theology brings a hard realism to social and political discussion, and warns against invidious comparisons which may betray a lurking self-righteousness. Heyne points out that there is greed in the capitalist arrangements, but not necessarily more than in alternative systems. This can be demonstrated from experience but is also a continuing religious insight in all social discussion. Theologically it is described as part of the continuing rebellion of man against God's intention that he care for his brothers and sisters. When people rather exploit each other, God's righteousness is present in the form of law to restrain evil and require justice.

The overcoming of the corruption is not achieved through moral progress but through the introduction of the order of redemption. The forgiveness of sin offered in the Gospel is, theologically viewed, God's destruction of corruption. In place of a community of the corrupt a new community of the forgiven arises. Corruption persists even within that community and will persist through history, but the fundamental reality of the new men and women of the community is that they are saints by faith before God. Not before men as empirically measured, but before God. "Simultaneously saints and sinners" was Luther's creative phrase. This is God's grace that He views them as saints even as they continue to be sinners. The new ethos which appears in this community has two dynamics: the new dynamic of love which imaginatively orients itself to the needs of the neighbor, and the old dynamic of corruption which persists.

In the discussion of nature and grace it is important to point out that the "natural" entities and processes in their essence are not corrupted by the Fall. Although there are large biblical hints that the whole cosmos groans, awaiting redemption, classical Christian theology has never identified evil with the created reality. Biblical writers do not evaluate the economic or political structures. They assume these to exist and to be part of the necessary ordering of things. It is mankind's actions within these structures which come under judgement, a judgement which is both within and beyond history as the interaction and reciprocities of history play themselves out. Thus, within the economic process, activities very much like those we all know are assumed to be taking place. Joseph cornered the corn market during the seven good years and made a fortune for Pharaoh while benefiting the Middle East during the seven lean years. If people do not work, they should not eat. The thief in the Christian community at Ephesus is admonished to quit his thievery and go to work so he may have something to give to those in need. Metaphors from the economic realm are frequently drawn on by the biblical tradition: "Forgive us our debts." "The wages of sin is death."

In the classical Christian tradition the notion of merit is quite important as a way of assessing behavior. Thus, in the Reformation teaching of justification, sinners are justified by the merits of Christ, because before the evaluation of God they have no merit. To the discomfort of Protestants the language of the New Testament at times suggests a relationship between good deeds and rewards in heaven. The whole notion of *suum cuique* and reward for meritorious work and behavior seems to be deeply rooted in the morality of our civilization from a very early time. Indeed, in Lutheran theology this feature is viewed as so strongly embedded that grace itself is seen as offensive to natural man, immoral. To get what you do not deserve seems contrary to all moral experience; yet to live by grace becomes the definition of the Christian as he lives before God. Can he live with and before men by grace as well? Yes and no.

In the ecstasy of the first Christian Pentecostal experience the author of Acts reports that the early Christians sold their goods and had all things in common. We hear nothing about the future of that movement in the Scriptures or in church history, unless St. Paul's later massive collection for the church in Jerusalem relates to a failed economic experiment.

Nor is there anything in the history of the monastic communities or mendicant orders to suggest that they were any more successful in creating new societies patterned on the distinctively gracious Christian imperatives though this was their intention. The more durable imperatives of nature seem always to have asserted themselves, and the equally durable presence of human corruption conferred a pattern of decline as well as renewal on the history of all these communities.

H. Richard Niebuhr has correctly described the Lutheran perception of the relationship between nature and grace to be a dialectical one. The new community of Christ lives in the created order without transforming it into a new society but penetrating it with vitalities aimed at getting God's work of sustaining the race done in the most humane way manageable. The dialectic produces tension within the lives of individual Christians, illustrated by certain hard cases always present in Lutheran ethical discussion. As an example consider the case of the Christian judge who must on the one hand convey absolution to his fellow Christian just convicted for crime, but at the same time must condemn him to the punishment set by law. Every individual must bear a similar tension as he or she lives out this dialectic.

This dialectic is not to be confused with another difficult one, that of the relationship between the personal and the impersonal. Despite the natural gravitation of the religious spirit to the realm of the personal, to the I-Thou relationship, this pair of categories does not equal that of grace and nature. The judge has a very clear I-Thou relationship with his fellow Christian criminal, though he may be acting strictly in terms of his "office" rather than of his "person." Stated from another perspective, Christian love is at work in the impersonal as well as in the personal realm. Christian pietism and similar movements have never understood that the care of institutions and the crafting of good legislation and the involvement in social struggle for justice, however this is finally discerned, is as much an activity of love as is the face to face activity of the Good Samaritan parable.

The rise of the Moral Majority to match the activities in the public realm of more liberally oriented Christian groups suggests that in the United States, where the Calvinist theocratic spirit is still strong, this insight is not totally lost. Yet Heyne's point, especially made with reference to the economic realm, is altogether valid, it seems to me. Ever since Toennies introduced the *Gemeinschaft-Gesellschaft* distinction into modern thought, social thinkers have tended to drive these categories apart. While the developments of modern mass society with its institutionalized impersonality may be liberation for many, they have also contributed to powerful centripetal forces producing what critics are calling the narcissistic or privatistic society. Heyne very properly asks for a reconsideration of the way in which a large-scale society must get its common work done, and to recognize that intelligent participation in the shaping of this common life, impersonal as especially the economic process may seem, is as much a vocation for the religious spirit as are the ways associated with intimacy and face to face relationships.

As a way of inaugurating a much-needed discussion of this matter, Heyne focuses on the role of rules in social and moral life, and this is the main contribution of his paper, in my judgment. The absence of such discussion in theological writing concerning economic injustice is, for Heyne, a grave flaw.

I agree with his assessment. We cannot underestimate both the importance and the difficulty of dealing with the topic. The well-being of our society is directly related to its functioning as a rule-coordinated body. In the legal world this is abundantly clear. The adversary system, for example, requires counsel to advocate zealously, and this zeal in turn requires the advocate to engage in somewhat repugnant activity, such as impugning the character or reliability of witnesses. With two parties zealously contending for the truth under rules which permit, indeed require, activities not countenanced in other situations, the theory is that through such combat the truth will emerge in the minds of a judge or twelve ordinary citizens. Similarly there is what one writer calls an internal morality of the law, the procedural rules which must be followed — though they do not appear to be self-evident or necessary at all times — if any of the substantive rules of law are to work effectively. And I fully agree that this realm of rules pervades all our activities, organized, associational or informal.

Certain problems arise, however, in connection with Heyne's paper. I do not know to whom he refers when he writes of people who want an end to rule-coordinated societies. The heydey of situation ethics is past. The specific target eludes my notice. A more difficult problem lies in the rather general use of the term "rules." I think greater specificity is required.

To discuss this it might be helpful to differentiate three kinds of rules. I shall illustrate these distinctions with reference to the act of driving an automobile. 1) *Directional rules* are guidelines on how to execute a project successfully toward a defined end. These are the rules which determine skillfulness in the technical act of driving. 2) *Game rules* define what it means for people to carry on a common activity. A driver drives on the right side of the road, stops for red lights, etc. 3) *Rules of natural regularities* refer to the patterns and dynamics in the natural and social world with which we must reckon in order to act effectively. A driver cannot drive at 50 mph around a curve designed for 25 mph passage. Finally, these rules become moral rules when they impinge on acting in a humane fashion or regarding others in a humane way.

Heyne speaks of the "rules of the game" when he uses the example of the bus driver to illustrate the importance of rules in society. The same concept is present when he speaks of capitalism as a political system, since it is a body of rules by which members of a society acknowledge themselves to be bound.

But the concept of game rule is not adequate to analyze the whole problem that Heyne has put before us. He speaks of American farmers following the simple rule to choose the option from which they expect the largest net revenue. But this is not simply a game rule. The example is discussed in terms of the problem of information and the argument is that this market mechanism is the best way to make decisions both with respect to the farmer's welfare and the consumer's. This is not simply following a game rule, it seems to me, but is better seen as acting in conformity to a natural regularity as defined by economic theorists. Respecting this rule is much the same as skillfully defining the kind of seed to plant, the amount of fertilizer to use and when to harvest.

This means that in making the decision to affirm a capitalist society, a decision is also being made about the most adequate description of economic reality as well as defining the game rules. Game rules and natural regularities are thus closely related, especially in light of the social concern that as many people as possible might have access to the game and be able to develop proficiency.

This approach to rules outlined above may make it possible to define more precisely what kinds of criticisms are being discussed when judgments are made concerning the economic system and economic injustice. Three kinds of problems seem to appear.

1. Discussion of economic justice is flawed when one attempts to define the game rules without paying adequate attention to the natural regularities. Much of Heyne's early discussion of problems of justice seems to criticize people for making criticisms without allowing economic reality to influence the way they define the game.

This seems especially important because people can come to believe utopian notions of what might be possible in society merely by altering the game rules. "Liberal" thinkers may not adequately consider economic limits; others may overlook such constraints as energy, resource or environmental factors.

2. The rules of the game need to be defined so that as many people as possible can participate equally in the game. Heyne makes a dubious assumption that people participating in the game have had a part in defining its rules. This is quite unclear; nor is it clear that the rules are defined so that all people can play who are eligible. Had we time, it might be interesting to review the justice problems discussed in the first part of the paper from this perspective.

   Moral considerations arise also with respect to those who do not or cannot play the game, people who cannot or will not work, say, and their dependants. It should be possible for society to identify this strata and provide subsistence income for them. (In smaller societies private charity might work better, especially given the more accurate and intimate knowledge and information about people's needs in such a society. In the larger, impersonal society, where information is a problem, a less personal system of statistical determination and administration is probably necessary.)

3. The moral issue may also lie at the level of directional rules. The knowledge of directional rules is necessary to developing the skills required to play effectively. This opens up questions of access to education.

One final comment is suggested by Heyne's discussion of the rules of the game and his comments on justice as promise. It may at times be a simple fact that people no longer possess an adequate image of the game to play. The image of the game by which they act might no longer be accurate, or the more accurate image may not motivate them, and may not meet their legitimate expectation. But that is another large issue, not for this paper.

Discussion

Edited by: Kenneth G. Elzinga

Richard Baepler: Paul Heyne is one of those very rare birds who was trained as a theologian and as an economist — and that is a great advantage at a conference like this. He has not particularly developed a theological position in his paper; and so one of the first things I did was to try to draw out, in broad outline, something of what I believe to be that theological position.

It is a Lutheran theological position — the theological tradition out of which, I think, both of us do our work. Paul now worships in the Episcopal church. Back in divinity school days at the University of Chicago, where we both studied, we had Dean Weaver, who had also joined the Episcopal church, and it was said about the Dean that, "You could take Dean Weaver out of Methodism, but you couldn't take Methodism out of the Dean." And, the same thing with Paul, I think. The thoroughly Lutheran approach to the question at issue, broadly outlined, is known familiarly as the "doctrine of the two kingdoms," coming from an image which Luther used, about God as king, ruling the world with two hands — the kingdom on the left (which is the world of ordinary, mundane experience). He guides that world — the world of history — with His left hand toward His own mysterious goals. Meanwhile, with His right hand, through the gospel, He renews it, and brings the future into the present.

And Christians are caught in both of these, living out of the kingdom on the right, fundamentally — getting their identity from that — but then coping and dealing, working out their vocation in terms of the kingdom on the left.

There are a lot of problems connected with this. The pathologies are probably well known: a certain quietism and passivity. It is certainly not (to use Roger Shinn's terms this morning), either a Puritan or Pietistic approach toward the world. Lutherans aren't so much interested in really changing the world according to any sort of model or ideal drawn from anywhere—certainly not from the Bible. Nor are they concerned, on the other hand, as Pietists would be, with only individual regeneration and making an impact on the world through the individual. There is a full recognition that the kingdom on the left is God's kingdom. The institutions that work there are the ways, the masks by which God carries on His work. There is no particular way in which a church can prescribe normative approaches in that kingdom on the left, but relies heavily on good lawyers, government people, and businessmen, working out their vocations—whether they are Christian or not—in a variety of ways and with a variety of interests.

And the value, I think, of this particular approach is that it recognizes the secular realm. It certainly gives full weight to the institutional realm. That is, Lutherans together with, I think, most liturgical Christians—Catholics, Episcopalians—respect institutions. Their own religious life is very much related to institutional forms, unlike perhaps Pietists, who seem to have a direct pipeline to God, and have intensive personal experiences with God.

The more liturgical churches relate to God in much more indirect, impersonal ways, through sacraments and things of this sort. And so there is a kind of predisposition among liturgical church people, such as Lutherans, to regard the realm of the impersonal as a vehicle of God's action, indeed of God's love; to participate in the realm of the impersonal with full knowledge of that; and to see how personal life can be renewed and sanctified precisely through impersonal means, including of course institutions—about which, and for whose design, there must be a great deal of care and craftsmanship.

I think this is then fairly clear in Paul Heyne's approach. He finds the test of world decisions, decisions as they take place, to be in the social and economic realm. It's a central theme, that one does not deal with the world except in terms of its own reality tests. And within this world, reason and experience are the key guides. Luther said, "Better have as a governor a good Turk, rather than a foolish Christian."

There is a very strong sense of historical development, so that Luther might well, were he living, suggest that there was a pre-capitalist period, a capitalist period, and there doubtless will be a post-capitalist period. The operative forces, as I say, are reason and experience. A notion of merit is very central to this. One gets what he deserves, and deserves what he gets, in mundane historical experience. Grace is not the operative principle in this realm. That notion of trying to organize communities by grace has had a persistent niche in Christian history— most notably in the monastic movement.

When you take the world as we experience it seriously, and try to determine the nature of institutions and make policy recommendations on that basis, then it seems to me you must be open to inviting people of all sorts—economists, including market economists—to make policy recommendations on the basis of evidence, which they indeed can collect and have collected, and to make proposals based on that evidence. And that is where, in the Lutheran tradition, theologians concerned with this question would begin. One is aware that the world is a busy, buzzing, complex place, and that we have enormous information problems for policy recommendation.

It takes a long while for social policy to work out its many different meanings—meanings which are often, as Kenneth Boulding reminded us, best exemplified in that political irony in which you hurt the people you intend to help, and help the people you intend to hurt. I think, again, Kenneth Boulding in his paper was very right in suggesting that we always keep our eyes open for the pathologies of every system and give good attention to them.

It seemed to me that the centerpiece of Paul Heyne's paper (which is full of all kinds of suggestive notions crying out for development) is his emphasis on the role of rules in theological writing concerning economic justice. And I agree fully with that. I do find some problems with the way in which he uses it however. For my part, I try to distinguish between directional rules, which are rules by which people simply learn how to do something, and game rules, which define what it means for people to carry on a common activity, and thirdly, rules of natural regularities which I think are very much involved in, what he calls, the "decision" to play the game according to capitalistic rules. I don't think that this is an artificially designed system of rules.

But there is, in the capitalist decision a commitment also to the way in which things really are. That is, call it the "market mechanism"; call it whatever you like—a commitment to certain regularities which are, I think, part of that decision.

Paul Heyne: I am grateful for Dick Baepler's explication of the theological system which I was taught, which undoubtedly "took" to some extent, and within which my argument fits rather well. I welcome it because I agree with all of it; but nothing in my argument depends upon it. I do not want to argue about Luther's two kingdoms. I want my claims to be evaluated without regard to whether Luther's doctrine of the two kingdoms is a cop-out, as many people have argued, or a profound insight; or whether there is a God, or not; or whether She cares about us, or not.

Now this is very important to me. It is central to my way of thinking; and again it illustrates the two kingdoms approach at work, I guess. Because, I am concerned about justice, I think that we have to pay attention to the foundations of justice. That task would be impossible in this Western world, if I had first to find a theological subfoundation. I think I can do it without theology; and I don't think I can do it with theology. So however much my theological education and religious upbringing may have shaped the development of my ideas (and I don't know how much they did—a lot, I'm sure) I don't want to talk about that.

There are two additional reasons why I don't want to talk about the theology of what I am saying here. One is that I don't want to say, or imply, or hint, "Thus saith the Lord," because I cannot do so without demeaning, or diminishing, or distorting my faith. I increasingly find that when I use my Christian faith as any kind of argument in a social analysis that I am putting forward, I feel that I need to take a shower afterwards.

The second is that I think theologically-grounded social analyses almost always deflect attention from what are, in fact, the key propositions in dispute. The function theological entry points actually serve is to divert attention from the real points at issue. They do some other bad things. They alienate those who disagree. When you say, "Thus saith the Lord," that's a pretty tough statement to deal with. They also foster an uncritical and self-righteous attitude among those who do agree.

So what I am proposing here is a way of thinking—a secular way of thinking, if you will. I am trying to coordinate the theory and practice of economics, and politics, and ethics. This paper is grounded in the conviction that agreement among the members of a society on the fundamental principles of justice is a prerequisite to the operation of Adam Smith's invisible hand. When Adam Smith says, "If everyone pursues his own interest, the public good will emerge," he means, *when the laws of justice are obeyed.* He makes that explicit a couple of times in *The Wealth of Nations.* I wish he had made it explicit more often. That deals with the very difficult question of why it is that, if the pursuit of self-interest in the so-called economic sphere leads to the public good, the pursuit of self-interest in parliament doesn't. The answer is, "Because, when people go down to parliament, they start violating the laws of justice."

Now that doesn't help very much, unless you can spell out something of what the "laws of justice" are. And here I believe that the concept of "rights" is enormously helpful as a concept that can integrate our thinking about economics, politics and ethics. Economic theory is being reformulated today on the basis of the concept of "property rights." Economic theory can be talked about very successfully around the fundamental notion that "everything that happens out there is a response to the actual property rights that people have." "Actual rights" explains economic theory, or unifies it. "Legal rights" can be used, I think, to coordinate political theory. And "moral rights," by which I mean the rights people ought to have, brings in the ethical question. Ethics is basic. The moral convictions of the members of this society are finally the deep substrata out of which everything else flows.

"Rights"—as a language—provides a way of talking about justice. It's not the only way, but it is the one I have found most useful. Now, what ties all of these together in my paper is the idea of promises. I conceive of rights in the context of "promises." I see a society as individuals bound together by promises that they have made.

In approaching this whole question, to make it very clear, I am taking an approach which I think Adam Smith took—the David Hume-inspired approach to the whole question of the foundation of property rights. What are the rights that people ought to have? Hume's approach was very conservative in the sense that he begins with the "rights," the "property rights" that people do in fact have, that you observe them having—as distinct from the Lockean approach which tries to find their origins. The Humean-approach avoids many of the problems that are tied up with the Lockean justification of property rights.

Robert Nozick is, I guess, a Lockean on the subject of property rights. But he makes the most brilliant critique of it I've ever read, in his *Anarchy, State, and Utopia*. So there are some problems with this Lockean notion. When I put a fence around some land, what do I acquire? The fence? The land inside the fence? The land immediately under the fence? The holes in which the fence posts are dug? And Nozick asks this, "And when I pour my can of tomato juice into the ocean, do I acquire the ocean, or do I waste my tomato juice?" (some laughter) This notion of property rights as justified by an original mixing of labour with unowned resources creates far more problems than it solves. It is not the way to go if we are interested in a historical-entitlement theory of property rights.

I do believe that every society, when the members of it are thinking clearly, will recognize that justice has to be defined in terms of history; in terms of the commitments we have made to one another and which we are now bound to keep, rather than in terms of some end state. In the first part of my paper, there is an attempt to show what I think is the essential emptiness and incoherence commonly found in discussions of justice, in terms of "end states."

The concept of social justice is very dangerous, because most of the people who use it don't know what they're talking about. They haven't thought through what they're talking about. And what they are saying implies things that they couldn't possibly want to accept.

But I think a society must be "just." And when we have specified the rules that make a society just, then we have talked about social justice. But I think we have to do it in terms of "rules." One cannot do it in terms of "final states."

Walter Block: I first want to make a remark about Paul Heyne's refusal to ground his economics in his theology. It's very reminiscent of a dear friend of mine who refused to come to this conference for reasons similar to that, Israel Kirzner. He is a man whom I admire greatly. And he, in effect, said something similar to Paul Heyne. He said, "Well here's economics; and here's theology; and never the twain shall meet."

Paul Heyne: I didn't say that.

Walter Block: Paul didn't say that, but what was said is reminiscent to me of Israel Kirzner's position. I think Paul is a moderate Kirznerian on this. Israel is the extremist on this question. I agree with Paul fully that justice is an integral part of the way society should operate. It's a crucial concept. Having said that, I have to differ sharply from his conception of justice. I agree that examining justice in terms of "end states" compared to "entitlements," to use Robert Nozick's terms, brings about great difficulties. If we have an end state view of property rights distribution, the difficulty is that it pretty much precludes any trade between consenting adults for these might result in income inequalities, or in divergences from the original distribution of income.

So, I think we have to go with "entitlement." However, I would ground it not on the Humean notion but on the Lockean notion, however imperfect. I think it's much more powerful and just than any other alternative.

Last week, Gregory Baum, a Marxist theologian, was here attending a Fraser Institute conference.* And for some strange reason, he and I really saw eye to eye on certain questions. We were in very close sympathy concerning the views of "liberation theology" and land theft perpetrated by the latifundi in the Third World. I approached it from a Lockean point of view. I know not from which view he approached it. I'll have to explore that with him one day.

But the point is that in the Lockean theory, as I understand it, the property rights are based ultimately, if you go back far enough, on mixing our labour with the land. If you try to ground it in any other criteria, property rights will be based on theft, or murder. Mixing our labour with the land is a much more just way to ground the entire system, which is based on property rights, than any other conception of property rights.

According to this theory of property rights, the peasants who tilled the soil are the rightful owners of the land. The conquistadores who conquered them stole their land. Their descendents, many of the large land owners in South and Central America, thus hold unjust title to their land, based on Lockean theory.

I do want to take issue very strongly with several conceptions of Paul Heyne's with regard to "justice" in his paper. From his paper I read:

> The employer may, if he wishes, pay the late arrivals as much as he is obligated to pay those who worked all day. (But that would be a matter of benevolence, not justice.) And it would surely be unjust for him to strike an average and pay five hours of wages to those who worked eight hours, and to those who worked but two.

Well, my immediate reaction to that is, justice consists of whatever he decides to do; and if that's what he decides to do and he can find someone to work for him, well then "by gum and by golly" that's just. It's true that the people who work eight hours are likely to leave his employ, and he's only going to keep people around who work two

---

*The proceedings of this conference will be published by the Fraser Institute under the title *Religion, Economics and Social Thought* – eds.

hours; but that's his problem. There is no violation of any kind of justice that I know of to have a voluntary contract between consenting adults on whatever exotic and eccentric kind of a basis can be imagined.

Secondly, in his discussion of the bus, I noticed three or four times in my copy of his paper, I kept saying, "Well, who owns the bus?" And my answer is whoever owns the bus, in justice, has the right to make any rule whatsoever that he wants. It's true he'll lose customers if he makes strange rules of the kinds that Paul points to, but that is the owner's right.

Roger Shinn: The paper says that critics of the market system are likely to be moved by the conviction that an impersonal social system is morally unacceptable and repeats a little later, these people believe economic justice requires the destruction of rule coordinated societies. I would have been inclined to put it exactly the other way around— that, many of the moral objections to a quite free market, in which exceptional need is taken care of by charity, are saying, "We want a more impersonal way of helping the unfortunate, the sick, and so on."

I go back to a comment made this morning about George Washington in relation to Rhode Island and Jews. He was not being nice to them by saying, "You've got some rights here." And some of us who are both appreciative and critical of the market would say, "We would like a system in which a sick person has a right—an impersonal right, to medical care—and does not depend upon charity as was the case when I was a youth, very often, of the doctor who will give some people free care, depending on personal whims.

Now I think one of the risks of this is the highly bureaucratized society that develops when you get a system of impersonal rules. And people are constantly asking for more rules to protect rights, and then complaining about bureaucracy. I think it's a very real problem. But, as we've been saying, all systems have their pathologies. But I would have been inclined to reverse Paul Heyne's judgement there.

Milton Friedman: I just want to bring into the discussion the comments of my old teacher to whom Paul Heyne referred this morning, Frank Knight. One of Frank Knight's favourite sayings was, "The search for justice will destroy the world." I think that is a very profound statement that needs to be considered carefully and not dismissed as a joke. What he meant as I interpreted him (and that's a very difficult thing to do, because Frank was a very sophisticated and complicated person, and nobody could profess to interpret him properly) was that "justice is in the eye of the beholder."

There are no really objective standards of justice. And there's no way other than force, ultimately, of mediating different claims of justice. It's a search for justice that animates Khomeini's Iran today. That is what it's about. That's what they regard as a "just" solution.

So, I believe that it is very dangerous to base any judgement of social policy upon the objective of searching for justice. Now you may say that we can get out of the problem by trying to avoid injustice, but that doesn't really get you out of it. It seems to me you have to substitute a very different ultimate value. As is clear from my own writings, I believe that freedom comes the closest to that kind of an ultimate value. And that freedom is very different from justice, in the sense that what freedom means is that each man shall seek justice, according to his own light provided he doesn't interfere with the ability of other people to do the same thing. To make "justice" the ultimate goal means that you have to use force; because, if your concept of justice disagrees with the other man's concept of justice, how do you mediate that? There is no way; it's not something you can strike a market bargain about. You fight over it.

So, I believe that, while I understand and sympathize very much with Paul's particular use of justice, and I agree with almost everything he says, Frank Knight was pointing to a pit that you ought to be careful not to fall into.

Walter Block: I wanted to comment on both Roger Shinn and Milton Friedman's points. With regard to Milton's point, take the latifundi in the Third World where, as far as I am concerned, the historical facts show that it was the conquistadores who, at one time, took over the land, kicked the peasants off, or allowed the peasants to stay there, but claimed ownership of it. And, on the other hand, you have a bunch of peasants who had, according to the Lockean theory, been the true owners of it. Now, if you say that there is no such thing as justice, and we must couch everything in terms of what is, then clearly the people who are working as peons there have no right to take over the land which I contend really should belong to them.

Milton Friedman: I didn't say there is no such thing as justice. I spoke of the "search for justice."

Walter Block: O.K. Well, if we listen to you and Knight and don't search for it, then we are left defending a system which is really based on theft. Suppose I were to go over to you, Milton, now, and grab your wallet; and then come back over here and keep it.

Milton Friedman: I wouldn't complain of that on grounds of injustice, but on the grounds that you were interfering with my freedom — which is a much more easily defined thing. And that's why I always say a free person shall be free to pursue his objectives, as long as he doesn't interfere with the freedom of others to do the same.

Philip Wogaman: I think what Paul Heyne provided for us is a definition of justice. Now, you may not want to call it that. It could have gone in the paper alongside some of the other theories of what justice is. I don't think it's an adequate explanation but at least it's a sufficient one. But I would observe Paul's statement that the search for justice means that ultimately you have to use force. Well, the search for freedom means that ultimately you have to use force. I think you're in the same boat conceptually, as what you're criticizing.

Kenneth Boulding: Fifty years ago, I was also a student of Frank Knight. I have the uneasy feeling that I stole all my best ideas from him. One possible edge towards resolution of this problem is the concept of the positive-sum game as over against the zero- or negative-sum game. That is, it's hard to come out against positive-sum games.

Economists have this very firm conviction that exchange is a positive-sum game. And I think they're 95 per cent right on this. There are problems of deception, and things of that nature. But on the whole, simply because of the veto power, there's a strong tendency for exchange to be a positive-sum game. And this is why we're fond of exchange and the free market, and all this stuff. But you cannot have exchange unless you have something to exchange which is your property. This is absolutely essential to any exchange. Yet the concept of property and the distribution of property, in a sense, is what justice is all about, isn't it?

The legitimation of this is extraordinarily tricky. I've really never felt I've ever solved this problem. I don't think the Lockean solution is adequate because there are all sorts of things you don't mix your labour with.

Now, one of my conservatisms, really, is that while exchange very frequently leads into positive-sum games, love always, or practically always does. There are pathologies of love, as there are pathologies of everything. But on the whole, benevolence is strongly positive sum. I build you up, you build me up. The more we are together, the happier we shall be.

And malevolence is purely a negative-sum game. I beat you down. You beat me down, and then we're all worthless. It seems to me that justice is moving towards the positive-sum forms of organization and away from the negative-sum ones.

Walter Block: There is a wallet right now in Milton's pocket. There is a question as to who is the rightful owner. I claim it. It's not even in his pocket now. It's being held up there. (laughter) It happens to be my wallet, I claim. He thinks it's his.

If there is no such thing as justice, or if justice is a very difficult issue to decide, we will never know whose wallet that is. And I think, ultimately, we'll only be able to fight about it. However, I think there is a better way. And that is the Lockean theory of property, which would indicate, roughly speaking, that wallet is his, and all the contents thereof.

Walter Berns: Locke's understanding of property has been referred to many times. I merely would like to point out that Locke's understanding of property consisting of the mixing of one's labour with some thing, is confined to the state of nature only; because that *thing* that one mixes one's labour with is part of the common heritage of mankind. It belongs to nobody. Nobody has a property right in it because nobody has yet appropriated it. It is only when one then mixes his labour with that which belongs to nobody that he acquires property in it. But that is the definition of property that is confined to the state of nature. And a different situation entirely applies when you have a sort of society, and when everything has been appropriated.

Edmund Opitz: Walter Block said something to the effect that if something appears to be unjust at the moment, you appeal to some longer experience of the practice of justice of the people. But the people we are talking about are not the people of some mythical "Rhubarbaria," but presumably, the English people and their tradition of justice. We are talking about the tradition shaped by the influences of Israel, Greece, and Rome, further molded by the centuries of European experience. Not merely tradition, but a particular tradition.

Another point I'd like to make is this: it seems to me that human beings, like all living things, want to go on living. And if something deters one from continuing his life, his freedom is impaired. It seems to follow that every person wants maximum freedom for himself to pursue his own goals. I can think of no exception. The worst dictator imaginable, whose goal in life is the extinction of the freedom of every individual on the planet, does not want anyone to interfere with his own freedom to pursue that particular goal.

What we are talking about, it seems to me, is not simply "individual freedom," but the phrase that the early Whigs, and Herbert Spencer, and others used: "equal freedom." We are talking about a "free society." A free society is one where everyone wants as much freedom for everyone else, to pursue their goals, as he demands for himself to pursue his — a society of "equal" freedom.

This, I think, is what Adam Smith had in mind with the phrase he used to distinguish his position from mercantilism. He spoke of his "liberal plan of liberty, equality, and justice," three words which I conceive to be denoting the same thing viewed from different angles — a society where every person is equal before the law. In such a society, every person has maximum liberty, but not complete liberty. He has maximum liberty to pursue his personal goals.

David Friedman: I would like to support both Walter Block against my father and my father against Walter Block, and attack Paul Heyne in the process. To begin with, I find it incomprehensible how my father can claim that there is any content in the statement, "I have a right to do what I like as long as I don't violate your rights," without some pre-existing idea of what my rights are. And the pre-existing idea of what my rights are, unless it just reads my "legal rights" (which, of course, I hope it doesn't), has to be founded on some idea of justice. So that it seems to me that he is, as far as I can tell, using meaningless expressions in order to avoid a problem merely because none of us knows how to solve it.

Now, the point where I would want to agree with my father and Frank Knight against Walter Block or at least make an argument on their side, goes back to the latifundi. It seems to me entirely possible (I don't know the actual case) that as a matter of abstract justice, if I were a judge in a court, I would agree that the peasants were in the right. But second, that it would be better for the world, including the peasants, if they forget about the past. Fighting over their claims to justice will get people killed. There is no particular reason to think that the most just people will win the war. Fighting tends to create unjust situations. So, it seems to me quite plausible to argue both that there is an abstract principle of justice, which in principle could be applied; and that as a matter of practical, social reality we accept what is, and work from there.

And that, then, gets me to my disagreement and agreement with Paul: it seems to me that he has the same problem my father does, a little bit further away. It's essentially the argument I've had with Jim Buchanan over the years. Jim has correctly observed that the standard libertarian talk about property rights simply sweeps the issue of how you get property in the first place under the rug. But all Jim has done is found a different rug to sweep it under. In talking about contract, Jim argues that a social contract, a voluntary unanimous social contract, justifies it.

But, of course, most of you don't regard it as a voluntary contract when somebody says, "Your money or your life." And therefore, in order to decide whether the contract is voluntarily agreed to, one must first know what belongs to whom. Otherwise, if I sign the social contract for fear that you would kill me if I didn't, it wasn't really voluntary. But we have to decide whether you had a right to kill me.

So, similarly, in Paul's case, I find it difficult to understand how you can get the whole thing out of promises, without first knowing what people own, and therefore what they are entitled to promise to do things with. And it's in that sense in which it seems to me that there is a gaping hole in his line of argument, or what I understand of his description of Hume's line of argument — a hole which, it seems to me, Locke makes some attempt, however unsuccessful, to fill.

Philip Wogaman: I am struck in reviewing what Paul Heyne has suggested here that each of his stated, and then rejected, notions may have some truth to contribute — including even the one that he identifies as the basic one; and also including the concept of freedom that Milton Friedman has put so much emphasis upon, but not defining it as justice. We could take time to sort out your discussion of equality, and need, and merit, as well as the discussion of promises. And I think that each of those points is pertinent to an adequate theory of justice. But then, what is the overall concept that brings coherence to it?

I'd like to nominate one which I think I could use to helpfully relate both the left and the right hands of God to each other, in one sense; but it can be stated entirely in secular terms, as well as theological. And that is to understand justice as the structure of society which assures the capacity of people to participate as recognized persons in society. Now, what that means, materially, is going to change; and people's perceptions of it will vary. I don't think one can arrive at a blueprint of justice that will fit now and forever. History changes; it moves. But that's what the public debate is all about; and therefore the quest for a kind of public philosophy really is a very important enterprise; and there should be a constant flow of argument within society over the substance of justice.

But, if one understands justice to be what I suggested, the guarantee of the "standing room" of every person within society, then that would help to illuminate why some important measure of equality should be observed, though there is no possibility of "perfect equality," even if we could define what it meant.

Need is of some great importance. And one can understand "relative need," as well as "absolute need." Merit has some role to play — certainly in criminal justice. The relationship between what one does, and what one gets as a result of doing it, is rather important and not to be washed out; and, clearly freedom is important. So it seems to me all of these values can be helpfully subsumed under that broader communitarian point of reference.

Arthur Shenfield: May I say a word about Roger Shinn's proposition, that if you generalize the duty to relieve distress by giving it to the whole of society, you then set up an impersonal rule. I think that's incorrect. In the first place, it's still "persons." It's still people who will be relieving that distress. And you can see that immediately when you say, "The trouble is that you've got to have a bureaucracy to do it."

But, the essential mistake there, in my opinion, is this: it misunderstands the nature of an impersonal rule. An impersonal rule doesn't tell anybody to do anything. An impersonal rule lays down the proposition that *if* you do anything, it has to be done according to certain principles. For example, the rule of law. The rule of law doesn't say that the government, or the state, must do anything whatsoever. But the rule of law says that anything the state or the government does, has to be done subject to such and such principles. So that wouldn't be an impersonal rule. It only looks, at first sight, to be impersonal because no particular single person is designated to relieve the distress.

Murdith McLean: I would like to comment on what Paul Heyne said in his paper. I find it very helpful. To some extent the procedure is understandable—that is, the procedure of starting off with candidates for a standard of justice; and finding that each one of them turns out to be inadequate and having to abandon them, saying helpful things along the way, especially about merit. But one might claim that in a way we are looking for the wrong thing. When we look for justice as a kind of rule book, that we can apply and will always tell us when we've got justice, we're likely to be... well, in fact, *certain* to be disappointed. We found that about every other concept. We are probably going to find it about justice, too.

The way we are going to decide what is a just situation (and also what is an unjust one) is by arguing about cases that we agree on—as to whether they are just or not. And we meet along the way, trying to use tags, like the ones that Paul Heyne has been investigating, as sort of handy, shorthand expressions to bring those cases to bear upon one another. For in the last analysis, the only way we are going to get anywhere in our discussion about justice, and injustice, is by starting off with cases that we all agree about, or don't agree about; and that's where we will find the "nitty gritty" really comes through.

Anthony Waterman: I am going to claim the chairman's right to say something at this point. It always struck me as being a very melancholy fact that in Part II of St. Thomas Aquinas's, *Summa Theologiae,* there are two adjacent volumes—one called "Justice," and the other called "Injustice." And the one called "Injustice" is more than twice as thick as the one called "Justice." (laughter)

Roger Shinn: I must reply to Arthur Shenfield. I just don't understand the idea that an impersonal law doesn't require me to do anything. It requires me to pay taxes, jury duty—all kinds of things. Someone should write an essay entitled, "The Search for Freedom Will Destroy the World" or "A Search for Liberty Will Destroy the World."

I am in a curious situation. I want freedom. I want justice; and I don't quite know what either of them is. But I am interested. The word "liberty" gives rise to two words, "liberationist" and "libertarian," which are just about opposite in social philosophies. I first got acquainted with the word "liberation" as a soldier, where to "liberate" the enemies' territory meant to liberate the cognac, and anything else you could carry around, and maybe the women, and so on.

David Friedman: The reason, it seems to me, that I have more reservation about the pursuit of justice than the pursuit of liberty, has to do with what I was saying to Walter Block earlier. That if by "justice" we are concerned with initial ownership of things, I think in the long run that isn't enormously important. In the U.S. at the moment, if you gave the country back to the Indians, in some fair way where you didn't give them the buildings that are built on it, but just the land; and divided it fairly evenly among the Indians, it would not noticeably affect the distribution of income in the U.S. It wouldn't much affect how well off I am, and so forth.

So it seems to me that starting with either a "just" or an "unjust" distribution of property, in a generation or two you end up in not very different circumstances, except for very extreme cases. Whereas if you have an unfree society, and accept the fact it's unfree, I don't see any reason to expect that the bad consequences of that will peter out over the years, in the same sense.

Walter Block: I would like to try to establish what I consider the libertarian theory of property rights. It starts with "self-ownership." There are only really three alternatives. Either we own ourselves, or one person owns us all; the problem with that is, why is it proper for one human being to own, as slaves, all other human beings? The third possibility is that we each own one, four and a half billionth of everybody. The difficulty with that is you'd have to have committee meetings before you could scratch your nose to get permission from your other owners.

If we start with the proposition that we each own ourselves, then we each own our labour. So, Ken Boulding's question is answered. We each start with owning our labour. If we own our labour, we can mix our labour with the land. If we mix our labour with the land, and we add capital, and we assume some sort of Nozickian entitlement theory of trade, and gifts, and luck, based on the initial property rights endowment, we answer Walter Berns' question of, "How can we apply this to a modern society?"

I fully agree with David Friedman's criticism of Milton, with regard to "freedom consists of people respecting other people's rights"; and if you cannot specify the "rights," the whole thing falls to the ground. However, when he joins Milton in attacking me, he is guilty of confusing the difference between normative and positive economics.

Milton and I were distinguishing ourselves on a "normative"

question. David replied in a "positive" vein, with which I happen to be in full agreement. That is, I agree that the Indians or the natives would probably be better off if instead of worrying about their lost endowments of property, they were just concerned with creating a libertarian society from hence forward; the property rights would wash out in probably weeks, if not years.

My point is still worth making. Those people owned that property. And now think of how we free market proponents appear to the liberation theologian, or to the people on the left. Here we are supposed to be defenders of property rights; and yet, grant me the facts of the case, massive theft has taken place; and we're giving them a positive statement with which I happen to agree: that this stolen property is economically unimportant. But I think it's very inadequate to give them that positive statement. What we have to make is the normative statement, too. Both. We have to say, "Yes, in justice, that property belongs to you." Namely, the free market advocate is not just in favour of the status quo, where blatant theft has taken place.

Milton Friedman: I want, first, before I get to this point, to clarify Frank Knight's view, because I think there has been a misunderstanding. Knight was not saying, and I wasn't interpreting him as saying, that there was anything wrong with people trying to establish for themselves a concept of justice. What was involved was not a search for justice in the sense of trying to reach a concept of justice, assuming that there is a concept of justice — not that at all.

What he was saying was something very different, and it really goes back to what essentially, in a way, David Friedman was saying at one point. What Knight was saying is that if you take the achievement of justice as a primary objective of social activity, if society's collective organizing principle and driving force is going to be the search for justice, that will destroy the world. That's what he was trying to say; and I think he's right for exactly the kind of reasons we were giving.

Now to turn to all of these other concepts about how it is logically inconsistent to talk about freedom, that one is really talking indirectly about justice, I happen, in the contrast that David was drawing, to side with Jim Buchanan, rather than with David. There is no way of getting to an ideal concept of a society that is going to correspond to what actually is. The tyranny of the status quo is overwhelming. It's very hard to move from there. What we are trying to do is to try to picture for ourselves the direction in which we would like to move from where we are, and what guiding conceptions should rule us in judging that issue. There I find the most helpful conception to be that of a group of people who unanimously decide on certain rules of the game under which they are going to operate.

When Walter Block wants to have my wallet, and he claims it's his property, I say, "O.K., you and I agreed to be members of this club." We agreed that when we became members of this club that certain rules would decide what is my property, what is your property, and we agreed on a method of adjudication, a certain set of courts. We'll go to that method of adjudication and try to decide. And I am not going to introduce the word "justice." Maybe, in the course of our originally agreeing on this set of rules, what caused us to agree on one set of rules rather than another was that we had certain common concepts of what was just or unjust.

One of the things that bothers me about so much of this discussion is that it goes around in sort of an endless circle. Each concept is imperfect; so you go to the next one. That's imperfect; so you go to the next one. And you keep going around that circle, and there is no exit from it. It seems to me that you exit from it by the standard procedure of science, by saying that for certain classes of purposes, we will treat the world as if it's like this, rather than like that. And outside of that, you're just in an endless cycle of disputation.

Walter Berns: We have a situation here where Phil Wogaman, for example, wants to use the word "justice," and Milton Friedman attempts to eschew the use of the word as if it were a four-letter word.

The following anecdote will indicate, I think, the origin of this. Milton, you may recall that at the University of Chicago, Mortimer Adler had this big series of great books, and the synopticon was a big index to the thing. One of the index entries was "justice."

This enterprise was physically located on the Mid-way Plaisance. I lived right next door to it. I had a friend who was working for Mortimer Adler. His job was to fill in the index on justice for Locke. He went and read Locke. He then went to Mortimer Adler and said, "Locke doesn't talk about justice." And Adler said in effect, "You are crazy. He is a political philosopher. Every political philosopher talks about justice. Look at Kant. Look at Plato. Look at Socrates and so on. Go back." He went back; and he read, and he read, and he read. He concluded that there was no reference to justice. And Mortimer Adler fired him. (laughter) Mortimer Adler was on the brink of a great discovery, at that point, and he failed to open his eyes.

Geoffrey Brennan: It seems to me that there is a point emerging here, which is really a major theme in Paul Heyne's paper. Paul is very close to Frank Knight, it seems to me, in this respect, because the Knightian point is a conviction that it's very important to have stable rules. Once one accepts that it's very important to have stable rules, for purely prudential reasons, it may not matter, particularly, what those rules are. This is something which in a way does distinguish economists and the way they think about the world, in a very important way from the way in which a lot of other people think about the world. And it is definitely caught up with the whole notion of "positive-sum" interactions, and the notion that once we have a set of stable rules, then we can get on with the real business, which is the business of undertaking transactions.

Walter Block: I couldn't agree more with Geoff Brennan and Milton and David Friedman in their positive statements. I emphasize that again. I couldn't agree more with them on their positive statements; however, they are failing to realize that there are other questions besides positive ones. Yes, if we have stable rules, if we have property rights' rules and they're stable, that will help maximize wealth.

But there is another question that they're ignoring — and that is, the normative question; or they're confusing the normative with the positive. This is a very different question — namely, suppose stable rules did not maximize wealth, or suppose you could be the dictator for a day, suppose you had your "druthers," what would justice require of you to do? That's a very different question. "What is just?" is a different question from "what maximizes wealth?"

Secondly, with regard to Milton and my wallet, suppose we went to court, and they gave me the wallet on the grounds that my beard is fuller than his. Would he then be tempted to inquire about justice?

Paul Heyne: I have seven points. Number one: everything Murdith said, I agree with. (laughter) Number two....

Murdith McLean: Very sound, Paul; very sound... (laughter)

Paul Heyne: Number two, I am asserting, as a matter of fact, that we are much more likely to establish tolerable justice by maintaining long established expectations, than by trying to correct injustices in the distant past.

Third point: "The search for justice may destroy the world." I agree, but the continuous effort to eliminate injustice will, and should, go on, through discussion, tolerant, yet committed.

Four: I used the phrase, Reinhold Niebuhr's phrase, "relative absolutism." That's how we have to go about it; as "relative absolutists." There is a standard for our claims about injustice; but none of us has it by the tail. We have got to talk to each other. Frank Knight wrote a lot about that, too—democracy is talking to one other.

Phil Wogaman suggested that justice might be a social system which assures the capacity of persons to participate. I think this is a good example of a hopelessly vague recipe—a recipe for endless strife, and continuous injustice. You have to check it out, test it out—what would it mean in practice?

Number five: Roger Shinn wanted to reverse my claim that "impersonal social coordination is seen as unjust." He claims that those suspicious of the market want an impersonal system, to make "charity" a "right," rather than a privilege. I deny that this is true; and I'd say it's an empirical question. For example, the church council in my city recently uttered a vast outcry over the new rule that people who took federal food would have to sign for it. Attempts to establish impersonal rules for the administration of aid to the poor, I find, are continually met by the "liberals" with outcries that this is "demeaning" the poor. They claim that they want impersonal rules, and that they want charity administered as a matter of right. The problem is that the statement, "Everyone has a 'right' to health care," turns out in practice to involve rules that cannot be administered both impersonally and in a way that people will accept.

Number six: Everything David Friedman said, I agree with; except that the hole in my system is gaping. The hole is not gaping; it is bottomless. (laughter) Now, that's important, because we keep going back, and back, and back, as far as we have to, in order to achieve agreement. There is no ultimate foundation.

And finally, I have here an article in yesterday's *Wall Street Journal* called "The Poverty Cycle." A welfare mother begets three welfare daughters, perpetuating life styles. It's a beautifully written piece but it's deeply disturbing. These are people who have gotten on the welfare system—the impersonal welfare system—and you realize that's not what they need. It's very clear, in this tragic case, that these women need a community of people who know them and would sustain them. Sustaining communities, of people who know and can really care for one another, are vitally important. Here is one of the great tragedies that I think my approach to injustice would help to remedy. It might help us to see the limits of what governments or markets, as necessarily impersonal systems, can do, so that we could get at the vitally important task, vitally important to the most unfortunate members of our society, of nourishing and sustaining small communities.

Chapter 10

Religion, Ethics and Politics in the 1980s

Edward R. Norman

I. THE NATURE OF THE MODERN STATE

Although for Church leaders, and to some external observers, opinion
seems to be most concentrated on deciding what exactly *is* the nature
of Christian ethics and politics, there is, at this time, a more fundamental reference that has to be made. For it is to the nature of the
modern state that reference is first necessary: to determine its ethical
capabilities and to evaluate the extent to which it is — as it is so often
described — secular. Clearly in a pure condition of things, Christians
could hardly find secular government satisfactory; they are people for
whom life on earth, and its structure and organization in social and
administrative units, is determined by the kingship of Christ — there
are known ends, which are unlikely to be compatible with the
organization of life around wholly materialist presuppositions. Yet
the historical separations of Church and State, in North America and
Britain, during the last two centuries, were originally the work of
Christians themselves. In the nineteenth century, they contended for
the creation of a neutral but still Christian state — one in which the
government would incorporate Christianity into the basis of law but
where no Church group or denomination would have priority over any
other. Their separation of Church and State was a mere device, recognizing the existence of a religious pluralism, but with no intention of

setting up what contemporaries would have called a "godless state," one with genuinely secular moral presuppositions. In the twentieth century, with the transfer of so much moral seriousness from religious to materialist agencies, the impulsion to separate religious considerations from the ends of government has been assumed by élites of non-Christian liberal opinion. It is they who have sought to give reality to the notion of secular government, and it is they who have, in the second half of the century, received unexpected support from liberal Christian leaders, themselves anxious to associate their faith with the human goals of secular moral seriousness. Indeed, the present advocates of a distinct Christian political activism, especially in the school of "Liberation Theology," are actually arguing for the creation of the kingdom of righteousness here and now on earth; but they are also looking for a secular scheme of government – perhaps even one conducted by philosophically committed Marxists – rather than for a Christian polity in the conventional sense of historical experience, a state run by Christian leaders and intended to lead its people into Christian ways of living. They are able to do this, of course, because they identify their understanding of Christianity with the political objectives of seeking to create conditions of social justice on earth. For them, the secular state has no problems: it is God's providential work, securing at the same time both the material benefits which give human dignity to men and also the institutional mechanisms that in theory allow men freedom of choice between competing beliefs and ethical positions. It is this premise, about human expectations in the political order, that I believe ought to be scrutinized rather critically.

The contemporary church on the role of the state

Leading Christian opinion has in recent years said an enormous amount to suggest that present claims to improved material living standards are founded upon false moral premises. In the *genre* of the Brandt Report, and the preceding acceptance by the churches of the contention that the existing distribution of wealth between the world's peoples is inherently unjust, there has been a recurrent call for Western societies to suffer a decline in their living standards. But this case was not founded upon a Christian denial of false material expectations but on secularized political concepts of social justice. It is, anyway, about the only area in which contemporary Christianity has pointed to the need for a new critical realism about the assumption that material improvement is what human life is all about. The main volume of debate within the Churches' leadership has been preoccupied with the supposed injustices of the distribution of wealth within existing societies; it has been characterized by an obsessive concern with material rewards and by a general and pervasive assumption that Christianity is primarily addressed to human needs and not to the cultivation of spirituality or personal moral quality. It is precisely because of this insistence on material needs, as the centre of its ethical vision for humanity, that received Christian opinion adds its weight — which in the developing world can sometimes be very considerable — to the heightening, not to the diminishing, of expectations within the populations. In political terms, too, this has led many Christians to contend that the only acceptable ethical tests for a satisfactory governmental or state structure are those calculated according to the satisfaction of material needs and the fulfilment of schemes of social justice based upon them. Hence the support of Christian opinion for radical change in the developing world, and for the adoption of a generally hostile attitude to what are thought of as non-progressive political forces within the Western nations. In the current rhetoric of Christianity, religion is conceived as being concerned essentially with human "liberation," itself seen as a political and economic condition. "Liberation" is a key word in the vocabulary of rising expectations, a word common to religious and secular idealists.

Hostility to capitalism, as the joint cause of raised material expectations and social injustice in the distribution of wealth, is generally part of this disposition. Despite the partisan judgements at play here, this part of the debate is in fact worthy of consideration. For the springs of capitalism do involve raising the expectations of the individual's material incentives. Those springs, however, are not ideological, as in contemporary political idealism, but are fixed according to market resources: they are the reward of labour and have to do with the very moral question of the obligation to work. Capitalism, that is to say, is arguably not a contributing element in the false material expectations of our Western societies; for where capitalism operates felicitously, the participants involved in the creation of wealth recognize that the expectations generated by capitalist incentive are intimately related to the resources available, and rise and decline accordingly. It is not capitalism, with its incentives dependent upon gain, that induces false expectations, but progressive ideologies, which teach men that existing social or political structures are to blame for their poverty. *There* is the cause of expectations that are artificially raised. Such ideologies suggest a solution that is not attained through increased labour or the initiative of the individual, but through simple collective morality—a political change in the way society is conducted. Societies in which this type of progressive idealism appeals most strongly are often those in which capitalism has just begun to deliver the goods: there are many Latin-American countries which illustrate the way in which a progressive élite within the intelligentsia converts the genuine material incentives wrought by capitalist developments into mass false expectations raised by political radicalism. Both in their association of Christianity with human material improvement, therefore, and in their critical scrutiny of the economic system of Western societies, contemporary Church leaders have laid down some strict and moralistic requirements for the modern state.

The state in the modern world

Let me now return to the nature of the modern state. A crucial distinction exists between historical political associations of the past, with their limited capabilities, and the modern experience of collectivist governments. Both the means of educating opinion, and the expectations men have of government, have expanded enormously, in response to the industrial and technological mechanisms of modern society and to the decay of the sense of social authority that traditional societies were able to enforce. The experience has been a liberating one, but it has also brought formidable problems of human organization and social control. In some parts of the world—unhappily in a majority of countries—these problems have been overcome, at least in part, by a return to the mechanisms of control characteristic of traditional societies: the Marxist states, and in some defined by militant nationalism, ideology has been so incorporated into the experience and capabilities of collectivism, that individual liberty has been substantially diminished. From this point of view, there is little to choose between a rigorously atheist collectivism, like the Soviet Union, or the quasi-theocracies of emergent Arab nationalism. In the West, on the other hand, the price of liberty has been a good deal of incoherence about the nature of human association and the practice of ordinary and necessary social discipline. With us, the tyranny of government has been replaced by the tyranny of opinion: the Western nations are internally motivated by a disorganized accumulation of educated élites, lobbyists, pressure-groups, and media-manipulation to a degree that makes many of the ordinary functions of government very difficult. But what most characterizes the resulting mixture is moral confusion — an inability to describe exactly what the ethical nature of the state is all about. During the last decade, the widespread respect paid to the notion of Human Rights has been able to perform the service of a sort of substitute moral definition of social organization. For reasons I shall suggest in due course, this has not been very satisfactory.

The plain fact about the modern state is that much of its machinery is of its nature secular. When the religious message of the New Testament is stripped down to a permanently applicable basis, it is seen to be concerned with relationships between men and God which are often rendered in terms of earthly relationships — in such things as personal honesty, sexual responsibility, respect for the spiritual value of life, and generosity with possessions. Now it is possible to translate these virtues into many forms of social organization, as the experience of the centuries has shown; but the modern collectivist state prescribes very precise and very inclusive conditions for social life. In such things as the provision of transportation infrastructures, money supply, the level of funding for scientific or technical research, and decisions about priorities in the relative expenditure of competing departments of state, for example, there can be no clear or uncontroversial translation of Christian precepts into the currency of modern government. Nothing is, in the end, value-free, however, and the collectivist state will actually behave, whatever the secularity of its machinery, only according to the values of those who move its components or who derive their own sense of social righteousness from resort to its resources. Hence the case for Christians to be *involved* with the modern state. That is a different condition of things, however, from claiming the authority of Christianity for the actual operations of the state that may from time to time achieve the respectability of becoming the repository of a broadly-based moral feeling.

II. MORAL PLURALISM AS A POLITICAL VALUE

Let me now turn to the nature of modern Western states — to the existence of a moral pluralism. Many Western leaders, if asked what actually *is* the cardinal value they would preserve against the unfreedom of the controlled societies, would speak about the area of choice reserved to citizens as individuals in society, about the morality of choosing values. The benefit they seek to preserve is the right *not* to have to conform to prescribed values in certain areas of social life. Here questions have to be put about the real existence of a moral pluralism within Western societies; about the extent to which, beneath all the praise of diversity, there is actually a pretty tightly prescribed area of what are regarded as non-negotiable ethical requirements. If society was genuinely pluralistic, for example, the collectivism of modern government could hardly operate as it does: the essential condition for the compelled morality at the basis of the welfare state is a consensus. It is assumed that compulsory taxation for the care of the sick, or compulsory education, are benefits beyond serious question. And there are, of course, areas of public concern about which there genuinely *is* a consensus. That does not amount to a pluralistic-society, but to one in which there is an establishment of liberal-humanitarian morality. What is the basis of that morality? Is it secular or religious in origin and orientation? Can it be changed, or is it to be regarded as sacral? The preference of public figures *not* to define the basis of social values in ultimate moral language does not make their social practices any less normative. As it happens they have in hand, in our day, the convenient doctrine of Human Rights, and there is a general assumption that the contents of Human Rights ideology is self-evident. This assumption needs very careful scrutiny — if only because, as revealed by the fate of the Helsinki Accords (to give but one example) there is not even agreement about the contents between East and West, let alone within Western pluralism. And the disagreement between East and West is not because there is a known body of Human Rights which one party cynically elects not to honour, for reasons of *realpolitik* or internal social control; for, beneath the deceptive common rhetoric of rights there is genuine divergence between collective and individualist understandings of moral choice of society.

The Church on pluralism

To the existence of a pluralistic society, the Churches have brought a set of attitudes that are indistinguishable from educated opinion in general, and thus have nothing additional to say about the moral capacities of the political order in reference to the pluralism. Though once the natural opponents of moral diversity, because of their guardianship of Revealed truth, the churches' acceptance of it has now passed beyond mere recognition to positive endorsement. "No one group can claim monopoly of the truth," according to a 1979 Report of the Board for Mission and Unity of the General Synod of the Church of England; "it is felt that all systems of belief and canons of behaviour must be seen in relation to others, and have therefore only relative, not absolute authority."[1] This assessment is actually in part true—but not for the reasons assumed in the Report. In their enthusiasm to promote the ideal of a multi-racial society, especially, the Churches have abandoned the notion of racial and cultural assimilation as a social goal, and have instead become to advocate self-conscious diversity. The supposition that Christianity, or any religious system, can provide the moral and uniform basis of contemporary society has also been abandoned by them. The rôle of the Churches is now seen, by themselves, as one among many, but with a prime duty to promote the interests of minorities. It is an odd blend of libertarian thinking and prescribed social moralism. There have been some recent signs of a reaction within the Churches' rank-and-file against the secularized attitudes of the leadership in such matters. The emergence of the so-called "moral majority" in the U.S. Presidential election of 1980 was an appeal for a Christian moral standard as the basis of law. The leaders of the major denominations were among the first to attack the "moral majority" for illiberal disregard of the other components of the moral pluralism. Their arguments were precisely those used by Victorian free-thinkers against the continuation of religious provisions in public life.

Now if this acceptance and promotion of moral pluralism in social life in fact derived from a genuine liberal pragmatism, it might have a very acceptable complexion; it might seek to support, in politics, those who did not wish to diminish the area of private choice and the area of enterprise—it might contend against those thorough collectivists who seek to impose their blue-print for secular redemption upon the general population. But the Churches' promotion of pluralism is actually ideological. It has positive characteristics. It has to do with opposition to traditional society, and with the moral necessity of obliging people to choose progressive alternatives. The area of agreed selection from within the diverse values is really very tightly circumscribed; the components of the moral pluralism have to be acceptable according to some strict criteria. It is rather like declaring an open selection for the players in a team game, but only allowing the members of one of the sides to be freely chosen. For within the field of choice, the Churches are on record as ruling out—as unsuitable for free selection—quite a number of positions. In the end, instead of a genuine pluralism of moral values, applicable to the political sphere, they actually, and for moral reasons, allow only universal democratic equalitarianism to be exercised within a non-sexist, multi-racial collectivist state. That may be a perfectly acceptable conclusion, but it is *not* the endorsement of plural values. Whatever their practice, however, Church leaders still declaim an ideal of moral pluralism for society on grounds of abstract justice.

Natural Law foundations of the Churches' stance

This discloses another odd feature. In their desire to promote the ideal of a multi-racial, multi-cultural society, churchmen had begun to contend that the competing values, secular and religious, are often in some way different insights into the Supreme Being. This is not a matter of Revelation but of observable moral laws, of the Divine expressed, often apparently anonymously, in a wide area of human experience, in many cultures. Contemporary churchmen, that is to say, are unconsciously promoting Natural Law as the authority for deriving some normative social truths. The Natural Law assumptions at the basis of contemporary Human Rights ideology have a comparable appeal — and are usually articulated with an equal innocence of their real pedigree in the history of political theory. Can authentic Christianity really associate itself with secular morality on a Natural Law basis with the precision that is now practiced? In reality, Christian leaders do not generally formulate the question that way, for they regard the main goals of Human Rights ideology as constituting a sort of agreed common content of the various outlooks of the pluralism of moral values in society, and, furthermore, as corresponding to the teaching of Christ. They assume, in the end, that Revealed and Natural truth are the same. Yet the contents of this vision have no particularly *religious* authority; it rests upon re-interpretations of the Bible according to the understanding of contemporary, secular moral seriousness. One of the most extraordinary features of the Christianity of our day is the extent to which its social and moral action, and the political forms which give them expression, in fact, rest upon secular premises. Let me give just one example. In the December, 1980, edition of the World Council of Churches' monthly journal, *One World,* there is an article denouncing the prostitution provided for businessmen visiting South East Asian cities. But the objections are not because of biblical teaching about fornication: they are because the practices at issue are what the article calls "sex imperialism"; they are the exploitation of women, a sign of what is condemned as "the subordinate role imposed on women generally." Much of the evidence comes from one Sister Mary-John Mananzan, a Catholic nun from the Philippines, who, at the Women's Conference on Human Rights, called by the World

Council of Churches in Venice, in 1979, had said: "We need a complete transformation of the economic system and of the consciousness of women in society." That may be very proper; but we are now a long way from the authority of religious tradition—and a very long way from the free choices of a genuinely pluralist society. In this third area of ethical and political questions, therefore, the Churches are offering no insights that are not to be found everywhere else.

III. THE CHRISTIAN AND THE STATE

So much for the diagnosis and for the description of existing attitudes. Christians *are,* however, involved in political action and have no way of not being—short of opting out of society altogether. The question now to ask, therefore, is exactly what the Christian contribution ought to be. I do not believe, and never have, that Christians should eschew political involvement. The burden of my Reith Lectures, in 1978, was to point out that Christian claims to religious authority for their political ideas are often ill-founded, and that the acceptance of secular morality as the grounds of political action has resulted in a serious secularization of Christianity itself. But Christians *are* concerned with politics—if for no other reason than that the enlarged area of competence of the modern collectivist state has come to incorporate aspects of personal conduct and choice which have always been the concern of religion. This is seen most clearly in education, for example, or in the care of the sick. These are matters which, from a religious point of view, have little relation to the morality of political theories but a close proximity to individual welfare. In addition, Christians can legitimately ask, as others do, what sort of society they want—in which to express or to transmit religious experience. I have, again, in the past contended along classical lines that the Churches as institutions are most appropriately restricted to the definition of general principles of human conduct, and that detailed applications in the political arena are best left to Christians as individuals. But that still, of course, means that the Christians involved in politics will need to be clear about the relationship of their religious understanding to the content of their social action.

Christian ideological agnosticism

I start, at this point, from the supposition that Christianity, as Revealed truth, and the ethics described in the New Testament, do not provide a blue-print for political society. I also observe that, through-out the preceding centuries, Christians have endorsed diverse modes of social authority and schemes of government, and have tended to represent each one as expressing authentic religious understanding. Hence the familiarity about the present consecration, by Church leaders, of Western bourgeois liberalism, or of collectivist socialism, as Christian politics. Now I also suppose that the pluralism of moral and political values in contemporary society is a real phenomenon and has qualities that should be recognized as beneficial. I do not mean by this — as Church leaders and liberal sages appear to mean — that plural-ism is *in itself* virtuous because no one can claim genuine authority for his knowledge of truth, but that diversity and relative choice pro-tect the individual (who if he is wise will be sceptical about absolute claims made on behalf of political values) from having blueprints for society enforced for ultimate moral reasons. Into the confusion of alternatives comes the Christian with his ordinary duty as a citizen to participate in the political order: the existing pluralism contains elements once derived from the long Christian inheritance, mixed up with, and usually now confused with, secular humanism, utilitarian values, and whatever else attracts the moral sense of the formulators of opinion. It is a grey area, where definitions are hazardous. Few, in-deed, attempt to describe with any precision the exact morality that lies at the basis of contemporary political association. But the Chris-tian enters the pluralism with insights which *are* precise — which *do* have a dogmatic basis in Revealed truth. His God is Incarnational: he entered human life in Christ not in order to declare that knowledge was an open question, but to claim allegiance. Like the Marxist ac-tivist in a Western democracy, the Christian is called to participate within the context of the moral pluralism. For the Marxist, truth is political truth: his ultimate purpose is the destruction of the pluralism itself as a political order and its replacement by the total ethical state, ordered according to an exclusive ideology. For the Christian, lacking a political scheme in his source of authority, the pluralism becomes a valid but secondary area of activity: his contribution is also precise, however — for him it is a doctrine of man and man's moral limitations that is exclusive, and with which he seeks to relativize the political con-text and to give it a rather diminished moral authority as the arbiter of man's destiny. The Christian points to the fallibility of men in political, as in all other, action; to the priority of emotional over reasoned impulsions in so many social calculations, and to the inabil-ity of political ideology to alter or to satisfy large areas of human experience. For the Christian in politics, therefore, the existence of the pluralism of values is to be regarded as a useful if historically fortuitous occasion to place men's political expectations within the austere confines of human spiritual capabilities. The pluralism is to be regarded as a device that protects individuals from the imperialism of ideas — from ideology. It is this concept which is unhappily denied in contemporary Christianity, with its apparently increasing preparedness to identify the essence of Revealed truth with human idealism, and to associate religious faith with merely political objectives. Alas, the present pluralism of Western moral values is almost certainly not stable. It represents an unusual interlude — in the widest perspective of human development — between monolithic social orthodoxies; a hiccup in the graph, from the breakdown of the unitary societies of the old world, before the Enlightenment of the eighteenth century and the liberalism of the nineteenth, until the new totalitarianisms of the future — already anticipated among a large section of the earth's peoples. The present time offers religion and politics a highly untypical and probably ephemeral opportunity to explore their relationships in a context of comparative moral freedom. Unhappily the religious leaders are already willing to represent *their* contribution in terms of political values. They are already preparing the ground for the political totalities that are to come.

Within the pluralism of values, of course, those who really believe in their own (as the Christians should) will seek the conversion of others to their own exclusivity. I have already suggested that a lot of the *rhetoric* of pluralism in contemporary discourse is actually bogus because beneath all the talk of diversity some values are regarded as normative in every situation. Provided the opportunity exists to change the ordering of values, however, through the manipulation of opinion within society (or through liberal education and the "media," to put it in less frank language), there is no great harm in that. In both England and America government is influenced in this way: ours are societies in which the pluralism works reasonably felicitously at present. The "false consciousness" of the people is formed by a sufficiently diverse body of opinion that a choice of values greater than is usual among mankind gets through.

Human moral ambiguity and Christian anti-Utopianism

Christians, being concerned with men's natures, with the emotional springs of action, will apply tests to political behaviour which derive from a knowledge of moral ambiguity. They know that, as in classical political theory – in Augustine, for example – government itself is provided by God in order to curb men's evil. Christians, therefore, will begin by asking about the moral characteristics of the individuals who are influential in political society as the way of determining the real essence of their contribution. They will do this not in order to exclude – for all men are corrupt in their inner beings, Jew and Greek alike, as St. Paul said – but in order to advertise the fact of human moral frailty as a preliminary to deflating the absolute claims of political virtue. They will not be impressed by a man's idealism, as contemporary society is, but by what he is like; they will, of course, be concerned about the contents of political programmes, but that concern will itself derive from their action as citizens within the pluralism, rather than as their peculiarly *Christian* contribution to civil society. How far we are from this sort of model is seen at the present time, when it is regarded as outrageously illiberal to discriminate in political or public life on grounds of what are thought of as a person's "private" beliefs. When Mr. Foot became Leader of the British Labour Party, for example, in 1980, I scanned the papers in vain to find any reference to his religious attitudes or opinions. It is an indication of the present terms of reference in English public life that it did not occur either to those who elected him, or to those who commented in the public prints upon the choice, to regard this as an important or proper area of inquiry. In the United States, at least, there is still a surviving tradition of Christians in public life scrutinizing the religious values of those to whom the welfare of society is entrusted.

IV. CONCLUSION

I am suggesting, therefore, that political ideas will be derived by both Christians and non-Christians from a shared area of pluralism of values, but that Christians have their own, unique contribution to make, in the shaping of political society, which is derived from religious tradition and authority. It informs them about human nature and is emphatically not to be regarded as an open matter within the pluralism. One of the consequences, at least in the circumstances of present society, is that Christianity ought to operate against the enlargement of state action in response to ideology, regarding that as a threat to the survival of un-politicized, non-secular values. I think, also, that Christianity should operate primarily through other units than the state—through family life and the inter-personal relationships that are the staple matter of the morality depicted in the Gospels, the face-to-face world of the parables. Christian action there, where it is expert, will then penetrate the political and wider social realms, where it has no directive programme but from whence the threat of secular moral exclusivity is most to be apprehended. Christianity influences the world indirectly, through the loyalty it claims in the witness to higher authority in the lives of those who comprise the flawed societies of men. To the grey world of the pluralism, the Christian brings a spiritual dimension from which to regard the same body of social knowledge available to everybody else. It is, again, one of the great failings of the contemporary Church, in my judgement, that it has for years now adopted its view of man from secular morality— only to find that, having surrendered its unique spiritual authority, no one bothers to take much notice of its declamation of the humanism it has substituted.

To the confused area of competing and diverse alternatives, Christians should bring a prior knowledge, exclusively maintained, not of the arrangement of society but of men and their natures. Within the pluralism, Christians cannot claim religious authority for the programmes and ideas which the relative values of their place and generation find most compelling. But they can argue for limitations in the moral competence of political ideology, as the most authentic contribution of those who are impressed with a sense that men's more fundamental and immutable instincts will express themselves in a wide variety of political schemes. In short: the Christian activist will confront the vaunted political moralizing of contemporary society with more durable criteria for being concerned with men and their social fate. He recognizes a context for human activity which diminishes men's sense of their own competence.

NOTE

1. *Evangelism in England Today.* A Report by the Board for Mission and Unity, GS 411, May 1979, p. 12.

Comment

Walter Berns

I. THE CHRISTIAN IN POLITICS

In his paper Dr. Norman addresses the question of the proper role or place of the Christian in the politics of the contemporary Western and pluralist (or, as I should prefer to say, liberal) state. Quite properly, in my opinion, he begins by analyzing the character of this state, for the role of the actor, so to speak, will be affected by the character of the setting in which he is to act. The essential characteristic of this setting, the modern liberal state, is, he says, and I agree, its secularism; that secularism will, in large part, determine what the Christian *may* do politically. What a Christian should do is also determined by *his* essential characteristic, which is his Christian faith.

This seems self-evident, but it is not, and is not so regarded by Dr. Norman. He recognizes that there are now powerful forces in the Christian churches who are engaged in what he regards, correctly I think, as improper political activity, and that that impropriety derives from a misguided understanding of what it means to be a Christian. He devotes a section of his paper to this subject, and his discussion of it is characterized by Christian forebearance and charity, or by generosity that I can admire but not imitate.

He, for example, points to an article criticizing the practice in Southeast Asia of providing businessmen with prostitutes; the basis of the criticism is not the biblical teaching against fornication but the radical feminist teaching against "sexual imperialism." Since the article appeared in a putative religious journal, *One World,* published by the World Council of Churches, he uses it to illustrate his point that the churches, in the process of accommodating themselves to the secular world, have themselves been secularized. That, I think, is true; but, to quote Winston Churchill, it is not exhaustive. If we judge the World

Council of Churches by its activities – and Dr. Norman himself points out that we should judge a man not by what he professes to be but, rather, "by what he is like" – it bears a remarkable resemblance to a political organization, and – judging it by the company it keeps – a left-wing revolutionary political organization. Much the same thing can be said of the National Council of Churches which gives financial support to various Marxist terrorist groups.

Is "secularization" an adequate term?

To say these organizations have been secularized conceals more than it reveals. The National Council of Churches, in its official teachings, says that the people of Tanzania, Cuba, and China are all privileged to live in societies spiritually, morally, and politically superior to that of the United States. So far as I know – and I looked and waited – it uttered not one word of official protest when martial law was imposed on Poland, yet it has been voluble on the subject of Chile. Dan Berrigan, nominally a Jesuit priest, returns from Hanoi uttering praises of the "many faces of Buddha," and couples this with ridicule of his own country for taking an "infant Jesus to its religious heart, changing His underpants on major feast days," and concludes by expressing his contempt for this "religion of infants." That New England and now New York divine, the Reverend William Sloane Coffin, heir to the furniture-store fortune, says he experienced "a very special feeling for the North Vietnamese," even as they were killing his fellow citizens.[1]

These church organizations and clergy have undoubtedly been secularized, but they have also been politicized. What is more, they have a pronounced propensity for communism and communist tyrants, and one should wonder why this is so. In the space available to me, I can offer only a provisional explanation: like alienated intellectuals generally – Norman Mailer, Susan Sontag, Mary McCarthy, and so many others – they have not been so much attracted to Marxism as repelled by the bourgeois character of the liberal democracies in which they live (and to which they all return). That bourgeois or prosaic character is an outgrowth of the secularization of the West which began in the 18th century.

This secularization of the West has deeper roots than Dr. Norman recognizes, or, at least, acknowledges in his paper. He says that the separation of church and state was "originally the work of Christians themselves," a "mere device" adopted as a way of "recognizing the existence of a religious pluralism." As a description of action on the political level, that is, I concede, accurate enough, although I would point out that the champions of separation in the United States — Madison, Washington, Jefferson, for example — were not Christians, except perhaps in the most nominal of senses. Madison was a Christian in the same way that the typical Englishman today is a Christian; I mean, the person who, when applying for school admission, jots down "C of E." Washington was a Mason. Moreover, he surely did not think the American government he helped to found would "incorporate Christianity into the basis of [its] law." In his famous answer to an Address from the Hebrew Congregation of Newport, Rhode Island, he wrote as follows:

> It is now no more that tolerance is spoken of, as if it was by the indulgence of one class of people, that another enjoyed the exercise of their inherent natural rights. For happily the government of the United States, which gives to bigotry no sanction, to persecution no assistance, requires only that they who live under its protection should demean themselves as good citizens, in giving it on all occasions their effectual support.... May the children of the Stock of Abraham, who dwell in this land, continue to merit and enjoy the good will of the other inhabitants, while everyone shall sit in safety under his own vine and fig-tree, and there shall be none to make him afraid.

And Jefferson, while calling himself a Christian, denied the divinity of Jesus Christ. He was, he said, perfectly willing to attribute to Jesus "every *human* excellence," and insisted that this was all Jesus ever claimed for himself. The so-called Christians thought otherwise, he said, because they had been corrupted by the Bible.

The secular foundations of the modern state

The American Founders insisted on a separation of church and state not primarily because they wanted to accommodate the varieties of religious beliefs, but because they held it to be a self-evident truth that all men were endowed with the natural rights of life, liberty, and the idiosyncratic pursuit of happiness.[2] In the words of the Declaration of Independence, government is instituted by men (not God) in order "to secure these rights," and a government so instituted is indeed one founded on "genuinely secular moral presuppositions." I would go further, the very idea of natural rights is incompatible with Christian doctrine and, by its formulators, was understood to be incompatible. In fact, Thomas Hobbes and John Locke were enemies of all revealed religions. It is important to recognize this fact when we attempt to delineate the proper role of Christians in the secular state.

Hobbes, the first natural rights philosopher, set out to find a way of excluding intellectuals and priests from politics, or more precisely, a way of depriving them of their political influence. Citing the authority of the books they have read or the word of God which they claim to understand better than others, these men exercise what Hobbes called "private judgment" respecting the justness of the laws. And "how many rebellions hath this opinion been the cause of, which teacheth that the knowledge whether the commands of kings be just or unjust, belongs to private men, and that before they yield obedience, they not only may, but ought to dispute them?"[3] Hobbes' solution to this problem took the form of an attempt to put, for the first time, moral and political philosophy on a scientific basis, so that the political conclusions drawn from them would be indisputable. Political science would have the degree of authority attributed by all thinking men to Euclidean geometry.

Now, according to Hobbes, we can have scientific knowledge only of those subjects "of which we are the causes,"[4] or, we can understand only what we make. But we do not make the natural beings, and, among them, man himself; which, for Hobbes, had the consequence that we cannot understand men's aspirations. Thus, if there was to be a political science, it would have to be non-teleological. It would have to take its bearings from men's beginnings, not their ends, because of their ends we can know nothing. (Which is why there is such disagreement concerning ends.) But observation allows us to know that men are governed by a passionate fear of violent death and the desire to preserve themselves. Being naturally subject to no law, men have a natural right to preserve themselves and to do whatever their preservation requires. This leads to a "war of every one against every one," and the life of man is "solitary, poor, nasty, brutish, and short." The solution to this is peace, and Hobbes's first and fundamental law of nature, a law discovered by men reasoning on their natural condition, is "to seek peace, and follow it."

The state as against the church

The second law of nature is that men lay down their right "to all things" in favour of the sovereign they create.[5] His job is to preserve peace and thereby better secure men's rights, but otherwise to leave men alone to pursue those individual ends that are not incompatible with the general peace. This was formulated in our Declaration of Independence as follows: to secure the rights of life, liberty, and the pursuit of happiness (idiosyncratically defined), governments are instituted among men deriving their just powers from the consent of the governed.

The trouble with the intellectuals and priests — for Hobbes, those pests — is that they claim to *know* what happiness is and seek to have government recognize it. The priests — or perhaps I should make it clear that I am referring to all religious denominations by using the word clergy — are especially inclined to do this. Their ability to defeat Hobbes's scheme depended on their ability to persuade the people to fear what Hobbes called "the power of spirits invisible" — that is, God — more than they feared violent death. Hobbes had to declare war on the clergy, for, as I once wrote, "so long as the power of the clergy remained intact, men would continue to offer the sovereign only a conditional obedience because they would fear eternal damnation more than the sovereign's laws."[6] To destroy the clergy's political power, Hobbes set out to undermine the authority of Scripture and especially of the New Testament, wherein the proof of Jesus' authority is supplied by "the multitude of miracles he did before all sorts of people." This was necessary, he said, because "where the miracle is admitted, the doctrine cannot be rejected." Thus, Hobbes wrote a critique of "miracles, and their use," and so did those other founders of liberal democracy, Locke and Spinoza.[7] Their efforts culminated in the constitutional principle we call the separation of church and state, which, as I have written, amounts to a "subordination" of religion. The clergy could be tolerated, but only if they were kept in their subordinate place. In that place they would be entitled, along with everyone else, to one vote each; in that place, they would be required, along with everyone else, to obey *all* the laws, even if the laws were incompatible with their religious tenets.

To repeat: The foundation of this new politics, which we know as liberal democracy, was wholly secular. To what extent its philosophical and political founders (Hobbes, Locke, Spinoza, Montesquieu, *et alia,* and Jefferson, Madison, and Washington, *et alia*) expected this new order to have to depend on organized religion to perform a civilizing role in it (to teach morality to its citizens) is a complicated subject I cannot explore here. I must say, however, without any supporting argument, that to a great extent it was expected that the commercial society, built on Lockean principles by way of Adam Smith, was intended to be a substitute for morality. (Thus, I take issue with Dr. Norman where he says that capitalism is "arguably not a contributing element in the false material expectations of our Western societies." Those expectations were not false—capitalism is the greatest producer of wealth ever invented—and it was not "progressive ideologies" that gave rise to them.[8])

The political role of the Christian

I turn now to Dr. Norman's specific suggestions concerning the political role of Christians in our secular Western societies. That as voters Christians should weigh the moral qualifications of candidates for public office, I find unobjectionable. His other prescriptions I find not objectionable but more difficult than he indicates. Like him, apparently, I am convinced there is a connection between stable families and a decent civil society, as well as between stable families and a religious orientation; I therefore think Christians, as well as Jews, for example, should oppose political action calculated to be detrimental to or destructive of the family; such action would include, but not be limited to, laws permitting abortion on demand and laws permitting the public display and distribution of pornography. Unfortunately, Christian action in opposition to such laws would come into conflict with principles of the secular state as these principles are now understood.

The Christian will be told that his efforts to forbid ready abortion constitute a violation of the separation of church and state insofar as he would impose on others his Christian beliefs respecting human life. He will meet similar arguments when he advocates school prayer and when he opposes homosexual "marriage," or, for one more example, when he challenges the right of parents, with the cooperation of hospital officials, to refuse medical treatment in order to save the life of a child born with Downs syndrome.

The fact is, Western societies are honeycombed with laws and practices (Sunday closing laws, for example) that are vestiges of a presecular age. As time passes and secularism gains more supporters, these laws and practices come under increasing attack, and the attacks frequently succeed because these vestigial laws and practices do violate the principle of separation of church and state, when that principle is strictly understood. Assuming that Christians will not be able to convert the heathen, thereby reducing the number of zealous secularists who file suits in the courts and lobby the legislatures, they should attempt to persuade jurists and legislators that the perpetuation of our free societies depends on the perpetuation of these vestigial laws and practices; that these laws and practices have a civilizing influence; that, in fact, a free but wholly secular society is impossible. Such instruction might begin by pointing to the growing crime rate and continue by offering the testimony of a few thinkers who, at the beginning of the secularizing movement, warned of its consequences.

Beyond that, I issue a warning of my own: the public sphere may, as George Grant has suggested, be beyond repair, and, therefore, activity devoted exclusively to repairing it would be unavailing. Besides, there is still a private realm in the Western liberal democracies, a realm in which we can tend to the salvation of our own souls. As a friend of mine has written, the existence of this private realm "makes corruption voluntary to an appreciable degree." It is a realm where the Christian churches can do good work.

NOTES

1. For the National Council of Churches, see its pamphlet series, *People and Systems* (Friendship Press, 1975), on the United States, Canada, Tanzania, Cuba, and the People's Republic of China. On the propensity of intellectuals for communist regimes, see Paul Hollander, *Political Pilgrims: Travels of Western Intellectuals to the Soviet Union, China, and Cuba* (New York and Oxford: Oxford University Press, 1981).

2. On the religious opinions of the American Founders, see Walter Berns, *The First Amendment and the Future of American Democracy* (New York: Basic Books, 1976), ch. 1 and sources cited.

3. Hobbes, *De Cive,* Preface to the Reader (New York: Appleton Century Crofts, 1949).

4. Leo Strauss, *Natural Right and History* (Chicago: The University of Chicago Press, 1953), p. 173.

5. Hobbes, *Leviathan* (Oxford: Clarendon Press, 1958), ch. 14.

6. Walter Berns, *For Capital Punishment: Crime and the Morality of the Death Penalty* (New York: Basic Books, 1979), p. 84.

7. Walter Berns, *The First Amendment...*, p. 22.

8. See *Federalist* 10 ("the first object of government [is] the protection of different and unequal faculties of acquiring property"); Locke, *Treatises,* II ch. 5, where Locke argues that in a properly governed state (in effect, a state that promotes unlimited acquisition) the increase of wealth over what God gives men in common will be tenfold, hundredfold, thousandfold, and, he finally ends up by suggesting, that what men can produce makes God's original bounty "almost worthless" in comparison (sec. 43); and Macaulay's essay on Bacon: The aim of the ancient philosophy, he wrote, as to raise us far above vulgar wants, whereas the aim of the modern—i.e., the seventeenth century—philosophy was to satisfy our vulgar wants. "The former was noble, but the latter was attainable."

Discussion

Edited by: Kenneth G. Elzinga

Walter Berns: Dr. Norman's paper is concerned with the "proper political role of the Christian in the secular state." He then proceeds to utter some criticisms of some political activity that is now engaged in by Christian theologians; and he attributes this improper activity to the secularization of some religious organizations. As he puts it, "In the process of accommodating themselves to the secular state, these organizations, themselves, have become secularized." I think that is certainly true with respect to some of these organizations. I would then go further to say that they have become secularized in a particular manner, or in a particular direction. They have become, in some cases, practically indistinguishable, in my view, from certain left-wing political organizations.

In my paper I point out the tendency on the part of some of these groups to criticize events in Chile, but, so far as I know (and I made a point of looking for this; and I have looked through the *New York Times* index), they say nothing about the events in Poland. That raises a question, which I treat very briefly in my paper, but in fact have written on elsewhere. I mention it here only because Dr. Norman has raised the question. "Why is this so?" Why should religious groups have a kind of propensity to exonerate communism and communist tyrants.

My opinion of that is (and this, I presume, would fall into the category of a sociological explanation), that they are not so much attracted to communism, or communist tyrants, as they are repelled by the bourgeois character of the world in which they live — the world of liberal democracies. And, in this respect, they share an attitude that is widespread among intellectuals generally. One of the things revealed by the poll conducted by the Roper organization is that the professors of theology in the seminaries have political views that are practically indistinguishable from the various humanists in the university faculties with which they are associated.

Now, this has an interesting cause, I think; because the life of liberal democracies, the "bourgeois life," is a prosaic life. By that, I mean precisely prosaic; it is not poetic. And it was intended to be that way. There is something unattractive to certain persons about that kind of life. This propensity expresses itself as a contempt for businessmen in their vulgarity, and for the kinds of things they do; and I can sympathize with that contempt. These people then tend to seek out the romance or the poetic character that is missing in the liberal democracies in which they live. They attribute it to the societies with which they are not associated, and about which they know very little. Out of this, comes this tendency to idolize Castro, Che Guevara, and Ho Chi Minh. Why is it that a Roman Catholic priest should come back extolling the virtues of Ho Chi Minh, at a time when Ho Chi Minh was killing his own fellow citizens, the Catholic priest's fellow citizens?

Now, that's an interesting subject. We can perhaps talk about it. I would encapsulate what I have to say on this by saying, as I have said in print, "One can not sing about business. One can sing and write poetry about God," which, of course, is one reason why almost all the choral music is liturgical music.

I learned about this in the days when I used to sing in the Cornell chorus, which was the Cornell Glee Club, and Cornell Choir, plus odds and ends from the faculty. At the time of the Cornell centennial, the president of the university, who was a vulgar man, called the director of choral music of Cornell and said, "Now, I presume that the chorus is going to participate in the activities of the centennial next year." And that was true. "Well, I hope that you will not sing some of that church music, but that you will sing Cornell music." (laughter)

Well, the prospect of two hundred voices, up on the stage with a large orchestra, singing "Far Above Cayuga's Waters" is an absurdity. We ended up singing, of course, Beethoven's "Missa Solemnis" on this occasion; because, if you have an assembly of this size, what can you sing about, except God?

Well, that is one subject. But, in my opinion, this secularization of liberal democracy has deeper roots than Dr. Norman, in his paper at least, acknowledges. It derives from the thought of political philosophers who were enemies — and I would stress that — they were enemies of Revealed religion.

Now I won't repeat here what I have said in my paper about Hobbes, and Locke, and the American Founding Fathers, who founded the first liberal democracy. But I would direct your attention to my discussion of the Declaration of Independence, which encapsulates, in a way, much of this.

The Declaration, after referring to the various rights that men have by nature, says, "To secure these rights, governments are instituted among men, deriving their just powers from the consent of the government." And these rights are the rights of "life, liberty, and the pursuit of happiness"; and it's a happiness that is idiosyncratically defined. That is to say, "privately defined." The government has *no right,* no right to define the happiness that will be pursued by the individuals within that society.

Now, the trouble with intellectuals and priests, according to the Founders, (or, for Hobbes, who referred to them as "pests"), is that they claim to *know* what happiness is. And they seek to have the government recognize it, and somehow pursue it in this public sense. And that causes the animosity between Hobbes' priests and lawyers, on the one hand, and civil society. So he sought an arrangement that would minimize their influence within civil society. And I discussed in my paper that the three principal political philosophers of liberal democracy who set down the foundation, the principles of it—Hobbes, Locke and Spinoza, each of them wrote a critique of miracles. Each of them wrote that critique for the purpose of undermining the authority of the clergy; and I indicate why they thought they could do that.

The consequence of this was that the clergy could be tolerated, in the civil society. But they would have only one vote each, and no other authority. And from there, we get into the problem of Archbishop Hunthausen.

One final statement here: The point I would stress is that the foundation of this new politics is *more* secular than Dr. Norman recognizes, it seems to me. The next question is whether a society built on such principles can sustain itself. Or to put this in terms of Locke, whether a Lockean society can be sustained, if it consists solely of Lockean men. And people like Rousseau, among others, said that is not going to be possible. That raises, then, the question as to whether the clergy do not have some role to play—a civilizing role to play—to make even a Lockean society possible.*

Geoffrey Brennan: As I understand it, and I might be misreading Walter Berns here, for somebody who feels himself to have strong libertarian tendencies, and to be a self-styled Christian, the sort of position that Walter is putting forth here is profoundly disturbing, to say the least. Because he seems to be arguing that Christianity and libertarianism are really incompatible, in some sort of fundamental, subliminal sense. Or that libertarianism logically requires a moral relativism, at least over an enormous range of issues—perhaps all those excluding the virtues of freedom.

I am reminded of an article in *Daedelus* by a colleague of Edward Norman's, Shirley Letwin, in which she attempts to argue a very strong connection between a certain strand of theological understanding, starting before Augustine and through to Hobbes, which is entirely faithful to liberal ideals. I cannot spell out the details of that line of argument, but I think it's important to acknowledge that, although Hobbes was anti-clerical, so were many Christians in important respects. Hobbes was in some ways anti-Aristotelian and anti-scholastic;

---

*Dr. Norman contributed a paper to the conference, but was unable to attend and therefore could not participate in the ensuing discussion—eds.

but I don't think that makes him anti-Christian. And I think one would have to be very careful of using Hobbes as evidence for the incompatibility of a libertarian position and a Christian position.

Ronald Preston: On this present matter, two things. One is, I'm not so worried when somebody sees a type of Christian attitude, or body, or institution, as indistinguishable from some secular one. I say to Christians, it's foolish to try to say something distinctive that nobody else could possibly have said—particularly in a plural society. It becomes extremely important that Christians should, as a contribution to helping societies work, find ways of saying things which are consistent with our own integrity, but also relate to positions held by others.

Many humanists in Western society are really Christian humanists. I am not trying to put a label on them that they wouldn't wish. They have come out of a Judeo-Christian-Greek civilization, where these things have been held together for centuries, and have taken over a common understanding of what it is appropriate to think about human beings, or how human beings ought to be treated, or how they ought to behave, which is consistent with the Christian view. So Christians and humanists often find themselves overlapping. And, personally, if I can find allies in some cause that I think important at the moment, then I am very happy to have allies wherever they may be.

The second related point is one that is being raised acutely by someone like Fred Hirsch in his book, *The Social Limits to Growth,* which I think is a very important book in its own way, and that is: where is the source of disinterested goodwill in advanced industrial societies? He asks this on the presumption that if there is not some source of this disinterested goodwill, in the end you cannot maintain the social fabric. Also, this argument is saying that traditional religion is disintegrated so that it is no longer a convincing source, that there is not enough left in religion—even in sectarian religion—to provide a sufficient supply of disinterested goodwill; that the kind of people who talk about economic philosophy, and so on, pay no attention to this, and do nothing to cultivate it, and even possibly undermine it. So we are left with something rather vague to fall back on, like a sense of "civic virtue," or something like that, as the only possible source we can see. The question is whether this is likely to be sufficient or not. This is a very important and serious question which anybody concerned with the stability and maintenance of the economic, social, and political institutions of an advanced industrial society must take seriously.

Paul Heyne: I have a point that bears on Walter Berns' speculation about why churchmen prefer politics of the left. I recount my own experience. I used to have strong leftist sympathies.

One of the reasons that I believed I had an obligation to be more sympathetic to the left than to the right was the principle that a Christian confesses his own sins; he doesn't call attention to the sins of others. I discovered, eventually, that I was fooling myself. Whether this autobiographical account applies to anyone else, I don't know; but I suspect it does. "I have sinned," is confession, and that's good because it leads to forgiveness. It opens the possibility for forgiveness. To say, "You have sinned," can also be good, provided you are willing to stay and follow that up. But to say, "You have sinned," and then to run away, is wrong. To say, "They have sinned," seems to me always to be inappropriate.

Now, here's the catch. What church groups like to do is say, "We have sinned." And what that actually means is that all those have sinned who don't agree that we have sinned. It sounds like *we* have sinned. It's actually *they* have sinned. I cannot read anybody else's motives. But I know I used to do this. I used to go to meetings where we would pass resolutions, "*We* deplore the racism of *our* society. *We...*"

President Kennedy's death had a traumatic effect on me; right after it I led a religious service in which "we" confessed our guilt. I later realized what I was doing there. I was really passing a strange sort of judgement on all kinds of groups in society of which I did not approve. I think there is something to that explanation of the "friendliness toward our enemies."

Walter Block: While we are reminiscing about why we used to be open to views on the left, I'd like to give my views on that. And I'd say in one sense, I have changed my mind. In another sense, I have not. Before I took up the study of economics, I used to be very leftist, very socialist oriented, because I believed that if the free market operated, the poor would get poorer, the rich would get richer; eventually the poor would all die; and the specter of poor, little, skinny children screaming with hunger just bothered me; and I figured it was time to be a socialist. Amazingly enough, I have learned. My experience was not President Kennedy's death, but was rather meeting Ayn Rand, and reading her books, which disabused me of that, and I started reading Hazlitt and Mises and Friedman, and, it was a downward path from then on.

There's another sense, though, in which I was and am still very sympathetic to the views of the left, and that is their passion for justice—not social justice, not "positive rights," or "rights to food, clothing, and shelter"; but rather the thing that we were talking about in the last session. They are taking up the cause of the native peoples in Canada and the United States who had their land stolen from them. The case of the peons who are forced to work on the latifundi in South America. Some leftists even support Malcom X's Republic of New Africa. This is the idea that when the blacks were set free, they should have been given the land on which they were forced to work. Instead, their rightful property was never returned to them, in any way, manner, shape or form. With the end of slavery, all they were given was a cessation of injustice. But, justice for many people on the left requires much more than that—namely a return of stolen property.

Many people on the left are not at all sympathetic to the marketplace, because they see it as a champion of the *status quo;* and they see the *status quo,* in many ways, as unjust. And that is why I think that many of them are sympathetic to Marxism; I think, tragically so. We have to really come to grips with and face this fact: that part of the reason our views on the free market are not seen as acceptable is because people interpret capitalism, or the free market, as businessmen grabbing property illegitimately. Advocates of free enterprise must make it clear that they favour the return of stolen property—even when such transfers would be at the expense of people calling themselves businessmen.

Arthur Shenfield: I think that Walter Berns' account of the reasons for the views of the churches, and clerics, is probably correct—perhaps more than that. One might put it higher. But it may possibly be wrong. Are we to assume, without considering it further, that these views and attitudes will never pass, that they are inherent in the character of churches and clerics, and therefore will go on and on without changing?

After all, as Paul Heyne has shown, in a previous paper,* that in the first half of the nineteenth century there were Christian economists and clerics who sang the praises of the free market economy. They didn't last, of course. It was a very brief phase in the views of the

---

*"Clerical *Laissez-Faire:* A Study in Theological Economics" in *Religion, Economics and Social Thought,* edited by Walter Block and Irving Hexham forthcoming from The Fraser Institute—eds.

churches and clerics. But if you talk to free market economists now, they will probably say to you that, though of course the ideas of the free market can hardly be found among politicians, journalists, and television pundits, at the deeper levels of opinion formation, these ideas are in the ascendant. For example, it is hard to find any economist of quality, of any standing, under the age of forty, who now believes in economic planning, or in Keynesianism for that manner. In short, the free market economists are winning. If they are winning, then we are really postulating that in perhaps another twenty-five years' time, the politicians, the television pundits, and journalists, will all have picked up their ideas; and once again, they will be truly in the ascendant. In that case, won't the clerics also, perhaps, follow? Aren't they also second hand retailers of ideas? Is it not possible that the pendulum will swing again? I am not forecasting this, but is it impossible?

James Wall: I particularly appreciate Walter Block's comment on compassion, because I recognize the church more there than I do in Walter Berns' view. I just don't recognize the church I know in his disquisitions about the National Council of Churches, and the various denominations being so pro-communist. I find that to be so extravagantly incorrect, as to not even be able to deal with it.

So, I think I ought to echo what Walter Block has said: yes, there may be a misunderstanding of the free market in that the churches feel the free market does not permit those who are in poverty to emerge from it. That may be the fault of the interpreters of the free market. It is certainly not a pronounced propensity for communism that makes the liberal churches concerned for the welfare of the poor.

I recognize what Walter Berns is citing here. I know that's a rather prevailing view that there's all kind of communist orientation in the various mainline churches. As indicated in my paper, the *Reader's Digest* has produced a hatchet job which they call, "Karl Marx or Jesus Christ?" which is incredibly inaccurate, incredibly Joe McCarthyist in its approach to the subject. It just isn't accurate.

Edmund Opitz: Businessmen tend to be a rather prosaic crowd compared to people in other occupations. In response to that, it's possible that we, who like to make free market affirmations, tend to overstate the case for the market. But the market's role is comparatively narrow. It is certainly not the arbiter of truth, beauty and goodness.

Consider the most popular play on Broadway — a box office success. The fact that the play makes money tells us nothing about its literary or dramatic merit. The fact that a book makes the best seller list week after week may have nothing to do with its literary merit — maybe quite the reverse. There are other canons of judgement that we have to employ to determine the literary merit of a novel, or poem, or drama, or whatever.

I believe in a free market for books; but I realize that if I were to judge the validity of economic ideas by the marketplace, the books of Galbraith and Samuelson sell in astronomical figures compared to the books of, say, Mises and Hayek. Nevertheless, I will maintain under oath that Hayek and Mises as economists are a million light years ahead of Galbraith and Samuelson.

So the market has the very narrow function to provide for our creaturely needs. It's something like (as I have said earlier) our digestive processes — very important in their own capacity, but I never was completely sold on the idea of D. H. Lawrence that the seat of our thought is the solar plexis, or anything of that sort. All I am saying is that the market we talk about as an important and essential element of a free society has a limited but nevertheless very vital role to play; and that there is room for other standards. It implies the necessity of other standards to test the truth, the goodness, the beauty of the things outside the realm of economic computation.

Geoffrey Brennan: Just a very small semantic point, but I think most often when people talk about totalitarianism, we keep slipping in the words (and I have heard Paul Heyne do it, I think, and Walter Block as well), "the left." Libertarians need to remind ourselves, the left and the right can be equal enemies. You know, there's a strong tradition of totalitarianism from the right, which I think is susceptible to the anxieties that Walter Berns is alluding to, and I think that we give a strange sort of bias to the remarks we make if we pretend that the only danger is from the World Council of Churches. To say that Poland or Russia is bad is not to justify South Africa at all. I think we have to be very even handed on this.

Walter Berns: I would like to reply to Jim Wall's point, because it challenges me. But it seems to me he attributes to me statements that I didn't make. I was rather specific, I thought, as to my accusations. I was referring, of course, precisely to Dan Berrigan; and I could have gone on then to raise the question as to why his Provincial didn't read him out of the order, or why they greeted him with open arms.

I made a specific reference to the National Council of Churches because they did indeed say what I attribute to them, that the people of Tanzania, Cuba, and China are all privileged to live in societies spiritually, morally, and politically superior to that of the United States. I didn't make any charges about the mainline churches, or of clergy in general. I made some specific charges here, and I will stand by them.

James Wall: Maybe we don't need to take a lot of time to keep saying this, but you cited one document that was published in 1975 that does not represent the official position of the National Council of Churches, as far as I know. Then you did say, this indicates a "pronounced propensity to communism." It just seems to me that sort of linkage is a bit of a strain. That was the only reason I was lifting that up.

Philip Wogaman: My desire initially was to speak essentially to that same point, and to say two things. First, that over a period of some twenty years, I have had a lot of contact with the National Council of Churches, serving on three of its substantial committees, and studying its work, making some use of its work, and, somewhat more removed, studying the work of the World Council of Churches. I find myself, sometimes, in a "lover's quarrel" with these organizations. I am sometimes in sharp disagreement with positions taken. Currently, I am involved in a little bit of back and forth with some people in the National Council of Churches over the infant formula issue, just as one example. But, I think were his paper to be printed in its present form, with these rather flat-footed statements, the impression is given that Walter Berns shares the view that these organizations, as a whole, really are defined by a strong propensity to support communism and communist tyrants. And I think that view is wrong.

It helps to understand the character of both the National Council of Churches and World Council of Churches. These are the responsible bodies of large numbers of substantial denominations. They are a creature of the mainline churches for the United States, in the case of the NCC; and the World Council of Churches, of course, involves churches everywhere. They bring into their life the tensions and the problems of a whole troubled world; and rarely does this come out very neatly. Sometimes it comes out rather conservatively. But I hope, before standing behind a statement like this, you will make sure that your database is a little broader than I think it is here.

The other point I wanted to raise, is on an entirely different front: on the role of the clergy and the secular state. I think I am in whole-hearted agreement that a secular state such as ours does not formally accord special status to clergy. It is "one person, one vote." But, of course, everybody is in a position to influence as many other votes as possible. Now, the archbishop of Seattle is not suddenly acquiring the opportunity to cast more than one vote against a nuclear submarine. No doubt his influence will be greatly magnified by the number of people who wish to give special weight to his views. But isn't that true of a lot of other people? That was true of John Wayne; that's true of Jane Fonda—to cite persons at opposite ends of the spectrum. Why on earth anybody would consider a movie star of right, or left, or centre, a fit guide in political matters is utterly beyond me. But large numbers of people do take them seriously; and I guess Machiavelli makes the point in a little different language, that anything really that can influence the "will" of people is potentially political.

A secular state is one that insists that *a priori* nobody's voice be weighted. And that probably is what you're saying. I just want to add that further expansive footnote on it.

David Friedman: I am not personally involved in any of these disputes about whether the National Council of Churches is or is not a minion of the devil. So I am curious about the facts; and I'd like at some point a response on the facts from the people on the, loosely speaking, pro-National Council of Churches side.

And the question is: Is it in fact true that the National Council of Churches has, in some sense, publicly and several times condemned the coup against Allende and that it has not publicly condemned the imposition of martial law in Poland? Is it in fact true that its public documents speak as though Cuba and China were reasonably civilized free countries—certainly not substantially worse than America—whereas South Africa is a terrible country?

If those statements are correct, then I would say that the description of it as "left leaning," or as "turning a blind eye to the evils of communism," or something like that, would be accurate. If not, it is not. It's a question of fact; and maybe someone can just answer with one word. Aside from all the interpretations, are these particular factual allegations correct?

James Wall: Not quite. First of all, as Phil Wogaman has already pointed out, the National Council is a small United Nations in the

U.S. with enormous and complicated representation. They have a very set rule that they will pass resolutions only under laborious procedures; and only resolutions that are officially adopted are considered official statements of the National Council. I cannot lift out documents. I do not think that the statements you've asked about are found in official NCC documents. The reference that is cited about Tanzania, Cuba and China, with which I suspect very few participants in the NCC would be sympathetic, apparently was in a study book of some sort. I'm not even sure where it was. It really cannot even be considered official. So, the answer to your question is, it's such an elaborate system in choosing resolutions, and approving resolutions, that I doubt that you would find one that would deal with any of those accusations you've just made.

Walter Berns: The statement with repect to the spiritual, moral, and political superiority of Tanzania, Cuba and China comes from the book cited — that was, an official book that was distributed under the aegis of the National Council of Churches, carrying the imprimatur of that organization; and I conclude that that is a position with which the Council has somehow associated itself.

With respect to the solidarity business, I did indeed look, as I indicated, through the *New York Times* index to see whether I had missed something; and I did not find any statement of the National Council of Churches condemning the events in Poland. Whereas I went back and found a whole series of official statements with respect to the Allende coup; and I draw conclusions from that fact.

What has the National Council of Churches, or the World Council of Churches, had to say about the plight of the various Christians in Lebanon? There has been support after support for PLO terrorism in one form or another. Now, I draw conclusions from that as well. And then I could also discuss El Salvador and the activities of the Maryknoll priests and nuns, and so forth and so on. And I come to a certain conclusion that, to put it this way, I sometimes wonder whether the mainline churches that collect our widows' mites are aware of what is being done with those widows' mites when a certain portion of them are handed over to the National Council.

Philip Wogaman: Well, to answer the Polish question: the president of the National Council of Churches, Bishop James Armstrong, has explicitly, publicly, and vigorously, condemned the invasion of Poland — that is, not the invasion, but the events in Poland. I don't

know what the character of statements may be on that. That would be
an interesting study.

Now two other quick points. One of them is I think I see a moral
distinction between commenting as a National Council of Churches,
on those areas of foreign policy where decisions taken by the United
States are pertinent, and those areas where they may not be. Some
kinds of things affecting, say, Czechoslovakia, or Poland, or the
Soviet Union may not be terribly pertinent to U.S. policy. They may
be, but I think that distinction needs to be borne partly in mind.

On the other point, I sit on the Committee of Religious Liberty of
the National Council of Churches. It is concerned with civil libertarian
questions—the protection of democracy in its various forms in the
United States. I can testify that in that committee, over a period of
years, there has been, what I take to be, a very even-handed support of
the right of people in our society—regardless of their point of view:
left, right, centre. Most of them are groups with which members of the
National Council of Churches wouldn't be terribly in sympathy, like
the Unification Church, for example. But where it is a matter of protecting their civil rights, it is felt by the National Council of Churches
that it has a responsibility to be protector.

Now, I guess my plea is: see the vastness in the diversity of this organization. Don't let a study book, or even one single range of questions, determine your attitude toward this large organization.

David Friedman: One thing I wanted to say goes back to the question
which Arthur Shenfield raised. To what degree is the hypothetical left-
wing bias of the church inevitable and natural? And there are two
things that I have wanted to say and haven't had a chance to raise.
They involve two writers I am very fond of—G. K. Chesterton and
C. S. Lewis.

Chesterton was, I would suppose, the most influential Catholic
apologist for a period of twenty years or so in England. He was also a
libertarian—a libertarian of a very peculiar sort. I would say a libertarian heretic. But, nonetheless, he was one of *our* heretics, not one of
somebody else's heretics. He clearly regarded his views as closely inte-
grated, and he attempted, unsuccessfully, to found a political movement which was in some sense a rather odd, and heretical, but nonetheless libertarian movement. So that suggests that there are poten-
tials, at least, for Christianity and libertarian views to go hand in
hand.

The other thing has to do with C. S. Lewis. It is my impression that he wasn't enormously interested in politics. What struck me about him was that his theology was, in a certain sense, profoundly libertarian. One of the most serious problems for a Christian apologist is to explain how it can be that the world is run by a benevolent and omnipotent God, and nonetheless it is full of pain, unhappiness, starvation, and so forth. And on that, Lewis's answer, as I interpret it, was that God is a libertarian. He could have made us all do virtuous things and be happy; however, he deemed that virtuous robots are inferior to imperfect free men; and he therefore chose to create, in some fundamental sense, a free society.

It would seem to me, from that viewpoint, one ought to be very sympathetic with the idea that we should imitate God's restraint, that we should try to persuade people to be virtuous, and be virtuous ourselves, but not go around saying to people, "You should be generous and I'll put you in jail if you're not." And in that sense, it seems to me, there are several pieces of evidence suggesting that Christianity, or at least some varieties of Christianity, could be very congruent with a libertarian approach.

Roger Shinn: As an abstract ethical principle, I think the church should not employ a double standard. If it is going to criticize violations of human rights, it should do it across the board, and not have any favourites.

I'd make two observations of a concrete form. First, in looking at the publications of church agencies, there should be a very scrupulous distinction between official teachings and documents circulated. Some church agencies circulate a variety of documents for educational purposes. Like the op-ed page of a newspaper, they are not official policy. Now, if the documents circulated are all on one side, that shows something too. But any selection better be a careful one, unless they are official pronouncements, of which there are rather few.

The other comment I'd make is that in practice, when my children were young and at home, I was much more critical of their misbehaviour than of a lot of kids around the neighbourhood who were misbehaving more than they. I expect my wife both to support me and criticize me more cogently than all the males around the neighbourhood. And at a certain point, the church feels a responsibility to criticize its own.

My own opinion is that the tyranny of North Korea is worse than that of South Korea; but it's my friends who are in jail in South Korea.

It's the American army that is visible in South Korea. I move around South Korea and see an image of my country and my church and so I talk more about violations of human rights in South Korea than in North Korea.

I think, concretely, there are reasons for this. In the case of North Korea, I just think I have no influence at all there. Again, consider the case of South Africa, where crimes are being perpetrated by a country that purports to be almost a theocracy, endorsed (well, less and less, I am glad to say) by clergy and by officials of the church. I think the church should pay more attention there than to the Soviet Union, where the leaders are declared atheists, and our opinion doesn't have any particular relevance. So, concretely, I think there is room for a certain occasionalism; though I believe we ought to check ourselves again and again against the universal principle.

Kenneth Boulding: Just one final word on this. Remember the wonderful remark of Pogo, the comic strip character, "We have met the enemy and he is us." This has struck me here. As you know, I have been a little uncomfortable here, really. This isn't the kind of group I am usually in; but I have had a good time, and it worries me, though I am no friend of socialist societies, and I am certainly no Marxist. I was a socialist until I read Marx at age 20, incidentally, and that cleared that up. (laughter)

And so I have a great deal of sympathy with the general position of this group; but I feel uneasy that we may be our own worst enemy. I think of contrasting the old National Association of Manufacturers and the National Industrial Conference Board, which commanded no respect among the economics profession, with the Committee for Economic Development. The CED has had a very remarkable impact on this country because, I think, it has standards of integrity, you see, which the NAM really didn't. And that's why the NAM was one of its own worst enemies, in that regard.

Now we have the same problem in my own Society of Friends. We don't have any clergy, in the type I belong to. But we do have the American Friends Service Committee, with which I have been having quite a row. I feel it has been captured by a rather alien ideology and it hasn't really worked out the real implications of its own faith. Part of the reason for this is what I call the Band-Aid complex. We are terribly afraid of being a Band-Aid. We want to solve all these problems, and really, really solve them once and for all. This is maybe a little spiritual pride. I think this is where some of the leftishness comes from, that is, from the feeling that you shouldn't just palliate. You should solve all these problems. When one feels that way, very often, well almost universally, one seems to me to do more harm than good. You get trapped in the inadequate use of the words, and inadequate ideologies or even inadequate theologies.

I think the question Walter Berns raised is very important. Another of my old teachers was Joseph Schumpeter. I still think his book *Capitalism, Socialism, and Democracy* is about the best book of the century on these things. Schumpeter was a great admirer of capitalism, but he thought it wouldn't last, because it couldn't really develop the legitimacies which would sustain it; these were derived from an earlier period.

I am not at all sure he was right about that. But on the other hand, the way you develop legitimacies is a very tricky question. Here again, as I was saying earlier, we have to be sensitive to the pathologies. We mustn't assume that anything is black and white here. Everything will have its problems; and we have to be very honest about this.

Ronald Preston: To return to Edward Norman's paper, he does, in the end, say that there is a political responsibility for Christians; but finally, towards the very end, he also says that the main thing that the Christian should do is to test the moral characteristic of individuals, to determine the essence of their contribution.

This seems to me to be the old, evangelical, simplification because we all know that Christians of impeccable moral integrity can be very blind to things that are under their nose. They can be very unjust and they can pursue mistaken policies. And often people whose moral character one has suspicions about, come up with policies which, in the situation under discussion, seem to be more adequate. So, I think it is very revealing that such an inadequate conclusion should come from this paper.

Walter Berns: I think there is a basic tension between Christianity and the libertarian society. I think, for example (in fact, I would assert), that the basis of this libertarian society we have is to be found in Hobbes; and that it is to be found in the notion of a state of nature; and a state of nature is simply incompatible with Christian doctrine — and from that, various things do flow.

But evidence, with respect to this tension, if not incompatibility (incompatibility, I think, is too strong a word, but the tension is there), is to be found in the behaviour of Christian churches. When liberal democracies came into the world, the Christian churches of Europe opposed them.

Ron Preston talked about the sources of goodwill; and that, I think, was in response to my point that the churches have to provide a civilizing function for these Lockean men — otherwise the Lockean society itself cannot exist. That is certainly something that I agree with altogether. Jefferson, towards the end of his life, said he hoped that every young man now alive would die a Unitarian. And I think what he had in mind was that very point.

Overview

John C. Bennett

I. INTRODUCTION

The project that gave rise to the Fraser Institute symposium and to the papers published in this volume was the result of concern on the part of those who strongly believe in the superiority of the market system, which some of them call "Democratic Capitalism," when they observe that there is quite a pervasive tendency in the churches, both Protestant and Catholic, to criticize that system. It is often said that these criticisms imply a preference for some form of socialism. Those who are responsible for this project seek to understand why here should be so much opposition in the churches to their ideological convictions and they have in their chapters attacked their theological critics.

Personal predispositions

I think that I should explain the place where I stand as I read these chapters. There is no uncertainty as to where Michael Novak stands as the author of *The Spirit of Democratic Capitalism* and of many articles on the subject in a great variety of journals. I was asked to write this overview because for more than forty years I have participated in the formulation of much of the thinking in Protestant ecumenical circles which is now in dispute. My presuppositions and the direction of my own thinking are in line with the moderate interpretations of the criticisms of capitalism which most of these writers regard as a threat to their own positions. I have taught Christian theology and ethics for many years and I have been influenced by both the American Protestant Social Gospel and by the Christian realism of Reinhold Niebuhr. I was in an earlier period a Christian socialist, preferring the label socialist Christian, but since about 1950 I have ceased to be a dogmatic socialist and am among those who, while agreeing with some of the socialist criticisms of capitalism, give weight to the pluralism and the incentives for efficiency and productivity which are characteristic of it, and also to the market as the best method of discovering what the desires of consumers are.[1]

Wogaman and the response

The only full length presentation of the position, which is the object of criticism in this book, is the paper by Philip Wogaman though its presuppositions are supported by Roger Shinn's interpretation of biblical ethics. I find Wogaman's paper to be an excellent statement of the criticisms of capitalism that are widespread among theologians and in corporate statements of churches, but I think Wogaman's critics exaggerate the extent to which he is committed to socialism as a total system. I shall say more about that later. I think that the paper that represents the best mediating position is the one by Kenneth Boulding. He has worked with the groups in the churches that have produced the criticisms of capitalism but he obviously has a firm commitment to the market system though, unlike most other writers in this book, he emphasizes the pathology in that system. There are raw materials for criticisms of the consumerism of capitalism and its effect on the quality of life in Mishan's chapter but he traces the sources of the evil that he recognizes to technology, rather than to capitalism and he is right in seeing the same tendencies in socialistic societies.

My comments on the tendency of critics to drive Wogaman more fully into the socialist camp than seems to me to be accurate lead me to call attention to some overlapping between the two sides which are in conflict in this book. Many of those who are the strongest defenders of capitalism accept elements of the welfare state even though they may do so more grudgingly than I would do. This is especially true of Novak's *The Spririt of Democratic Capitalism* which was written to achieve the same result as was the intention of the initiators of this project. Walter Block in his very polemical comments on Wogaman's views does make some concessions in supporting services by government which society needs but which the market cannot effectively provide. He greatly stresses the limited role of government but opposes what he calls "free market anarchism." I find no place in what he writes for what in the United States is called by conservatives "the safety net" which provides maintenance and medical care and other life-supporting services to the "truly needy." Perhaps in Canada this is so taken for granted that it does not need to be stated. In the United States the safety net admitted in principle has so many holes in practise that emphasis on a more adequate safety net is central in the political debate. Dr. Block is so afraid of any governmental encouraging of equality that he backs off from any redistribution of wealth that is not voluntary. The other critic of Wogaman, Professor Cooper, is another mediator and he says that democratic capitalists claim the New Deal. He goes so far as to say that "If Wogaman means by 'democratic socialism' the mixed economies of Western Europe and Israel, for example, then we could all be democratic socialists." That goes beyond the views held by many other writers but this is in line with much that Novak says in his book: i.e., that it is difficult to distinguish modern democratic socialism from democratic capitalism.[2]

Some theological motifs — the relevance of sin

There is throughout this book an interesting mixture of religious or theological motifs and economic-political motifs. Most of the writers who are critical of the teachings in mainline churches are themselves committed Christians and in various ways their theological views influence their economic-political judgements. I detect a strain in several of the papers of a rather conservative Lutheranism that reflects the "two realms" doctrine interpreted in a dualistic fashion in contrast to the view of many contemporary Lutherans who stress the interaction, even inter-penetration of the two realms.[3] One sees these effects in the tendency to emphasize action by individual Christian citizens and to play down action by churches, in the tendency to accuse those who stress Christian social action of Utopianism involving failure to recognize the limits of human action because of the depth and universality of sin, and to criticize especially Christian commitment to secular goals. What is most emphasized in some cases is criticism of what are believed to be distortions of Christian faith itself. Those who have this as their main interest are not necessarily Lutherans in denominational connection. Probably Edward R. Norman more than any other writer focuses on what he regards as false understandings of Christian faith itself.

Christian teaching about human finiteness and the depth and pervasiveness of sin can be used to support both opposing tendencies in this book. One of the chief sources of differences of view is the perception that one has of the relative importance of the diverse uses of this aspect of Christian teaching. It can be used to defend the view that the creativity and the dynamism of capitalism depend on the motive of seeking one's own advantage on many levels including the search for profit in the technical sense. Socialists may have been too confident that less self-centred motives such as the desire to serve and the creative urge itself would be sufficient to make the economy dynamic and innovative. There are other selfish motives such as seeking for social approval or prestige or power and the question would be raised by critics of the emphasis on profit without limit that there may be diminishing returns from this motive after a person has achieved considerable financial success. On the other hand, Christian teaching about sin warns against the concentrations of private power that are not accountable to the public. Yet that same warning can be used against centralization of power in the state.

Reinhold Niebuhr always used the Christian teaching about human nature against the Utopian tendency in Marxism but, while he abandoned his earlier belief in a socialist system he was always left of centre in his criticisms of the practices of capitalism, and he gave support to the general tendencies in the churches which are opposed in this book. I think that he never abandoned the belief that systems of justice should stand under the criticism of the idea of equality, that while there should be no attempt to develop complete equality by regimentation, the burden of proof was on inequalities.

I think that one general conclusion that can be drawn is that Christian teaching about finiteness and sin provides warnings against both a consistent socialism and a consistent faith in the market economy. Roger Shinn quotes Archbishop Temple's statement that "the art of government in fact is the art of so ordering life that self-interest prompts what justice demands." That is a good application of Christian realism but Temple was himself a moderate socialist and one of the inspirers of the teaching in the churches critical of capitalism. Reinhold Niebuhr often spoke in these terms using the idea that self-interest needed to be "beguiled" into serving the common good. Yet those who speak about sin warn about the tendency of capitalism to intensify self-interest and to tempt those who hold private economic power to abuse their power.

II. SOURCES OF THE CRITICISMS OF CAPITALISM IN THE CHURCHES

I am puzzled that some of these writers feel that they have to go out of their way to explain the trend in the teaching in the churches which troubles them. As an extreme example I refer to Professor Brennan who thinks that the "church will direct its preaching to players in politics rather than the economic game" because according to his ingenious argument the political game is cheaper than the economic game. I think that both Wogaman and Shinn point to the ultimate sources of the theological criticism of capitalism in biblical teaching about justice and in the emphasis of Jesus upon the victims of society. Believers in the near moral self-sufficiency of capitalism contend that these sources do not give support to the criticism of capitalism if its capacity for productivity for the benefit of the whole society is adequately appreciated. However, as many Christian thinkers have considered the actual human results of the industrial revolution under capitalist auspices they came to the conclusion that the human cost had in reality been far too great and that either there must be drastic reforms of capitalism or movement toward some form of socialism.

The Catholic tradition on capitalism

Roman Catholic thought, while it rejected Socialism because of its Marxist connections, because of fear of over-emphasis on central control by the state, never fully accepted the presuppositions and structures of capitalism. From the encyclicals of Leo XIII in the last decades of the nineteenth century to the encyclicals of John XXIII, Paul

VI and John Paul II there was a development of thought that became more and more deeply critical of capitalism. I think that the encyclical of Paul VI, *Populorum Progressio,* is probably the most radical in its implications. In his Letter celebrating the 80th anniversary of the chief social encyclical of Leo XIII, entitled *Octogesima Adveniens* Pope Paul went so far as to maintain neutrality as between a reformed capitalism and socialism. Previously the Catholic rejection of socialism had often meant political opposition to moderate socialist parties in Europe. Catholic response to the oppressive effects of a combination of feudal and capitalistic institutions in Latin America gave rise to Liberation Theology which has great strength in many Latin American countries and has been an inspiration to Christian thinkers both Catholic and Protestant on other continents.[4]

The Protestant position

Protestantism in contrast to Catholicism is often believed to have given religious and moral support to capitalism but late in the nineteenth century much Protestant thinking moved away from this. Most of the best known Protestant theologians in the first half of this century were Christian socialists. That was true of Karl Barth, Paul Tillich, Reinhold Niebuhr for several decades, Walter Rauschenbusch, the chief theologian of the American Social Gospel, and Archbishop William Temple. I do not know that Emil Brunner, who had more influence on this continent than Karl Barth, ever considered himself a socialist but he was a very strong anti-capitalist, saying of capitalism that it was "irresponsibility developed into a system."

In one of the most important volumes on Christian social ethics in the first half of this century, *The Divine Imperative,* Brunner said the following about capitalism:

> Capitalism is such a perversion of the divine order of creation, that we would feel obliged to assert its economically ruinous character even if — certainly the contrary is the case — all the experts were to say the opposite. An economic system which contradicts the divine order to such an extent *must* prove the ruin of the people; this is a fact which none can gainsay. Here we are dealing not with technical questions but with the fundamental ethical question: can we as Christians affirm a system which, as such, in its very foundations, is opposed to morality?[5]

I quote Brunner, a Swiss Protestant, because for several decades he was one of the most influential Protestant theologians in this country, and socially more conservative than the others whom I have named. Any Protestant who was studying theology in Western Europe or North America a generation ago, unless he was in a very conservative theological school, would have studied one or more of these thinkers.

The conference that met in Oxford on "Church Community and State" in 1937 summarized very widely held ecumenical positions and it prepared the way in its thinking on economic ethics for the first Assembly of the World Council of Churches that met in Amsterdam in 1948. The Oxford Conference refused to identify the Christian faith with either capitalism or socialism but it offered four criticisms of what it called "the economic order of the industrialized world" which in effect meant capitalism. These four criticisms are all expressed by Wogaman in his own way. I mention them to indicate how pervasive this kind of thinking was as early as 1937 and hence its presence today calls for no ingenious explanations. They are as follows: the tendency of this economy to enhance acquisitiveness; its tendency to create what are called "shocking inequalities"; its tendency to develop what is called the "irresponsible possession of economic power"; its tendency to frustrate the sense of Christian vocation both because participants in the economy realize that they are working for someone's profit and not directly for the public good and because too often they are unemployed. The Amsterdam Assembly substantially repeated these four criticisms of capitalism, using that label as Oxford did not do, and added to them the statement that "It has also kept the people of capitalist countries subject to a kind of fate which has taken the form of mass unemployment."[6]

The Assembly also criticized communism more fundamentally than it criticized capitalism but it also said that "Christians who are beneficiaries of capitalism should try to see the world as it appears to many who know themselves excluded from its privileges and who see in communism a means of deliverance from poverty and insecurity." The Assembly faced both directions in its criticisms. On the one hand it criticized the "new forms of injustice and oppression" in communist nations. On the other hand it said that some of the false teaching of communism, especially its atheism, are in part a reaction to the chequered record of a professedly Christian society." No representative Christian teaching has given religious support to communism. The Liberation Theologians now, and Reinhold Niebuhr and many others in the 1930s, have appropriated in a selective way some aspects of the Marxist analysis of society but they have not given positive religious support to communism as a political system. They have in some situations tolerated it under necessity.

I have gone into all of this, which is supported by much of the historical material in the companion volume, to show two things. First, that those who are committed to the claims for the market economy are correct in realizing that very pervasive teaching in the churches is critical of any views of the system which tend to regard that system as morally self-sufficient. Second, to show that, when those who support the market economy attempt to account for this teaching, their explanations do not take account of the depth of its sources.

III. ONE AGREEMENT IN PRINCIPLE: ECONOMICS AND ETHICS

There is one agreement in principle among all these writers: economics and ethics should not be separated. Most agree that religion is important as inspiration and support for the moral life including some moral disciplines in economic life. Differences appear in various aspects of the argument—in ethical priorities; in particular prudential judgements concerning the social effects of economic institutions and policies; in ethical judgements concerning such matters as the relation between merit and income; in perceptions that result from one's location in society. One characteristic difference of perception and of judgement is between those who stress the support for freedom in capitalism and those who stress more the victims of the way in which economic agents use their freedom. In both cases the judgements are ethical judgements.

Roger Shinn introduces this subject in his discussion of the relation between theology and social decisions, theology with its ethical implications. He calls attention to the two sides of Adam Smith and says that he sees continuity between *A Theory of Moral Sentiments* and *The Wealth of Nations*. He also quotes a strong passage from Keynes in a letter to William Temple: "There are practically no issues of policy as distinct from technique which do not involve ethical considerations." Shinn adds that "ethical language is conspicuous in the regular columns in *Newsweek* of Milton Friedman and Lester Thurow." The socialist economists with which any of us have dealings in the West make strong appeals to ethics. The Marxist pretense to represent pure science is disproved by Marx's own furious moral denunciations of the human effects of capitalism.

The paper by Mishan defends capitalism as the protection of freedom and he provides the raw material for one of the most popular criticisms of capitalism: the effects of its exaggerated stimulus of ever more lavish consumption on the quality of life. He traces this to technology rather than to capitalism as such and he indicates that socialist economies have a similar tendency. But what he sees causes others to raise moral questions concerning what seems to be a predicament of capitalism — namely, that without continuous economic growth which stimulates ever-increasing consumption there is no chance to have what anyone regards as "full employment." There is the related moral question of the use in developed countries of resources that are needed for life itself in other parts of the world.

IV. JUSTICE AND EQUALITY

The centre of the debate that pervades these papers can best be explored under the general heading of "justice and equality." All of the writers believe in justice as a criterion for economic life but I doubt if I ever realized how diverse interpretations of the meaning of justice can be until I read these chapters! The defenders of capitalist assumptions shy away from ideas of economic equality as a distortion of the idea of justice and of economic health in society. When we try to get a viable conception of how justice is related to grace, merit, need, impersonal rules, incentives, fellowship between groups and much else we seem to end up in a quagmire. I think that anyone who addresses these issues can learn from Professor Heyne's paper as a check list of questions to be considered as we try to think clearly. There is a danger from my point of view that it may lead us to fail to see the forest for the trees, that it may cause us to miss the main issues while discussing interesting debating points.

Professor Heyne does well in indicating that we do have clearer ideas of injustice than of justice. We may be led to talk about justice because actual human conditions are so clearly wrong that the very stones cry out. This wrongness in terms of what happens to people becomes identified with injustice. In the background there are positive but vaguer ideas of what justice means and these receive surer content as we try to overcome what some of us at least designate as examples of injustice. In the United States at the present time it is not difficult to find examples of this wrongness that I regard as unjust. For example we learn that about a fifth of American children are living under conditions which are officially regarded as conditions of poverty.[7] I realize that poverty is a relative matter but this idea can be exaggerated when we estimate what housing and food and medical care cost poor people in the United States as compared with what they may cost in monetary terms in some other countries. Another example: the families of several million unemployed workers in the United States have no medical insurance since that had been related to their jobs. It is true that some social provisions for medical care are present but often these people do not find them available. Literally millions of people (I am thinking of families of the unemployed) who formerly had not been poor probably avoid going to a doctor early enough to prevent their health from needlessly deteriorating. One may debate statistics about the number of people involved but there is no doubt that the number is shocking and is a sign of the pathology, to use Boulding's term, of the market system when it is too much trusted to supply medical care. The United States is the only industrialized democracy in which such a situation exists and in part this is because of the market ideology of the medical profession itself.

Several times in these papers the argument is made that what some of us are seeking as a matter of justice in Western countries does not help people who are worse off in the Third World. There are great dilemmas in that context. I seek better conditions for those who are suffering from what I regard as injustice in my own country; but this does not help those who are greater sufferers in Bangladesh. And this fact should arouse my ethical and very human concern. If citizens of a Western country could do as much by their influence on public opinion and by their votes for people in other countries as they can for people in their own country the immediate moral dilemma would be in practice greater. I haven't seen in the chapters in defense of the market very much interest in taking steps that would lead to greater intercontinental economic justice.

Thinking about justice

I think that we can begin our thinking about justice with the traditional conception of giving all persons and groups their due. Yet that provides no content because it does not tell what anyone's due is. Justice should be seen not as the application of existing rules or the adjusting of existing structures to a static conception of what is anyone's due but as a dynamic process which takes account of new perceptions of what the due of any person or group of persons is. We have seen a series of revolutions in this matter. For Aristotle the due of some persons was slavery. That was recognized by law in the United States, amazingly as it seems now, until about 125 years ago. There have been revolutions in what was believed to be the due of industrial workers in the West, of non-white people, of the people who were subjects of Western empires, and today we see the early stages of such a revolution in regard to what is the due of women. The exact measurement of what is just in particular situations may be difficult to determine precisely but those who believe in the democratic side of democratic capitalism can hardly say that these revolutionary changes were in the wrong direction. The fact that most of humanity has been in a position to make few claims until recent generations is the great reality. The dynamism of justice has been the overcoming of what was wrong or unjust in that reality. In each country people are at different stages in this process and it is always possible to raise precise questions about merit and about new injustices. One significant passage in these chapters by defenders of the market system is the statement of Professor Heyne that "defenders of capitalism do their cause a disservice, I believe, when in their eagerness to establish the moral legitimacy of capitalism they undertake to argue that people deserve, as a consequence of their merit, whatever they receive in a competitive capitalist economy." We may reflect in that context on the fact that while a fifth of American children are in poverty, hundreds of thousands of people were reaping great profits as the stock market advanced four hundred points. Think of the contrast between those two worlds and the lack of communication between them!

The burden of proof

Underlying all of these revolutionary changes in regard to the due of various segments of humanity there is the rightful claim, to many theoretically disturbing though seldom denied in principle, the claim of all human beings because they are human to the opportunity to develop their capacities, and to possess the political rights of all other human beings in their society. To accept this claim in principle is to go far in the recognition of the need for systems of justice to be under the pressure of the ideal of equality. I am not speaking of complete coerced equality. Such a way of thinking of equality would involve an enormous amount of regimentation and a major preoccupation of most people would be to find ways of beating the system. Such a system of equality would smother many forms of freedom and there would be little space for creative diversity. Also, the defenders of the market economy are right in thinking that it would undermine needed incentives for innovation, productivity, efficiency and risk. The possibility of improving the economic situation of oneself and one's family is a good, but the fact that it is a good does not mean that without limit the more of it there is the better. There are other more creative motives but I think that the critics of the market system should not deny that the advantage motive has an essential place. There are limits to the degree of inequality that it justifies but when we perceive some of the human effects of particular inequalities it is essential to take action to redistribute wealth to counteract these undesirable human effects. It is in this sense that systems of justice should be under the pressure of the ideal of equality. Put more strongly: there should be a burden of proof on inequalities.

Equality as the pinnacle of justice

Reinhold Niebuhr is sometimes wrongly claimed as a "neo-conservative" who would be happy with all that is being said in defence of democratic capitalism by many papers in this book. One point of difference between him and those chapters can be seen in the fact that he never abandoned this position about equality expressed in his major work: *The Nature and Destiny of Man*. The following passage summarizes his views:

> Equality as a pinnacle of the ideal of justice implicitly points toward love as the final norm of justice; for equal justice is the approximation of brotherhood under the conditions of sin. A higher justice always means a more equal justice. Special privilege may be frowned upon more severely by those who want it than by those who have it; but those who have it are uneasy in their conscience about it.[8]

I do not know how many contemporary North Americans of great wealth have an uneasy conscience about it but certainly there is evidence that both religious motives and motives influenced by democratic experience have caused many such people to divest themselves

of large parts of their wealth philanthropically, often through foundations over which they have at least shared control with others. One can
criticize this way of redistributing wealth as involving too much arbitrary power but it reveals that there is a widespread conscientious
awareness that ownership of such wealth has dubious moral justification.

John Rawls in his very influential philosophical volume, *The
Theory of Justice,* by an intellectual route quite different from that
taken by the theologians and churches comes out at a similar position.
He too believes that there should be a burden of proof on social and
economic inequalities. He says that these "are just only if they result in
compensating benefits for everyone, and particularly for the least advantaged members of society."[9] This is not very different from "the
preferential option for the poor."

Equality of opportunity

Believers in democratic capitalism usually believe in equality of opportunity for all persons in the society. I doubt if any of these authors
would deny that in principle. They usually say: "equality of opportunity and not equality of results." What is seldom said or even
perceived is that equality of opportunity does not exist if the conditions under which children live are beyond a certain point unequal.
Probably there is an advantage in not being too rich! But in the
earliest years malnutrition permanently injures the mental capacity of
children. There are many inequalities which neither economic nor
political institutions can overcome such as having or not having paren-
tal love. I am fascinated by a development in the thought of George
Will whose conservatism has been expressed in innumerable journals
for many years. In an article in *The New Republic*[10] he says the following: "Conservatives rightly stress equality of opportunity rather
than equality of outcomes. Conservatives are, therefore, fond of the
metaphor of a footrace: all citizens should be equal at the starting line
of the race of life. But much that we have learned about early-child-
hood development suggests that 'equality of opportunity' is a much
more complicated matter than most conservatives can comfortably
acknowledge. Prenatal care (which the 'right to life' movement should
regard as something of a 'right'), infant stimulation, childhood nutri-
tion, and especially home environment — all these and other influences
affect the competence of a young 'runner' as he or she approaches the

academic hurdles that so heavily influence social outcomes in America." He concludes by saying that "'equality of opportunity' can be enhanced by various forms of state action." Such considerations require redistribution of wealth to an extent that family maintenance on which children depend (often the maintenance of a single parent family) is essential if there is to be equal opportunity. The deserving children of people who are regarded as "undeserving poor" should have as much consideration by society as the children of those of us who have written in this volume and of our readers. Children should not be sacrificed because of the weaknesses, moral or otherwise, of their parents. This happens on a large scale in the United States. Remedies here are examples of dynamic justice that raises up neglected or exploited people who lack economic "merit" to a new and higher external level of life. This may not easily fit the ethics of the market but it does fit the democratic side of democratic capitalism.

The preferential option for the poor

The religious imperative that we see the world first of all as it is experienced by the disadvantaged support this concept. As Roger Shinn says in his chapter: "Churches in our own society characteristically represent the more stable and at least the moderately privileged social groups; but when they remember their historic faith, they feel responsibility to represent the less privileged." This is expressed in the Roman Catholic watchword that is heard around the world: "preferential option for the poor." There will always be tension between this view of the world and that which is often regarded as the right rule for successful capitalism: make sure that well-to-do investors have more wealth to invest because in time everyone will benefit. In a democratic society there will always be an uneasy relationship between these two perspectives. Religious and democratic imperatives should prevent the second perspective from blacking out the first. This conflict will continually give rise to important political debates. At present these are a considerable part of the substance of domestic politics in the United States. Reinhold Niebuhr has repudiated some elements of his *Moral Man and Immoral Society,* but there is one passage that is true for us which I am sure that he never repudiated: "Who is better able to understand the true character of a civilization than those who suffer most from its limitations?"[11] One phrase that recurs in this book, "the politics of envy," is most inappropriate when those who have already "made it" criticize morally those who struggle politically for minimal justice, not only for themselves but also for a community of neighbours whose plight is similar.

V. CHRISTIANS AND POLITICS

There is no more polemical rejection of the positions often held in the churches which trouble the defenders of the market economy than the chapter by Edward Norman. His attack is directed chiefly against Christian involvement in secular politics. He admits that Christian citizens should assume political responsibilities and this is especially true on matters that affect individual welfare including education and the care for the sick. Dr. Norman has much to say about a fundamental theological contribution to politics with which I agree. He emphasizes tests of political behaviour which are derived from a knowledge of moral ambiguity. No one has stressed this more than Reinhold Niebuhr who has been the inspirer of many of us who come to opposite conclusions from Dr. Norman on many contemporary issues. Dr. Norman seeks to move from revealed truth to political action directly and to bypass political decisions which are shared with secular movements in a pluralistic society. He sees in the tendency to identify with secular movements for particular objectives the secularizing of the church and of one's views of Christianity itself. He wants to emphasize chiefly politics as a means of curbing "men's evil" and I believe that this is where we should very often see Christian political responsibility.

While one can agree with many of Dr. Norman's views about the Christian contribution to politics and the nature of the political process, Dr. Norman's quarrel with the positions in the churches against which he is arguing has to do with judgements concerning what the evil is that needs most to be curbed and concerning the direction in which Christian political action often moves. It is true that Christians often lose their sense of ambiguity when they are involved in movements on the left but when Christians either by advocacy or by political neutralism or passivity support the dominant powers in society they are not even regarded as political. Their unawareness of ambiguities is not even noticed.

Is there a Christian politics?

In a pluralistic society there cannot be "Christian politics" except in the form of exclusive sectarian politics that seek to preserve purity in separation from all secular alternatives. The "Christian politics" of any state that claimed to be a "Christian state" would today be a great distortion whatever we may think of "Christian civilizations" at their best before the rise of modern pluralism. Even under Roman Catholic auspices the "Christian state" has lost its claims with the Catholic affirmation of religious liberty for all and with Catholic commitment to a transforming social justice guided in immediate political decisions by broadly based natural law shared, often under another name, with non-Christians. Yet the ultimate source of the commitment in the case of Catholics and other Christians is the Gospel itself. In this context the movement from revealed truth to political action is indirect. It depends on technical and practical judgements concerning the actual social situation and concerning what the available political alternatives are and which of them has the greatest promise. There is a difference between people who recognize the ambiguity in this process and those who psychologically, if not theoretically, tend to make absolute claims for the positions to which they come, absolute claims with a full Christian sanction. But the fact that many Christians move in this uncritical way because of the pressures of their situation and the emotional needs generated by political struggle in which they are engaged should not prevent the Church from preferring one political direction rather than another. The Church should keep reminding its members of the ambiguity of human choices. To remain on the sidelines because of the temptations that accompany involvement is to give actual support to those now in power.

The leftist orientation

Dr. Norman brings out what is often regarded as the most severe criticisms of tendencies in churches. It is that both the Roman Catholic church and mainline Protestant churches that belong to the World Council of Churches give moral support to leftist movements in the Third World. It is true that they are responsive to movements which are often branded as leftist. These churches regard themselves as part of a world-wide ecumenical community and they are very much aware that in many countries more radical transformations involving the changing of the centres of power are desirable than are approved by defenders of the market economy in North America. They do not write off all revolutionary movements because they are influenced by a selective use of Marxism. Marxism has become in many places the language and the agent of needed revolutions. Within churches there is no support for Marxism as a hardline absolutistic system and obviously there is no support for the traditional Marxist view of religion often not shared by secular Marxists.[12] But the fact that some revolutionaries, both Christian and secular, have used Marxism as a tool for the analysis of their societies and have been guided by Marxist criticism of capitalism is not a reason for rejecting them. Democratic capitalists have little to offer people who need to displace those who now have power over them by revolutionary means. If capitalists begin by admitting the need of such radical change they may later help in the reconstruction of those societies. As a start the mild reformism of democratic capitalism is not likely to be enough. I know that there will be a strong disagreement with these sentences by many writers in this volume but I think that they fairly represent what many people in the ecumenical community think about some situations. In many other situations they have no relevance at all.

Christianity and revolution

Even where they have relevance Christian thinking keeps a sense of transcendence, of divine judgement on all human striving and all human achievements. A very representative series of statements about revolution came out of a conference held in Zagorst, near Moscow, in 1968.[13] This conference was not influenced by its Russian environment! It consisted of thinkers from all continents, both Catholic and Protestant, and was held under the auspices of the World Council of Churches. A section of its report was a theological interpretation of revolution. It began by emphasizing the conviction that we should see in some revolutions the emerging of "a new sense of human dignity" in which the Christian Gospel has played no small part. It warns against "sacralizing either the status quo or the revolution." It warns against the "fury of self-righteousness" generated by the "self-justification" produced by revolutions. It says about violence "that Christians should do all in their power to exercise the ministry of reconciliation to enable the revolutionary change to take place non-violently or if this is not possible, with a minimum of violence." But it also says that we must recognize that "some Christians find themselves in situations where they must, in all responsibility, participate fully in the revolution with all its inevitable violence." In such situations "they will need the understanding, sympathy, and prayer of their Christian brethren."

There is a considerable group of Christians who are absolute pacifists and who could not agree with that report. They are today more than ever influential in the churches and more than ever they cause people to put the burden of proof on all claims that violence can be justified. It is difficult to see how other people can in principle oppose the possibility of revolutionary violence when they support an immense build-up of armaments and allow their government to support counter-revolutionary violence in Central America. Certainly we need to apply Dr. Norman's dictum about moral ambiguity to all activities of Christians in situations that call for revolution.

The world-wide ecumenical community includes many people who are so satisfied with the main lines of the economic situation that they are tempted to think that any change would be for the worse. It also includes many people, a much larger number of people, who suffer as victims of the dominant institutions and powers and who are tempted to believe that any change would be for the better. The churches should identify themselves especially with the needs and aspirations of the latter group but they should help them to be critical of all ideologies and to find ways to change the conditions of their lives that turn the struggle for justice into channels that will be free from new oppressions.

Economics and the Jewish tradition

A most interesting series of chapters deal with the attitude of Jews toward economic systems. Milton Friedman presents perhaps the most powerful defense of capitalism in this book in the course of his examination of the tendency of Jews to be anti-capitalist in spite of his view that this position is against their interests. Two other chapters by Jewish writers also defend capitalism but provide more room for modifications of the action of the market for social purposes.

Readers who are affronted by the anti-capitalistic teaching of theologians and of religious institutions because they regard this teaching as bad economics, socially destructive, and as misrepresenting their own religion will find most of this book reassuring and heart-warming.

NOTES

1. In 1948 I published a book entitled *Christianity and Communism* in which I said that there were the following three elements in capitalism that should have a place in any adequate alternative to communism: recognition of the importance of incentive; many independent centres of economic initiative; and having segments of the economy left to impersonal and automatic forms of regulation instead of their being planned from a centre with great concentration of power. I mention this to indicate that as long ago as 1948 I had some things in common with democratic capitalism! (Chapter on "Christianity and the Major Alternatives to Communism" — *Christianity and Communism* — Associate Press, 1948) A later edition in 1970 was entitled *Christianity and Communism Today.*

2. Michael Novak, *The Spirit of Democratic Capitalism,* New York: Basic Books, 1982, pp. 251-252.

3. See Karl H. Hertz, editor: *Two Kingdoms and One World,* Minneapolis: Augsburg, 1976, for an account of developments in the Lutheran thinking about the "two realms."

4. See chapter by Gregory Baum in the companion volume. *Religion, Economics and Social Thought,* edited by Walter Block and Irving Hexham to be published by the Fraser Institute in 1985.

5. Emil Brunner, *The Divine Imperative,* Philadephia: The Westminster Press, 1947. p. 426.

6. See J. H. Oldham (Editor) Oxford Conference — Official Report, Willett, Clarke & Co., 1937. pp. 75-112.

7. Mrs. Alice Rivlin, Director of the Congressional Budget Office reported the proportion of children who are poor is now almost 20 per cent (*New York Times,* April 29, 1983). The Census Bureau of the Labor Department reported that 22 per cent of children under six live in poverty. (*Los Angeles Times,* Dec. 13, 1982).

8. Reinhold Niebuhr, *The Nature and Destiny of Man,* Vol. II, New York: Scribner's, 1943, pp. 254-5.

9. John Rawls, *The Theory of Justice,* Cambridge, Mass.: Belknap Press, 1971, pp. 14-15.

10. George Will, "In Defense of the Welfare State," *The New Republic,* May 9, 1983.

11. Reinhold Niebuhr, *Moral Man and Immoral Society* New York: Scribner's, 1932, p. 157.

12. It may not be widely known but Castro is the only communist head of

state who has renounced the official Marxist teaching about religion. He made this very clear in a speech to the Jamaican Council of Churches on October 20, 1977 saying that there is no essential conflict between Christianity and the revolution. The Italian Communist Party officially takes this position. A European witness to this who is especially interesting in this respect is Milan Machoverc, author of *A Marxist Look at Jesus* (Fortress Press, 1976). *Christians and Marxists* (Eerdmans, 1976) by Jose Miguez Bonino, the leading Protestant theologian in Latin America in its discriminating treatment of Marxism would counteract the simplistic ideas about Marxism that dominate public life in the United States.

13. About forty theologians from seventeen countries were present. As a participant it interested me that the draft of this section of the report primarily was the work of two persons: Andre Dumas, a French theologian who had in his background memories of the French Revolution and M. M. Thomas, the most influential Christian interpreter of Christian social ethics in India, author of *The Christian Response to the Asian Revolution* (S.C.M. Press, London 1968). What they produced was strongly approved by the group as a whole. One of the most careful studies of the ethics of revolutionary violence was the work of a commission, appointed by the World Council of Churches, which carried on a two-year study of the subject. It concluded with a difference of opinion because of the presence of absolute pacifists on the commission but it states well the views of those who have seen in their own experience no alternative to revolutionary violence. The report is published in *The Ecumenical Review* (October 1973). After many years of the discussion of this subject I come to three conclusions: (1) Only those who are pacifists in relation to international war can rightly be absolutists in rejecting revolutionary violence in all possible situations; (2) revolutionary violence in most situations is likely to be counterproductive and the burden of proof on its advisability should be heavy; (3) a major responsibility of the churches is to counteract the temptations after the revolution to self-righteous vindictiveness, to create new forms of oppression.

Overview

Michael Novak

Introduction

Whereas in the companion volume* in this series the major essays emphasize the teachings on economics of four major *religious* traditions (Catholic, Protestant, Jewish and Islamic), the present volume moves closer toward *political* and *economic* specifics. Once again, so many good points have been raised that a commentator feels hopelessly inadequate. It seems sensible, therefore, to follow the outline of the current volume, dealing first with some matters of general theological background, and then with the thisworldly specifics. Near the end, I comment briefly on the individual papers. I have tried to make the current overview continuous with the one presented in the companion volume, in such a way that the reader who chances solely on this one will find it standing on its own two feet, while readers of the companion will grasp its continuity without undue repetition.

I. THEOLOGICAL ISSUES

Two words which cause theologians particular trouble in discussing the liberal tradition in economics are "self-interest" and "acquisitiveness." Let us begin with these, then mention several others.

Self-interest

When an economist uses these words, he means "autonomous choice."

---

*This refers to *Religion, Economics and Social Thought,* edited by Walter Block and Irving Hexham forthcoming from The Fraser Institute — eds.

He says nothing at all about the moral content of that choice; in the eyes of the economist, that frame is deliberately kept empty. Self-interest means *whatever* a person has chosen, whether it is sanctity or truth, pleasure or material benefit. The concept is as general and empty as possible, in order to be universalizable.

The very same word, however, has quite different meanings in theology. In Islamic and Jewish traditions, for example, "self-interest" does not typically have negative connotations. It is understood as an elemental commonsense duty to oneself, quite reasonable and basic. In this context, the commandment "Love thy neighbor as thyself" has a sound basis. A fundamental and proper love of self (including love for one's family and community, one's duties and one's vocation) is no cause for moral uneasiness. In the Christian tradition, however, "self-interest" has acquired a pejorative connotation. There are two reasons why this is so. First, Christianity strives to go "beyond the law." The impulse to go beyond the counsels of common sense (easily misunderstood as "the counsels of the flesh" or "the counsels of this world") introduces a potentially heretical ambiguity into Christian judgement that may, perhaps, best be expressed as Christian perfectionism. Under this impulse, which is not necessarily orthodox, Christians often feel obliged to reject (or to disguise) self-interest as too imperfect, too flawed, too self-enclosed. Secondly, the Christian understanding of love, especially as *agape* (self-sacrificial love), seems to some Christians to be *opposed* to self-interest or self-love. A Christian should be like Christ, who was "a man for others." An appeal to self-interest seems, in this symbolic network, directly contrary to the Christian appeal to the denial of self-interest in order to love God and neighbour. A full discussion of these complex ideas would require too much space. But, clearly, "self-interest" is an expression which, in the tradition of Christian symbolic language, has reverberations which are lacking in the context of economics and in many non-Christian theological traditions.

When Adam Smith speaks of the "self-interest" of the butcher and the baker, for example, it should be noted that this "self-interest" is not likely to be individualistic merely. The butcher tolerates the blood and the baker bears the heat, typically, not for themselves alone but for their families and their dependants, and in the light of a future which only their children may enjoy. Many are the parents who have sacrificed themselves to gain advantages for their children and for others.

Care must be taken in the theology of economics to unpack the misleadingly simple concept of self-interest, so as to specify its exact
moral meaning in each and every context. Without such care, quite
conflicting meanings may frustrate understanding. Thus, Dean Wogaman, in his essay, questions whether businessmen work for charity, as
George Gilder says (using a special meaning for the word) or for personal advantage. Erik Erikson has developed the concept of "basic
trust" (which he does not scruple to relate to biblical love) to mean a
psychological attitude toward reality which permits the self to reach
out, to act, to take risks, to create new events — as opposed to psychological withdrawal, mistrust, inability to affirm, and self-enclosure.[1]
"Basic trust," Erikson believes, is the root impulse of creativity, love,
faith, and affirmation. This, I think, is what Gilder is getting at. The
opposite to the creator of new wealth is the miser, the hoarder, the
frightened and isolated Scrooge. The Belgian sociologist of economics, Leo Moulin[2] holds that one reason why Judaism and Christianity were indispensable conditions for the discovery of capitalism is
that they taught human beings that creation is good, that God is good,
that humans are made in the image of the Creator — and, therefore,
that they should be bold, free, inventive, exploratory, and creative.
When Dante wrote of "the love that moves the sun and all the stars,"
he similarly used "love" in this general meaning of affirmation, movement, act.

Thus, theologians and economists would do well to study the depths
hidden behind that word "self-interest." It is a word of many meanings
and profound associations. Unexamined, it causes unnecessary mischief.

Acquisitiveness

R. H. Tawney, the socialist historian, was the decisive force in naming
the fundamental motive of capitalist economic activity acquisitiveness; he did not do so for friendly reasons.[3] But this word confuses
two quite different motivations. Truly, the miser is acquisitive,
hoards, holds, wants to possess. This is quite opposite to the motive of
the investor, the entrepreneur, and the inventor. Two key words in a
capitalist civilization are "new" and "improved." Business reaches out
to create new things and often fails. Technological obsolescence is
characteristic of dynamic capitalist advances. It is not *having* that
characterizes the capitalist spirit, but *venturing* and *creating*. Putting
money in the bank, or burying it in the ground, are not distinctively

capitalist acts; nor is the grasping acquisition of money. Quite the opposite. The capitalist ideal is to invent, to invest and to produce new wealth. It is true that there are—there always have been—speculators who do not create. That is neither specific to a capitalist order nor its defining characteristic. What does define a capitalist order is, rather, the habit of abstaining from consumption and from miserly hoarding, in order to invest in creative ventures which produce new wealth in a sustained way—which new wealth is then again similarly invested. As Max Weber saw, the goal of the capitalist spirit is not to live sumptuously or even comfortably, as pre-capitalist persons of commerce did, but to create ever new wealth in a systematic way. The capitalist spirit appeared to Weber distinctively new because of its emphasis upon the future rather than the past, because of its corresponding "thisworldly asceticism," because of its spiritual rather than materialistic focus.[4] *Acquisitiveness* names this spirit very badly, indeed.

Profit

The semantic confusion is just as great with "profit." Most persons intuitively confuse profit with mark-up. They further intuitively confuse profit with cash taken out of the business by owners or managers. They think that the capitalist spirit is "Buy cheap, sell dear," and that profits "go into the pocket" of those who make them. In actual fact, profit is another word for development. Not to earn profit is to be economically stagnant or going backwards—spending more for an economic activity than its return. In our day, perhaps as many as half of all persons paid more than $30,000 a year are engaged in activities of government, teaching, research, and other not-for-profit activities which earn no profit. No wonder many have an inadequate conception of profit; they have no experience in earning it in a sustained, creative, venturesome way. If they did, they would see that most profit is a cost of doing creative, productive work. Some of it goes to retire the loans used to start up a business (a magazine, for example). Some of it is invested in improving the product or in finding new markets for it (as in direct mail to find new subscribers). By far, the largest proportion of profit is reinvested. Typically, only a small proportion of it is used in paying dividends to the original investors (to whom the business is in debt) and in raising salaries. One may say that dividends and salaries go "into someone's pocket," but often that money, too, is reinvested.

One may say, of course, in retort, that this is how "the rich grow richer." (It does not seem to be true in any democratic capitalist society over time that "the poor get poorer.") Yet as John Stuart Mill pointed out in *The Principles of Political Economy,* there is a keen difference between wealth and capital.[5] Wealth alone is unproductive, either hoarded or used for consumption. Capital is that portion of wealth which is reinvested in productive activities, which creates not only new employment, new goods and new services, but further new wealth as well. Wealth may or may not be socially useful. But capital provides many social benefits in the form of new employment, new goods, new services, invention, and new wealth. It also provides the funds which are paid into non-profit activities and taxes. As we have seen, it is also the source of funds for the research and development on which future prosperity depends.

Those who are in favour of doing away with, or confiscating, profits are necessarily in favour of halting development and the production of new wealth. If they retort that their wish is rather to "socialize" profit, by sharing it with all citizens directly or by yielding all profit to the state, they subordinate the economic system to the political system. Their view seems to be that this subordination serves the common good. Such experiments have been widely tried. The fundamental idea is Marxist. Even if adapted to democratic socialist purposes, its actual consequences for the common good need to be assessed. I myself discern no evidence that such a conception actually does serve the common good. It seems to lead to the daily impasses of politics and the economic unproductivity of political processes. Since profit is another way of saying economic growth, those democratic socialists who favour economic growth have withdrawn their objections to profit in principle, and argue only about the most creative way to maintain and to assign it. About this, 160 nations of the world have been engaged in national experiments. Empirical surveys are in order. Profit, in any case, is best understood as the margin of new wealth created by the efficient investment of old.

The market

In theological circles, the word market has been surrounded by many symbolic overtones. It is treated as a question of faith or ideology, as if some trust "the magic of the marketplace" and some do not, as if to support the use of markets in economic activities were a matter of "ideological bias" which one either shares or resists. In addition, some seem to harbour fears about the market, as if through it, if it is left free and untrammelled, things will be out of control, no one will be in charge, irrationality and abuse will spread, anarchy will ensue, the strong will take advantage of the weak, etc.

Of course, there is no single "the market." There are only many particular markets. A market is often imagined as a place, like the "marketplace" of a medieval town. In practice, a market — for home computers, say — is an aggregation of those who want to purchase home computers now and those who manufacture and distribute them for sale. A short while ago, no such market existed. Markets come and disappear (although antiquarians sometimes keep some markets going long after fashion passes by). Some are large, especially those designed for potentially every family and person, and some are small, especially those for very expensive or highly specialized goods or services. Some markets are easy, some quite difficult, to find or to establish. Some goods and services are not marketed. Air, though indispensably good, did not have a market in John Stuart Mill's time, although he foresaw its potential marketability in activities in places where air was absent. Sometimes the word market is used metaphorically, as in "the free market of ideas" or even "the market for religious belonging in a pluralistic society." In such cases, one does not mean literally that persons "purchase" ideas or religious belonging. Yet even such items of the spirit must be "exchanged" from person to person and are subject to autonomous choice; hence the metaphor.

Non-market forms of allocation

There are ways to distribute goods and services other than through free exchange and autonomous choice. Goods and services can be commanded, assigned, distributed through political dictate. Whether political distribution is achieved by totalitarian power or by democratic majorities, however, it must also be conducted bureaucratically if the number of recipients is large. Such distribution will also always have two other features. It will never be subject to the autonomous choice of the supplier or the recipient, but to political command. And it will never be the result of a voluntary exchange.

Most democratic socialists have come to see the merit of markets as technical devices which have two advantages. Free exchange in markets yields instantly available information about supply and demand that no set of planners can arrive at on their own. Secondly, markets act quickly and efficiently to match those who desire with those who supply, with as few obstacles in the way as possible. These arguments are pragmatic. Typically, democratic capitalists have a further reason for preferring, wherever possible and, if in doubt, by giving the benefit of the doubt to market mechanisms. The reason is that markets respect the political nature of human beings — their autonomous choosing and their capacities for voluntary action — better than politicized command mechanisms, even if democratic, do.

Finally, it is difficult to see what "political liberty" and even "political dissent" can mean in practice in a command economy, whether totalitarian or democratic. When every aspect of economic life is governed by political command, even if democratically arrived at, in what space in the real world of human activities can dissenters function? Economic activists, both those with genius in economic activities and those with simply ordinary economic capacities, must necessarily be frustrated when their activities are subject to command by others. Majorities can be as tyrannical as individual tyrants. Decisions reached by committee are not always as penetrating, original, or wise as those reached by the individual.

Markets and democracy

For this reason, it seems "not to be an accident" (to use the Marxist phrase) that, after 150 years of vast and international experimentation, there are still no examples of thoroughly socialist societies which are also democratic. Perhaps it can be done. I remain skeptical, since I cannot imagine any *concrete institutions* through which democracy can be truly socialist. A margin of autonomous choice and voluntary exchange — a market — seems indispensable. Democratic socialism means rule by majorities, not simply in large issues of state but in every significant detail of economic life. How can the tyranny of majorities be prevented? By which institutional mechanisms? How can dissent be practiced by dissenters, or tolerated by majorities? Will dissenters really be free to act contrary to political command?[6] Once the principle of political command is extended over economic activities, such activities are no longer subject to autonomous choice, personal originality, or personal achievement. The inevitable result must be psychological apathy.

For this reason, I believe Dr. Wogaman was wrong not to have argued against the alumnus of his college mentioned in his essay, now the leader of an African state, who asserts that he desires to build a democratic polity together with a socialist economy. Of course, such a leader is free to try; presumably, he was elected to try. Not only is his project bound to lead to economic stagnation and deprivation, however; it is bound as well to make political democracy empty of all active economic content. People may vote, but they will have little or no economic autonomy. What sort of liberty is that? What creativity, invention, or personal exertion may be expected from that? Such an ideologue will do what he will do; all the evidence of recent history is against him. I wish Dr. Wogaman had saved him grief.

Markets and the Christian vision

Theologically, which device for distributing goods and services — the market or political command — is most concordant with the Christian vision of the human being? I have no hesitation in saying that it is the market. Voluntary exchange and autonomous choice are critical both for religious liberty and for freedom to preach the Word. One can imagine a democratic socialist state maintaining the "bourgeois" institutions of human rights, including religious liberty. (Will political command limit the newsprint available to the religious press?) But I cannot imagine political command over economic activities being in harmony with Christian views of autonomous choice and individual liberty. That would be too like the *ancien regime* in which, often enough, prince-bishops gave economic commands.

Nonetheless, command economies do offer religious leaders the prospect, lost in bourgeois democratic capitalist societies, of suffusing every aspect of economic life with Christian values, through control over the processes of political command. A *Christian* democratic socialist state does seem to some attractive. If Christian leaders could exert moral authority over democratic socialist leaders (or entire peoples), they would have it within their power to create Christian commonwealths by command. Even absent such direct ecclesiastical control over Castro and the Sandinista junta, some religious leaders, as Walter Berns points out, hold that the command economies of Cuba and Nicaragua are morally superior to the market economies of the United States, Canada, Japan, and Western Europe. The authoritarian impulse seems strong, perhaps because it is disguised by the word "democratic."

II. ECONOMIC ISSUES

In summary, there is need for theological sophistication about concepts like self-interest, acquisitiveness and basic trust, profit, and markets. But several specific economic issues are frequently brought up by religious leaders, as if there was general agreement about them — pollution, the use of scarce resources, unemployment, and poverty.

On such issues, persons in religion often merely repeat the conventional wisdom of the moment, even though that conventional wisdom is, typically, wrong. The notes that follow have the modest purpose of showing that the issues are, at the very least, more complicated than is commonly supposed, and that persons of sound judgement must give a hearing both to the prosecution and to the defense.

Speaking as prosecutors, some religious leaders make several arguments against contemporary capitalist societies: that the environment is being destroyed; that basic resources are being squandered; that unemployment is structural; and that the poor, especially children, are not receiving compassionate support. There are, of course, other charges. These are the ones most often alluded to in these two volumes.

Ecology

Are modern capitalist societies more polluted than traditional societies? Smokestacks and auto exhausts suggest yes; so do beer cans in national parks. But consider the cheap supply of drinking water, the hygiene of modern plumbing, the operating rooms of modern hospitals, the irrigation of farmlands and the scientific control of erosion, the virtual elimination of disease-bearing parasites and insects, the diminishment of scores of diseases and epidemic dangers, and many other advances in human compatibility with nature. On these measures, contrast capitalist with traditional (or socialist) societies. As the river Thames is today cleaner than at any time since before Shakespeare's day, so recent environmental science has made great strides in improving the quality of air and water. The disappearance of the horse and wagon has done wonders for the hygiene of city streets, as have indoor plumbing and systematic garbage disposal. Perhaps the best measures of the compatibility of democratic capitalist societies with their environment are increased longevity, decreased infant mortality, and other such standards. Every advance, of course, brings new problems; every problem, a new advance. In putting down modern societies, prosecutors ought to recall quite vividly the ecological hazards of a hundred years ago.

Resources

The prosecution alleges that irreplaceable resources are being expended wantonly. What the prosecution fails to specify is what "irreplaceable" resources have been used by humans since the beginning. Nearly all the things which we today call resources were not known to be resources fifty, one hundred or two hundred years ago, oil, for example. The first oil well was drilled in Titusville, Pennsylvania in 1859; the first in the Middle East in 1909. Oil was useless stuff until human mind invented a use for it. So with all the modern forms of energy: the ignition mechanism for anthracite coal; natural gas; electricity; electrical batteries; nuclear energy. In Julian Simon's trenchant phrase,[7] the ultimate resource is the human mind, which finds in humble and long-neglected materials unprecedented utilities.

For centuries, the human race ignored oil. The most dramatic metaphor for poverty was "poor as a Bedouin." Only relatively recently was "the oil age" conjured forth by human invention. And after oil? One thing we know is that the earth (from its inner centre) is alive with energy. Nature moves; it changes. (Cf. Aristotle's *Physics*.) To imagine resources running out is to imagine the human mind standing still. It is typical, moreover, to forget to calculate relative costs. As a much-used resource becomes more scarce, it tends to become more costly (like oil). This makes substitutes more attractive and forces all users to alter their priorities. It also makes harder-to-obtain sources of supply economical, thus adding to available reserves. In a word, whoever uses the word "natural resource" should always add to it three qualifying characteristics: recognized as a resource at time T; rendered a resource by human invention; and commonly available at price P. These qualifications cut through many mystifications.

Unemployment

Under conditions of familial subsistence living, parents typically welcome many offspring and (often) unattached relatives as "extra hands" and "familial security." Under conditions of a free market in labour services, workers (and the vast majority of all citizens in modern societies are employees, not proprietors of their own employment) seek free contractual arrangements to exchange their time and effort for recompense. In the former case, unemployment (through flood, drought or other catastrophe) may mean starvation. In the latter case, a mismatch between available jobs and the supply of workers may create "structural unemployment." The cure for this cannot be to lop off the unemployed; the obvious remedy is to create more jobs. Thus, widespread unemployment suggests to democratic capitalists an examination of business conditions; why is the economy not creating sufficient jobs? Democratic socialists, by contrast, look to the state, at least as "the employer of last resort." In either case, while labour is prior to capital as a final cause—the economy is for human persons, not human persons for the economy—capital is prior to labour in job formation: First, somebody must put up the money, even before labour produces values sufficient to repay labour costs. One may compute the amount of capital which must be invested to supply one job; it typically far exceeds the costs only of labour since it includes many other costs as well (materials, plant, equipment, taxes, transport, insurance, and the like). In this sense, at least, the problem of unemployment points to the deeper problems of productive investment, capital formation, savings, invention, and the entrepreneurial spirit. This is true whether the state or a non-statist economic system supplies the capital. A stagnant economy produces few new jobs. Jobs which do not produce at least as much of their costs pull any single firm (and the economy as a whole) toward stagnation.

Employment trends in the U.S.

But the actual picture in the United States, for example, does not match the conventional wisdom. The conventional wisdom holds that the U.S. is "losing" jobs. On the contrary. the number of persons actually employed in the United States has been increasing even though population growth has been slowing. Consider the following table (numbers in millions):[8]

	U.S. Adult Population:	Full-time Employees (Civilian):	Unemployed Seeking Work:
1950	106.2	58.9	3.3
1960	119.1	65.8	3.9
1970	139.2	78.7	4.1
1980	169.3	99.3	7.6
1983(Sept.)	176.3	103.6	10.4

At present, a higher percentage (65 per cent) of Americans ages 18–65 are employed in the labour market than ever before in U.S. history. This is largely, of course, due to the proportion of adult women entering the work force. In addition, immigration into the U.S. during the 1970s reached figures comparable to the greatest migrations of past decades.[9] The work ethic—at least in the sense of the desire for gainful employment—is not only alive and well in the United States but at an all-time high.

From 1970 to 1983, despite recessions and "stagflation," the U.S. economy generated 25 million new jobs. As of September, 1983, there were 103 million Americans in full-time employment and 10 million unemployed.[10] Demographers estimate that by the end of the 1980s, the U.S. will have to create more than 21 million new jobs."[11] This task will be difficult, but not beyond that of the 1970s. From then on, the sequel to the "baby boom" suggests a labour shortage.

The state's role

A good society values full employment as the best sort of self-reliance, family stability, and general well-being. Reliance on the state to attain this high goal has consequences. Among these consequences are: inflation; diminished private-sector investment; a drop in productivity; slackness in invention; dependency; and a downward cycle of national decay.

Furthermore, the developed nations would seem to have some obligation to allow the simpler economies of the developing world to absorb some growing portion of the world's industrial production. For the developing nations need to be able to rely upon their own industrial systems rather than upon subsistence agriculture, if they are ever to reach adequate employment. This means that the economies of the developed world must shift their own priorities to new invention and new areas of employment. In practice, of course, world markets are moving roughly and slowly in this direction. "Comparative advantage" adds persuasive arguments that this will remain the case.

Thus, some critics of capitalist economies move in self-contradictory directions. First, they urge the developed nations to do more for the less-developed nations. But then, they say, do not "export jobs." This is like offering band-aids but no real project for industrial development. In actual fact, manufacturing jobs in the United States now count for a mere 23 per cent of all jobs.[12] This proportion is likely to fall further, not without benefit to other nations. In 1945, the U.S. produced 53 per cent of the gross world product. With the resurgence of Western Europe, Japan, and other nations, this total has fallen to 22 per cent—not because the U.S. is producing less, but because others are producing so much more. This shift will certainly continue, to the benefit of the entire world.

Poverty and welfare

In 1982, the U.S. Census Bureau reported that 34.4 million persons (of 234 million) had cash incomes below $9,862 for a non-farm family of four.[13] Such poor persons in aggregate, however, fell only $45 billion short of sufficient cash income to have raised all of them above this official poverty line.[14] In addition, non-cash benefits like food stamps ($22 billion in 1982), housing subsidies and other allotments were supplied to overcome the "poverty shortfall" (the amount necessary to raise all above the official poverty line). The composition of the U.S. poor also deserves treatment.

Composite Portrait Poor in the U.S. (in thousands)[15]

White	23,517
Black	9,697
Hispanic	4,301
Under 15 years	11,587
Over 65 years	3,751
Single female heads of households	3,434
Persons living alone	6,458
Urban	21,247
Rural	13,152

Among the white poor in particular, a significant proportion lives in relatively non-cash economies, in areas (Maine, Montana, Iowa, etc.) in which a low cash income does not necessarily signify dire need. Moreover, as the table above shows, 15.3 million of the poor were too young or too old to be in the market economy themselves. Even of those between the ages of 15–65, about 19 million, nearly 3 million were ill or disabled; almost 3.4 million were mothers with young children; 9 million worked for pay during at least part of 1982; another 1.3 million were looking for work.[16] The vast majority of the poor are, therefore, truly dependent and in need of assistance. As we have seen, the "poverty shortfall" — $45 billion — is not an insuperable sum. Indeed, far more than that is currently being expended to eliminate poverty. What, then, is wrong with the *design* of social expenditures, that they prevent this relatively simple task (in monetary terms) from having been long since accomplished?

Welfare and families

There is a more painful question. The number of single-parent (almost always female) households is growing in direct correlation with welfare expenditures intended to *strengthen* families. Among whites, a full 12 per cent of households is now headed by a single female (up from 9 per cent in 1965). Among blacks, the number is 42 per cent (up from 24 per cent in 1965). Almost half of all black youngsters now grow up in female-headed households.[17] If one assumes that the father is the normal teacher of economic disciplines and skills, and the normal source from whom the young gain introduction to employment, the future looks even more bleak, since one can see ahead still further dramatic increases in the number of the poor. It is wrong to "blame the victim." But it is not wrong to question a so-called welfare system which seems to be generating a pattern of family break-up unprecedented in history.

On this point, one would expect religious leaders to shed some light for social policy analysts. Instead, most seem to ignore the facts and to abdicate responsibility.

By contrast, intact black couples have reached income levels at 80 per cent of those of comparable white couples.[18] The correlation of poverty with family break-up — the so-called "feminization of poverty" — is extreme, especially among blacks and Hispanics. (Many female-headed white households are middle-class or above). Those who care about poverty and welfare are led inexorably then to concern for the strength of families. On this intimate matter, the state may be more than usually incompetent. At the very least, though, the state can *cease* doing those things which seem to give incentives to family break-up. Why should teenagers be systematically offered an incentive for becoming pregnant and independent, in the form of welfare cheques, housing assistance, food stamps, and other benefits *in their own name?* No doubt, such young persons, after the fact, need assistance. But it ought not to come in the form of a systematic incentive. As matters stand, if their behaviour is beyond reproach, they receive no assistance; if they create a dependent family, they are given assistance. Assistance given through neighbourhood centres able to offer instruction, child care, meals, and companionship might better meet both criteria: of compassion and wisdom.

A good society must help those in need. But it ought to do so with moral and politically wise criteria, offering incentives for socially creative behaviour, discouraging dependency. Religious thinkers, in particular, have an obligation to defend the integrity of the families of the poor. Nearly all intact families escape poverty, and few that fall into poverty remain in it long.[19] Female-headed families now constitute the single largest—and newest—category of the poor. It is a tragedy, caused not by an act of God but by acts of state. It must soon be addressed.

III. PARTICULAR COMMENTS

I would like to enter into many of the fascinating individual debates between the major authors and their respondents. But to do so intelligently would require many pages. Regrettably, a few observations must suffice. Neither religion nor economics is a sphere for simple, self-evident propositions on which unanimous agreement is to be expected. Moreover, the illation from religious belief to economic practice is not clear and deductive, straight and easy. Even supposing that two devout and learned Christian scholars have similar theological principles for social ethics and even a reasonably similar vision of the good society, it does not follow that they will both perceive the present economic situation, or make probable judgements about future consequences of economic policies, in the same way. It may even happen that two such persons may share the same theological vision and the same economic leanings and *still* disagree strenuously about a particular economic policy; this happens frequently enough in cabinet meetings and at faculty seminars. Sharp disagreement in prudential judgements, not only about particular matters of fact but about large-scale policy decisions, often enough strains the relations between even the wisest and best of colleagues.

In the four sets of essays (and comments) in this volume, I kept wanting to say "good point," "not at all," "not quite right." Each of us has a favourite vocabulary for discussing these matters and sees error lurking in alternative formulations. The distance between some essayists and some commentators is often so vast that it is hard to focus on the several *salient* differences between them. Instead, often enough, the ground keeps shifting from point to point. Patience is required to stick to one issue at a time. Little by little, year by year, the arguments may be drawn more tightly, as one issue after another is settled.

Thus, virtually all the contributors to this volume do favour *some* of the elements of democratic capitalism (the device of markets, some forms of private property; differential incentives; a democratic polity; a limited government, concerned in key respects for the general welfare; and pluralism in moral-cultural life). Virtually all also concede the legitimacy of certain of the reforms at times introduced into history in the name of democratic socialism (some forms of regulation of markets and property; some concern for equality not only before the law but also in opportunity, education, and the like; some forms of assistance to the poor and the dependent needy; and resistance to totalitarian forms of socialism, whether of the Nazi or the Soviet type). When it comes to *defining* democratic capitalism and democratic socialism, differences remain (although patience and generosity of mind can usually dispel definitional wrangles). And, of course, when it is time to judge the present situation or to offer projects of reform, differences become more acute — but properly so, and sometimes surprisingly so.

The Wogaman and Opitz papers

The discussions between Wogaman, Cooper and Block, for example, and between Opitz and Wall, will make the *next* discussions in this area easier. Wogaman is a gentle democratic socialist, as it were a democratic capitalist with a democratic socialist vision. Opitz tends toward the libertarian side of democratic capitalism, but intelligently so and with a mind open to facts and argument. The two essayists stand at opposite poles, but of the same bi-polar reality: the political system has its proper rights and duties, as does the economic system. Wogaman favours the political, Opitz the economic. In this dialectic, the comments by Cooper, Block and Wall set some limits to the questions raised by Wogaman and Opitz. The way is now open, not so much for mediators, as for a more precise statement of one or more disputed points.

I would press Wogaman, for example, to face some of the objections to current welfare and poverty programs which have led other democratic socialists to become (as they are called) "neo-conservatives." That would illuminate what he means by democratic socialism in the U.S. context. I would press Opitz to define his own proposals for U.S. welfare and poverty programs, to the same purpose. One might then take a Third World experiment in "socialism" and try to define the issues in *that* context.

The Shinn paper

The paper by Roger Shinn, with the comments of Shenfield and McLean, helps to prepare us for the "slippage" and ambiguities typically encountered when one begins with theological principles and passes by way of "middle axioms" toward quite complex concrete judgements. One problem not sufficiently addressed is that the current of public ideas has a special power at any given time. The active "political culture" of the U.S., for example, is very much smaller than that of the voters as a whole. The power to define the issues is more than half the game, and this power today inheres in the political reporters (as David Halberstam shows in *The Powers That Be*), who can give governments fits. Moral discernment sometimes requires one to fight against the conventional wisdom of the political culture, even more sharply than to address one particular issue. For the political culture may embrace a *systematic* illusion, whose cumulative impact exceeds that of any one particular issue.

The "neo-conservatives," for example, especially editors like Norman Podhoretz and Irving Kristol, have come to prominence precisely for "breaking ranks" with the dominant political culture, which first nourished them. This challenge at the root of political perception may be more significant, in the end, than any particular tactical victory. That was also the broad effect of Reinhold Niebuhr's "biblical realism" during the 1940s. Thus, religious thinkers have an obligation to challenge the prevailing systems of perception; they need to reflect on *which* establishment they are challenging, which supporting. For the conventional wisdom of the political culture no longer is controlled by political leaders; to some large degree, it is controlled by leading figures in the media and the universities. When Lyndon Johnson saw Walter Cronkite take an adversarial position on the Vietnam war, it is said, he clicked off the set and realized he would have to resign, it was over.[20]

Brennan, Mishan, and Martin

The essays by Brennan and Mishan, with comments by Meiselman, Boulding, David Friedman, and Elzinga range even more broadly than the others. I think they make too little of a central point. Without a certain kind of ethos, and a certain set of institutions in the political economy (protection of patents as private property, e.g.), both "institutional choice" and the invention and creativity symbolized in the word "technology" still slumber in the bosom of underdevelopment. One can talk about the *problems* of free, inventive societies — their morals and their madness. One cannot forget how recently the world was slumbering, as a great vast portion of it still is.

David Martin's essay is brilliant, as we have come to expect, and the energetic comments by Roberts and Preston help him even to sharpen it. I wonder, though, about the religious passions that today stir even those who think themselves the most secular. For there are today many highly *politicized* religious passions, which Michael Harrington celebrates in *The Politics at God's Funeral,* in which he as it were substitutes "socialism" (as he defines it) for "God."[21] The world seems full of religious passion in this supposedly secular age. Much of it takes the vision of the political city in this world as its heaven. One hears nuns speak of a "conversion to peace," as if the politics of peace were not politics but religion. More impressively, "secular" professors now talk the same way. Nuclear blast has merely replaced hellfire and brimstone; the sermon is the same: Repent, and give what you have to the poor.

Friedman vs. Levine

The argument among Jews seems not quite so perfectionist as that among Christians. Milton Friedman, Herbert Frankel and Aaron Levine, although disagreeing, do so in a tone of voice quite different from that of a parallel Christian dispute. We speak too glibly of "Judaeo-Christian" and "Jewish Christian," and Christians too glibly ignore Torah and Talmud, isolating "the Jewish prophets" in false light and for non-Jewish uses. More attention must be paid to the pragmatic, thisworldly, clear-eyed sense of reality a Christian often finds — to his relief — among Jews. The *Jewish* side of "Judaeo-Christian" needs far closer attention, not least in matters of political economy. Irving Kristol says some arresting things on this point in the concluding essays of *Reflections of a Neo-Conservative.* [22]

Heyne and Norman

Finally, Heyne and Norman, and the comments by Baepler and Berns, drive the complexities of using religious ideals in discussions of political economy to helpful depths. Much more is at stake, we finally see, than we first thought. It is easy enough to be in favour of a "pluralist" society. But do Christians really mean *pluralist,* or do they mean a *Christian* society with certain escape hatches for marginal dissenters? If it is necessary to fashion political economies by Christian principles, what happens to genuine pluralism — to *non*-Christian principles? And, as Dr. Norman asks, what is left of Christianity if *that* is how we interpret its mission? These last essays are, properly, very disturbing.

Taken together, these two volumes establish an enormous agenda of work yet to be done.

NOTES

1. See Erik Erikson, *Identity: Youth and Crisis* (New York: Norton, 1968), pp. 91–107; and *Insight and Responsibility* (New York: Norton, 1964), chap. 4.

2. See Leo Moulin, *L'Aventure Europeenne* (Brussels: De Tempel, 1972), chaps. 4–7.

3. R. H. Tawney, *The Acquisitive Society* (New York: Harcourt, 1920).

4. Max Weber, *The Protestant Ethic and the Spirit of Capitalism* (New York: Charles Scribner's Sons, 1958), chap. V: "Asceticism and the Spirit of Capitalism."

5. John Stuart Mill, *Principles of Political Economy,* ed. J. Laurence Laughlin (New York: D. Appleton and Co., 1888), chap. III: "Of Capital."

6. While the socialist Robert Heilbroner does not wish to jeopardize such liberties and rights, he is candid about the prospect of diminished liberties under democratic socialism: "... under socialism, every dissenting voice raises a threat similar to that raised under a democracy by those who preach antidemocracy. Because socialist society aspires to be a *good* society, all its decisions and opinions are inescapably invested with moral import. Every disagreement with them, every argument for alternative policies, every nay-saying voice therefore raises into question the moral validity of the existing government, not merely its competence in directing activities that have no particular moral significance. Dissents and disagreements thereby smack of heresy in a manner lacking from societies in which expediency and not morality rules the roost." Robert L. Heilbroner, "What is Socialism?" *Dissent* (Summer 1978): 347.

7. Julian L. Simon, *The Ultimate Resource* (Princeton, N.J.: Princeton University Press, 1982).

8. U.S. Bureau of Labor Statistics, *Employment and Earnings,* October 1983, Table A-1.

9. According to the director of Demographic Research and Policy Analysis at the Population Reference Bureau, "the number of immigrants to the United States rose dramatically during the 1970s and may once again be as high as the first decade of this century, when about 9 million people entered the country." Leon F. Bouvier, "Immigration at the Crossroads," *American Demographics* 3 (October 1981): 17.

10. *Employment and Earnings,* October 1983, Table A-1.

11. "Employment in the 1980s," *American Demographics* 4 (November 1982): 46.

12. U.S. Bureau of the Census, *Statistical Abstract of the United States: 1982–83,* 103d ed. (Washington, D.C., 1983), Table 652.

13. U.S. Bureau of the Census, Current Population Reports, Series P-60, No. 140, *Money Income and Poverty Status of Families and Persons in the United States: 1982,* July 1983, Table 14.

14. Spencer Rich, "'Poverty Gap' Put at $45 Billion," *Washington Post,* October 19, 1983.

15. *Money Income and Poverty Status of Families and Persons in the United States: 1982,* Table 14.

16. Ibid., Tables 14, 17, 18.

17. *A Dream Deferred: The Economic Status of Black Americans* (Washington, D.C.: Center for the Study of Social Policy, 1983), p. 29.

18. See U.S. Department of Commerce, Bureau of the Census, Current Population Reports Series P-60, No. 145, *Money, Income and Poverty,* Status of Families and Persons in the United States: 1983 (Washington, D.C.: U.S. Government Printing Office, 1984), Table 1.

19. A decade-long study of the poverty population conducted at the University of Michigan found that from 1969 to 1978 only about 3 per cent of individuals were poor during all ten years, while about 17 per cent were in poverty for two years and 39 per cent were in poverty for one year. See Martha S. Hill, "Some Dynamic Aspects of Poverty," in M. S. Hill and J. N. Morgan, ed., *Five Thousand American Families—Patterns of Economic Progress* Vol. 9 (Ann Arbor, Michigan: Institute for Social Research, University of Michigan, 1981), pp. 116–120.

20. See Austin Ranney, *Channels of Power* (New York: Basic Books/American Enterprise Institute, 1983), pp. 4–5.

21. See Kristol's essay, "Christianity, Judaism and Socialism," in *Reflections of a Neo-Conservative* (New York: Basic Books, 1983), pp. 315–326.

22. Irving Kristol, *Reflections of a Neo-Conservative,* New York: Basic Books, 1983.

Index

DATE DUE

GAYLORD   #3523PI   Printed in USA